THE VIENNA GESTAPO, 1938–1945

AUSTRIAN AND HABSBURG STUDIES
General Editor: Howard Louthan, Center for Austrian Studies, University of Minnesota

Before 1918, Austria and the Habsburg lands constituted an expansive multinational and multiethnic empire, the second largest state in Europe and a key site for cultural and intellectual developments across the continent. At the turn of the twentieth century, the region gave birth to modern psychology, philosophy, economics and music, and since then has played an important mediating role between Western and Eastern Europe, today participating as a critical member of the European Union. The volumes in this series address specific themes and questions around the history, culture, politics, social and economic experience of Austria, the Habsburg Empire, and its successor states in Central and Eastern Europe.

Recent volumes:

Volume 33
The Vienna Gestapo, 1938–1945: Crimes, Perpetrators, Victims
Elisabeth Boeckl-Klamper, Thomas Mang and Wolfgang Neugebauer

Volume 32
Imagining Bosnian Muslims in Central Europe: Representations, Transfers and Exchanges
Edited by František Šístek

Volume 31
More Than Mere Spectacle: Coronations and Inaugurations in the Habsburg Monarchy during the Eighteenth and Nineteenth Centuries
Edited by Klaas Van Gelder

Volume 30
Estates and Constitution: The Parliament in Eighteenth-Century Hungary
István M. Szijártó

Volume 29
Antisemitism in Galicia: Agitation, Politics, and Violence against Jews in the Late Habsburg Monarchy
Tim Buchen

Volume 28
Revisiting Austria: Tourism, Space, and National Identity, 1945 to the Present
Gundolf Graml

Volume 27
Empty Signs, Historical Imaginaries: The Entangled Nationalization of Names and Naming in a Late Habsburg Borderland
Ágoston Berecz

Volume 26
Men under Fire: Motivation, Morale and Masculinity among Czech Soldiers in the Great War, 1914–1918
Jiří Hutečka

Volume 25
Nationalism Revisited: Austrian Social Closure from Romanticism to the Digital Age
Christian Karner

Volume 24
Entangled Entertainers: Jews and Popular Culture in Fin-de-Siècle Vienna
Klaus Hödl

For a full volume listing, please see the series page on our website:
http://berghahnbooks.com/series/austrian-habsburg-studies.

The Vienna Gestapo, 1938–1945

Crimes, Perpetrators, Victims

Elisabeth Boeckl-Klamper, Thomas Mang and
Wolfgang Neugebauer

Translated by John Nicholson and Nick Somers

First published in 2022 by
Berghahn Books
www.berghahnbooks.com

© 2022, 2025 Elisabeth Boeckl-Klamper, Thomas Mang and Wolfgang Neugebauer
First paperback edition published in 2025

All rights reserved. Except for the quotation of short passages
for the purposes of criticism and review, no part of this book
may be reproduced in any form or by any means, electronic or
mechanical, including photocopying, recording, or any information
storage and retrieval system now known or to be invented,
without written permission of the publisher.

Library of Congress Cataloging-in-Publication Data

Names: Boeckl-Klamper, Elisabeth, 1956- author | Mang, Thomas Franz, author | Neugebauer, Wolfgang, 1944- author
Title: The Vienna Gestapo, 1938-1945 : crimes, perpetrators, victims / Elisabeth Boeckl-Klamper, Thomas Mang, and Wolfgang Neugebauer ; translated by John Nicholson and Nick Somers.
Other titles: Gestapo-Leitstelle Wien 1938-1945. English
Description: New York : Berghahn Books, 2022. | Series: Austrian and Habsburg studies ; volume 33 | Includes bibliographical references and index.
Identifiers: LCCN 2021028805 (print) | LCCN 2021028806 (ebook) | ISBN 9781800732599 (hardback) | ISBN 9781800732605 (ebook)
Subjects: LCSH: Germany. Geheime Staatspolizei. Staatspolizeileitstelle Wien. | Holocaust, Jewish (1939-1945)--Austria--Vienna.
Classification: LCC HV8202.V5 B6313 2022 (print) | LCC HV8202.V5 (ebook) | DDC 363.2/30943613--dc23
LC record available at https://lccn.loc.gov/2021028805
LC ebook record available at https://lccn.loc.gov/2021028806

British Library Cataloguing in Publication Data
A catalogue record for this book is available from the British Library

ISBN 978-1-80073-259-9 hardback
ISBN 978-1-83695-053-0 paperback
ISBN 978-1-83695-186-5 epub
ISBN 978-1-80073-260-5 web pdf

https://doi.org/10.3167/9781800732599

Contents

List of Figures and Charts	vii
Acknowledgements	ix
Notes on Text and Transliteration	xi
List of Abbreviations	xii
Glossary	xvi
Introduction	1
Chapter 1. The Gestapo as the Central Terror Instrument of the Nazi Regime	9
Chapter 2. Establishment of the Gestapo in Austria and of Its Regional Headquarters in Vienna	24
Chapter 3. Hotel Metropole: Headquarters of the Vienna Gestapo	47
Chapter 4. The Gestapo in the Network of the SS and Political Structures – Organization of the Vienna Gestapo	63
Chapter 5. The Officials and Employees of the Vienna Gestapo	83
Chapter 6. Working Procedures and Methods of the Vienna Gestapo	114
Chapter 7. Informants and Cell Spies – 'Radio Games'	140
Chapter 8. Denunciations	151
Chapter 9. Mass Arrests	162
Chapter 10. The Vienna Gestapo and the Persecution of the Jews	174

Chapter 11. Persecution of the Catholic Church and Other
    Religious Bodies   209
Chapter 12. Suppression of Organized Resistance   232
Chapter 13. Suppression of Non-organized Resistance   267
Chapter 14. Oberlanzendorf 'Labour Education Camp'   296
Chapter 15. Vienna Gestapo Officials on 'External Deployment'   308
Chapter 16. End-Phase Crimes   324
Chapter 17. The End of the Vienna Gestapo   332
Chapter 18. Prosecution of Vienna Gestapo Officials   337
Summary and Conclusion   358

Bibliography   371
Index   389

Figures and Charts

Figures

3.1	The former Hotel Metropole, headquarters of the Vienna Gestapo 1938–45.	49
5.1	An office in Hotel Metropole, showing Josef Auinger with his staff.	92
5.2	Rosa Friedl, secretary in the Vienna Gestapo intelligence section.	95
5.3	Group of Vienna Gestapo officials, probably in front of Huber's office as IdSuSD.	96
5.4	Franz Josef Huber, head of the Vienna Gestapo 1938–44.	104
5.5	Karl Ebner, deputy head of the Vienna Gestapo 1942–44.	107
6.1	Vienna Gestapo official Franz Rudischer.	128
9.1	Gestapa 'protective custody' order for the Socialist resistance fighter Rosa Jochmann.	169
10.1	Josef Löwenherz, director of the Vienna Jewish Community; photo taken during the raid of 18 March 1938.	181
12.1	Burgtheater actor and Gestapo informant Otto Hartmann before the Vienna Volksgericht, 1947.	234
12.2	Resistance activist Franz Josef Messner.	236
12.3	Otto Ernst Andreasch, leader of the Vienna League of Mischlings.	248
12.4	Tortured to death by the Gestapo: Soviet civilian forced labourer Nikolaj Baran.	259
13.1	Socialist resistance activist Ella Lingens.	281

15.1 Shooting of Jewish men in eastern Europe (photograph found on Felix Landau when he was arrested). 314

15.2 Vienna Gestapo official Friedrich Kranebitter, head of the Verona Gestapo from January 1943. 315

18.1 Johann Sanitzer before the Vienna Volksgericht, January 1949. 352

Charts

Vienna Gestapo organization charts (GVPs, abbreviated in schematic form):

4.1 1st Vienna Gestapo GVP, 1938–41. 75

4.2 2nd Vienna Gestapo GVP, 1942–44. 77

4.3 3rd Vienna Gestapo GVP, 1944–45. 79

Acknowledgements

For the production of the original German-language publication, its translation into English and research work, generous financial support was provided by the Future Fund of the Republic of Austria (Zukunftsfonds der Republik Österreich), for which we express our sincere thanks to the fund's former and present presidents Kurt Scholz and Herwig Hösele, and its secretary general Margit Dumfahrt. For a further grant we thank the National Fund of the Republic of Austria for Victims of National Socialism (Nationalfonds der Republik Österreich für Opfer des Nationalsozialismus). In our research, we received invaluable assistance from the Documentation Centre of Austrian Resistance (Dokumentationsarchiv des österreichischen Widerstandes, DÖW) and its director Gerhard Baumgartner, and from staff of the Austrian Research Agency for Post-War Justice (Forschungsstelle Nachkriegsjustiz: Winfried Garscha, Claudia Kuretsidis-Haider, Siegfried Sanwald), which is closely associated with the DÖW, and at all stages of the project we were the beneficiaries of highly competent support given by DÖW staff, in particular Dr Christa Mehany. We are obliged to the director and relevant staff members of the Municipal and Provincial Archives of Vienna (Wiener Stadt- und Landesarchiv) and the Austrian State Archive (Österreichisches Staatsarchiv) for making relevant archive holdings available to us. In this regard we also extend our thanks to foreign archives, in particular the Federal Archives (Bundesarchiv), Berlin, and the Archives of the Republic of Slovenia, Ljubljana. For valuable input and for allowing us to consult documents in their possession, we offer sincere thanks to our historian colleagues Hans Schafranek, Peter Pirker, Hans Hautmann (†), Manfred Mugrauer, Josef Vogl and Wilhelm Mensing. We are likewise indebted to John Nicholson and Nick Somers for their English translation, and we thank Matthäus Zinner for kindly adapting three German diagrams for the English edition. We wish to express our special gratitude to the publisher of the original German edition, Heribert Steinbauer – who as a child witnessed the Vienna Gestapo conducting searches at his family home – for generously ceding the rights for the English edition to Berghahn Books. We thank Marion Berghahn for agreeing to include our book in her catalogue, and her staff members Sulaiman Ahmad, Chris Chappell, Mykelin Higham and Caroline Kuhtz for their attentive and conscientious work in seeing the present volume through to publication.

Notes on Text and Transliteration

In some cases, Russian names are not transliterated according to an English-language system but, rather, as they appear in the archival sources (e.g. 'Ostarbeiter' such as Iwan Schelasko, Igor Truskowski and others). Likewise, the ß is retained in German names (e.g. Seyß-Inquart).

Police and SS ranks have been left in German. For a list of the Gestapo ranks and corresponding SS ranks, see Chapter 5, n. 49. Military ranks have also been left in German. For British equivalents, see Wikipedia.

Vienna is divided up by 'district' ('Bezirk'). The 1st district is the inner city within the Ring, which is surrounded by the 2nd to 9th districts. Outside these are the 10th to 23rd districts. Under the National Socialists, the city borders were expanded to form the Reichsgau of Vienna, with three further districts.

Of the many words and expressions rendered in German, the great majority are jargon or colloquialisms specific to the Nazi regime, for example, *Wehrkraftzersetzung, Ostarbeiter, Rassenschande* or 'Altreich'. When these are not put in quotation marks, this is not to suggest that they form part of normal German discourse.

ABBREVIATIONS

AdR: Archiv der Republik / Archive of the Republic (of Austria).

AEL: Arbeitserziehungslager, literally 'work education camp', de facto a Gestapo concentration camp.

AVA: Allgemeines Verwaltungsarchiv / General Administration Archive – part of the ÖStA.

ARS: Archives of the Republic of Slovenia.

BA Berlin: Bundesarchiv / Federal Archives (Berlin).

BDM: Bund Deutscher Mädel / League of German Girls – female section of the Hitler Youth.

BdSuSD: Befehlshaber der Sicherheitspolizei und des SD / Commander-in-Chief of the Security Police and SD (in a given area).

BMF: Bundesministerium für Finanzen / Federal Ministry of Finance (Austria).

CV: Österreichischer Cartellverband – Austrian union of Catholic university fraternities, for students and graduates.

DAF: Deutsche Arbeitsfront / German Work Front.

DAW: Diözesanarchiv Wien / Diocesan Archive, Vienna.

d. G.: des Generalstabs / on the General Staff (Austrian Army).

DM: Deutschmark – German currency 1948–91.

DÖW: Dokumentationsarchiv des österreichischen Widerstandes / Documentation Centre of Austrian Resistance.

EG: Einsatzgruppe – 'deployment group'; see Glossary.

EK: Einsatzkommando – 'deployment commando unit', subunit of an EG.

FSB: Federalnaya sluzhba bezopasnosti Rossiyskoy Federatsii / Federal Security Service (Russian Federation).

GDR: German Democratic Republic (East Germany).

Gestapa: Geheimes Staatspolizeiamt / Secret State Police Office (Berlin).

Gestapo: Geheime Staatspolizei / Secret State Police.

GVP: Geschäftsverteilungsplan – literally 'business distribution plan', organizational chart; see Glossary.

HJ: Hitler-Jugend / Hitler Youth – youth organization of the Nazi state.

HSSPF: Höherer SS- und Polizeiführer / Higher SS and Police Leader.

IBV: Internationale Bibelforscher-Vereinigung / International Association of Bible Students – i.e. the Jehovah's Witnesses.

IdSuSD: Inspekteur der Sicherheitspolizei und des SD / Inspector of the Security Police and SD (in a given area).

IfZ: Institut für Zeitgeschichte München / Institute for Contemporary History, Munich.

i. G.: im Generalstab / on the General Staff (German army).

IKG: Israelitische Kultusgemeinde / Jewish Community (of Vienna).

Juva: Judenvermögensabgabe / Jewish Assets Tax – a special property tax for the Jews, introduced after the November Pogrom of 1938.

KdSuSD: Kommandeur der Sipo und des SD / Commander of the Sipo and SD (in a given area).

KJV: Kommunistischer Jugendverband / Communist Youth League.

KPD: Kommunistische Partei Deutschlands / Communist Party of Germany.

KPÖ: Kommunistische Partei Österreichs / Communist Party of Austria.

Kripo: Kriminalpolizei / Criminal Investigation Police.

KVG: Kriegsverbrechergesetz / War Criminals Act (Republic of Austria, 26 June 1945).

KZ: Konzentrationslager / concentration camp.

LG: Landesgericht, Landgericht / Regional Court – in the Nazi period 'Landgericht' (as in Germany), otherwise 'Landesgericht' for Austria.

MLW: Mischlingsliga Wien / Vienna League of Mischlings.

NARA: National Archives and Records Administration.

n.d.: no date.

NKVD: Narodnyiy Komissariat Vnutrennikh Del / People's Commissariat for Internal Affairs.

NS: nationalsozialistisch / National Socialist.

NSDAP: Nationalsozialistische Deutsche Arbeiter-Partei / National Socialist German Workers' Party (the Nazi party).

NSKK: Nationalsozialistisches Kraftfahrkorps / National Socialist Motor Corps.

O5: Cross-party resistance group (O5 = *Oe*sterreich, *e* being the fifth letter of the alphabet).

OLG: Oberlandesgericht / Higher Regional Court.

Orpo: Ordnungspolizei – literally 'Order Police', the regular uniformed police.

OSS: Office of Strategic Services (US).

ÖStA: Österreichisches Staatsarchiv / Austrian State Archive.

ÖVP: Österreichische Volkspartei / Austrian People's Party (founded 1945).

PAAA: Politisches Archiv des Auswärtigen Amts / Political Archive of the Foreign Ministry (Germany).

PCF: Parti communiste français / French Communist Party.

POEN: Provisorisches Österreichisches Nationalkomitee / Provisional Austrian National Committee – cross-party resistance group 1944–45.

RAD: Reichsarbeitsdienst / Reich Labour Service.

RGBl.: Reichsgesetzblatt / Reich Law Gazette.

RH: Rote Hilfe / Red Aid.

RM: Reichsmark.

RMI, RMdI: Reichsministerium des Innern / Reich Ministry of the Interior.

RS: Revolutionäre Sozialisten / Revolutionary Socialists.

RSHA: Reichssicherheitshauptamt / Reich Security Main Office.

RSt: Reichsstatthalter / Reich Governor – normally the same person as the NSDAP Gauleiter.

RStGB: Reichsstrafgesetzbuch / Reich Penal Code.

SA: Sturmabteilung – literally 'Storm Division' (of the NSDAP), 'Stormtroopers', 'Brownshirts'.

SAH: Sozialistische Arbeiterhilfe / Socialist Workers' Aid.

Schupo: Schutzpolizei – literally 'Protection Police' – part of the Orpo.

SD: Sicherheitsdienst des Reichsführers-SS / Security Service of the Reichsführer-SS – i.e. the SS Security Service.

SDLA Wien: Sicherheitsdienst Leitabschnitt Wien – the SD in Vienna.

SDAP: Sozialdemokratische Arbeiterpartei / (Austrian) Social Democratic Workers' Party (1889–1934).

SED: Sozialistische Einheitspartei Deutschlands / Socialist Unity Party of Germany (GDR).

SG: Sondergericht / Special Court.

SHAEF: Supreme Headquarters Allied Expeditionary Force.

Sipo, Sich. Pol.: Sicherheitspolizei / Security Police (Gestapo and Kripo).

SOE: Special Operations Executive (Great Britain).

SPÖ: Sozialdemokratische Partei Österreichs / Social Democratic Party of Austria (1945–91: Sozialistische Partei Österreichs).

SS: Schutzstaffel – literally 'protection squad'.

Staatspol. Abt.: Staatspolizeiliche Abteilung / State Police Department.

Stasi: Staatssicherheitsdienst / State Security Service (GDR).

StGBl.: Staatsgesetzblatt / State Law Gazette.

TA: Travail Allemand or Travail Anti-Allemand – section of the French Resistance founded by the PCF, so called because its work was directed at German soldiers.

V-Mann, V-Leute: Vertrauensmann, Vertrauensleute – literally 'confidence man / person', i.e. informant, informants (of both sexes).

VG, Vg: Volksgericht / People's Court (1945–55).

Vg: Verbotsgesetz / Prohibition Act (1945, amended 1947).

VGH: Volksgerichtshof / People's Court (NS), 1934–45.

Vugesta: Verwaltungsstelle (or Verwertungsstelle) für das Umzugsgut jüdischer Emigranten bei der Gestapo Wien / Vienna Gestapo Office for the Administration of Removals Goods of Jewish Emigrants – only Vienna had an office of this kind.

WStLA: Wiener Stadt- und Landesarchiv / Municipal and Provincial Archives of Vienna.

ZK: Zentralkomitee / Central Committee (of the KPÖ).

ZStL: Zentrale Stelle der Landesjustizverwaltungen zur Aufklärung nationalsozialistischer Verbrechen (for short, Zentrale Stelle der Landesjustizverwaltungen Ludwigsburg) / Central Office of the State Justice Administrations for the Investigation of National Socialist Crimes – located in Ludwigsburg, Germany.

GLOSSARY

'Alter Kämpfer': literally 'old fighter', 'veteran'. In the Austrian context, member of the NSDAP before the Austrian prohibition of the party in 1933 and during the years of prohibition.

'Altreich': German Reich in its 1937 borders (without Austria). Similarly, 'Reich-German' and 'Reich Germans' ('Reichsdeutsch', 'Reichsdeutsche') refer to Germans from the 'Altreich'.

Einsatzgruppen (EGs): special operation units formed from the Sipo and SD with the purpose of murdering Jews and other groups of the population in occupied Eastern Europe, divided up into 16 Einsatzkommandos (EKs).

'Funkspiele': literally 'radio games', disinformation transmitted by Allied parachute agents under pressure of torture.

Geschäftsverteilungsplan ('business distribution plan', GVP): The GVPs regulated the organizational structure of Gestapo offices and regional headquarters, on the pattern of the structure of the Gestapa, or from 1939, the RSHA.

Gestapo-Leitstelle: 'Gestapo regional headquarters' (23 in the German Reich).

Gestapostelle: regular Gestapo office, subordinate to a Gestapo-Leitstelle.

Gestapo branch office: subsidiary office of a Gestapo Leitstelle or regular office.

Heimtücke: literally 'insidiousness, malice, treachery' (against the regime). The 'Heimtückegesetz' was the common term for the law against 'insidious utterances' ('heimtückische Äußerungen').

'illegals': Austrian NSDAP members/activists during the prohibition years 1933–38.

Ostmark: Nazi designation for Austria as annexed in 1938, from 1942 officially the 'Alpine and Danube Gaus' (strictly speaking, 'Reichsgaus'): 'Vienna' (expanded), 'Lower Danube' (seat of government in Vienna, Gau capital Krems), 'Upper Danube' (Linz), Tyrol-Vorarlberg (Innsbruck), Styria (Graz), Salzburg (Salzburg).

Reichsstatthalter: Reich Governor. Normally the RSt was also Gauleiter, i.e. both Reich Governor and NSDAP leader for a given Gau/Reichsgau.

'Rücküberstellung' (remand): To ensure that detainees reported to the courts were not sentenced too leniently or did not go free after being acquitted, the Gestapo usually applied to the courts for the defendants to be returned to them ('remanded'). See the section 'Referrals to State Prosecutors and Courts, Applications for Remand' in Chapter 6.

'Sonderbehandlung': 'special treatment', official Nazi cover term for extra-legal killings, usually carried out in concentration camps.

'verschärfte Vernehmung': 'enhanced interrogation' (official Gestapo cover term for torture).

'Wehrkraftzersetzung': 'undermining military morale', offence introduced in 1938, potentially carrying the death sentence, applied for the prosecution of conscientious objectors, defeatists et al.

'Ostarbeiter': 'Eastern worker/s', forced labourers deported from the occupied territories of Eastern Europe (strictly, those from the Soviet Union).

Introduction

The secret state police of the National Socialist regime – Geheime Staatspolizei, or Gestapo for short – has become a byword for the secret police in totalitarian systems. The expression 'Gestapo methods' has gone into common parlance as a damning political insult. The Vienna Gestapo was the most important instrument of Nazi terror on Austrian soil. It was responsible for combating all forms of resistance, organized and non-organized, and played a leading part in the persecution of the Jewish population. It treated all who violated Nazi norms with unrelenting severity, and was particularly brutal towards foreign forced labourers.

Founded in 1938 with the official full name 'Geheime Staatspolizei – Staatspolizeileitstelle Wien', it was the biggest Gestapo office with the exception of the central head office in Berlin: until 1939 the secret state police office (Geheimes Staatspolizeiamt, Gestapa) and thereafter Amt IV of the Reich security main office (Reichssicherheitshauptamt, RSHA). The word 'Leitstelle' in the Vienna Gestapo's official name literally means 'leading office', and it is translated in the present volume as 'regional headquarters'. With a staff of over nine hundred, the Vienna Gestapo was numerically the largest Gestapo 'Leitstelle' in the German Reich, and bigger than Berlin or Prague. It was also second to none in the number of arrests it made, which amounted to around fifty thousand. The arrestees were commonly subjected to brutal interrogations and torture before being either committed to concentration camps or handed over to the courts to be tried. The area of competence of the Vienna Gestapo extended over the eastern part of annexed Austria – that is to say, over the former federal provinces of Vienna, Lower Austria and (north) Burgenland – and the parts of former Czechoslovakia incorporated into the Reichsgau 'Lower Danube' (Niederdonau). It had a total population of over 3.5 million, which was more than half the population of Austria at the time (1939 census: 6.65 million inhabitants, 6.88 million including the incorporated territories). On account of the Reich's new borders with (rump) Czechoslovakia (or, after the latter's occupation, with the Protectorate of Bohemia and Moravia and with Slovakia) and Hungary, the Vienna Gestapo acquired further important responsibilities and tasks, especially as it was also in charge of the border police and its stations and border posts. Writing the history of the Vienna Gestapo – including the post-war prosecution (or non-prosecution) of its former officials – is thus an important task, to which it is hoped that the present volume will be a valuable contribution.

There are numerous publications on the Nazi police machinery in the 'Altreich' (i.e. Germany in its pre-1938 borders): with regard to the Gestapo, see among others the seminal studies by Gerhard Paul/Klaus-Michael Mallmann and Robert Gellately, and the admirably concise account by Carsten Dams/Michael Stolle.[1] On the Gestapo in Austria, by contrast, there are only a few. In 1991, Franz Weisz presented an extensive doctoral thesis on the Vienna Gestapo, which was meritorious for its recording and analysis of important source materials, in particular the post-war trials of Vienna Gestapo officials by the Vienna Volksgericht, and this performed important preparatory work for the present volume. However, because of its lack of analyses and historical contextualization, Weisz's thesis had, to a large extent, the character of a voluminous, unstructured and uncommented collection of material, and therefore could not be published.[2] Important findings concerning central figures of the Vienna Gestapo have been provided in the degree dissertation and doctoral thesis of Thomas Mang, his dissertation being on the head of the section colloquially known as the *Judenreferat* ('Jewish section') Karl Ebner, and his thesis on Vienna Gestapo head Franz Josef Huber.[3] These studies also shed light on the part played by the Vienna Gestapo in the deportations of Jews from Vienna from February 1941, which is still insufficiently recognized, and the strategy of 'reinsurance' successfully implemented by Ebner and Huber, which enabled these two heavily incriminated Gestapo officials to survive the prosecutions of the post-war era. Two further Vienna University degree dissertations have been devoted to important Vienna Gestapo officials: one by Christine Cézanne-Thauss on intelligence section head Lambert Leutgeb, and the second on the department head Othmar Trenker.[4] A number of thoroughly researched studies on the Vienna Gestapo's system of informers have been published by Hans Schafranek, who has presented and analysed the devastating impact of the infiltration of undercover agents into the ranks of the resistance groups.[5]

In this connection, finally, mention must be made of the research studies published by the Dokumentationsarchiv des österreichischen Widerstandes (Documentation centre of Austrian resistance, DÖW) and publications by Wolfgang Neugebauer, which primarily focus on the resistance but at the same time provide a great deal of information about the activity of the Vienna Gestapo.[6] An extensive source base has been created through the digitalization and partial publication on the DÖW website of the Vienna Gestapo's identification card index ('Erkennungsdienstliche Kartei', preserved at the Wiener Stadt- und Landesarchiv) and the online publication of the Vienna Gestapo daily reports (now only accessible to institutions under licence, see Bibliography);[7] however, while these sources are relevant for research into resistance and repression, and were duly utilized for the present publication, they provide hardly any information on the internal structure of the Vienna Gestapo, or on the individuals responsible for its crimes.

Our interest in Gestapo research was the result of decades devoted to the subject of resistance and repression in the Nazi period. In the course of her many years as DÖW archivist, Elisabeth Boeckl-Klamper evaluated all the Gestapo documents archived or acquired for archiving there, and played a leading role in the creation of the newly designed memorial room and exhibition in the Leopold Figl-Hof apartment block at the site of the former Vienna Gestapo headquarters on Morzinplatz, also acting as editor for its website and publication.[8] In addition to the above-mentioned studies, Thomas Mang has published biographical accounts of Franz Josef Huber and Karl Ebner, the two most important officials of the Vienna Gestapo.[9] Wolfgang Neugebauer conducted and published numerous studies on Nazi terror during his many years as director of the DÖW, focusing particularly on the Gestapo's role in the suppression of resistance; in addition, as honorary professor of contemporary history at Vienna University, he lectured and supervised several degree dissertations and doctoral theses on the Gestapo. Our goal – on the basis of our knowledge and the current findings of research in Austrian and foreign archives and other international research – was to compose as comprehensive as possible an account of the Vienna Gestapo in the years 1938–45, with a presentation and analysis not only of the victims of persecution and repression but also of the structures, organization and individuals actively involved on the Gestapo side, and with at least a rough picture of what became of the perpetrators in the post-war period.

The present volume starts by presenting the development of the Gestapo into the Nazi regime's central instrument of repression, culminating in the foundation of RSHA in Berlin, and the process of fusion – promoted by Reichsführer-SS Himmler – of the security police (Sicherheitspolizei, or 'Sipo' – i.e. the Gestapo and the criminal investigation police (Kriminalpolizei, or 'Kripo')), the regular uniformed police or 'order' police (Ordnungspolizei, or 'Orpo'), and the SS. The section on the RSHA (and its forerunner agency the Gestapa) is relevant in that in 1938 the Vienna Gestapo was modelled exactly on the Berlin office, the structure of which was laid down in a 'business distribution plan' (Geschäftsverteilungsplan, GVP), and when the GVP changed in 1942 and 1944, the changes were also implemented in Vienna. Notwithstanding the dominance of the Berlin central offices, which at the beginning at least appointed 'Reich Germans' to leading positions in the Vienna Gestapo, the present volume gives detailed consideration to the active part played by Austrian National Socialists (who until March 1938 were members of a prohibited political party and thus 'illegals') in the overthrow of the Vienna police and to the recruitment into the Gestapo of officials of the pre-annexation Austrian police, with particular attention to the additional incorporation of Gestapo officials into the SS. The Vienna Gestapo staff structure is investigated on the basis of statistical data, with consideration given to the role played by women on the Gestapo staff.

One special aspect of the study is the presentation of the criminal methods employed by the Vienna Gestapo, including the systematic use of torture to extract confessions and coerce victims into betraying fellow resisters, and committals to concentration camps; in this context, a special chapter is devoted to the most efficient method of suppression used by the Vienna Gestapo, namely, the extensive deployment of informers. Another special focus is laid upon denunciations. As a contribution to the ongoing debate on this subject, the extent of denunciation and the composition of the denouncers are analysed in order to assess the place and importance of denunciation in this historical context.

A number of substantial chapters focus on the fate of the Vienna Gestapo's victims, the most important categories being political and religious opponents and resistance fighters, Jews, young oppositionals, persons stigmatized as 'asocials', and last but not least the foreign forced labourers, who have hitherto been wrongly neglected in Gestapo research. In connection with this group, a special chapter is devoted to the '(forced) labour education camp' (Arbeitserziehungslager, AEL) of Oberlanzendorf, which was de facto a Vienna Gestapo concentration camp. Furthermore, an ample account is given of the Vienna Gestapo's part in the persecution of the Jews, which in some publications has been underestimated in comparison with that of the 'Central Office for the Emigration of Jews in Vienna' established by Adolf Eichmann; in particular, an account is given of the critical initiative undertaken by Gauleiter Baldur von Schirach in collaboration with Vienna Gestapo head Franz Josef Huber that led directly to the deportations.

Particular attention is also devoted to the history of the building on Morzinplatz that served as the Vienna Gestapo headquarters – from the construction of the Hotel Metropole in 1872/73 through to its seizure in 1938 and final destruction from direct hits in the bombing of 1945. In the relevant chapter, a lengthy section is devoted to the two most prominent figures to have been detained at Morzinplatz – former Austrian federal chancellor Kurt Schuschnigg and the banker Louis Rothschild. Equally detailed attention is paid to the first transport of Austrians to Dachau in 1938 and to later mass arrests, notably before the outbreak of war in 1939 and after the assassination attempt and resistance operation of 20 July 1944. In the concluding chapters, accounts are given of the part played by the Vienna Gestapo in the end-phase crimes of 1945 – for example, the murder of captured American pilots – and of the end of the Vienna Gestapo regional headquarters, which was given up without a fight, its protagonists retreating or going underground after taking all possible measures to destroy evidence of their deeds. Finally, the volume concludes with a critical account of the way in which the Austrian and German judiciary and the denazification bodies dealt with the crimes of the Vienna Gestapo and its officials.

The volume also considers five key issues of Gestapo research:

1. The 'Gestapo myth' – that is to say, the idea cultivated and propagated by Himmler and Heydrich of the security police being ubiquitous and all-powerful. It has played an important role in modern Gestapo research (Paul/Mallmann 1995, Gellately 1990, and others). While the deconstruction of this myth is in itself right and good, it does run the risk of tending to make light of or underestimate the work carried out by the Gestapo. It was thus an important concern for us to examine the effectiveness and efficiency of the Gestapo, its 'success', which we have done principally in relation to its suppression of resistance.

2. Denunciations. As a result of certain far-reaching interpretations, denunciations from the general public have been perceived as being of high importance for the evaluation not only of the Gestapo but of the Nazi regime as a whole. In particular, this has led to a tendency to relativize the dictatorial character of the Nazi regime (by invoking the existence of a 'nationalsozialistischer Volksstaat' or 'National Socialist people's state'). The extent of such denunciations, the social and political categorization of the denouncers, and the contexts in which the denunciations were made are thus important thematic areas for the present study.

3. Austrian perpetrators. Not only was the proportion of Austrians amongst Nazi perpetrators generally played down in the post-war era but apologias, such as that of Vienna Gestapo deputy head Karl Ebner, made light of their crimes by claiming that the Austrian Gestapo officials were far more moderate than their German colleagues. In the present publication, the subject of Austrian perpetrators is thus not considered merely in terms of statistics: attention is also given to the questions of whether it is possible to demonstrate differences in the procedures followed by Austrian and German officials, whether the distinction was of any relevance at all in practice, and to what extent tensions or conflicts developed.

4. 'Reinsurance'. The leading officials of the Vienna Gestapo, Franz Josef Huber and Karl Ebner, both pursued the strategy of 'reinsurance' by giving favourable treatment to prominent detainees, especially from the Catholic-conservative camp, with a view to guaranteeing their own sur-

vival after the end of the Nazi regime. A special section is devoted to the presentation and analysis of this – ultimately successful – strategy.

5. Women perpetrators? Researchers into National Socialism are increasingly using the gendered term 'TäterInnen' ('male and female perpetrators'), which tends to imply that women had a substantial share in the crimes of the Nazi regime, and even to put them on the same level as the men. By contrast, this volume establishes the actual number of women who worked for the Vienna Gestapo and their position in the hierarchy, and investigates the occasional instances of women participating in criminal acts.

When it came to the collapse of the Nazi regime, the leading Vienna Gestapo officials sought to erase all evidence of their crimes by setting about destroying the entire body of files, which they almost succeeded in doing. Fortunately for historians, however, the great majority of the Vienna Gestapo daily reports were in fact preserved, as copies were always sent to other NS authorities – not just to offices in Vienna but also to central offices in Berlin, where the Allies subsequently took possession of them and where they are now preserved in the German federal archives. An important secondary body of source material is provided by the records of the NS courts (VGH, Vienna OLG, Vienna SG; see list of abbreviations), as these often contain surveillance records, the findings of police investigations, accusations made by the Vienna Gestapo when reporting individuals to the prosecutors, and sometimes the testimonies of Gestapo officials. Arguably the most important source for the history of the Vienna Gestapo is the records of the post-war Vienna Volksgericht (People's Court, 1945–55), which are preserved in the Wiener Stadt- und Landesarchiv (WStLA). The documents relating to the police's investigations and preparatory research provide information on the organizational structure, training of officials, and administration of the Vienna Gestapo, and not least on its methods as it went about tasks ranging from the processing of complaints and the evaluation of informers' reports through to the systematic use of torture during interrogations. The judgments, statements of defendants and witnesses, and records of the main court proceedings combine to provide a comprehensive picture, which nevertheless for obvious reasons calls for critical interpretation. An important complementary source was the 'Gau files' of the NSDAP (the Nazi party) held in the Austrian state archives, which provided essential information, in particular on the biographies of individual Gestapo officials. Another source that turned out to be relevant was the archival holdings of Department I, state police department, Vienna police headquarters (Abteilung I, Staatspolizeiliche Abteilung, Bundespolizeidirektion Wien), which contain not only the – sadly few – extant original documents of the Vienna Gestapo, but also documents about the Vienna Gestapo drawn up after 1945 by the

Austrian state police; immediately after the collapse of the Nazi regime, these two holdings of documents formed the basis for the tracking down and detention of former Vienna Gestapo officials.

At the German federal archives, the holdings of the RSHA and the former US Berlin Document Center were particularly revealing sources for the present study. Another foreign state archive that – surprisingly – turned out to be an important source of information was the archives of the Republic of Slovenia in Ljubljana, which holds a number of key documents on Vienna Gestapo officials stemming from police investigations and court proceedings in former Yugoslavia, in particular against Lambert Leutgeb, head of the Vienna Gestapo intelligence section. Important documents relating to the participation of the Vienna Gestapo and its head Franz Josef Huber in the preparations for the mass deportation of Vienna's Jewish population were found in the 'Austria Collection' of the Institute for Holocaust Research at Yad Vashem. From the National Archives and Records Administration, Washington DC, the most relevant items were the microfilms of the Vienna Gestapo's daily reports, which were in fact published many years ago. Since then, all the extant Vienna Gestapo daily reports have been made available online ('Deutsche Geschichte im 20. Jahrhundert Online', access now only possible under licence and to institutions).

Even in a volume of this length, it has not been possible to deal with all aspects of the subject thoroughly. Among the aspects insufficiently explored are the activities of the Vienna Gestapo units responsible for espionage and counter-intelligence, of the Gestapo branch offices, and of the border police stations and border posts; furthermore, the crimes committed by Vienna Gestapo officials in the occupied territories of Europe have been accorded little attention by historians and are dealt with here only through a number of representative examples. Other subjects requiring further research include the inadequate judicial prosecution of Vienna Gestapo officials, likewise presented here only in case studies relating to certain important figures, and the reintegration of former Gestapo officials into Austrian society after the waning of the anti-fascist spirit, characteristic of 1945.

Notes

1. Paul and Mallmann, *Die Gestapo – Mythos und Realität*; Paul/Mallmann, *Die Gestapo im Zweiten Weltkrieg*; Gellately, *The Gestapo and German Society*; Dams and Stolle, *Die Gestapo*.
2. Weisz, 'Die Geheime Staatspolizei'.
3. Mang, 'Retter, um sich selbst zu retten'; idem, 'Nicht in der Lage'.
4. Cezanne-Thauss, 'Lambert Leutgeb'; Pichler, 'Dr. Othmar Trenker'.
5. See especially Schafranek, *Widerstand und Verrat. Gestapospitzel im antifaschistischen Untergrund*.
6. See, among others, DÖW, *Widerstand und Verfolgung in Wien*, and Neugebauer, *Der österreichische Widerstand*, translated as *The Austrian Resistance 1938–1945* (Vienna, 2014).

7. http://www.doew.at/erinnern/personendatenbanken/gestapo-opfer (last accessed on 31 May 2021); Bailer and Form, 'Tagesrapporte der Gestapo-Leitstelle'.
8. 'Gedenkstätte für die Opfer der Gestapo Wien'.
9. Mang, *'Gestapo-Leitstelle Wien'*; idem, *Die Unperson*.

Chapter 1

THE GESTAPO AS THE CENTRAL TERROR INSTRUMENT OF THE NAZI REGIME

The Gestapa – Germ Cell of the Gestapo

After their takeover of power in the German Reich on 30 January 1933, the National Socialists immediately sought to gain control over the whole police apparatus. However, this goal could not be achieved simultaneously in all the federal states ('Länder') of the Reich: first, the Nazis had to take control of the Prussian police, which with its manpower of fifty thousand was the strongest of all the federal state forces. To this end, on the same day, 30 January 1933, Hermann Göring, as the second most powerful figure after Hitler, was appointed Reich commissioner for the Prussian interior ministry and thus also chief of the political police. The Prussian secret police thereby created was to become the germ cell of, and subsequently the binding model for, the secret state police (Geheime Staatspolizei, Gestapo) later organized uniformly throughout the Reich; in fact, 'Geheime Reichspolizei' was even one of the proposed names for it.[1]

With the so-called Reichstag Fire Decree of 28 February 1933,[2] the basic rights contained in the Weimar Constitution were suspended and the foundations laid for National Socialist police law. The 'permanent state of legal emergency' in the battle 'between the National Socialist state and its mortal enemies'[3] had begun: not for nothing did the jurist and political scientist Ernst Fraenkel describe the decree as the 'constitutional charter of the Third Reich'.[4] The first Gestapo law of 26 April 1933 and the establishment of the secret state police office (Geheimes Staatspolizeiamt, Gestapa) brought about a further and essential extension of the powers of the political police. By this time, the Gestapo, under the direction of Göring's protégé Rudolf Diels, had thus already acquired the status of a special authority; furthermore, it was placed directly under the control of Göring, now prime minister of Prussia.

Shortly after the takeover of power, the realization of the potential of a political police force under the aegis of the Nazi state led to a power struggle between the various institutions involved. Göring wanted to extend his Prussian political police uniformly throughout the Reich, which conflicted with the interests of Reich interior minister Wilhelm Frick. What Frick envisaged was a 'centralized Reich police into which, however, the Prussian political police was also to be integrated'. One way or the other, the Gauleiters and heads of government of the federal states feared that the centralization of the political police would reduce their powers. One particularly serious problem was that of the SA (Sturmabteilung, assault division), which not only laid claim to be the official Nazi 'Wehrmacht' (armed force) and thus successor to the Reichswehr but was also 'apparently presenting its reign of terror in the unauthorized concentration camps as the activity of a state police force'.[5]

That final outcome – the creation of a unified political police for the whole Reich under the leadership of Heinrich Himmler – was essentially the result of the overthrow of the SA in the operation of 30 June 1934 in which Hitler had Ernst Röhm and other SA leaders murdered, with a leading role being played by Himmler's SS. Subsequently – 'in recognition of its outstanding services' – the SS was separated from the SA, to which it had formerly belonged, and given the status of an NSDAP organization in its own right.

The Gestapo's critical contribution to the rapid erosion of constitutional norms came principally through its possession of a special executive instrument of its own in the form of 'Schutzhaft' or 'protective custody', which enabled it to arrest suspects and hold them in detention without a court ruling.[6] Given that the Gestapo had other police bodies at its beck and call, it could mobilize hundreds of police officers at short notice. As a result, it arrested over thirty thousand people between March and June 1933, mainly Communists, Social Democrats and trade unionists.

Originally, the duration of protective custody was limited to three months, and there was, in theory at least, the possibility of appealing against its imposition. However, even the Reichstag Fire Decree enabled protective custody to be imposed for an unlimited period and with no right of appeal. A year later – by which time Himmler was head of the Prussian political police and Reinhard Heydrich head of the Gestapa – the Gestapo's monopoly over protective custody was confirmed. Neither the NSDAP, the SA nor the SS had the power to take people into protective custody. As a rule, the imposition of protective custody meant committal to a concentration camp. A later decree defined it as a 'coercive measure of the secret state police' against people 'who by their behaviour endanger the security of Volk and state'.[7]

The jurist and 'Gestapo ideologist-in-chief' Werner Best defined the competence of the Gestapo as covering tasks concerned with 'police investigations in matters of high treason, state treason and explosives [i.e. sabotage] and related to other criminal attacks on party and state. However, more important than the prosecution of offences committed is their prevention'.[8] The Gestapo was thus not just a law enforcement body acting in the service of the judiciary: its terror was founded above all on its preventive policing tasks.

The Privilege of a Space to Operate Outside the Law

The victims of the Gestapo had no legal security at all, because arrests and concentration camp committals did not require proof of an offence or criminal behaviour: mere suspicion was enough. The Gestapo operated in a space outside the law – it possessed, to quote Ernst Fraenkel, 'a competence over competence, independent of the courts'.[9] On this basis, the Gestapo developed into an organ that had the authority to monitor and revise court judgments but was itself free from any control: if someone was convicted by a court of law, but in the eyes of the Gestapo too leniently sentenced, it took the prosecution into its own hands, committing the convicts to concentration camps or ordering their execution.

The third Gestapo law of 10 February 1936 ratified the establishment of the Gestapa as an autonomous special authority, and the political police became a constitutive component of the Nazi state. Paragraph 1 defined the task of the Gestapo as, 'to investigate and combat all activities dangerous to the state [*staatsgefährlich*] throughout its territory, and to collect and evaluate the results of those investigations'. As the Gestapo researchers Dams and Stolle point out, the use of the word *staatsgefährlich* as opposed to *staatsfeindlich* (hostile to the state) 'allowed for a broad scale when defining one's opponents'.[10] The power to define who was to be regarded as *staatsgefährlich* lay solely with the Gestapo. The vision of the police as an 'internal Wehrmacht' outside the law had won the day: the incorporation of the political police into the state administrative structure and its subordination to the legal system – as had been the case until then, at least de jure – was now turned on its head.

The Nazi understanding of law was now no longer based on the protection of the individual and the equality of all citizens before the law but on the priority of protecting the (supposed) interests of the *Volksgemeinschaft* (ethnic community). Paragraph 7 of the third Gestapo law made it crystal clear: 'Decisions and regulations of the Geheime Staatspolizei are not subject to review by the administrative courts'. As a result, in its dealings with political opponents, the Gestapo acquired powers similar to those of the judiciary. In no circumstances was it to be obstructed in its freedom of action by 'unpolitical' organs such as courts. For Reichsführer-SS Heinrich Himmler – by Hitler's decree of 17 June 1936 also chief of the German police in the Reich ministry of the interior – the police did not derive its powers 'from individual laws but ... from the tasks entrusted to it by the leadership. On this account, its powers may not be hampered by formal obstacles'.[11]

It was above all Werner Best who had the task of safeguarding the Gestapo against rival authorities and defending its position as an autonomous institution, unfettered by norms. For a time Heydrich's deputy at the Gestapa, Best was an unconditional and unscrupulous disciple of Nazi ideology. At the same time, he was a brilliant jurist who represented the prototype of a new leadership elite that contrasted strongly with the senior functionaries of the 'Kampfzeit' prior to 1933. Instead of the 'liberalistic' view of life, with its emphasis on the protection of the individual, Best championed the *völkisch* view: 'The *völkisch*-organic worldview does not see the original (primary) reality of human life in the individual human being ... but in the Volk'.[12] The purpose of the state was to preserve the 'power of the Volk' (*Volkskraft*) and promote its development. The state's activity was expressed by the 'will of the Leader' (*Führerwille*), which was binding, lawful and just, without regard for formalities.

From the Normative State to the Prerogative State

The arrogation of traditional state functions in accordance with the ideology of the NSDAP necessitated a complete reinterpretation of the classical concept of a constitution. The task of the constitution was no longer to order the rights and duties of the individual but to regulate the organism of the Volk as a whole. This no longer had anything to do with 'law' or 'justice' but, rather, with what Best called a 'primal and pre-legal creative and formative will'. Even today, the role model for a dictatorship is that of law proceeding from the 'people', personified by a quasi-democratically legitimized 'leader' figure.

This transformation is vividly illustrated by the example of the Gestapo: in a very short time, under political pressure, what had been an institution of the 'normative state' (Ernst Fraenkel) – and as such bound by the principles of the separation of legislature, executive and judiciary and of lawgiving – mutated into an institution of the National Socialist 'prerogative state'.[13] As Best apodictically put it, 'the normative legal regulation of the means to be used by a political police force [is] just as impossible as it is to foresee every kind of attack that could be made by enemies of the state ... at any time in the future'.[14] To put it more simply, any legal limitation on the Gestapo's methods was unthinkable, because it had to be prepared to react flexibly to 'every kind of attack'. In the fight against the 'enemy within' – like the Wehrmacht in the battle against the 'enemy without' – it had to be freed from 'all fixed and invariable legal forms' if it was to fulfil its task. In other words, the Gestapo was to act in a 'norm-free' space in order to protect the functions of the norm-bound state. By fighting the 'destructive forces' without being inhibited by statutory norms, the Gestapo enabled the state to act in accordance with the norms when dealing with the Volk's 'positive forces'.

The deriving of police law from '*völkisch* laws of life' constituted the ideological foundation for the terror measures of the SS/police machinery – right through to the extermination of European Jewry. Hostile, 'degenerative' elements within the German Volk or other peoples were obstacles to the vision of a 'healthy *Volksgemeinschaft*' and thus had to be eliminated.

While Wilhelm Stuckart, state secretary in the Reich interior ministry and co-drafter of the Nuremberg Laws, referred to the Jews as the 'ferment of decomposition',[15] Heydrich talked of the 'residue of an infection' that had to be eliminated, meaning thereby the remains of 'Jewish, liberal and Masonic' influence, which were summarized in his mind in one single enemy, namely, Judaism, the goal of which 'for ever remains … domination of the world'.

Like Best, Heydrich also invested hard thought in establishing an enemy stereotype for the Nazi mind, noting that according to the 'liberalist-democratic' way of thinking, *Staatsfeinde* (enemies of the state) had been those who were combated by the rulers of state. Changing governments and power-holders thus had – in accordance with the colour of the respective government – changing *Staatsfeinde*. But it was quite different with National Socialism, which knew only one kind of enemy, the 'enemy of the Volk', the *Volksfeind*.[16]

Himmler made a distinction between two types of *Volksfeind*, namely: 'People who on account of degeneration of either body or soul have separated themselves from the natural structures that make up the *Volksgemeinschaft*, and … people who as the instruments of [our] ideological and political enemies are striving to demolish the unity of the German Volk and destroy its state power; against these enemies of Volk and state the Gestapo wages its unremitting battle'.[17]

Thanks to the deliberate vagueness of the term *Volksfeind*, the Gestapo was able to arbitrarily define all manner of organizations and groups as enemies of the state – even without them doing anything *volksfeindlich* – and thus as enemies to be fought and destroyed. In the paranoid world of National Socialism, the list of *Volksfeinde* was a very long one, ranging from Communists, monarchists, 'politicizing churches' and homosexuals through to Jewry as the 'main enemy of the German Volk'.

The organizational chart ('Geschäftsverteilungsplan', literally 'business distribution plan', GVP) of Department II (Gestapa) of the political police office of 1 January 1938 gives an impression of the breadth of anti-opposition activities, which even extended into the ranks of Nazi organizations (Unit II H 2); this GVP's essential structure was to remain the definitive model for the Gestapo GVP as it changed in the course of the following years:

Section II A: Communism, Marxism, Soviet Russians, foreign subversion

Unit II A 1:   Communism
Unit II A 2:   Marxism
Unit II A 3:   Soviet Russians
Unit II A 4:   Evaluation of all manifestations of Communism worldwide
Unit II A 5:   Passport forgery

Section II B: Confessions, Jews, Freemasons, emigrants, pacifists

Unit II B 1:   Political Catholicism
Unit II B 2:   Protestant movement
Unit II B 3:   Emigrants
Unit II B 4:   Jews, Freemasons

Section II C: Reaction, opposition

Unit II C 1:   Former centre and right-wing parties, monarchism, nobility, societies and associations, paramilitary groupings (*Freikorps*)
Unit II C 2:   Black Front, Stennes movement, Sperr-Kreis (monarchist resistance movement in Bavaria), Jungdeutscher Orden (Young German order), Tannenberg-Bund

Section II D: Protective custody

Section II E: Economy

Unit II E 1:   Politico-economic affairs
Unit II E 2:   Politico-agricultural affairs
Unit II E 3:   Sociopolitical affairs
Unit II E 4:   Societies

Section II F: Card index, staff files, evaluation of political reputation

Section II G: Assassinations, surveillance, arms, troublemakers, identification service, 24-hour duty office, special tasks

Section II H: Party members

Unit II H 1:   Other affairs not covered by II H 2
Unit II H 2:   SA, SS, NSKK, Hitler Youth, BDM, DLV, Feldjägerkorps, Bündische Jugend

Section II J: Foreign police forces, dealings with foreign police

Section II P: Press

Unit II P 1:   Home press

Unit II P 2:	Foreign press
Unit II P 3:	Cultural politics, Catholic and Protestant press, sects, film, theatre
Section II S:	Homosexuality and abortion
Unit II S 1:	Homosexuality
Unit II S 2:	Abortion

The ministry of justice and certain parts of the corps of judges so inclined could do very little to resist Himmler's successful drive for the Gestapo to be given 'judiciary-like' forms and means in their dealings with political opponents. Although in the Weimar Republic the judgments against the left-wing camp had in principle been more severe than against the right wing, the judiciary's attempt to resist the growth in the Gestapo's power potential through more rigorous judicial practice only put it even more firmly on the defensive. Hitler's decision not to allow legal representation to defendants in Gestapo protective custody proceedings put a definitive end to resistance within the judiciary, which had in any case been modest: 'The Führer has prohibited the calling in of lawyers,' wrote Reichsführer-SS Himmler to the Reich minister of justice in 1935, 'and has instructed me to inform you of his decisions'.[18]

Amalgamation of Police and SS: Dismantling the State Monopoly on the Use of Force

The ambitions of Himmler and Heydrich, in the pursuit of which they were very largely able to count on Hitler's support, went much further than the intermediate goal of establishing a state secret police unimpeded by legal constraints. Their ultimate goal was a centralized structure unified throughout the Reich, and a police force with one homogeneous ideological orientation, entirely independent of all other authorities in the German Reich.

The definitive decision for the centralization of the police had been made as early as 1936 with Himmler's appointment as chief of the German police, which vastly increased his power and that of his SS. He was now in control of the entire German police including the criminal investigation police (Kriminalpolizei, Kripo), the 'protection police' (Schutzpolizei, Schupo) and the rural police (Gendarmerie). As a result, he was able to extend the competence of the political police, which until then had been restricted to the prosecution of political offences, to deviant social behaviour and to aligning the entire police machinery with the racial ideology of the SS, under oath. This created the conditions required for the police to focus entirely on the task of guaranteeing the 'health of the German ethnic body [Volkskörper]' – which was indeed the critical justification, supported by Hitler, for the amalgamation of the police and

NSDAP machinery. Ulrich Herbert interprets this fusion of party and state tasks, which was intended by Werner Best to be a 'general empowerment of the political police', as a 'constitutive component of the National Socialist Führer state'.[19]

Himmler's vision of a state defence corps (Staatsschutzkorps) implied the operational and above all the ideological amalgamation of the security police (Sipo, i.e. Gestapo and Kripo) – that is to say, a state institution – with the SS, an NSDAP organization. This was a process unthinkable under any democratic constitution. It 'was characterized by the combination of the "normative" and the "prerogative" state, the fusion of the adopted civil service apparatus with an ideologically elitist organization, and the ever-closer interlocking of the legal and the ideological legitimization of terror'.[20]

Most members of the Sipo bore civil service titles, were paid according to the law governing civil servants, and were subordinate to the Reich interior minister Wilhelm Frick, who naturally resisted the privatization of his police by Himmler's SS. Himmler, however, with Hitler's support, had no trouble in thwarting Frick's ambition of incorporating the Sipo into the overall framework of a centralized police force. Writing in a Festschrift in honour of Frick's 60th birthday, Himmler stated – with unmistakable irony – that 'although considerable work' admittedly still had to be done, 'under Reichsminister Frick, a unified executive and security force for the German Reich has been created for the first time in a thousand years'.[21]

Finally, as a gesture of goodwill towards Frick, the matter was regulated through the meaningless compromise formulation contained in the full designation of Himmler's office: 'Reichsführer-SS and Chief of the German Police in the Reich Ministry of the Interior'. In practice, however, this in no way implied that Himmler or Heydrich's Reich security main office (RSHA) were subordinate or answerable to Frick. In terms both of personnel and the institution itself, there was from the beginning a strict separation between the RSHA and the ministry, until finally, on 24 August 1943, Himmler himself became minister of the interior.

The monopoly on the use of force held by the state and its police had now definitively passed to the SS, the 'private army of a political party'.[22] The idea of the state had been eroded to a historic low: from the Platonic-Aristotelian idea of a state that does not consist in power and domination but facilitates 'the best, perfect life', via the state as the holder of the 'monopoly over the legitimate use of force' (Max Weber), through to the privatization of this monopoly by the Nazis.

That Gestapo and Kripo officials should become members of the SS was something that was expressly desired and indeed actively promoted, with the aim of furthering the amalgamation of the police and NSDAP machinery. Whoever fulfilled the 'conditions for admittance to the SS – which were reduced for this case – could be given an SS rank corresponding to his current civil service rank. However, Himmler was emphatic that nobody was to be compelled to join the SS: 'I want an admission only if ... the man applies freely and voluntarily [and] fits racially and ideologically into the SS'.[23]

After the war, nevertheless, many former Sipo officials sought to save their necks by claiming that admission to the SS had been compulsory, describing the 'rank alignment' through which they had received an SS rank as something that happened automatically. However, the historian Robert Gellately states that SS ranks could be awarded in alignment with police ranks 'in a second, separate procedure', as a kind of promotion. This was the actual 'rank alignment', which 'involved much more than being merely co-opted into the SS'.[24]

On admission, Gestapo and Kripo officials were attached to the security service of the SS (Sicherheitsdienst, SD) and wore the diamond-shaped SD flash on their uniform sleeve. Heydrich justified this allocation in terms of the intended division of labour between Gestapo and SD: 'The Gestapo [Staatspolizei] is to be assisted in its tasks by the party organization of the security service of the Reichsführer-SS, which does not possess executive powers. ... While on the one hand the Gestapo's tasks are tactical and executive in kind, the SD, on the other, has the task, which is to be carried out through intelligence and investigative activities, of providing the strategic foundations for leading the movement and thus the state'.[25] Furthermore, the SD was to be developed into the 'inner elite' of an ideological 'state defence corps', as the scientific and theoretical 'brain trust'[26] of the Nazi leadership – and thus to stand in strong contrast to the political hooliganism of the initial years of the 'movement', and in particular the rabid and violent antisemitism of the SA. In any case, the SD was intended to play a special role in the Sipo and SS amalgamation process.

In personnel terms, the very names of the newly created posts of 'Inspector of the Sipo and SD' (IdSuSD) and 'Higher SS and Police Leader' (HSSPF) were indicative of the close cooperation between Sipo and SD – as indeed was Himmler's title 'Reichsführer-SS und Chef der Deutschen Polizei'. The inspectors were, as Heydrich's 'personal authorized commissioners', to represent 'the Gestapo, Kripo and SD ... vis-à-vis the central authorities and command posts of the Wehrmacht and offices of the NSDAP'.[27] As such they were 'one of the most important instruments in the Reich for securing the fusion of Sipo and SD'; Heydrich considered their creation to be an 'indicator of the efforts ... to develop and consolidate the position of Sipo and SD within the Nazi power structures'.[28]

The creation in 1937 of the post of HSSPF was of still greater significance for the amalgamation of police and party machinery. Like the inspectors, the HSSPFs were allocated to the military districts (Wehrkreise, finally twenty-one in number) corresponding to the regional divisions of the Wehrmacht. They were directly subordinate to Himmler, who could also issue them orders via a second command chain, which likewise bypassed any authorities at the RSHA, following which the HSSPFs then passed orders on to, for example, their respective inspectors.[29]

Peter R. Black writes that one of the HSSPFs' principal tasks – the monitoring of ideologically motivated measures ordered by Hitler such as 'the deportation and elimination of Jews, Roma and other real or supposed enemies of Germany'[30] – related above all to the conquered territories in the East – that is to say, areas where there were no established state or party structures, and where these measures were carried out on a large scale and with devastating consequences. In the 'Altreich' and 'Ostmark' (former Austria), where there were solidly established structures of state and party machinery, the tasks of the HSSPFs were more representative in character. This was particularly relevant in the case of the career of Ernst Kaltenbrunner, who as HSSPF of Military District XVII (Vienna, Lower Danube, Upper Danube) found himself in a state of 'obscurity, political impotence and boredom'[31] – until 1943, that is, when he became head of the RSHA.

The Reich Security Main Office: Terror Centre and 'Institution of the War'

In September 1939, shortly after the beginning of the war, the efforts to advance the amalgamation of the police with the SD were given an institutional superstructure in the form of the successor organization to the Gestapa, the Reichssicherheitshauptamt (RSHA, Reich security main office). While the task of the Gestapa had above all been the suppression of internal political opponents such as Communists and Social Democrats, the RSHA can justifiably be described as an 'institution of the war'.[32] Its realization in actual practice was the result not so much of long-term conceptual thinking as of the urgent need to create an organizational framework for the wartime deployment of Gestapo and SD officials. As Wildt has put it, 'Gestapo rule in the occupied territories radicalized [entgrenzte] the practices of the RSHA', also with respect to the 'number of people that the RSHA defined as "opponents" and "enemies". When the Germans conquered Poland, more than three million Jews fell under their control'.[33] No documentary evidence exists to show that before the war any thought had been given to the fate of these people at all.

The RSHA was not simply a central authority that issued orders to the Gestapo regional headquarters (*Leitstellen*) and regular offices (*Stellen*), which were organized, to scale, in exactly the same way as the RSHA itself was. From the very beginning it was a central office of terror, and the offices under it were its branches. What Wildt calls the 'dissolution of boundaries' (*Entgrenzung*) with regard to the tasks of the RSHA not only related to the extent of the territory under Nazi rule but also to 'the number of victims terrorized, driven out, deported and murdered', and, not least, to 'the practices used by the RSHA to implement its own policies, with the radicalization of measures all the way up to systematic genocide'.[34] The prototype of Heydrich's 'fighting administration' (*kämpfende Verwaltung*) was 'the ethnic cleansing in the annexed western Polish territories as well as the liquidation of the "Jewish-Bolshevik leading strata" in the Soviet Union'.[35]

A clear indicator of the extent of the 'dissolution of boundaries' with respect to the territory under the authority of the RSHA is given by the number of Gestapo regional headquarters and offices, with particular reference to the occupied territories. In 1939, out of a total of sixty-four Gestapo offices (including 'Leitstellen'), eleven were located outside the 'Altreich' (six of these in annexed Austria); in 1941 the figure was twenty-six out of a total of sixty-seven. But by the end of 1944, as a result of the mass posting of Gestapo staff to the occupied territories, the number of offices in the 'Altreich' had sunk to twenty-five. At this point, of the 31,374 Gestapo staff members, around '75 per cent ... were tied up in "security police operations" outside the Reich borders of 1937'.[36]

Michael Wildt describes the RSHA as a 'mobile, flexible organization ... of a new type: extremely capable of adapting to circumstances ... and of creating new departments and dissolving old ones'.[37] An example of this is provided by the GVPs, which were applied according to exactly the same scheme at all Gestapo offices, regulating the distribution of tasks and areas of competence down to the smallest detail.

These GVPs were changed four times in a space of six years,[38] on each occasion necessitating major interventions in the organizational structure of the individual Gestapo offices. Over and above the additional bureaucratic work, the redistribution and renaming of the sections and departments created competency-related problems and thus inter-staff conflicts at the Gestapo offices. However, far from being an expression of latent dissatisfaction, these measures were in fact typical of the strategy of 'organized chaos' with which Himmler, by changing the command hierarchies or creating short cuts within them, sought to increase the efficiency with which his orders were carried out: 'The constant delimitations of competency kept the power structure of the Third Reich in a permanent state of movement. But this dynamic must not be taken to imply ... that the matter of competencies tended to get increasingly chaotic. The chaos served exclusively to advance the swift and efficient realization of the goals of the Nazi leaders.[39] Heydrich too was concerned that fusion with the Sipo should not result in his SD becoming what he called a 'bürokratischer Beamtenladen' (bureaucratic civil service shop), demanding with absolute clarity: 'Despite amalgamation ... maintain the fighting line'.[40]

Under the conditions of war, it finally proved impossible to achieve the ultimate goal of the RSHA, namely, to transfer the state's sovereign rights into the hands of a party organization through the amalgamation of police and SS. Although Himmler wished this process of fusion to be crowned with the institution of a 'state defence corps', the law he envisaged in order to fulfil this wish was never passed. It was not even possible to achieve 'the desired uniformity of career structure, training and remuneration'. Although the RSHA remained an incomplete torso, 'the objectives of the new institution were unambiguous ... maintaining the racial purity of the Volk's body and repelling or exterminating an enemy defined in *völkisch* terms. Unfettered by any legal restrictions, it was the law enforcement authority of the racist *Volksgemeinschaft*'.[41]

The only instance of the concrete organizational amalgamation of Sipo and SD was the creation of the mobile task forces known as 'Einsatzgruppen' (literally, 'deployment groups', EGs) and their component parts, 'Einsatzkommandos' (EKs) and 'Sonderkommandos' (special commando units), each of which was composed of a Gestapo, a Kripo and an SD unit, complemented with squads of regular police and Waffen-SS.

Units of this kind were deployed as early as the occupation of Austria (Einsatzkommando Österreich), of the Sudetenland (September 1938) and of the 'Czech rump' (March 1939); however, the EGs only became organizations of systematic mass murder in the course of the offensives against Poland, Yugoslavia and the Soviet Union.[42]

Organizational Structure of the RSHA

From 1936, the security police main office (Hauptamt Sicherheitspolizei, headed by Reinhard Heydrich) and the order police main office (Hauptamt Ordnungspolizei, Kurt Daluege) were subordinate to Himmler as Reichsführer-SS and chief of the German police. While the Sipo was made up of the Gestapo and Kripo, the Orpo consisted of the 'protection police' (Schutzpolizei or Schupo), the rural police (Gendarmerie), the technical emergency services (Technische Nothilfe), and the fire protection and local police. This structure changed in 1939 with the establishment of the RSHA, which was divided up by *Amt* (office or department); these were seven in number, representing functional groups of the Sipo and SD. While the seats of office of the RSHA were on Wilhelmstrasse and Prinz-Albrechtstrasse, the Orpo main office was at the Reich ministry of the interior.

The GVP valid on 1 March 1941, which in the opinion of Vienna Gestapo deputy head Karl Ebner 'proved its worth in the working context', offers a clear picture of the organization and divisions of the RSHA:[43]

In *Amt I/Personnel*, Gestapo and Kripo officials and SS officers in the SD were trained for their functions before being appointed to their posts; this office was also responsible for the SS officers' schools (SS-Führerschulen).

Amt II/Organization, Administration, Law was concerned with, among other things: assessing whether individuals were 'hostile to Volk and state'; confiscation of assets and 'expatriation' (deprivation of citizenship); and matters related to arms, aircraft and motor vehicles, including the construction of gas vans.

Amt III/Areas of German Life [Deutsche Lebensgebiete] (SD Domestic) was strongly ideological in orientation. Department III B, 'Volkstum' ('Volk-dom'), containing Section III B 3, 'Rasse und Volksgesundheit' (race and the health of the Volk), was described by Heydrich as 'the most important group' of all. Amongst further important areas covered were 'Reichsaufbau' (development of the Reich), with tasks related to educational and settlement policy and appointments in the economy and in science and scholarship, and, furthermore, the intelligence-related reports 'Meldungen aus dem Reich'.

Amt IV/Investigating and Combating Opponents evolved from the security police main office of the Gestapa, and was the central office of the Gestapo within the RSHA. It was divided into five groups:

Group IV A   Opposition
Group IV B   Ideological opponents
Group IV C   Card indexes, protective custody
Group IV D   Occupied territories
Group IV E   Counter-intelligence

Each group was divided into sections: in Group IV A, for example, there was Section IV A 1 (Communism, Marxism, etc.), and in Group IV B there was Section IV B 4 (Jewish affairs), with Adolf Eichmann as section head.

The distribution of groups and sections in the GVP was changed and extended in the two GVPs that followed (1942 and 1944). In 1942 a sixth group was added, Group IV F (passports and foreign police forces); in 1944 there was an extensive restructuring, because as the war proceeded the sections concerned with Gestapo operations in the occupied territories became increasingly important. However, this last GVP was never fully implemented at the Vienna Gestapo.

Amt V/Crime-Fighting, as the office of the Reich criminal investigation police, was concerned with 'preventive crime-fighting' and was the central office for investigation and tracking; it pursued and deported Roma and Sinti and committed homosexuals to concentration camps. In Section V D 2 (Forensic institute of the security police), procedures were developed for Nazi 'euthanasia' (murder), gas vans, and poison munitions.

Amt VI/SD Foreign had the task of processing and evaluating political information from abroad, with the various sections being devoted to various geographical areas. 'The SD's most intensive foreign intelligence work occurred in Vienna, where Wilhelm Höttl and Wilhelm Wanek (Group VI E South) had a diverse network of informants reporting on political and economic relations in south-eastern Europe.'[44]

Amt VII/Ideological Investigation and Evaluation had a range of tasks that went beyond those of traditional police work: it was concerned with the ideological investigation of opponents on a scientific basis – with a strongly antisemitic orientation. It was the central institution for the confiscation (or robbery) of – principally Jewish – collections, and of archives and libraries in the occupied territories.

Notes

1. Best, 'Die Geheime Staatspolizei', 127.
2. RGBl. I, 1933, 83, Verordnung des Reichspräsidenten zum Schutz von Volk und Staat (Decree of the Reich President for the Protection of People and State) of 28 Feb 1933.
3. Herbert, *Best*, 152.
4. Fraenkel, *The Dual State*, 3.
5. Herbert, *Best*, 133. By 1934, the NSDAP army known as the SA had grown to four million members, a considerable number of whom were armed; for comparison, the Reichswehr was, in accordance with the Versailles peace treaty, only one hundred thousand strong.
6. For the content of the following, see Mang, 'Juristen in der Gestapo'.
7. [Zwangsmaßnahme der Geheimen Staatspolizei … die durch ihr Verhalten den Bestand und die Sicherheit des Volkes und Staates gefährden] From the Protective Custody Decree ('Schutzhafterlass') of Reich interior minister Frick of 25 Jan 1938.
8. [… der polizeilichen Ermittlungen in Hoch- und Landesverrats- und Sprengstoffsachen, sowie bei sonstigen strafbaren Angriffen auf Partei und Staat. Wichtiger aber als die Ahndung bereits begangener Delikte ist ihre vorbeugende Verhinderung.] Best, 'Die Geheime Staatspolizei', 125.
9. [gerichtsfreie Kompetenz-Kompetenz] Fraenkel, *The Dual State*, 88–89, quoted in Davy, *Die Geheime Staatspolizei in Österreich*, 20.
10. [Der Begriff 'staatsgefährlich' statt 'staatsfeindlich' ließ einen weiten Spielraum bei der Gegnerdefinition.] Dams and Stolle, *The Gestapo*, 7 (*Die Gestapo*, 19).
11. [nicht aus Einzelgesetzen, sondern … aus den ihr von der Führung gestellten Aufgaben her. Ihre Befugnisse dürfen deshalb nicht durch formale Schranken gehemmt werden.] RGBl. I, 1936, 487/88.
12. [Die völkisch-organische Weltanschauung sieht nicht im Einzelmenschen …, sondern im Volk die ursprüngliche (primäre) Wirklichkeit des Menschentums.] Best, 'Rechtsbegriff und Verfassung', 152.
13. Linck, *Der Ordnung verpflichtet*, 13.
14. [eine gesetzliche Normierung der von einer politischen Polizei anzuwendenden Mittel … so wenig möglich wie es unmöglich ist, jede Art von Angriffen der Staatsfeinde … für alle Zukunft vorauszusehen] Best, 'Rechtsbegriff und Verfassung', 152.
15. [Ferment der Dekomposition] Quoted in Pfundtner, *Dr. Wilhelm Frick*, 38.
16. Heydrich, 'Die Bekämpfung der Staatsfeinde', 121.
17. [Menschen, die aus physischer oder seelischer Degeneration sich aus den natürlichen Zusammenhängen der Volksgemeinschaft gelöst haben und … Menschen, die als Werkzeuge der weltanschaulichen und politischen Feinde bestrebt sind, die Einheit des deutschen Volkes zu sprengen und seine staatliche Macht zu zerstören; gegen diese Volks- und Staatsfeinde führt die Geheime Staatspolizei ihren unablässigen Kampf.] Heinrich Himmler, 'Aufgaben und Aufbau der Polizei des Dritten Reiches', quoted in Pfundtner, *Dr. Wilhelm Frick*, 129–30.
18. [Der Führer hat die Hinzuziehung von Rechtsanwälten verboten und mich damit beauftragt, Ihnen seine Entscheidungen zur Kenntnis zu bringen.] Letter from Himmler to the Reich ministry of justice, 6 Nov 1935, quoted in Herbert, *Best*, 571.

19. Herbert, *Best*, 162.
20. Ibid., 191.
21. Heinrich Himmler, 'Aufgaben und Aufbau der Polizei des Dritten Reiches', quoted in Pfundtner, *Dr. Wilhelm Frick*, 130.
22. Dahm, 'Der Terrorapparat', 153.
23. [Ich wünsche nur dann eine Aufnahme, wenn der Mann sich ... wirklich freiwillig meldet (und) rassisch und weltanschaulich in die SS passt.] Letter from Himmler to Kaltenbrunner of 24 Apr 1943, quoted in Wildt, *An Uncompromising Generation*, 151–52 (*Reichssicherheitshauptamt*, 259).
24. Gellately, *The Gestapo*, 57, n. 5 (*Die Gestapo*, 74–75).
25. [Die Staatspolizei wird in ihren Aufgaben unterstützt durch die nicht mit Exekutivbefugnis versehene Parteiorganisation des Sicherheitsdienstes des Reichsführers-SS .... Während einerseits die staatspolizeilichen Aufgaben taktischer und exekutiver Natur sind, hat andererseits der Sicherheitsdienst nachrichten- und forschungsmäßig die Aufgabe, strategische Grundlagen für die Führung der Bewegung und damit des Staates zu liefern.] Heydrich, 'Die Bekämpfung der Staatsfeinde', 121–23.
26. See Herbert, *Best*, 190.
27. BA Berlin, R 58/241, sheets 220ff.
28. Banach, *Heydrichs Elite*, 174.
29. See Birn, *Die höheren SS- und Polizeiführer*.
30. Black, *Ernst Kaltenbrunner*, 106.
31. Ibid., 126.
32. Wildt, *An Uncompromising Generation*, 165; on the RSHA in this connection, see ibid., chap. 6, 'Structure and Staff', 165–214 (*Reichssicherheitshauptamt*, 283–415).
33. Ibid., 198 (363).
34. Ibid., 166 (284).
35. Ibid., 213 (415).
36. Paul, 'Kämpfende Verwaltung', 68.
37. Wildt, *Reichssicherheitshauptamt*, 284 (see also *An Uncompromising Generation*, 166).
38. According to Ebner, only three GVPs were put into practice at the Vienna Gestapo, see the section 'The Vienna Gestapo GVPs' in Chapter 4.
39. Birn, *Die höheren SS- und Polizeiführer*, 397.
40. [Trotz Zusammenschmelzung ... Erhalt der kämpferischen Linie.] Note in Heydrich's hand in the margin of a letter from Best of 1 Mar 1939 suggesting that the SD should be integrated into the Sipo, and its members made civil servants. Quoted in Wildt, *An Uncompromising Generation*, 159 (*Reichssicherheitshauptamt*, 270). The subsequent dispute on this point was what led to Heydrich breaking with Best.
41. Wildt, *An Uncompromising Generation*, 164 (*Reichssicherheitshauptamt*, 281–82).
42. See, among many others, Krausnick/Wilhelm, *Die Truppe des Weltanschauungskrieges*; Benz/Graml/Weiß, *Enzyklopädie des Nationalsozialismus*, 440.
43. [arbeitsmäßig gut bewährt] On the following, see Wildt, *An Uncompromising Generation*, chap. 6, 'Structure and Staff', 165–214 (*Reichssicherheitshauptamt*, 283–415).
44. Wildt, *An Uncompromising Generation*, 209 (*Reichssicherheitshauptamt*, 404).

Chapter 2

ESTABLISHMENT OF THE GESTAPO IN AUSTRIA AND OF ITS REGIONAL HEADQUARTERS IN VIENNA

Planning, Preparation and Measures Undertaken by the Central Authorities in Berlin

By the time it came to the annexation of Austria in March 1938 (the 'Anschluss'), the Gestapa and the SD main office (SD-Hauptamt) had long been intensively occupied with preparations. How concrete the preparations for the building up of the Gestapo in Austria had been is indicated by a 133-page SD exposé that foresaw a personnel requirement of 2,059, which turned out to accord fairly exactly with the actual numbers of staff in the subsequent years.

These plans were clearly drawn up by experienced police jurists with the help of Austrian police officials who had fled to Germany, and with a wealth of intelligence information supplied by Austrian 'illegals' (i.e. Austrian Nazis during the NSDAP's prohibition in Austria, 1933–38). As well as being extremely precise, the plans varied in their details from region to region – and were systematically implemented following the annexation.[1]

Franz Josef Huber, later head of the Vienna Gestapo, had worked in the Bavarian political police as head of Section II 1 C ö – 'ö' being the abbreviation for Austria – from as early as 1933, following which he continued in the same field in the 'newly founded Department II 1 H'[2] of the Gestapa from 1934. The Gestapa GVP of 1 January 1938 cites Huber as head of Section II C (Reaction, opposition, Austrian affairs). Huber later confirmed that this was why he was transferred to Vienna and that he 'had already been concerned with Austrian affairs in Munich and Berlin'.³

From 1935 to 1936 there were several former Austrian police officials working in Section II C who had fled to Germany to escape imprisonment for involvement in Nazi activities, amongst them Hubert Kern, Karl Hemetsberger,⁴ and Humbert Achamer-Pifrader. The exceptionally ambitious Achamer-Pifrader was extremely well connected, not only with his mentor Otto Steinhäusl but also with Heinrich Himmler and Reinhard Heydrich. In combination with his good contacts with (covert) Nazi-minded circles within the Austrian state and police machinery, these connections soon enabled Achamer-Pifrader to make his mark in Section II C as an expert on Austrian affairs (as head of Unit II C 3, Austrian refugees). Immediately after the annexation he was appointed deputy head of the Vienna Gestapo under Huber. Achamer-Pifrader's good friend Rudolf Mildner, likewise an 'Austrian refugee', continued to work with the Bavarian political police until he became deputy head of the Linz Gestapo following the annexation.⁵

Hubert Kern, a jurist, had been a member of the Hitler Youth since 1924 and of the NSDAP since 1932; he was an official at the Vienna police headquarters (Polizeidirektion Wien) until 1934, when he was dismissed from police service for his activities as a Nazi. During his period at the Gestapa, where he principally collected material about members of the Austrian government,⁶ those with whom he was in constant contact for intelligence purposes included his elder brother Anton Kern, who likewise was a jurist, an NSDAP member from 1931, and until March 1936 an official at various Vienna police stations. In 1936, Anton Kern was dismissed from state service for his activities as a Nazi, and sentenced by a court of law, but he was granted an amnesty at Christmas of that year. Until the annexation, he played a leading role at the top level of the illegal Austrian NSDAP; thereafter he worked for a short time on building up the Vienna Gestapo before finally taking over as head of Department III (Staff) of the Ordnungspolizei in April 1938.⁷

On 14 March 1938, Hubert Kern was transferred from his Berlin post to the Vienna Gestapo, where he played a leading role in the initial build-up phase as head of Department I (Personnel); moreover, he was promoted to the second-highest rank in the Gestapo regional headquarters hierarchy, Regierungsrat.⁸

Similarly, Adolf Eichmann, who had grown up in Linz, had left Austria when the NSDAP was made illegal, and offered his services with the SD in Berlin. By his own account, shortly before the annexation of March 1938 he was involved in preparing Hollerith punched cards with thousands of names of 'persons, organizations, newspapers and periodicals, authorities, schools, etc.' in Austria – though he himself, of course, just 'cut cards and punched holes'.⁹ Based on lists drawn up at the Gestapa, this 'Austria card index' was a comprehensive 'wanted' list of all individuals and institutions suspected of being opponents of National

Socialism; later, similar lists and indexes were prepared for other countries that had been or were due to be occupied.[10]

As day broke on 12 March 1938, one day before the 'reunification of Austria with the German Reich', Himmler landed at the Vienna-Aspern airfield, accompanied by Sipo and Orpo heads Heydrich and Daluege, as well as further high-ranking SS officers and police and Gestapo officials. On the same day, Huber and Achamer-Pifrader were flown to Munich, as they had originally been intended to arrive in Vienna 'with the marching troops',[11] and thence to Vienna.

The takeover of the Austrian police was initiated without delay, with two special staffs being created: one entrusted with the task of building up the security police (Sipo – i.e. the Gestapo and Kripo), and one with responsibility for regular, uniformed police (Ordnungspolizei, Orpo for short, consisting essentially of Schupo and Gendarmerie).

On 14 March, the NSDAP newspaper *Völkischer Beobachter* was able to report that 'under the command of Reichsführer-SS Heinrich Himmler ... all measures [are being taken to] make the police in Austria what it has long been in the Reich, namely, a reliable National Socialist instrument of power, closely bound to the Volk and firmly in the Führer's hand'.[12] On 15 March, the territorial organization of the Gestapo in Austria was mapped out by the 'special staff of the chief of the security police [Heydrich]' at its first, provisional seat of office in the Hotel Regina, not far from the Ring in Vienna's 9th district:[13] the Gestapo regional headquarters (Staatspolizeileitstelle) was to be in Vienna, with regular Gestapo offices (Staatspolizeistellen) in Linz, Salzburg, Eisenstadt, Innsbruck, Klagenfurt and Graz. On the same day, Huber was appointed head of the Vienna Gestapo, with Achamer-Pifrader as his deputy.

On the very next day, the entire Austrian police was sworn in under allegiance to Hitler. With the enactment, published on 18 March 1938, of the Law on the Reunification of Austria with the German Reich (Gesetz über die Wiedervereinigung Österreichs mit dem Deutschen Reich), Himmler as Reichsführer SS and chief of the German police was authorized by Reich interior minister Frick 'to undertake such measures as are necessary for the maintenance of security and order, [even if] beyond the legal limitations otherwise laid down for this purpose'.[14]

Heydrich's decree of 18 March 1938 on the 'Organisation der Geheimen Staatspolizei in Österreich'[15] contained more specific provisions about the tasks and regional responsibilities of the Gestapo on Austrian soil:

> The Vienna Gestapo regional headquarters is to be established with its seat in Vienna. It takes over the entire political police tasks of the hitherto existing General Directorate for Public Security and the police headquarters and its security directorate in Vienna ... The hitherto existing security directorates or commissariats of Linz, Graz, Salzburg, Klagenfurt, Innsbruck, Eisenstadt are to become Gestapo offices, at the

same time taking over the political departments of the respective police directorates. The tasks of the hitherto existing security directorate of Bregens [sic] are to be taken over by Innsbruck Gestapo office.[16]

The typing errors, which are uncharacteristic of Heydrich's decrees, are a telling indication of the urgency with which the measures were to be carried out.

Just as the Gestapo offices in the federal provinces were given the same regional competences as their predecessor bodies, the Vienna regional headquarters was given responsibility for Vienna and Lower Austria. Furthermore, it was authorized to 'issue instructions to and demand reports from the Gestapo offices'. With regard to their relation to the Gestapa – that is to say, to Heydrich himself – the Vienna Gestapo and the provincial Gestapo offices were obliged to submit reports directly to Heydrich, who could also give them orders directly. This was by no means, as has sometimes been suggested, a conscious restriction of the powers of the regional headquarters. It was simply an example of Himmler and Heydrich's practice of creating short cuts in chains of command, which they considered would result in a more efficient implementation of the measures they ordered.[17]

The same decree also regulated the Gestapo's relations to other authorities. As head of the Vienna regional headquarters, Huber was given an additional function as 'political security adviser to the state secretary for security', namely, Ernst Kaltenbrunner, who had been appointed to the post shortly after the annexation.[18] However, Heydrich imposed a massive limitation on the post's functions, which for the following four years was to significantly weaken the position of Kaltenbrunner – from September 1938 also HSSPF 'Danube' – and force him into a predominantly representative role: although Kaltenbrunner was 'authorized to issue instructions to the Gestapo in the country [former Austria]', he could do so only 'insofar as they do not conflict with orders of [Himmler] or his authorized representatives. In cases of doubt, a decision shall be obtained from the central Reich authority'.[19]

A comment made by Huber during his denazification proceedings in 1949 reveals how little authority Kaltenbrunner had over the Vienna Gestapo in practice, and over Huber as his 'political security adviser': 'I was the designated head of the future Staatspolizei-Leitstelle ... My superior was Kaltenbrunner as Staatssekretär für das Sicherheitswesen in Österreich. Later, the Reichsstatthalter, Josef Bürckel, was officially also head of the Austrian police. In reality, however, I received my orders directly from what was to become the Reichssicherheitshauptamt'.[20]

With the decree issued on 22 March by Heinrich Müller,[21] acting inspector of the Sipo and SD (IdSuSD) for SD-Oberabschnitt 'Austria' (later 'Danube'), the organizational building up of the Gestapo in Austria began at the second, provisional seat of office at Herrengasse 7 (1st district of Vienna, inner city), under SS-Sturmbannführer Heinrich Seetzen.[22] The tasks related to coordinating the

Sipo and Orpo were undertaken by Gustav Adolf Nosske, head of the Gestapo office in Frankfurt an der Oder.[23] In the same decree of 22 March 1938, Müller transferred 'his Gestapo-related tasks to the Vienna Gestapo regional headquarters',[24] at which point Huber took over the IdSuSD's supervisory function over the Gestapo, thus launching the period of almost seven years during which he was his own official supervisor as head of the Vienna Gestapo.[25]

A further decree issued by Heydrich on 23 March 1938[26] announced the names of those appointed to be heads (and deputy heads) of the Gestapo regional headquarters and offices in Austria. The appointees were almost without exception Nazis from the 'Altreich', especially if one includes the Austrians Achamer-Pifrader and Mildner, who – as already mentioned – had been in Germany since 1936 and 1935 respectively. They were as follows:

Staatspolizeileitstelle Wien

> Head: SS-Obersturmbannführer Huber
> Deputy head: SS-Obersturmbannführer Dr Pifrader
> Address: Hotel Metropol [sic], Morzinplatz, Vienna I

Staatspolizeistelle Linz

> Head: SS-Sturmbannführer Dr Rasch[27]
> Deputy head: SS-Sturmbannführer Dr Mildner[28]
> Address: Landhaus, Promenade, Linz …

Staatspolizeistelle Graz

> Head: SS-Sturmbannführer Schulz
> Deputy head: Dr Delphin
> Address: Paulustorgasse 8, Graz …

Staatspolizeistelle Salzburg

> Head: SS-Untersturmführer Müller
> Deputy head: Revierinspektor Dr Trenka
> Address: Kurfürstenstrasse 1, Salzburg …

Staatspolizeistelle Klagenfurt

> Head: SS-Obersturmführer Dr Isselhorst
> Deputy head: tba
> Address: Landesregierung, Arnulfplatz 1, Klagenfurt …

Staatspolizeistelle Innsbruck

> Head: SS-Untersturmführer Dr Harster

Deputy head: Dr Spann
Address: Herrenstrasse 1, Innsbruck …

Staatspolizeistelle Eisenstadt

Head: SS-Untersturmführer Bovensiepen
Deputy head: tba
Address: Landhaus, Eisenstadt

In October 1938 the Eisenstadt Gestapo office was dissolved, Burgenland being divided up between the Reichsgaus of Lower Danube and Styria, and for secret police purposes between the Gestapo regional headquarters in Vienna and the Gestapo office in Graz. The Eisenstadt Gestapo office was converted into a border police station ('Greko', short for Grenzpolizei-Kommissariat) of the Vienna regional headquarters.

On 1 April 1938 the staff of the 'Hauptamt der Sicherheitspolizei und des Gestapa' were informed in a circular from Heydrich[29] that the 'inspector of the Sipo and the Gestapo regional headquarters in Vienna … [had] moved into their new official premises, Hotel Metropol [sic], Morzinplatz, Vienna I'. This top-class luxury hotel, which the Nazis had wasted no time in seizing for their own use, was to become the permanent headquarters of the Vienna Gestapo, and for the following seven years was an address synonymous with the full force of Nazi terror on Austrian soil. In an article in the SS paper *Das Schwarze Korps*, Heydrich made it unmistakably clear what opponents of the National Socialist regime in Austria would have to expect: 'The supreme law, the supreme judge over all interventions into personal freedom and property, and, when necessary, over life and death, is the Führer – in Austria as elsewhere'.[30]

Even as early as 18 March 1938, Werner Best[31] had instructed the relevant sections of Gestapa 'without delay … to make a compilation of all the cases of penal offences (especially high treason and state treason) and subversive activity … stemming from Austria, or with traces leading to Austria or proceeding from Austria into the Reich'.[32] On the basis of these 'blacklists' and the Gestapa 'Austria card index' mentioned above, between fifty and seventy thousand Austrians were arrested in the first six weeks after the annexation, some of whom were released after only a few days but others were kept in detention for years. 'In this course of events, it was particularly disastrous for opponents of the Nazis that on 12 February 1938, Hitler and Schuschnigg had agreed in Berchtesgaden on responsibility for security being transferred to the (still clandestine) National Socialist Arthur Seyß-Inquart, as it led to all the police records of the Schuschnigg regime, in particular those regarding the illegal left, falling into the hands of the new authorities.'[33]

Role of the Illegal Austrian National Socialists in Setting Up the Vienna Gestapo in 1938

The Nazi Putsch in the Vienna Police

The annexation of Austria in March 1938 and concomitant establishment of the Vienna Gestapo as the most important instrument of Nazi terror in Austria by no means came about solely as an external act of force on the part of German armed forces and powerful police formations. Important roles were also played by Austrian members of the NSDAP – not only 'illegal' activists and sympathizers in the Austrian police but also Nazi-oriented Austrian police officials who had fled to the Reich and been appointed to posts in the police apparatus there. Following the annexation, they helped the new German authorities by facilitating the swift build-up of organizational structures, as well as the immediate and efficient repression of political opponents and persecution of the Jews.

Only a short time after Chancellor Schuschnigg's radio speech on the evening of 11 March in which he announced his resignation, members of various Austrian NSDAP formations – first and foremost SS and SA men in scruffy old clothes – occupied both the general directorate for public security (Generaldirektion für die öffentliche Sicherheit),[34] which had its seat in the ministry of the interior, Herrengasse 7, and at the Vienna police headquarters, Schottenring 11. At both locations, NSDAP members and sympathizers 'secured' files and card indexes, and carried out a first wave of arrests of well-known anti-Nazi officials and employees.[35]

Although the Vienna chief of police (Polizeipräsident) and state secretary for security Michael Skubl had instructed the commandant of the Vienna security guard (Sicherheitswache), Emil Michall, to prevent NSDAP members and sympathizers – if necessary by force of arms – from forcing their way into the ministry of the interior, Michall did not obey the order, in recognition of which he was awarded the '13 March 1938 Commemorative Medal' shortly after the annexation.[36]

Within the building, the course of events was now determined by ministry officials who were members of the hitherto illegal NSDAP, or were close to it. One of these was the administrative police official Heinrich Demschik, who had been appointed to a post in the general directorate for public security in 1937, and after the annexation joined the Vienna Gestapo to work in Department III, Counter-intelligence. Demschik succeeded in laying his hands on the keys to room 111, which contained the files concerning the illegal NSDAP in Austria, and room 118, with Oberst (Colonel) Maximilian Ronge's 'espionage card index', and in arresting the officials responsible for maintaining them.[37]

After Reichsführer-SS Heinrich Himmler had announced that he would arrive in Vienna in the early hours of 12 March 1938, in the course of the night, following an order from the Austrian SS leader Ernst Kaltenbrunner, rooms were prepared at the ministry of the interior for Himmler and his immediate staff.[38]

At around 8 P.M. the Vienna police headquarters on Schottenring was occupied by non-uniformed SA men, who immediately arrested the head of the state police department, Ludwig Weiser. At 10.31, the swastika flag was unfurled on the front of the building.[39]

The night hours saw more and more members of the Austrian police coming out as Nazis, both at the general directorate for public security and at the Vienna police headquarters, where Ferdinand Schmidt – as he later boasted a few weeks later – 'played a leading part in the seizure of power … and in the arrest of individuals who had been pillars of the outgoing regime [Systemträger]'.[40] Schmidt, who had worked as a fully trained jurist at the Vienna police headquarters since 1930, and in this capacity as an adviser on banking and currency matters for the economic police, had not only been a member of the Hitler Youth from 1924 to 1928 but also a co-founder of the Nazi student fraternity at Vienna's Hochschule für Welthandel (University of World Trade, forerunner of the present-day Vienna University of Economics and Business). He joined the Nazi party in 1928. After the prohibition of the NSDAP in Austria in 1933, Schmidt succeeded in keeping his political ambitions under wraps, although he remained in regular contact not only with NSDAP comrades who had fled to Germany but also with the influential economic expert SS-Gruppenführer Wilhelm Keppler. On 14 September 1937, Keppler, who had been one of Hermann Göring's closest economic advisers for the 1936 four-year plan, was appointed by Hitler to deal with all NSDAP-related matters in Austria, and as such was instrumental in the preparations for the annexation.[41] Schmidt provided Keppler with numerous proposals for the safeguarding of foreign exchange reserves and home currency. In order to prevent capital flight, in the night of 11 March 1938 Schmidt ordered the closing of Austria's borders. On 14 March, he became the only Austrian civil servant to be appointed to high-ranking office at the newly created Gestapo regional headquarters in Vienna, as head of Department II, 'Exekutive' (i.e. police).[42]

In the early hours of 12 March 1938, following the arrest of Ludwig Weiser the previous evening, further leading Austrian police officials were arrested and held in detention at the police headquarters: Ministerialsekretär Franz Nagy, Hofrat Rudolf Manda, Ernst Rossmanith, Polizeirat Heinrich Hüttl, Polizeirat Leopold Buchsbaum, and others.[43] Some of them were detained and interrogated by men who only hours before had been their subordinates. Kriminaloberinspektor Franz Grünn, for example, was arrested at his apartment at 3 A.M. that night by three policemen and an NSDAP man, and interrogated at the police headquarters by the criminal investigator Rudolf Jirousek, who had until then been inferior to Grünn in rank.[44] Jirousek was one of the members of the Vienna police who had been intensely active in the illegal NSDAP between June 1933 and February 1938. Not only was he a member of the group of 'illegal' policemen operating under the cover name 'Ortsgruppe Gersthof', but he was also in underground contact with Section II C of the Gestapa in Berlin (more specifically, with Franz Josef Huber and Humbert Achamer-Pifrader, and others), to whom he supplied extensive information about the Austrian police.[45] After the annexation, Jirousek became a Vienna Gestapo official, and member of a 'special commission' that assessed the political reliability of civil servants entering the Gestapo and Kripo.

For roughly a week, chaos reigned in the police headquarters: not only had various NSDAP formations stationed themselves there and were locking up and maltreating individuals at their own discretion, but hitherto 'illegal' police officials were arbitrarily putting politically disagreeable colleagues into detention.[46]

In the night 11/12 March, more and more officials of local police stations came out as NSDAP members. One particularly notable example was Josef Auinger of the police station of Ottakring (16th district), who after the annexation was to become a section head at the Vienna Gestapo (Section II A 2, responsible for the Social Democrats). Immediately after Schuschnigg's speech, Auinger ordered the arrest of well-known opponents of National Socialism. Among his victims were Paul Springer, who as a Communist had already been severely maltreated by Auinger before 1938, and Josef Paul, a colleague of Auinger's at Ottakring police station.

Josef Paul was apprehended by SA men at his apartment in the early hours of 12 March and put into detention at Ottakring police station, where he found himself in the company of his colleagues Adolf Popelka and Josef Thaler from the police station of Mariahilf (6th district). On the same day he was transferred to the police prison on Rossauer Lände. There he shared a cell with, amongst others, the future federal chancellor Leopold Figl; on 1 April 1938, both were on the first transport of Austrians to Dachau.[47]

By the time Reichsführer-SS and chief of the German police Heinrich Himmler had landed at the airfield of Vienna-Aspern in the early morning of 12 March 1938, the Austrian police was already firmly in Nazi hands.

Nazi Networks in the Police Machinery

Even before the annexation, parts of the Austrian police had sympathized with the National Socialist ideology or with Nazi Germany. For example, Josef Weidinger, who was a Kriminalsekretär in Section II B 4 ('Jewish affairs') of the Vienna Gestapo from 1938, had joined the NSDAP as early as 1931. A member of the Vienna security guard (Sicherheitswache) from 1920 and of the state police from 1934, he was taken into detention twice in the years of the NSDAP's prohibition but was released both times for lack of evidence. In 1943, Weidinger stated that before the prohibition there were 54 'fee-paying members' of the NSDAP and 40 sympathizers amongst the 120 criminal investigators of the security guard.[48] And Johann Hoi, a leading 'illegal' in the Vienna police between 1934 and 1938 and after the annexation a member of Section II C (Legitimism) of the Vienna Gestapo, even claimed in a letter to the Reich treasurer of the NSDAP in Munich that during the prohibition years he had headed a group of Nazi police officials eight hundred strong.[49] Even though these numbers may well have been exaggerated, they do indicate that there was a strong Nazi presence in the police apparatus before the annexation.

A considerable number of members of the police had been actively involved in the Austrian National Socialists' attempted putsch of 25 July 1934. On the previous day, several criminal investigation officials had met to discuss plans at a hostelry in Penzing (14th district of Vienna).[50] Amongst those present were Konrad Rotter, Karl Hirt, Franz Toyfl, Josef Garhofer and Johann Hoi, all of whom (except Rotter, who died in 1936) entered the Gestapo in 1938. At the meeting, Hoi outlined the plans for the occupation of the federal chancellery, the apprehending of members of the council of ministers, the transfer of the federal president from Carinthia to Vienna, and the occupation of the Austrian broadcasting company RAVAG (Radio Verkehrs AG) and Bisamberg broadcasting station. His own task, Hoi said, was to allocate posts to the 'comrades' scheduled to take part in the putsch – and, if all went well, to put himself at the service of Otto Steinhäusl, who was intended to become the new police chief.[51] Steinhäusl, who headed the Salzburg police headquarters from 1922 and the Vienna security office from 1932, had maintained intensive close relations with the NSDAP since 1923; in the 1920s his protégés included the future high-ranking Gestapo functionaries Rudolf Mildner and Humbert Achamer-Pifrader.[52] After the abortive putsch of 1934, Steinhäusl, who had not been involved but was party to the plans, was taken into detention, and in 1935 sentenced to seven years' imprisonment; however, he was released in 1936 under the Austro-German Agreement of 11 July. On 14 March 1938, on the initiative of Austrian SS leader Kaltenbrunner, he was appointed acting chief of the Vienna police.[53]

The Vienna criminal investigators Konrad Rotter, Johann Pöllhuber, Franz Rudischer and Franz Kamba, who had taken an active part in the occupation of the federal chancellery, fled to Germany in order to escape the imminent threat of arrest. In Munich, once their political reputation had been checked in a camp established for Austrian Nazis, they were taken on under cover names in the newly created special departments ('Sonderdezernate') II 1C and II 2C of the Bavarian political police. Immediately after the annexation, Pöllhuber and Rudischer were transferred to Vienna to work on the establishment of the new Gestapo regional headquarters; Kamba was likewise moved to Vienna, to be head of the NSDAP Gau main office.[54]

In the years up to 1938, the criminal investigators Hirt, Toyfl, Garhofer and Hoi,⁵⁵ all likewise involved in the putsch, played important roles in building up a network of Nazi-minded officials (and sympathizers) within the Austrian police. They gave warnings to members of the network under threat of house searches, helped 'party comrades' in danger of arrest to flee to Germany, and saw to it that incriminating material disappeared from police files.

The activities of the illegal Nazis benefited from the at times extremely amateurish working methods of the Austrian authorities. When, for example, as noted above, the police official Heinrich Demschik was transferred to the general directorate for public security in 1937, his task was to work on the card index of Austrian National Socialists. Immediately, Demschik communicated all the relevant information not only to the head of the Austrian NSDAP, Hauptmann Josef Leopold, but also to the Gestapa.⁵⁶ The extent of the Nazi presence in the Austrian police is illustrated by a letter of 1935 from the NSDAP's refugee assistance department in Munich. In the letter it is pointed out that the political record of Austrian Nazis fleeing to Germany was to be checked 'with the help of party comrades at present working for the Austrian security authorities', and that an 'information service [had been set up] to this end'.⁵⁷

The 'comrades' at the Austrian security authorities maintained direct contacts not only with the NSDAP refugee assistance department but also with the Bavarian political police and the Gestapa office II C, which was responsible for 'Reaction and opposition' and all matters relating to Austria. Since 1934 it had been headed by Franz Josef Huber, who had previously been with the Bavarian political police and was to become head of the Vienna Gestapo.⁵⁸

For Austrian Nazis who had fled to Germany, activities with the Bavarian political police, and in particular with the Gestapa office II 1 C, were of the greatest importance for their future political careers. Firstly, by gathering valuable experience in the security police field, gaining expertise in routine procedures, and above all demonstrating their political loyalty, they qualified themselves to participate in the building up of the Sipo in Austria. Secondly – even more importantly for their political careers – their work in Germany enabled them to cultivate contacts with office-holders in even the highest echelons of the Reich government and the NSDAP. For example, Humbert Achamer-Pifrader, who had risen to become the 'Austria expert' in Unit II C 3, was one of the Gestapo members who flew from Munich to the Austrian capital with Franz Josef Huber on 12 March 1938, and was thus one of the police staff who immediately embarked on building up the Vienna Gestapo.

By March 1938, both in Germany and in Austria, a number of mutually overlapping and interlinked networks of Austrian police officials had developed that spied not only on the Austrian police (from within) but also on the Austrian government (from without). And as Walter Schellenberg recalled in his memoirs, 'Our secret service work in Austria itself was not very difficult', as 'the

[Austrian] sources [flowed] so abundantly that we were positively overwhelmed with material', and 'innumerable National Socialists who had fled Austria provided us with the necessary contacts'.⁵⁹

The activities not only of 'illegal' police officials in Austria but also of Austrian Nazis in Germany contributed to accelerating the structural planning for the establishment of the Gestapo in Austria. By the time of the annexation, this planning had very largely been completed and was put into print by the SD security main office (SD-Sicherheitshauptamt) in the form of a 133-page exposé under the programmatic title 'The Austrian security system and its integration into the security police of the Reich following the incorporation [into the Reich] of Austria (the Südmark)'. That this fundamental document gave such a detailed and knowledgeable account of the local and traditional structures of the Austrian police is a clear indication that Austrian members of the Gestapa were involved in its drafting, as is corroborated by a passage outlining future assessment commissions that were to effect a 'strict screening' of officials being taken over from the Austrian police. In this passage it is emphasized that when selecting the members of the commissions – which did indeed come into being after the annexation – 'particular consideration should be given to Austrian SS officers, who not only know the officials concerned but are also familiar with the general situation [in the police] from their own experience'.⁶⁰

This makes it clear that thought was already being given to future positions for those who had been active in the Bavarian political police, the Gestapa, or the illegal NSDAP in Austria. During the building up of the Gestapo in Austria, these well-interconnected and mutually supportive cliques, which enjoyed good contacts with influential members of the Sipo and Gestapa, not only constituted a substantial pool of politically reliable personnel but also expected and laid claim to key positions as a reward for their political commitment.

First Measures Regarding Political Staff

When Heinrich Himmler and his staff landed at Aspern airfield on 12 March 1938, they were welcomed by prominent Austrian Nazis such as Ernst Kaltenbrunner, leader of the Austrian SS, and Austrian NSDAP office-holders, notably its head Hubert Klausner, its political head Odilo Globocnik, and its organizational head Friedrich Rainer; also present was Vienna police chief, Michael Skubl, whose removal from office and detention Himmler ordered that same morning.⁶¹ As mentioned above, the Germans accompanying Himmler – amongst them the Sipo chief SS-Gruppenführer Reinhard Heydrich, Orpo chief General Kurt Daluege, Gestapa head Heinrich Müller, and head of Department I/1 (Staff Office) at the SD-Hauptamt, Walter Schellenberg – initially moved into the Hotel Regina, as did Humbert Achamer-Pifrader.⁶²

In the course of the day, they were joined by Ferdinand Schmidt and Otto Steinhäusl, who were no strangers to Himmler and his staff, and were predestined for high-level involvement in the establishment of the Nazi security police in Austria. Not only were they long-standing active NSDAP members with many contacts to influential state and party office-holders, but they could also boast extensive knowledge of the staff structures and specific traditions of the Austrian police. While Schmidt, according to his own account, was invited 'to function, with a number of other Austrian colleagues ... as mediators and legal advisers to the Berlin police staff who had settled at the Hotel Regina', Steinhäusl, on Kaltenbrunner's initiative, was appointed acting chief of the Vienna police.[63]

During the afternoon of 12 March, the great majority of the German task force – with the exception of Himmler and his closest collaborators, who stayed at the Hotel Regina – moved into rooms prepared for them in the general directorate for public security at the ministry of the interior. There, under the direction of Walter Schellenberg, divided up into 'Einsatzkommandos' (task units, EKs) made up of German officials not only from the police but also from the SD, they started working through all the secret police documents and Austrian police staff files that had been 'secured' by illegal members and supporters of the NSDAP.[64] In so doing, they paid particular attention to the files from the 'special office' of Oberst Maximilian Ronge,[65] who had masterminded (albeit without great success) the suppression of the illegal National Socialists, and to the files relating to the trials of the murderers of federal chancellor Engelbert Dollfuß in 1934. While a part of this stock of files – in particular the files relating to the abortive putsch of 1934 – was sent to Berlin, where its 'evaluation' by the SD lasted several months, the remainder was transferred in April to Departments II and III of the Vienna Gestapo.[66] The German EKs were supported by jurist civil servants of Department I of the general directorate for public security, who – with the exception of those who had been arrested – had been ordered to perform this supporting role by Otto Steinhäusl. The fact that Steinhäusl was acting police chief enabled him to second officials to various German EKs from the Austrian state police and Kripo, and from the security guard.[67]

Through the acquisition of the secret police documents of the general directorate, the EKs at a stroke came into possession of, among other things, the entire body of files relating to the illegal activities of the Austrian Socialists and Communists. This having been said, even before 1938 the intelligence machinery of the Austrian National Socialists had supplied extensive information about the Austrian left movement to Berlin, where some weeks before the annexation, Gestapo and SD staff had drawn up lists and card indexes containing the names of Nazi opponents from all parts of the political spectrum and of prominent Jewish figures from the worlds of art, culture, scholarship and commerce. As noted above, among those who worked on drawing up these information banks was Adolf Eichmann, at that time a member of SD-Department II 112 ('Jews'):

> We made a record of the Jewish functionaries and Freemasons in all ideological fields. We sat there like schoolboys at their desks and wrote out the index cards; then they were ordered alphabetically and put into the index under the respective letters, and things that could wait were put on one side. And with this card index material, the first wave of the SD hastened off to Austria.[68]

In the evening hours of 12 March 1938, SD 'commando groups' began to make arrests on the basis of these lists and card indexes. In many cases, however, they arrived too late, as the arrests had already been made by Austrian Nazis. In the first – chaotic – days after the annexation, the arrestees were put into detention in the ministry of the interior's in-house prison, in rooms at the police headquarters on Schottenring, in the police prison on Rossauer Lände, and in various local police stations.[69]

About a week after the annexation, Ferdinand Schmidt was summoned to Herrengasse 7, where Huber, in the presence of his deputy Humbert Achamer-Pifrader and Heinrich Müller, entrusted him with the acting headship of Department II ('Exekutive') of the Vienna Gestapo:

> Huber assured me ... that he was endeavouring to find a building for his new entity as quickly as possible. Until then, however, the machinery would have to operate on a number of tracks. The staff of leaders and operatives, and a special commando unit from the Reich, would have their seat in the Herrengasse, while the secret police apparatus hitherto on Schottenring would be transferred to the new Gestapo headquarters as Department II.[70]

After a further ten days, Huber informed Schmidt that the future seat of the Vienna Gestapo would be the erstwhile Hotel Metropole, and that he [Schmidt] should now organize the move.

By this time, there was already a cloud over the relations between Schmidt and Huber. In 1945, Schmidt stated before the Vienna VG that he had very soon experienced 'difficulties and disagreements' with Huber, who had become 'more and more unpleasant and irritable'. In fact, in the few weeks that had passed since the annexation, Schmidt had been compelled to recognize that as head of Department II not only his powers but also his career opportunities were limited. For example, the section heads of Department II, who were to a large extent 'Reich Germans', were not answerable to him but to Huber. Schmidt remained acting head of Department II during the first weeks after the move to the former Hotel Metropole, but as an established expert on economics and foreign currency enjoying good relations with Wilhelm Keppler, who at that time and until June was in Vienna as Göring's economic adviser, he quickly realized that private business offered him more interesting and considerably more lucrative prospects. Schmidt finally left the service of the Vienna Gestapo in the summer of 1938.[71]

The days following 12 March saw the arrival in Vienna of further high-rank Gestapo officials from the 'Altreich', who were to assume the headship of important sections of the Vienna Gestapo, though some only for a matter of weeks. Amongst these were Karl Haselbacher (Section II B until June 1938),[72] Kurt Christmann (Section II H),[73] Heinz Rux (Section II D),[74] Josef Meisinger (Section II G), Rudolf Lange (Section II B from July 1938),[75] and Heinz Rennau, who was appointed head of Department III (Border police, counter-intelligence, high treason and state treason, and surveillance of consulates and other foreign representations).[76]

Regional and Supraregional Competencies of the Vienna Gestapo

The Vienna Gestapo regional headquarters was initially given branch offices in Wiener Neustadt and Sankt Pölten. Another branch office was set up in Znaim (Znojmo, southern Moravia), which from 1 October 1938, following the Munich Agreement and the cession of the Sudetenland to the German Reich, belonged to the Reichsgau 'Lower Danube'. Later, a further branch office was established in Zwettl.

The border police, over which the Gestapo had been given control in 1937, was located at border police stations and their affiliated border posts. The Vienna Gestapo's border police stations were at Eisenstadt and Lundenburg (Břeclav, south-eastern Moravia, likewise acquired as a consequence of the Munich Agreement); there was also a border police station for Vienna, which was located at the Vienna Gestapo headquarters on Morzinplatz. Border police stations set up at Gmünd and Mistelbach were closed down after only a short time. The Vienna Gestapo's border police stations initially had a total of fifteen affiliated border posts,[77] which were finally reduced to eight: Bruck an der Leitha, Kittsee, Sauerbrunn, Lundenburg, Aspern Airfield, Engerau (Petržalka), Marchegg and Vienna-Reichsbrücke.[78]

The Vienna Gestapo's area of influence spread over the two Reichsgaus of Vienna and 'Lower Danube' ('Niederdonau', including northern and middle Burgenland and the incorporated parts of south Moravia). The Gau of 'Greater Vienna', created by the National Socialists through the incorporation of ninety-seven Lower Austrian communes, had an area five times larger than the city of Vienna before the annexation and, according to the census of 17 May 1939, a population of over 1.9 million. As the Vienna Gestapo's area of competence also included 'Lower Danube', it had a total area of 24,706.86 km^2 and a population of 3,627,652,[79] which was more than half of the Austrian population at that time.

Through the person of Franz Josef Huber, however, the competencies of the Vienna Gestapo regional head office extended far beyond the Gaus of Vienna and Lower Danube. Huber was one of only three border police inspectors in the German Reich and, as Border Inspector II (South-East) for military districts XVII and XVIII, he was responsible for border control at the frontiers to Slovakia, Hungary, Yugoslavia, Italy and Switzerland.[80] From 1 April 1944 he was also responsible for the protection of customs borders, after this task had been entrusted to the Gestapo.

The paucity of archival sources makes it impossible to confirm the indication that Huber assumed the function of secret police head in Hungary after the occupation of that country in March 1944.[81] In this connection, however, it is conspicuous how frequently Vienna Gestapo officials were deployed to Einsatzgruppe F (Hungary), which was formed at Mauthausen in March 1944 and was eight hundred strong.[82] In all, thirty-two staff from groups IV A 'Combating opponents', IV D 'Occupied territories' and IV E 'Counter-intelligence' were deployed to Hungary to serve in Einsatzgruppe F, and six to Einsatzgruppe H (Slovakia).[83] Furthermore, it is clear from Hungarian sources that Huber spent several periods of time in Hungary after the occupation.[84] There, his task was most likely to support the head of the Hungarian security police, Péter Hain, with whom he had been in close contact since 1938, in the creation of a 'Hungarian Gestapo' on the German model. In collaboration with the 'Sondereinsatzkommando Eichmann', Hain was responsible for the deportation of over four hundred thousand Hungarian Jews to Auschwitz. Huber himself quoted his tasks as border police inspector to explain his frequent spells in Budapest.[85]

In 1939, a year after the annexation of Austria, the Vienna Gestapo – with a total staff of 842, including the employees as well as the officials, who were civil servants – had more personnel than any other Gestapo regional headquarters in the whole German Reich. As its head, Franz Josef Huber was promoted to the civil service rank of Oberregierungs- und Kriminalrat after only two years (as opposed to the normal period of five years), on the grounds that 'Vienna has the largest and one of the most important Gestapo offices in the Reich'.[86] By comparison, the Berlin regional headquarters had only 719 officials and employees, in spite of having a considerably larger population in its area of competence.[87] At its peak, the total number of personnel at the six Gestapo offices (Vienna, Linz, Graz, Salzburg, Klagenfurt, Innsbruck) in the territory known as the 'Alpine and Danube Gaus' was around 2,000, compared to around 2,200 in the whole of occupied France at the end of 1943.

An insight into the composition of the Vienna Gestapo is provided by the 'Estimated balance of the planned revenue and expenditure of the security police for the financial year 1940, Part III' issued by Heydrich on 30 July 1940.[88] While the number of administrative police officials at the Vienna Gestapo (128)[89] was slightly lower than that in Berlin (135), the number of criminal investigation officials (473)⁹⁰ was slightly higher than Berlin (468). The total number of posts provided for in the budget was higher for the Vienna regional headquarters (604) than for Berlin (589), and considerably higher than for the Düsseldorf regional headquarters (384), which like Berlin also had a larger population in its area than Vienna. At the Vienna Gestapo, auxiliary work was performed by staff without civil servant status, who in 1940 numbered 175 employees and 48 manual workers. Only 'Amt IV/Gestapo' of the RSHA – with 857 established posts in 1940 and 1,100 in 1942 – had a larger staff than the Vienna regional headquarters.⁹¹ The figures for 'ongoing expenses' in 1940 also give an indication of the dimensions of the Vienna regional headquarters, amounting to RM 648,000 as compared with Berlin's total of RM 268,680.

The estimated balance for the financial year 1942⁹² makes it clear that the staff of the Vienna Gestapo continued to grow and to remain disproportionately large in comparison with other regional headquarters:

- Administrative police officials: Vienna 135, Berlin 133, Frankfurt am Main 48, Düsseldorf 80.
- Criminal investigation officials: Vienna 560, Berlin 505, Frankfurt am Main 165, Düsseldorf 374.
- Total number of established posts in 1942 (excluding non-civil servants): Vienna 704, Berlin 651, Frankfurt am Main 156, Düsseldorf 457.

In 1942, the number of established Gestapo posts in the Alpine and Danube Gaus – that is to say, 704 at the Vienna regional headquarters, 70 at the Salzburg Gestapo office, 219 at Innsbruck, 205 at Klagenfurt, 110 at Linz, and 193 at Graz – amounted to a total of 1,501, excluding the non-civil servants.

A number of explanations can be advanced for the size of the Vienna Gestapo staff. The fact that the number of personnel at the Prague regional headquarters (812 as of 1 September 1941) was also well above the average strongly suggests that the secret police presence was generally intended to be stronger outside the original borders of the German Reich than within.⁹³

A further explanation – not least with regard to the comparative numbers of personnel at the Vienna and Berlin Gestapo headquarters – could be related to the fact that since 1933 the secret police of the German Reich had systematically repressed (and, by 1938, to all intents and purposes suppressed) all resistance to the Nazi regime. In Austria, by contrast, the repression of political opponents from the Communist, Social Democrat and conservative camps only began five years later, when it was carried out all the more uncompromisingly. Finally, the size of the Vienna Gestapo staff resulted from the considerable number of its branch offices and border police stations and border posts. In addition, the Kripo, which as part of the Sipo worked in close collaboration with the Gestapo, had branch offices in Sankt Pölten, Wiener Neustadt and

Znaim, and local offices in Baden bei Wien, Berndorf, Krems, Lundenburg and Neunkirchen.

Finally, consideration may be given to one further, albeit speculative, line of thought. In view of the German Reich's plans for expansion to the East, it is possible that the Vienna regional headquarters was from the very outset intended to fulfil a strategic role as a hub or vanguard station, as could possibly be suggested by Kaltenbrunner's activities to promote the destabilization of Czechoslovakia and his alleged building up of a south-eastern Europe espionage organization,[94] and, as mentioned above, by Huber's constant activities in Hungary.

Notes

1. DÖW 14 890 (from the holdings of the Military Archive of the GDR, now in the BA), 'Das österreichische Sicherheitswesen und dessen Einbau in die Sicherheitspolizei des Reiches nach einer Eingliederung Österreichs (der Südmark)'; see also Ramme, *Der Sicherheitsdienst*, 100.
2. ZStL 110 AR-Z 70/76, sheets 121–22, denazification files for Franz Josef Huber. This is confirmed by an internal Gestapa communication of Heydrich's of 23 Mar 1938 concerning the closing down of a 'Special Service for Austria' ('Sonderdienst Österreich'), BA Berlin, R 35, sheets 621–22.
3. IfZ München, ZS 735, 7738/89, sheets 24–51, interview with Franz Josef Huber, 3 June 1970, in which Huber confirmed that he was occupied with, among other things, 'obtaining intelligence from Austria [and] classification of the information from Austria'.
4. WStLA, Vienna LG, Vg 6e Vr 56/51, VG proceedings against Karl Hemetsberger. The Gendarmerie (rural police) official Hemetsberger, who fled to the German Reich after being arrested several times for illegal Nazi activity, was employed as a criminal investigator at the Gestapa from 1936 to 1938 and was moved to the Vienna Gestapo in 1938. On his involvement in the murder of General Zehner, see Chapter 9.
5. ÖStA, AdR, Gau file no. 180 169, Dr Rudolf Mildner; Gafke, *Heydrichs Ostmärker*, 108 and 148.
6. ÖStA, AdR, Gau file no. 235 218, Dr Hubert Kern; WStLA, Vienna LG, Vg 4c Vr 4424/47, VG proceedings against Hubert Kern, letter from the Vienna police headquarters to the Vienna public prosecutors, 23 June 1947.
7. WStLA, Vienna LG, Vg 8b Vr 7411/48, VG proceedings against Anton Kern, curriculum vitae of Anton Kern, n.d.
8. WStLA, Vienna LG, Vg 4c Vr 4424/47, VG proceedings against Hubert Kern, questioning of the accused before Linz District Court, 20 Sept 1947.
9. [ich schnitt und lochte] Eichmann in his so-called 'Erinnerungen' ('Recollections'), published from 12 Aug 1999 in the daily newspaper *Die Welt*.
10. Wanted lists of this kind existed for Great Britain and the Soviet Union, see Röder, *Sonderfahndungsliste UdSSR*.
11. ZStL 110 AR-Z 70/76, sheet 122.
12. *Völkischer Beobachter*, 14 Mar 1938, 10.
13. BA Berlin, R 58/621, sheet 22, handwritten draft entitled: 'Sonderstab des Chefs der Sicherheitspolizei Wien, Hotel Regina SS-Oberführer Joost [sic]'. The writer was Heinz Jost, from 1939 SS-Brigadeführer and head of Amt III in the RSHA.

14. [die zur Aufrechterhaltung der Sicherheit und Ordnung notwendigen Maßnahmen auch außerhalb der sonst hierfür bestimmten gesetzlichen Grenzen zu treffen] RGBl. I, 1938, 262.
15. BA Berlin, R 58/241, fiche 3, sheets 127–30. Heydrich's decree formed the basis for the official founding document, 'Organisation der Geheimen Staatspolizei in Österreich' (G. Bl. f. Ö. no. 47/1938), a circular decree of Himmler's of the same day, 18 Mar 1938. On this see Pfeifer, *Die Ostmark*, 262ff.
16. [Die Staatspol.-Leitstelle Wien wird mit dem Sitze in Wien errichtet. Sie übernimmt die gesamten politisch-polizeilichen Aufgaben der bisherigen Generaldirektion für die öffentliche Sicherheit und der Pol.-Direktion und Sicherheitsdirektion in Wien … Die bisherigen Sicherheitsdirektionen bzw. Kommissariate Linz, Graz, Salzburg, Klagenfurt, Innsbruck, Eisenstadt werden Staatspol. Stellen. Sie übernehmen gleichzeitig die Aufgaben der politischen Abteilungen der Pol.-Direktionen. Die Aufgaben der bisherigen Sicherheitsdirektion Bregens [*sic*] werden von der Staatspo.-Stelle [*sic*] Innsbruck übernommen.] In October 1938, the Eisenstadt Gestapo office was closed in the course of the partition of Burgenland, when the secret state police responsibilities were shared out between Lower Austria and Styria, that is to say, between the Vienna Gestapo regional headquarters and the Graz Gestapo office. The area of competence of the Innsbruck Gestapo office extended over Tyrol and Vorarlberg from the beginning.
17. [die Staatspol.-Stellen mit Anweisungen zu versehen und von den Staatspol.-Stellen Berichte anzufordern] See the section 'The Reich Security Main Office' in Chapter 1.
18. BA Berlin, NS 19, FC, 1695, decree of the Reichsführer-SS, SS-Personalhauptamt, of 21 Mar 1938, by which Kaltenbrunner was promoted from SS-Standartenführer to SS-Brigadeführer (police rank: Generalmajor der Polizei) with immediate effect and, additionally, entrusted 'with the leadership of SS-Oberabschnitt Österreich'.
19. [berechtigt, den Behörden der Geh. Staatspol. im Land Weisungen zu erteilen / soweit dem nicht Anordnungen des RFSSuChdDt.Pol. im RMdI oder seiner Beauftragten entgegenstehen. In Zweifelsfällen ist die Entscheidung der Reichszentralbehörde einzuholen.] 'RFSSuChdDt.Pol. im RdI' stood for 'Reichsführer-SS und Chef der Deutschen Polizei im Reichsministerium des Innern', that is to say, Himmler, with Heydrich as his principal 'authorized representative'.
20. ZStL, KHN/HKM, sheet 122, denazification files for Franz Josef Huber.
21. BA Berlin, R 58/261, sheet 334, quoted from Banach, *Heydrichs Elite*, 178. Heinrich Müller ('Gestapo-Müller'): 1900–1945 (disappeared), career in the office of the Munich chief of police, 1934 appointed by Himmler and Heydrich to the Gestapa in Berlin, Heydrich's deputy in the Hauptamt Sicherheitspolizei ('Gegnerbekämpfung') of the Gestapa, 1939 head of Amt IV (Gestapo) in the RSHA, 1942 participant in the Wannsee Conference on the 'final solution of the Jewish question'. He was involved in practically all the decisions relating to the crimes of the Gestapo.
22. See also Weisz, 'Gestapo in Österreich', 439–62.
23. Herbert, *Best*, 195.
24. BA Berlin, R 58/261, sheet 334, quoted from Banach, *Heydrichs Elite*, 178.
25. Müller's successors as 'IdS u. SD im SD-OA Donau', that is to say, in military districts XVII and XVIII (Walter Stahlecker from 1 July 1938, Otto Rasch from 2 June 1939, and Herbert Fischer from 12 Oct 1939) only performed this function for short periods (BA Berlin, R/601 1815). Stahlecker led Einsatzgruppe II (for Moravia) in March 1939, Rasch led Einsatzgruppe I (for Bohemia) in the occupation of rump Czechoslovakia (circular letter of Heydrich of 24 Mar 1939, BA Berlin, R 58/241, sheet 154). In September 1939 Fischer led Einsatzgruppe III in Poland (Wildt, *Reichssicherheitshauptamt*, 351). Only in January 1941 was Huber appointed acting IdSuSD in Military District XVII (headquarters in Vienna), and only definitively appointed in October 1941 (letter from Heydrich to the SS-Personalhauptamt of 2 Oct

1941, NARA, SS-Personalhauptamt files, A 3343 880-118A). Nevertheless, it can be assumed that, in accordance with Müller's transferral of tasks, Huber in fact performed the duties of inspector in the Vienna Gestapo area.

26. BA Berlin, R 58/241, fiche 3, sheet 129, addresses of the offices of the secret state police in Austria.
27. Otto Rasch, from June to October 1939 IdSuSD for military districts XVII and XVIII (Vienna and Salzburg). In 1941, as leader of Einsatzgruppe C, he gave the orders for the massacre of over 30,000 Jewish men, women and children at the ravine of Babi Yar near Kiev. See Klee, *Personenlexikon*, 480.
28. Rudolf Mildner, from August 1939 Gestapo head in Salzburg, 1941 Gestapo head in Kattowitz/Katowice and head of the political department of the Gestapo in Auschwitz, from December 1944, as commander of the Sipo and SD in Vienna, de facto head of the Vienna Gestapo. Klee, *Personenlexikon*, 412.
29. BA Berlin, R 58/621, fiche 1, sheet 39.
30. [Oberstes Gesetz, oberster Richter über alle Eingriffe in die persönliche Freiheit, das Eigentum und, wenn es notwendig werden sollte, über Tod und Leben ist auch in Österreich der Führer.] Heydrich, 'Aufbau und Entwicklung der Sicherheitspolizei im Lande Österreich', 3.
31. Werner Best, Heydrich's deputy as head of the Gestapa.
32. [unverzüglich ... alle Fälle strafbarer Handlungen (vor allem Hoch- und Landesverrat) und staatsfeindlicher Tätigkeit, die ... ihren Sitz in Österreich hatten oder deren Spuren nach Österreich oder aus Österreich in das Reich führten, zusammenzustellen.] BA Berlin, R 58/621, sheet 20, Kleiner Verteiler für das Geheime Staatspolizeiamt, 18 Mar 1938.
33. Neugebauer/Schwarz, *Stacheldraht, mit Tod geladen*, 7.
34. The Generaldirektion für die öffentliche Sicherheit was established in the federal chancellery (Bundeskanzleramt, BKA) as Austria's supreme security authority by a decree of the BKA of 23 Sep 1930. Under Federal Chancellor Engelbert Dollfuß, a regulation of 13 Jun 1933 established a security directorate (Sicherheitsdirektion) for each federal province, all subordinate to the BKA.
35. See WStLA, Vienna LG, Vg 3a Vr 4769/46, VG proceedings against Heinrich Demschik, confirmation by Josef Hoi, 24 Jan 1940, judgment against Heinrich Demschik, 25 Jan 1949; Vg 4c Vr 2657/46, VG proceedings against Ferdinand Schmidt, written statement by Ferdinand Schmidt, n.d.
36. ÖStA, AdR, Gau file no. 85 500, Emil Michall.
37. WStLA, Vienna LG, Vg 3a Vr 4769/46, VG proceedings against Heinrich Demschik, judgment, 25 Jan 1949.
38. WStLA, Vienna LG, Vg 4c Vr 2657/46, VG proceedings against Ferdinand Schmidt, written statement by Ferdinand Schmidt, n.d.
39. Report in the *Mittagsausgabe* newspaper on the Nazi takeover of power in the police, 12 Mar 1938, quoted from DÖW, *'Anschluß' 1938. Eine Dokumentation*, 301. Ludwig Weiser remained in 'protective custody' from March 1938 to October 1939 (DÖW 20000/W306).
40. [führend an der Machtergreifung in der Polizeidirektion und Verhaftung der früheren Systemträger] ÖStA, AdR, Gau file no. 87 309, Dr Ferdinand Schmidt.
41. Keppler was involved in the annexation of Austria in that he carried out Göring's instructions in Vienna; until June 1938 he acted as 'Reichskommissar in Österreich' (Reich commissioner in Austria), see Schafranek, *Söldner, für den Anschluss*, 321.
42. ÖStA, AdR, Gau file no. 87 309, Dr Ferdinand Schmidt. After resigning from the Gestapo, Schmidt went into private business, where his positions included that of works manager for the firm Kontropa (previously Bunzl & Biach).
43. WStLA, Vienna LG, Vg 4c Vr 2657/46, VG proceedings against Ferdinand Schmidt, written statement by Ferdinand Schmidt, n.d.

44. WStLA, Vienna LG, Vg 11h Vr 559/45, VG proceedings against Rudolf Jirousek, testimony of Franz Grünn, 16 Jan 1948.
45. ÖStA, AdR, Gau file no. 280 825, Rudolf Jirousek.
46. WStLA, Vienna LG, Vg 4c Vr 2657, VG proceedings against Ferdinand Schmidt, written statement by Ferdinand Schmidt, n.d.
47. https://www.doew.at/erinnern/biographien/erzaehlte-geschichte/haft-1938–1945/josef-paul-der-erste-transport (last accessed on 22 May 2021). Paul Springer was also in the first transport of Austrians to Dachau, see Neugebauer/Schwarz, *Stacheldraht, mit Tod geladen*, 12ff.
48. WStLA, Vienna LG, Vg 11f Vr 2564/47, VG proceedings against Josef Weidinger, curriculum vitae of Josef Weidinger, 1 Jan 1943.
49. ÖStA, AdR, Gau file no. 8757, Johann Hoi, letter dated 22 May 1942.
50. WStLA, Vienna LG, Vg 1h Vr 5071/46, VG proceedings against Karl Prieler, judgment, 27 Feb 1947; WStLA, Vienna LG, Vg 4c Vr 3533/47, VG proceedings against Josef Garhofer, testimony of Karl Prieler, 2 Nov 1948.
51. DÖW 19 836.
52. Gafke, *Heydrichs Ostmärker*, 105–6.
53. For greater detail, see Graf, *Österreichische SS-Generäle*, 321–22; Weisz, 'Steinhäusl Otto', 184.
54. ÖStA, AdR, Gau files no. 96 823, Johann Pöllhuber, no. 338 867, Konrad Rotter, no. 305 186, Franz Kamba; Schafranek, *Söldner*, 78–79 and n. 24.
55. Although Hoi was dismissed from police service in 1936 on account of his NS activities, he remained in contact with his 'illegal' former colleagues in the police.
56. WStLA, Vienna LG, Vg 3a Vr 4769/46, VG proceedings against Heinrich Demschik, judgment, 25 Jan 1949.
57. Schafranek, *Söldner*, 78–79.
58. WStLA, Vienna LG, Vg 3a Vr 4769/46, VG proceedings against Heinrich Demschik, judgment, 25 Jan 1949; ÖStA, AdR, Gau file no. 235 218, Dr Hubert Kern; Gafke, *Heydrichs Ostmärker*, 332–33; Mang, 'Gestapo-Leitstelle Wien', 115.
59. Schellenberg, *Aufzeichnungen*, 51.
60. [scharfe Siebung / insbesondere österreichische SS-Führer berücksichtigt werden müssen, die sowohl die Beamten als auch die Verhältnisse aus eigener Anschauung kennen] DÖW 14 890, n. 1.
61. *Der Nürnberger Prozess*, vol. 20, 20, testimony of Michael Skubl, 13 June 1946 (*The Nuremberg Trials*, 154th day).
62. Schmidl, *Der 'Anschluss' Österreichs*, 109. Hotel Regina was a popular meeting place for Austrian National Socialists. Even on 10 March 1938, leading Nazis including Seyss-Inquart and Globocnik had met there, along with the Nazi-minded 'Volkspolitische Referenten' of the Fatherland Front, in order to discuss future political developments.
63. WStLA, Vienna LG, Vg 4c Vr 2657/46, VG proceedings against Ferdinand Schmidt, written statement by Ferdinand Schmidt, n.d.
64. Weisz, 'Gestapo-Leitstelle Wien', 38ff.
65. Oberst Maximilian Ronge, Austria-Hungary's last head of military intelligence, was reactivated after his retirement in 1933 and made head of the secret police special office (Sonderbüro). After being arrested in March 1938, he was interned at Dachau from 1 April to August of that year.
66. Schellenberg, *Aufzeichnungen*, 52–53.
67. Weisz, 'Gestapo-Leitstelle Wien', 39ff.
68. [Wir saßen wie Schulbuben auf den Bänken und schrieben die Karteikarten; dann wurden sie nach Alphabet geordnet, buchstabenweise eingereiht und Dinge, die noch Zeit hatten, zur Seite gelegt. Mit diesem Karteimaterial 'rauschte' die erste Welle des SD nach Österreich

ab.] Quoted from Hachmeister, *Die Gegnerforscher*, 192. See Stadlbauer, 'SS-Einsatzgruppen-führer Erich Ehrlinger', 182–227.
69. Weisz, 'Gestapo-Leitstelle Wien'.
70. Ibid.
71. WStLA, Vienna LG, Vg 4c Vr 2657/46, VG proceedings against Ferdinand Schmidt, written statement by Ferdinand Schmidt, n.d.
72. Karl Haselbacher, b. 1904, jurist, was head of Dezernat II at the Gestapa from 1936. From July 1938 he was head of Kiel Gestapo office, and from September 1939 Düsseldorf. In June 1940 he was appointed BdSuSD in Belgium with his headquarters in Brussels. He was killed in an accident in September 1940.
73. Kurt Christmann, b. 1907, jurist, was the SS winter sports adviser. In 1938 he was transferred to the Innsbruck Gestapo and from 1939 he was head of the Salzburg Gestapo. From August 1942 he was leader of EK 10a of EG D, in Krasnodar, after which he was head of the Gestapo offices in Klagenfurt and Coblenz.
74. Heinz Rux, b. 1907, jurist, was made head of the Salzburg Gestapo only a few months after the annexation. After the outbreak of war he assumed command of EK 2, EG II, in occupied Poland. Subsequently, as a member of the Sipo and SD, he was active at various SD stations in Germany. In 1944 he was deployed to Oberkrain (Upper Carniola, Slovenia) to fight partisans. In 1945 he was taken prisoner by the British and committed suicide on 8 May in Vellach.
75. Rudolf Lange, b. 1910, jurist, was deployed to the Gestapo offices in Stuttgart, Weimar, Erfurt and Kassel in autumn 1939. In 1941 he became head of staff for EG A and for a time was head of EK 2, which by December 1941 had murdered around sixty thousand Latvian Jews and Jews deported to Latvia. As KdSuSD in Latvia, Lange in person gave the orders for mass shootings on the periphery of Riga.
76. WStLA, Vienna LG, Vg 4c Vr 1223/47, VG proceedings against Karl Ebner, interrogation of Ebner at the Vienna LG, 12 July 1947. Rennau was transferred to the RSHA at the end of 1941 and later became head of the Gestapo office in Brünn/Brno.
77. BA Berlin, R 58/4207, 1 (undated). Border police posts: Vienna (Reichsbrücke-Hainburg, Aspern-Flughafen, Berg), Gmünd (České Velenice/CSR, Neu-Nagelberg, Grametten), Mistelbach (Retz, Haugsdorf, Laa an der Thaya, Drasenhofen, Lundenburg/Břeclav/CSR, Marchegg).
78. BA Berlin, R 58/717 (undated – end of 1942 or later, as the head of the Vienna Gestapo Franz Josef Huber appears in the document bearing the title 'SS-Brigadeführer und Generalmajor der Polizei', which he was accorded on 9 Nov 1942).
79. BA Berlin, R 58/717.
80. ZStL, 110 AR-Z 70/76, sheet 123, interrogation of Huber, 3 Oct 1961: 'In my capacity as IdSuSD, I was also used as inspector of border police in military districts XVII and XVIII. This area encompassed the whole border from Lundenburg to Lindau'.
81. Letter of 16 Dec 1947 from the Munich police chief Franz Xaver Pitzer to the 'Spruchkammer' (civilian denazification court) of the Garmisch-Partenkirchen internment camp where Huber was held.
82. WStLA, Staatspol. Abt. Pol. Erhebung, A 1/1, Nachrichtenblatt der Staatspolizeileitstelle Wien 1944 – see among other issues that of 1 Nov 1944. In 1944 the advance of the Soviet armed forces prompted the formation of the EGs F (Hungary), G (Romania) and H (Slovakia); Einsatzgruppe G was not put into operation. See, among others, Indelárová, *Finale der Vernichtung*.
83. Archives of the Republic of Slovenia, AS 1931, 811, sheets 2107–324, Vienna Gestapo personnel card index, undated post-war transcript with original photos.
84. Szita, *Verschleppt, verhungert, vernichtet*, 81.
85. ZStL, 110 AR-Z 70/76, sheet 123.

86. BA Berlin, R 2/12154, sheet 96, quoted from Banach, *Heydrichs Elite*, 242, letter of 28 Dec 1939 from the Reich ministry of the interior-S I V3a to the Reich ministry of finance. See also Mang, *'Gestapo-Leitstelle Wien'*, 12–17.
87. Kohlhaas, 'Die Mitarbeiter', 224.
88. [Kassenanschlag über die planmäßigen Einnahmen und Ausgaben der Sicherheitspolizei für das Rechnungsjahr 1940, Teil III] BA Berlin, R 58, microfilm 528.
89. Vienna Gestapo administrative police officials, 1940: 1 Oberregierungsrat, 1 Regierungsrat, 3 Polizeiräte, 1 Polizeioberinspektor Gr. [Gruppe, (salary) group] A 4 b 1, 6 Polizeioberinspektoren Gr. A 4 b 2, 2 Polizeiinspektoren Gr. A 4 c 1, 28 Polizeiinspektoren Gr. A 4 c 2, 7 Polizeiobersekretäre, 2 Polizeisekretäre Gr. A 5 b, 32 Polizeisekretäre Gr. A 7 a, 32 Polizeiassistenten, 1 caretaker, 12 assistants.
90. Vienna Gestapo criminal investigation officials, 1940: 1 Oberregierungs- und Kriminalrat, 2 Regierungs- und Kriminalräte, 6 Kriminalräte, 44 Kriminalkommissare, 6 Kriminalinspektoren, 40 Kriminalobersekretäre, 164 Kriminalsekretäre, 60 Kriminaloberassistenten Gr. A 7 c, 150 Kriminaloberassistenten Gr. A 8 a.
91. Rürup, *Topographie des Terrors*, 55.
92. BA Berlin, R58/94.
93. Sládek, 'Standrecht und Standgericht', 326.
94. Black, *Ernst Kaltenbrunner*, 117; BA Berlin, R 58/241, sheet 326. At the International Military Tribunal, Kaltenbrunner claimed that he had built up a 'pretty large espionage service' based in Austria for work in South-East Europe. However, the 'Auswertungsstelle Südost' (evaluation office for the south-east) established for this purpose in Vienna was closed down by a circular from Heydrich on 21 Apr 1941.

Chapter 3

HOTEL METROPOLE

Headquarters of the Vienna Gestapo

History of Hotel Metropole

Hotel Metropole was built between 1872 and 1873 according to plans by the architects Ludwig Tischler and Carl Schumann on Franz-Josefs-Kai – the address Morzinplatz 4 did not exist until 1888.[1] Both Tischler and Schumann worked for Wiener Bau-Gesellschaft, established during the development of the Ringstrasse by renowned architects such as Heinrich von Ferstel and Karl von Hasenauer.[2] The original reason for the construction of Hotel Metropole had to do with the Vienna World's Fair due to take place in 1873, which was not only the first such event in the German-speaking world but also, with over fifty thousand exhibitors, the biggest show of its type until then. Several large luxury hotels were built in Vienna at the time to accommodate the anticipated twenty million visitors.

Hotel Metropole was commissioned and owned by the Hotel-Aktien-Gesellschaft Metropole, established on 2 January 1872 with a capital of 3 million gulden for the purpose of building a 'hotel appropriate for the present time on a suitable site on Franz-Josef-Quai'.[3] Among the members of the first supervisory board of Hotel-Aktien-Gesellschaft Metropole were Graf (Count) Adolf Dubsky, Hermann Flesch, Baron Lazar Hellenbach, Alexander Lippmann, Graf Georg Stockau, Maximilian Weiss and Baron Franz von Wertheim, an Austrian industrialist and tool supplier by appointment to the court (k. k. Werkzeuglieferant). The members of the first supervisory board, and the vast majority of the Hotel-Aktien-Gesellschaft shareholders registered between 1873 and 1920,[4] were all members of a class of capitalists and rentiers who had made their fortunes and achieved social recognition in the second half of the nineteenth century through hard work and a willingness to innovate and take risks.

The six-floor Hotel Metropole was completed in just sixteen months on a site of 950 square klafter,[5] and opened on 20 April 1873, eleven days before the start of the World's Fair. It was a deluxe hotel with 365 elegantly furnished rooms, some with their own bathroom, which could be rented on their own or connected to form apartment suites. It had several restaurants, reception rooms, kitchens, utility rooms, reading rooms and a magnificent two-storey lobby dominated by a majestic double staircase. On the ground floor were a large number of small premises opening onto the street, for rent as boutiques, offices, and the like. On the square in front of the hotel a garden was laid out and a coffee pavilion built.[6]

Just a few weeks after the opening of Hotel Metropole, the stock exchange crash of 9 May 1873 ('Black Friday') ended the boom of the 'Gründerjahre'. The subsequent depression and cholera epidemic that broke out that summer meant that the expected visitors largely stayed away. Although the ambitious expectations of Hotel-Aktien-Gesellschaft Metropole regarding the influx of visitors were not completely met,[7] in the following years the hotel acquired not only a very good reputation but also a wealthy clientele, including the American author Mark Twain, who spent eight months at the Metropole in 1897/98 with his daughters Clara and Jean.

The First World War and the collapse of the Austro-Hungarian monarchy also left their mark on Hotel Metropole. The flow of visitors practically dried up on account of the war, and in 1918 the hotel's restaurant operations had to be closed because of food shortages.[8] But from 1920, Hotel-Aktien-Gesellschaft Metropole was once again profitable, not least because the massive devaluation of the krone made Vienna into an inexpensive travel destination for foreigners.

In 1925, Markus Friediger, who owned hotels in Munich, Berlin and Garmisch-Partenkirchen, became the majority shareholder (98 per cent) of Hotel-Aktien-Gesellschaft Metropole. Friediger, who under the Nuremberg Laws was considered a Jew (as were his wife Hedwig and their three children), began to experience financial difficulties during the 1920s on account of the growing influence of the National Socialists. This process intensified after Hitler came to power in 1933. To bolster up his German assets, Friediger was increasingly forced to withdraw capital from Hotel-Aktien-Gesellschaft Metropole; for example, he pledged 25 per cent of his shareholding to his Austrian-born brother-in-law Ernst A. Klein, a businessman in Munich, who had joined the supervisory board in 1925.

In 1937, Friediger was ultimately forced to sell all of his shares in Hotel-Aktien-Gesellschaft Metropole to the industrialist Robert Feix. Born in Vienna,

Feix was the proprietor of the Cologne company Opekta GmbH, which made pectin-rich gelling agents for jams and fruit jellies. When Feix took over the shares, Hotel-Aktien-Gesellschaft Metropole had a nominal share capital of 3 million schillings, divided into twenty thousand shares worth 150 schillings each. Of this amount, 60 per cent was owned after 1937 by Robert Feix, 20 per cent by unknown shareholders and a further 20 per cent by a minority group. Within this latter group, 10 per cent of the shares were held by Elisabeth Klein,[9] widow of Ernst Klein, who had died on 5 January 1936, and 10 per cent by two other shareholders.[10]

Feix, who was also classified as a Jew under the Nuremberg Laws, entrusted the management of the hotel to Emil Wohl, head of the Vienna branch of Opekta GmbH. The hotel was still doing well in 1937: although Austria's economic situation was anything but rosy, Hotel Metropole not only registered 75,228 overnight stays that year but also had a staff of between 150 and 180 employees, depending on the season.[11]

Hotel Metropole and the Annexation of Austria

On 25 March 1938, Josef Stachelberger, who before the annexation of Austria by the Nazis had worked in various hotels and restaurants in Austria and other

Figure 3.1. The former Hotel Metropole on Morzinplatz, from 1938 to 1945 the headquarters of the Vienna Gestapo. Photo June 1940. © Österreichische Nationalbibliothek, Bildarchiv und Graphiksammlung. Used with permission.

countries, was appointed provisional administrator (Kommissarischer Verwalter) of Hotel Metropole.[12] The following day, 26 March, the hotel was seized for the benefit of the German Reich.[13]

Hotel Metropole offered several advantages as the headquarters of the Gestapo in Vienna. First, it was under 'Jewish' ownership, all shareholders being Jewish, and could thus be seized 'without any problem'. The main shareholder of Hotel-Aktien-Gesellschaft Metropole, Robert Feix, had also been targeted by the Gestapo in Germany before the annexation. He had hitherto vehemently and above all successfully resisted the threatened 'Aryanization' of Opekta GmbH in Cologne. In Austria, he had attracted the attention of the illegal Nazis not only as a 'Jewish' hotel owner, but also because of his political views. He was a committed legitimist – a supporter of those who regarded Otto von Habsburg as the only rightful Austrian head of state and who were therefore considered enemies of the Nazi regime. On 27 March, a day after the seizure of the hotel, Feix was arrested in Berlin 'at the request of the Vienna Gestapo'.[14] Accompanied by a Berlin Gestapo official, he then flew to Vienna, where he was detained, along with the future federal chancellor Bruno Kreisky and others, in a cell in the police prison at Rossauer Lände 7–9 (9th district).[15] He was accused of engaging in subversive activities by giving Otto von Habsburg, who was wanted by the Nazi regime, RM 5,000 to purchase a motor car and paying for its transport to Belgium.[16] Hugo Hoffmann, the Gestapo official who accompanied Feix from Berlin to Vienna, stated in 1949 that a telephone operator from Hotel Metropole had reported him for legitimist activities right after the annexation. The telephone operator had been listening into his telephone conversations for some time and had heard, among other things, that Feix had given Otto von Habsburg a motor car.

The absence of relevant source material makes it impossible to determine whether this telephone operator actually existed or whether it was a device by the Vienna Gestapo to have Feix arrested. He was ultimately released from detention at the end of May 1938, and the assets of Hotel-Aktien-Gesellschaft Metropole were seized by the Gestapo.[17] In 1943 he was interned at Dachau concentration camp on charges of 'foreign exchange offences', and his company Opekta GmbH was expropriated. He was liberated from Lochau satellite camp in 1945.[18]

Markus and Hedwig Friediger, the former main shareholders of Hotel-Aktien-Gesellschaft, were deported from Cologne to the ghetto in Riga on 7 December 1941, where all trace of them was lost. Their son Karl Friediger, also a legitimist, escaped first to Czechoslovakia, where he contacted Karl Burian's resistance group. He provided Burian with the building plans of the hotel, which the resistance group were planning to blow up.[19] In 1939, Friediger escaped via Paris and Lisbon to the United States, where he worked for the OSS.[20] Elisabeth Klein, Ernst Klein's widow, who lived in an apartment in the Metropole, was with her son in London at the time of the annexation. Her daughter Annemarie Böhm, née Klein, had to move out of the apartment after the family jewellery had been seized by the Gestapo. The Klein family escaped thereafter to the United Kingdom and Australia.[21] The fate of the other minor shareholders of Hotel-Aktien-Gesellschaft Metropole has not been established to date. Emil Wohl, who managed Hotel Metropole until the annexation, was able to flee to England.

Apart from the possibility of rapid seizure, Hotel Metropole was ideal as the future headquarters of the Gestapo for two further reasons. It was conveniently located close to the police prison at Rossauer Lände, where most of the Gestapo detainees were held. As they had to be brought for interrogation to the Gestapo headquarters, it was important that they were imprisoned nearby. A further advantage was the fact that the over three hundred hotel rooms could be converted quickly and at relatively small expense into offices for the Gestapo officials and employees. From 1 April 1938, the building at Morzinplatz 4 was the official headquarters of the Vienna Gestapo.[22]

The conversion of the interior commenced after the Nazi plebiscite of 10 April 1938. The former guest bedrooms were transformed into offices, with furniture being provided partly from seized Jewish assets and partly from the hotel's own inventory. The first floor was occupied mainly by members of Department I of the Gestapo, responsible for personnel and material, including wage accounting, the provision of uniforms and building maintenance. On the second floor were the offices of Gestapo head Franz Josef Huber (room 243) and his deputy and members of Section II A (later IV A). The offices of Section II B (later IV B), and within it Unit II B 4 (Jews) – the infamous *Judenreferat* ('Jewish section', later IV B 4) – were on the third floor. On the ground floor, the former reading and recreation rooms were converted into a porter's lodge, the main Gestapo filing room and ten detention cells.[23] Further cells were installed in the basement in 1943, where Allied parachutists in particular were interned for months. Several rooms on the fifth floor were reserved for 'prominent' detainees. It was here that Kurt Schuschnigg and Louis Rothschild were interned in 1938–39. From 1943, the parachutists arrested by the Gestapo were interned there and forced to participate in *Funkspiele* (disinformation by means of fake radio messages).

While people who were summoned by the Gestapo for a reprimand, questioning or testimony, or who came in the hope of obtaining information about the fate of interned family members, used the main door on Morzinplatz 4, arrestees were taken for interrogation by the former tradesmen's entrance in Salztorgasse. This was done because the staircase from there up to the fifth floor was enclosed by a cage that prevented arrestees from committing suicide by throwing themselves down the stairwell.

At the end of March 1938, Josef Stachelberger, the 'provisional administrator' of Hotel Metropole, and the 143 employees were faced with unemployment.

They were assured at a staff meeting that they would be given equivalent posts elsewhere and that in the meantime their wages would be paid by the Gestapo; but a few weeks later, on 11 May 1938, Stachelberger was obliged to inform the staff on behalf of Kriminalrat Josef Meisinger[24] that their employment would be terminated on 30 June 1938 and that they would only be paid until that date. When the staff representative appealed to Meisinger, the latter replied that he did not recognize staff representatives. An appeal to Reichsführer-SS Himmler was also unsuccessful.[25] Josef Stachelberger continued to run the bar until 6 May 1938 and was able to work thereafter in various restaurants.[26]

On 10 November 1938, the Vienna Gestapo noted in a letter to the Landeshauptmannschaft (regional administration) of the Reichsgau Lower Danube that 'title to the building ... has passed to the German Reich and it has been made available to the Gestapo as its official headquarters (offices) in Vienna'. It further emphatically decreed: 'This building is no longer a hotel'.[27]

The 'Special Detainees' Kurt Schuschnigg and Louis Rothschild

During the night of 11 March 1938, the apartment of Kurt Schuschnigg, the Austrian federal chancellor who had been forced to resign, was surrounded by armed civilians and SA men. The ex-chancellor, his fiancée and his father, who were also in the apartment, which was in an annexe of Belvedere Palace at Landstrasser Gürtel 3, were not allowed to leave. In the morning, Schuschnigg attempted in vain to call his successor Arthur Seyß-Inquart, who just the evening before had 'guaranteed' his safety. On 14 March, the new chancellor informed Schuschnigg through a former state secretary that it was 'undesirable' for him to contact anyone outside his home. The former Austrian federal chancellor was under house arrest, guarded by Viennese police officials and SS men, who in the following weeks took pleasure in grossly insulting the occupants, threatening to shoot them and tormenting them at night with noise and floodlights.

On 26 March, when the initial 'Anschluss euphoria' had dissipated and the new police structures were already being established, Schuschnigg was interrogated for the first time in his own living room by four SS members and Gestapo officials. The interrogation was led by Humbert Achamer-Pifrader, at this time already deputy head of the Vienna Gestapo, who asked him in particular about his assets and his contacts with monarchist circles, Louis Rothschild, and Cardinal Theodor Innitzer.[28]

After this interrogation, Schuschnigg remained under house arrest, but without any information about his future fate. On 30 May, officials from the Gestapo headquarters returned, again led by Achamer-Pifrader, together with Othmar Trnka (later Trenker), who was responsible at the time for personal safety, including Hitler's security at Hotel Imperial.[29] After Schuschnigg had been ordered by Achamer-Pifrader to pack clothing, he was taken by him and Trenker in a car with curtained windows to the Gestapo building on Morzinplatz, where he was interned on the fifth floor in a former drying room, while his father and fiancée were allowed to go free.[30]

The Historical Commission of the Reichsführer-SS and the Extraordinary Constitutional Court

The decision to intern Schuschnigg at the Gestapo headquarters had already been made on 25 April 1938, when Sipo chief Reinhard Heydrich telexed Gauleiter Bürckel approving Schuschnigg's internment there. This step by Heydrich was closely connected with the order issued the same day by Reichsführer-SS Himmler that a commission be formed to investigate the failed putsch by the Austrian Nazis on 25 July 1934.

Accordingly, the Historische Commission des Reichsführers-SS was set up to reconstruct the reasons for the failed putsch from the point of view of the SS, and to determine the 'culprits on both the Nazi and the opposition side'. It was also to 'identify ... and determine the persons responsible for the severe punishments imposed on SS men in Austria', and to investigate 'Schuschnigg's constitutional and possibly criminal transgressions'.[31]

In May 1938, Heydrich appointed SS-Gruppenführer Wilhelm Koppe[32] to head the commission, SS-Standartenführer Franz Alfred Six, the inland head of the SD, to coordinate its work, and SS-Standartenführer Steinhäusl to 'handle the proceedings'. Franz Josef Huber, head of the Vienna Gestapo, was also one of the members of the commission.

In the same month, Hitler decided to have charges against Schuschnigg preferred in an 'extraordinary constitutional court' and to have the ex-chancellor prosecuted 'according to Austrian law'. The law on the establishment of a 'constitutional court' was passed on 17 August 1938. After Schuschnigg's conviction, 'all major politically incriminated persons and heads of the "Christian corporate state"' were also to be tried in such a court.

On 14 June 1938, when the former federal chancellor was already interned at Morzinplatz, an 'Arbeitskommando' (work commando) headed by Six started its work. The group was provided with three rooms, some safes, office material, two shorthand typists and a few assistants.[33]

The planned show trial of Schuschnigg – whose conviction was a foregone conclusion – was intended to give the appearance, above all to other countries, of respect for the rule of law. After all, the defendant was a former Austrian federal chancellor. Unlike other top functionaries of the authoritarian corporate state, even the Nazi regime could not simply intern him in a concentration camp, at least not at this particular time.

As Schuschnigg was to be questioned extensively by the members of the 'Arbeitskommando' in the Gestapo building, it was logical for him to be interned there as well. The Gestapo headquarters was also deemed suitable for the ex-chancellor's internment because his presence there could largely be kept secret and, above all, his physical integrity could also be guaranteed. In order to give the appearance of adherence to the rule of law, it was essential that the ex-chancellor appear before the 'extraordinary constitutional court' in relatively good physical condition.

Kurt Schuschnigg at Morzinplatz 4

Along with Louis Rothschild, who was also interned on the fifth floor of the Gestapo headquarters, Kurt Schuschnigg was one of the first 'special detainees' (*Sonderhäftlinge*) of the Nazi regime.[34] This group, which grew considerably in the course of the war, included politicians such as the former French prime minister Léon Blum, officers such as Charles de Gaulle's brother-in-law Alfred Cailleau, and clergymen such as Martin Niemöller, as well as members of the Stauffenberg family and other 20 July 1944 conspirators. These 'special detainees' were held prisoner under comparatively mild conditions at various locations including remote hotels, castles and separate barracks in concentration camps. Although they were detained for quite diverse reasons, they were all hostages of the Nazi regime, and their survival, in spite of the relatively mild detention conditions, was by no means certain.

Everything connected with Schuschnigg's detention was not only 'Geheime Reichssache' (secret Reich business), but also exclusively 'Chefsache' (a matter for Himmler himself). Every detail, however small, of his imprisonment had to be reported to Berlin and presented both to Gestapo head Müller and Reichsführer-SS Himmler, even minutiae such as an addition to the guard regulations stating that Schuschnigg was to 'take a bath every Saturday ... in the early evening in a bathroom on the fourth floor'.[35]

Apart from Gauleiter Bürckel, who however 'left all measures against Schuschnigg to the Gestapa's discretion', only the top echelons of the Sipo were entrusted with dealing with the Schuschnigg matter: Himmler, Heydrich and Müller in Berlin; the leading Gestapo officials – Franz Josef Huber, Humbert Achamer-Pifrader, Othmar Trenker and Rudolf Lange – in Vienna; and the state secretary for security matters in Austria and head of the SS-Oberabschnitt 'Danube', Ernst Kaltenbrunner.[36] There was extensive correspondence between Vienna and Berlin until Schuschnigg's transfer to Munich on 29 October 1939 – mostly in the form of 'Blitzfernschreiben' (lightning telexes) – offering a relatively good idea of the conditions in which the ex-chancellor was detained. It also clearly shows how much Schuschnigg suffered from his situation, in spite of the relatively mild treatment, to the extent that he even considered suicide.[37]

Schuschnigg was allowed to move freely in the room where he was imprisoned, which contained a bed, table, chair, wardrobe and washbasin, but he was forbidden to stand at the window. SS guards were posted in his room and in front of it, mostly young Austrian and German SS men, some of whom tormented Schuschnigg by forcing him to carry out cleaning tasks and the like. In September 1938 Himmler ordered that the SS men be replaced by regular uniformed police officials.[38] The corridor outside the room where Schuschnigg was imprisoned could be entered only by the guards – who were changed every two hours – or by anyone identified by a password, which was changed every day.[39]

Letters to and from the ex-chancellor were checked by Achamer-Pifrader or Lange, and letters to him were often withheld.[40] Until summer 1939, Schuschnigg had to pay for his food, which was obtained from the canteen on the ground floor.

His wife Vera – the marriage ceremony had taken place in Schuschnigg's absence at the Dominican church in Vienna on 1 June 1938[41] – was allowed to visit him once a week for ten minutes, and to bring him books, fruit and cigarettes. Vera Schuschnigg was under observation at times by the Gestapo, who kept a file on her 'in the safe of the deputy head [Pifrader]'.[42]

In August 1938 Schuschnigg mentioned the possibility of suicide to his wife, which the guard in the room immediately reported. Thereafter the guards posted in the room were instructed in particular 'to watch Schuschnigg closely when he is shaving'.[43] Achamer-Pifrader also banned Vera Schuschnigg from continuing to bring fruit and cigarettes because of the possibility that 'relatives or friends of Schuschnigg would use the opportunity to give him poison so that he would not have to stand trial'.[44] Achamer-Pifrader also immediately informed SS-Standartenführer Müller that 'if his current state of health does not change … Dr Schuschnigg, who has now been detained for three months, will probably have to be hospitalized in the near future. The SS doctor has determined that Schuschnigg is organically healthy but extremely nervous. He has prescribed a medicament for the nerves'.[45] On 1 September 1938, Achamer-Pifrader requested in a telex to SS-Standartenführer Müller that the ex-chancellor be transferred to the 'Altreich'. He repeated the request on 5 September, noting that he 'could no longer take responsibility for Schuschnigg to the same extent as before'.[46]

It would not have been in the regime's interests for Schuschnigg to commit suicide, not only because the planned show trial would no longer be possible, but also because, as Huber stressed in a letter to SS-Standartenführer Müller, 'the standing of the German Reich would be damaged'.[47] The remarkable number of measures taken to prevent the former federal chancellor from committing suicide seems almost absurd considering the countless victims put to death by the Nazi regime.

For example, on 13 October 1938 Himmler ordered that with immediate effect Schuschnigg was to be examined weekly on Saturdays by a 'suitable doctor' and that the results of the examination were to be telexed to him that same day.[48] The medical reports sent every week from the Vienna Gestapo to the Gestapa give a good idea of Schuschnigg's critical mental state. On 25 October 1938, for example, it was stated that 'the patient' made 'an extremely neurasthenic impression', that 'he sat restlessly on the chair when speaking' and was 'close to tears'.[49] On 9 December 1938, Achamer-Pifrader informed SS-Standartenführer Müller about Schuschnigg's 'depressive mood' and the utterance during the weekly examination that he 'would like nothing more than a lethal injection, which he would prefer to a slow end'.[50]

When Schuschnigg began increasingly to lose weight, the guards were instructed to keep a precise list of the food he ate, as it was feared that by starving 'his strength in general ... will deteriorate to such an extent that he will have to be hospitalized', and 'should Schuschnigg be released at some point it will be said that we ... stood by as he slowly starved'.[51] On 20 February 1939, Huber finally ordered 'that Schuschnigg is to be fed with immediate effect at the cost of the state'.[52]

Although for political rather than humanitarian reasons, the Gestapo wished not only to ensure that the ex-chancellor remained healthy but also to keep his detention at the Gestapo headquarters secret. When the kitchen closed there in summer 1939, Achamer-Pifrader telexed Müller with the suggestion that Schuschnigg's meals be obtained from a nearby restaurant. In order to conceal the recipient's identity, he recommended that the restaurant be told 'that they are for the commander of the guards'.[53] Achamer-Pifrader's suggestion was approved by the Gestapa, albeit on the condition 'that the reason for the meals remains secret at all costs', and that 'the new regulation is closely monitored'.[54]

However, Schuschnigg's detention at the Gestapo headquarters did not by any means remain secret, as is illustrated by two almost tragicomic incidents. On 24 December 1938, a bunch of lilacs was delivered by the Fossati flower shop to the duty room of the Gestapo building with a request that it be given to Schuschnigg. The request was not carried out; on the contrary the flower shop was put under investigation immediately after the holidays. It came to nothing, however, because no one could remember who had purchased the lilacs or commissioned their delivery. In March 1939, Gräfin Elisabeth Kerssenbrock appeared at the duty room at Morzinplatz 4 with a large bouquet of flowers 'to cheer up Federal Chancellor Schuschnigg'. The flowers were not accepted and the woman was told that her behaviour was a provocation and that 'only because of her age' (she was sixty years old) would they 'refrain from further measures'.[55] A file was opened on her forthwith in Section II F 2.

Louis Rothschild and the Nazi Lust for the Witkowitzer Bergbau- und Eisenhüttenwerk

Baron Louis Rothschild, the only member of his family still in Vienna at the time of the annexation, was arrested on 12 March 1938[56] and interned under dreadful conditions in the first few weeks after the annexation at the police prison on Rossauer Lände. Rothschild was one of the prominent detainees who were 'presented for viewing' to influential Nazis by the coal merchant and SA man Franz Towin and his accomplices. The prisoners handled by Towin and his associates were not only grossly insulted but also had to allow themselves to be photographed in certain positions. Rothschild was shown together with Leopold Kunschak, a leading official in the Christian-social workers' movement. These photos were later distributed in Nazi circles.[57]

After a few weeks, Hermann Göring ordered that Louis Rothschild be transferred to the Gestapo headquarters nearby. Göring realized that Rothschild was an important bargaining chip in the future 'Aryanization' of the Rothschild assets. As the person responsible for the Four-Year Plan, Göring not only wanted to seize the Rothschild family assets in Austria but also above all to get hold of the Rothschild mining and ironworks in Moravia, the Witkowitzer Bergbau- und Eisenhüttenwerk. This was of great significance for the armaments industry, giving Germany control of 30 per cent of crude steel production, 30 per cent of coal production and 40 per cent of pig iron production in Czechoslovakia.

To preserve Germany's reputation, Rothschild, whose fate was followed closely abroad, above all by the many branches of his family, was to be interned, like Schuschnigg, in relatively humane conditions. He was also to be made available to various official representatives, including those from the property transaction office (Vermögensverkehrsstelle) and the Reich trustee from the Reich ministry of economic affairs, as the 'Aryanization' of the extensive and above all diverse Rothschild assets were proving complicated, not least because the three Rothschild brothers had shares in both Austrian and foreign businesses. It was difficult to estimate the real value of the Rothschild family assets in Austria, and the Nazi economic experts also had particular difficulty in untangling the complicated ownership situation of the avidly coveted Witkowitzer Bergbau- und Eisenhüttenwerk. It took some time before they realized that the Rothschilds had successfully sold the lion's share in the ironworks before the 1938 annexation to a British trust controlled by the family. It was only after the occupation of 'rump Czechoslovakia' in March 1939 that the plant, which was formally held by the British, was effectively incorporated into Reichswerke Hermann Göring. In early May 1939, an agreement was finally concluded between the Reich ministry of economic affairs and the Rothschild agent about transferring title of all of the Rothschild assets throughout the Reich territory, including the art collections, to the German Reich. Louis Rothschild was finally released in July 1939, and by a roundabout route he managed to escape to the United States.[58]

There are few records of Louis Rothschild's internment. His name appears only twice in the correspondence between the Gestapa in Berlin and the Vienna Gestapo. The first time is in a telex from Achamer-Pifrader on 1 September 1938 to Heinrich Müller, with the request 'to transfer Dr Schuschnigg and Rothschild to the Altreich, as under the circumstances it is impossible in the long term to continue to keep them here',[59] and a second time is in connection with Himmler's visit to Rothschild and Schuschnigg.

Visit of the Reichsführer-SS to Kurt Schuschnigg and Louis Rothschild

Himmler visited the Gestapo headquarters in Vienna on 12 December 1938 accompanied by SS-Gruppenführer Ernst Kaltenbrunner, state secretary for security, SS-Standartenführer Franz Stahlecker, Sipo inspector in Austria, and SS-Gruppenführer Karl Wolff.[60] While Achamer-Pifrader, as deputy of the absent Gestapo head Huber, was still being informed of Himmler's presence, the Reichsführer-SS and his entourage went straight to the fifth floor to visit Schuschnigg and Rothschild. No details of this visit exist except for the fact that afterwards Himmler ordered the detainees' rooms to be made more comfortable, and for them to be provided with a wireless. On the same day, Achamer-Pifrader ordered Rudolf Lange, 'possibly by arrangement with Dr Siegl [= Siegel] from II H/S',[61] to provide the rooms with the necessary furnishings, 'as at 4 p.m. the inspector [Stahlecker] will be coming in person to check that the order of the Reichsführer-SS has been carried out, so that he can report back to Berlin today'.[62]

The two detainees were evidently of great value to Himmler for political and propaganda reasons. But the refurnishing of the rooms did not proceed as rapidly as ordered, because it was not until 7 January 1939 that Huber was informed in a letter from Department II that 'the detainees' rooms on the fifth floor … have been carpeted and, in accordance with the prisoners' wishes, provided with tables and chairs. Pictures, when requested, have been obtained'.[63]

In February 1939, Heinrich Müller was also informed of the new furnishings in the two rooms, with carpets, bedside tables, rugs, clothes racks, typewriters and a three-piece suite in each room. Louis Rothschild was also allowed to acquire two hotplates at his own expense, which would indicate that he cooked for himself.

The End of the Historical Commission of the Reichsführer-SS and Schuschnigg's Transfer to Munich

When Louis Rothschild was released from custody in July 1939, important decisions about Kurt Schuschnigg's fate had also been made. They were closely connected with the activities of the historical commission of the Reichsführer-SS. After the commission had started work, old conflicts that had been painstakingly suppressed after 1934 soon resurfaced within the Austrian Nazi party, and between the SS, which had in fact been largely responsible for the June 1934 'Röhm purge', and the SA leadership. When it also became more and more apparent during the commission's work that Hitler himself had at least known about the purge – which he vehemently denied in 1934 – he personally ordered that the investigations be suspended and that all involved be sworn to the strictest secrecy and silence.

After the Vienna 'Arbeitskommando' had written its 'final report on the activities of the work commando of the historical commission of the Reichsführer-SS' of 27 January 1939, the commission was disbanded by Himmler in March 1939. An (unsigned) letter of 15 March 1939 to SS-Gruppenführer Koppe also stated that Hitler had decided that while the planned trial should not take place, 'no decision has yet been made … about the fate of Schuschnigg, who will continue to remain in custody'.[64]

As the Nazi leadership feared that, were he to be released, Schuschnigg could offer 'important support for émigrés',[65] initial consideration was given in April 1939 to releasing the exchancellor from Gestapo imprisonment but then placing him and his wife under house arrest in Gera.[66] This idea was quickly discarded, however, and on 30 June 1939 a telegram was sent by the Gestapa to the Vienna Gestapo stating that the Reichsführer-SS had ordered that 'an arrangement [is] currently being made for the detainee Schuschnigg to be allowed to live with his wife, and that while Frau Schuschnigg should under no circumstances be regarded as a co-prisoner, she should be subject to certain conditions. It is hoped that this new arrangement can be implemented by September/October at the latest'.[67]

As part of the 'new arrangement', the Gestapa sent an order to Achamer-Pifrader on 14 August 1939 that 'in all matters regarding Dr Schuschnigg in future … the code name "Dr Auster" is to be used'.[68] On 19 August 1939, SS-Standartenführer Müller informed Huber that 'the construction work for accommodating Dr A. in a concentration camp (with the possibility of his living with his wife) has already begun'. Huber was apparently in a hurry to get rid of his 'special detainee', because in early September he was already asking the Gestapa – pointing out that twenty-four officials were required to guard Schuschnigg – how long 'Dr Auster … will remain in Vienna'.

On 29 October 1939, Schuschnigg, accompanied by Achamer-Pifrader, Ebner and two further officials, was taken by car to the Gestapo prison in Munich.[69] After intermediate stops in Dachau and Flossenbürg concentration camps, he was ultimately transferred on 8 December 1941 to Sachsenhausen, where he lived with his wife and daughter, born on 28 March 1941, in a special section of the camp.

Although the surviving files of the historical commission of the Reichsführer-SS indicate that a 'supplementary report on the Schuschnigg constitutional affair' had been drafted, neither this nor the questioning of Schuschnigg on the events of 25 July 1934 can be traced.

While the conditions under which Kurt Schuschnigg and Louis Rothschild were held differed considerably from those of other detainees and prisoners, the associated psychological pressure should not be underestimated. It is striking that the Vienna Gestapo was the only executive body in these two cases, albeit without any leeway in its actions, as the decisions were made at the highest level by Himmler, Hitler, and others.

Notes

1. Between 1860 and 1863, Karl Treumann built a temporary wooden theatre on this site on Franz-Josefs-Kai, which was destroyed in a fire in June 1863.
2. *Compass 1870*, 474.
3. WStLA, Geschäftsbericht der Hotel-Actien-Gesellschaft Metropole, 1873, Handelsgericht Wien, A44-B-Registerakten: B1, 42, Hotel Metropole.
4. Shareholders included Josef Mauthner, Moritz Strakosch, Baron Franz Mayr-Melnhof and Count Adolph Dubsky.
5. 1 square klafter = 3.597 m².
6. WStLA, Handelsgericht Wien, A44-B-Registerakten: B1, 42 Hotel Metropole, annual report of Hotel-Actien-Gesellschaft Metropole, 1873.
7. Ibid., annual report of Hotel-Actien-Gesellschaft Metropole, 1874.
8. *Reichspost*, 29 Nov 1918, 6.
9. Elisabeth Klein, born 12 Feb 1891, mother of Annemarie Böhm, née Klein, born 11 Feb 1919, and Gottlieb Klein, born 2 Jun 1921. At the time of the annexation of Austria, Elisabeth and Gottlieb Klein were in London. The Klein family managed to escape to Australia; private archive of Doris (Dymia) Schulze, Vienna.
10. WStLA, Handelsgericht Wien, A44-B-Registerakten: B1,42 Hotel Metropole, written statement by Robert Feix to the Vienna public prosecutor's office, Jan 1938.
11. ÖStA, AdR, Bestand Liegenschaften, box 388, 1355, letter from the NSDAP Betriebszelle to Gauleiter Bürckel, 26 Mar 1938.
12. WStLA, Vienna LG, Vg Vr 2008/46, indictment of Josef Stachelberger.
13. WStLA, Gebäudeakt Wien 1, Morzinplatz 4, Innere Stadt Einlagezahl 306.
14. Hessisches Hauptstaatsarchiv Wiesbaden 518/8586, statutory declaration by Hugo Hoffmann to the reparation chamber of Frankfurt am Main regional court in the Feix restitution case, 4 June 1949.
15. Kreisky, *Erinnerungen*, 214.
16. From 1929 until the start of the Second World War, Otto von Habsburg lived at Steenokkerzeel near Brussels.
17. Hessisches Hauptstaatsarchiv Wiesbaden 518/8586, statutory declaration by Hugo Hoffmann to the reparation chamber of Frankfurt am Main regional court in the Feix restitution case, 4 June 1949.

18. Hessisches Hauptstaatsarchiv Wiesbaden, 461, 32805/1-6, statement by Feix, n.d., in the investigation of Walter Fischer et al.: offences against the businessman Robert Feix before the restitution chamber of Frankfurt am Main regional court.
19. See the section 'Catholic-Conservative and Legitimist Resistance' in Chapter 12.
20. http://historicum.jku.at/HABIL/Beer.html (last accessed on 20 Oct 2017).
21. Private archive of Doris (Dymia) Schulze, Vienna.
22. DÖW 3663, letter from the head of the Sipo to all heads of departments and sections of the Sipo headquarters and the Gestapa, 1 Apr 1938.
23. WStLA, Bundespolizeidirektion: Staatspolizeiliche Abteilung, A1-Polizeiliche Erhebung: 23-Gestapo Wien, telephone list of the Gestapo regional headquarters, Vienna.
24. Josef Albert Meisinger, born 14 Sep 1899 in Munich, was already involved in the Hitler putsch in 1923 and joined the NSDAP and SS in 1933, where he progressed to become SS-Standartenführer. As a former member of the Bavarian political police, he had very good contacts with Heinrich Müller and Franz Josef Huber. From 1941 to 1945 he was transferred to Tokyo as a punishment. He was executed as a war criminal in Poland in 1947.
25. ÖSTA, AdR, Bestand Liegenschaften, box 388, 1355, letter from Josef Stachelberger to the property transaction office (Vermögensverkehrsstelle) in the ministry of economic affairs and labour, 4 July 1938.
26. WStLA, Vienna LG, Vg Vr 2008/46, indictment of Josef Stachelberger.
27. [das Gebäude ... in das Eigentum des Deutschen Reiches übergegangen und der Geheimen Staatspolizei als behördlicher Dienstsitz für die Staatspolizeileitstelle Wien zur Verfügung gestellt worden ist. ... Mit einem 'Hotel' hat dieses Haus nichts mehr zu tun.] DÖW 7968.
28. Schuschnigg, *Austrian Requiem*, 58–62 (*Requiem in Rot-Weiß-Rot*, 118–22).
29. WStLA, Vienna LG, Vg 1h Vr 7459/48; for Othmar Trenker, see chapters 4 and 18.
30. Schuschnigg, *Austrian Requiem*, 63–64 (*Requiem in Rot-Weiß-Rot*, 125).
31. [jene Personen fest ... stellen und festsetzen, welche für die gegen SS-Männer in Österreich gerichteten schweren Bestrafungen verantwortlich sind / die verfassungsrechtlichen und etwaigen kriminellen Verfehlungen Schuschniggs] Steiner, *Die Erhebung*, 16; Hachmeister, *Der Gegnerforscher*, 31–32; cover letter by Heydrich of 9 Dec 1938 regarding the transfer of the file to Reichsführer-SS Himmler, quoted from Steiner, *Die Erhebung*, 16.
32. Karl Heinrich Wilhelm Koppe, born 1896 in Hildesheim, and a member of the NSDAP, SA and SS from 1930, enjoyed Heinrich Himmler's particular confidence. At the time he was inspector of the Sipo and SD in Saxony, and head of the Gestapo in Dresden. On 26 Oct 1939, after the invasion of Poland, he was appointed HSSPF in the Warthegau, where he was responsible for the killing of disabled people and Jews. Subsequently, as HSSPF in the Generalgouvernement (Poland), he played an instrumental role in the extermination of the Jews there. He disappeared after 1945 until his arrest in 1960. The criminal proceedings against him were adjourned in 1964 'for health reasons'.
33. Letter from SS-Standartenführer Franz Alfred Six to the inspector of the Sipo in Austria, SS-Obersturmbannführer Franz Stahlecker, undated, quoted in Steiner, *Die Erhebung*, 15; Hachmeister, *Der Gegnerforscher*, 35.
34. On 'special detainees' (*Sonderhäftlinge*), in Nazi jargon also cynically known as 'prisoners of honour' (Ehrenhäftlinge), see Koop, *In Hitlers Hand*.
35. ÖStA, AVA Reichsstatthalter, Staatspolizeileitstelle Wien, Asservat 98/2 Dr Schuschnigg, memo of the Vienna Gestapo, n.d.
36. Ibid., memo of the deputy head of the Vienna Gestapo, 17 Apr 1939.
37. However, Schuschnigg does not mention this at all in his memoirs.
38. Schuschnigg, *Austrian Requiem*, 65 (*Requiem in Rot-Weiß-Rot*, 126ff.); ÖStA, AVA Reichsstatthalter, Staatspolizeileitstelle Wien, Asservat 98/2 Dr Schuschnigg, telex from Achamer-Pifrader to SS-Standartenführer Müller at the Gestapa, 5 Sep 1938.

39. ÖStA, AVA Reichsstatthalter, Staatspolizeileitstelle Wien, Asservat 98/2 Dr Schuschnigg, guard regulation of 8 Sep 1938.
40. Some of these are to be found today in ÖStA, AVA Reichsstatthalter, Staatspolizeileitstelle Wien, Asservat 98/2 Dr Schuschnigg.
41. Schuschnigg was represented at the marriage ceremony by his brother Arthur Schuschnigg, and the witnesses were his father and the sacristan; see ÖStA, AVA Reichsstatthalter, Staatspolizeileitstelle Wien, Asservat 98/2 Dr Schuschnigg, memo of the Vienna Gestapo regarding Vera von Schuschnigg, née Gräfin Czernin, divorced Fugger von Babenhausen, 20 June 1938.
42. ÖStA, AVA Reichsstatthalter, Staatspolizeileitstelle Wien, Asservat 98/2 Dr Schuschnigg, letter from the Vienna Gestapo to SS-Standartenführer Müller at the Gestapa, 18 Jun 1938.
43. Ibid., memo of the Vienna Gestapo, 20 Aug 1938.
44. Ibid., report by Humbert Achamer-Pifrader to the head of the Vienna Gestapo, 29 Aug 1938.
45. Ibid., telex from Humbert Achamer-Pifrader to Heinrich Müller at the Gestapa, 1 Sep 1938.
46. Ibid., telex from Achamer-Pifrader to SS-Standartenführer Müller at the Gestapa, 5 Sep 1938.
47. Ibid., express letter from the Gestapo headquarters to SS-Standartenführer Müller at the Gestapa, 17 Feb 1939.
48. Ibid, telex from the Gestapa to the Vienna Gestapo, 21 Oct 1938.
49. Ibid., report of SS-Hauptsturmführer Dr Waegner, duty doctor, and Standortarzt der SS-Verfügungstruppe Wien, 25 Oct 1938.
50. Ibid., lightning telex from the Vienna Gestapo to SS-Standartenführer Müller at the Gestapa, 9 Dec 1938.
51. Ibid., express letter from the Vienna Gestapo to SS-Standartenführer Müller at the Gestapa, 17 Feb 1939.
52. Ibid., telex from the head of the Vienna Gestapo to SS-Standartenführer Müller at the Gestapa, 23 Feb 1939.
53. Ibid., telex from the Vienna Gestapo to SS-Standartenführer Müller at the Gestapa, 12 Aug 1939.
54. Ibid., telex from the Gestapa to SS-Obersturmbannführer Achamer-Pifrader, 1 Aug 1939.
55. Ibid.
56. Louis Rothschild's brothers Eugene and Alphonse had escaped to Paris and Switzerland respectively; see Heimann-Jelinek, 'Die "Arisierung"', 356.
57. WStLA, Vienna LG, Vg 6b Vr 2724/46 (DÖW 20 029).
58. Heimann-Jelinek, 'Die "Arisierung"', 358–62.
59. ÖStA, AVA Reichstatthalter, Gestapo-Leitstelle Wien Asservat 98/2 Dr Schuschnigg, letter from Pifrader to SS-Standartenführer Müller at the Gestapa, 1 Sep 1938 (DÖW 19 314).
60. Karl Friedrich Otto Wolff was (later) SS-Obergruppenführer and general in the Waffen-SS, head of the Reichsführer-SS personal staff and SS liaison officer to Hitler.
61. This Gestapo section headed by Viktor Siegel was responsible for the seizure of Jewish assets.
62. ÖStA, AVA Reichstatthalter, Gestapo-Leitstelle Wien Asservat 98/2, Dr Schuschnigg (DÖW 19 314).
63. Ibid., letter from Department II to the head of the Vienna Gestapo, 7 Jan 1938.
64. Steiner, *Die Erhebung*, 8ff., 35ff., 49.
65. Ibid., letter to SS-Gruppenführer Koppe, 15 Mar 1939.
66. ÖStA, AVA Reichsstatthalter, Staatspolizeileitstelle Wien, Asservat 98/2 Dr Schuschnigg, memo of the Vienna Gestapo, 17 Apr 1939.
67. Ibid., telex from the Gestapa to the Vienna Gestapo, 30 Jun 1939.
68. Ibid., express letter from the Gestapa to the Vienna Gestapo, 14 Aug 1939.
69. Schuschnigg, *Austrian Requiem*, 177–79 (*Requiem in Rot-Weiß-Rot*, 375–76).

Chapter 4

THE GESTAPO IN THE NETWORK OF THE SS AND POLITICAL STRUCTURES

Organization of the Vienna Gestapo

After the annexation of Austria in March 1938, the Vienna Gestapo found itself at the centre of an institutional structure typical of the often opaque chain of command emanating from the Reichssicherheitshauptamt (Reich security main office, RSHA), enabling good cooperation with the office of the local Gauleiter/Reichsstatthalter (Reich governor), the administrative authorities and the Wehrmacht. Especially on account of the multitude of offices held by its head Franz Josef Huber, the Vienna Gestapo had a special status unparalleled in the German Reich. Huber's close relationship with his protector Reinhard Heydrich and his long-standing friendship with Heinrich Müller meant that he had the benefit of a shortened chain of command, often bypassing Ernst Kaltenbrunner, who as an HSSPF was his official superior. Huber's unique dual role as head of the Vienna Gestapo *and* inspector of the security police and SD, which effectively meant that in the former position he was answerable to himself, offered him the necessary latitude to expand the Vienna Gestapo into a highly powerful, efficient and violent organization.

This chapter looks at the position of the Gestapo in general – and the Vienna Gestapo in particular – within the network of the SS and the political structures, the relationship it developed with the SS security service (SS-Sicherheitsdienst, SD), and the way it held its own among the competing intelligence systems within the German Reich.

Himmler's 'Generally Authorized Agents': The Higher SS and Police Leaders

The tasks of the Höhere SS- und Polizeiführer (HSSPFs, higher SS and police leaders) were originally defined for the event of mobilization and war, but were later to evolve into fundamentally different patterns of deployment. The essential function of the HSSPFs was 'political administration'[1] and safeguarding the political interests of Himmler and his SS and police. As Ruth Bettina Birn has observed: 'The HSSPFs served not only to extend Himmler's power externally but also to consolidate it internally'.[2]

The work of the HSSPFs in the occupied territories and behind the front – their original assignment – was of decisive importance, particularly in the extermination the Jewish population and in combating resistance,[3] but their duties in the 'Altreich' and the Alpine and Danube Gaus did not extend much further than routine and representative functions. Birn notes that 'in the Reich ... the HSSPFs' responsibilities were more restricted [than in the occupied territories]. They acquired scope for independent action in disciplining foreign workers and in air raid protection'.[4] For the most part, however, they dealt with internal SS procedures, particularly the ideological monitoring and welfare of the families of SS members.

The HSSPFs were personally selected by Himmler and were directly answerable to him as 'authorized agents'; like the upper echelons of the SS, they were also assigned to the military districts (Wehrkreise) – for example, Kaltenbrunner as HSSPF 'Danube' to Military District XVII. They exemplified Himmler's intention of 'keeping the power structure of the Third Reich in permanent motion by constant shifting of responsibilities'.[5] Regardless of the chain of command and hierarchies, Himmler's instructions always had priority, which Himmler exploited extensively, not only because it was in his nature but also with a view to ensuring the rapid and efficient implementation of important decisions via flat hierarchical structures.

The HSSPFs had relatively little say in routine procedures, and were barely involved in Gestapo activities,[6] but the chain of command for special assignments – bypassing the RSHA – went directly from Himmler to the HSSPFs, with the RSHA being informed only 'for intelligence purposes'.[7] Inevitably, such special assignments from Himmler to the HSSPFs related in particular to actions in the occupied territories and the theatres of war.

By contrast, the position of the HSSPFs in relation to the authorities in their regional military districts is more difficult to determine. The official chain of command was Reichsstatthalter/Gauleiter > HSSPF > military district commander (in the 'Altreich', still Reichsstatthalter/Gauleiter > minister > Regierungspräsident). Himmler ordered the HSSPFs to attend NSDAP, state and Wehrmacht events.[8]

Officially, the HSSPFs were therefore subordinate to the Reichsstatthalter/Gauleiter – Kaltenbrunner, for example, to Baldur von Schirach in the Reichsgau of Vienna and to Hugo Jury in 'Lower Danube' (Niederdonau). Officially, however, Himmler was also 'subordinate' to the Reich minister of the interior, which in practice was meaningless. Just as Himmler, in conflict situations, was always 'personally and directly' answerable to Hitler, bypassing the minister of the interior, the HSSPFs' 'personal and direct' subordination to Himmler always had priority. On the other hand, Kaltenbrunner was not subordinate to Schirach or Jury in their functions as Reich defence commissioners (Reichsverteidigungskommissare)[9] in Military District XVII, but to Himmler in his function as Reich commissioner for the consolidation of German nationhood (Reichskommissar für die Festigung deutschen Volkstums).

Both the Vienna Gestapo and SD-Oberabschnitt 'Danube' were answerable to the chief of the Sipo and SD *and* to the HSSPF in Military District XVII. While Heydrich could issue instructions directly to the Gestapo, bypassing the HSSPF, Kaltenbrunner, as an HSSPF, was required to pass on his instructions to the Gestapo through the regional inspector of the security police and SD (Inspekteur der Sicherheitspolizei und des SD, IdSuSD). The subordination of the IdSuSDs to the HSSPFs was not clear, however, as demonstrated by Heydrich's designation of the IdSuSDs as 'senior colleagues of the HSSPFs, who [the HSSPFs] are also responsible for the military districts'.[10] As Huber exercised the functions of both IdSuSD and head of the Vienna Gestapo in Military District XVII in personal union, conflicts with Kaltenbrunner as HSSPF were inevitable from the outset.

Heydrich's 'Personal Authorized Agents': The Inspectors of the Sipo and SD

The original task of the IdSuSDs was formulated by 'Reich and Prussian minister of the interior' Wilhelm Frick on 20 September 1936 in the instructions for inspectors of the security police, but these were anything but precise, and more in the style of a memorandum or hierarchy description:

> The particular duties of the security police demand the closest and most understanding cooperation with the central departments of the general and internal administration of the provinces and Länder, and with the Gauleiters of the NSDAP and the Wehrmacht. … The inspectors … are to promote this cooperation … [and] are personally and directly subordinate to the Oberpräsident and state minister of the interior, and are to follow their instructions.

In the next sentence, however, comes the decisive limitation: 'Should these instructions be irreconcilable with the general and particular orders and guidelines of the chief of the security police [Heydrich], and should no agreement be reached, the head of the security police is to be consulted for a decision'.¹¹

The IdSuSDs were part of the chain of command within the RSHA, and directly answerable to its head – first Heydrich and then, from 30 January 1943, Kaltenbrunner. Their function as driving forces in the operational and, above all, ideological fusion of the Sipo and SD was of central significance, particularly for Heydrich.

As 'personal authorized agents of the head of the security police and SD', the IdSuSDs represented the Gestapo, Kripo and SD 'with respect to the central authorities, Wehrmacht commands and NSDAP offices'. In their direct relationship with the Sipo authorities, however, they had no material right to issue instructions, and their duties with respect to the Gestapo and Kripo offices were restricted to coordination and supervisory functions.¹² Ebner, who also deputized for Huber as inspector, described Huber's duty effectively as one of 'visiting offices … although he only did so once every three to four months. … Huber never had an office in the inspectorate [Theresianumgasse 16–18, 4th district] but only at the Gestapo headquarters, and the inspector's advisers came to the Gestapo headquarters with their files'.¹³

Like the HSSPFs, the inspectors were officially subordinate, 'personally and directly', to the representatives of the state such as the Reichsstatthalters and the ministers of the interior (of the respective Länder of the 'Altreich'). But also like the HSSPFs, they had an overriding escape clause, by which Himmler and Heydrich eliminated any possible obstacle to their freedom of action from the outset. Paradoxically, this maxim also applied to the relationship between the HSSPFs and the IdSuSDs in their military districts:

> The inspectors of the security police and SD are to follow the instructions of the higher SS and police leaders insofar as they do not conflict with the instructions of the chief of the security police and SD. If this is the case, the inspector of the security police and SD is to notify the higher SS and police leader immediately, and consult with the chief of the security police and SD. … The inspectors of the security police and SD are the personal agents, both externally and internally, of the chief of the security police and SD within their mandates, and the personal supervisors, advisers and trainers of the members of the security police and SD under their command.¹⁴

The authority of the HSSPFs with regard to the Gestapo was also ultimately weakened through the rider 'insofar as it does not conflict with the orders of the RFSSuChdDt.Pol. in the RMdI [i.e. Himmler or Heydrich as his deputy] or his agents. In the case of doubt, the Reich central authority is to be consulted'.¹⁵

Whether the formal subordination to the heads of the administrative authorities was practised to the letter or not depended on the people involved: the inspectors acted in a free area deliberately created by Himmler and Heydrich outside the administration and its official channels. Here, as with the HSSPFs, it should be noted that Himmler and Heydrich counted on the personal persuasive powers of their SS leaders, and gave them the possibility to use these powers through seemingly contradictory hierarchical structures.

The inspectors were assisted by a comparatively small staff of ten, including the heads of the Gestapo and Kripo and the head of the SD-Leitabschnitt at his headquarters.[16] They were to 'devote at least half of their time to inspection of subordinate offices outside the location of their headquarters'.[17]

In the inspector's absence, he was represented 'by the head [of the Gestapo or Kripo office or SD-Leitabschnitt] with the most senior SS ranking'. In the case of SS-Oberabschnitt 'Danube', Huber's deputy as inspector should have been SS-Standartenführer and Regierungsdirektor Hans Karl Kaphengst, head of the Kripo in Vienna. Huber ignored the service instruction, however, and appointed Ebner, already his deputy as head of the Vienna Gestapo, as deputy inspector.[18] Ebner's function is confirmed by a memo from Rudolf Mildner, who stood in for the indisposed Huber as Gestapo head and inspector from June 1944. When Mildner was 'summoned' for a bogus meeting to the military district headquarters and held for a short time in connection with the events of 20 July 1944, he explicitly described Ebner, who had also been summoned, as 'deputy inspector'.[19]

Apart from his tendency to delegate, as far as possible, routine work, be it as Gestapo head or inspector, the ever-mistrustful and vigilant Huber tolerated only absolutely loyal employees in his immediate vicinity.[20] Ebner was ideally suited to this role of 'right-hand man': years of experience, a precise method of working, sensitivity in dealing with (Austrian) staff, personal loyalty to Huber to the point of total subordination, and above all a work rate that frequently exceeded the limits of his physical ability.

The declaration of a state of emergency after the war had entered the territory of the Reich in 1944 entailed institutional changes for the inspectors. Their regional spheres of authority, which until then had coincided with the SS-Oberabschnitte, were adapted on Himmler's order to align with the boundaries of the Nazi Gaus. While the Gestapo heads were given the new official title 'Kommandeur (commander) of the Sipo and SD', the inspectors became 'Befehlshaber (commander-in-chief) of the Sipo and SD'. As part of this process, on 1 December 1944, Huber, for example, was appointed 'Befehlshaber of the security police and SD in Military District XVII', while at the same time being relieved of his duties as head of the Vienna Gestapo.[21]

The Vienna Gestapo within the SS and Administration Network

Regarding the place of inspectors in the command structure of the RSHA, HSSPFs and local administrative authorities, there was one important exception, unique in the entire Reich and occupied territories: Franz Josef Huber, who was inspector of the security police and SD in Military District XVII *and* head of the Vienna Gestapo.[22] A letter of 2 October 1940 from Heydrich to the main personnel office of the SS (SS-Personalhauptamt) shows that at this time Huber was already performing the functions of an inspector, albeit on an acting basis.[23] His official appointment, confirmed by Heydrich, did not take place until 1941,[24] but it can be assumed that he already had the position of 'provisional' or 'acting' inspector from March 1939. Moreover, Heinrich Müller, in his position as acting IdSuSD in SS-Oberabschnitt 'Danube', had already handed over 'his functions with regard to the Gestapo' to Huber a few days after the annexation of Austria.[25]

Heydrich's order of 12 June 1941 that 'to avoid duplication ... the main tasks of the Gestapo offices' were to be transferred 'to the inspectors of the security police and SD' was thus of no relevance at all to Huber. By virtue of his dual function, he had long been able to avoid this kind of 'duplication'. Only the order that 'the former main functions of the Vienna Gestapo ... were to be shared between the inspectors in Vienna [district XVII] and Salzburg [XVIII]' meant that Huber's tasks as inspector were limited to Military District XVII. This process had nothing to do with Huber personally but was merely part of the systematic alignment of the inspectorates with the military districts.[26]

Thus, for almost seven years, Huber not only headed the largest of the fifty-nine Gestapo main offices in the German Reich and occupied territories, but as IdSuSD in the Reichsgaus of Vienna, Lower Danube and Upper Danube he was effectively his own boss for almost as long. His other official functions demonstrate the extent to which he and, through him, the Vienna Gestapo were enmeshed in the SS and administrative power structure. Huber was political adviser to the two Reichsstatthalters, Schirach and Jury, and Schirach's deputy as Reich defence commissioner in Military District XVII, as well as 'general representative' of Rudolf Querner, Kaltenbrunner's successor as HSSPF of SS-Oberabschnitt 'Danube'. As an inspector, Huber was answerable to the HSSPF, and in Querner's absence therefore had no one checking on him.[27] Huber was also formally responsible for the 'Central Office for Jewish Emigration in Vienna' (Zentralstelle für jüdische Auswanderung in Wien), although in reality he delegated practically all the relevant tasks to his deputy Ebner. In his function as inspector of border police II (south-east), the customs and border protection unit affiliated to the Gestapo, he was in charge of a further important inspectorate whose influence extended far beyond that of the Vienna Gestapo.

As IdSuSD and thus as his own superior, Huber was able to manage the Vienna Gestapo without significant local consultation – for example, with Kaltenbrunner as HSSPF or with the SD in Vienna – in accordance with direct instructions from the RSHA and its head Reinhard Heydrich. It was thanks to Heydrich that Huber had risen to become a multiple Nazi functionary with unparalleled official authority and power. In his defence plea written while in prison, Ebner, Huber's deputy as head of the Vienna Gestapo,[28] stated: 'An accumulation of offices of this type was very rare, if not unique. It reflected the particular faith that the chief of the security police and SD in Berlin placed in Huber'.[29]

The main task of the Vienna Gestapo in relation to the five regular Gestapo offices in the Alpine and Danube Gaus – Linz (Reichsgau 'Upper Danube'), Graz, Salzburg, Innsbruck (Reichsgau 'Tyrol-Vorarlberg') and Klagenfurt – was to coordinate Gestapo measures. These Gestapo offices had a duty to report only because Huber, as head of the Vienna Gestapo and 'political adviser to the central authority within the internal administration responsible for the Gestapo district', had to be 'informed of reports to them of major incidents'. Otherwise, Huber could only request reports from subordinate Gestapo offices, or take over certain cases himself under exceptional circumstances.[30]

But 'to avoid duplication' Heydrich also decreed on 12 June 1941 that these competences be transferred to the inspectors of the security police and SD. This did not imply any restriction in competences for Huber or the Vienna Gestapo, as Huber was both Gestapo head and inspector in Military District XVII.

Gestapo, SD and Competing Intelligence Services

The Gestapo and the SD occupied central positions in the National Socialist power structure. As described in Chapter 1, the Gestapo had already established itself in 1936 as an autonomous special authority and a constituent component of the Nazi state, with a clearly defined mandate and competences. By contrast, the SD, although founded in 1931, developed only slowly under the leadership of Werner Best 'from a dilettante minor organization to a serious intelligence service'.[31] Early on, the original idea of the SD as a central police institution, as a 'nucleus of a completely new political police force',[32] could not be implemented because of a financing problem, as in that case the SD would no longer have been regarded as an NSDAP organization and would not have had any access to party funds.

As Himmler and Heydrich were not satisfied with the idea that the SD should be merely an intelligence service and 'Reich polling institute', Best ultimately concentrated on developing the SD into the 'internal elite' of an ideologically defined 'state security corps'. The problem therefore arose of effectively connecting the SS, which saw itself as a 'pillar of the National Socialist movement called upon to shape political will',[33] with the security police, whose members consisted mainly of officials who had served the Weimar Republic, in conformity with the NSDAP line.

Heydrich therefore wanted to replace Sipo officials with members of the SD, who could not, however, compete with Sipo officials trained in the latest police and forensic methods. In a decree issued on 4 July 1934, Himmler had already confirmed that the SD had 'no police powers', and that fundamentally 'the police should combat opponents of National Socialism, and the SD should identify enemies of the National Socialist idea'.[34] As the future was to show, this principle was never systematically implemented, and competences were constantly exceeded, resulting in conflicts between the rival institutions. The Funktionsbefehl (function order) issued by Heydrich on 1 July 1937,[35] in which the competences of the Gestapo and SD were redefined, failed to fully eliminate the conflict potential. Heydrich stated that the SD and Gestapo should form 'a unified whole ... in the results of their work' and that their relationship should not be one of 'rivalry or superiority and subordination but of complementarity with the avoidance of duplication'. The regulation whereby the SD was responsible for 'all general and fundamental questions' and the Gestapo for 'all individual incidents (in which state police enforcement is applicable)' was once again emphasized in the Funktionsbefehl.

The cooperation between the Gestapo and SD by no means developed to the disadvantage of the SD: 'The SD's institutional advantage lay in its close connection with the political police, which as an expanding instrument of rule was increasingly assuming regular police functions. In this way, the SD managed to acquire information and competences that would have been unavailable to it as a party institution'.[36] But when it came to pure police tasks – such as the arrest of suspects – the SD was completely reliant on cooperation with the Gestapo.

There was also cooperation between the Gestapo and SD on the level of personnel, as illustrated in a letter from the Vienna SD to Huber, which announced the transfer of five SS applicants or SS members of the SD, students at Vienna University, as 'candidates for leading positions' within the Sipo.[37]

The largely smooth cooperation between the Vienna Gestapo and the SD in Vienna resulted essentially from Huber's control over both institutions and his own interest in this cooperation. As will be discussed in Chapter 10, those conflicts that did arise were almost exclusively in the cooperation with the 'Central Office for Jewish Emigration' and, above all, with Adolf Eichmann, initially its titular deputy head but, in reality, its head. Conflicts regarding responsibility for the 'Jewish question' were by no means limited to the special situation in Vienna, where the future model for the systematic looting, forced emigration and deportation of the Jewish population was first institutionalized through its application to Vienna's almost two hundred thousand Jewish inhabitants.

Cooperation between the Gestapo and SD with regard to 'Jewish policy' was fraught with problems from the outset. The SD was not content merely to have ideological competence but sought to claim all aspects of the 'Jewish policy' for itself:

> While the considerable information deficit [as compared with the Gestapo] put it at a great disadvantage, particularly in the early phase, the SD was able to overcome this in mid-1937 when, to 'avoid duplication', Heydrich assigned it an equal function alongside the Gestapo and, on Werner Best's instruction, the Gestapa made the extensive

files in its Jewish section available to it. ... In autumn 1937 the Gestapa transferred parts of its record-keeping and hence essential elements of its special knowledge in the 'Jewish question' to the SD.[38]

During the subsequent persecution and extermination of the Jews, a clear distinction became evident between the way it was approached in the 'Altreich' and in the jurisdiction of the Vienna Gestapo. In the 'Altreich', implementation was the exclusive responsibility of the Gestapo, while in Vienna the central office and thus the SD were mainly responsible. The conflicts were caused, not least, by Eichmann's insistent attempts to expand his own competences.[39] In his dual function as Gestapo head and IdSuSD, Huber was also head of the central office, but he was, to a large extent, able to stay clear of the rivalry between it and the Gestapo. His antisemitism was allegedly so extreme that when he was present 'Jews were not allowed to appear at Morzinplatz'.[40] He himself stated that he did not once visit the central office or speak with Eichmann,[41] but delegated his supervisory and command function almost completely to Ebner, head of the 'Jewish section' at the time of the mass deportations. As described in detail in Chapter 10, there can nevertheless be no doubt that Huber was the second local initiator of the first deportation of the Jews of Vienna in February 1941, alongside Reichsstatthalter/Gauleiter Baldur von Schirach. Through his personal access to Heydrich and Müller, the RSHA deportation orders were received directly by Huber and not the central office for Jewish emigration, which was subordinate to him. While the deportations (until March 1943) were organized by the central office, the 'Jewish section' at the Vienna Gestapo had overriding authority for the persecution of the Jews remaining in Vienna.

The third Gestapo law of 10 February 1936 meant that Himmler's reorganized police structure 'prevailed and established itself against all competing and rival power groups'.[42] However, this general authorization of the political police at best meant that rivalries were shifted to a lower level or, as Best put it, 'department rivalries replaced party rivalries'.[43] A typical example of this was the regime's rival intelligence organizations. As knowledge, and the power it offered, played a decisive role in the Third Reich power structure, it was of importance from the outset but also offered potential for rivalries and conflict, which – as in the case of the conflict between the Gestapo and the Wehrmacht intelligence service (Amt Ausland/Abwehr, the 'Abwehr') – could only be settled by Hitler himself.

Shortly after the National Socialists came to power in Germany, conflict arose through the growing independence of the Gestapo in police counter-intelligence and counter-espionage: 'Himmler and Heydrich wanted gradually to take over full responsibility for counter-intelligence'. It was only after Hitler's intervention and the appointment of Wilhelm Canaris, whom Heydrich knew personally, as head of the Abwehr that the respective competences were defined. 'Thereafter, counter-espionage remained, along with foreign intelligence and active espionage and sabotage, with the Abwehr, while the investigation and prosecution of state treason [Landesverrat], and the areas of work safety and of border and aliens police [Grenz- und Ausländerpolizei] became the responsibility of police counter-intelligence at the Gestapa'.[44] As the war progressed, and with the massive use of foreign forced labourers, the 'aliens police' role of the Gestapo grew steadily in importance until it formed the main focus of its activities.

Because conflicts continued to arise in spite of this fundamental decision regarding intelligence-gathering by the Gestapo and the military, an agreement was ultimately reached by which the military was given priority, in particular in the field of counter-espionage: 'In the treatment of individual cases, the interests of the secret service [Geheimer Meldedienst] and counter-espionage have priority over police counter-intelligence'.[45] This established once and for all that police counter-intelligence was subordinate to the Abwehr/Ausland, but 'police counter-intelligence remained a department of the Gestapo, with which the Abwehr was required to cooperate … as the Abwehr had no policing rights and was in any case reliant on the Gestapo when it came to arrests. According to this agreement, the SD was to take over political intelligence'.[46]

Although the Gestapo cooperated closely with the Abwehr in some areas, the activities of the two organizations were quite separate in others. Following the events of 20 July 1944, for example, high-ranking members of the Abwehr office in Vienna participated in Operation Valkyrie in Military District XVII without the Gestapo's knowledge. These included Oberst Rudolf Graf von Marogna-Redwitz, head of the Vienna office of the Abwehr from March 1938 to April 1944, his deputy Oberstleutnant Kurt Fechner, Generalmajor Erwin von Lahousen, until 1943 head of Department II of the Abwehr, and Oberst Otto Armster, head of the Abwehr office in Vienna from April to July 1944.[47]

Another rival to the police intelligence was the SD. In the early 1930s, when various Nazi bodies such as the SA, the Deutsche Arbeitsfront (DAF; German labour front) and Göring's 'Forschungsamt der Luftwaffe' (Luftwaffe research office) had their own intelligence services, Himmler ordered Heydrich to develop the SD because he did not want to fall behind them. Its original task was to collect information on political opponents, but also on rivals within the Nazi party, particularly the SA.[48]

Gradually, however, some of the SD's tasks were ceded to the Gestapo, and after 1937 the task of the SD in Germany was 'to collect information … on the public mood and evaluate it for the Meldungen aus dem Reich';[49] the SD reports were received by leading NSDAP officials two or three times a week. As they were relatively frank about the increasingly critical attitude to the regime as the war progressed, Goebbels and Martin Bormann ordered a reduction in the reporting in 1944 on account of 'defeatism'. By contrast, the SD foreign intelligence service (from 1939, RSHA Department III) continued to grow until 1944, becoming a hugely powerful organization. It had 6,482 full-time SD members and a network of around 30,000 informants.

There were also conflicts and overlaps – particularly with regard to radio and telephone monitoring – with Göring's Forschungsamt, 'one of the most efficient secret intelligence services',[50] which only shared its information with a small select leadership group. Huber in Vienna described the Forschungsamt as an institution 'that obtained intelligence … in particular by wiretapping. … The Forschungsamt was headed by Göring, who jealously … checked that the results … were not made available to the Gestapo. I draw this conclusion because there was also a branch of the Forschungsamt in Vienna, which never provided me with intelligence except on matters directly connected with my area of operation'.[51] Huber's telephone was also tapped by the Forschungsamt, as Heydrich confirmed to Huber with the 'wry comment' that 'his [Huber's] wife's social contact' with the 'wife of the Hungarian consul general' and 'the soap, a rabbit or a fish' that she received from that source was perhaps 'a little too obvious'.[52]

Finally, Hitler's order of 12 February 1944 'on the creation of a unified German secret intelligence service' led to the fusion of the police and military intelligence services. 'Gestapo offices that had not hitherto fought radio and parachute agents [assumed] this task [from the Wehrmacht] but not the Vienna Gestapo, which had been carrying out this task since May 1942'.[53] The Forschungsamt retained its independence until it was transferred in early 1945 to the RSHA, thus coming under the influence of the SS.

Quite apart from the rival intelligence services in different institutions, there were also internal conflicts within the Gestapo, as some sections sought to use their own staff for their specific intelligence requirements. A typical example from the Vienna Gestapo is Section II B (Ideological opponents), whose responsibilities included members of 'politicizing churches'. The work of the churches intelligence service IV A 4 (N), established by section head Karl Ebner, included wiretapping and letter censorship, the use of informants at masses, meetings and confessions, and photographing participants in processions. In spite of the existence of a separate intelligence section, II N (after 1942, IV N) in the RSHA GVP, the Gestapo church intelligence service with four members (Ferdinand Joksch, Franz Ebhardt, Inge Norde and Maria Paheimer) existed until autumn 1944.[54]

Lambert Leutgeb, head of Section II N from April 1940, commented on the result of this uncoordinated intelligence work by the individual sections with their own informants: 'When I … took over this unit on 1 April, there were no suitable people available at all'. Leutgeb established his own network of informants, with the assistance, among others, of former members of the Austrian state police 'except for church affairs, which was very difficult, [as] the church unit collected its own intelligence but did not go about it properly'.[55]

The main significance of the Vienna Gestapo intelligence section was in the recruitment and deployment of its network of agents: 'Towards the end of the war [it had] five regular staff and over 170 informants'.[56] Leutgeb described the

Vienna Gestapo intelligence service trivially as merely a collection point 'where all intelligence ... be it from the party or its organizations ... was ... collected and possibly verified'. In addition, 'a few SS officers ... were seconded to it from the Gestapo. ... They visited the NSDAP district heads [Kreisleiter] at least once a week and collected the intelligence that had been received there'.[57]

The Vienna Gestapo GVPs

The Gestapo 'business distribution plan' (Geschäftsverteilungsplan, GVP) for a given period described mandates and competences down to the smallest detail. GVPs were used identically in all Gestapo offices like blueprints of the Gestapa (and later the RSHA) systems, and updated when required. The organizational structure of the Vienna Gestapo underwent considerable changes as a result, because three or four different GVPs were used in the course of six years: 1938–41, 1942–44 (with additions in 1942 that are sometimes regarded as a separate plan) and 1944–45. According to Karl Ebner, the last plan was only partially implemented in Vienna.[58]

The associated reorganization and renaming of departments, sections and units inevitably produced friction, competence problems and hence personal conflicts. The apparent dissatisfaction and confusion were, in fact, part of the strategy of 'organized chaos' typical of Himmler's leadership. To prevent bureaucratic overload and 'work-to-rule', Himmler continuously stirred things up, bypassed established chains of command, and made his feared on-the-spot decisions. Whether he increased the effectiveness of 'his' Gestapo is questionable. According to those involved, his interventions were more likely to be counterproductive – as Kaltenbrunner's adjutant Wilhelm Höttl put it, it was 'a typical example of the situation in the Third Reich, where one hand often didn't know what the other hand was doing'.[59]

The GVPs were not merely efficient internal Gestapo charts. Implicit in their structure was a systematic classification of the enemy: former classifications of the 'National Socialist ideological rhetoric'[60] such as 'Communists' or 'Jews' became concrete offender categories, defined groups of 'enemies of the state'. According to Bernward Dörner, the GVPs represented 'a systematic bureaucratic reflection of the enemy categorization of the SS ideology'.[61]

First GVP: 1938–1942

The GVP for the first period of the Vienna Gestapo remained in force from March 1938 to April 1942. During this time the Gestapo office was divided into three departments:

Gestapo, SS and Political Structures – Organization of the Vienna Gestapo | 75

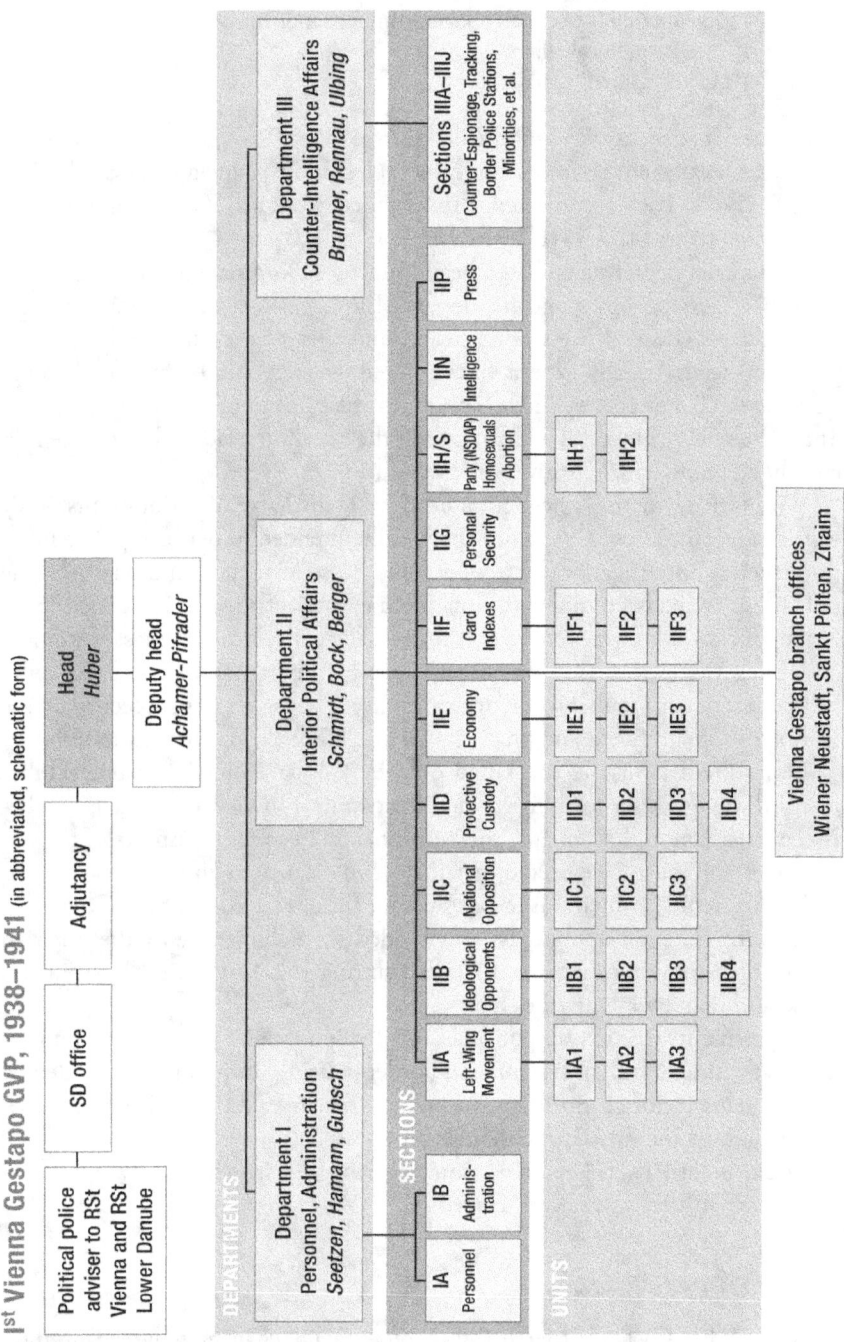

Chart 4.1. 1st Vienna Gestapo GVP, 1938–41. Chart created by the authors.

- I Organization, personnel, budget, administration and legal
- II Interior political affairs
- III Counter-intelligence affairs

The three departments were subdivided into sections (Referate) and units (Sachgebiete). Department II, for example, had ten sections, named successively II A, II B, II C, etc. Each section had various units. Section II A, for example, had three units, named II A 1, II A 2 and II A 3.

Each of the departments had a head, directly subordinate to the head of the respective Gestapo office and his deputy. The department heads in turn were the direct superiors of the section heads, and they of the unit heads. The department heads, usually experts in their field, were appointed by the Gestapa/RSHA, which lent corresponding weight to their positions in the organization. They generally held weekly meetings with their section heads, who reported on current activities and were given instructions.

Within this structure, the section heads were in charge of various units. They were senior officials who were not specifically intended to perform police functions such as interrogations, but who could do so at their own discretion. The unit heads were also senior staff, but the members of their units tended to be Kripo officials, who were responsible for actually carrying out the tasks assigned.

During this period, Huber's deputy was Humbert Achamer-Pifrader, who had been sent with Huber to Vienna from the Gestapa. He was succeeded by the German Wilhelm Bock, and finally by Heinrich Berger, another Austrian jurist.

Department I was always staffed only by Germans, and ultimately Huber reserved the headship for himself (and his deputy). In view of the tensions between Austrians and Germans, the personnel and economic aspects of the Vienna Gestapo must have been of particular importance to him.

Department II, which was responsible for the effectiveness of the Gestapo in suppressing 'internal opponents', was headed for a short time by the Austrian Ferdinand Schmidt, who was succeeded during this first period by Wilhelm Bock, and then by Heinrich Berger.

Department III was responsible for foreign affairs (primarily counter-espionage) the informant system, and border policing. It was initially headed by the Germans Heinrich Brunner and Heinz Rennau, and then, until the end of this period, by the Austrian Richard Ulbing.

Department III was 'separated from the other departments. It was sealed off by grating, and access to it was barred'.[62]

Second GVP: 1942–1944

The new RSHA GVP of 1 March 1941 brought major changes in the organization of the Vienna Gestapo. The former Department I was split into Department I

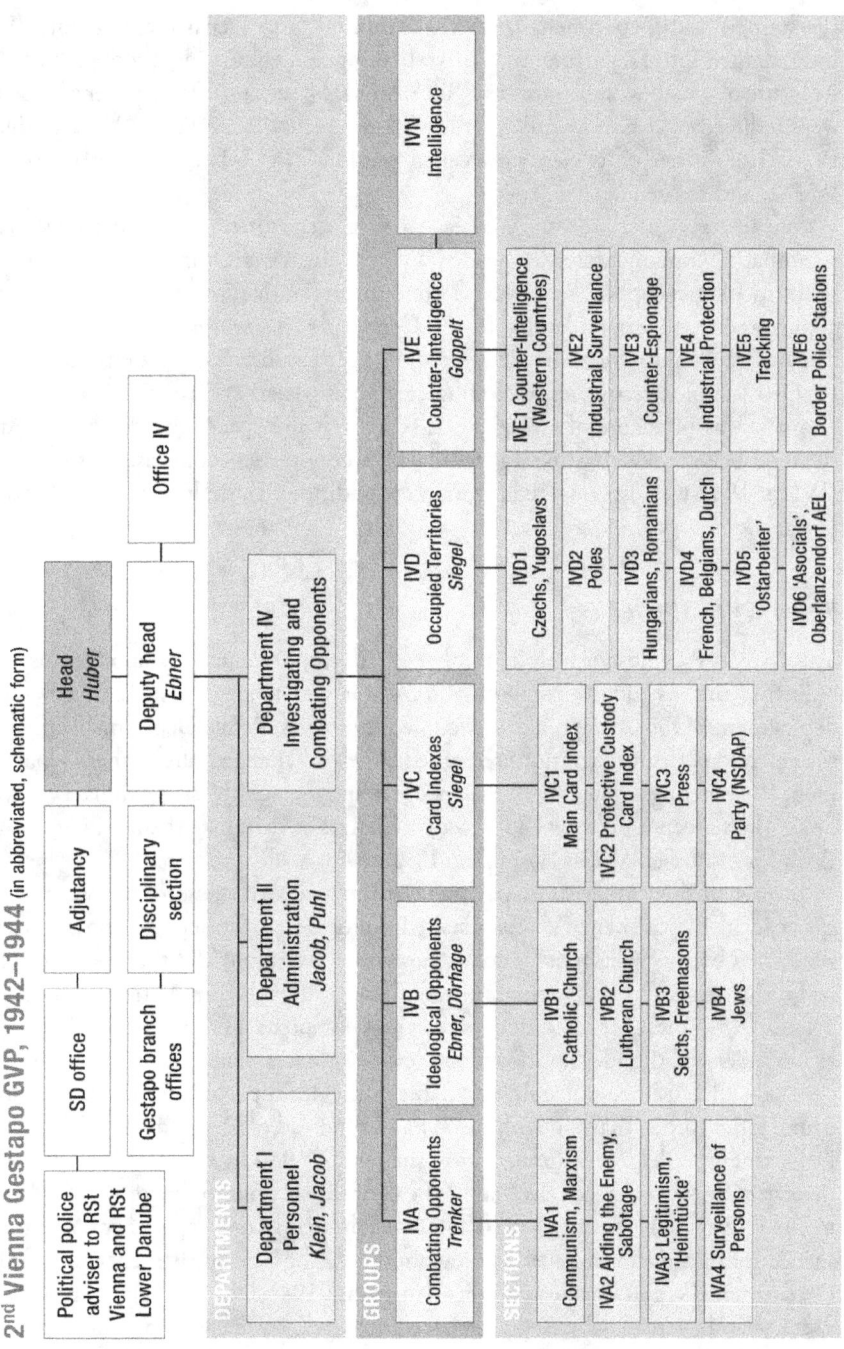

Chart 4.2. 2nd Vienna Gestapo GVP, 1942–44. Chart created by the authors.

(Personnel) and Department II (Administration), and Departments II and III were merged into Department IV (Investigating and combating opponents), the structure of which was the same as RSHA Amt IV (Gestapo). The former sections were reduced to five, now called 'groups' and labelled IV A, IV B, IV C, IV D, IV E. The former units were now called 'sections', IV A 1, IV A 2, or IV B 1, IV B 2, and so on.

The five groups IV A to IV E each had a 'department group head'. IV A (Combating opponents) was headed by the Austrian Othmar Trenker, and IV B (Ideological opponents) by Karl Ebner from South Tyrol, and then, after his appointment as Huber's deputy, by the Germans Hans Dörhage and Rolf Rack. The Austrian Viktor Siegel headed Group IV C (Records, protective custody) and IV D (Occupied territories, including foreign workers) and the German Hugo Goppelt was in charge of Group IV E (Counter-intelligence, border posts). At the level below the department group heads were the section heads. This second GVP of 1942 was also enlarged through the addition of a sixth group IV F (Passports, aliens police).

Third GVP: 1944–1945

This last GVP could not be fully implemented in the Vienna Gestapo, because – reflecting the restructuring of the RSHA – it was tailored particularly to the deployment of the Gestapo in the occupied territories. While Department I (Personnel) and II (Administration) remained largely unchanged, the former Department IV was consolidated, with the groups being replaced by six sections, IV 1 to IV 6. The sixteen units now had lower-case letters to designate them – in Section IV 2, for example, IV 2 a, IV 2 b and IV 2 c.

Instead of the former six 'department group heads' of the second GVP, a single head of Department IV was installed. Later, when former Gestapo officials were tried by the Volksgericht, colleagues giving testimony did their best not to reveal the name of this department head, because after the International Military Tribunal in Nuremberg had designated the Gestapo as a criminal organization, all members of the Gestapo from the level of department head upwards were deemed collectively responsible, and liable to the death penalty. Ebner claimed in court, for example, that Huber himself had been head of Department IV. In fact, Department IV had been headed until the end of 1944 by Othmar Trenker and thereafter by Viktor Siegel: 'In May 1944 all of the sections in the former Departments II and III were consolidated and concentrated in one department, and the special status of Department III was abandoned. The new department was called Department IV and was headed until Christmas 1944 by Oberregierungsrat Dr Trenker and thereafter by Regierungsrat Dr Siegel'.[63] Trenker's appointment on 1 May 1944 as head of Department IV was indirectly confirmed in a circular of that date by Huber, interpreting the application of the new GVP to the

Gestapo, SS and Political Structures – Organization of the Vienna Gestapo | 79

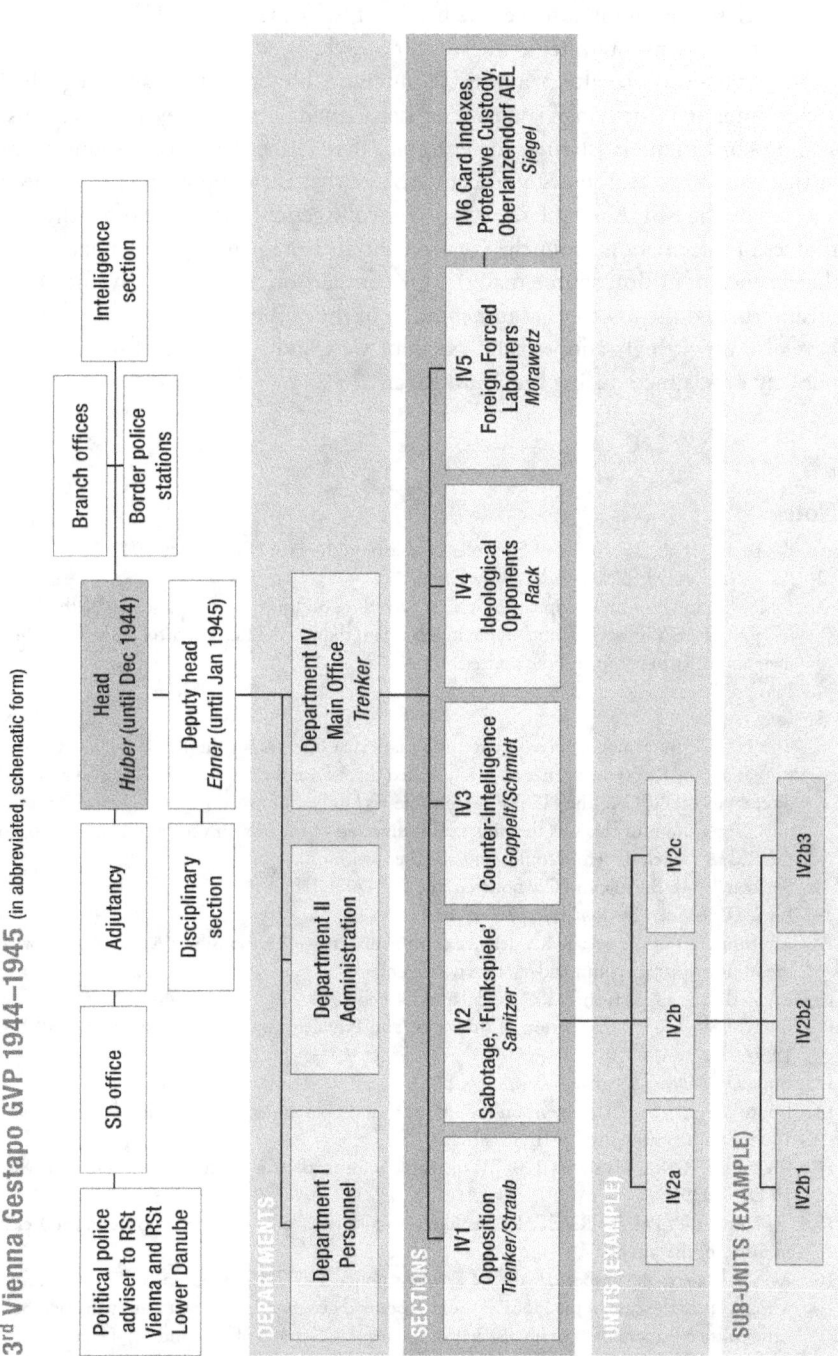

Chart 4.3. 3rd Vienna Gestapo GVP, 1944–45. Chart created by the authors.

Vienna Gestapo: 'In his absence, the head of Department IV will be represented by SS-Sturmbannführer, Regierungsrat Dr Siegel'.[64]

With the death penalty as a possible outcome, Ebner, Trenker and Siegel had a vital interest in denying having been department heads. They invented misleading constructions, stating, for example, that Huber had sole responsibility, or that they were 'temporary replacements', or that their appointment had been rejected by the RSHA. As the records of the Volksgericht trials were often the sole sources of information about the Gestapo and its headquarters in Vienna, and in the absence of critical source material for comparison, historians have not only misinterpreted the *pro domo* argumentation of the perpetrators but in some cases have also unwittingly adopted the 'point of view and self-image of the Gestapo publicly proclaimed during the Third Reich'.[65]

Notes

1. BA Berlin, R 58, 241, order of Himmler establishing the HSSPFs, 21 May 1941.
2. Birn, *Die höheren SS- und Polizeiführer*, 398.
3. Ibid., 17: 'In all of the occupied territories, including occupied Norway and the Netherlands in 1940, the HSSPFs were much more independent than in the Reich territory. They had their own authority to command the police.'
4. Ibid., 397.
5. Ibid.
6. The HSSPFs were not involved in routine matters. Orders from the RSHA – for example, to Gestapo or Kripo departments – were issued directly, and these departments also reported directly to the RSHA. The HSSPF responsible was to be 'informed for intelligence purposes' only. The reason for this was the direct subordination of the HSSPFs to Himmler and not to the RSHA, which therefore could not issue them with orders.
7. For details, see Buchheim, 'Die höheren SS- und Polizeiführer'.
8. Birn, *Die höheren SS- und Polizeiführer*, 310.
9. After the start of the war, Reich defence commissioners were responsible, in consultation with the military district commanders, for civil defence.
10. BA Berlin, R 58, 241, sheet 283, circular of 24 Feb 1941.
11. Ibid., sheets 67–69, instruction of the Reich and Prussian minister of the interior of 20 Sep 1936.
12. Birn, *Die höheren SS- und Polizeiführer*, 82.
13. Estate of Karl Ebner, statement on the structure and operations of the Vienna Gestapo 1938–1945, photocopy owned by Thomas Mang.
14. BA Berlin, R 58, 241, sheets 220–21, instruction for inspectors of the security police and SD, 19 Dec 1939.
15. 'RFSSuChdDt.Pol. im RMdI': Reichsführer-SS and chief of the German police in the Reich ministry of the interior.
16. As SD leaders, the inspectors of the security police and SD headed an SS-Oberabschnitt, which – as in the case of the HSSPFs – corresponded geographically to a military district. SD-Abschnitte corresponded to the districts of the regular Gestapo offices, and SD-Leitabschnitte to those of 'Gestapo-Leitstellen' (regional headquarters), such as Vienna (BA Berlin, R 58, 241,

sheet 191, order of the chief of the security police and Sicherheitshauptamt of 23 Sep 1939 on the organization of the SD and security police).
17. BA Berlin, R 58, 241, sheets 220–21, instruction for inspectors of the security police and SD, 19 Dec 1939.
18. Karl Ebner, statement on the structure and operations of the Vienna Gestapo 1938–45, photocopy owned by Thomas Mang. In a document written while in prison, Ebner described himself as 'honorary employee [Ehrenamtlicher Mitarbeiter] of the inspector of the security police and SD in Vienna', having 'received notification of his appointment from Huber in autumn 1942'. Evidently, he was attempting to conceal his de facto activity as 'deputy inspector'.
19. Gedenkstätte Deutscher Widerstand (memorial to the German resistance), Berlin, permanent exhibition, document 116ff.
20. 'At a very late stage, he [Huber] also once explained to me his reason for "keeping" me [in Vienna]. Vienna was a sensitive area – he didn't want any intriguers around him' (Karl Ebner, statement on the structure and operations of the Vienna Gestapo 1938–45, 77, photocopy owned by Thomas Mang).
21. NARA, SS-Personalhauptamt A 3343 880-118A, letter from Kaltenbrunner to the SS-Personalhauptamt, 1 Dec 1944. As Kommandeur of the security police and SD, Rudolf Mildner, Huber's acting successor as head of the Vienna Gestapo, was officially subordinate to Huber as BdSuSD.
22. There is only one other known case of an IdSuSD simultaneously exercising the function of a Gestapo head, which was in Military District IV, Dresden, albeit only briefly in 1941–42.
23. NARA, SS-Personalhauptamt A 3343 880-118A: 'I request that SS-Standartenführer Franz Josef Huber be promoted with effect from 9 November 1941 to SS-Oberführer. SS-Standartenführer Huber currently performs the functions of the inspector of the security police and SD in Vienna. Signed Heydrich SS-Obergruppenführer'.
24. ZStL 110 AR-Z 70/76, sheet 120, testimony of Franz Josef Huber, 3 Oct 1961.
25. See the section 'Planning, Preparation and Measures' in Chapter 2.
26. BA Berlin, R 58/241, sheet 311. A similar letter of 22 Jan 1942 announced the deferred transfer of the main functions of the Kripo departments to the inspectors (BA Berlin, R 58/241, sheet 323).
27. BA Berlin, R 58, microfilm 711, telegram from Rudolf Brandt, personal assistant to Himmler, of 18 Jul 1943 to Rudolf Querner, HSSPF 'Danube': 'Obergruppenführer! The Reichsführer-SS agrees to the transfer of representation to SS-Brigadeführer and Generalmajor der Polizei Huber'.
28. For Huber and Ebner, see also Chapter 5, 'Personnel Structure', and Chapter 18.
29. Karl Ebner, statement on the structure and operations of the Vienna Gestapo 1938–45, 143, photocopy owned by Thomas Mang.
30. BA Berlin, R 58, no. 243, sheet 291, instruction for Gestapo headquarters, 15 May 1940.
31. Herbert, *Best*, 142.
32. Ibid., 188.
33. Best, *Die Deutsche Polizei*, 107, quoted in Herbert, *Best*, 189.
34. Quoted in Aronson, *Heydrich*, 196.
35. 'Gemeinsame Anordnung für den Sicherheitsdienst des Reichsführer-SS und die Geheime Staatspolizei' of the chief of the RSHA and the chief of the police, 1 Jul 1937, BA Berlin R 58/39; see also Stadlbauer, *Erich Ehrlinger*, 142–43.
36. Wildt, *Die Judenpolitik des SD*, 62–63.
37. Archives of the Republic of Slovenia, AS 1931/821, sheet 26.
38. Matthäus, 'Konzept als Kalkül', 134.
39. See Mang, *'Gestapo-Leitstelle Wien'*, 64–74.

40. WStLA, Vienna LG, Vg 12g Vr 1223/47, sheet 90, testimony of Wilhelm Bienenfeld (from 1939 to 1942 deputy head of the IKG/Council of Elders) in the trial of Karl Ebner, 7 Dec 1948.
41. In a private letter to Ebner, Huber stated that he himself 'never gave any orders for deportation, never visited the central office and never dealt personally with Eichmann' (letter from Huber to Ebner, July 1964, estate of Karl Ebner, photocopy owned by Thomas Mang).
42. Herbert, *Best*, 180.
43. BA Berlin, NL 23, 176, quoted in Herbert, *Best*, 184.
44. Herbert, *Best*, 181–82.
45. IfZ, Zs 207, quoted in Herbert, *Best*, 578, agreement between CSSD (chief of the security police and SD, Heydrich) and the OKW (Oberkommando der Wehrmacht), 21 Feb 1936.
46. Buchheit, *Der deutsche Geheimdienst*, 250.
47. For the events of 20 July 1944 in Vienna, and subsequent arrests, see the section 'Mass Arrest after 20 July 1944' in Chapter 9.
48. The description of the SD's original intelligence mandate as a kind of 'Third Reich Gallup Institute' (Wildt) and its subsequent development to become an integral component of the system of terror, in particular the *Einsatzgruppen* in the East, has produced something of an unbalanced historical assessment of its activities; see Wildt, *An Uncompromising Generation*, 140–48 (*Reichssicherheitshauptamt*, 239–51).
49. Benz/Graml/Weiss, *Enzyklopädie des Nationalsozialismus*, 728.
50. Ibid., 465.
51. IfZ, ZS 735, sheet 30, record of a conversation with Prof. Harold Deutsch, 3 Jun 1970.
52. Ibid.
53. Weisz, 'Die V-Männer der Gestapo-Leitstelle Wien', 338–57.
54. Archives of the Republic of Slovenia, AS 1931, 809, sheet 482.
55. Ibid., AS 1931/809, 104-72/ZA, sheets 677–78.
56. Schafranek, 'Drei Gestapo-Spitzel', 250–77.
57. Archives of the Republic of Slovenia, AS 1931/809, 104-72/ZA, sheet 677.
58. While Weisz speaks of four different GVPs, Ebner, whose competence in this matter is difficult to deny, mentions only three: 'There were three different business distribution plans (plans for short) between 1938 and 1945, namely plan I from 1938 to 1942, plan II from 1942 to 1944, and plan III from 1944 to 1945. ... Plan II worked well, while plan III produced both personnel and material difficulties. This plan was not fully implemented'. Karl Ebner, statement on the structure and operations of the Vienna Gestapo 1938–45, 57, 65ff. (photocopy owned by Thomas Mang).
59. ÖStA/KA, NLS, B/1226, NL Höttl, folios 1–21, typescript entitled 'Von Heydrich zu Kaltenbrunner – die Rolle Eichmanns', probably preliminary work for Wilhelm Höttl's memoirs.
60. Broszat, 'Nationalsozialistische Konzentrationslager'.
61. Dörner, *'Heimtücke'*, 63.
62. WStLA, Vienna LG, Vg 12g Vr 1223/47, Dr Karl Ebner, 'Wolfsberger Dossier'.
63. WStLA, Vienna LG, Vg 12g Vr 1223/47, Karl Ebner, 'Wolfsberger Dossier'. In 1946, when interned by the British in Wolfsberg, Ebner wrote a twenty-page dossier 'as the senior and highest-ranking member of my office in Vienna available after 1945'. It was intended as mitigating evidence for the use of Rudolf Merkel, who was defending the Gestapo at the Nuremberg tribunal. Because Ebner was not aware at the time that Gestapo members of the rank of department head and above were liable to the death sentence, he incriminated himself and others: 'In early 1942 ... three departments were divided up: Section IV A (Left-wing movement) headed by Dr Trenker, Section IV B (Ideological opponents) headed by Dr Ebner ...'.
64. Archives of the Republic of Slovenia, AS 1931/808, sheet 440.
65. Schmiechen-Ackermann, 'Der "Blockwart"', 579.

Chapter 5

THE OFFICIALS AND EMPLOYEES OF THE VIENNA GESTAPO

Personnel Structure of the Gestapo: Cliché and Reality

The work of the Gestapo demanded not only a specific organizational structure but also a personnel structure that differed from the structures usual for regular criminal police work. While Heinrich Müller, head of Amt IV (Gestapo) at the RSHA, attached great importance to police training and experience, for Himmler and Heydrich ideological reliability as demonstrated by membership of the NSDAP and SS tended to be the decisive criterion: 'Combating enemies of the state calls for unconditional espousal of the National Socialist idea. The men of the Gestapo must be absolutely aligned in their mental attitude. They must feel as if they belong to a fighting corps. That is the reason why very many Gestapo officials are also SS officers or SS men'.[1]

There are no reliable data regarding the selection criteria or number of officials from the Prussian political police recruited into the Gestapo on this basis after the Nazis came to power in 1933. According to Dams/Stolle, 'there is much to suggest that around half of the Prussian [political] police force was not transferred to the Gestapo'.[2]

In spite of the criteria specified by Himmler and Heydrich, the 'generally very young men' in the Gestapo (over 80 per cent of them were under forty in 1940)[3] were by no means all predisposed or ideologically confirmed members of the NSDAP. Gerhard Paul describes them as an 'explicitly unsoldierly generation group' whose main motivations were 'career ambitions' but also 'financial and proletarianization fears', and he quotes as an example the situation of Prussian probationary judges (Gerichtsassessore) at the end of 1932, when half of the four thousand judges in this position were unemployed.[4] And to quote Michael Wildt:

> In none of the young men who later assumed leadings posts at the RSHA do we find at the beginning of the National Socialist regime any indication of an 'eliminatory antisemitism' or a readiness for mass murder merely waiting to be unleashed. ... Nevertheless, only a few years later many of these men ... were responsible ... for the murder of tens of thousands of Jewish men, women and children.[5]

They were 'neither technocratic killing machines nor socially marginalized underlings, but on the contrary above-averagely intelligent, self-confident and energetic ... young men, with their own political ideas, coming rather from the middle to upper ranks of German society than from marginal groups and lower classes'.[6] They were by no means all 'callow and raw', as Edward Crankshaw characterized them.[7]

In a collective biography, Gerhard Paul made an empirical investigation of the origins, education and careers 'of all heads of the sixty Gestapo offices existing in 1938–39 in the Altreich, Austria and occupied Czechoslovakia'. According to Paul, 95 per cent of the Gestapo heads had a high school leaving certificate (Matura/Abitur), 87 per cent had law degrees, and half of all Gestapo heads had doctorates.[8] Of the 221 members of the RSHA examined, two-thirds had studied at university and half had doctorates – the largest group in law, followed by German and history.[9]

Most members of the Gestapo were representatives of the 'Kriegsjugend' generation, who had experienced the First World War as children and so did not possess the 'front experience' valued by the Nazi regime. But like many members of their generation, they were highly motivated as a result, and compensated for having been unable to meet this requirement by strongly supporting National Socialism. Even if they were not yet completely committed to the Nazi idea, their age made it reasonable to assume that their attitude to the ideology of the state and party could still be shaped.

Within the party, particularly among 'Alte Kämpfer' (veterans), there were considerable misgivings about the ideological reliability and unconditional commitment of this elite group, no doubt combined with a good portion of social envy.[10] The objections were above all aroused by the demand by Werner Best, who headed the organization and personnel departments at the Gestapo central headquarters, that Gestapo heads should have a law degree – if possible, a doctorate. This selection principle meant that, from the outset, very few old members from the early days of the struggle were likely to be sufficiently qualified for leading positions. As 'SS veterans capable of filling higher official positions were few and far between, specialists had to be sought who could be put into SS uniforms'.[11]

In spite of some bitter resistance, Best's personnel policy prevailed, with the initial support of Heydrich – a remarkable achievement, because the mistrust of the judiciary and of jurists extended to the top of the Nazi regime. Hitler was known to have little or no interest in the judiciary and a personal aversion to jurists – as he is supposed to have said, 'What do legal reservations mean when something is necessary in *völkisch*-political terms? It is not because of but rather in spite of lawyers that the Volk lives'.[12] Himmler was popularly quoted in Gestapo circles as having said that Best had 'soiled his Gestapo with lawyers'.[13] It was only after Best demanded that all applicants for leading positions in the Gestapo, Kripo and SD should have a law degree and stated that there should always be many more jurists than 'specialists' that Heydrich also withdrew his trust: 'The primary general training must be the SS-related training for Sipo and SD; the jurist is one of the specialists'.[14]

In contrast to the Gestapo staffing structure as it actually was – and not just at the leadership level – the cliché of the typical Gestapo figure in a 'black leather coat' as the sinister symbol of Nazi terror still lives on, supported by the mass media. However, this focus on the rank-and-file within the Gestapo personnel structure – conjuring up the idea of primitive, sadistic thugs – is only part of the reality.

These official torturers did exist, their activities euphemistically described as 'enhanced interrogation' (*verschärfte Vernehmung*). For them, physical violence was a matter of daily routine, and they also carried out their evil practices at the Vienna Gestapo. This gave rise to the paradoxical situation that, with the exception of a few notorious examples, it was the representatives of the Gestapo rank-and-file who were to determine its future historical image rather than those really responsible for its murderous efficiency. There were few Gestapo leaders 'who did not bear direct or indirect responsibility for the mass murders by the Einsatzgruppen, the deportation and extermination of European Jewry or the oppressive policies in the countries occupied by Germany'.[15]

Below the leadership level, in the Gestapo penal and administrative services, the personnel were generally well educated and experienced in modern police and forensic investigation methods, contributing in this way to the Gestapo's overall 'efficiency'.

Recruitment of Personnel for the Vienna Gestapo in and after 1938

By the afternoon of 12 March 1938, talks had begun between leading German police functionaries and Nazi-minded Austrian police under the leadership of Otto Steinhäusl, the designated chief of police of Vienna, to discuss the future personnel structure in the police force. Both the development of the security police (Sipo) in Austria and the head and deputy head of the Vienna Gestapo, Franz Josef Huber and the Austrian Humbert Achamer-Pifrader, had already been fixed by the Gestapa in Berlin.[16] The German Gestapo officials Heinz Seetzen and Heinrich Brunner headed Department I (Administration) and Department III (Counter-intelligence) at the new Vienna Gestapo headquarters, respectively. The Austrian Ferdinand Schmidt became head of Department II (Executive), before moving in July 1938 to private industry, to be succeeded by Wilhelm Bock, former head of the Gestapo in Lübeck, who was in charge of Department II from August 1938 to May 1941 and also acted during this time as Huber's deputy after Achamer-Pifrader had been transferred. All of these leading officials, with the exception of Huber and Bock, were jurists. Whereas there were only two Gestapo or department heads from Austria after the annexation and in 1938–39, half of the subordinate section (Referat) head positions in Department II were immediately filled by Austrians. Sensitive areas, such as Section II B, which also included the special unit 'Jews', were headed by Germans, with the exception of the period 1939 to 1942, when the Austrian Karl Ebner was in charge. The Reich-German section heads Karl Haselbacher and Rudolf Lange came from middle-class backgrounds, were relatively young and had attended university. Both had belonged to *völkisch* student fraternities and were the most typical representatives of the leadership class in the National Socialist security structure ideally sought by Himmler and Heydrich ('fighting administration'). Both were also heads of Unit (Sachgebiet) II B 4 (Jewish section), which until 1941–42 had the most staff of all units. For both Haselbacher and Lange, the positions in Vienna were merely springboards for their future careers in German police departments in occupied Europe.[17]

Whereas the Vienna Gestapo leaders sent in from the Gestapa are well documented, considerable problems are encountered when researching the personnel structure of the lower levels of the Gestapo hierarchy. The fact that there are no full personnel lists for Vienna makes it extremely difficult to identify the names of Gestapo employees. There are some telephone and room lists, but they are merely evidence for particular points in time, and the names represent only a fraction of the entire staff.[18] For example, neither Josef Wendl, who was a mobile gas van driver in Byelorussia from 1942 to 1943, nor Friedrich Kranebitter, head of sections II K and II G from 1939 to 1942 and head of the Gestapo in Verona from 1943, appear in the surviving lists.[19] Apart from the 'daily reports' and investigation files used between 1938 and 1945 in Nazi criminal proceedings, and some tiny remnants that survived by chance (today preserved at the DÖW or Wiener Stadt- und Landesarchiv), all original Vienna Gestapo files were destroyed. Researchers have at their disposal only the files of the German Bundesarchiv (Federal Archives) and the fragmentary 'Gau files' ('Gauakten', NSDAP records for the Gau of Vienna), and, as a secondary source, the records of criminal proceedings conducted by the Volksgericht against members of the Vienna Gestapo after 1945. In considering these documents it should be taken into account that both the defendants and most of the witnesses (former Gestapo officials – in other words former colleagues of the defendants – were questioned in all of the trials) were at pains not only to deny any responsibility and to present themselves as merely small cogs in a huge machine, but they also appear to have succeeded in coordinating their testimonies, frequently steering the trials in their favour as a result.

To date it has been possible to determine the names of around 400 officials and employees of the Vienna Gestapo, of whom some 230 can be firmly identified from the sources. Because of the limited source material, some of the quantitative and qualitative statements about the personnel structure of the Vienna Gestapo are therefore based on estimates and extrapolations.

A reliable source for the personnel strength of the Vienna Gestapo is provided by Sipo funding requests at the Bundesarchiv in Berlin, albeit only for the years 1940 to 1942.[20] They indicate that in 1940 the Vienna Gestapo had just under 830 staff. By 1942 the number of employees had risen to over 900; thereafter, the personnel numbers were reduced because of the war, and in 1944 the Vienna Gestapo is estimated to have had just under 490 employees.[21]

Between 1938 and 1945, the policing departments (in other words, Departments II and III, or Department IV after II and III were merged in 1942) together accounted for the largest share of the staff. Department II had 419 employees between 1938 and 1942 and was thus the largest department, and the two departments together had 667 employees in 1942. In 1944, Department IV had only 360 employees, but they still accounted for just under 74 per cent of the total payroll.[22]

Within Department II, Section II B (Ideological opponents) with just under 100 staff, and Section II A (Left-wing movement) with around 75, were the largest sections between 1938 and 1942.[23] Within the sections in Department II, the individual units had different staffing levels, which also varied over time. For example, Unit II B 4 (Jews) in Section II B had 60 staff in 1939, but by 1943, when only a few Jews were left in Vienna, there were only 29. In Section II P (Press), which was of lesser importance to the Gestapo, the staff remained constant at the relatively low level of around 20.[24]

Gestapo Officials: 'Alte Kämpfer', 'Illegals' and Careerists

In the first weeks after the annexation, around 320 officials of the former Austrian state police and criminal investigation police (Kripo) were transferred to the Gestapo, where they made up just under 50 per cent of the entire personnel.[25] Nearly 40 per cent of the remaining Gestapo officials were recruited from the Vienna security guard (Sicherheitswache).[26] Only a relatively small number came to the Gestapo from the rural police (Gendarmerie) or non-police professions.[27] The latter included mainly cleaners, drivers and telephone operators, occasionally also long-standing 'illegals' (that is to say, Austrians who had been NSDAP members before 1938) such as Karl Macher, who quickly rose to the rank of Kriminalkommissar. Born in 1911, Macher broke off his law studies and in 1932 joined the NSDAP. He was arrested several times for National Socialist activity, and is a good example of the 'failures' described in older research as typical candidates for employment in the Gestapo. This image did in fact apply in some cases, but Macher, who was transferred in 1941 to Radom (Poland), where he was significantly involved in the murder of the Jewish Council of Tomaszów,[28] was an exception among the officials of the Vienna Gestapo. Not least on account of the chaotic situation in Vienna during the first weeks after the annexation, the new authorities were most interested in getting the new Gestapo headquarters up and running. The Gestapo therefore did not primarily recruit non-police personnel, such as members of the Austrian Legion who had returned from the 'Altreich', but experienced members of the police, who had expertise, service know-how and the classic professional virtues of hard work, dedication, ambition, obedience and competence. From the Nazi point of view this was less of a problem, as the Austrian police force had long been infiltrated by 'illegal' National Socialists, who had carried out an internal 'purge': many police officials who were known to oppose the Nazis or who were considered Jewish or related to Jews had already been arrested on the night of 11 March.[29] It is most likely that the social values, sense of order and notions of police service of members of the Austrian police did not differ greatly from those of their colleagues in the 'Altreich'. In view of the traditional authoritarian manner – mistreatment of arrestees had occurred in Viennese police stations even before the annexation[30] – many police officials no doubt even welcomed the 'enlarged' scope for action, and were at least willing to turn a blind eye to the brutal reprisals typical of the Gestapo.

Most of the police officials taken over by the Gestapo hoped for rapid career advancement and for material benefit from the introduction of the Reich Remuneration Law (Reichsbesoldungsgesetz).[31] In particular, those who had been active in the illegal NSDAP between 1933 and 1938 and prosecuted for it expected to be rewarded through 'preferential' promotion. The Second Implementing Provision of the Regulation on the Introduction of the Reich Remuneration Law in Austria of 7 February did indeed provide for 'preferential' advancement of former 'illegals'.[32] Thus, for example, time spent as a 'Politischer Leiter' (political leader) or simply as a member of the NSDAP, SA, Hitler Youth or SS before 12 March 1938 was counted as years of service towards acquisition of the status of civil servant with unlimited tenure.[33] Immediately after the annexation, many officials therefore claimed to have been 'illegal Nazis' and thus to deserve the status 'Alter Kämpfer' ('old fighter', i.e. an NSDAP member before the 1933 prohibition and thereafter). In Ottakring police station, which at the time had around forty Kripo officials, a list was posted on the evening of 11 March 1938 for 'illegals' to enter their names. The next morning there were twenty names on the list, including that of Josef Auinger.[34] The expectations of the police officials were generally fulfilled, at least in the lower echelons of the Gestapo hierarchy. Thus Josef Miksch, born in 1893, who had worked originally on his parents' farm and joined the police in 1920, transferring to the criminal investigation police in 1925, was not only recruited by the Vienna Gestapo but also obtained a permanent post and promotion to Kriminalobersekretar on account of his 'illegal' party membership.[35]

To be recognized as an 'illegal' or 'Alter Kämpfer', the commitment to the illegal NSDAP had to be proved, which was only really possible for police officials who had been dismissed or had fled to the Reich on account of their political activities. Most of the police officials who had been active between 1933 and 1938 in the banned NSDAP had understandably been afraid of losing their jobs, and had therefore only acted under cover and together with like-minded colleagues. If an official now wanted to be recognized as having been an 'illegal' and gain promotion, his attitude when the movement was prohibited[36] had to be confirmed in writing by party comrades or colleagues whose status as 'illegals' was undisputed; this was the case, for example, with Johann Hoi, and also Franz Kamba, the Gauhauptstellenleiter (head of the NSDAP office for the Gau of Vienna). Kamba himself claimed to have issued over two hundred 'Alter Kämpfer' certificates for Austrian Gestapo officials in his NSDAP function.[37] According to the statement made by former Gestapo official Ernst Schwertführer to the Volksgericht in Vienna, five to six hundred such certificates were issued.[38] After 1945, all former Gestapo officials claimed in their statements to the Volksgericht that the certificates had been issued exclusively on the instructions of police chief Otto Steinhäusl. Steinhäusl was said to have feared a massive 'invasion' of German police, and wanted to prevent this by ensuring that as many Austrian officials as possible were declared to have been 'illegal' party members and hence politically reliable.[39] In 1953, the former Gestapo official Karl Prieler even went as far as claiming that there was a 'Steinhäusl order' to counter the 'excessive infiltration of Reich-German officials into the Vienna police'.[40] When the former Kripo official Josef Dworak stated to the Volksgericht that he had declared himself as an 'illegal' because of pressure from his colleagues,[41] Johann Rixinger, a former official in the 'Jewish section' who had been called as a witness, emphatically refuted this claim. He declared openly that 'neither I nor to my knowledge other officials, including Josef Dworak, [were] forced to take this step ... I did so because I hoped for more rapid promotion and other material advantages'.[42] Karl Amler was one of the few former Gestapo officials to state to the Volksgericht that he had allowed himself to be 'illegalized' so as to 'get on'.[43] Steinhäusl could no longer be questioned on this matter, because he had died of cancer in 1940.

Among the police officials who claimed after the annexation to have been 'illegals', the distinction between committed National Socialists, fellow travellers and rank opportunists is no doubt blurred. It is possible that in some cases certificates regarding supposed 'illegal' activity were issued on the basis of personal sympathies, contacts or cronyism, or – as some officials claimed after 1945 – in return for a donation to the NSDAP.[44] But even if the Gestapo officials coming from the Austrian police had no formal connection with the NSDAP because of the ban from 1933 to 1938, all of those who tried so vehemently after 1945 to trivialize their affiliation to the 'illegal' NSDAP must have shown a certain degree of ideological support or sympathy for National Socialism for them to be certified as 'Alte Kämpfer'. The persistent attempts and absurd arguments employed after 1945 to deny 'illegality' were in many cases due to the fact that membership of the illegal NSDAP before 13 March 1938[45] was often the only offence that the defendants could be proved to have committed on the basis of the available sources, particularly the 'Gau files'.

Incorporation of Gestapo Officials into the SS – Police and SS Ranks

Most Gestapo officials who did not claim after the annexation to have been 'illegals' quickly joined the NSDAP or SS, although neither was obligatory for Sipo officials.[46] According to a decree issued by the Reichsführer-SS on 23 June 1938, 'officials of the Sicherheitspolizei may join the Schutzstaffel of the NSDAP if they meet the general requirements for the SS'.[47] If the applicants for SS membership met the recruitment criteria, which were not as stringent for Gestapo or Kripo officials, in a second distinct step they could be promoted to an SS rank equivalent to their police rank.[48] This alignment of ranks 'involved much more than being merely co-opted into the SS'[49] and was seen as a promotion for special merit.

After 1945, however, all former Gestapo officials claimed in their statements to the Volksgericht that membership of the NSDAP or SS was obligatory or 'automatic'. For example, the jurist Richard Ulbing, who joined the police force in 1923 and the Vienna security directorate (Sicherheitsdirektion) in 1930, and after the annexation headed Section D (Foreign workers) in Department III of the Vienna Gestapo, claimed in his plea for clemency to the federal president in autumn 1956 that he had been 'officially ordered' to fill out an application form for membership of the SS.[50] Deputy head Karl Ebner asserted in his trial before the Volksgericht that his membership of the SS, where he ultimately held the rank of Obersturmbannführer, was 'automatic' and occurred without his involvement.⁵¹ And Otto Schleiffer, one of the most brutal thugs in the Vienna Gestapo, justified his membership of the NSDAP and SS by stating that at a roll call in May 1938 Huber had stated 'that it was a duty of every police official, and in particular every Gestapo official, to join the NSDAP and SS'.⁵² There was no doubt considerable peer group pressure within the Vienna Gestapo to join the NSDAP and SS, but this was prompted in the first instance by the assumption and fear of individual Gestapo officials that, for example, they would have difficulties at work if they failed to join, or would miss possible career advancement or would be considered outsiders by their colleagues.

There are no known cases to date of an Austrian Gestapo official being dismissed because he had refused to join the NSDAP or SS. It is highly likely, however, that non-membership would have been an obstacle to advancement, as former Gestapo official Anton Wartha stated after 1945.⁵³ The great influence of career ambitions on personal decisions by Gestapo officials is illustrated indirectly by the testimony of Karl Ebner. He 'justified' his leaving the Catholic Church by claiming he was forced to do so, although admitting bluntly that one could 'not become an SS officer or take the SS officer examination without leaving the church. Without this, promotion, even in accordance with the normal civil service framework, was impossible'.⁵⁴

Age and Social Structure of Gestapo Officials – Female Gestapo Employees

The vast majority of Vienna Gestapo officials below the level of section head, occupying a position as unit head or unit member and holding the rank of Kriminalsekretär, Kriminaloberassistent or Kriminalassistent, were born between 1900 and 1910. Practically all of them came from lower-middle-class backgrounds and had originally learned a different trade. Weidinger, for example, was a qualified waiter,⁵⁵ and Karl Amler a metal printer.⁵⁶ Only a few had the university entrance qualification (Matura), and some had served for a few years in the armed forces before or after 1918. A common feature of all the biographies studied to date is that the strongest motivations for joining the police force, in most cases in the early 1920s, were fear of unemployment and the desire for job security. Interestingly, however, only a few of those studied were in fact ever unemployed. At the level of section head, a number of Gestapo officials – Josef Auinger and Friedrich Kranebitter are two examples – stand out in that they completed law degrees while working in the police force but never held positions commensurate with their qualifications before 1938. As for the age structure, according to Franz Weisz, the largest group in the Gestapo between 1938 and 1942 was aged between thirty and thirty-five, with 40.58 per cent of the employees of Departments II and III being in this age group. Between 1942 and 1944 the proportion in this age group dropped to 24.35 per cent, while in the same period the over-forty age group increased. This can be explained first by the natural ageing process but also by the fact that younger officials in particular were posted elsewhere, at least for certain periods.⁵⁷

One striking feature is the above-average number of jurists in the Vienna Gestapo. Originally there were twenty-six Austrian and ten German jurists, whereas even the largest offices in the 'Altreich' had only two or at most three. The establishment of such a large office, the introduction of Reich-German laws, regulations and practices, and not least the complex agenda, including the expropriation of monasteries and the plundering of Jewish property, called for qualified personnel. The number of jurists later dwindled, particularly as a result of transfers, and from 1943 there were only three (Austrian) jurists, albeit in absolutely key roles: Karl Ebner, Othmar Trenker and Viktor Siegel.⁵⁸

The Vienna Gestapo was not an exclusively male domain. Between 1938 and 1942 there were an estimated 17 per cent women on the payroll. During the war their number increased, on account of transfers and secondments of male colleagues, to over 30 per cent. Regarding this increase, it should not be forgotten, however, that by 1944 the total Vienna Gestapo payroll had dropped

Figure 5.1. An office in Hotel Metropole, showing the Vienna Gestapo official Josef Auinger (centre) with his staff. © Dokumentationsarchiv des österreichischen Widerstandes. Used with permission.

to just under 490 employees. In absolute terms, this meant that between 1938 and 1944 the number of women effectively only rose from around 140 to 170.[59]

The vast majority of female Gestapo employees were transferred directly after the annexation from the Austrian state police. This was the case, for example, with Hildegard Rock, who together with seven other typists took up a new position on 1 April 1938 in Section II B (Church, Freemasons, Jews).[60] Later on as well, there was a reluctance to take staff from the employment office, and most female workers were recruited from the former Austrian security services.[61]

Female Gestapo employees were employed exclusively for subordinate office tasks in support of their male colleagues. They managed the extensive card index and filing system, typed interrogation reports dictated by male section officials, and operated the telex machines and telephones. Apart from these simple clerical tasks, women were also employed as cleaners. They always had a male supervisor, and could not become civil servants or assume leading positions.[62] The largest proportion of female employees between 1938 and 1942 was to be found in Department I (Administration): of 145 employees, 39 were women. At the same time there were 99 women among the 650 employees of the two police departments II and III, although the proportion of women differed from section to section: while women made up 25 per cent – 5 out of 20 – of Section II P (Press and cultural affairs) and were also in the majority – 10 out of 19 – in Section II D (Protective custody), there were no women at all in the special Section III F (Tracking).[63]

Female Gestapo employees are mentioned only occasionally in the available source material, mostly in lists of names. After 1945 very few women who had served in the Gestapo were investigated in Germany and Austria. Although the International Military Tribunal in Nuremberg classified the Gestapo as a criminal organization, simple office workers, stenographers, porters, messengers and others performing routine non-official tasks were excluded from the indictment.[64] With the exception of Rosa Friedl, who will be discussed in greater detail later, female ex-employees of the Gestapo did not therefore stand trial before an Austrian Volksgericht. They appear in the records of the Volksgericht proceedings only as witnesses – as was the case with Hildegard Rock, who was a secretary in the 'Jewish section' – or in the testimonies of former victims.

The male-centric structure of the Gestapo meant, among other things, that women were not involved in the physical violence inflicted on detainees. After 1945, however, surviving Gestapo detainees stated in the Volksgericht proceedings that women were often present as typists during the interrogations, and not only witnessed but also sometimes expressly approved of the brutal maltreatment. Several witnesses reported, for example, that the typist Elisabeth Obernosterer frequently encouraged the violent Gestapo official Karl Perger to maltreat prisoners, saying: 'The dog's lying! Hit him!'[65] According to one witness, the typist Hildegard Fritsch behaved in a similar fashion.[66]

The women who guarded the female internees from 1944 at Oberlanzendorf 'labour education camp' (Arbeitserziehungslager, AEL) had closer contact with prisoners. Dr Fritz Gerscha, a physician transferred to the Gestapo-run camp, testified to Sankt Pölten local court in 1947: 'There were two Polish and two German female guards'.[67] The 'Poles' were presumably *Volksdeutsche* (ethnic Germans). It is not possible to determine the (service) relationship of the women guards to the Gestapo. The assaults on prisoners were committed by male guards. Emilia Ploi, who was interned in the camp for two weeks in 1944, testified in 1947 to the Vienna LG (regional court) that she had had her hair pulled during a dispute with the head of the women's camp and was reported to the camp commandant Karl Künzel, who maltreated her even more roughly.[68]

The sources available to date suggest that female employees of the Vienna Gestapo were not transferred to the East, for example to serve with the Sipo in Litzmannstadt (Łódź); nor were they directly involved in the deportation of Austrian Jews, unlike in the 'Altreich', where female Gestapo employees conducted body searches in the assembly camps. Nevertheless, the female employees of the Vienna Gestapo did not just carry out various forms of 'unpolitical' office work, as Hildegard Rock and Rosa Friedl claimed in their statements after 1945. These women worked for a central terror and repression instrument of the Nazi regime and were thus part of it. They knew about the criminal nature of the regime and the consequences of their work for those who fell foul of the Gestapo. Women who managed the 'protective custody' card index, for example, knew not only that there were concentration camps but also that many inmates perished there, often within the shortest time. In the narrow corridors of the Gestapo building they saw prisoners' relatives waiting and their desperate attempts to obtain information about the fate of a loved one, as well as the prisoners themselves, who would stand for hours outside the rooms where they were to be interrogated, often facing the wall with their arms raised.[69] Hildegard Rock testified in detail after 1945 about the role of the Gestapo during the November Pogrom of 1938, and in the expropriation, looting and deportation of the Jewish population; and before 1945 she must have been basically aware of the fate of the Jews.[70] Rock, who was born in 1910 and joined the police force in 1930 after attending school and commercial college, denied any involvement in the Gestapo crimes, claiming typically: 'I didn't do anything'. She did not demonstrate the slightest remorse for her work in the Gestapo but complained at being treated like a dangerous criminal.[71] Gertrude Pichler, another typist in the 'Jewish section', who testified in the trial of Karl Zeitlberger, one of the most brutal thugs in that unit, denied having witnessed the maltreatment of prisoners: 'I never saw the defendant [Zeitlberger] maltreating prisoners, nor did he swear at them'.[72] Rosa Friedl, secretary in Section N, made very similar claims.

As far as we know, Friedl was the only female employee of the Vienna Gestapo to be investigated after 1945 under Section 3 of the War Criminals Act[73] (i.e. on account of her work in the Gestapo and her membership of the 'illegal' NSDAP). Born on 19 October 1899 in Vienna, she joined the NSDAP in 1932 and worked for the party during the years when it was prohibited. With a letter of recommendation from the NSDAP, which described her as 'one of our most reliable and trustworthy members, who has selflessly made herself available to our party at all times',[74] she joined the Gestapo in May 1938, where she worked at first as a typist in Unit II A 3 (Russia returnees) and later in Section N (Intelligence). According to her own account, she initially performed simple clerical work but later – not least owing to her political reliability – worked relatively independently. She took down reports by informants and also arranged for their payment. When she was questioned after 1945, she was very circumspect. She only admitted what was provable from surviving documents, and emphasized that she had never reported anyone or harmed them through her work. Even when she was arrested on 13 July 1945, she still managed to destroy incriminating material. The police official who arrested her reported that there was a fire burning in the stove and 'she could easily have burned documents before opening the door'. The Vienna LG ceased investigation of her activities on 18 December 1945, and she was released.[75]

The fact is that while female Gestapo employees did not have any police functions or authority, they still contributed through their work to the functioning of the Gestapo, despite the fact that their daily activities provided them with clear evidence of the consequences for Gestapo victims.

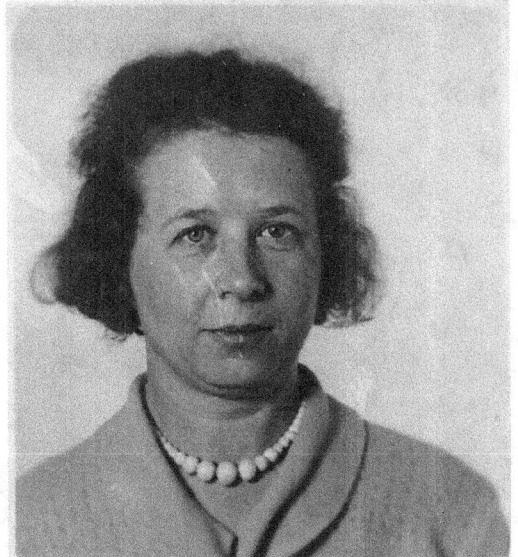

Figure 5.2. Rosa Friedl, secretary in the Vienna Gestapo intelligence section. Police photo after 1945. © Dokumentationsarchiv des österreichischen Widerstandes. Used with permission.

Personnel Continuity and Rotation – Demotion of Huber and Ebner

The heads of the regular and regional Gestapo offices were the most prominent examples of the mass of staff strategically manoeuvred by the SS leadership: the strict rotation principle, permitting only very rarely a period in office of over two years, was intended to prevent the formation of personal attachments and loyalties at the local level. Moreover, with the establishment of EGs, special commando units, and new Sipo departments in the occupied countries of Europe as the core of an unparalleled persecution and extermination regime, it was vital to have ideologically committed Gestapo and SD personnel without moral or humanitarian scruples. With regard to the principle of rotation, Huber's uninterrupted leadership of the Vienna Gestapo from March 1938 to the end of 1944 was an absolute exception.

The large payroll over a long period and the lower turnover of personnel in Vienna in comparison with other Gestapo regional headquarters were due to Huber. However, there were also objective factors in his favour that made the importance and geopolitically exposed situation of the Vienna Gestapo apparent to the Gestapo leadership in Berlin, including: the much stronger resistance

Figure 5.3. Group of Vienna Gestapo officials, probably in front of Theresianumgasse 16–18, Huber's office as IdSuSD, before July 1941, some wearing the grey service-dress uniform of the Waffen-SS. Front row: second from left Karl Ebner, third from left Franz Josef Huber. © Archives of the Republic of Slovenia. Used with permission.

to the regime compared with the 'Altreich', in particular from the Communists; pro-Habsburg separatist tendencies among the bourgeoisie; the position at the border of the Reich to states such as Czechoslovakia and Yugoslavia, which were identified as the next victims; the increasing number of 'Eastern workers', who were deemed to be dangerous; the operations of Allied commandos; and finally, the approaching front in 1945.

'Huber's personnel policy was not anti-Austrian', said his deputy Ebner in a post-war statement. In view of constant feuds and rivalries between Austrians and Reich Germans, he was at pains to surround himself with unconditionally loyal staff. This led to the formation of a permanent group of leading employees – first and foremost his long-standing deputy and personal friend Karl Ebner.[76]

Unlike their Reich-German colleagues, the Austrian officials were not eager to be transferred or seconded.[77] With a few exceptions – such as Josef Auinger, who headed SS-Sonderkommando 7b of Einsatzgruppe B in Byelorussia from July to October 1942 – the Vienna Gestapo officials transferred to *Einsatzgruppen* and Sipo offices in eastern and south-eastern Europe were mainly those in subordinate positions, and their secondments were usually for a limited period. In 1939, for example, Josef Dworak was transferred for several months to the Gestapo in Brünn (Brno), and Johann Weitschacher to the Gestapo in Mährisch-Ostrau (Ostrava).[78] In 1940, Otto Schleiffer was transferred for some months to Saarburg in Lothringen (Lorraine), where he was responsible for the establishment of the Gestapo there and was involved, to use his own words, in 'cleaning up the language mix at the France-Lothringen border' (i.e. the expulsion of the French-speaking population).[79] In March 1944, before the occupation of Hungary by German troops, when Einsatzgruppe F was formed, there was a larger secondment of thirty-two members of staff from sections IV A and IV E in Vienna.[80]

Although the Vienna Gestapo with Huber as long-term head and Ebner as his deputy had relatively constant leadership (and also a constantly lengthy payroll) in comparison with other Gestapo regional headquarters, continuity in office was not the case at the lower levels. The sections and units – and after 1942 the departments – were not headed continuously by one and the same person. Unit II B 4 (the 'Jewish section'), for example, was headed as follows:

April to June 1938	Karl Haselbacher (German)
July 1938 to June 1939	Rudolf Lange (German)
July to September 1939	Wilhelm Vogel (German)
October 1939 to April 1942	Karl Ebner (Austrian)
April to December 1942	Josef Schindler (German)
January 1943 to April 1944	Rudolf Rack (German)
May 1944 to April 1945	Christian Nicoll (German)

As the case of Nicoll shows – he was unit head in Section II C (National opposition) from 1941 to 1942, and head of Section IV A 3 (Left-wing movement, sabotage) from April 1942 to April 1944 – it was quite common for personnel to be transferred internally. Johann Rixinger was an exception: like many other officials at the Vienna Gestapo headquarters he was also seconded for several months to Brünn/Brno in 1939, but returned to the 'Jewish section' and remained there until April 1945. It was no doubt thanks to his good personal relationship with Ebner that he was transferred only once at Morzinplatz.

This period of continuity at the top level ended in 1944–45, when first Huber – gradually – and then Ebner – abruptly – were stripped of their authority. The driving force behind these moves was Ernst Kaltenbrunner, appointed head of the RSHA in January 1943. As Höherer SS- und Polizeiführer (higher SS and police leader) 'Danube' with his office in Vienna, he had been ignored previously by Huber, who was officially subordinate to him. Now he could wreak his revenge. When Huber simulated a heart attack at Easter 1944, SS-Standartenführer Rudolf Mildner was ordered by the RSHA to stand in for him in his 'official duties' from June of that year.[81]

Mildner, a Sudeten German, had worked in the Austrian police before moving in 1935 to the 'Altreich', where he made a career for himself in the Gestapo, and 'was well known as a fanatical National Socialist and an absolute firebrand'.[82] As Sipo head in Kattowitz (Katowice) in 1941–42, he is said to have had 350 members of a Polish resistance group publicly executed as a deterrent.[83] As part of the restructuring in the third GVP, Kaltenbrunner made Mildner Kommandeur (commander) of the Sipo and SD in Military District XVII on 1 December 1944, thus also taking over Huber's (now vacant) position as head of the Vienna Gestapo, while Huber was shunted out of the way to the theoretically senior but largely non-influential post of Befehlshaber (commander-in-chief) of the Sipo and SD in Military District XVII.[84]

Huber's fall from power also ended the dominant position of his deputy Karl Ebner, whose 'reinsurance' endeavours were not lost on other Gestapo officials. The new head Mildner had incriminating material and accusations fabricated against Ebner by the in-house disinformation expert Johann Sanitzer, and pressed charges for 'undermining military morale' *(Wehrkraftzersetzung)*, 'protecting prisoners' and 'several cases of corruption'. Ebner was arrested in his office at Morzinplatz on 9 January 1945 and sentenced to death by the supreme SS and police court (Oberstes SS- und Polizeigericht) in Munich, which was in session in Traunstein, for offences under Section 5.1.1 *(Wehrkraftzersetzung)* of the special wartime criminal law regulation (Kriegssonderstrafrechtsverordnung).[85] In the confusion at the end of the war, the sentence was not carried out.[86]

While the RSHA appointed the (Reich-German) Kriminaldirektor Franz Straub, previously head of the Gestapo in Brussels, to assist Mildner as a man of radical action with special authority, the position of important Austrian officials in Vienna – particularly Viktor Siegel, Lambert Leutgeb and Johann Sanitzer – remained unaffected. Only Othmar Trenker – according to his own statement on account of insufficient severity in Operation 'Gitter' (following the events of 20 July 1944) – was relieved of his post as head of Department IV in October 1944 and transferred to the RSHA.[87]

German-Austrian Conflict Potential at the Vienna Gestapo

After the annexation there was a veritable inrush of Gestapo officials from the 'Altreich' to Gestapo posts within the Sipo in Austria. Heydrich's deputy Werner Best was obliged to issue a circular ordering that all transfer applications be submitted to him for consideration.[88] With Heydrich's support, Franz Josef Huber, who headed the Vienna Gestapo from March 1938 and who was already familiar with the Austrian police and local situation through his years of experience at the Gestapa, ultimately ensured the gradual reduction of staff from the 'Altreich'.[89] For quite a number of younger and ambitious Reich-German officials, such as Rudolf Lange and Karl Haselbacher, the posting to Vienna was in any case only a springboard to greater responsibilities and higher positions created in the wake of Nazi expansion in Europe.

Because of the inadequacy of the source material, it is only possible to estimate the number of officials from Germany who served, mostly for just a limited period, in the Vienna Gestapo. In spite of the lack of sources, the claim by Austrian officials after 1945 that there was an 'invasion of Prussian officials' after the annexation can be regarded as an exaggeration.[90] First, in view of the manpower shortage, the German police leadership would hardly have been in a position to replace Austrian officials with Germans; second, Austrian police officials – quite apart from the widespread ideological sympathy for National Socialism in their ranks, which was well known to the Gestapa in Berlin even before the annexation – were of considerable importance for the efficient pursuit of opponents on account of their specific local knowledge. A typical example is Lambert Leutgeb, who from 1936 to 1938 had already worked in the intelligence service of the Austrian state police against Social Democrats and Communists; after being taken over by the Gestapo in March 1938, he developed the network of informants into the most powerful instrument of the Vienna office.

From 1938 to 1945, the proportion of Vienna Gestapo employees from Germany fluctuated between 8 and 16 per cent, with the greatest proportion in the first two years of Nazi rule, tapering off thereafter.[91] It is striking that in the first two years at Morzinplatz there were considerably more German than Austrian officials in leading positions – that is, head, deputy head, and department heads. However, as early as 1941, the German officials Wilhelm Bock and Heinz Rennau, who headed departments II and III, were replaced by the Austrians

Heinrich Berger and the previously mentioned Richard Ulbing. Ulbing joined the NSDAP on 1 May 1938; he was appointed head of Department III on 1 May 1941 and transferred, probably to Lemberg (Lviv) or Paris in 1942. After the war he lived 'with friends in West Germany' and did not return to Austria until 1956, where he was not prosecuted further for his activity as a Gestapo official.[92]

Because of the fragmentary source material, it is impossible to determine the precise number of Austrians and Germans from section head down – unit heads and officials in the different sections and units – not least because these officials often moved from one unit to another to cover the changing workload. Moreover, they were frequently transferred to other Gestapo offices, often for several months, and the merger of departments II and III provided for by the 1942 GVP to form Department IV is a further complicating factor. Between 1938 and 1942, for example, 3 of the 92 officials in Section II A (Left-wing movement) were German, 12 of 119 in Section II B (Ideological opponents) and 2 out 88 in Section II C (National opposition). During the same period, Section II D (Protective custody) had 19 members, one of whom was German. Sections with no German Gestapo officials included Section II F (Card index and records) and II P (Press and cultural affairs).[93]

Unsurprisingly, the predominance of Reich Germans, especially in the sought-after higher positions, soon led to frictions and conflicts, above all in the first years after the annexation. These conflicts resulted as well from the clash of two different civil service cultures, the Reich-German and the Austrian, within the historical framework of traditional prejudices going back centuries on both sides. Karl Ebner, Huber's 'permanent deputy' and the senior and longest-serving official in the Vienna Gestapo, was more familiar than anyone with the personal conflicts of this initial period; in a dossier he wrote after his arrest by the British occupying powers, Ebner discussed this problem in detail, blaming the Germans for the tensions that arose: 'With a generosity hitherto unknown in them, with inexperience and ignorance of the country and its people, and in many cases unencumbered by even the most rudimentary policing skills, the Reich Germans were mistrustful of the Austrians, including old party comrades, and claimed that they lacked energy. But the Reich Germans were without doubt in the stronger position, and they let it be known most emphatically. The Austrians got very down in the mouth'.[94]

In the weeks and months after the annexation, Austrian officials sent anonymous letters to Berlin complaining of discriminatory treatment by 'Reich-German instructors', the 'excessive' workload and 'low ranking'. One of them, stemming from Linz police circles, was read by Kurt Daluege, head of the Ordnungspolizei (regular police), who prompted the Gestapa to demand an explanation of the situation from Huber, and pointed out that the anonymous letters were suspiciously similar to 'subversive Communist writings'. In his reply of 17 February 1939, Huber not only categorically rejected investigations by the Gestapo but gave a frank and non-ideological assessment of the bad atmosphere:

> With few exceptions, the officials coming from the Altreich to the Ostmark ... are not well viewed or tolerated. The particular mentality of the inhabitants of the Ostmark makes them prone to criticize openly and make personal comments, with membership of the Altreich being often referred to in particularly crass terms. Interventions by the party ... have helped to create an untenable situation. With my knowledge of the real situation, I can state quite categorically that these reports should not under any circumstances be seen as subversive Communist writings.[95]

The letter from the Gestapa to Huber also indicated that the German-Austrian confrontation since the annexation was not just present within the police force but was probably a general phenomenon. In the military training sector as well, 'the inhabitants of Vienna are apparently resentful ... of the treatment of Ostmark soldiers by Reich-German trainers in Vienna. ... Instances [can be] observed every day of soldiers ... being referred to as "Austrian swine". For that reason, it is said, there is a certain ill humour among the troops'.

The relationship between German and Austrian Gestapo officials was adversely affected not only by the different mentalities and by German arrogance, but also by personal rivalries. Some of the Austrian Gestapo officials were soon frustrated that they were not being given leading roles as they had hoped but, at least for a time, were subordinate to Germans who bossed them around. Even important former 'illegals', such as the Vienna police chief Otto Steinhäusl and the NSDAP Gauhauptstellenleiter Franz Kamba no doubt followed this development with misgivings. They and other old Nazis were increasingly forced to recognize that many hopes and expectations that they had harboured regarding the Third Reich were illusory. The idea held by many Austrian Nazis that Austria, or rather they themselves as supporters of National Socialism, would have a 'special role' to play within the Third Reich and would be able to exercise a certain amount of independence proved to be completely misjudged, and many of these high-ranking Austrian Nazis perceived this as an insult to their self-esteem. Hopes for a betterment of their material situation and generous compensation for disadvantages experienced during the period of 'illegality' were also dashed. Johann Hoi, for example, who was one of the most active 'illegals' between 1934 and 1938, and had been dismissed from the police for that reason, was only a unit head. The introduction of the Reich Remuneration Law produced material gains for employees of the Vienna Gestapo, but they were not as great as expected. Steinhäusl and Kamba were therefore probably also interested, at least to some extent, in ensuring that their Austrian colleagues were not 'short-changed'. In a political assessment on the jurist Otto Kolb, which was of importance for Kolb's civil service career, Kamba certified that he had 'always been a strong nationalist' and 'sympathetic to national socialism ... without being politically active', whereas an NSDAP assessment on the occasion of his application for membership had judged him to be 'politically indifferent'.[96] With this support, Kolb, unit head in Section II E (Economic affairs), was admitted to the SS in 1939 and to the NSDAP in 1940, and ultimately promoted on 29 May 1941 to the rank of Regierungsrat. A year later he was transferred to the Gestapo in Breslau (Wrocław), where in June 1944 a superior described him not only as hardworking and thorough but also possessing 'a good interrogation technique', which was saying a lot given the Gestapo's customary methods.[97]

All these tensions, frictions and conflicts for posts and competences should not be overestimated, however, because they did not affect the efficiency of the Gestapo's work and nor did they diminish the widespread ideological approval of the Nazi regime on the part of Austrian Gestapo officials.

'Reinsurance'

As it became clear that the 'final victory' propagated by the Nazi regime was not going to materialize, more and more Nazis, even in the regime's highest echelons, took to making contingency plans through a survival strategy known as 'reinsurance' (*Rückversicherung*). This expression – like 'Blitzkrieg' or 'organisieren' – is an example of what Victor Klemperer memorably called the *lingua tertii imperii* (LTI, language of the Third Reich), and the very fact that it has passed into the German language in this general sense suggests that the practice was widespread. It involved deliberate measures undertaken in the hope that they could be used later to mitigate accusations of collaboration in Nazi crimes.[98] The methods depended on the extent of the involvement in and knowledge of the crimes that had been committed, the practical possibilities and, lastly, the willingness to take risks.

As a first step in the practice of 'reinsurance', practitioners had to distance themselves more or less clearly from their obligations of loyalty to the regime. Even Heinrich Himmler, in what is probably the most extreme example of 'reinsurance', sought through Count (Graf) Folke Bernadotte, president of the Swedish Red Cross, to establish contact with Eisenhower, commander-in-chief of the Allied forces in Europe, so as to conduct peace negotiations on his own, releasing all Scandinavian concentration camp inmates for that purpose. Adolf Eichmann's proposal to Joel Brand,[99] to exchange ten thousand trucks for a million Jews, may be seen as an attempt by Himmler to escape the noose by profiling himself as a 'saviour of the Jews'. Himmler's relative leniency towards the former mayor of Vienna, Karl Seitz, who was involved in the 20 July 1944 plot, may also be seen in this light.

Ernst Kaltenbrunner stated at the Nuremberg military tribunal that in February 1943 he had already suggested 'moving towards a change in policy towards the churches so as to win over the Vatican as an initial mediator of peace', and that he had been 'in contact with Mr Dulles'.[100] Kaltenbrunner took out a final 'reinsurance policy' shortly before the end of the war: at the urging of miners and resistance fighters, he helped to prevent the dynamiting of a salt mine in Altaussee containing precious works of art looted from various European countries.

A particularly effective form of 'reinsurance' was the offer by incriminated members of the Nazi secret services to make their expert knowledge available to the Allies. Reinhold Gehlen was a typical example of this method: in his strategically important position as head of the Foreign Armies East department in the army general staff, and thus responsible for espionage in the East, his 'reinsurance' was as good as guaranteed. From 1946, he was co-head with the CIA of the Gehlen Organization named after him,[101] and his staff were recruited mainly from the SS, SD, Gestapo and Abwehr. For similar reasons, the US Counter Intelligence Corps (CIC) was interested in the Viennese Wilhelm Höttl, Kaltenbrunner's adjutant in Vienna and, from 1943, head of the intelligence service in Department VI of the RSHA. He had apparently built up an 'invasion network in Eastern Europe', which would provide the US secret service with information about activities in eastern Austria, the zone occupied by the Soviets.[102] As will be shown later, the activities of Huber and Sanitzer in combating espionage and parachute agents in the Vienna Gestapo also attracted the interest of foreign secret services – in Huber's case, with extremely advantageous results for him.

More commonly, 'reinsurance' took the form of resistance activities of various types – failing to carry out orders or to impose sanctions, and engaging in sabotage or agent operations. Alternatively, it could involve activities deliberately aimed at rescuing individuals persecuted by the regime, a particularly ambivalent form of 'reinsurance' practised by Huber and, above all, Ebner in the Vienna Gestapo.

'Reinsurance' through illegal official aid for persecuted individuals is in a different category from other forms of obstruction of state interests. An act of resistance such as the refusal to obey an order has a different moral dimension to giving direct assistance to someone at risk. Both can be motivated by the idea of self-preservation, but the calculated effect being sought acquired a new moral dynamic through the act of saving a victim. For victims and persecutees, of course, the motivation of the person who rescued their property, health, dignity and life was completely irrelevant: the cold calculation behind the 'reinsurance' thus became incidental to the morality of the act.

Moreover, a personal contribution to rescuing a victim was not even absolutely necessary. The main thing was the degree to which the person in question was perceived as a rescuer in the victim's eyes. As the case of Ebner shows, his contribution in a number of cases was practically non-existent or consisted solely in carrying out Huber's orders. He nevertheless managed to achieve the desired effect through skilful self-profiling as the person responsible for the rescue – aided by the fact that the Gestapo was an organization whose structures and mechanisms were completely opaque for the victims.

The way 'reinsurance' worked successfully in practice can be illustrated through the cases of the leading protagonists in the Vienna Gestapo, namely Franz Josef Huber and Karl Ebner.

Franz Josef Huber's Passive and Active Strategy of 'Reinsurance'

Through his protector Heydrich and long-standing friend Heinrich Müller ('Gestapo-Müller'), the head of the Vienna Gestapo had excellent contacts to the RSHA. He must have known early on and at first-hand about the course of the war and the extermination of the Jews. It is therefore striking that Huber, although as IdSuSD he was head of the central office for Jewish emigration, avoided any personal contact with this office, distanced himself above all from any activities connected with the deportation of Jews from Vienna, and handed over full responsibility to his deputy Ebner: 'I myself did not issue any deportation orders and I never entered the central office for Jewish emigration [but writing 'Abwanderung' for 'Auswanderung', see endnote] or dealt personally with Eichmann ... The responsibilities of the head of the Vienna office were so extensive that responsibility ... had to be shared ... with the permanent deputy. My permanent deputy [Ebner] had primary responsibility for the affairs of Section II B (Jews, churches, etc.)'.[103]

Even if this statement was written with a view to self-exoneration, Huber had clearly been at pains while in office to give the impression through overtly passive behaviour that he had nothing to do with the deportation of Jews from Vienna

Figure 5.4. Franz Josef Huber, head of the Vienna Gestapo 1938–44. © Archives of the Republic of Slovenia. Used with permission.

or other Gestapo crimes: 'Huber recognized the impending collapse in time, and through skilful behaviour distanced himself from criminal activities'.[104]

To further reinsure himself, Huber began to simulate illness, increasingly so towards the end of the war, with the result that his deputy Ebner headed the Vienna Gestapo on his own for months on end. When Huber suffered a 'serious heart attack' at Easter 1944, his arch-enemy Kaltenbrunner, who suspected him of shamming, sent Himmler's personal physician to Vienna, who was also apparently deceived and wrote that he was 'in need of convalescence'. Ebner was not taken in by his boss's 'serious heart attack': 'Huber became ill at Easter 1944. As he was already driving his car himself at the end of April, he cannot have been very sick'.[105] The continuing story of his illness indicates that at no time after April 1944 did Huber function fully as head of the Vienna Gestapo.

Apart from the tactic of avoiding responsibility through passiveness and distancing, Huber also pursued an active form of 'reinsurance': 'It was, of course, impossible to oppose legally binding orders, but it was quite possible to limit damage on occasion ... Even in my office, I was able to help people of all shades, including Jews'.[106]

The 'reinsurance' strategy of intervening to help victims of the Gestapo was a tactic more often employed by Huber's deputy Ebner, but as Gestapo head, Huber had additional possibilities, which he employed very purposefully. In the few interventions mentioned by him, in some cases confirmed by Ebner, it is interesting that the recipients of his aid were almost exclusively members of the Jewish cultural scene in Vienna. In a letter to Ebner in 1964 he asked the rhetorical question: 'Who ... is aware that I intervened personally for individual Jews and without further question released the assets of the Jewish wife of Hans Moser and of the brother-in-law of Leo Slezak by the name of Schlesinger? Who remembers the case of Generalmusikdirektor Krips? Or the release of Alice Strauss, Grete Painsiepp [sic] and other Jewish women?'[107] Huber also claimed to have rescued the property of the famous opera singer Lotte Lehmann, who emigrated in 1933 to the United States in protest at Göring's demand that she participate in Nazi cultural activities.[108]

It is clear that it was not moral scruples that prompted the Vienna Gestapo head to go so far as to intervene even in the case of Jewish victims. His efforts cannot be compared in any way with private 'rescue resistance'[109] – that is, high-risk attempts to hide fellow Jewish citizens in order to protect them from deportation. For Huber it was the 'expiry date' of the regime – at the latest following the now undeniable disaster at Stalingrad – that prompted him to help Jews in order to provide himself with ammunition for his post-war exoneration. And he had good reason to do so: after Baldur von Schirach, who was the driving force, he was the second most important local protagonist of the deportation and extermination of the Jewish population of Vienna.[110]

A further example of Huber's active 'reinsurance' was his late and surprising interest in the Gestapo's counter-sabotage intelligence operations and in the Allied parachute agents captured by the Gestapo, who were to be 'turned' and used to send false radio messages.[111] Huber calculated that his expert knowledge, which would be of interest to the Allies, and his gentle treatment of their agents would be useful as 'reinsurance' against prosecution for crimes committed in his almost seven years in office. And he was right: 'After the war Huber [was] not only approached by the Russian intelligence service but also urged to cooperate by American officers in the internment camp'.[112]

After his time in the Nuremberg-Langwasser US internment camp, Huber was classified in 1948 in a 'Spruchkammer' (civilian denazification court) hearing as a lesser offender, and thus sentenced to only one-year probation and a fine of DM 500. In spite of several requests by the court, the Austrian authorities failed to submit any incriminating material; it was only later – albeit unsuccessfully – that Austria demanded Huber's extradition. As a US secret service officer stated, he had 'only ... good information about Huber's activities in Austria. ... Franz Huber was not a supporter of the Nazi party ideology. He carried out his police tasks as fairly and reasonably as possible'.[113]

The final paragraph of the grounds for the decision totally exonerated one of the main criminals of the Nazi regime on the territory of former Austria: 'The accused [is] not part of the group ... who committed crimes against humanity. The ... evidence clearly shows that he did not support the Nazi tyranny, and that on the contrary ... he protected many people whom he should have been persecuting ... and without doubt averted much harm'.[114]

Karl Ebner, 'Reinsurance' Virtuoso

Karl Ebner's change from a careerist strategy to one of 'reinsurance' can be dated on the basis of two statements to the post-war VG focusing on early 1943, after the destruction of the Sixth Army in Stalingrad: 'Dr Ebner, who before 1943 was in favour of a radical approach to enemies of state, particularly Jews, then had reservations about the simplest of measures that he had previously absolutely insisted on being carried out'.[115] And Michael Stern – from 1938, legal consultant of the Jewish community and in this capacity in constant contact with the Vienna Gestapo – said when questioned by the VG that 'regarding his [Ebner's] attitude to Jews, from 1943 he was in fact the one who prevented or attenuated a series of measures against the Jews and the churches'.[116]

As Huber had delegated responsibility to Ebner except for some representative functions, Ebner was able to plan and implement his 'reinsurance' measures independently and with great care. Unlike Huber, his approach was exclusively an active one. For Ebner, who in complete contrast to his boss may be described as a workaholic – his wife constantly complained about how much he worked and that he regularly failed to come home 'until the middle of the night'[117] – reporting sick and delegating responsibility were simply not options. Ebner's active 'reinsurance' consisted on the one hand in being dilatory with the bureaucracy, preventing inquiries and having files disappear, and on the other hand in direct intervention for people at risk or already detained. The degree to which he acted on Huber's instructions can be determined in only a few isolated cases.

Ebner based his 'reinsurance' activities on two criteria: first, the 'reinsurance' potential of those for whom he intervened, and second, the minimization as far as possible of the risk to himself. Practically all the interventions concerned victims from the higher social classes, whose status, education and political credibility could be helpful 'afterwards': 'Ebner's list' – that is to say, the people on whose behalf he intervened – contains the names of numerous clergymen, including high-ranking church dignitaries, and above all members of the Austrian Cartellverband (CV), which Ebner had joined as a student. The others he chose to intervene for appear at first glance to be random: major industrialists, landowners, lawyers, notaries and artists, such as the actor Hans Moser and the conductor Josef Krips. And yet there were common features: membership of a certain social class, prominence and hence guaranteed public awareness – and a correspondingly high dividend for Ebner's personalized 'reinsurance'.

Figure 5.5. Karl Ebner, deputy head of the Vienna Gestapo 1942–44. © Wiener Stadt- und Landesarchiv. Used with permission.

When it came to people arrested for active resistance, Ebner refrained from intervening – even in favour of clerics.[118] As he had already been involved as a police official before 1938 in combating left-wing opposition, it is not surprising that he never intervened for individuals belonging to the Communist or Marxist resistance. There are also only three known cases of his specific intervention to prevent Jews from deportation.[119]

Ebner's calculation for obtaining the maximum effect with the minimum effort paid off. Ultimately, it was the twenty-five defence witnesses who testified in his post-war trial who saved his neck: 'The court was of the unanimous opinion that the fact that the defendant saved the lives of countless persons should be taken particularly into account as a reason for refraining from pronouncing a sentence of death'.[120] However, in view of the procession of defence witnesses, the presiding judge could not resist passing a comment at one juncture: 'If I understand you correctly, all you did at the Gestapo was to help people who were not in agreement with the Nazi regime. And you were paid for that?'[121]

It is difficult to interpret the sometimes conspicuous behaviour of lower-ranking Gestapo officials when interrogating prominent representatives of the political opposition. As dealt with in detail in Chapter 9, even notorious thugs exercised manifest restraint when dealing with public figures such as the Social Democratic politicians (and future federal presidents) Theodor Körner and Adolf Schärf. It is hard to determine whether this behaviour, which, thanks to positive testimony, in some cases resulted in more lenient sentences in post-war trials, can be regarded as a planned form of 'reinsurance'. It might be true occasionally of Gestapo officials who knew of the significance of the people being interrogated. Otherwise, it may be assumed that the elite functionaries in the Gestapo – above all Huber and Ebner – gave appropriate instructions for leniency, and that the torturers followed these orders and showed restraint. Under no circumstances can the attempts, above all by leading Gestapo functionaries, to ensure their exoneration 'afterwards' by protecting individual selected victims conceal the fact that the Gestapo terror machinery continued without interruption until the end. The extent of the Gestapo crimes should be measured not by the few who were spared but by the many who were killed.

Notes

1. [Zur Bekämpfung der Staatsfeinde gehört das bedingungslose Erfassen der nationalsozialistischen Idee. Die Männer der Staatspolizei müssen absolut gleichgerichtet in ihrer geistigen Haltung sein. Sie müssen sich als kämpferisches Korps fühlen. Das ist der Grund, warum sehr viele Beamte der Staatspolizei gleichzeitig SS-Führer oder -Männer sind.] Heydrich, 'Die Bekämpfung der Staatsfeinde', 121–23.
2. Dams/Stolle, *The Gestapo*, 6 (*Die Gestapo*, 18).

3. Herbert, *Best*, 582; the ninety-two people examined were RSHA department and section heads, Gestapo heads and deputies.
4. Paul, *Ganz normale Akademiker*, 243.
5. Wildt, *An Uncompromising Generation*, 10 (*Reichssicherheitshauptamt*, 25–26).
6. Herbert, *Best*, 15.
7. Crankshaw, *Gestapo*, 21; see also Kohlhaas, 'Die Mitarbeiter', 219.
8. Paul, *Ganz normale Akademiker*, 236ff., 240.
9. Wildt, *An Uncompromising Generation*, 38 (*Reichssicherheitshauptamt*, 74–75).
10. Paul, *Ganz normale Akademiker*, 244.
11. Leopold von Caprivi, *Erinnerungen*, unprinted manuscript, parts as Zs 307 in IfZ, quoted in Herbert, *Best*, 187.
12. [Was sollen juristische Bedenken, wenn etwas volkspolitisch notwendig ist? Nicht dank, sondern trotz der Juristen lebt das Volk.] Quoted in Wildt, *An Uncompromising Generation*, 152 (*Reichssicherheitshauptamt*, 260).
13. WStLA, Vienna LG, Vg 12i Vr 1223/47, VG proceedings against Karl Ebner.
14. [Tragende Allgemeinausbildung muss die SSmäßige Sich.Pol. u. SD Ausbildung sein, der Jurist gehört zu den Spezialisten.] Letter from Heydrich to Best, 1 Mar 1939, quoted in Wildt, *An Uncompromising Generation*, 159 (*Reichssicherheitshauptamt*, 270).
15. Herbert, *Best*, 195.
16. See the section 'Planning, Preparation and Measures' in Chapter 2.
17. See the section 'Activities of Unit II B 4' in Chapter 10.
18. The problem is that it is not always possible to determine whether these lists are really from the Nazi period or were drawn up after 1945 during police or judicial investigations.
19. Kranebitter (see Chapter 15) was involved in serious crimes in 1942 as commander of the Sipo and SD in Kharkhiv (Ukraine), and in 1943 as head of the Gestapo in Verona. Section II K was established in 1939 shortly after the war began to take over some of the work of Section II G (Personal security) – explosions, fires, accidents, etc. – especially those with a political background or involving sabotage. From early 1941, Section II G took over this work in its entirety, and II K was closed.
20. BA Berlin, R 58, microfilm 528.
21. Weisz, 'Gestapo-Leitstelle Wien', Tables, 24.
22. Ibid., 136.
23. Ibid., 25.
24. Weisz, 'Gestapo-Leitstelle Wien', 1811–12.
25. WStLA, Vienna LG, VG proceedings against Anton Wartha, Vg 11h Vr 887/47, testimonies of Karl Ebner and Johann Sanitzer, 2 Dec 1947.
26. Weisz, 'Gestapo-Leitstelle Wien', Tables, 24.
27. Ibid., 1985.
28. At the end of 1942, Macher was transferred to Greece, and in April 1945 he was involved in the murder of foreign forced workers in Stein; see WStLA, Vienna LG, Vg 1g Vr 7463/46, judgment against Karl Macher; and Graz LG, 4 Vr 912/69, judgment against Karl Macher, 10 May 1970.
29. See the section 'Role of the Illegal Austrian National Socialists' in Chapter 2.
30. See Neugebauer, 'Repressionsapparat und -maßnahmen', 311–12.
31. The Reich Remuneration Law was not implemented until summer 1939; see Weisz, 'Gestapo-Leitstelle Wien', 1094.
32. ÖStA, AdR, Gau file no. 4346, Josef Auinger.
33. Weisz, 'Gestapo-Leitstelle Wien', 1082–83.
34. WStLA, Vienna LG, VG proceedings against Karl Amler, Vg 1c Vr 1672/45, testimony of Florian Roth, 19 Sep 1945.

35. WStLA, Vienna LG, VG proceedings against Josef Miksch, Vg 1a Vr 1659/45, judgment, 20 May 1946.
36. See, for example, the relevant form in: ÖStA, AdR, Gau file no. 4346, Josef Auinger.
37. WStLA, Vienna LG, VG proceedings against Josef Weidinger, Vg 11f Vr 2564/47, testimony of Franz Kamba in the main hearing, 29 Mar 1949.
38. WStLA, Vienna LG, VG proceedings against Johann Rosanits, Vg 4c Vr 4650/47, testimony of Ernst Schwertführer, 27 Jul 1949.
39. WStLA, Vienna LG, VG proceedings against Hubert Kern, Vg 4c Vr 4424/47, testimony of Karl Ebner, 12 Mar 1948.
40. WStLA, Vienna LG, VG proceedings against Johann Rixinger, Vg 11g Vr 1866/46, testimony of Karl Prieler, 1 Jun 1954.
41. WStLA, Vienna LG, VG proceedings against Josef Dworak, Vg 7c Vr 430/46, questioning of the defendant, 27 Sep 1945.
42. Ibid., testimony of Johann Rixinger, 27 Sep 1945.
43. WStLA, Vienna LG, VG proceedings against Karl Amler, Vg 1c Vr 1672/45, statement by the defendant in the main hearing, 13 Jun 1947.
44. WStLA, Vienna LG, VG proceedings against Josef Dworak, Vg 1a Vr 430/46, testimony of Johann Rixinger, 27 Sep 1945.
45. According to Section 10 of the Prohibition Act (Verbotsgesetz) of 1945, any person over the age of eighteen who ever belonged to the NSDAP or one of its organizations (SA, SS, NSKK, NSFK) between 1 July 1933 and 13 March 1938, or was recognized as a result of activity for the National Socialist movement as 'Altparteigenosse' (veteran party member) or 'Alter Kämpfer' was declared guilty of the crime of high treason, punishable by imprisonment of five to ten years; see http://www.nachkriegsjustiz.at/service/gesetze/gs_vg_10.php (last accessed on 16 Mar 2018).
46. See Kohlhaas, 'Die Mitarbeiter', 230.
47. [Angehörige der Sicherheitspolizei können auf Antrag in die Schutzstaffel der NSDAP aufgenommen werden, wenn sie die allgemeinen Bedingungen der SS erfüllen.] Mitteilungsblatt des RKPA, Oct 1938, in WStLA, Vienna LG, VG proceedings against Friedrich Kranebitter, Vg 4c Vr 6171/48.
48. The police ranks corresponded to the SS ranks as follows (followed by annual salary in RM): Ministerialdirektor, Generalmajor der Polizei: SS-Brigadeführer (RM 6,000–19,000); Ministerialdirigent, Oberst der Polizei: SS-Oberführer (16,000); Regierungs- und Kriminaldirektor, Oberst der Polizei: SS-Standartenführer (8,400–12,600); Oberregierungs- und Kriminalrat: SS-Obersturmbannführer (7,000–9,700); Regierungs- und Kriminalrat: SS-Sturmbannführer (4,800–8,400); Kriminalrat: SS-Hauptsturmführer (4,800–7,000); Kriminalinspektor (up to 15 years of service): SS-Obersturmführer (3,900–5,300); Kriminalinspektor: SS-Obersturmführer (2,800–5,000); Kriminalobersekretär: SS-Untersturmführer (2,300–4,200); Kriminalsekretär: SS-Untersturmführer (2,350–3,500); Kriminaloberassistent: SS-Hauptscharführer (2,000–3,000); Kriminalassistent: SS-Oberscharführer (2,040); Kriminalassistentenanwärter: SS-Unterscharführer (1,410–1,980). Wilhelm, *Polizei im NS-Staat*, 256.
49. Gellately, *The Gestapo and German Society*, 57, n. 52.
50. ÖStA, AdR, Gau file no. 38 653, curriculum vitae of Richard Ulbing; WStLA, Vienna LG, VG proceedings against Richard Ulbing, Vg 4c Vr 648/48, plea for clemency, Sep 1956.
51. Mang, *Die Unperson*, 68.
52. WStLA, Vienna LG, VG proceedings against Otto Schleiffer, Vg 2a Vr 1272/45, undated curriculum vitae of Otto Schleiffer.
53. WStLA, Vienna LG, VG proceedings against Anton Wartha, Vg 11c Vr 887/47, statement by the defendant in the main hearing, 26 Oct 1948.
54. Ibid., testimony of Karl Ebner, 26 Oct 1948.

55. ÖStA, AdR, Gau file no. 240 744, Josef Weidinger.
56. WStLA, Vienna LG, VG proceedings against Karl Amler, Vg 1c Vr 1672/45, statement by Karl Amler to Vienna police department, 10 Aug 1945.
57. Weisz, 'Gestapo-Leitstelle Wien', 1973.
58. Karl Ebner, 'Wolfsberger Dossier'; see also Chapter 18; and Mang, *Juristen in der Gestapo*, 138–46.
59. Weisz, 'Gestapo-Leitstelle Wien', 1929–30.
60. WStLA, Vg 4c Vr 1223/47, VG proceedings against Karl Ebner, testimony of Hildegard Rock, 28 Jan 1946.
61. Weisz, 'Gestapo-Leitstelle Wien', 1353; WStLA, Vg 4c Vr 1223/47, VG proceedings against Karl Ebner, written statement by Karl Ebner.
62. See Kohlhaas, 'Weibliche Angestellte der Gestapo 1933–1945', in Krauss, *Sie waren dabei*, 149.
63. Weisz, 'Gestapo-Leitstelle Wien', 1930–31.
64. See Kohlhaas, 'Weibliche Angestellte der Gestapo', 149.
65. WStLA, Vienna LG, Vg 11 Vr 2628/46, VG proceedings against Anton Perger, testimony of Karl Schall to Vienna police department, 22 Feb 1946.
66. WStLA, Vienna LG, Vg 8e Vr 623/55, VG proceedings against Josef Handl, testimony of Moritz Margulies to the Vienna LG, 22 Jun 1945.
67. WStLA, Vienna LG, Vg 3b 4750/46, VG proceedings against Karl Künzel, testimony of Fritz Gerscha to Kreisgericht Sankt Pölten, 11 Feb 1947, referring to his attached written report.
68. Ibid., testimony of Emilia Ploi to the Vienna LG, 10 Mar 1947.
69. Heinrich Himmler was also surprised at the large number of waiting prisoners when he made an unannounced visit to the Gestapo headquarters on 12 Dec 1938; see DÖW 19 314.
70. WStLA, Vienna LG, VG proceedings against Karl Ebner, Vg 4c Vr 1223/47, statement by Hilde Rock to Vienna police department, 28 Jan 1946. From 1 Apr 1938, Rock was secretary to Karl Ebner, who became an officer in the 'Jewish section' immediately after the annexation, and was head of Section II B from 1939 to 1942.
71. WStLA, Vienna LG, Vg 4c Vr 1223/47, VG proceedings against Karl Ebner, testimony of Hildegard Rock, 28 Jan 1946.
72. WStLA, Vienna LG, 20a Vr 731/55 (reopening of VG proceedings Vg 4 Vr 5597/47), record of the main hearing, 21 Nov 1956; see also Chapter 10.
73. According to Section 3 of the War Criminals Act, anyone who tortured or seriously mistreated a person during the National Socialist tyranny out of political spite or through the use of official or other force, is liable to imprisonment of five to ten years, and ten to twenty years if the offence seriously damaged the victim's health; see http://www.nachkriegsjustiz.at/service/gesetze/kvg2.php (last accessed on 28 Mar 2018).
74. ÖStA, AdR, Gau file no. 4442, Rosa Friedl.
75. WStLA, Vienna LG, VG proceedings against Rosa Friedl, Vg 3 Vr 5048/45, decision of 18 Dec 1946.
76. Mang, *'Gestapo-Leitstelle Wien'*, 114ff.; Mang, *Die Unperson*, 67ff. Huber was a controversial figure in Nazi circles on account of his work with the Munich police before 1933, when he had been responsible for opposing the Nazis.
77. Karl Ebner, statement on the structure and operations of the Vienna Gestapo 1938–45, 68 (photocopy owned by Thomas Mang).
78. WStLA, Vienna LG, VG proceedings against Johann Weitschacher, Vg 12d Vr 4490/47, statement by the defendant in the main hearing, 11 Mar 1948.
79. WStLA, Vienna LG, VG proceedings against Otto Schleiffer, Vg 1a Vr 1272/45, statement by the defendant to the state police, Vienna police headquarters (Staatspolizei, Polizeidirektion Wien), 27 Jun 1945; for typical examples, see Chapter 15.

80. See Chapter 15.
81. ÖStA, AdR, Reichsstatthalter Wien, Organisationsreferat, box 193, memo from Regierungspräsident (Dellbrügge) to Reichsleiter (von Schirach), 13 Jun 1944.
82. ZStL, 110 AR-Z 4/1961, letter by STA Wien, 17 Nov 1960.
83. *Der Nürnberger Prozess*, Digitale Bibliothek, vol. 20, 3985, letter from the Generalstaatsanwaltschaft Kattowitz, 2 Dec 1941.
84. NARA, SS-Personalhauptamt, A 3343 887-118A, lightning telegram from Kaltenbrunner, 1 Jan 1944; see Mang, *Die Unperson*, 166.
85. ÖStA, AdR, Gau file no. 4353, Karl Ebner, Ebner's plea for clemency to Himmler, submitted by Ebner's lawyer Erich Führer; see Mang, *Die Unperson*, 170ff.; Weisz, 'Gestapo-Leitstelle Wien', 2129. Ebner claimed to have been sentenced to death 'three times over'.
86. For details, see Mang, *Die Unperson*, 170–75.
87. Pichler, 'Dr. Othmar Trenker', 91, 95ff.
88. BA Berlin, R 58/621, sheet 33, memo of 24 Mar 1938 from Werner Best deputizing for Heydrich, distributed with a 'large mailing list' at the Sipo and Gestapa headquarters.
89. Mang, *'Gestapo-Leitstelle Wien'*, 121–22.
90. WStLA, Vienna LG, VG proceedings against Johann Rosanits, Vg 4c Vr 4650/47, statement by the defendant, 26 Nov 1948.
91. Weisz, 'Gestapo in Österreich', 450.
92. WStLA, Vienna LG, proceedings against Richard Ulbing, 31 Vr 892/56, curriculum vitae, 14 Jun 1941, and plea for clemency, Sep 1956.
93. Weisz, 'Gestapo-Leitstelle Wien', 1944ff.
94. WStLA, Vienna LG, VG proceedings against Karl Ebner, Vg 12g Vr 1223/47. Ebner wrote this document in the camp in Wolfsberg (hence its name 'Wolfsberger Dossier') at the instigation of Rudolf Merkel, the defence lawyer for the Gestapo at the Nuremberg military tribunal, who had sought the advice of experienced Gestapo jurists, as a last unsuccessful defence strategy.
95. BA Berlin, R 58/2231, sheets 225ff.
96. ÖStA, AdR, Gau file no. 11926, Otto Kolb.
97. BA Berlin, R 9361-III 557288 and R 9361-III 536957.
98. For details, see Mang, 'Retter, um sich selbst zu retten'.
99. Member of a Jewish aid organization who attempted, after the German occupation of Hungary, to rescue Jews from deportation to Auschwitz.
100. *Der Nürnberger Prozess*, Digitale Bibliothek, vol. 20, 13379. Allen W. Dulles headed the US Office of Strategic Services (OSS) in Switzerland.
101. From 1956: Bundesnachrichtendienst (federal intelligence service).
102. Höttl, *Einsatz für das Reich*, 220ff.
103. From an 'admission' that Huber wrote in his defence in 1964 when he (unnecessarily) feared new charges against him, and sent to Ebner for his perusal (estate of Karl Ebner, photocopy owned by Thomas Mang). It is interesting to note the way Huber distanced himself even terminologically from everything concerned with the activities of the central office (Zentralstelle für jüdische *Auswanderung*) by writing 'Abwanderung', thus implying that he had 'forgotten' the name of the terror institution of which he had been head.
104. ZStL 110 AR-Z 70/76 I, sheets 118–19, Franz Josef Huber denazification file.
105. Estate of Karl Ebner, statement written in prison around 1952 on the judgment of the Vienna VG of 11 Dec 1948, 56 (photocopy owned by Thomas Mang).
106. ZStL, 110 AR-Z 70/76 I, sheet 123, Franz Josef Huber denazification file, record of interrogation in Memmingen, 3 Oct 1961.
107. Estate of Karl Ebner (photocopy of letter owned by Thomas Mang). Leo Slezak was a Heldentenor at the Vienna state opera, Alice Strauss the daughter-in-law of Richard Strauss,

Margarete Painsipp an art historian. Huber had an affair with the Vienna state opera diva Danitza Ilitsch, which presumably prompted some of his interventions.
108. WStLA, Vienna LG, VG proceedings against Karl Ebner, Vg 12g Vr 1223/47, sheets 118–19, statement by Guido Soklic in the main hearing, 8 Sep 1948.
109. Lustiger, *Rettungswiderstand*.
110. See Mang, *'Gestapo-Leitstelle Wien'*.
111. See also Chapter 7.
112. ZStL KHN/HKM, sheet 119, Franz Josef Huber denazification file.
113. Ibid., sheet 125ff.
114. Ibid., sheet 7.
115. WStLA, Vienna LG, VG proceedings against Karl Ebner, Vg 4b Vr 1223/47, sheet 119, statement by Lambert Leutgeb; see Mang, *Die Unperson*, 156.
116. WStLA, Vienna LG, VG proceedings against Karl Ebner, Vg 4b Vr 1223/47, sheet 137, testimony by Michael Stern, 6 Sep 1947.
117. Interview by Thomas Mang with Ebner's daughter Ingrid Leierer-Ebner, 23 Jul 1998.
118. There is no evidence to indicate that Ebner intervened in cases such as those of the Augustinian canon Karl Roman Scholz, the nurse Helene Kafka (Sister Maria Restituta), the curate Anton Granig, the Franciscan Guardian Wilhelm Pieller or the Franciscan Provincial Eduard Steinwender. Scholz and Sister Maria Restituta were guillotined (at the Vienna LG) and Granig, Pieller and Steinwender were shot in the last days of the war in the prison at Stein an der Donau.
119. Detailed information in Mang, *Die Unperson*, 147ff.
120. WStLA, Vienna LG, VG proceedings against Karl Ebner, Vg 12g Vr 1223/47, judgment, 11 Dec 1948.
121. [Wenn ich Sie recht verstehe, haben Sie bei der Gestapo nichts anderes mehr getan, als Leuten zu helfen, die mit dem Naziregime nicht einverstanden waren. Und dafür sind Sie bezahlt worden?] *Arbeiter-Zeitung*, 7 Dec 1948.

Chapter 6

WORKING PROCEDURES AND METHODS OF THE VIENNA GESTAPO

Like all Gestapo offices and regional headquarters, the Vienna Gestapo was also responsible for executing orders from its superiors in Berlin: Reichsführer-SS Heinrich Himmler; chief of the Sipo and SD Reinhard Heydrich; and the Gestapa or its successor organization the RSHA with its Amt (department) IV headed by Heinrich Müller. It was bound by their decrees, orders, regulations and written and telephone instructions. Occasionally, as was the case with the delicate matter of the imprisonment of ex-federal chancellor Schuschnigg at Morzinplatz, Reichsführer-SS Himmler demanded daily reports on the implementation of his instructions. The Vienna Gestapo also had to report promptly on mass arrests, such as the one targeting Communists and Socialists before the outbreak of war in 1939, the one against Jehovah's Witnesses in 1940, and the one after the 20 July 1944 plot.[1] Appointments and other personnel questions such as promotions and the recruitment of members to the SS remained the responsibility of the central offices in Berlin.

In practice, however, the members of the Vienna Gestapo still had considerable scope in their actions. This applied not only to the head Franz Josef Huber, who as inspector of the Sipo and SD in Military District XVII was practically his own boss, and his deputy Karl Ebner, who effectively headed the Vienna Gestapo for extended periods on account of Huber's long absences and lack of diligence. Department (*Abteilung*), section (*Referat*), and even unit (*Sachgebiet*) heads could also act independently in some cases. Even low-ranking Gestapo officials could thus ignore the restrictive provisions regarding 'enhanced interrogation' (*verschärfte Vernehmung*), the official Gestapo euphemism for torture. Their superiors turned a blind eye to such infringements – or even ordered them – and it is likely that their superiors in Berlin were not exactly sticklers for the rules either. Between 1940 and 1945, only two cases came before the SS and police court (SS- und Polizeigericht) for prisoner maltreatment by officials of the Vienna Gestapo; one case ended with an acquittal and the other one was dismissed. Conversely, prisoners were occasionally afforded preferential treatment, especially in the 'Jewish section', mostly in return for some other service. A method frequently employed was to put files aside or 'lose' them. Between 1940 and 1945, four cases of preferential treatment for prisoners and five cases of corruption came before the SS and police court, with one death sentence being pronounced.[2]

Routine Bureaucracy

In contrast with secret police departments in other countries (such as the Stasi in the GDR), the Gestapo was by no means a huge organization and so was incapable of fully monitoring the population or groups opposing the Nazi regime. A considerable proportion of the nine hundred or so Vienna Gestapo staff were involved not with operational tasks, such as monitoring, investigating and 'dealing with' opponents, but with bureaucratic tasks such as records, reports and statistics, personnel files, building management, receiving and dealing with complaints, writing indictments for public prosecutors' offices, documenting and photographing arrestees, and arranging transports to prisons and concentration camps.[3] Apart from this work, which was performed by men, there were the secretaries, cleaners and other auxiliary workers, most of whom were women. The details of routine administrative tasks such as personnel management, awards, accounting and building management need no further discussion here; however, they are listed and described at length in Franz Weisz's doctoral thesis 'Gestapo-Leitstelle Wien'.

Records and Card Indexes

'The Gestapo's various [card-]index systems', note Gestapo researchers Carsten Dams and Michael Stolle, 'formed the bureaucratic linchpin of the persecution, documenting information about the opponents of the Nazi state.'[4] One significant aspect that should not be underestimated is the detailed registration and photographing of newly arrived prisoners. The Vienna Gestapo's systematic identification card index (Erkennungsdienstliche Kartei) formed an important basis for the Gestapo's work, because it made it possible to keep tabs on the immense number of present and former detainees. Every day, up to five hundred people were summoned to Morzinplatz for questioning or taken there after being arrested. Karl Ebner, deputy head of the Vienna Gestapo, euphemistically called this *Parteienverkehr* (office hours, as in municipal departments). Over 50,000 people must have passed through the workings of the Vienna Gestapo;[5] more than 17,000 arrestees are recorded in the daily reports – which have not survived in their entirety, and are in any case by no means a complete record – with names, dates, offences and other relevant details. The Vienna Gestapo identification files in the Wiener Stadt- und Landesarchiv and the DÖW's digitally accessible database list over 11,000 prisoners.[6] The difference between this number and the 17,000 names in the daily reports and the 50,000 or so total arrestees may be explained by the fact that the Gestapo did not bother to create identification files for 'foreign and Eastern workers', most of whom were transferred to camps, or include them in the daily reports.[7] A considerable number of Gestapo photos were lost during and in the aftermath of the liberation of Vienna.

The three 'classic' police photos were normally taken of each prisoner – full-face, profile, and half-profile – but rarely full-body. Sometimes signs of maltreatment are visible on the photos.[8]

The form used to request photographs specified the name of the recording official and Gestapo department or section, along with the name, date of birth and admission of prisoners and their 'offender class'. The spectrum covered all forms of opposition and non-conformist behaviour: from work-shyness and 'asocial' behaviour, listening to enemy broadcasts, forbidden relations with POWs and *Fremdarbeiter* ('foreign workers', i.e. foreign forced labourers) and homosexual relations through to violations of the anti-Jewish regulations, Communist or subversive (*staatsfeindlich*) activities, and the planning of treasonable acts. Particular attention was paid to the efficient recording of the identity. On the A5 envelopes with the person's fingerprints there was also a personal description with twelve categories of characteristics to facilitate the task. The appropriate description needed only to be underlined: the face could be 'delicate', the forehead 'receding', the earlobes 'wedge-shaped', and the nose, variously, 'concave, straight, convex, hooked' or 'bumpy'.[9]

During its project to record the names of victims of political persecution between 1938 and 1945 (Namentliche Erfassung der Opfer politischer Verfolgung 1938–1945), the DÖW has been able to discover the date of arrest, camp transfer, and fate of over 5,000 people, and has so far established the deaths of 1,362.[10]

The Vienna Gestapo Daily Reports

Among the most important tasks of the Gestapo was the strictly regulated and regular reporting to the superior office on all major events. The office in question was the Geheimes Staatspolizeiamt (Gestapa) in Berlin, or (from September 1939) its successor organization Amt IV (Department IV) of the newly created

Reichssicherheitshauptamt (RSHA, Reich security main office), both headed by SS-Gruppenführer Heinrich Müller. Müller's superior and the most powerful man after Reichsführer-SS Heinrich Himmler was SS-Obergruppenführer Reinhard Heydrich, chief of the Sipo and SD and head of the RSHA. Heydrich already played an important role in the establishment of the Gestapo in Austria,[11] and occasionally intervened directly in its work – as in the case of General Wilhelm Zehner. For example, after discussion with Ernst von Weizsäcker, state secretary in the ministry of foreign affairs, Heydrich decided on 5 July 1938 that most of the Austrians still in detention should be released on account of foreign policy considerations.[12]

Initially, the Vienna Gestapo had a higher status than the other Gestapo offices in Austria in that it could issue instructions to and demand reports from them. Between 1940 and 1944, the Gestapo offices in the 'Alpine and Danube Reichsgaus', as Austria was now called, worked directly on orders from Berlin without the involvement of the Vienna Gestapo and reported directly to Berlin. However, as inspector of the Sipo and SD in Military District XVII, 'Vienna' (i.e. northern Austria), Huber was informed about all major incidents.[13]

Every two or three days, the Vienna Gestapo sent a daily report to the Gestapa/RSHA (and other Nazi offices such as that of the Vienna Gauleiter/Reichsstatthalter) with details of arrests, seizure of newspapers, books and other printed material, and other matters of relevance. Reports are available for the period September 1938 to February 1945. By the end of the Nazi regime, some 810 reports had been sent to the central office in Berlin with regular information on the following issues: left-wing opposition such as the KPÖ and other Marxist groups, the conservative and monarchist opposition (Fatherland Front), the Catholic movement and political Catholicism, opposition (civil disobedience, defiance, insidious utterances, listening to foreign radio broadcasts), NSDAP and its units, Jews, homosexuals, press, sects, economic questions, foreign workers, and other matters (e.g. seizure of foreign newspapers). In the surviving daily reports, 17,277 individuals are mentioned with the offences they were accused of, the date of arrest, and any police measures taken.[14]

The Gestapo's categorization of arrestees mentioned in the daily reports reflects the tasks of the Vienna Gestapo. Apart from combating and suppressing organized political opposition and individual resistance, one of their main tasks was also the maintenance of the forced labour required by the war, and the surveillance and monitoring of the steadily growing number of foreign workers, the vast majority of whom were forced labourers.

These reports usually included monthly statistics on arrests and the numbers of detainees in 'protective custody' in the area of the Vienna Gestapo. There were sometimes situation reports and more detailed accounts of important issues, such as the uncovering of large resistance groups. For example, on 3 January 1939, Unit II A 1 provided a report on Communist propaganda activity in

1938, followed by an undated situation report for the period January to March 1939.[15] The report for a meeting in Vienna on 28 March 1944 of the 'N and IV A 1 experts on the Ostmark' effectively presented a summary of the measures taken by the Vienna Gestapo after 1938 against Communist resistance, in which the Vienna Gestapo boasted of having arrested 6,300 Communist party members.[16]

From 1943, the Vienna Gestapo produced an information sheet 'for official use only' announcing regulations, decrees and so on, and reporting on major personnel matters (transfers, secondments, awards, officials dying on duty or in the war, and the like).[17] The Vienna reports were incorporated in the activity reports of the Berlin central offices. In an RSHA report of 20 February 1940 on a decline in Communist writings in the 'Altreich' and an increase in leaflet propaganda by the KPÖ, for example, there are details of 'inflammatory publications' in the 'Ostmark', and the tracking down and destruction of the KPÖ's technical apparatus at the end of 1939.[18]

The value of the Gestapo reports as source material for academic research is disputed,[19] but their regular appearance from 1938 to 1945 and the tens of thousands of names and dates of Nazi victims make them indispensable, especially for research on resistance.

Surveillance and Arrests

Suspected activists in larger, widespread and important resistance groups were subject to days or weeks of permanent surveillance (tailing) so as to identify as many contact persons as possible. The results of this activity, carried out alternately by several officials, were then used in the interrogations and presented to the public prosecutor's office and courts as evidence. For example, a surveillance report in October 1939 by Karl Albrecht from Unit II A 1 on the resistance fighter Marie Hofmann, a member of a Communist student group, contains minute-by-minute details of whom she met, how long they spoke, and which premises they visited. This surveillance report formed part of the indictment by the prosecutor general in Vienna, and is a component of the Vienna OLG record.[20]

Informants and denouncers played a decisive role in the identification of resistance fighters. The relevant section within the Vienna Gestapo (Section N), headed by Johann Sanitzer from 1939 to 1940 and Lambert Leutgeb from 1940 to 1944, had a host of between four hundred and six hundred informants, who systematically infiltrated resistance groups and reported on them.[21] In some cases, agents provocateurs were also active, with the aim of radicalizing the groups being spied upon and of provoking violence so as to incriminate the resistance fighters even further.

As soon as a resistance network was largely identified, the Gestapo men would pounce on it brutally and suddenly. They used extreme force when making arrests and did not shy away from employing firearms, often already starting to rough up their prisoners during the arrest and transport. A letter by the Innsbruck Gestapo of 23 April 1945 contained the following order concerning the arrest of resistance fighters: 'Arrests are to be carried out ruthlessly with immediate application if necessary of the special regulations for the use of firearms'.[22] Shots were fired, for example, when the Communist resistance fighter Josef Sasso, put in place in Austria by the French secret service, attempted to escape during his arrest at his parents' home in Winzendorf in April 1944, in the course of which the Gestapo official Johann Potzinger was shot dead.[23]

Arrests were usually accompanied by house searches, which often took place on mere suspicion and without the need for a court search warrant. Apartments and houses were turned upside down and suspicious material seized; it was not uncommon, particularly in Jewish homes (see the section 'Looting of Jewish Assets' in Chapter 10), for Gestapo officials to appropriate valuables and interior furnishings for themselves.

More than 50,000 people were arrested by the Vienna Gestapo. In his doctoral thesis, Franz Weisz calculated that there were 47,348 arrests between September 1938 and June 1944; of these, around 35,000 were connected with the sector related to 'economic affairs and offences by foreign workers'.[24] As mentioned, only a small proportion of the arrests of forced labourers were entered in the identification card index or daily reports. The figures do not include the mass arrests after 11 March 1938, the 6,547 Jews arrested during the November Pogrom of 1938, the over 1,000 Jewish men arrested and detained at the Prater football stadium in September 1939, or any of the approximately 48,000 Jews deported to concentration camps, ghettos and extermination camps between October 1939 and March 1945 by the Vienna Gestapo and the central office for Jewish emigration.

Radicalization, Interrogation and Maltreatment

The 'radicalization spiral' in the Gestapo's work identified by Gestapo scholars Gerhard Paul and Klaus-Michael Mallmann[25] also existed in Austria. The first surge in radicalization in the 'Altreich' in 1933 with the offensive against the German Communist party was mirrored in Austria by the mass arrests and attacks immediately after the annexation, not just by the Gestapo in this case but to a large extent also by members of the Austrian Nazi movement seeking vengeance and redress. The Gestapo stepped up its offensive against Communist activists after the start of the attack on the Soviet Union in June 1941, and maltreatment and torture became increasingly frequent in the interrogations.

The second intensification of brutality and barbarity identified by Paul and Mallmann, namely the extermination of the Jews in the East from 1941, also reverberated within the Vienna Gestapo, not least because quite a number of Gestapo officials had served in the East. These included Humbert Achamer-Pifrader, Huber's deputy as head of the Vienna Gestapo in 1938, and commander of Einsatzgruppe A in 1942–43; Rudolf Mildner, Huber's successor, who had earlier been head of the SS summary court at Auschwitz; and Josef Auinger, head of the Sankt Pölten office and, in 1942, leader of SS-Sonderkommando 7b in Einsatzgruppe B.[26] The systematic mass murder of Jews, partisans, political officers in the Red Army, and Soviet civilians by the EGs and EKs made up of members of the SD and Sipo, and the knowledge of these acts within the Gestapo, also helped to eliminate any remaining scruples that Gestapo members may have had when dealing with detainees back on their home ground.

A further intensification of Gestapo methods throughout the Reich took place with the enormous increase in forced labour, particularly regarding labourers from Eastern Europe, who were not only paid less but also persecuted with far greater brutality. Of the fifty thousand arrests by the Vienna Gestapo, over twenty thousand concerned foreign civilian labourers, who were sent to concentration camps for the smallest breaches of work discipline or other Nazi regulations. Public executions of 'Ostarbeiter' (forced labourers from the Soviet Union) by the Gestapo, which were quite frequent in the 'Altreich', were more of a rarity in Austria. But the Vienna Gestapo did not lag behind when it came to the brutality of interrogations – including torturing to death – and the number of concentration camp committals.[27]

The fourth and last phase of the radicalization spiral took place in connection with the 'end-phase war crimes' (*Endphaseverbrechen*). Allied pilots who had been shot down were murdered by the Vienna Gestapo, and Vienna Gestapo officials were implicated in the operations of various Nazi summary courts through their investigations, brutal interrogations and presence at executions – for example, at the execution of three Austrian officers on 8 April 1945 in Vienna-Floridsdorf, and at the executions in Sankt Pölten and Krems in Reichsgau 'Lower Danube' (Niederdonau).

In spite of the deconstruction in recent research of the 'Gestapo myth' and of the idea cultivated by Himmler and Heydrich, and still prevalent until well after the war, of an 'omnipotent, omnipresent and omniscient' Gestapo,[28] it should not be forgotten that the effectiveness and efficiency of the Gestapo's work, the 'success rate' in combating Nazi opposition, was very high. Not only did the Gestapo track down thousands of individuals who criticized the Nazi regime, listened to forbidden broadcasts, helped those persecuted or in other ways infringed Nazi regulations, but it also destroyed most of the organized resistance, at least until 1943–44. The Gestapo achieved this by using traditional police methods, but even more so by employing practices common in totalitarian dictatorships, including physical violence and intimidation in interrogations, surveillance of suspects, the use of informants against resistance groups and the exploitation of information from denouncers. Hans Schafranek has determined that informants constituted the decisive factor in the 'successes' of the Vienna Gestapo.[29]

From 1938 to 1940 the Gestapo and Nazi judiciary were more lenient with regard to resistance fighters than they were to be later. Women were not treated as harshly as men, because they were often regarded merely as female appendages to male resistance fighters. For example, Marie Hofmann (later Tidl by marriage), who belonged to a Communist student organization and was arrested by the Vienna Gestapo on 19 November 1938, states that she was not tortured, whereas torture was probably used to extract a confession from her boyfriend, the student Siegfried Köhl. Hofmann, who denied all accusations, was acquitted by the Vienna OLG in 1940 for lack of evidence and, in spite of a 'protective custody' order and a Vienna Gestapo application for remand (*Rücküberstellung*), was released, escaping committal to a concentration camp as a result.[30]

Numerous eyewitness accounts and the trials of Vienna Gestapo officials before the Volksgericht testify clearly to the extreme brutality used. Maltreatment, torture to obtain confessions, and excessive punishments were the rule rather than the exception. In the words of Jean Améry, himself tortured by the Gestapo in Belgium in 1943, 'torture was not an accidental quality of this Third Reich, but its essence'.[31]

Franz Weisz's doctoral thesis describes the Vienna Gestapo's various torture methods in detail.[32] They ranged from long and frequent interrogations, with the prisoner being obliged to stand or squat for extended periods, to threats, insults and humiliation, and deprivation of food, liquids and tobacco (in the case of smokers) and brutal physical violence – punching and slapping, kicks in the abdomen, being beaten with rubber truncheons, whips, blackjacks and steel rods, primarily on the soles of the feet, back and buttocks. Particularly recalcitrant prisoners were very often hung up on chains (with their hands tied behind their back) and left for hours, often being beaten into the bargain. Sometimes prisoners were tortured with spotlights and strong light, or with electrodes and burning cigarettes. Holding prisoners under water until they lost consciousness or applying thumbscrews were further techniques in use.

The torture was quasi-legalized by central regulations on what was officially known as 'enhanced interrogation', for example in a decree by the chief of the Sipo and SD of 12 June 1942 signed by Gestapo head Müller, which was communicated to all the relevant members of the Vienna Gestapo both orally and in writing. Those liable to *verschärfte Vernehmung* were enumerated by Berlin: 'Communists, Marxists, Jehovah's Witnesses, saboteurs, terrorists, members of resistance movements, parachute agents, asocials, Polish and Soviet slackers or work-shirkers'. All other cases required the authorization of the chief of the

Sipo. Permission for the 'enhanced interrogation' was to be obtained from a higher level, namely Huber or his successor Mildner, and supervised by a doctor if more than twenty lashes were to be inflicted. In practice, the Gestapo staff tended to ignore these regulations, which was tolerated, if not even encouraged, by their superiors. Sometimes the torturers would check with their section head. Doctors were never summoned, and from 1942 the Gestapo leadership even found it unnecessary to have a medical officer on the premises at Morzinplatz.[33] After the July 1944 assassination attempt and until the collapse of the regime in April/May 1945, the restrictions on torture methods, which were not enforced in any case, were relaxed even further. The authorization was now issued by the section or unit head, and in the final phase the decentralized Gestapo offices acted without any authorization procedure whatsoever.[34] The risk of being disciplined or prosecuted for maltreating prisoners was almost non-existent. In a statistic compiled by Franz Weisz of cases coming before the SS and police court in Vienna, there are only two involving Vienna Gestapo staff, in 1943 and 1944; one case was dismissed (probably against Rudolf Hitzler) and the other ended in acquittal.[35]

The following examples give an idea of the human dimension of these dry statistics. The Gestapo showed extreme brutality, for example against members of the KJV, because their sabotage of the military – until 1942 they had distributed the illegal newspaper *Der Soldatenrat*, above all among Wehrmacht soldiers – was considered to be particularly dangerous. The chemistry student and soldier Walter Kämpf, one of the leading KJV functionaries, who was executed in 1943, warned in a secret message about Gestapo informants within the KPÖ and denounced the Gestapo methods:

> The Gestapo uses medieval torture to make everyone spill the beans. ... Regierungsrat Höfler – the swine beat me up and left me hanging by my hands. He made Fritzl (he has only one, defective, kidney) drink eight litres of water then threatened him with another five, brought (him) to the Liesl [police prison on Elisabethpromenade, now Rossauer Lände] and showed him his mother through the peephole, who would not be released until he confessed. Then he spilled the beans ... I pretended to break down, cried and gave them false information.

The KJV functionary Oskar Klekner, arrested in 1942, tortured by the Vienna Gestapo and executed in Vienna on 2 November 1943 at the age of twenty after being sentenced to death by the VGH, took responsibility for his actions in a secret message to his mother:

> After an interrogation that went on without interruption from 5 P.M. on Friday until 8 A.M. on Saturday, I couldn't go on any longer and then I confessed. Mother, please believe that I did everything humanly possible to take all the responsibility myself and not to incriminate anyone else. But I had no choice. If someone says that I betrayed people, then I can only wish that once in their lives they get to know how the

Gestapo works. Those who do know will forgive me, because they are well aware that the Gestapo gets everyone to talk in the end.[36]

The most brutal interrogations were carried out by Section IV A 2 (from May 1944, Section IV 2) headed by Johann Sanitzer, responsible for sabotage and for parachutists and agents, and by the Gestapo official Rudolf Hitzler in the 'Ostarbeiter' section. 'Pressured to get results' by his superior the Reich-German Kriminalrat Oskar Wendzio,[37] Hitzler, who although an 'Alter Kämpfer' had not advanced very far in his career, was described in the judgment by the Volksgericht in Vienna as the 'most evil torturer' ("ärgster Schinder") in the Gestapo. Even his superiors Richard Ulbing and Karl Ebner mentioned his 'brutality' in a reference: 'Presumably as a result of the burden of work and his desire to exhaust every possibility for convicting enemies of state, a certain tendency to brutality was noted, which always produced the desired result'.[38]

Although Stefan Palmer, former director of the police prison, who saw the prisoners sent to him by Hitzler, described him in his testimony as a 'sadist', the post-war Volksgericht (VG) came to a different conclusion in its judgment. Hitzler was not a 'sadist', because he was interested only in extorting confessions – afterwards he was a 'normal person' again and was even friendly towards individual torture victims. In any event, the motives of this Gestapo man were clear to the VG: Hitzler's fanatical support for the National Socialists, his desire to remove all opponents of the regime by any means possible and his 'blind obedience' resulted in the complete suppression of any humane values or law-abiding instincts. Added to this was the personal ambition to advance in the Gestapo through 'results' (confessions, the elimination of resistance groups, preparations for summary court trials in 1945).[39] This mixture of political fanaticism, unscrupulous brutality and personal ambition was probably typical of many Gestapo men.

Johann Sanitzer, who as a section head was further up the Gestapo hierarchy, was interested not only in extracting confessions, investigating the supporting structure and arresting further incoming parachutists, but also in 'turning' prisoners and using them to participate in *Funkspiele* – the transmission of misleading radio messages to the Allies. Through disinformation supplied by Wehrmacht sources, the idea was to deceive the Allies about military operations and to encourage them to send more parachute agents to the country.[40]

Sanitzer stopped at nothing and encouraged his underlings to use extreme brutality, also having innocent family members arrested, maltreated and sent to concentration camps. In the VG judgment against Johann Sanitzer in Vienna, the torturing of prisoners by Sanitzer's staff was documented in detail. Only a few cases can be mentioned here. Concerning Rupert Grissinger, arrested on 25 March 1943 on account of his link to the Communist parachutist Hermann Köhler, the VG judgment ran as follows:

When he entered the defendant's office on Morzinplatz, the defendant Sanitzer asked Grissinger the question 'What are you doing here?' and hit him on the left and right side of his face, while other Gestapo officials kicked him. Sanitzer gave the sign for torture and said to his officials: 'Let's get on with it!' Grissinger was now severely beaten ... with straps, sticks and rubber truncheons. The maltreatment lasted, with interruptions, until 2 P.M. on the following day. ... To escape this torment, Grissinger jumped out of the window of the fourth-floor interrogation room in an attempt to commit suicide. ... It was only on the third day that the 'enhanced interrogation' could be continued. On that day his hands and feet were bound and he was hung up with his head forced through his legs, and beaten, punched in the face and kicked, including in the lower abdomen. ... The tortures inflicted on Grissinger and Köhler were repeated on Johann Brunner, who was imprisoned in mid-October 1943. ... Gregor Kersche ... was maltreated in the same way. The maltreatment was such that Kersche couldn't sit or lie down. ... Johann Brunner's daughter was also detained and subjected to the most severe maltreatment.[41]

When it came to the violent treatment of defenceless detainees, the Gestapo officials in Wiener Neustadt and Sankt Pölten, and at the Eisenstadt border police station and Engerau (Petržalka) border post, were hardly any better than their Viennese colleagues. For example, Ernst Gabriel and Josef Wild, members of an anti-Fascist youth group in Deutschkreutz, were so severely maltreated by Gestapo officials in Eisenstadt and Vienna that they died as a result. As Gabriel's mother testified in court, air had been pumped into her son's lungs with the result that he vomited blood for a long time afterwards.[42] At the summary trials in the last weeks of the war, in Reichsgau Lower Danube in particular, the death sentences pronounced on resistance fighters were based above all on confessions extracted from the accused, with Gestapo officials Rudolf Hitzler and Johann Röhrling demonstrating particular brutality.[43]

It was not only Communist resistance fighters who were maltreated by the Gestapo. Many activists from other resistance groups were also victims of these brutal methods. Jakob Kastelic, head of a large conservative Catholic group betrayed by the agent provocateur Otto Hartmann and arrested in July 1940, wrote in a secret message of the Gestapo's sophisticated interrogation techniques. Walter Caldonazzi, a leading activist in the resistance group led by the curate Heinrich Maier and Franz Josef Messner, who was arrested in February 1944 and executed in January 1945, complained to his girlfriend in a message smuggled out of prison on 26 November 1944: 'In my second twelve-hour interrogation, they threatened to arrest my girlfriend, parents and all acquaintances if I continued to deny everything. I couldn't have borne the knowledge of you and Herta being detained as hostages, so I confessed to things that I hadn't even done'.[44]

Our study of countless Gestapo and court documents reveals that barely any prisoners could long withstand the inhuman pressure exerted by the Gestapo. It was already an exceptionally heroic feat to refrain from confessing and revealing the names of colleagues for days or weeks, in this way enabling them to escape or go into hiding.⁴⁵

In many cases the Gestapo maltreatment caused serious physical and psychological damage. Among the long-term health impairments following maltreatment listed by Weisz in his dissertation are loss of teeth and jaw injuries, loss of hearing, impaired vision, broken bones (cheekbones, jaws, noses, ribs), kidney, heart and lung damage, blood clots and wounds in the head, impairment of the shoulders, paralysis and balance problems.⁴⁶ Several such cases are documented alone in the VG judgment against Johann Sanitzer. It states with regard to the tortured resistance fighter Johann Brunner: 'Black and blue bruises on the buttocks, back and thighs, and an injury to the coccyx that took around two years to heal were the consequences of this terrible maltreatment'. It said of parachutist Albert Huttary: 'As a result of the injuries caused by the maltreatment, Huttary was unable to sit or lie on his back for eight weeks'.⁴⁷

Josef Auer, a member of the Communist resistance group in Hainburg, was so brutally beaten at the Engerau border police post in early 1942 by Gestapo officials, including Walter Hinker, a thug with the nickname 'the butcher', that he suffered a broken elbow, thigh, ribs and other injuries, and after his release he was no longer able to work.⁴⁸ Adele Nitsche, who was pregnant when she was arrested in October 1944 for 'activity hostile to the state', was kicked so hard in her lower abdomen by members of Unit IV A 2, including the notorious thug Karl Wolf, that her unborn child was killed and she was obliged to abort it. The long-term consequences were cited in a medical report in 1946: jaw injury, impaired vision, chronic gastritis and parametritis following the abortion, nervous disorder, chronic lower abdominal pain. 'The disorders', noted the medical officer, who also described her as having 'serious health damage', 'are due mainly to the maltreatment suffered while in prison'.⁴⁹

In many cases, the severe maltreatment also produced psychological damage such as trauma, PTSD, depression and chronic nervous disorders. As prisoners who could no longer be interrogated were not released or transferred to normal hospitals, the Gestapo put these prisoners in the (high-security) punishment block of the Steinhof mental hospital, where they were not allowed to be released or visited, and were available to the Gestapo at any time. For example, the Communist resistance fighter Theresia Meller, whose nerves were at breaking point, was transferred to Steinhof in May 1944 to stabilize her condition. In October of that year, she was sentenced to death by the VGH and executed in January 1945. The lawyer Karl Wanner, who in 1942, with his legitimist resistance group, had joined the Antifaschistische Freiheitsbewegung Österreich (anti-Fascist freedom movement of Austria), was arrested on 8 February 1943 and severely maltreated. He was transferred by the Gestapo to the psychiatric hospital for three months for treatment, and remained there in Gestapo detention until he was freed in April 1945. By contrast, because Steinhof's reputation not only as a 'madhouse' but also as a Nazi 'euthanasia' clinic would have been damaging to the Gestapo, the Gestapo official Walter Münch, arrested in 1944 because of contacts with the resistance and with mental impairment due to maltreatment during interrogations, was not transferred there but to the university psychiatric and neurological clinic. Moreover, when victims of torture and other crimes suffered the kind of psychological damage that is frequently diagnosed today, it was largely ignored after the war by medical officers and experts.[50]

Murders, Suicides and 'Executions'

If possible, the tortured prisoners were kept alive, not out of humanitarian considerations but to avoid bureaucratic and legal difficulties – with death certificates, for example – and also to be able to continue the interrogations. If the Gestapo wanted to get rid of prisoners/detainees, they were transferred to concentration camps, mostly Mauthausen or Auschwitz, and murdered there. As part of the project to list the names of victims of political persecution, the DÖW has identified at least twenty people who died directly during police detention; furthermore, some perished in pre-trial detention following maltreatment by the Gestapo.[51]

A list of causes of death, although incomplete, reveals the following statistic for fifteen prisoners being detained by the Gestapo: two through gunshot wounds, five beaten to death, two suicides, five through other physical maltreatment, and one through denial of medicaments. Of the victims, ten were from the left-wing resistance and five were Jews or forced labourers.[52]

Most of the prisoners who died as a result of maltreatment had been interrogated by Section IV A 1 (formerly II A 1, 'Communism').[53] The Viennese tram conductor Franz Kokta, who kept Communist funds in safekeeping, was arrested on 3 December 1941 and died in detention on 13 January 1942. The apprentice wood-turner Franz Rouca from Vienna was imprisoned by the Gestapo on 6 April 1943 for Communist activity, because he had listened to radio broadcasts from Moscow, and died twelve days later.[54] Johann Lang, a member of the Communist resistance group in Hainburg, had been so severely beaten during an interrogation by members of Unit II A 1 that he died in hospital following two haemorrhages.[55] In Section IV B 4 ('Jewish section', formerly II B 4), Alexander Pick, a diabetic and member of the Vienna league of Mischlings (Mischlingsliga Wien) resistance group, died because the Gestapo official Karl Zeitlberger refused to allow him his daily insulin injections.[56]

The DÖW naming project has identified 4,313 concentration camp victims, many of them transferred by the Vienna Gestapo.[57] Thus, the railway worker Josef Brenner, who had already been sentenced to six months' imprisonment in 1934 for participation in the February fighting, and was active after 1938 as treasurer of the Communist party cell at Vienna's North Station and as a liaison with the district Communist party organization, was arrested by the Vienna Gestapo on 2 December 1941 and transferred to Mauthausen, where he was shot on 16 July 1942. The tram conductor Albert Dlabaja from the Favoriten depot, who was active in the KPÖ and Rote Hilfe, was arrested in 1939 by the Vienna Gestapo and killed on 16 April 1941 at Flossenbürg concentration camp. Otto Wehofschitz, a worker at the Simmering railway works, was arrested in December 1941 as a functionary of the KPÖ, transferred by the Gestapo to Mauthausen on 14 July 1942 and shot there two days later.[58]

Quite a few prisoners who had been tortured or were threatened with imprisonment committed suicide – not only to escape further torture but so as not to divulge the names of their fellow combatants. Franz Weisz concludes that between 1939 and 1944 at least ten prisoners attempted suicide in the building on Morzinplatz, but only successfully in two cases. Half of the cases occurred in the Vienna Gestapo units responsible for combating left-wing movements and parachute agents, where the most brutal torturing took place.[59]

The first maltreatment leading to a prisoner's suicide took place in 1938. On 23 June that year, the registry office of St Stephen's Cathedral announced the death of the van driver Franz Gollner, place of death 'Vienna I, Gestapo building, Salztorgasse, pavement'.[60] The Communist resistance fighter Josef Fohringer knew what was in store for him when the Gestapo came to arrest him on 31 October 1941, because he had already been detained several times before and also interned in Buchenwald in 1939–40. During the house search, he jumped out of the window and died immediately.[61] The railway worker Leopold Tischer was arrested on 19 January 1942 for KPÖ activity and died in Gestapo custody five days later. His death certificate says 'death by hanging, suicide'.[62] Like her father Johann Brunner and the other supporters of the KPÖ parachutist Gregor Kersche, the Communist resistance fighter Rosa Grossmann was brutally tortured by the Sanitzer group and jumped over a banister before a further interrogation session; she survived with multiple injuries.[63] Sanitzer attempted through severe maltreatment to force the KPÖ functionary Josef Angermann, who had deserted to the Red Army on the Eastern front and returned to Vienna as a parachute agent, to send fake radio messages to the Moscow headquarters. Angermann grabbed a bayonette from a guard in the interrogation room and stabbed himself in the neck; he died on 8 January 1944 from the wounds he had inflicted on himself.[64]

In some cases, the Gestapo was able to conduct 'executions' without trial; in the Nazi terror jargon, extrajudicial killings such as these were designated euphemistically as *Sonderbehandlung* ('special treatment'). Directly after the outbreak of war in September 1939, Sipo chief Heydrich had ordered 'the brutal liquidation' of 'underminers of military morale'; on his instructions, they were to be 'eradicated by the most ruthless methods'.[65] For example, twenty detained members of the Czech section of the KPÖ were transferred by the Gestapo on Himmler's orders to Mauthausen, and shot there without a trial 'during special treatment'.⁶⁶ This practice was extended and intensified in reprisals against foreign forced labourers, particularly Poles and *Ostarbeiter*. Those who refused to work, attacked employers or supervisors, or had relations with German (Austrian) women could be sentenced to death by the Gestapo (with the authorization of the superior authority). Thus, in April 1942, members of the Vienna Gestapo branch office of Sankt Pölten strung up the Polish forced labourer Stefan Andreanczik on a pear tree in the garden of a farmer by the name of Wohlmuth in Untereichen, Neulengbach district. As a deterrent, all Poles and other foreign workers employed on farms in Neulengbach district were forced to visit the spot of the extrajudicial execution. The reporting gendarmerie official stated that this 'administration of justice' was not well received by the local inhabitants.⁶⁷ No details are available about the execution for sabotage of an *Ostarbeiter* in Hirtenberg by members of the Wiener Neustadt Gestapo led by Kriminalrat Franz Rudischer. Foreign forced labourers from camps in Hirtenberg and Enzesfeld were forced to witness the execution.⁶⁸ According to the sources available to us, such executions were not as common in the area of the Vienna Gestapo as they were in other places, such as Cologne or Braunschweig.⁶⁹

Figure 6.1. Vienna Gestapo official Franz Rudischer, who directed, among other things, the 'execution' of an *Ostarbeiter*. © Dokumentationsarchiv des österreichischen Widerstandes. Used with permission.

As far as we know, the Vienna Gestapo did not carry out any 'executions' directly at Morzinplatz, apart from the usually unintentional deaths of prisoners through severe maltreatment, and the suicides. As mentioned, prisoners who were not handed over to the Nazi judiciary but were to be liquidated because they were of no further use to the Gestapo, having confessed or being Jewish resistance fighters, were transferred to concentration camps, mostly with the instruction 'special treatment' (i.e. to be killed). For example, Theodor Rakwetz and his 19-year-old son of the same name, parachute agents from the Soviet Union, were killed immediately after their transfer to Mauthausen on 15 and 14 October 1944, respectively.[70] A large number of *Ostarbeiter* who were in breach of contract or were active in the resistance were sent to Mauthausen and killed there.

Political opponents from the time before 1938 were also dealt with in concentration camps if they were not brought to trial or if the sentence was not sufficient for the Gestapo. The retired prison director Karl Richter was arrested on 1 August 1941 'because he had participated in 1933 in the maltreatment of an imprisoned National Socialist who died as a result of his injuries'. Richter was sent to Mauthausen, and from there to the Hartheim 'euthanasia' centre, where he was put to death on 14 October 1942.[71]

Referrals to State Prosecutors and Courts, Applications for 'Remand'

After the investigations and interrogations had been completed, the Gestapo reported those individuals and members of resistance groups who had not been transferred to concentration camps to the public prosecutor's office. The Vienna special court (Sondergericht, SG) and its public prosecutor's office had jurisdiction for *Heimtücke* (insidious utterances), 'radio offences' and the like; 'high treason' and *Wehrkraftzersetzung* (undermining military morale) went to the prosecutor general in Vienna or the chief Reich prosecutor (Oberreichsanwalt) at the Volksgerichtshof, which then pressed charges with the Vienna OLG, special senates, or VGH. While the investigating Gestapo officials and denouncers testified in the main court hearings, informants – by agreement between the Gestapo, public prosecutor's office and courts – were not called upon to testify. The summary report by the Vienna Gestapo of 28 March 1944, mentioned earlier, proudly announced that as a result of its referrals, 364 death sentences had been pronounced by the VGH and Vienna OLG on Communist party members and 293 had been carried out. Between 1938 and 1945 as a whole, well over half of the 814 death sentences pronounced against Austrian resistance fighters for 'planning high treason' originated with the Vienna Gestapo.[72]

To ensure that detainees were not sentenced too leniently by the courts, or did not go free after being acquitted, the Gestapo usually applied to the court for them to be returned or 'remanded' (*Rücküberstellung*). This meant that if the prisoners were acquitted, they had to be transferred back to the Gestapo, which in many cases meant their being sent to a concentration camp.[73] Thus after being acquitted by the Vienna OLG on 16 June 1943 for 'organizing a Red Help [Rote Hilfe] collection at his place of work to support the relatives of an imprisoned Communist', the car-body painter Gottfried Bevelaqua was remanded to the Vienna Gestapo and interned at Dachau until the end of the war. The office clerk Franz Josef Mika, born in 1903, was arrested on 23 June 1941 for KPÖ activity and sentenced on 23 July 1942 to three years' imprisonment. On completion of his sentence, he was remanded to the Gestapo and sent to Dachau in 1944, from there to Natzweiler concentration camp/Leonberg commando, and finally on 11 March 1945 to Bergen-Belsen, where he perished.[74] When the architect and Communist resistance fighter Margaret(h)e Schütte(-Lihotzky) was referred to the VGH on 17 December 1941, Section II A 1 of the Vienna Gestapo applied at the same time for her to be remanded. In this case the application was not followed up because she remained in prison until the end of the war.[75]

Concentration Camp Committals

The terror exercised by the Gestapo and other police formations only reached its culmination through combination with the institution of the concentration camp – that is to say, with the state forced labour camps and in some cases extermination camps, to which the Gestapo was able to commit detainees without trial on the basis of a 'protective custody' order obtained from the Gestapa or (from 1939) the RSHA in Berlin. This competence, insisted on and claimed by Heydrich, meant that the Gestapo had precedence over the judiciary regarding the course of action.[76] It is unclear what criteria the Gestapo used to determine who was to be handed over to the judiciary for criminal prosecution and who was to be committed to a concentration camp under a 'protective custody' order. While the decision appears in some cases to have been arbitrary, there were certain cases in which transfer to a concentration camp was preferred – for example, with parachute agents or 'turned' detainees who were still usable, or in cases where activities hostile to the state were suspected but insufficient evidence was available for judicial prosecution. Then there were the large number of political opponents arrested as a precaution in 1938–39, and those apprehended in large-scale arrests ordered from Berlin (Himmler, RSHA), such as the round-up after 20 July 1944. By virtue of the Thirteenth Regulation to the Reich Citizenship Law of 1 July 1943, Jews were not to be prosecuted by the courts but dealt with by the SS and police.⁷⁷ This meant that, from this time, Jewish resistance fighters were generally deported to concentration camps after the Gestapo was finished with them. The regulation affected most members of the widespread Communist resistance group that had returned from France to Austria in 1942–43. For example, the Spanish Civil War veteran Walter Greif, born in 1911, who was ordered back by the head of the KPÖ abroad in November 1942 with false papers as a French civilian worker, was arrested by the Vienna Gestapo on 28 August 1943, deported to Auschwitz and shot, according to eyewitnesses.⁷⁸

In the case of Allied parachutists, the entire support network – not only those sheltering them but also innocent family members – were arrested, often brutally maltreated and transferred to concentration camps. Thus, nine relatives of Albert Huttary, who deserted on the Eastern front and returned to Austria in early 1944 as a Soviet parachutist, were sent to concentration camps by the Gestapo. Huttary's mother, father and aunt perished, while Huttary himself survived in Theresienstadt. The roadworker Vinzenz Christian and his son Gustav, who sheltered the parachutist Georg Kennerknecht in 1943, although not informed of his mission, died in prison or a concentration camp, while Christian's wife Theresia survived Ravensbrück.⁷⁹

As indicated by the thousands of 'protective custody' orders, the mere suspicion of an attitude 'hostile to the state' was sufficient for transfer to a concentration camp. For example, the Gestapa order of 5 January 1940 against RS functionary Franz Heigelmayr, who had already been imprisoned for several months between 1934 and 1938 for political reasons, read simply: 'According to the Gestapo investigation, he endangers the existence and security of Volk and state through his behaviour, being strongly suspected of working for the RS and hence of planning acts of high treason'.⁸⁰

Quite a few concentration camp inmates did not survive long after their liberation. For example, the commercial clerk Josef Pürrer, member of a Communist resistance group in Kottingbrunn, who was transferred to Dachau after sentencing in 1941, died in Kufstein on 28 May 1945, a month after being liberated.⁸¹ Most of the Catholic-conservative opposition imprisoned in 1938–39, including the future ÖVP politicians Leopold Figl and Fritz Bock, were released under strict conditions, but many were rearrested later on for resistance activities. Numerous imprisoned Socialists, including Franz Heigelmayr, mentioned earlier, and the future minister of transport Otto Probst, were also released from concentration camps and drafted into the Wehrmacht. Most Communist activists were interned until the end of the Nazi regime. The only ones to be released – at least until 1939 – were Jewish prisoners with emigration visas.⁸²

Many concentration camp inmates were victims of 'Aktion 14f13', a purge ordered by Himmler against political undesirables or sick concentration camp inmates no longer able to work, who were transferred to the Hartheim or Bernburg 'euthanasia' centres.⁸³ Thus, the apprentice lathe operator Josef Gruber, who had fought on the side of the Republicans in the Spanish Civil War and was transferred by the Vienna Gestapo to Dachau in 1941, was killed at Hartheim on 6 February 1942 in 'Aktion 14f13'. Similarly, the Spanish Civil War veteran Johann Strasser, who had been sent to Dachau in 1941, was transferred to Hartheim on 2 March 1942 and was registered in Dachau as having 'died of heart failure as a result of pneumonia' on 16 April 1942.[84]

The Gestapo also had its own camps and prisons, such as Reichenau near Innsbruck, the Kleine Festung in Theresienstadt, and the Vienna Gestapo's own Oberlanzendorf AEL, where prisoners could be detained without formalities, and where quite a few perished in the process.[85]

Cooperation with the SD, Orpo, Wehrmacht, Administration and Counter-intelligence Officers in Companies

The SS security service (SD) had close links with the Vienna Gestapo – not least by virtue of the close links between Heydrich (as head of the RSHA) and Huber (as head of the Vienna Gestapo) – but, as discussed earlier, there was also a certain rivalry. After the annexation, the SD, a domestic and foreign secret service with political ambitions and a network for spying both within the population and on the NSDAP, its branches and other institutions, also developed a network of paid and unpaid workers in Austria, as well as having numerous informants. Prominent informants and SD recruiters included Professor Kurt Knoll, rector of the Hochschule für Welthandel (university of world trade), Paul Heigl, director general of the Austrian national library, the ethnologist Hugo Bernatzik, the Burgtheater actor Eduard Volters, and Helmut Wobisch, a member of the Vienna Philharmonic.[86] Through the fusion of the Sipo and SD effected by the establishment of the RSHA in 1939, the SD also gained influence over the Gestapo and Kripo, and played a decisive role in particular in the persecution of the Jews in Austria, and later in occupied Europe.[87] Right at the beginning, when the Germans entered Austria, the SD 'Einsatzkommando Österreich' from Berlin, under Franz Alfred Six, murdered Wilhelm-Emanuel Freiherr von Ketteler, a Catholic opponent of the Nazis and a member of the German legation in Vienna, on Heydrich's orders on 12 or 13 March 1938 – that is to say, before the founding of the Vienna Gestapo.[88]

The various SD offices regularly reported on their activities, and submitted situation and mood reports, albeit mostly in quite general terms, with none of the specific detail or precision of the Gestapo reports. A surviving list of informants of the SD headquarters in Eisenstadt (Burgenland, then in 'Lower Danube') reveals that even in this small area there were around one hundred SD informants, including ten women. Most SD informants there were in high positions – as academics, teachers, civil servants or gendarmes (rural police) – and came from the illegal Nazi movement in Burgenland before 1938.[89] It has been shown that the SD informants and officials also assisted the Gestapo in persecuting resistance fighters. For example, Heinrich Kunnert, SD head in Eisenstadt, informed the Gestapo immediately when he learned from an SD informant, the gendarme Andreas Mikler, of the landing of a four-man US parachute unit in October 1944. During the arrests resulting from this information, Josef Prieler, municipal employee in Schützen, was shot by the Gestapo on 1 December 1944.[90]

Because of the relatively low numbers of staff, the Gestapo was reliant on the collaboration of other police formations or authorities, and other institutions.[91] The Gestapo leadership expected 'the most extensive cooperation and support of all state bodies'. 'In the case of the local and district police organs,' said one decree, 'this cooperation is not a voluntary duty but one decreed by the Reichsführer-SS'.[92]

From 1937, the border police were directly subordinate to the Gestapo, not least because border controls played an important role in combating escaped 'enemies of state', foreign agents, and smuggling. The border police locations functioned as outposts of the Gestapo offices. After various restructuring operations, the Vienna Gestapo had border police stations in Lundenburg (Břeclav) and Eisenstadt, as well as one at the headquarters on Morzinplatz; in addition, there were border police posts at Bruck an der Leitha, Kittsee, Sauerbrunn, Lundenburg, Aspern-Flughafen (airport), Engerau, Marchegg and Vienna-Reichsbrücke (on the Danube).[93] At these locations too, detainees were interrogated, maltreated and transferred to the Vienna Gestapo headquarters or to concentration camps. The border police station in Eisenstadt was generally referred to as the 'Eisenstadt Gestapo'.[94]

Although the criminal investigation police (Kripo), as part of the Sipo, had the same hierarchical status as the Gestapo, in practice it also had the function of assisting the Gestapo. For example, members of the Kripo in Bremen were made available to the Gestapo there when the latter was required to detach most of its officials for the annexation of Austria in March 1938.[95] Added to this was the fact that the Kripo in Vienna was subordinate to Huber as regional inspector (later 'Befehlshaber') of the Sipo and SD. Given that Huber (or, later, his successor Mildner) was also head of the Vienna Gestapo, this clearly put the Gestapo in a dominant position. In September 1939, Heydrich ordered that the persecution of homosexuals be transferred from the Gestapo to the Kripo,[96] while the persecution of Roma was part of the Kripo's mandate from the outset. It was responsible for the 'gypsy camp' in Lackenbach, and organized the deportation of Roma. In this way, and through its operations against supposed 'asocials' and the ruthless persecution of 'professional criminals' (through preventive detention), the Kripo was also deeply implicated in Nazi crimes.[97]

The Ordnungspolizei (regular police, Orpo), which included the uniformed Schutzpolizei (Schupo) and the Gendarmerie (rural police), assisted the Gestapo in, for example, making mass arrests, surrounding suspicious buildings, and transporting prisoners. In a mass arrest organized by the Vienna Gestapo, the fugitive Fritz Sonnenschein, a '1st-degree Mischling', was killed in a shoot-out with the Schupo on 30 December 1944.[98]

To save on manpower and to keep staff for more important tasks, the Gestapo entrusted the Vienna Schupo with guarding the prominent prisoners Kurt (von) Schuschnigg and Louis (Freiherr von) Rothschild on the fifth floor of the building on Morzinplatz.[99] The Gestapo scholars Klaus-Michael Mallmann and Gerhard Paul believe that it was through the assistance of the regular police that the 'aura of the omniscience and omnipresence of the Gestapo was made credible'.[100] The Orpo infrastructure and its presence in the tiniest places considerably increased the Gestapo's scope. Dams and Stolle conclude that it was 'the interplay between the decentralized persecution network and the centralized Gestapo apparatus' that 'made the Gestapo's investigations successful'.[101]

Resistance fighters in the Wehrmacht were arrested by the military police – that is to say, the Geheime Feldpolizei or Feldgendarmerie – and normally handed over to the Gestapo. NSDAP offices, mayors, local and regional councils, juvenile departments, and so on were recruited to assist the Gestapo, being requested, for example, to provide 'political assessments' or information about the reputation of suspects. NSDAP officials and organizations were also often the first contact for denunciations. Closer collaboration developed in particular with the relevant offices of the Vienna city council in combating 'asocial' juveniles after the Vienna Gestapo took over the 'labour education camp' (Arbeitserziehungslager, AEL) of Oberlanzendorf established by the city of Vienna.

The relationship with the leaders of the regional authorities – for the Reichsgau of Vienna the Reichsstatthalter/NSDAP Gauleiter Josef Bürckel and (from 1940) Baldur von Schirach, and Hugo Jury in the Reichsgau Lower Danube – was generally informal and unproblematic. Gestapo head Huber was the adviser on 'political police' to the office of Reichsstatthalter Schirach (with address Morzinplatz 4) and his representative as Reich defence commissioner in Military District XVII or (from 1942) in the Reichsgau of Vienna. Huber's tasks in the Reichsgau included not only responsibility for the Sipo but also reporting on the political police, dealing with associations, meetings and press matters where they were of interest to the political police, and collaborating in all matters with a political police component – for example, in policing, schooling, church and commercial matters. The link with the Gestapo was through the 'Zentralbüro' of 'Reichsleiter' Baldur von Schirach – a hitherto little known but important office.[102] It was headed (until he was killed in an air raid at the end of 1944) by Herbert Müller, who signed himself as 'Obergebietsführer' (of the Hitler Youth). He had already worked for Schirach at the Hitler Youth headquarters, dealing on his behalf with particularly sensitive matters. For example, a meeting chaired by Müller took place in his office on 12 February 1941 with Alois Brunner from the 'central office for Jewish emigration in Vienna', Karl Ebner from the Vienna Gestapo 'Jewish section' and representatives of the city of Vienna and the NSDAP Gau leadership, at which important details of the first deportation of Viennese Jews to the 'Generalgouvernement' (Poland) on 15 February were arranged.[103] The further collaboration between the Vienna Gestapo and Schirach on 'Jewish matters' can also be seen from a memo from the central office stating that 'the resettlement of Jews will be headed by the Gestapo'; petitions by deported Jews were passed on without comment to the Vienna Gestapo.[104]

Huber faced a difficult situation through the long-term conflict between Schirach and the SD headquarters in Vienna, whose head, SS-Sturmbannführer Friedrich Polte, was accused by Schirach of spying on him and putting him in a bad light in Berlin through unfavourable reports. In an unparalleled demonstration of power in March 1941, the Reichsstatthalter expelled the SD head from the Reichsgau of Vienna – according to Karl Ebner 'the only instance in the Reich territory'. Huber, who as IdSuSD was Polte's superior, did not wish to endanger his relationship with Schirach, and simply left Polte in the lurch.[105]

Large industrial companies had counter-intelligence officers (*Abwehrbeauftragte*), usually dependable supporters of the regime. They also provided important assistance to the Gestapo, in particular with the rapid increase in the number of foreign forced labourers, who were seen as a security risk. For training and control purposes, from October 1942 Vienna Gestapo head Huber issued a special confidential 'circular' to the counter-intelligence officers, and established an 'industrial security' section within the Gestapo, responsible for communication with the 'political police counter-intelligence officers', who were required to 'report directly' to the Gestapo. The communication focused on combating spies, saboteurs and foreign resistance groups, who did indeed attempt to destroy the German war machinery.[106] Regarding the treatment of Soviet prisoners of war, in one circular Huber recalled an OKW (Oberkommando der Wehrmacht) decree of 24 March 1943, which illustrated the cold-bloodedness of both the Wehrmacht and the Gestapo: 'Ruthless and energetic measures are ordered in cases of insubordination, refusal to work and negligence, particularly in the case of Bolshevist rabble-rousers: obstruction or active resistance is to be suppressed immediately through force of arms (bayonet, truncheon or firearms, no sticks). ... Fugitive Soviet prisoners of war are to be fired at immediately, without warning'.[107]

Notes

1. See Chapter 9.
2. Weisz, 'Gestapo-Leitstelle Wien', Tables, table no. 35, 41.
3. See comments on 'daily bureaucracy' in Paul, 'Kontinuität und Radikalisierung', 168ff.
4. Dams/Stolle, *The Gestapo*, 61 (*Die Gestapo*, 73).
5. Weisz, 'Gestapo-Leitstelle Wien', Tables, synopsis no. 2, 193.
6. The card index, whose existence the Vienna police and ministry of the interior still denied to the DÖW in the 1970s, was 'discovered' in 2000 in the Wiener Stadt- und Landesarchiv by Thomas Mang while working on his dissertation. With the archive's cooperation, the entire card index, including photos, was digitized by the DÖW in 2001 and stored in a database, a large part of which is accessible online (http://www.doew.at/erinnern/personendatenbanken/gestapo-opfer, last accessed on 24. May 2021).
7. See the section 'Repression of Foreign Forced Labourers' in Chapter 12.
8. See, e.g., the identification photos of Nikolaj Baran (Figure 12.4), a Soviet civilian worker who was tortured to death. He was photographed a second time after his violent murder.
9. http://www.doew.at/erinnern/personendatenbanken/gestapo-opfer/die-erkennungsdienstliche-kartei-der-gestapo-wien (last accessed on 21 Aug 2016).
10. Bailer et al., 'Die Gestapo', 163–90.
11. See Heydrich, 'Aufbau und Entwicklung der Sicherheitspolizei', 3–4.
12. Neugebauer/Schwarz, *Stacheldraht, mit Tod geladen*, 49–50. See also the section 'Concentration Camp Committals', this chapter.
13. Bailer et al., 'Die Gestapo', 165.
14. The daily reports of the Vienna Gestapo, most of which are at the DÖW, were published on the Internet (Bailer/Form, 'Tagesrapporte', now only accessible under licence and to institutions), and consist of 741 daily reports and 5,742 pages. Around seventy reports have disappeared. The gaps relate above all to the first months and the last weeks of the Nazi regime. For various strategic or bureaucratic reasons, quite a few arrestees were not included in the daily reports; this confidentiality applied above all to Allied parachutists and their networks. Nor were most of the detained forced labourers recorded in the daily reports.
15. DÖW 4112, 1578.
16. DÖW 5080.
17. WStLA, Bundespolizeidirektion Wien: Staatspolizeiliche Erhebung, A1-Polizeiliche Erhebung 24/Gestapo Wien 2.5.1.9. Kon. 24.
18. DÖW 1453, RSHA report on 'inflammatory' Communist propaganda, 26 Feb 1940.
19. See, e.g., Eckert, 'Gestapo-Berichte', 204–7.
20. DÖW 7759, OLG Wien OJs 165/40.
21. For details, see Schafranek, *Widerstand und Verrat* (2017), 30ff. For example, the surveillance of the KPÖ network built up around the central functionary Erwin Puschmann, whose right-hand man was the informant 'Ossi' (Kurt Koppel), is well documented.
22. DÖW 5210.
23. NARA, KV2/2656, detailed interrogation report of Johann Sanitzer, Gestapo, Vienna, Section IV 2, Jul 1945. SCI Unit A, Salzburg, Austria, Headquarters Co. 'A', 2677 Regiment, Office of Strategic Services. We are grateful to Peter Pirker for providing a copy of this document. See also Freihammer, 'Dem NS-Regime nicht untergeordnet'.
24. Weisz, 'Gestapo-Leitstelle Wien', Tables, tables no. 2 and 3, synopsis no. 2, 192–93.
25. Mallmann/Paul, 'Die Gestapo', 638–39.
26. See, e.g., article in Klee, *Personenlexikon*, and the corresponding Wikipedia entries.
27. See the section 'Repression of Foreign Forced Labourers' in Chapter 12; and Chapter 14.
28. Paul/Mallmann, *Die Gestapo – Mythos und Realität*, 4.

29. Schafranek, *Widerstand und Verrat* (2017). See also chapters 8 and 9.
30. For details, see Tidl, 'Marie Hofmann-Tidl', 30–31; DÖW, *Widerstand Wien*, vol. 2, 214. Georg Tidl attributes this relatively unusual release to the intervention by the defence lawyer Walter Riehl, a veteran of the Nazi movement in Austria.
31. Améry, *At the Mind's Limits*, see the chapter 'Torture', 21–40, here 24.
32. Weisz, 'Gestapo-Leitstelle Wien', 1474–656.
33. WStLA, Vienna LG, Vg 11c Vr 586/47, statement by Karl Ebner in the main proceedings against Johann Sanitzer, 11 Jan 1949.
34. WStLA, Vienna LG (DÖW 20 642), Vg 12a Vr 612/46, decree by the chief of the Sipo and SD regarding enhanced interrogation, 12 Jun 1942; ibid., judgment against Rudolf Hitzler, 19 Mar 1948; statements by Heinrich Wohl and Johann Sanitzer in the main proceedings against Rudolf Hitzler, 9 Mar 1948.
35. Weisz, 'Gestapo-Leitstelle Wien', Tables, table no. 35, 41.
36. Rizy/Weinert, *Korrespondenzen*, vol. 1, 66.
37. Oskar Wendzio, Freikorps combatant, NSDAP member since 1932, did not join the SS until 1944, but was promoted the same year at the request of the head of the Vienna Gestapo to the rank of SS-Sturmbannführer. BA Berlin, SS-Führerpersonalakten, 236-B, letter from RSHA to SS-Personalhauptamt, 31 Mar 1944.
38. BA Berlin, ZR 602 A (R 2091), Vienna Gestapo service reference, 17 Jul 1940.
39. WStLA, Vienna LG (DÖW 20 642), Vg 12a Vr 612/46, judgment against Rudolf Hitzler, 19 Mar 1948. See the section 'Repression of Foreign Forced Labourers' in Chapter 12.
40. Weisz, 'Gestapo-Leitstelle Wien', 2290–98.
41. WStLA, Vienna LG, Vg 11c Vr 586/47, judgment against Johann Sanitzer for high treason, torture and maltreatment, 17 Jan 1949.
42. WStLA, Vienna LG, Vg 1a 1175/49 (copy: DÖW 12 586), testimonies of Pauline Gabriel and Maria Wild to Oberpullendorf Bezirksgericht, 30 Jan 1947; see also DÖW, *Widerstand Burgenland*, 178–83.
43. See DÖW, *Widerstand Niederösterreich*, vol. 2, 494–514.
44. Rizy/Weinert, *Korrespondenzen*, vol. 1, 66–67.
45. The Communist resistance fighter Josef Meisel, arrested and tortured on 17 March 1943, said nothing about fellow resistance members still at large, with the result that the next arrests of resistance fighters did not take place until three months later. DÖW 8475, Vienna Gestapo daily reports, 27–31 Aug 1943. See Meisel, *'Jetzt haben wir Ihnen, Meisel!'*.
46. Weisz, 'Gestapo-Leitstelle Wien', 1619–56.
47. WStLA, Vienna LG, Vg 11c Vr 586/47, judgment against Johann Sanitzer for high treason, torture and maltreatment, 17 Jan 1949.
48. WStLA,LG Wien, Vg 4c Vr 7620/47, trial of Walter Hinker (DÖW 19 860), statement by Josef Auer at the security directorate of Lower Austria (Sicherheitsdirektion für das Land Niederösterreich), 5 Sep 1947, and expert opinion of Dr Leopold Gerzner, 31 May 1949.
49. DÖW 20 100/4661 (KZ-Verbandsakten), medical report of 9 Jul 1946.
50. Weisz, 'Gestapo-Leitstelle Wien', 1643–50.
51. Bailer et al., 'Die Gestapo', 179.
52. Weisz, 'Gestapo-Leitstelle Wien', 48, table no. 41.
53. Ibid., 1622.
54. www.doew.at/erinnern/personendatenbanken/gestapo-opfer (last accessed on 21 Aug 2016).
55. WStLA, Vienna LG, Vg 4c Vr 7620/47 (copy: DÖW 19 860), trial of Walter Hinker, statement by Johann Knaus at Vienna police department, 24 Jul 1947.
56. WStLA, Vienna LG, Vg 4c Vr 5597/47 (copy: DÖW 19 841), trial of Karl Zeitlberger, statement by Alexander Pick's mother Maria Pick to the investigating judge of LG Vienna, 10 Nov 1947; see also the section 'Vienna League of Mischlings' in Chapter 12.

57. Bailer/Ungar, 'Die Zahl der Todesopfer politischer Verfolgung', 122–23.
58. www.doew.at/erinnern/personendatenbanken/gestapo-opfer (accessed on 17 Nov 2017).
59. Weisz, 'Gestapo-Leitstelle Wien', 1623, and Tables, table no 43.
60. DÖW 20 000/3277 (KZ-Verbandsakten), certificate of Standesamt Dom- und Metropolitanamt St. Stephan, 23 June 1938.
61. www.doew.at/erinnern/personendatenbanken/gestapo-opfer (last accessed on 21 Aug 2016).
62. Ibid.
63. WStLA, Vienna LG, Vg 11c 586/47, judgment by Vienna VG against Johann Sanitzer for high treason, torture and maltreatment, 17 Jan 1949; see Fischer, *Das Wichtigste ist, sich selber treu zu bleiben*.
64. Weinert, 'Er starb für Österreichs Freiheit'; www.doew.at/erinnern/personendatenbanken/gestapo-opfer (last accessed on 15 Oct 2016). According to his mother Maria Angermann and fellow prisoner Josef Sasso, Angermann was shot by a guard while attempting to escape, see Weisz, 'Gestapo-Leitstelle Wien', 1622, and n. 1107.
65. Quoted in Gerhard Wysocki, 'Lizenz zum Töten', in Paul/Mallmann, *Die Gestapo im Zweiten Weltkrieg*, 237–38.
66. *Völkischer Beobachter*, Vienna edition, 10 Nov 1941; DÖW 5080.
67. DÖW E 19 289, report of Gendarmerierayonsinspektor N.N. Böhmer to Neulengbach 'Gendarmeriepostenkommando' (rural police commando unit) regarding the execution of the Polish civilian worker Andreanczik, 11 Dec 1945. A picture of an execution of two Polish 'Fremdarbeiter' by the Innsbruck Gestapo at the camp of Kirchbichl in autumn 1940 can be found in DÖW, *Widerstand Tirol*, vol. 1, Illustrations, no. 19. See in general Weitz, 'Verbotener Umgang mit Kriegsgefangenen'.
68. DÖW E 19 290, report of Hirtenberg border police to the Vienna LG regarding the murder of foreign workers, 11 Jun 1946.
69. See Paul/Mallmann, *Die Gestapo im Zweiten Weltkrieg*, 237–54, and eidem, *Die Gestapo – Mythos und Realität*, 402–16.
70. www.doew.at/erinnern/personendatenbanken/gestapo-opfer (last accessed on 21 Aug 2016).
71. DÖW reference library, Vienna Gestapo daily report no. 1 of 1–3 Aug 1941; www.doew.at/erinnern/personendatenbanken/gestapo-opfer (last accessed on 11 Mar 2017); see the section 'Arrests in March/April 1938' in Chapter 9.
72. DÖW 5080; Bailer/Ungar, 'Die Zahl der Todesopfer politischer Verfolgung'.
73. The court record normally contains the application for remand, or evidence of the defendant being remanded.
74. www.doew.at/erinnern/personendatenbanken/gestapo-opfer (last accessed on 18 Oct 2016).
75. http://www.doew.at/cms/download/934c7/rueckstellungsantrag.pdf (last accessed on 18 Oct 2016).
76. See Gellately, 'Allwissend und allgegenwärtig?', 58ff.
77. *Reichsgesetzblatt* 1943, 372.
78. www.doew.at/erinnern/personendatenbanken/gestapo-opfer (last accessed on 18 Oct 2016).
79. Ibid.; Neugebauer, *Austrian Resistance*, 108, 124–25.
80. www.doew.at/erinnern/personendatenbanken/gestapo-opfer (last accessed on 18 Oct 2016).
81. Ibid.
82. Neugebauer, *Austrian Resistance*, 40.
83. See Grode, *Die 'Sonderbehandlung 14f13'*.
84. www.doew.at/erinnern/personendatenbanken/gestapo-opfer (last accessed on 18 Oct 2016).
85. For details, see Lotfi, *KZ der Gestapo*, and Chapter 14.
86. Archive of the Republic of Slovenia, AS 1931/821, 106 36, 628–42.
87. See, in general, Boberach, *Meldungen aus dem Reich*; Ramme, *Der Sicherheitsdienst der SS*.
88. Stadlbauer, 'Ehrlinger', 188 and n. 988; Hachmeister, *Der Gegnerforscher*, 10–20.

89. For details, see Wilhelm, *SD-Hauptaußenstelle und Volkstumsstelle Eisenstadt*, 93–94.
90. Heinrich Kunnert, who was sentenced after 1945 only for registration fraud (false information about Nazi membership), later made a career with the aid of the BSA and SPÖ in Burgenland. See Neugebauer/Schwarz, *Der Wille*, 124ff; www.doew.at/erinnern/personendatenbanken/gestapo-opfer (Jack Taylor); text of debriefing of Lt Jack Taylor on 30 May 1945, quoted in: https://www.jewishvirtuallibrary.org/the-dupont-mission-october-1944-may-1945 (last accessed on 25 May 2021); for details, see the section 'Murder of Crew Members of Downed Allied Aircraft' in Chapter 16.
91. Gerhard Paul notes that this aid was also provided to the Gestapo in Würzburg; Paul, 'Kontinuität und Radikalisierung', in Paul/Mallmann, *Die Gestapo – Mythos und Realität*, 170ff.
92. [Diese Mithilfe ist bei den Polizeiorganen in der Kreis- und Ortsinstanz keine freiwillige, sondern eine auf Erlass des Reichsführers SS beruhende Verpflichtung.] Quoted in Dams/Stolle, *The Gestapo*, 82 (*Die Gestapo*, 95).
93. BA Berlin, R 58/4207, 1 (undated), and R 58/717 (undated, c. late 1942).
94. See, e.g., DÖW, *Widerstand Burgenland*, 411ff.
95. Nitschke, 'Polizei und Gestapo', 316, n. 44.
96. See the section 'Persecution of Homosexuals' in Chapter 13.
97. See Wilhelm, *Die Polizei*, 94ff.
98. WStLA, Vienna LG, Vg 4c 5597/47, trial of Karl Zeitlberger (copy: DÖW 19 841), report by Ernst Sonnenschein, 26 Aug 1947.
99. See the section on 'The "Special Detainees"' in Chapter 3.
100. Mallmann/Paul, 'Allwissend, allmächtig, allgegenwärtig?', 996.
101. Dams/Stolle, *The Gestapo*, 83–84 (*Die Gestapo*, 96).
102. *Handbuch Reichsgau Wien*, 1941, 75. For details, see Schwarz, 'Der Ballhausplatz 2', 297, 302–7. Schirach called himself officially, and in official correspondence, 'Reichsleiter' (of the NSDAP) – no doubt a more prestigious title than his official titles Reichsstatthalter and NSDAP-Gauleiter.
103. DÖW 1456, memo, 12 Feb 1941; see also Mang, *Die Unperson*, 88–90.
104. ÖStA, AdR, Reichsstatthalter Wien, Organisationsreferat, Karton 195, Amtsvermerk, 10. 4. 1941; see also the section 'Activity of the Gestapo' in Chapter 10.
105. BA Berlin, ZB 7061, sheet 174; Mang, '*Gestapo-Leitstelle Wien*', 218–24. Polte, later head of SD-Abschnitt Berlin, was sentenced to death and executed in Belgrade in 1946 for his participation in the Sipo and SD Einsatzgruppe in Yugoslavia from April to July 1941.
106. DÖW 20 333/2, circulars no. 1 and no. 2 of the head of the Vienna Gestapo, 21 Oct 1942 and 25 Dec 1943 [correct: 1942].
107. [Rücksichtloses und energisches Durchgreifen bei Unbotmäßigkeit, bei Arbeitsverweigerungen und Nachlässigkeit in der Arbeit, insb. gegenüber bolschewistischen Hetzern, ist zu befehlen: Widersetzlichkeit oder aktiver Widerstand muss sofort mit der Waffe (Bajonett, Kolben u. Schusswaffe, keine Stöcke) restlos beseitigt werden. … Auf flüchtige sowj. Kgf. ist sofort ohne vorherigen Haltruf zu schießen.] DÖW 20 333/2, Circular no. 8 of the head of the Vienna Gestapo, 25 Oct 1943, 5.

Chapter 7

INFORMANTS AND CELL SPIES
'Radio Games'

Informants, Cell Spies, Agents Provocateurs – the Gestapo's Most Potent Weapons

Large areas of the Gestapo's investigative activities did not require it to have surveillance structures of its own. Through denunciations and reporting, it received notifications of anti-regime statements, listening to foreign radio broadcasts, 'defilement of the race' (*Rassenschande*), 'asocial' behaviour and much more. When the regime's power base was threatened through political activities, however, the Gestapo operated proactively and took preventive measures. These threats derived in particular from political resistance groups, foreign agents and activists smuggled in by them, and, to an increasing extent, perceived dangers from the masses of foreign workers brought by force to the German Reich. In his testimony before the Nuremberg military tribunal, Werner Best, the Gestapo's 'chief ideologist' and Heydrich's sometime deputy, said that 'an in-house intelligence service was developed only when organized groups were suspected, for example, in the illegal Communist party or in enemy intelligence services, for espionage purposes. In those cases, agents or similar means were used in an attempt to track down and expose these groups'.[1]

The Gestapo counter-espionage activities were deadly in their efficiency. The Vienna Gestapo used paid 'V-Leute' (*Vertrauensleute* – informants who enjoyed special confidence) and agents provocateurs against the politically organized resistance, managed by Section IV N (Intelligence). In this way, the large Communist, Socialist and Catholic-conservative resistance groups were exposed by just a handful of informants: the KPÖ functionary Kurt Koppel, the RS functionaries Hans Pav and Eduard Korbel, and the Burgtheater actor Otto Hartmann operating in the Scholz group.[2]

Through Koppel (code name 'Ossi'), who worked as liaison officer for several central functionaries in the KPÖ, had contacts abroad, and with the aid of his girlfriend Grete Kahane (code name 'Sonja') also spied on the KJV, the Gestapo was informed of all important events, connections and people in the KPÖ. Surveillance, arrests and brutal interrogations that forced even leading functionaries (such as Karl Zwifelhofer) to collaborate provided the Gestapo with further information resulting in huge mass arrests. According to the Gestapo, no fewer than 536 Communists, including 42 top functionaries and 105 other officials were arrested from October 1941 onwards, and 112 detainees were handed over to the VGH, which sentenced most of them to death for 'preparation for high treason' (*Vorbereitung zum Hochverrat*). The large Styrian provincial group built up by Herbert Eichholzer, Karl Drews and Franz Weiss, and the 'Czech section of the KPÖ', as the Gestapo called it, were victims of Kurt Koppel's betrayal. According to Hans Schafranek, Koppel and Kahane alone were responsible for over eight hundred Gestapo victims.[3]

One single informant, the Burgtheater actor Otto Hartmann, sufficed to uncover the Catholic-conservative Freedom Movements led by Karl Roman Scholz, Jakob Kastelic and Karl Lederer, resulting in two hundred arrests and the execution of twelve resistance fighters.[4] Even in 1947, Lambert Leutgeb, who headed Section IV N at the Vienna Gestapo from May 1941 to November 1944, euphemistically praised the work of his informant with the code name 'Burgler': 'Hartmann was well established in the monarchist groups of the Austrian Freedom Movement, and brought very nice and good information. Thanks to this information, it was also possible to intervene successfully in some cases'.[5]

Leutgeb, who was born in Lower Austria in 1895, was already working in the intelligence service of the Austrian state police in 1936 combating Social Democrats and Communists, and had built up his own network of informants. In March 1938, he placed this expertise at the disposal of the Vienna Gestapo. 'When I became head of this section [II/N] on 1 April after having headed the investigation team since early March 1940, there were no useful informants available.'[6] Leutgeb fell back on his old network and continued to expand it.

The informants and agents provocateurs usually came from the same political and social milieu as the members of the resistance groups they were spying on, and were integrated in these organizations: 'Their greatest asset was their intimate knowledge of the specific circumstances and practices, and the trust accorded to them by the people working in this milieu on account of the informants' past'.[7]

Hans Schafranek, Diana Albu, Franz Weisz and Christine Cézanne-Thauss[8] have written in detail about the recruitment, utilization and methods of the Gestapo informants in Vienna, and have also investigated the lives of individual informants such as Otto Hartmann. It would appear that most members of the political resistance groups could only be persuaded by force to betray their former comrades. Schafranek reckons that 'around two-thirds of the Gestapo informants for whom biographical information is available worked involuntarily for their employers, at least initially'.[9] The pressure ranged from 'enhanced interrogation' to solitary confinement, as well as the threat of committal to a concentration camp or execution. The threat of reprisals against family members was another effective means of persuading victims to join the perpetrators. To save their own lives and protect their families, many were willing to accept the offer of working for the Gestapo. Between 1938 and 1945, 'at a cautious estimate between four and six hundred informants worked for the Vienna Gestapo'.[10]

For members of the active political resistance, the refusal to accept the option of spying for the Gestapo was usually tantamount to a death sentence – through the consequences of torture, the deadly chicanery of a concentration camp, or the guillotine of Nazi justice. Those who accepted the offer could hope at least for a postponement of this prospect, the dropping of criminal charges or release from a concentration camp or Gestapo detention.

The small number of Jews who worked as Gestapo informants did not have any special status – as 'honorary Aryans', so to speak – that would have exempted them from the provisions of the Nuremberg Laws. They merely received 'temporary protection as long as the Gestapo required their services'.[11] The story of Rudolf Klinger, the most important Jewish informant of the Vienna Gestapo, will be narrated in connection with the betrayal of the resistance group around Kurt and Ella Lingens.[12]

What motivated those informants, estimated by Schafranek as numbering around one-third of the total, who worked for the Gestapo despite their lives not being in danger? In his statement before the Belgrade military tribunal in 1947,[13] Lambert Leutgeb confirmed that a large number of people volunteered their services to the Gestapo for reasons other than the threat of violence. In only a few cases were they likely to have been prompted by support for the Nazi ideology. More commonly, there was a material incentive and also a desire for recognition that tempted them to enter into their dangerous dependence on the Gestapo. Leutgeb mentions among his informants: a priest, who gained access to secret directives issued by the offices of the Archbishop of Vienna; a doctor of philosophy, who was to spy on monarchist resistance groups in aristocratic circles and among the high clergy; and two women 'without a profession', who spied in the Grand Hotel in Vienna and the casino in Baden.

Among the fifty-nine Gestapo informants described, often in detail, by Leutgeb, there were eighteen workers who had been arrested by the Gestapo on account of their contacts with the KPÖ or the former Schutzbund, two of whom were also members of the political resistance. Of the other forty-one, it is unlikely for the most part that the Gestapo was obliged to use violence to persuade them to become informants. Even if Leutgeb's list is not representative of the entire Gestapo informant network in Vienna, it is useful to examine it as a basis for discussion of the relationship between coerced and voluntary recruitment.

Research on this subject suffers, however, from a 'considerable dearth of sources',[14] not least for internal Gestapo reasons. Informants could not testify against their victims in court, as the Gestapo would then have 'burned' their informants, not only breaking their cover but also endangering their lives; instead, just the interrogation reports were presented in evidence. Moreover, pursuant to the decree of the Reich ministry of the interior of 12 October 1944 on the 'destruction of official documents', the Gestapo managed practically everywhere to cover up its paper trail. In Vienna, the files were first burned 'in the boilers at Morzinplatz' and then, after the Gestapo headquarters were damaged in an air raid in March 1945, in the 'light well of the building at Riemergasse 7'.[15]

With regard to the incriminating and fraught issue of informants, Mallmann also rightly asserts that post-war resistance research, with its 'emotional projection of goodness onto its subjects', tended to 'minimize … the phenomenon'.[16] The idea that many former opponents of the Nazi regime had become agents and spies of the regime, even if in most cases it was under threats to their existence, was simply too embarrassing.

Two separate files were established to hide the identity of the informants, also initially from competing intelligence services. One was kept only by the intelligence section, and contained personal details and identification records, information about political and professional background, nature and circumstances of recruitment, area of work as agents, and finally a 'peer assessment' of 'efficiency' and motivation. The second file contained index cards with the code names of the informants to be used in any correspondence. Complete information about a particular informant could thus only be obtained by consulting both files: 'As these dossiers rarely survived, the standard practice of encryption means that historians know only of the existence, for example of "V72", but nothing of the person's identity that would give an idea of their motivation or position'.[17]

In view of the dearth of source material in this highly secret area of the Gestapo's work, Leutgeb's interrogation protocol, discovered in 2011 by Thomas Mang in the Archive of the Republic of Slovenia, gives surprising insights, and reveals that the Vienna Gestapo kept meticulous detail in the personal records on its informants. Above all, Leutgeb's statements provide revealing information about the cover names, personal details, origins, recruitment and activities of the informants in his section. The undated fifty-three-page protocol, the first eighteen pages of which are signed by Leutgeb, no doubt came about in connection with his extradition to Yugoslavia by the Soviet Union. Cézanne-Thauss states that Leutgeb was arrested in 1946 by the Soviet military authorities. In the same year, the Austrian authorities instigated criminal proceedings, which were suspended on 1 July 1947 with Leutgeb's extradition. He was charged by the Belgrade military tribunal with 'activities against Yugoslav resistance groups on the territory of former Austria [and], according to unconfirmed reports, ... [was] sentenced in November 1948 to ten years' imprisonment'. He was deported four years later to Austria, and was no longer prosecuted there.[18]

Among the fifty-nine informants named by Leutgeb, there were eighteen workers, eleven civil servants, eight self-employed persons and professionals, seven middle- and high-level salaried workers, six members of the intelligence section, four only indicated as members of the KPÖ, two women without details of their profession, a student, a 'countess', and a 'Russian guards officer'. Like practically all previous information about Gestapo informants in Vienna, these details also come from post-war court records – when the informants themselves were charged or testifying as witnesses. But no one had more detailed inside knowledge of the workings of the intelligence section and the informant network than the section head Lambert Leutgeb. As he was 'directly subordinate to the Gestapo head [Huber]',[19] he effectively had the status of a head of department.

With few exceptions, his statements about the fifty-nine informants are neither incriminating nor exonerating, in the style of an objective internal peer assessment. He does, however, praise Otto Hartmann, because he produced 'good and nice information', and levels criticism at Michael Bankovic, 'because there was the danger that he was also working for the enemy'. 'Nice information' (*schöne Meldungen*) was probably the normal expression used in Gestapo circles, but it might also have been chosen deliberately by Leutgeb when questioned so as to minimize the significance of the operations. In fact, this 'nice information' made critical contributions to the elimination of entire resistance groups and to the deaths of many individuals.

In his statements about the brothers Leopold and Josef Koutny – workers arrested by the Gestapo as members of the KPÖ – Leutgeb says they could be 'recruited' ('geworben') or 'acquired' ('gewonnen') because they could otherwise have expected 'a very heavy sentence' from the VGH. It was 'only after three or four months' that they were both 'passed on to the intelligence services for further handling'. Here, too, Leutgeb is evidently using a rhetorical tone to conceal his recruitment methods. In the 'three to four months' they were almost certainly subjected to 'enhanced interrogation', threats and reprisals – until they could be 'acquired' for the intelligence section. It is clear that Leutgeb's statements about informants given to the tribunal in Belgrade were an attempt to play down his own role, or to trivialize it as the professional exercise of 'normal intelligence work'.

The following summarizes Leutgeb's statements about the 'most successful' Gestapo informant, Kurt Koppel (direct quotes in inverted commas):[20] Kurt Koppel, cover name Konrad Hans Klaser: '172 cm tall, slim, dark, thick, wavy hair, wears thick glasses, has an eye disease. He looks Jewish. He is a first-degree Jewish Mischling'. Employed by the Austrian federal police in 1936 as an informant against the young Communists; in Spain in 1938 on behalf of the KPÖ 'to participate in the fight against Franco'; in 1939 as a stateless person applied for a passport at the German consulate general in Paris and presented 'a report on perceptions'; after examination by the Gestapa, assigned to the Vienna Gestapo; seconded in autumn 1940 by the Reich security main office (RSHA) for an operation in Bratislava (Pressburg); in mid-1941 to Zagreb (Agram); in 1944 as an informant for the RSHA, Department VI E, in Vienna. 'After Vienna was cleared out, he left with the RSHA VI E … As I heard by chance at the Gestapo in Vienna … he headed for Spain.'

Cell Spies – Informants Disguised as Fellow-Sufferers

One of the few well-documented Vienna Gestapo informants is the Communist resistance fighter Karl Zwifelhofer. He is a prime example of the Gestapo method of breaking the physical and mental resistance of an enemy of the regime through enormous pressure, and forcing him to become an informant. Zwifelhofer, a Communist since 1920, attended the Lenin School in Moscow, and from 1933–34 was a member of the highest KPÖ executive bodies – that is, the central committee and Politbüro. After being held at Wöllersdorf internment camp in 1934 for his work in the KPÖ, he joined the International Brigade in the Spanish Civil War at the end of 1936, and with the rank of lieutenant advanced to become head of the Austrian cadre office in Albacete. After living in Paris, Zwifelhofer returned illegally to Vienna in 1940 and participated in the development of a KPÖ underground organization. Having already attracted the Gestapo's attention in December 1938 as a member of the 'Communist movement' with the code names Georg Mott and Faber,[21] he was arrested with his brother Leopold Zwifelhofer on 5 April 1941. Like his brother, he was sentenced to death for 'preparation for high treason', the sentence being confirmed as a matter of course by Reich minister of justice Otto Georg Thierack, and 'executioner Reichhart' was commissioned to carry out the sentence. At this very late moment, however, the Vienna Gestapo sent a request to Berlin for 'a delay in the performance of the execution' to enable Zwifelhofer to be interrogated, claiming that it was interested in his 'participation in a meeting of the Comintern secretariat in Moscow … and the timetable of the Lenin School'. The Gestapo used the anticipation of imminent execution experienced by the 'returned' KPÖ functionary to 'turn' him. He was to 'spy on newly arrived arrestees in the cells of the police prison on Elisabethpromenade, and through the promise of favourable treatment to break their spirit of resistance so that they would be willing to confess to anything'.

Zwifelhofer was an example of a special kind of informant, the 'cell spy' (*Zellenspitzel*). He pretended to be a particularly 'experienced' prisoner and attempted to build up a relationship of trust with his fellow-prisoners. The plight of the victims, who were thankful for any kind of attention, was thus exploited in a particularly devious manner. Zwifelhofer's performance as a cell spy was so 'successful' that the Vienna Gestapo once again turned to Berlin. Karl Ebner informed the RSHA by telegram that Zwifelhofer's information about the Comintern and Lenin School had been verified, and that Ebner proposed 'to arrange with the senior Reich prosecutor (Oberreichsanwalt) at the VGH that Zwifelhofer's execution be stayed for an indefinite time, and that Zwifelhofer himself be transferred provisionally to a concentration camp until further instruction from this office'.[22]

The lengths the Gestapo went to in procuring Zwifelhofer's services by having him spared execution are understandable considering the results the venture brought. As a cell spy, he betrayed no fewer than seventy-three interned Communist resistance fighters. As with other 'turned' Communist functionaries, the prospect of a pardon or at least a postponement of execution was the decisive motive for Zwifelhofer to become a cell spy and betray his former fellow combatants. Zwifelhofer's death sentence was ultimately commuted to life imprisonment.[23] 'Tribute' was paid to Zwifelhofer's conversion from top Communist functionary to turncoat in a brochure of the Reich propaganda office of the NSDAP in Vienna.[24]

Kurt Koppel, mentioned earlier, was also employed for a short time as a cell spy but was discovered by his 'fellow detainees'. After the message 'Ossi is a spy' had been found on cell walls and plates at the police prison on Elisabethpromenade (Rossauer Lände), he was no use any more as a prison spy and had to be removed from Vienna.

After the annexation of Austria, Friedrich Schwager, who had already been arrested for illegal KPÖ activity in 1936, became active again in Communist resistance groups and was arrested in 1941. He escaped from his prison cell but was recaptured and sentenced to death. As a Gestapo informant, he now spied on comrades interned in Viennese prisons. While he himself survived Mittelbau-Dora concentration camp, the confectioner's assistant Georg Strecha, who had only supported Schwager by providing him with money and food, was sentenced to death by the VGH for 'preparation for high treason', and executed on 21 November 1944 at the Vienna LG. The railway post office clerk Josef Blaschek, who had helped Schwager when he had been on the run, suffered the same fate on 30 August 1944. The KPÖ functionary Josef Meisel, who returned from French exile to work in the Austrian resistance, only to be arrested in May

1943 by the Vienna Gestapo and brutally maltreated to force a confession, described in his autobiography how Schwager had asked him to turn informant while he was interned by the Gestapo. After 1945, Schwager became an SED functionary in East Germany, which did not abandon him in spite of vehement protests by the KPÖ.[25]

Other important KPÖ functionaries, such as Julius Günser and Myron Pasicznyk, made full confessions, on the basis of which many of their former fellow combatants were arrested by the Gestapo.[26] However, their confessions were not rewarded by the Gestapo. The student Julius Günser, who had also fought in Spain and who had returned to Austria from France in late 1942 with Meisel and other members of the Communist resistance, perished at Mauthausen on 15 February 1945; Myron Pasicznyk was transferred to Gross-Rosen concentration camp on 16 January 1942 and from there to Dachau, where he died on 22 October 1943.[27]

Parachute Agents and 'Radio Games'

Allied agents who had parachuted over their operating area were usually arrested directly on landing, or after a period of observation with their contacts.[28] According to an order by Heydrich, they were to be 'handcuffed whenever possible immediately after arrest'. They were also to be 'gagged and … their bodies, clothes and bags searched in every case, because experience has shown that the captured parachutist is under instructions to commit suicide with a handgun or cyanide pills'.[29]

After they had fallen into the hands of the Gestapo, the parachute agents were forced to engage in 'radio games' (*Funkspiele*) – that is, to provide their home intelligence services with disinformation, mostly regarding troop movements, by sending fake messages. Johann Sanitzer,[30] of the Vienna Gestapo's Section IV A 2 (Aiding the enemy, sabotage; later IV 2), was adept at 'turning' detainees with an extremely effective mixture of brutality and subtlety, and claimed that no one was more successful than he was with 'radio games'. In 1948 he wrote in prison that he was 'still proud … of, at Christmas 1944, having been responsible for a quarter of the radio communications with the enemy, and of being far ahead of all other departments in Germany and the occupied territories'.

Sanitzer justified his routine use of torture by arguing that 'they were spies, who passed on information to a radio operator in safe hiding. To rapidly disable this radio operator, who controlled air raids, I had to obtain confessions in this way to prevent the accomplice from causing further harm. I therefore had no qualms about making one individual suffer to reduce the suffering of a city with a million inhabitants'.[31] Karl Ebner, the Vienna Gestapo deputy head, confirmed in testimony that Sanitzer had used torture on several occasions: 'In his section it was routine. ... I believe he needed six, twelve, twenty-four strokes to achieve the desired outcome'.[32]

Not only a large number of Communist activists coming from the Soviet Union, usually dropped by British aircraft, but also agents and parachutists from the Western Allies and their contacts and supporters in Austria fell victim to Sanitzer. The former Social Democrat member of the Lower Austrian provincial parliament (Landtag) Heinrich Widmayer was the liaison person with the Austrian section of the British wartime secret service, SOE. His contact, Alexander Hochleitner, turned out to be a double agent working for Sanitzer. On 23 October 1944, Widmayer and the courier Maria Matzner, a Socialist from Graz, were arrested and badly beaten up by the Gestapo. Widmayer survived in the Small Fortress Gestapo prison in Theresienstadt.[33]

The Communist resistance fighter Josef Sasso, recruited by the French secret service (probably the Direction générale des études et recherches, DGER) from a POW camp, was parachuted into Austria as a spy with Karl Brezina from an RAF aircraft at the end of 1944. On his arrest by Vienna Gestapo officials at his parents' home, shooting broke out in which the Gestapo man Johann Potzinger was shot dead. Sasso was then badly maltreated, but the 'radio game' instigated by Sanitzer (in order to have further agents sent, and disinformation spread) with the French secret service was unsuccessful. Sasso was transferred to a concentration camp for 'liquidation', but, like Widmayer, he survived in the Small Fortress Gestapo prison in Theresienstadt.[34]

Gestapo head Franz Josef Huber, 'who was very interested in Sanitzer's work', was effectively the department head of this section, alongside or above the officially appointed Othmar Trenker. He wanted to acquire expert knowledge because he suspected, not unjustifiably, that the victorious (Western) Allies would be interested in intelligence information, above all in connection with the USSR. As part of this 'reinsurance', Huber ordered 'turned' Allied agents to be given preferential treatment, and allowed them to use the public air raid shelter at the church of St Ruprecht, whereas 'the detainees in the Gestapo prison were ordered by Huber to remain locked up during air raids'.[35] When Morzinplatz was hit by a bomb, making it impossible to operate 'radio games' from there, they were continued in the villa belonging to the interned resistance fighter Franz Josef Messner at Hasenauerstrasse 61 in Währing (18th district), not far from Huber's official residence. Sanitzer, who was also thinking of 'reinsurance', noted on the detainee transport list: 'For special use and therefore to be offered every facility'. According to Sanitzer, the detainees were neither executed 'as ordered by Berlin, nor did I have them transferred to concentration camps like the detainees in the house prison'.[36] The same cannot be said of parachute agents who were of no further use, such as Theodor Rakwetz and his son of the same name, as well as numerous individuals who helped and billeted them, who were transferred by Sanitzer to concentration camps, where most of them perished.[37]

Notes

1. *Der Nürnberger Prozess*, Digitale Bibliothek, vol. 20, 25496–7 (*The Nuremberg Trials*, vol. 20, 191st day, 31 July 1946), statement by Werner Best.
2. For details, see Schafranek, *Widerstand und Verrat* (2017); also Albu/Weisz, 'Spitzel und Spitzelwesen', 169–208; Schafranek, 'V-Leute und "Verräter"', 300–49.
3. Schafranek, *Widerstand und Verrat* (2017), 422–23; DÖW, *Widerstand Wien*, vol. 2, 107; Neugebauer, *Austrian Resistance*, 87ff.
4. Ibid., 151.
5. [Hartmann war in den monarchistischen Gruppen der österreichischen Freiheitsbewegung verankert und brachte von dort sehr gute und schöne Meldungen. Auf Grund dieser Meldungen konnte auch in einigen Fällen erfolgreich eingeschritten werden.] Archive of the Republic of Slovenia, Ljubljana, AS 1931/846, 104 73/ZA, 163, undated interrogation report.
6. Ibid., AS 1931/809, 104-72/ZA, 677.
7. Mallmann, 'Die V-Leute der Gestapo', 271.
8. Schafranek, *Widerstand und Verrat* (2017); Albu/Weisz, 'Spitzel und Spitzelwesen', 169–208; Cézanne-Thauss, 'Lambert Leutgeb'.
9. Schafranek, 'Drei Gestapo-Spitzel', 274.
10. Albu/Weisz, 'Spitzel und Spitzelwesen', 175.
11. Steiner/von Cornberg, 'Willkür in der Willkür', 162.
12. See the section 'Repression of Persons Rendering Assistance to Jews' in Chapter 13.
13. Archive of the Republic of Slovenia, AS 1931/846, 104-72 ZA, 113–65.
14. Mallmann, 'Die V-Leute der Gestapo', 273.
15. ZStL 110 AR-Z 4/1961, sheet 26, report from district criminal inspector Josef Mikusch to the Vienna police headquarters (Polizeidirektion Wien), 10 Oct 1945.
16. Mallmann, 'Die V-Leute der Gestapo', 274.
17. Ibid.
18. Cézanne-Thauss, 'Lambert Leutgeb', 126ff.
19. Archive of the Republic of Slovenia, Ljubljana, AS 1931/808, 104-72/ZA, 451.
20. DÖW 51 840 (copy of entire document); for details, see Mang, 'Er brachte sehr gute und schöne Nachrichten', 165–94.
21. BA Berlin, R 58/1081, vol. 2, Nov–Dec 1938, Fiche 2, Vienna Gestapo daily report no. 1 of 1–2 Dec 1938.
22. Schafranek, 'V-Leute und "Verräter"', 336–37.
23. After the war, Karl Zwifelhofer fled to the US occupation zone but was soon arrested and handed over to the state police in Vienna, where he died. His brother Leopold Zwifelhofer, who had also agreed to work as a Gestapo informant, died in April 1945.
24. Geppert, *Im Namen des Volkes*.
25. Meisel, *'Jetzt haben wir Ihnen, Meisel!'*, 118ff.; www.doew.at/erinnern/personendatenbanken/gestapo-opfer (last accessed on 16 Aug 2016).
26. Meisel, *'Jetzt haben wir Ihnen, Meisel!'*, 129ff.; DÖW 8232.
27. http://www.doew.at/erinnern/biographien/spanienarchiv-online/spanienfreiwillige-g/guenser-julius; https://nachkriegsjustiz.at/aktuell/pasicznyk.html (both last accessed on 15 Aug 2016).
28. DÖW, *Widerstand Wien*, vol. 2, 436; WStLA, Vienna LG, Vg 11c 586/47, protocol of the questioning of Johann Sanitzer before Salzburg district court, 15 Jun 1956.
29. BA Berlin, R58, 9803, express letter from Heydrich regarding the 'deactivation of parachute agents, terrorists and saboteurs', 6 Jun 1942.
30. For details on Sanitzer, see also chapters 7 and 19.

31. WStLA, Vienna LG, Vg 2b Vr 586/47, questioning of Johann Sanitzer, 14 Oct 1946.
32. ZStL 110 AR-Z 4/1961 II, sheets 214–15, testimony of Ebner in the investigation of Johann Sanitzer.
33. Pirker, *Subversion deutscher Herrschaft*, 266 ff.
34. Detailed interrogation report of Johann Sanitzer, Gestapo, Vienna, Section IV 2, July 1945. SCI Unit A, Salzburg, Austria, Headquarters Co. 'A', 2677 Regiment, Office of Strategic Services, The NARA, KV2/2656. A copy of this document was made available to us by Peter Pirker; see also Freihammer, 'Dem NS-Regime nicht untergeordnet'.
35. WStLA, Vienna LG, Vg 2b Vr 586/47, questioning of Johann Sanitzer, 14 Oct 1946.
36. Mang, *'Gestapo-Leitstelle Wien'*, 172ff.
37. See the section 'Murders, Suicides and Executions' in Chapter 6.

Chapter 8

DENUNCIATIONS

Status in Academic Research

The 'success' of the Gestapo was based in many areas on reports and denunciations that came either from other police units and Nazi bodies or, to a large extent, from individual citizens. Denunciation in the Nazi era has become a high-profile issue in academic research, as far-reaching conclusions can be drawn from it about the overall character of the Nazi regime. The sociologist Karl-Heinz Reuband has observed a paradigm shift 'that emphasizes the role of active collaboration by the public in maintaining totalitarian political systems'.[1] The Canadian historian Robert Gellately coined the term 'self-policing society' as a characteristic feature of the Nazi state. With reference to this, Gerhard Paul and Klaus-Michael Mallmann, editors and authors of several seminal works on the history of the Gestapo, talk of 'society engaging in auto-surveillance' ('gesellschaftliche Selbstüberwachung') and a 'denunciation society'.[2]

By contrast, Bernward Dörner of the Center for Research on Antisemitism in Berlin claims that the abundance of denunciations in Gestapo and judicial files has led to an overemphasis of this phenomenon, giving the impression that 'the population consisted almost entirely of denouncers'. He argues that there was probably an extremely large proportion of offences that went unreported, and that 'only a minority of the population were willing to report "insidious utterances"'.[3] Carsten Dams and Michael Stolle even reckon that 'most illegal remarks' were not reported, and that the actual number of offences was 'probably several hundred times higher than all the denunciations combined'.[4] The view of the British historian Richard J. Evans is just as striking: 'Denunciation was the exception, not the rule, as far as the behaviour of the vast majority of Germans was concerned'.[5]

In the light of our decades of research into the suppression of resistance fighters and opponents of the Nazi regime, the critique of the 'Gestapo myth'[6] by Gellately, Paul, Mallmann and other authors needs to be partially relativized, at least as far as it applies to the Vienna Gestapo, because it tends to underestimate the Gestapo. It is true that with its relatively small infrastructure, compared with the Stasi in the GDR, the Gestapo never achieved the omnipotence or omnipresence that were attributed to it by the regime and its opponents, and which formed the basis for the 'myth'. Without the collaboration of 'Partei- und Volksgenossen' (comrades from party and Volk), the Gestapo could not have worked as successfully or as effectively as it did. However, the denunciations were confined essentially to individual resistance, 'insidious utterances' and 'undermining military morale', 'radio crime', and economic crimes and violations of the anti-Jewish regulations. In Austria at least, they were almost never in connection with organized political resistance. The Communist works groups were not denounced (as would have been quite feasible) by fellow-workers, and the same was true of the Catholic-conservative and legitimist resistance and rural resistance.[7] The combating and extensive elimination of the organized resistance were not based on reports from the population or internal betrayal. On the contrary, the 'success' of the Gestapo was due to the systematic use of informants ('V-Leute'), the extraction of confessions by force, and to other police methods characteristic of dictatorships. In this area the Gestapo was by no means merely 'reactive', operating on the basis of denunciations and reports, but proactive in its identification and elimination of political opponents of the Nazi regime.[8]

Particularly during the war, the Gestapo gave absolute priority to combating organized resistance, partisans and enemy agents, and non-compliant foreign forced labourers. General surveillance of the population for utterances critical of the regime, listening to forbidden broadcasts or infringements of Nazi regulations would have overstretched its resources; in that area, the Gestapo was reliant to a large extent on denunciations. The dense network of Nazi organizations – NSDAP, SA, SS, SD, DAF, NSBO (NS factories organization) and others – throughout the entire Reich territory, including Austria, and present in all classes of the population was of great assistance to the Gestapo.[9] Without their aid, large-scale prosecution of these infringements of the Nazi norms would have been impossible. In our view, however, it would be an exaggeration to claim that denunciations were absolutely necessary to shore up the regime's authority. The Nazi regime would not have been shaken if critical utterances (for example, jokes about Hitler or other Nazi leaders) or listening to foreign broadcasts had been tolerated more, and prosecuted less intensively and with less severity. At the same time, the denunciations and resultant prosecution had a deterrent and intimidating effect, and resulted in a kind of 'public self-censorship'.[10]

The Gestapo and Denunciations

The well-known saying 'Der größte Lump im ganzen Land, das ist und bleibt der Denunziant' (roughly, 'there is nothing worse than a denouncer'), attributed to the author of the German national anthem Hoffmann von Fallersleben, meant that even during the Nazi era denouncers were not well thought of. Even the Nazi authorities had an ambivalent view of denunciation; to paraphrase the saying Plutarch attributed to Emperor Augustus, they loved treachery but not the traitor. On the one hand, they needed voluntary reports so as to uncover opponents of the Nazis, but on the other they did not wish to encourage the many privately motivated denunciations, because they clogged up the system unnecessarily.[11] Deputy Gestapo head Karl Ebner is recorded as having said to his wife and daughter: 'The worst thing about Vienna was the ratting'.[12] To control the flood of denunciations, Sipo chief Heydrich issued a decree on 3 September 1939 stating that 'denouncers who for personal reasons make unjustified or exaggerated reports about their fellow citizens ... are to be suitably dealt with at once, through a strong reprimand or, in particularly malevolent cases, committal to a concentration camp'.[13] In a further decree relating to denunciations in parallel with divorce proceedings, Heydrich instructed the Gestapo offices in 1941 'first to verify "exactly" the motive behind the report and ... before taking down an affidavit to ask whether divorce proceedings have been instigated or are planned'.[14] As Bernward Dörner notes, 'the first task facing the Gestapo in cases of "insidious utterances" was to identify groundless and irrelevant reports, and to concentrate on the prosecution of "serious cases"'.[15]

Alongside infringements of the anti-Jewish laws, the most common denunciations concerned anti-regime statements (dealt with as 'insidious utterances' or 'undermining military morale') and listening to foreign broadcasts ('radio crime').[16] The Gestapo officials responsible could exercise considerable discretion: they could content themselves with a reprimand, but they could also report cases to a special court (Sondergericht, SG) or the VGH, or apply for 'protective custody' and internment in a concentration camp. Although there was an agreement between the Gestapa, the 'Führer's chancellery' and the Reich ministry of justice that the results of investigations into 'insidious utterances' were to be referred to the judiciary – in the case of Vienna to the chief public prosecutor's office at the Vienna regional court (Landgericht, LG) – the flood of reports after the introduction of the 'Heimtückegesetz' (the law on, among other things, 'insidious utterances') in Austria in 1939 meant that the head of the relevant Vienna Gestapo unit decided at his own discretion which cases were to be reported to the SG, which were to be dismissed for lack of 'subversive relevance', and which were to be punished by a fine, reprimand or placing in 'protective custody' in a concentration camp. The last-mentioned was ordered when the individual already had an incriminating political record or was related to a Jew.[17] In any event, after acquittal or dismissal of the case, detainees were remanded to the Gestapo, which made the final decision on the person's fate. As all reports of 'political offences' ended up with the Gestapo and were processed and prejudged by it, it had priority in determining the course of 'justice' and was the 'decisive investigating instance'.[18] Contrary to the rule of law, by which the judiciary controls the administration and the police, the Gestapo had more power than the judiciary.[19]

Within the Vienna Gestapo, Unit II C 2 (1938–42), Section IV A 3 (1942–44) and Unit IV 1 b (1944–45) were responsible for dealing with anti-regime statements, the latter also covering conservative opposition and various resistance groups. These units were headed by Regierungsrat Hubert Kern (1938–39), Polizeisekretär Oskar Schmidt (until 1942), Regierungsrat Josef Auinger (1942) and Kriminalrat Christian Nicoll (from 1942). The fact that the 'insidious utterances' unit in the Vienna Gestapo was not considered important can be seen from the fact that in spite of the number of files it dealt with, it had a staff of only eight or nine.[20]

The much less common offence of 'radio crime' (listening to foreign broadcasts, forbidden after October 1939) was dealt with by units II A 1, IV A 1 (1942–44) and IV 1 a (from 1944). Section II A was headed from 1939 to 1944 by Othmar Trnka (Trenker). He stated in court that only three officials dealt with the investigation of radio offences. The Gestapo was therefore particularly reliant on denunciations in this area.[21]

Although a large number of people were arrested by the Vienna Gestapo on the basis of denunciations, the figure was still lower than those established for German cities. In his study of the Gestapo in Krefeld, Eric A. Johnson estimated that around 1 to 2 per cent of the adult population of that city were denouncers.[22] By this reckoning, there should have been between 36,000 and 72,000 denouncers within the jurisdiction of the Vienna Gestapo, which was not the case. Winfried Garscha, head of the Austrian research agency for postwar justice (Forschungsstelle Nachkriegsjustiz), has determined that the Volksgericht in Vienna investigated 10,800 people – 7,800 men and 3,000 women – for the crime of denunciation (Section 7, War Criminals Act (KVG)).[23] This figure corresponds more or less to the 7,000 to 8,000 denunciation proceedings identified by Franz Weisz from the VG records.[24] The leading Gestapo official Othmar Trenker stated to the Vienna VG that there were 3,000 denunciations per year, which would make around 13,500 for the years 1940 to 1945.[25] The discrepancy may be explained by the fact that not all denouncers could be prosecuted after 1945. It may also be assumed that not all of the reports received by the Gestapo led to judicial proceedings and sentences, and hence to consequences for the person denounced.

For example, the Catholic priest Josef Christelly from Orth only received an official reprimand after making a reference to the church regulations regarding cremation at the burial of a fallen soldier. As this 'offended some of those present', it was reported to the Gestapo, who however clearly regarded it as an entirely trivial matter.[26]

Denouncers: Motives and Milieus

In view of the divergent interpretations by historians, it is important to identify who the denouncers were and what prompted them. It makes a qualitative difference whether the denouncers represented a cross-section of society, which would indicate general approval of the regime of terror, or whether most of them were members of the NSDAP or Nazi organizations and institutions.

Regarding anti-Jewish denunciations, Vienna Gestapo deputy head Karl Ebner stated after the war that 50 per cent of anti-Jewish reports had come from NSDAP members, 25 per cent from other organizations and 25 per cent from the general public.[27] The historian Heimo Halbrainer from Graz has determined that in Styria 48 per cent of the denouncers were prompted 'primarily by their loyalty to the system', and only 28 per cent were not members of the NSDAP.[28] A similar picture emerges from studies of the Reich-German territories, which indicate that the large majority of denouncers were not mere 'members of the Volk' but 'party comrades' and Nazi sympathizers.

All authorities and NSDAP offices were obliged to report anti-regime statements and communications from the population to the Gestapo. Very few denunciations were made straight to the Gestapo; the vast majority came via block, cell, local group and district leaders of the NSDAP and functionaries in Nazi organizations.[29] 'The widely ramified network of institutions', writes Bernward Dörner, 'thus created a practical structural "denunciation framework" for the public'.[30]

There are several typical examples to illustrate this. On 14 September 1939, in the Ottakring district of Vienna, Theresia P. was listening to a foreign news broadcast. Two NSDAP members, Johann Schneider and Josef Spindelberger, who were patrolling 'by order of local group leader Braunhirschen', heard a radio broadcast in French coming from the apartment and reported it to the local NSDAP group. Theresia P. was arrested by the Gestapo and convicted by the Vienna SG.[31] In another instance, on 16 January 1945, the NSDAP Vienna city councillor Thomas Kozich reported a conversation he had overheard in the

Rathausstüberl restaurant, in which the Burgtheater actor Franz H., his wife Paula and a friend welcomed the Allied air raid on the police and Gestapo headquarters. They were arrested by the Gestapo and sentenced to imprisonment for 'radio crimes' and 'insidious utterances'.[32] The cook Frieda B., an NSDAP member since 1931, felt 'obliged' to report her former employer, among other things for saying that 'our Führer deserves to be strung up'. Finally, Oberregierungsrat Erwin Obenaus, 'with legitimist sympathies and an enemy of the Nazi state', was denounced and then arrested by the Gestapo in late May 1940 for 'listening to foreign broadcasts'; on 14 August 1940 he was sentenced by the Vienna SG to eighteen months' imprisonment.[33]

Gestapo official Heinrich Wohl testified to the VG in Vienna that reports reaching the Gestapo from Nazi offices had highest priority: 'All reports from NSDAP offices had to be dealt with first, otherwise the district [NSDAP district office] would intervene. A large number of reports came via the party'.[34]

The denouncers can be identified because they were generally obliged to testify in the Nazi court hearings and could also be indicted after 1945 by the Austrian judiciary under the War Criminals Act. The motives for denunciation, in many cases by neighbours, were sometimes personal, with divorce, the end of a relationship, dismissal from work and similar grounds often providing the incentive. Other denunciations were simply the result of political spite and Nazi fanaticism. The need to feel important also played a role.[35]

Spontaneous discussions and arguments in taverns, on public transport or in shops sometimes gave rise to denunciations. After the war, Alfred Bodenstein, formerly a Vienna Gestapo official in Unit II A 1 (later Section IV A 1), which dealt with radio crime, stated that written reports 'from all classes of society' mostly had 'spiteful or vengeful motives'.[36] For example, the retired Major Erwin Fürer, a legitimist, was denounced by a woman who had formerly shared his convictions, arrested by the Gestapo in February 1942 and sentenced by the Vienna SG to two years' imprisonment because during a bridge game he had called Hitler the 'greatest traitor in the world'.[37]

The writer Aloisia Helia was arrested by the Gestapo on 27 April 1942 for 'offensive remarks about the Führer' and sentenced on 26 September 1942 to eighteen months' imprisonment for 'an offence under the Heimtückegesetz'. The judgment states that she was denounced by a taxi driver: 'The defendant began to complain, saying literally: "That swine [Hitler] does nothing but complain about the Jews. He's all-powerful, I know, but he's just a stupid decorator's assistant". The witness did not respond to the defendant but drove her to Böcklinstrasse 35 and, after she had got out of the car, called the arrest unit to have her apprehended'.[38]

The tobacconist Gisela Stanicz (also Stanitz) from Eisenstadt was involved in a conversation with a Kriminalsekretär from Eisenstadt border police station sent to spy on her, in which, according to the charge, she made 'subversive utterances': 'You know, the way the National Socialists went after the Jews right after the change, I said to myself, that's not right. That way, Hitler just turns people into animals, and the whole world will turn against us'. Stanicz, who was arrested on 18 August 1941 by the Eisenstadt border police, was convicted under the 'Heimtückegesetz' by the Vienna SG and imprisoned until 2 March 1942.[39]

Without a complete evaluation of the Gestapo daily reports and the records of the Vienna SG, it is not possible to settle the disputed question in research literature as to whether denunciations took place primarily within the milieu of those involved or whether it was vertical, from bottom to top, or whether there were more denunciations in the 'lower class' than in the 'upper class'. Mallmann and Paul speak of a 'lower-class phenomenon'.[40] We are not convinced by Robert Gellately's claim that 'upper-income groups and the nobility for the most part did not need to utilize the police, since they had other and more effective avenues through which to exercise social power'.[41]

In our view, there were denunciations in all classes of society – and members of the nobility, entrepreneurs and large property owners were not immune to it. For example, the concert pianist and composer Ladislaus Döry von Jobbahaza was denounced by an acquaintance, Graf (Count) Paul Seilern, an employee at the NSDAP Gau headquarters, and arrested by the Gestapo on 29 January 1943. Döry, who described himself as a legitimist and had been a member of the Heimwehr and Paneuropa-Union, stated 'repeatedly that "Austria's economic and cultural life is dying" and that Austria could be freed only "by getting rid of Hitler", whom he described as a "power-hungry despot" and an "upstart seeking to plunder countries". When the conversation turned to the Führer, he always called him "swine" or "Schweinehund"'. Ladislaus Döry von Jobbahaza was sentenced to death by the VGH on 7 October 1943 for 'undermining military morale'; the execution was stayed on the intervention of the Hungarian legation, and Döry remained in prison until May 1945.[42]

Dr Josef Riese, Oberstabsarzt (medical staff officer) in the Wehrmacht and senior consultant at the hospital of the Barmherzige Brüder, was arrested by the Vienna Gestapo on 21 January 1944 after being reported by the university professor Bruno Schussnig and subsequently transferred to the Wehrmacht investigation department; he had said in conversation that 'Nazi Germany will collapse in 1944' and that he himself wanted 'to do everything to speed up this collapse'. As a military doctor, it was reported, he had deliberately delayed the healing of wounded soldiers so as to postpone their return to the front.[43]

According to the Gestapo report, Baroness Nadine Drasche-Wartinberg, a landowner from Ebreichsdorf and member of a large industrialist family, responded to the 'Nazi salute' by the Bessarabian Germans quartered in her castle with 'vulgar and insulting words', and was arrested by the Gestapo on 21 January 1944 for 'an offence under the Heimtückegesetz'.[44]

According to the VGH decision, the car dealer Rudolf Kozian, arrested by the Vienna Gestapo on 9 December 1943, had in early November 1943 made 'extremely defeatist comments to the wife of a wounded soldier, insulted the Führer and said that the Viennese didn't care whether they lived under Hitler, Stalin or Churchill, and also attempted to prevent his son from continuing to serve at the front'. He was sentenced to death for 'undermining military morale', and executed at the Vienna LG on 8 November 1944.[45]

Regional studies have refuted the assertion made in some older publications that women made more denunciations than men.[46] Women were underrepresented both as denouncers and defendants in post-war denunciation trials. Most denouncers were men.[47] Winfried Garscha has determined that 72 per cent of the investigations by the Vienna VG involved men.[48] The study of the files of the Vienna SG by Herbert Dohmen and Nina Scholz reveals that 29 per cent of denouncers were women, but they do not exclude the possibility that in some denunciations instigated by women the actual reporting to the Nazi offices was done by their husbands.[49]

Denunciation as Death Sentence

Antisemitism, which was aimed at Jews, Jewish 'Mischlings' and those who helped the Jews, considerably intensified both the nature and the extent of persecution. Directly after the annexation of Austria in March 1938, a wave of antisemitic denunciations occurred, expressed above all in the form of countless reports to Reichskommissar Bürckel.[50] While Jewish 'Mischlings' were still generally put on trial, in accordance with the Thirteenth Regulation to the Reich Citizenship Act of 1 July 1943, 'punishable actions by Jews' were dealt with only by the police.[51] This meant in practice that Jews arrested by the Gestapo for trivial offences such as not wearing the Jewish star were committed to concentration camps or assigned for deportation from Vienna to an extermination camp. Whereas 'insidious utterances' and 'radio crime' by 'Aryan members of the Volk' were punished by prison sentences – provided that there was not an additional political background – the denunciation of Jews usually resulted in death.

For example, Leo Rogowoj from Odessa, who was living in Vienna, was sentenced on the basis of a denunciation in 1941 to fifteen months' imprisonment because he lived together with an 'Aryan' woman ('defilement of the race'). After completing his sentence on 9 August 1942, he was remanded to the Gestapo. He was deported on 5 October 1942 to Maly Trostinec extermination camp and murdered there a few days later.[52]

The radio dealer Oskar Beck from Leopoldstadt (2nd district), a 'first-degree Mischling', attracted attention on account of a relatively harmless utterance about the Nazi terror. In April 1943 he commented to the retired post office worker Therese Draxler in her apartment: 'Do you realize that every woman who goes to work is sending a soldier to his death?' The private denunciation was passed on by the NSDAP block leader to the Rembrandtstrasse NSDAP group, who gave it a racial-political spin: 'Beck is a first-degree Mischling but behaves like a full Jew and is a spiteful opponent of the party and the state'. The denunciation reached the Gestapo via the NSDAP district office II. Beck was arrested and indicted by the chief public prosecutor's office in Vienna. The death sentence pronounced by the VGH for 'undermining military morale' was carried out on 20 October 1943 at the Vienna LG.[53]

This route from the block leader to the NSDAP offices, and from there to the Gestapo and public prosecutor's office, was a common one, not least because many denouncers were hesitant to make a report directly to the Gestapo and preferred to report, often verbally, to an NS block leader. Sometimes, these Nazi functionaries did not pass on reports to the Gestapo but, rather, dealt with such disparagingly termed *Meckerer* (moaners) themselves.[54]

The Jew Stella Kubs, who was arrested by the Gestapo in June 1941 after being denounced, and was sentenced by the Vienna SG to two years' imprisonment for listening to and disseminating foreign radio news, was transferred by order of the Reich ministry of justice in December 1942 to the Gestapo, and murdered at Auschwitz on 31 January 1943.[55]

Possibly the most tragic denunciation took place in a family milieu. Rosa Schwarz had separated from her Jewish husband and started a relationship with an SS man. When her husband refused a divorce, she denounced him in 1943 for earlier KPÖ activity. Michael Schwarz was arrested by the Vienna Gestapo and deported to Auschwitz on 25 June 1943, where he perished on 25 November of that year. Thereafter, the seven children from this 'mixed marriage', who lived not with the 'Aryan' mother but the Jewish father, were deported to Theresienstadt. Rosa Schwarz was sentenced by the Vienna VG to five years' imprisonment for this fateful denunciation within the family.[56]

These denunciations demonstrate that not only the Nazi movement as such but also Nazi terror had a firm footing within the population. NSDAP members in particular – but not exclusively – denounced a large number of people, primarily Jews and those who verbally criticized the regime, with devastating consequences for the victims. However, our research does not indicate that denouncers were in the majority or that there was a 'denunciation society'. In our view it would be an exaggeration and inappropriate, at least for Austria, to conclude from the large number of denunciations that the Nazi regime was not a regime or dictatorship but a 'National Socialist people's state' ('nationalsozialistischer Volksstaat') – as historian Götz Aly called it at the Vienna presentation of the book by Eric A. Johnson on the Gestapo in Krefeld and Cologne.[57]

Notes

1. Reuband, 'Denunziation', 219.
2. Gellately, *The Gestapo*; Paul/Mallmann, *Die Gestapo – Mythos und Realität*, here 9–10, 629ff.
3. Dörner, 'NS-Herrschaft und Denunziation', 61–64; similarly, Reuband, 'Denunziation', 219–34.
4. Dams/Stolle, *The Gestapo*, 81–82 *(Die Gestapo*, 94).
5. Evans, *The Third Reich in Power*, 114.
6. See esp. Gellately, *The Gestapo*; Paul/Mallmann, *Die Gestapo – Mythos und Realität*.
7. See the relevant chapters in Neugebauer, *Austrian Resistance*, based on the examination and evaluation of all the high treason trials relating to Austria by the VGH and Vienna OLG, and all the Vienna Gestapo daily reports from 1938 to 1945. Weisz, 'Gestapo in Österreich', 459, bases his counterclaim – that there were many denunciations of resistance groups – merely on the unsubstantiated written comments of the Gestapo official Karl Ebner in his VG trial.
8. Schafranek, 'V-Leute und "Verräter"', 300–49; details in idem, *Widerstand und Verrat* (2017); see also Chapter 7 above.
9. According to the 1939 census of 6.65 million inhabitants, the NSDAP had around 700,000 members in Austria; to be added to this is a considerable number of members of NSDAP satellite organizations.
10. See also Reuband, 'Denunziation', 232–33.
11. Diewald-Kerkmann, 'Denunziantentum und Gestapo', 302–5; Reuband, 'Denunziation', 223–24 and n. 14.
12. [Das Schlimmste in Wien war das Vernadern.] Interview by Thomas Mang with Ebner's daughter, Ingrid Leierer-Ebner, 5 Mar 1998, quoted in Mang, *'Gestapo-Leitstelle Wien'*, 35. Ebner was himself the victim of a denunciation, and was sentenced to death in 1945 by an SS and police court; see the section 'Reinsurance' in Chapter 5.
13. BA Berlin, R 58/243, 204, decree of chief of the Sipo Heydrich to all Gestapo offices, 3 Sep 1939.
14. BA Berlin, R 58/243, 317–18, decree of chief of the Sipo Heydrich to all Gestapo offices, 24 Feb 1941.
15. Dörner, *'Heimtücke'*, 27.
16. Dörner, 'NS-Herrschaft und Denunziation', 55–69.
17. Weisz, 'Gestapo-Leitstelle Wien', 284ff.
18. Dörner, 'Heimtücke', 328.
19. See Fraenkel, *Der Doppelstaat*, 69.
20. Archive of the Republic of Slovenia, Ljubljana, AS 1931/808, box with GVPs of the Vienna Gestapo 1938–44; see also Weisz, 'Gestapo-Leitstelle Wien', 293ff., 597ff. According to Weisz, the unit responsible for insidious utterances was II C 3 but in the 1942 GVP it was given as II C 2. The different department, section and unit names, generally equivalent to those in the Gestapa and RSHA, changed in the 1942 and 1944 GVPs.
21. Müllner, 'Schwarzhörer und Denunzianten', 49ff., 81–82; WStLA, Vienna LG, Vg 8554/46 (copy: DÖW 19.791/3), statement by Othmar Trenker, 5 Jan 1949.
22. Johnson, *Nazi Terror*, 367 *(Der nationalsozialistische Terror*, 395–96).
23. Garscha, 'Organisatoren und Nutznießer', 114–15.
24. Weisz, 'Gestapo in Österreich', 459.
25. WStLA, Vienna LG, Vg 8554/46, statement by Othmar Trenker, 5 Jan 1949.
26. DÖW reference library, Vienna Gestapo daily report no. 4 of 24–30 Nov 1944.
27. Mang, *'Gestapo-Leitstelle Wien'*, 48.
28. Halbrainer, *Der größte Lump*, esp. 121ff.
29. Dams/Stolle, *The Gestapo*, 76 *(Die Gestapo*, 89).
30. Dörner, *'Heimtücke'*, 322–23.

31. DÖW 15 486, judgment of the Vienna SG against Theresia P., 11 Jan 1940.
32. WStLA, Sondergericht Wien, SHv 8107/47, judgment of 16 Feb 1945, and SHv 8172/47, judgment of 30 Mar 1945. Kozich was sentenced to ten years' imprisonment in 1947 under Section 7 KVG and Section 11 VG.
33. DÖW reference library, Vienna Gestapo daily report no. 1 of 1–3 June 1940; WStLA, SG Vienna, SHv 6557/47, judgment, 14 Aug 1940.
34. WStLA, Vienna LG, Vg 8554/46, testimony of Heinrich Wohl to the Vienna VG, 7 Jan 1949.
35. The doctoral thesis by Christian Müllner contains numerous examples of private denunciations: Müllner, 'Schwarzhörer und Denunzianten', 304ff.
36. DÖW 19795/2, 59, application by Alfred Bodenstein to the state office for internal affairs in Vienna for removal from the Nazi registration list and reinstatement as criminal officer, 14 Jun 1945.
37. www.doew.at/erinnern/personendatenbanken/gestapo-opfer (last accessed on 9 Dec 2016).
38. DÖW 5733c, Vienna Gestapo daily report no. 1 of 1–2 May 1942; www.doew.at/erinnern/personendatenbanken/gestapo-opfer (last accessed on 9 Dec 2016).
39. DÖW 5732d, Vienna Gestapo daily report no. 10 of 22–24 Aug 1941; www.doew.at/erinnern/personendatenbanken/gestapo-opfer (last accessed on 9 Dec 2016).
40. Mallmann/Paul, *Herrschaft und Alltag*, 233.
41. Gellately, *The Gestapo*, 158.
42. DÖW 4197; www.doew.at/erinnern/personendatenbanken/gestapo-opfer (last accessed on 9 Dec 2016); autobiographical manuscript in the archive of the Institut für Zeitgeschichte München, http://archiv.ifz-muenchen.de/vtrech.FAU?sid=2400E90E&dm=1&RO_ZEILE_1=Ladislaus%20D%F6ry (last accessed on 25 May 2021).
43. DÖW 8478, Vienna Gestapo daily report no. 7 of 25–27 January 1944.
44. DÖW reference library, Vienna Gestapo daily report no. 9 of 22–23 January 1941; www.doew.at/erinnern/personendatenbanken/gestapo-opfer (last accessed on 9 Dec 2016).
45. DÖW 4039; www.doew.at/erinnern/personendatenbanken/gestapo-opfer (last accessed on 9 Dec 2016).
46. For example, the East German author Helga Schubert, *Judasfrauen*; also Gerhard Paul, 'Deutschland, deine Denunzianten', in *Die Zeit*, 10 Sep 1993, 56.
47. Dörner, 'NS-Herrschaft und Denunziation', 58–61; Diewald-Kerkmann, 'Denunziantentum und Gestapo', 301–2.
48. Garscha, 'Organisatoren und Nutznießer'.
49. Dohmen/Scholz, *Denunziert*, 220–21.
50. For details, see Safrian/Witek, *'Und keiner war dabei'*.
51. https://de.wikisource.org/wiki/Dreizehnte_Verordnung_zum_Reichsb%C3%BCrgergesetz (last accessed 25 May 2021)
52. http://www.doew.at/personensuche (last accessed on 6 Dec 2016); for details, see Dohmen/Scholz, *Denunziert*, 204–11.
53. DÖW 4168; DÖW, *Widerstand Wien*, vol. 3, 459–60.
54. Reuband, 'Denunziation', 222.
55. DÖW reference library, Vienna Gestapo daily report no. 6 of 13–15 Jun 1941; WStLA, SG Wien, SHv 5950/47; DÖW 20.000/K895, letter from the Vienna police headquarters to the municipal department Magistrats-Abteilung 12 (victim welfare), 23 Sep 1954.
56. For details, see Dohmen/Scholz, *Denunziert*, 9–31; DÖW reference library, Vienna Gestapo daily report no. 6 of 16–19 Apr 1943; http://www.doew.at/personensuche (last accessed on 4 Jan 2017).
57. Johnson, *Nazi Terror*; Götz Aly quoted in Austria Presse Agentur (press agency) press release of 31 Oct 2001 (APA 035 5 II 049 AI); see also Reuband, 'Denunziation', 219–34.

Chapter 9

MASS ARRESTS

The Gestapo by no means restricted its activities to investigating and combating resistance fighters and regime opponents. It also aimed to neutralize potential or supposed political opponents, even if they had not committed 'subversive' acts. This preventive repression applied particularly to functionaries and politicians belonging to former political parties. The first mass arrests took place in March and April 1938, immediately after the annexation, and also involved a large number of Jews; subsequently, the Vienna Gestapo was also instrumental in the committal and deportation of Jews to concentration camps. Likewise, on orders from Berlin, the Gestapo rounded up political opponents before and at the beginning of the war in 1939, and after the assassination attempt on Hitler of 20 July 1944.

Arrests in March/April 1938

The agreement made by Hitler and Schuschnigg in Berchtesgaden on 12 February 1938 to transfer responsibility for security to the (still clandestine) National Socialist Arthur Seyß-Inquart proved particularly fateful for opponents of the Nazis, because all police records of the Schuschnigg regime, particularly those regarding the illegal left, thereby fell into the hands of the new authorities. We know today that lists of Austrians to be arrested already existed in Berlin, drawn up on the basis of information and documents received from illegal NSDAP members in the police in Austria. Such lists were subsequently drawn up for other occupied countries as well.[1]

Moreover, the Gestapo was able to rely from the outset on the support of the Austrian National Socialists, who on their own initiative had already begun to arrest well-known opponents of Nazism all over Austria during the takeover of power in the night of 11/12 March 1938. The 'spontaneous' terror by the local Nazis was in places so massive that it had to be reined in by the political leaders, who wanted a controlled transition. Thus, Sipo and SD chief Heydrich complained to Vienna Gauleiter Bürckel on 17 March 1938 that 'in recent days members of the party have committed large-scale attacks in a completely undisciplined manner'; there was no reason for such 'unauthorized action' because the Gestapo had 'started its work immediately after the troops had entered the country'. Heydrich announced that there would be repercussions 'with the most severe means' and 'merciless rigour' against 'such criminal activities'.[2] In late April 1938, after further arrests and maltreatment of political opponents – in this case members of the Heimwehr – in some Lower Austrian towns (Amstetten, Schwechat, Himberg, Zwölfaxing), the Gestapo intervened and interned some SA members. In a telephone message of 26 April 1938, the Vienna Gestapo instructed all police departments in Lower Austria to immediately report 'unauthorized seizures, excesses and other attacks by the party and its structures on opponents of the NSDAP' and 'to prevent such attacks and excesses in future'.[3] This rigorous approach was aimed not at maintaining law and order but at ensuring the Gestapo's power monopoly and preventing uncontrolled acts by the Nazi movement. Ultimately it was also about safeguarding seized assets for the National Socialist state.

The first mass arrests after the occupation principally affected representatives of the defeated 'Fatherland' regime (corporate state), Communists, Socialists, prominent Nazi critics in cultural and media circles, and Jews. The figures cited for internments within the first six weeks range, entirely plausibly, from 50,000 to 76,000; a precise determination will never be possible, however, because no records exist of many of the arrests by NSDAP, SA, SS and Hitler Youth functionaries, particularly at the local level. Several thousand arrestees remained in detention for a considerable time or were transferred during 1938 to concentration camps, mostly Dachau. The majority were released after a few days or weeks – though many were arrested again later.[4]

By December 1938, 20,793 individuals had been taken into 'protective custody'.[5] These mass detentions were generally accompanied by maltreatment, insults, robbery and other attacks. In some cases, political opponents were murdered or driven to suicide as a result of fear of maltreatment by the Gestapo and committal to a concentration camp. The best-known suicides are those of the writer Egon Friedell, the former Heimwehr leader and federal minister Odo Neustädter-Stürmer, and the former Heimwehr leader and vice-chancellor Major Emil Fey, who had played a questionable role in the putsch of July 1934.

The Vienna Gestapo was directly involved in the death of General Wilhelm Zehner, until 11 March the state secretary of defence, who was particularly hated by the National Socialists on account of his attempts to defend Austria. The general was to be arrested during the night of 10 April 1938 by two Gestapo men, Josef Junker and Johann Mösslacher, but was shot in the attempt. The order to arrest Zehner was apparently telephoned directly by Sipo chief Heydrich, who was in Vienna at the time, and passed on by the Gestapo duty official, Karl Hemetsberger, an illegal Austrian National Socialist who had fled to the German Reich and joined the Gestapo there, to subordinates, also members of the NSDAP and SS. By massively intimidating the witnesses, the Gestapo attempted to pass off the death as suicide, but in view of the unambiguous testimony of Zehner's wife Maria and their maid Stefanie Forster, as well as the unusual personal intervention by Heydrich, his death at the hands of the Gestapo officials is the more plausible version.[6]

All of these measures were intended on the one hand to immediately eliminate the leaders of the political opposition, but also to create a general atmosphere of fear so as to deter any resistance or oppositional acts.

The 'VIP Transport' to Dachau

In comparison with elaborate and drawn-out trials, which in the case of prominent defendants (as in the case of the Reichstag fire trial in 1933) also attracted international interest, the transfers to concentration camps by means of 'protective custody' orders from the Gestapo were simpler, less conspicuous and more rapid. For the vast majority of Austrian arrestees, some of whom were in makeshift prisons such as schools, the nearest concentration camp was Dachau. During 1938, arrestees were also interned in Buchenwald.

The choice of Austrian detainees to be sent on the first transport to Dachau was made by the recently established Vienna Gestapo. There is no report available, but the lists drawn up by Section II D on the allocation of detainees to railway compartments have survived.[7] According to Ludwig Soswinski, who was deported at the time, the allocation was carried out by an illegal Viennese Nazi named Hackl, who had worked as an Oberpolizeirat for the Gestapo in Berlin before 1938.[8]

The transport was organized by Polizeimajor Johann Herzog. According to a report by the Vienna Kripo of 1 April 1938, the deportees were assembled in the police prison on Elisabethpromenade (which gave the prison its nickname, 'Liesl', now Rossauer Lände) and taken in nine closed vehicles to the Westbahnhof, from where the train departed for Dachau. 'The transport', said the report, 'left a marked psychological impression on all security guard officials as a result of the presence in it of their own former supervisors and superiors'.[9]

The make-up of the first transport of Austrians to a concentration camp basically reflected the political affiliations of the (almost exclusively male) detainees at the time: supporters of the Schuschnigg regime, Socialists, Communists and Jews. The Nazi terror in March and April 1938 was directed primarily against Jews and representatives of the corporate state, who were deemed responsible for the persecution of illegal National Socialists between 1933 and 1938, and with whom Austrian Nazis had personal scores to settle. Most of those arrested for political reasons were politicians and functionaries of the Fatherland Front, ministry and police staff, Christian Social trade unionists, monarchists and former Heimwehr leaders. As these measures, and the accompanying propaganda, were also intended to persuade Social Democrat workers to support the Nazi regime, very few Social Democrats or Revolutionary Socialists were arrested at this time. Those who were arrested were all politicians and left-wing regime opponents who before March 1938 had advocated concerted action and armed resistance to countering the Nazi threat.

The 150 detainees in the first Dachau transport can be broken down approximately as follows:[10] sixty-three – so well over a third – were Jews (as defined by the Nuremberg Laws); about a third were supporters of the corporate state (half of them as political functionaries and half as members of the police and judiciary); and around 10 per cent were Socialists and Communists. There are some overlaps in this classification, as some of the political detainees were of Jewish origin, a double stigmatization that normally entailed a greater risk. A particularly large proportion of the Jewish arrestees were politically active journalists, writers and artists. Most of the detainees – all but fifteen – were from Vienna. Roma and other groups were not deported to concentration camps until later.

Among the best-known conservative politicians were: Leopold Figl, director of the Bauernbund; Alfons Gorbach, leader of the Fatherland Front in Styria; Oberst Walter Adam, secretary general of the Fatherland Front; Fritz Bock, the movement's propaganda director, later minister of trade and vice-chancellor; Josef Reither, governor of Lower Austria; Richard Schmitz, mayor of Vienna; Ludwig Draxler, former minister of finance; and Johann Staud, president of the corporate state trade union, who died at Flossenbürg concentration camp in 1939. The members of the police and judiciary included: Baron Emanuel Stillfried, commandant of the internment camp ('Anhaltelager') of Wöllersdorf; Oberst Franz Zelburg, Styrian security director; retired Major General Maximilian Ronge, former head of espionage intelligence; Josef Gerö, public prosecutor and future minister of justice; and Alois Osio, senior regional court judge responsible for several political death sentences against opponents of the regime, who was murdered in January 1939 at Buchenwald. It was no coincidence that the senior civil servant Robert Hecht was one of the first Austrians to perish at Dachau – by suicide on 30 May 1938. He was of Jewish origin and had advised Federal Chancellor Dollfuß on the adoption of an authoritarian course and the establishment of the corporate state in 1933–34. Hecht was also used in Nazi propaganda to present the 'Christian corporate state' as having been 'Jewish'.

The best-known of the Social Democrats were Robert Danneberg, former Vienna city councillor for financial affairs, and Major Alexander (von) Eifler, leader of the Republikanischer Schutzbund. With many other refugees, Danneberg reached the safety of Czechoslovakia by train on the evening of 11 March 1938 but, like all others with an Austrian passport, was sent back to Vienna by the Czech authorities. Danneberg, who for the Nazis was the epitome of the 'Jewish Marxist labour agitator', was transferred from Dachau to Auschwitz during the 'purging' of Jews from German concentration camps in October 1942, and was murdered there in December of that year.

Desider Friedmann (president of the Vienna Jewish community), Jakob Ehrlich (vice-president) and Robert Stricker (former president of the Zionistische Landespartei, and member of the constituting national assembly in 1919/20) were deported to Dachau as leading representatives of Austrian Jewry; none of them survived. Among the Jewish detainees was also the first Austrian to die at Dachau; on 28 April 1938, four weeks after his arrival, the spice importer Johann Kotanyi was driven to commit suicide.[11]

All reports speak of insults and maltreatment by the accompanying SS personnel already during the transport. 'Lazy, Jewified and clericized coffeehouse rabble' is an example of how the Austrians were commonly described by the SS. In what was presumably the first report on the VIP transport, published in Shanghai in 1940, the journalist and writer Mark Siegelberg (listed as Dr Max Siglberg), wrote that 'Austrian gemütlichkeit' vanished when they got to the Westbahnhof, and everything was organized 'with a well-nigh admirable Prussian precision, intensity and speed'. The SS men who welcomed the detainees with such brutality at the railway station were members of the notorious SS-Totenkopfstandarte 1 'Oberbayern', who acted as guards at Dachau. The assaults by the SS continued on the train journey to Dachau, causing the death of one detainee and reaching a first high point on arrival at the concentration camp.[12] The Dachau admission book for 1938 lists almost eight thousand Austrians, most of them Jewish.[13]

A year later, evidently for foreign policy reasons, most Austrian Catholic-conservative detainees were released before the outbreak of war in 1939, albeit subject in many cases to restrictions (such as the obligation to report to the police). Some were arrested later by the Gestapo for resistance activities, and again deported to concentration camps. Jewish detainees were released in 1938–39 if they undertook to leave Germany and could produce visas for recipient countries, which were very difficult to obtain on account of the immigration restrictions in many states.[14]

The VIP transport on 1 April 1938 was merely the prelude to further historically unparalleled repression, deportation and mass murder, particularly of Jews.

For example, two 'Jewish transports', each carrying six hundred, left for Dachau on 31 May and 3 June 1938. Given that the Austrian Jews were very largely concentrated in Vienna, the Vienna Gestapo will have played a significant role in their persecution.

Mass Arrest before the Outbreak of War in 1939

Apart from the arrest of individual resistance fighters and groups as part of the Gestapo's routine work, the large-scale round-up of all those in Gestapo A 1 card indexes throughout the Reich, ordered by Sipo chief Heydrich as early as 27 September 1938,[15] did not take place until just before the outbreak of war. On 22 August 1939, the Vienna Gestapo carried out a sudden 'special action against leading Communists and Revolutionary Socialists' in Vienna and Wiener Neustadt, as Vienna Gestapo head Huber telexed to Gestapo head SS-Oberführer Müller in Berlin two days later. In Vienna alone, sixty-seven Communists and forty-four Revolutionary Socialists (RS) were arrested, and it was announced that 'a larger number of other supporters [Mitbeteiligte]' were to follow. In a further report by Vienna Gestapo Section II A 2 of 3 September 1939, forty-seven arrested RS functionaries, including at least two women, were listed by name.[16] The Gestapo did not normally interrogate or maltreat the political opponents arrested as a precautionary measure during large-scale operations, but simply created identification files and transferred them after a few days to concentration camps, mainly Buchenwald and Ravensbrück.

Among the arrestees was the trade union functionary and future second president of the Nationalrat (parliament) Friedrich Hillegeist, who on 3 March 1938 led a delegation of representatives of the illegal Freie Gewerkschaften (free trade unions), which unsuccessfully offered to cooperate with Federal Chancellor Schuschnigg in combating the Nazi threat. He was interned from 12 March to the end of June 1938 in Vienna, and from 1 September 1939 until the end of April 1940 in Buchenwald; also for another month after the assassination attempt on Hitler in 1944.[17] The leading illegal trade union functionary (and future chamber of labour president) Karl Mantler was interned in Buchenwald on 7 September 1939, where he remained until the camp was liberated on 11 April 1945.[18] He was co-author of the 'Aufruf und Programm der demokratischen Sozialisten vom Buchenwald' (Buchenwald manifesto for peace, freedom and socialism) of 16 April 1945. The illegal metalworkers trade unionist (and future minister for social affairs) Karl Maisel, who was deported to Buchenwald on the same transport, was also interned until 1945, while the RS functionary and future minister of transport Otto Probst was consigned to penal battalion (Strafbataillon) 999 in 1943.[19]

Probably the best-known woman from the group of left-wing activists arrested in August 1939 was the RS functionary (and future long-standing chairperson of the SPÖ women and freedom fighters) Rosa Jochmann, one of the most important female politicians in the history of Austrian social democracy. She worked illegally during the time of the corporate state from 1934 to 1938 as a leading functionary in the RS, was imprisoned several times, and continued her political activity after March 1938 as a member of Sozialistische Arbeiterhilfe (Socialist workers' aid – SAH).

In the reasons (see illustration, under 'Gründe') given in the Gestapa's 'protective custody' order of 14 December 1939 signed by Heydrich, it is stated that she 'endangers the existence and security of Volk and state' in that 'she is urgently suspected of continued Marxist activity today and, if released, gives cause to fear that she will continue her subversive activity'. Rosa Jochmann was transferred in March 1940 to Ravensbrück women's concentration camp, where she was interned until the camp was liberated in 1945, acquiring a legendary reputation as 'block elder' because she stood up boldly for her fellow internees, and received punishments on several occasions for doing so. Two other RS functionaries, Rudolfine Muhr and Helene Potetz, were arrested with her on 22 August 1939 and transferred to Ravensbrück.[20]

Before and after the start of the invasion of the Soviet Union on 22 June 1941, there were no large-scale arrests ordered from Berlin, in spite of which every Vienna Gestapo daily report in June and July of that year mentions the arrest of anything from ten to forty Communist resistance fighters.[21]

Mass Arrest after 20 July 1944: Operation 'Gitter'

As is well known, the putsch by senior Wehrmacht officers and allied civilian opponents of Hitler led by Oberst (Colonel) Claus Schenk von Stauffenberg on 20 July 1944 was initially successful in Paris and Vienna, where Wehrmacht officers cooperating with the conspirators in Berlin were able to take power and imprison some of the local Nazi leadership for a time. Stauffenberg, Hitler assassin and the main organizer of the attempt, had sent a telex on the evening of 20 July ordering the arrest of leading Nazi politicians, SS and Gestapo heads, and concentration camp commandants, and the occupation of Gestapo and SD offices. In Vienna, NSDAP deputy Gauleiter Karl Scharizer, the HSSPF of Military District XVII Rudolf Querner, police chief Leo Gotzmann, Rudolf Mildner (acting Vienna Gestapo head in place of Huber) and deputy head Karl Ebner were disarmed and detained for some hours in the military district headquarters on Stubenring. This was an embarrassing episode for the Vienna SS and Gestapo in that their leading functionaries simply let themselves be arrested, and did not become suspicious or even attempt to oppose the putschists. It was only after it became known that

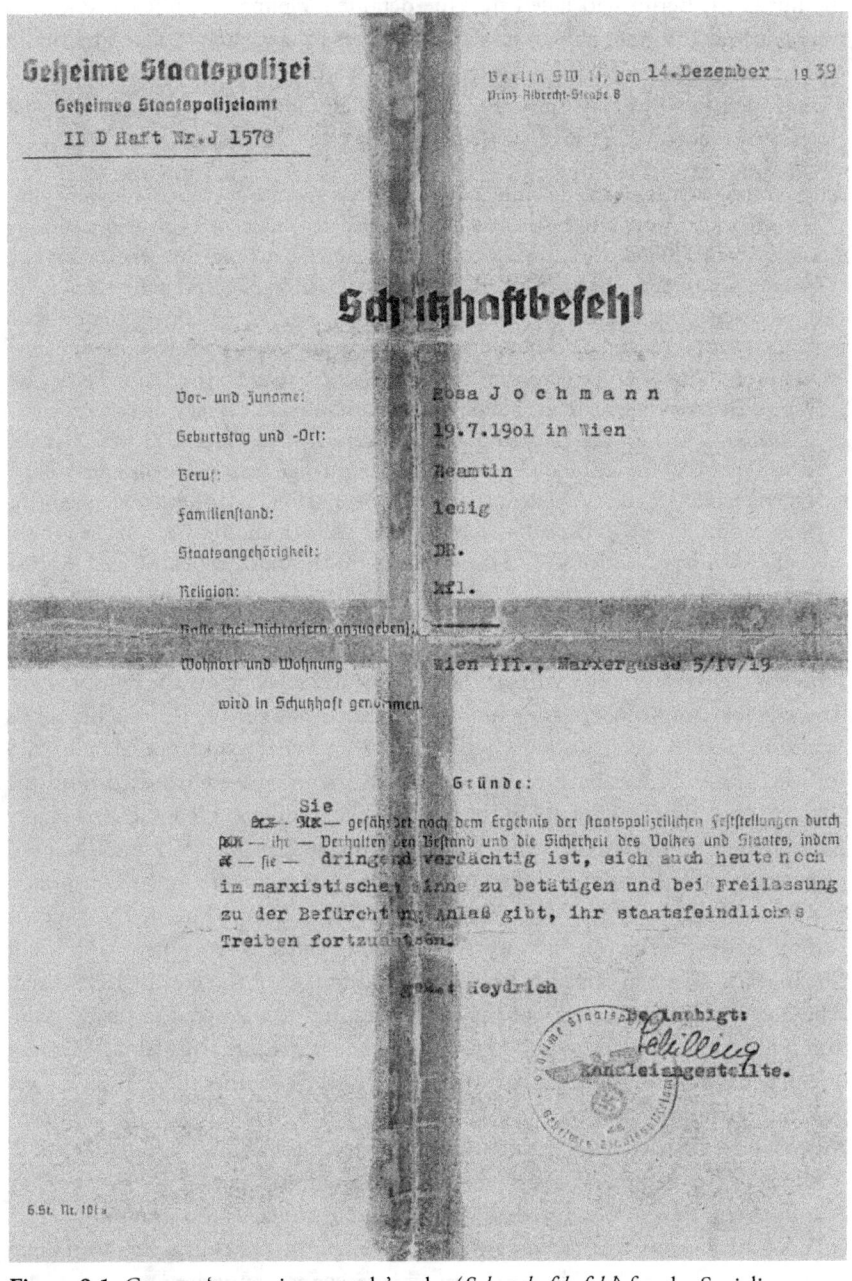

Figure 9.1. Gestapa 'protective custody' order (*Schutzhaftbefehl*) for the Socialist resistance fighter Rosa Jochmann, 14 December 1939. © Dokumentationsarchiv des österreichischen Widerstandes. Used with permission.

the putsch in Berlin had failed that the detained Vienna SS and police leaders were released and were able to take the measures immediately ordered by Berlin against the conspirators.[22] The Gestapo heads, who had been put out of action for a time, attempted to play down and conceal their failure. Thus, Rudolf Mildner stated in a report to the RSHA written directly after the events:

> I went with Dr Ebner to the military headquarters and was taken to a room by some Wehrmacht officers and held there. I attempted to obtain an explanation but my request was refused. My demand to be taken immediately to the general was also refused. I was [ordered] by an Oberstleutnant to name the concentration camps in his inspectorate [sic]. I refused to give any information. After around three-quarters of an hour I was taken to the commanding general's deputy, who explained the situation to me on the basis of the telexes for the Wehrmacht that had arrived from Berlin. We were then allowed to leave the building without restriction. At the same time, deputy Gauleiter Scharizer and Gau propaganda director Alfred Frauenfeld were also detained in the Wehrmacht building on Stubenring, along with SS-Obergruppenführer Querner, HSSPF, and the police president. The entire Sipo and SD were alarmed. The Wehrmacht initially occupied military objects. Esebeck and the head of the general staff in Military District XVII, Oberst i.G. Heinrich Kodré, credibly stated that the orders from Berlin were genuine, and that as soldiers they were obliged to obey them without question.[23]

Hitler and Himmler ordered merciless and brutal revenge on the conspirators. The participating officers – including Oberstleutnant i. G. Robert Bernardis from Linz, and Oberst Rudolf Graf Marogna-Redwitz, who from March 1938 to February 1944 was head of the Abwehr in Vienna – were expelled from the Wehrmacht, convicted by the VGH in show trials, and executed. General Hans-Karl Freiherr von Esebeck, commander of Military District XVII, and the head of general staff Oberst Heinrich Kodré, who, as participants in the conspiracy, had issued Stauffenberg's 'Walkyrie' orders in Vienna, were interned in concentration camps.[24] The Vienna city commanding officer Generalleutnant Adolf Sinzinger, a National Socialist from 1925 and holder of the Gold Party Medal, who had not been initiated into the conspiracy and had ordered the arrest of SS and police functionaries in good faith, was discharged and arrested. The former Vienna mayor and chairman of the SDAP Karl Seitz and the former Lower Austrian governor Josef Reither, who had been designated as 'political officers' for Military District XVII in a telex to Military District XVII headquarters in Vienna by Generaloberst Erich Hoepner, appointed 'commander-in-chief' by Stauffenberg, were also arrested and transferred to concentration camps. Hauptmann Carl Szokoll was the only person involved in the conspiracy to remain undiscovered and to be able to continue his resistance activities.[25]

The elimination of close relatives of the involved resistance fighters threatened by Hitler and Himmler did not take place in such a radical form, but a large number were interned. In particular, the children of the families were taken away and had to be painstakingly searched for after the liberation. Among the Austrian participants affected by this repressive measure was Oberstleutnant Robert Bernardis, whose family were in Linz. Oberst-leutnant in Linz.[26]

The Nazi regime used this resistance activity as a pretext for the long-planned round-up of political opponents, in particular Social Democrats, trade unionists and Communists, but also Christian-conservative politicians. As part of the operation 'Aktion Gitter' (also 'Aktion Gewitter') ordered by Reichsführer-SS Himmler, an estimated five thousand people were arrested all over the Reich on 22 and 23 August 1944, and were mostly transferred to concentration camps. Among many others, the Social Democrat politicians Heinrich Schneidmadl, Oskar Helmer and the future federal presidents Theodor Körner and Adolf Schärf were arrested by the Vienna Gestapo along with Christian Socials such as Lois Weinberger and Felix Hurdes.

As some Gestapo officials were already thinking of their 'reinsurance' (for the time after the looming defeat of the Nazi regime), they refrained from maltreating some detainees whom they hoped could be useful for that purpose. They were correct, as many of these arrestees did testify in their favour after the end of the Nazi regime.[27] Among the Gestapo officials to act in this way were the notoriously brutal thugs Johann Neuffer and Karl Wolf, who showed restraint in their treatment of the well-known Lower Austrian Social Democrat politicians Oskar Helmer and Heinrich Schneidmadl. At the VG trials after 1945, both testified in favour of the Gestapo officials, who as a result received relatively lenient sentences.[28] Adolf Schärf, who was arrested by the Graz Gestapo on 22 August 1944 by order of the Vienna Gestapo, testified in court that he had been treated 'courteously and decently' on the two occasions he was interned.[29] Governor Josef Reither and mayor Karl Seitz also testified that they had been treated 'correctly' by the Gestapo official Adolf Anderle. Anderle, born in 1904, NSDAP member since 1930 and SS-Hauptsturmführer, who as an associate of Sanitzer had maltreated many detainees, received a disproportionately lenient sentence as a result.[30]

The former Social Democratic mayor of Vienna, Karl Seitz, got off relatively lightly despite there being serious charges against him, and the conspirators had in fact planned to make him political officer for Military District XVII. After a period at Ravensbrück he was interned in Plaue, Thuringia. A letter from Reichsführer-SS Himmler to his massage therapist Felix Kersten, who seems to have spoken up for Seitz, indicates that the elderly Social Democrat politician, who was not initiated into the plot, was spared by the VGH in spite of the charges against him.[31]

These individual instances of calculated preferential treatment should not disguise the fact that until May 1945 the Vienna Gestapo continued to persecute political opponents, deserters and defeatists, Jews, forced labourers and other 'enemy groups' with great brutality.

Notes

1. Neugebauer/Steiner, 'Widerstand und Verfolgung in Österreich', 86–108; see, e.g., 'Fahndungsbuch UdSSR 1941' (1941 USSR wanted persons list), http://www.dhm.de/datenbank/dhm.php?seite=5&fld_0=20055750 (last accessed on 23 June 2016).
2. *'Anschluss' 1938*, 440.
3. DÖW E 19 829; see DÖW, *Widerstand Niederösterreich*, vol. 2, 494–506.
4. See Stadler, *Österreich*, 26–27; Schmidl, *Der 'Anschluss' Österreichs*, 232–33; Neugebauer/Steiner, 'Widerstand und Verfolgung', 92ff.
5. NARA, microcopy T 84 R13, 39752, Vienna Gestapo daily report of 10–12 Dec 1938.
6. WStLA, Vienna LG, Vg 6e Vr 56/52 (copy: DÖW 19 877); according to his own statement (ÖStA, AdR, Gau file no. 339.022, Karl Hemetsberger) Hemetsberger had been an NSDAP member since 1932 and had worked for the Gestapa in Berlin until 1938; see also Angetter, *Gott schütze Österreich*; Zehner, 'Mord oder Selbstmord?'.
7. DÖW 532, report of the Vienna Gestapo, 1 Apr 1938.
8. Interview with Ludwig Soswinski, DÖW, collection 'Erzählte Geschichte', no. 19/2; DÖW 532, report of the Vienna Gestapo, 1 Apr 1938.
9. Ibid.
10. The classification is based on verbal and written recollections and many discussions with the detainees Ludwig Soswinski, Erich Fein, Fritz Bock and Hermann Lackner.
11. For details of the sources for these people, see Neugebauer/Schwarz, *Stacheldraht, mit Tod geladen*, 24ff.
12. Ibid., 39ff.
13. DÖW 12 800, copy of Dachau admission book; Ungar, *Die Konzentrationslager*, 191–209.
14. Neugebauer/Schwarz, *Stacheldraht, mit Tod geladen*, 49–50.
15. DÖW 1576, quoted in DÖW, *Widerstand Wien*, vol. 2, 43–44.
16. DÖW 1580, quoted in ibid., 52ff. A page with nine names is missing from the list.
17. www.doew.at/erinnern/personendatenbanken/gestapo-opfer (last accessed on 29 Jun 2016).
18. DÖW 4488, ID for Karl Mantler, issued by the camp commandant and camp committee of the former Buchenwald concentration camp, 13 May 1945; Röll, *Sozialdemokraten im Konzentrationslager Buchenwald*, 323.
19. https://de.wikipedia.org/wiki/Otto_Probst; http://www.dasrotewien.at/probst-otto.html (both last accessed on 26 July 2016).
20. https://de.wikipedia.org/wiki/Rosa_Jochmann; http://www.dasrotewien.at/seite/jochmann-rosa; https://de.wikipedia.org/wiki/Helene_Potetz; https://de.wikipedia.org/wiki/Rudolfine_Muhr; Rosa Jochmann, Rudolfine Muhr, http://www.doew.at/result (all last accessed on 13 June 2021); DÖW 11 052.
21. DÖW reference library, Vienna Gestapo daily reports, June–July 1941.
22. For details, see Jedlicka, *Der 20. Juli 1944*, 54ff.
23. Mang, *Die Unperson*, 165. In the report, Mildner confusingly wrote 'in *seinem* Inspektorat'. He presumably meant either 'my inspectorate', or 'his military district', which were geographically equivalent.
24. See the biographies in the German resistance memorial centre, http://www.gdw-berlin.de/nc/de/vertiefung/biographien/ (last accessed on 23 June 2016).
25. Telex from the head of the Heimatführungsstab Generaloberst (Erich) Hoep(p)ner to Wehrkreiskommando XVII in Vienna regarding the appointment of the 'political officer' and other functionaries, 20 Jul 1944; telex from the head of the RSHA Ernst Kaltenbrunner regarding the arrest of participants in the 20 July plot; both documents quoted in Jedlicka, *20. Juli 1944*, 169–70.

26. https://de.wikipedia.org/wiki/Robert_Bernardis#cite_note-7 (last accessed on 23 June 2016); details in Glaubauf, *Robert Bernardis*.
27. For details, see Mang, *Die Unperson*. See also the section 'Reinsurance' in Chapter 5.
28. Weisz, 'Gestapo-Leitstelle Wien', Notes, 594, n. 94; ibid., 620, n. 141. These estimates by Franz Weisz are based on statements by the accused Gestapo officers to the VG.
29. WStLA, Vienna LG, Vg 4c 3533/47, testimony of Adolf Schärf, 30 Sep 1947.
30. BA Berlin, RS A 0078 Adolf Anderle; WStLA, Vienna LG, Vg 2a Vr 831/48 (DÖW 19863/1), testimony of Josef Reither, 11 Dec 1947, and Karl Seitz, 9 Jan 1948.
31. Letter of 21 Mar 1945 from Reichsführer-SS Himmler to (Felix) Kersten regarding the treatment of Seitz, arrested after 20 July 1944, quoted in Jedlicka, *20. Juli 1944*, 171.

Chapter 10

THE VIENNA GESTAPO AND THE PERSECUTION OF THE JEWS

Establishment of Unit II B 4, the 'Judenreferat' ('Jewish Section')

The jurist Karl Haselbacher from the 'Altreich' was commissioned to establish and head the 'Jewish section' of the Vienna Gestapo, officially named Unit II B 4 (sometimes also II B 4J) and part of Section II B (Ideological opponents). Haselbacher, born on 7 April 1904 in Neu-Dieringhausen, was an expert, in spite of his youthful age, in anti-Jewish persecution. He joined the NSDAP on 1 May 1933 and was recruited in July of that year by the Prussian state ministry, where he was involved in the implementation of the Law on Restoration of the Civil Service, which had been adopted in April 1933. This law was not only designed to eliminate politically undesirable officials but it also already contained an 'Aryan paragraph'. On 1 January 1934, Haselbacher was transferred as a Regierungsassessor to the Gestapa, Section II F 2, which was responsible for 'Jews, Emigrants and Freemasons'. In December 1934 he joined the SS and, as a member of the Gestapo, was assigned to the security service of the SS (SD), which at that time was already endeavouring to exert increasing influence on the Nazi state's anti-Jewish policy.[1] In this dual position, Haselbacher was an example of the way in which Werner Best, Heydrich's deputy and administrative head of the Gestapa, was attempting to amalgamate not only the functions but also the staff of the security police (Sipo) and the SD. As a member of the Sipo, Haselbacher presented a paper in early 1936 at a training conference in Bernau for heads of the 'Jewish sections' of the SD Ober- und Unterabschnitte (higher and lower districts of the SS/SD) on 'practical experience in combating Judaism',[2] and was able to present himself as an expert in the field. In early 1937, when the SD was unmistakably demanding equal status with other state and party authorities in the 'solution of the Jewish question', Haselbacher suggested that the list of members of Jewish organizations held by the Gestapa be made available for the SD to deal with it. In summer 1937, not only was this suggestion put into practice, but the SD's competence was also considerably enhanced through the instruction by Best that all the work of the Gestapa 'Jewish section' should be transferred to the SD.[3]

In Vienna, Haselbacher became head not only of Unit II B 4 but also of the entire Section II B, which dealt with the persecution of 'ideological opponents', including 'churches, sects and Jews'. He was also head of Section II E, which prosecuted economic and foreign exchange crimes. This section was heavily involved between 1938 and 1940 in the systematic looting and expropriation of the Jews. The extreme paucity of source material makes it impossible to reconstruct exactly when Haselbacher took up his position in Vienna. It is highly likely that he arrived in the city, like Horst Freytag,[4] the Gestapa Jewish affairs consultant, shortly after 11 March. Apart from high-ranking Sipo officials, leading representatives of the SD also arrived in Vienna at that time: on 12 March, for example, Franz Six,[5] who had headed Central Department II 1 of the SD since 1937, his deputy Erich Ehrlinger,[6] and Herbert Hagen, who had headed SD Department II 112 (Jewish affairs) since the end of 1937. Adolf Eichmann, who had since 1935 been a member of SD Section II 112 responsible for observing Zionist organizations, arrived in Vienna on 16 March.[7]

Activities of Unit II B 4 until the November Pogrom of 1938

The decree of 15 March 1938 issued by Sipo chief Reinhard Heydrich on the organization of the Gestapo in Austria also marked the start of the establishment of the 'Jewish section' in the Vienna Gestapo. While the relevant leading officials from the 'Altreich', such as Haselbacher, Freytag and Otto Kuchmann, had offices until 1 April 1938 in the former general directorate for public security (Generaldirektion für die öffentliche Sicherheit), the officials transferred from the Austrian state police and criminal investigation police worked initially in offices at the former police headquarters at Schottenring 11. By 1 April 1938, the sections headed by Haselbacher were occupying rooms in the former Hotel Metropole, where he and other high-ranking Nazis had been living since their arrival in Vienna. Unit II B 4, which at this time had a staff of seventy-five and eight secretaries,[8] was now responsible for the prosecution of all offences (allegedly) committed by Jews, particularly those in connection with the specifically anti-Jewish special regulations.

Immediately after the annexation, the Gestapo began to arrest Jews in the political, business and cultural milieu in accordance with lists that had been drawn up at the Gestapa since 1935.[9] A surviving undated list with the names of Viennese (Jewish) lawyers 'designated by name for transfer to Dachau', and with comments such as 'smuggler', 'dangerous race defiler' and 'shameless usurer', suggests that these lists were compiled before the annexation or in the days immediately afterwards with the energetic support of local Nazis.[10]

The SD, which was also heavily involved in the preparations and radical intensification of anti-Jewish persecution before 1938, came with its own lists to Vienna. It had had the Austrian Jews in its sights since at least 1937. For example, Herbert Hagen, at the time a member of Central Department II 1 (Ideological assessment) of the SD, noted in a memo on 9 June 1937 following an internal department meeting that by order of Franz Alfred Six, head of Central Department II 1 of the SD, a file was to be compiled with the 'leading foreign Jews, with particular attention to the Jews in Austria'. Just before the annexation, on 9 February 1938, Adolf Eichmann, who helped to put the file together, received the order to obtain 'information of all kinds on Judaism in Austria'.

Although, as an NSDAP organization, the SD had no police powers, there is nevertheless documentary evidence that it interrogated people arrested by the Gestapo. A memo by Herbert Hagen, who was in Vienna at the time, indicates that many Jews were arrested 'at the instigation of II 112'.[11] As a letter of 15 July 1938 shows, the SD, or more specifically Department II 112, was also 'interested' in interrogating prisoners. The SD announced its particular 'interest', for example, in interrogating Desider Friedmann and Robert Pelzer. Friedmann, a jurist and member of the Zionistischer Landesverband für Österreich, since 1932 president of the Vienna Jewish community (Israelitische Kultusgemeinde, IKG) and since 1934 Staatsrat in the federal state of Austria, had been held in the police prison on Rossauer Lände since 16 March 1938 and had 'already been interrogated variously by SS-Untersturmführer Eichmann'. The letter indicates that Eichmann wanted to question him again 'regarding the connection of Jews to English political circles'. Robert Pelzer was to be questioned by Department II 112 because he was chairman of the Austrian human rights league, and the SD wanted to hear about the 'connection of this league with Jews, and vice versa'.[12]

In the weeks following the annexation, however, most of the arrests of Jews in Vienna were carried out not by the Sipo or SD but by members of Austrian Nazi formations (NSDAP, SS, SA and the like). Hundreds of Jews were victims of brutal excesses, humiliation rituals, looting and mass arrests. The new authorities were uneasy about these excesses, as much of economic value was destroyed, but they barely intervened. In their view, the expropriations and maltreatment – like the political and economic pressure they were exerting – were also helpful ways of making Austrian Jews feel unsafe and encouraging them to emigrate.

One of the best-known victims of these attacks was the Austrian journalist, writer, dramatist, theatre critic and cultural philosopher Egon Friedell, who threw himself out of a window of his third-floor apartment in Währing (18th district) on 16 March 1938 after two SA men had rung his doorbell.[13]

In addition to arrests and seizures, one of the first tasks of the 'Jewish section' was to transfer the victims of unauthorized arrests, who had been locked up in the first weeks after the annexation in various police prisons and emergency detention centres such as schools and local NSDAP offices, to the police prison on Rossauer Lände and to take their details. This was done in close cooperation with Section II D, built up by Karl-Heinz Rux and taken over in December 1938 by the Austrian official Josef Hess. This section was responsible for transports and the internment of arrestees in prisons and concentration camps.[14]

Of the thousands of Jews arrested in the first weeks after the annexation by members of the NSDAP and its organizations, and by police authorities not attached to the Gestapo, in most cases no record was made of who arrested them, or why. In close cooperation with Unit II B 4 and Section II D, these arrestees were now interrogated, officially documented and transferred to concentration camps – in 1938, mainly Dachau and Buchenwald. The first transport of Austrian internees ('VIP transport') to Dachau on 1 April 1938 was already organized by Section II D.[15]

Although Karl Haselbacher as head of Section II B and Unit II B 4 was not officially replaced by Rudolf Lange until June 1938,[16] Lange had already been in Vienna since April, as indicated in a letter of 9 April 1938 from SD Department II 112.[17] Karl Ebner, the future head of Section II B and deputy head of the Vienna Gestapo, described Lange as a 'radical supporter of the ideological principles of National Socialism'.[18] Although it should not be forgotten that, when questioned by the police and court after 1945, Ebner attempted to blame the officials from the 'Altreich' for all major actions of the Vienna Gestapo and to minimize his own responsibility, his characterization of Lange was accurate. Lange was born on 18 April 1910 in Weisswasser, Prussia, studied law in Jena, and in 1928, like his colleague Karl-Heinz Rux, became a member of the Germania fraternity. He joined the SA in 1933, where he was described as 'completely reliable'. In 1936 he held the position of assessor at the Gestapa and was transferred to the Gestapo on 1 September 1937, and in the autumn of that year he joined the SS and NSDAP.[19] From 1941, Lange played a leading role in the murder of Latvian Jews and Jews deported to Latvia, and was one of the fifteen participants in the Wannsee Conference.

Karl Ebner claimed after 1945 that there had been tensions between Lange and the subordinate Austrian members of his section.[20] Lange was 28 years old when he became head of Section II B of the Vienna Gestapo. For the long serving Austrian officials, who had climbed the career ladder of the state police and criminal investigation police rung by rung, it was probably not easy to accept this young, brash, out-and-out supporter of the National Socialist ideology as their superior. Given the fact that central positions within the Vienna Gestapo were occupied by German officials, Austrian Gestapo staff also feared for their own career prospects. Personal rivalries, animosities and resentment were inevitable. However, this does not mean that there were political differences or conflicts between the German and Austrian officials regarding the aims of the 'Jewish section'. Practically all its members, most of whom had lower-middle-class backgrounds, had been transferred to the Gestapo from the Austrian state police or criminal investigation police. Karl Ebner and Johann Rixinger, both of whom were soon to become important members of Unit II B 4, had been active in the illegal NSDAP before 1938. The Austrian members of the section clearly had a positive attitude to the Nazi regime, because police officials considered politically 'unreliable' were not transferred to the Gestapo after the annexation but dismissed or transferred to other service branches.[21] The members of Unit II B 4 saw themselves as part not of a criminal organization but of a legitimate state authority. Their lack of a sense of injustice, the long-standing antisemitism anchored in the social consciousness, and their desire to demonstrate that they were as efficient and ideologically sound as their superiors and colleagues from the 'Altreich' quickly led to the abandonment of all humanitarian qualms with regard to Jewish detainees. Psychological pressure, threats, gross insults, dehumanizing language and physical maltreatment were used customarily during interrogations in the 'Jewish section' to achieve the desired result as rapidly as possible. Emil Tuchmann, responsible from 1939 for all health matters in the IKG, testified in the trial of Karl Zeitlberger, one of the most brutal thugs in the Vienna Gestapo, that many of the Gestapo prisoners admitted to the (Jewish) Rothschild hospital had shown signs of serious maltreatment, including the use of knuckledusters and the like.[22] In view of their positions, leading officials such as Ebner and Rixinger had no need to use physical violence themselves, but they permitted and even encouraged maltreatment on the part of their subordinates.

The first major operation against the Jews (*Judenaktion*), conducted with great zeal by Rudolf Lange, took place on 24 May 1938. On that day, the 'Jewish section' sent an order to all local Viennese police stations to arrest 'undesirable' Jews for transfer to Dachau.[23] This series of arrests was almost certainly agreed with the Gestapa. Because of the absence of source material, it is not possible to determine whether the idea originated in Vienna, but this is quite conceivable, given the heated antisemitic mood and the ambitiousness of Lange, who was for the first time in his career actively involved in the persecution of Jews. Officials from all sections were recruited for the well-planned arrests. Interrogation forms had to be filled out in triplicate at the police stations and sent daily by courier to the Vienna Gestapo, Unit II B 4, room 314 – Otto Kuchmann's office. The first transport to Dachau with 602 arrestees took place as early as 31 May 1938; a further 600 Jewish arrestees followed on 3 June 1938.[24] The mass arrests and concentration camp transports were designed to speed up the emigration of Jews from Austria, which at this point was being encouraged by the Nazi regime as the 'solution to the Jewish question'.[25]

Many Jews were arrested in the first months after the annexation on the pretext that they had committed some ordinary criminal offence. Denunciations and defamation by members of the public played a not insignificant role. Businessmen were frequently accused of 'foreign exchange offences' or 'misappropriation of assets', and doctors of performing abortions.[26] Thus the taxi driver Karl Wottawa denounced two unknown Jews to the duty office of the Vienna Gestapo for misappropriation of assets, merely because he had driven them shortly beforehand to Gentzgasse 132 and Weimarerstrasse 5 (both 18th district) where they had each unloaded two suitcases. The accusation was passed on from the duty office to Section II B and Unit II B 4.[27] Paul Pollak, who before the annexation had been senior medical officer of the Vienna police, was arrested for (alleged) 'abortion for gain'.[28] At the instigation of the commission formed within the police by former illegal Nazi members to verify the political reliability of certain colleagues, he was discharged from the police service immediately after the annexation. On 1 October 1938, Pollak was deported to Buchenwald and from there to Auschwitz, where he was liberated in January 1945.[29]

In cases of alleged 'misappropriation of assets' or 'foreign exchange offences', the 'Jewish section' worked closely with Section II E – which dealt among other things with 'bogus transactions' by Jews – in arresting and looting the assets of prominent members of the business community with Jewish origins. One member of this section, which was also responsible for the persecution of 'asocials', was Viktor Siegel, who rose to become section head in 1941. Section II P, responsible for press affairs, cooperated with the 'Jewish section'; it was headed from the annexation until February 1939 by the German Gestapo official Ernst Weimann, and from March 1939 to April 1942 by the Austrian Alfons Rosse-Blaschko.[30] It monitored how Jews were presented in the press, in literature, publishing, art and culture, in films, and in theatres and other places of public entertainment, and it seized and destroyed 'undesirable' literature. In November 1938, for example, the Gestapo conducted an operation against Jewish bookshops in Vienna, during which fifty bookshops were closed and further 'controls' of bookshops announced.[31]

After the Nazi plebiscite on 10 April 1938, a slew of anti-Jewish 'laws' and decrees entered into force, above all the Nuremberg Laws introduced on 20 May 1938. The regulation promulgated on 23 July 1938 regarding compulsory identity cards (*Kennkarten*) obliged Jews when dealing with official or NSDAP offices to indicate 'without being asked' that they were Jews by presenting their identity card, which had a 'J' stamped on it. From 17 August 1938, Jews who did not have a recognizable Jewish name were forced to adopt the additional name 'Sara' or 'Israel', which from January 1939 were a required component of every signature and document.[32] Violations of these regulations, which included 'defilement of the race' (*Rassenschande*), 'failure to stamp the identity card' and 'failure to use the additional name', were sanctioned by Unit II B 4 with punishments ranging from a few weeks' detention to committal to a concentration camp. It also sanctioned infringements of the employment bans, for example for Jewish doctors, whose licences to practise were revoked throughout the entire German Reich with effect from 30 September 1938.[33]

Role of the Gestapo and SD in the Expulsion of Austrian Jews

Maltreatment, humiliation, expropriation and social marginalization quickly made it clear to the Jews of Vienna that escape abroad was the only possibility for avoiding the increasingly intolerable situation. But in order to leave, numerous hurdles had first to be surmounted. Apart from the fact that it was extremely difficult to obtain an immigration visa for a particular country, there were all kinds of bureaucratic impediments. Only when all taxes, levies and debts had been paid did 'Austrian citizens of the Jewish race', as Unit II B 4 already noted in a circular on 22 March 1938, obtain a 'special endorsement' in their passports that there was 'no impediment to emigration'.[34] The police stations were authorized by Unit II B 4 to issue endorsements in passports until June 1939. In the circular signed by Humbert Achamer-Pifrader – presumably because Haselbacher had not yet officially taken up his position as head – the border police stations and border posts were explicitly ordered to monitor this measure. These border units were answerable to Section III G of the Vienna Gestapo, headed directly after the annexation by Heinrich Rennau (also Renau), and later by Fritz Preiss and Hugo Goppelt, all three from the 'Altreich'.[35] It was responsible for all border matters and worked closely with the 'Jewish section' – for example, when Jews were caught trying to pass the frontier illegally or an organization helping Jews to escape was rounded up.[36]

The emigration and departure of the Austrian Jews suited the Nazi regime perfectly. In particular, from an early date the SD saw forced emigration as the 'solution to the Jewish question', made it the main aim of their anti-Jewish policy, and thus saw it as 'its task to establish this option as a principle of Nazi policy'.[37] Since 1936, it had carried out systematic (pseudo-scientific) studies and analyses of the economic and social situation of German Jews, the history of Judaism and the political role of Jews in various countries.[38] Zionist organizations were also targeted and meticulously studied by SD Department II 112 (Jews) – where Adolf Eichmann worked – to assess their utility in encouraging emigration. In January 1937, Eichmann presented a memo entitled 'On the Jewish Problem' in which he suggested the creation of a 'central office' that would carry out 'all emigration work within Germany' for the purpose of 'de-Jewing Germany'.[39]

The specific situation in Vienna after the annexation, marked by excesses and by confusion with regard to competences within the state administration apparatus, enabled SD Department II 112 to implement its concepts for 'solution of the Jewish question' quite rapidly.[40] Immediately after his arrival in Vienna, Eichmann, who had been writing training material on Judaism and Zionism in the SD since 1935 and was regarded as an 'expert' on Jewish and Zionist organizations,[41] set out ambitiously to put his department's anti-Jewish policy into practice.

On the SD's initiative, the Vienna IKG was dissolved on 18 March 1938 after a raid, and its functionaries were arrested; participants in the raid included Eichmann and Otto Kuchmann, a 'Reich-German' official in the 'Jewish section'.[42] After its reopening with the new name 'Jewish Community of Vienna' on 2 May 1938, it was under the complete control of the Gestapo and SD, and became 'the prototype for a Jewish administration under Nazi control and a precursor of the later Jewish councils'.[43] From now on, the IKG was forced to announce all anti-Jewish measures within the Jewish population. It was also required, with the assistance of foreign aid organizations, to obtain visas and foreign exchange, thus playing a significant role in the expulsion of the Austrian Jews.[44]

Under Eichmann's guidance, the central office suggested in 1937 by the SD was established with the full name Zentralstelle für jüdische Auswanderung in Wien (Central Office for Jewish Emigration in Vienna). It was later to become a model for Berlin, Prague and Paris.[45] It brought together all institutions dealing

Figure 10.1. Josef Löwenherz, director of the Vienna Jewish Community; photo taken during the raid of 18 March 1938. © Dokumentationsarchiv des österreichischen Widerstandes. Used with permission.

with forced emigration, such as the IKG and the tax authority, rationalizing both the bureaucratic administration and the systematic looting of Jewish assets. The central office was officially answerable to the IdSuSD in Austria, a position held from May 1938 to June 1939 by Walter Stahlecker. In reality, however, it was controlled until 1939 by Eichmann, and thereafter by Alois Brunner and others.[46] The establishment of the central office 'consolidated all emigration work in the Ostmark in the hands of the SD'.[47] In this way, the SD carved out a key position for itself in the future anti-Jewish policy of the Nazi regime. This does not mean, however, that the SD was in competition with the Gestapo or – as Karl Ebner claimed after 1945[48] – was superior to it. On 1 July 1937, Heydrich's 'function order' had already essentially defined the relationship between the Gestapo and the SD, which was not to be one of 'competition or superiority and subordination',[49] but of 'mutual complementarity'. While the SD was to deal with all 'basic questions (in which the executive powers of the police were not affected)' regarding 'churches, pacifism, press, right-wing movements, economic affairs and Judaism', the Gestapo was to handle all 'individual cases (in which the executive powers of the police were involved)'. Thus, the SD was responsible for the 'basic handling of the Jewish question' and hence the planning of the Jewish policy, while the Gestapo was responsible for all policing measures. This internal division of labour did not in any way 'weaken' the Gestapo: on the contrary, 'the assignment to the SD of responsibility for Jewish policy strengthened the political police as an executive authority and terror instrument'.[50]

In spite of the function order and the close connection between the SD and the Sipo, there were recurrent frictions between the two. However, these related only to individual areas of responsibility and not to political objectives. From the outset, for example, the Gestapo supported the 'illegal'[51] refugee transports to Palestine by enabling refugees to obtain emigration papers and foreign exchange. Eichmann and the SD originally objected to such transports but ended up tolerating them. When the first ones left Vienna on 9 June 1938, both Eichmann and Lange from the Vienna Gestapo were at the railway station. Also present was Erich Rajakowitsch,[52] articled clerk in the law office of Dr Heinrich Gallop, who had 'close connections with the Gestapo'. In his memoirs, Charles J. Kapralik, until 1939 head of the foreign exchange department in the IKG, recounts that the work of Rajakowitsch and the Gallop office in the first weeks after the annexation consisted in obtaining passports and emigration papers for wealthy Jewish families, for which they charged large fees. In reality, it is likely that the Gallop law office, which claimed to act by agreement with the Gestapo,[53] paid considerable bribes to members of Unit II B 4 so as to be able to 'speed up' emigration so 'successfully'. Bribery and corruption within the 'Jewish section' were commonplace right up to 1945. Only rarely were officials taken to task for it.[54] Not least on account of this lucrative 'side business', it was no doubt difficult for the 'Jewish section' in the Vienna Gestapo to accept the fact that from August 1938 the administration of the forced emigration was to be in the hands of the central office. There was a certain rivalry between Lange (Gestapo) and Eichmann (central office), but it did not cause major problems or have any effect on the treatment of the Jews.

Even after the establishment of the central office, Unit II B 4 remained responsible until June 1939 for correspondence with other authorities and offices connected with emigration and for checking the emigration papers of Jews in detention. This latter meant that the IKG or relatives of a detainee had to apply to the Gestapo for release as soon as visas were available; for example, in a letter of 10 January 1939 to the Vienna Gestapo, room 314 (Otto Kuchmann's office), the IKG asked for the release of Rudolf Feigenbaum, as he was now in possession of a 'limited immigration visa for Switzerland and an affidavit for the United States of North America'.[55]

The checking of detainees destined for concentration camps led to recurrent problems between the Gestapo on the one hand and the central office and Eichmann on the other. One conflict in early 1939 lasted several weeks. The ones who suffered most were the representatives of the IKG, who received contradictory instructions from the two institutions. In early June, a meeting finally took place between Gestapo head Huber and an unnamed representative of the central office in which the respective competences of the central office and the Gestapo were precisely defined. On 2 June 1939, the Vienna Gestapo informed Gauleiter Bürckel by express letter that with effect from 1 June 1939 the central office for Jewish emigration would be responsible for 'all public business that has arisen to date in connection with Jewish emigration'. The letter went on to say that, with immediate effect, the central office would take over all correspondence regarding emigration with authorities and offices, and the 'verification of the emigration papers of Jews in protective custody ... whom it [the central office] will make ready for emigration'.[56] This agreement should not be seen as a reduction in the competence of the Vienna Gestapo but, in view of the impending outbreak of war, a further definition of the distribution of labour between the Gestapo and the SD.

Activity of Unit II B 4 from the November Pogrom to the Start of Mass Deportations

The attack by the 17-year-old Herschel Grynszpan on the German diplomat Ernst vom Rath in Paris gave Reich propaganda minister Joseph Goebbels and the NSDAP a pretext to initiate a pogrom by the Nazi movement against Jews 'throughout the Reich' in the early hours of 10 November 1938. The role of the Gestapo in this action was determined by Gestapa head Heinrich Müller. That night he sent a lightning telegram to all Gestapo offices instructing them to ensure that: synagogues were only set on fire if there was no danger of the fire spreading to neighbouring buildings; Jewish businesses and apartments were 'only' to be destroyed but not looted; archive material of the Jewish community was to be seized but not destroyed; and above all, as many Jews, especially wealthy ones, were to be arrested as could be held in the available detention centres.[57]

In Vienna all members of Section II B and some from the Kripo headquarters in Vienna were involved in this *Judenaktion*, as Karl Ebner's secretary Hildegard Rock testified after the war.[58] Altogether 6,547 Jews within the Vienna Gestapo's jurisdiction were arrested. They were interned initially in 'emergency detention centres' such as schools and seized monasteries, where they were subject to terrible maltreatment, leading in some instances to attempted suicide. Subsequently, 3,989 of the arrestees were transferred to Dachau. In spite of Müller's instructions, considerable looting was carried out by the SA, Hitler Youth and NSDAP officials during the pogrom, which in Vienna was not restricted to this 'Night of Broken Glass' (*Kristallnacht*) but lasted several days. In his report on the *Judenaktion*, Josef Trittner, head of the SD-Unterabschnitt 'Vienna', criticized the undisciplined behaviour of members of the NSDAP, SA and Hitler Youth: 'In any event, unannounced house searches in SA and NSKK centres and in their leaders' homes would lead to astounding discoveries'.[59] Assets such as cash and jewellery seized by NSDAP members were to be delivered to a depot on the ground floor of the Vienna Gestapo.[60] A special subunit within Unit II B 4 was set up to deal with the seized assets. According to Hildegard Rock, this unit sent jewellery worth RM 1 million to Berlin, where it was apparently auctioned off 'cheaply'.[61]

After the November Pogrom, Jews were excluded from business and economic life. Regulations such as a ban on visiting cinemas, theatres and dance performances[62] forced them increasingly into social isolation. The Gestapo punished infringements of these regulations severely, mostly following denunciations to NSDAP offices.

From summer 1939, the Nazi regime began to recruit Jews for minimally paid forced labour. They were only allowed to perform auxiliary tasks, and were employed above all in road engineering and earth excavation, or waste disposal. At the same time, the Jewish inhabitants were gradually herded into 'collective housing' (*Sammelwohnungen*).[63] Both these operations were closely monitored by the Gestapo 'Jewish section'. Through its cooperation with the residency registration office (Einwohnermeldeamt), Unit II B 4 had a list of all Jews living in Vienna, which was continuously updated when anyone moved, emigrated or died. The list was further enlarged directly after the outbreak of war as a result of an order by Ebner to Josef Löwenherz, director of the Jewish community, to create file cards of all males between the ages of 20 and 45 living in Vienna, showing, among other things, their former profession, particular skills, ability to work, emigration destination, whether support was received from the IKG and the amount of this support.⁶⁴ The list provided valuable information for both forced labour and deportations.

Directly after the invasion of Poland, Heydrich ordered the arrest of all male Jews who were either Polish nationals or stateless with a right of residence in Poland. In early September 1939, Unit II B 4, like the entire Section II B, headed since June 1939 by Karl Ebner, arrested over a thousand Jews and interned them in the Prater football stadium. Among the victims of these arrests were also 122 people arrested by the Gestapo on 10 September in an IKG old people's home, all but one of whom were between 74 and 85 years of age. The IKG wrote a letter to the Gestapo on 12 September with the unsuccessful request for the release of these old people.⁶⁵ On 30 September the internees were transferred to Buchenwald, where most of them died within a few months.⁶⁶

The outbreak of war speeded up the disenfranchisement and persecution of the Jewish population. Jews were now only allowed to leave their homes at certain times,⁶⁷ and had to shop in separate stores for Jews (*Judengeschäfte*), which represented a massive reduction in their individual freedom of movement. These restrictive orders were almost inevitably infringed, leading to sanctions – both individual and collective – by Unit II B 4. For example, it forbade Jews in general from entering Karmelitermarkt in Leopoldstadt (2nd district) when the market was open, after a Jewish woman had asked an 'Aryan' woman to buy a pickled herring for her.⁶⁸

In late September 1939 the Gestapo also implemented a decree of the RSHA ordering the seizure of all wirelesses owned by Jews.⁶⁹ The wireless sets had to be handed into the local police station, from where they were brought to the Gestapo and then sent 'either to the Wehrmacht or to Berlin'.⁷⁰

The Gestapo as the Body Controlling the IKG

Among the most important tasks of the Gestapo was to control the IKG after its reopening on 2 May 1938. The IKG and individual departments had to write a weekly report on their activities to the Gestapo, and later also to the central office for Jewish emigration. In his memoirs, Charles Kapralik, head of the IKG foreign exchange department, recalled that 'everything [had to be] reported to the duo Kuchmann and Eichmann', who in his estimation differed from the Gestapo 'Jewish section', which was more interested in simply tormenting the Jews, while Eichmann was in favour of 'uncompromising but rapid emigration'.⁷¹

Director Löwenherz was frequently summoned to Unit II B 4, where he was informed – almost always orally – about future anti-Jewish measures, which he had to announce within the community.⁷² On other occasions he was confronted by various accusations made against the IKG or the Jewish population.

On 5 and 6 September 1939, for example, Löwenherz was summoned to Ebner, who reproached him concerning the increase in reports of 'improper behaviour' by Jews, such as forbidden visits to parks and coffee houses.[73] By order of the Gestapo, the IKG also had to provide detailed reports of the duration and course of every trip abroad by its representatives to obtain foreign exchange from Jewish aid organizations. It was also required to report the arrival of all representatives of foreign Jewish aid organizations. They were monitored by the Gestapo, and a Gestapo official was always present at meetings with the IKG. For example, on 20 May 1938 Otto Kuchmann and another unnamed Gestapo official participated in a meeting between representatives of the IKG and James Bernstein, authorized agent of the Jewish organization Hicem. At this meeting Löwenherz asked for permission to contact the American Joint Distribution Committee. In the following years, this organization not only alleviated the economic difficulties of the Jews in Austria through donations but also, and above all, supported the forced emigration by making foreign exchange available.[74]

Immediately after the annexation, the Gestapo also monitored the IKG finances. The IKG, as well as being compelled to report all financial transactions to the Gestapo in writing, also had to accept 'auditing visits', as on 25 November 1940. On this occasion, Ebner, Rolf Günther[75] and Alois Brunner[76] together checked the various IKG departments. Afterwards, Löwenherz was ordered to cut the number of employees, including not only administrative personnel but also teachers, doctors, nurses and kindergarten workers, by one hundred, and to reduce the salaries of the remaining employees, and the pensions received by retirees.[77]

The IKG had to obtain permission from the Gestapo for all financial transactions, regardless of whether they concerned the recruitment of employees or the establishment of soup kitchens, old people's homes or retraining courses.[78] Wilhelm Stern, a courier for the IKG, recalls that issuance of food ration cards also had to be approved by the Gestapo: 'I was often at the Gestapo on Morzinplatz because we had to have food coupons for all institutions, such as the old people's home, soup kitchen and hospital, signed off by the Gestapo'.[79] In the 'Jewish section', Otto Kuchmann was responsible for dealing with IKG requests, such as the request on 9 January 1939 to establish a home for up to fifty-five elderly people at Grosse Schiffgasse 3, Leopoldstadt.[80] He was succeeded by Johann Rixinger.

Kuchmann and Rixinger were also responsible within Unit II B 4 for supervising the IKG hospital (Rothschild-Spital). This was the only hospital available to Jews after Löwenherz was informed by the head of the 'Jewish section' in summer 1938 that Jewish patients were to be removed immediately from hospitals because 'Aryan nurses could not be expected to care for Jewish patients'.[81] Just under a year later, the Gestapo appointed SS doctor Eduard Sponer, who had also on occasion examined Kurt Schuschnigg, as 'supervising physician' at

Rothschild-Spital. This was a perfidious appointment in that the IKG thus even had to pay Sponer for his harassment of the doctors and nurses there. Within the IKG, Emil Tuchmann was responsible for all health matters. He also had to provide the Gestapo with monthly reports and appear in person in the event of the occurrence of infectious diseases or complaints against health system employees.[82] Karoline Schwarz, a nurse at Rothschild-Spital, reported when questioned by the Austrian state police in 1946 that the Gestapo frequently raided the hospital.[83]

After the November Pogrom, the Gestapo had to deal with numerous requests from the IKG for the reversal of measures such as the closure of apartments, the termination of rental agreements and the closure of soup kitchens and trade schools; similarly, requests were submitted for the return of passports, documents, seized travel money and the like. When Löwenherz visited the Gestapo on 24 November 1938 on this matter, he was informed that the IKG was required to present a report within a few days on the eviction of Jews from apartments in the vicinity of Morzinplatz. Löwenherz also had to deal with a particularly sensitive situation when he was summoned to Kuchmann in January 1939 and confronted with a photo from the *Daily Mail* of 16 December 1938 showing the arrival of a Kindertransport at the English port of Harwich. The harmless caption read: 'These children, who have come from Vienna on a Kindertransport from Austria, are very tired and will be housed in England'. Kuchmann threatened to cancel further transports if news of the Kindertransports were to appear again in the foreign press.[84]

On 1 November 1942, by when the deportation of Austrian Jews had practically been completed, the IKG was dissolved and transformed into the 'Ältestenrat der Juden in Wien' (council of elders of the Jews in Vienna), which was also supervised by the 'Jewish section'.[85]

Activity of the Gestapo from the Start of Mass Deportations to the End of the War

In April 1942, when the mass deportation of Austrian Jews was already well under way, a new organization plan (GVP) for the Vienna Gestapo entered into force, in which Unit II B 4 was renamed IV B 4. Its agenda remained unaffected by this reorganization. Its staff, which had consisted of sixty employees in 1938, was reduced in 1942 to twenty to twenty-five, and in 1944 to a mere ten to twelve. With the new organization plan, Karl Ebner was appointed as deputy to his personal friend Franz Josef Huber.[86] Section IV B was headed from September 1942 to February 1944 by Hans Dörhage, and then until April 1945 by Rolf Rack, a 'Reich German' like Dörhage. Both were described by IKG employee Wilhelm Bienenfeld as 'particularly anti-Jewish'.[87]

From 1942, the head of Unit IV B 4 was Johann Rixinger, who after Kuchmann's recall in 1939 had increasingly taken over the unit's affairs. Rixinger, who joined the Kripo in the 1920s and later transferred to the state police, knew his superior Ebner from the time before 1938, when they were both at the police station in Favoriten (10th district).[88] As Ebner's close associate, Rixinger had a relatively large radius of operation. By agreement with Ebner, he could decide not only whether charges against Jews were acted on or ignored, but he was also an authorized signatory. His signature was required for every single transfer to a concentration camp. Rixinger therefore shared responsibility for all of the committals to concentration camps, whether as a 'punitive measure' or, from 1943, in connection with deportations in the framework of the Shoah.[89]

After 1945, Ebner and Rixinger attempted to conceal the involvement of the Gestapo and their own collaboration in the murder of Austrian Jews by presenting the deportations to ghettos and extermination camps as the sole responsibility of the 'Central Office for Jewish Emigration'. In fact, the Vienna Gestapo – and from June 1939 Unit II B 4, headed by Karl Ebner – was already involved in or at least aware of the preparations for the 'Nisko transports';[90] after the occupation of Poland, Sipo chief Heydrich had ordered Adolf Eichmann to organize the establishment of a 'Jewish reservation' near the town of Nisko, at the border with the Soviet Union. On 17 October 1939 a meeting took place between Eichmann, Ebner and a representative of Reichskommissar Bürckel to discuss the organization of several transports from Vienna to Nisko. Ebner offered 'to assign his entire staff to the resettlement, and to take the necessary steps to register the Jews', and suggested that all Jews interned in a concentration camp or prison, as well as the stateless people interned in the Prater football stadium, be 'attached' to the planned transports.[91] In October 1939, 1,584 men were deported to Nisko in two transports. The experiment had to be abandoned, however, because the Nazi leadership had other political priorities in 1940.[92]

The 'evacuation to the East', as the deportations were euphemistically called in Nazi jargon, was once again a focus of the NS regime towards the end of 1940. At a meeting with Hitler on 2 October 1940, Baldur von Schirach, the new Reichsstatthalter and Gauleiter of Vienna, urged that fifty thousand Jews be deported to Poland to 'solve' the housing shortage in Vienna. Hitler complied with this request by the Vienna NSDAP, and decided that 'the 60,000 Jews still living in the Reichsgau Vienna should be expelled into the Generalgouvernement while the war is still in progress'.[93] Gauleiter Schirach passed on this order from Hitler to Franz Josef Huber, head of the Vienna Gestapo, who announced the impending 'evacuation' of Viennese Jews in a letter sent to the Vienna police chief Leo Gotzmann, Adolf Eichmann in the RSHA, and the NSDAP leadership of the Vienna Gau.[94] Earlier, on 1 February 1941, on instructions from Huber, Karl Ebner, head of the 'Jewish section', had informed IKG director Josef Löwenherz in the presence of Alois Brunner from the central office for Jewish emigration that some of the Jews living in Vienna were to be resettled in the Generalgouvernement. Ebner also sketched the procedure for future deportations, namely that the central office would be responsible for drawing up a list of the Jews to be considered for each of the transports, and for organizing the transports.[95] Until the end of 1942 it not only drew up the deportation lists but also organized the collection of the victims from their apartments, and the administration of the collection points (*Sammellager*). Although the central office was without a doubt the main organizer of the deportations until 1942, this does not mean that the Vienna Gestapo and its 'Jewish section' was not involved. After March 1941, Huber had also been inspector of the Sipo and SD in Military District XVII (i.e. Vienna, Lower Danube and Upper Danube), and was thus also the superior of the central office. The departure time of the deportation trains, the number of people and the destination were noted in the Vienna Gestapo's daily reports.[96] It should be emphasized here that this active collaboration in the deportation of the Jewish inhabitants of Vienna, leading to the death of the majority of the forty-eight thousand deportees, was probably the most serious crime committed by the Vienna Gestapo and its head and deputy head Franz Josef Huber and Karl Ebner.

Vienna Gestapo officials were also involved in the practical preparations for the transports. Shortly before the deportation trains departed, the victims at the collection points had to hand in their food ration cards, documents and valuables in what were euphemistically known as 'takeovers' (*Kommissionierungen*). This often gave rise to rough treatment by the SS men, who also unashamedly helped themselves to the deportees' assets. Also present at these 'takeovers' was a member of the Gestapo, to whom the victims gave the keys to their apartments with an address label attached, along with a detailed list of their assets.[97] The furniture and all assets were sold by the Gestapo, who used the proceeds to cover the costs of the 'resettlement' and the 'final solution of the Jewish question'.[98] Until the end of 1941, the Gestapo also dealt with requests to the Gauleiter for 'deferral' of the deportation, which were passed on to the Gestapo as the competent authority.[99] The applicants were usually people who had obtained an emigration visa at the last moment, or were very old or frail (some even blind), or could claim to have performed special services; however, even a positive reply – which was in any case very rare – would merely represent a postponement of the deportation. For example, Siegfried Kolisch, a First World War captain who had been wounded and awarded numerous decorations, and was also head of the Bund jüdischer Frontkämpfer (association of Jewish veterans), received a 'deferral' in 1941 but was deported with his mother to Theresienstadt in 1943.[100] The 'Jewish section' kept a special file on these 'protected Jews',[101] and of the IKG functionaries and their relatives.

When the deportations started, further decrees and regulations came into force that visibly stigmatized the Jewish inhabitants and imposed even greater restrictions on their lives. From 1 September 1941, Jews over the age of 6 had to wear a 'Jewish star' on their clothing and affix it to the front door of their apartments.[102] They were not allowed to use public telephones (their private telephones had been dismantled previously), trams, buses or the urban railway system; nor were they permitted to purchase daily newspapers, send letters or packages to the ghettos in the occupied territories of Eastern Europe, or make enquiries to the Red Cross. By 1939, Jews had already been prohibited from visiting the Prater and most of the parks in Vienna; and from early 1942, they were also forbidden from entering the Vienna Woods, the Bisamberg Hills on the other side of the Danube, and the Freudenau racecourse. According to the Gestapo's daily reports, infringements of these anti-Jewish provisions – until the second half of 1941 – were punished by 'lenient' periods of detention. After this time, however, practically all offenders who were defined as 'full Jews' according to the Nuremberg Laws and had 'committed offences' were deported after completing their period of detention. For example, Georg Radler and Fritz Jokl, both 17 years old, and Georg Gottesmann, 14 years old, received a punishment of three days' detention at the end of August 1941 because they had been caught in the Prater.[103] They were deported soon afterwards: Fritz Jokl on 23 October 1941 to Łódź, and Georg Radler on 3 December 1941 to Riga. The fate of Georg Gottesmann is unknown.[104]

From 1942 the Gestapo 'Jewish section' passed on all 'offenders' to the central office, for 'evacuation' (*Evakuierung*), as the deportations were called in official Nazi jargon. When the deportations began, the number of 'offenders' in connection with the anti-Jewish decrees and regulations rose suddenly. Many people attempted to avoid deportation either by escaping abroad, mostly to Hungary, by not wearing the 'Jewish star',[105] by going into hiding, or by claiming to be 'first-degree Mischlings' or 'Aryans'. Jews caught committing such offences were immediately transferred by Unit IV B 4 to the central office for 'resettlement in the Generalgouvernement' or 'evacuation'. This was the case, for example, with Kurt Löwidt, who had attempted to escape to Hungary,[106] Flora Schön, who had gone into hiding and had been living without registering in an empty store,[107] and Alfred Schireno, who was arrested by the Gestapo at the end of February 1942 for 'not wearing the Jewish star and illegal restaurant visits'.[108]

By the end of September 1942, the mass deportations of Austrian Jews had practically been completed. On 31 December 1942 there were only 7,989 Jews left in Vienna.[109] Apart from a few hundred IKG employees, they were mostly Jews married to non-Jews ('arisch versippt') or *Geltungsjuden* (i.e. deemed to be Jews under the Nuremberg Laws).[110]

After the central office for Jewish emigration was closed in March 1943, the further deportations of the Jews remaining in Vienna were organized by Unit IV B 4. They included IKG employees, who were deported in 1943–44, and those who had hitherto succeeded in hiding but had now been discovered, as well as *Geltungsjuden* and Jewish partners from mixed marriages (*Mischehen*) who had committed 'offences'.[111] After 1945, Ebner and Rixinger claimed that Unit IV B 4 had received the names of deportees from Department IV of the RSHA.[112] These assertions should be questioned, however, not least as Wilhelm Bienenfeld mentioned explicitly in the main proceedings against Rixinger on 3 October 1947 that although the 'evacuation' order came from Berlin, it stated only 'the required numbers but not the names'. According to Bienenfeld, the lists of names of Jews to be deported were compiled by Unit IV B 4 based on a register there of the Jews still remaining in Vienna.[113] This procedure was common practice in the 'Altreich'.[114]

The Gestapo submitted the names of those to be deported to the council of elders so that it could 'reclaim' any people who were urgently needed. The council was forced to do this when, for example, the Gestapo wanted to deport all the nurses, because otherwise the hospital would have had no care personnel. The IKG did not provide 'replacements' for those it had 'reclaimed'; according to Bienenfeld, replacements were 'once again drawn from the Gestapo card index'.[115]

The people listed for deportation were either sent a letter instructing them to report to the collection point, or they were fetched by Gestapo officials. Rixinger was responsible for obtaining tickets for the transports, organizing food and assigning guards.[116] Until the departure, the people remained at the collection point, where the 'takeovers' were also carried out by members of Unit IV B 4. At this point, the victims had to hand over to the Gestapo officials their remaining goods and chattels and the keys to their apartments, and could also give reasons for being exempted from deportation.[117] For 'full Jews' this was usually a forlorn hope, and with few exceptions all of them were deported by 1945. Most of the 'protected Jews', whose deportation until then had been 'deferred', were now deported. The latter included Johann Friedländer, who had been highly decorated in the First World War and rose to the rank of Feldmarschallleutnant in the First Republic. He was deported on 19 March 1943 with his wife to Theresienstadt, and was murdered on the death march from Auschwitz to Pless (Pszczyna) in January 1945.[118]

During this time, it was Johann Rixinger who was mainly responsible for deciding whether or not someone should be deported.[119] In his VG trial in 1946 he was able to produce (several) Jewish witnesses who claimed that they had been relatively well treated by him or that he had rescued them or their relatives from deportation. Among the latter was Karl Güttl, a coal merchant in Vienna, whose (Jewish) wife was arrested in Hungary in 1942 and was to be deported. Güttl intervened with Rixinger, who, according to Güttl, noted in the Gestapo file that Güttl's wife had been 'transported to Poland' but arranged for her to be released from the collection point. In view of the corruption among Gestapo officials, it is highly likely that Güttl bribed Rixinger either with money or coal, which was strictly rationed at the time. Güttl later showed his gratitude: when

Rixinger was released from prison in 1952, Güttl employed him in his company until 1965.[120]

Like Ebner, Rixinger sought to 'reinsure' himself – in other words, to generate defence witnesses for the time after the approaching end of the Nazi regime. Emil Tuchmann also confirmed that after 1943 Rixinger was more conciliatory towards the council of elders. For example, in 1944 he exempted the thirteen doctors at the Rothschild hospital from wearing the 'Jewish star' so that they could seek out an air raid shelter without being attacked or spat at.

Rixinger was apparently counting on the fact that people who could testify to his brutality, insensitivity and cynicism would not survive. However, he could not have expected that Gerda Mayer, for example, would return from Theresienstadt, as she did. She was the daughter of a German officer and had a 'non-Aryan' mother. As she was married to a 'full Jew', she and her 5-year-old child were also considered 'full Jews'. The family asked Rixinger in vain to have their deportation 'deferred'. When a non-Jewish friend of the family attempted to intercede, Rixinger said cynically: 'It was her choice. She married a Jew and so she has to go'.[121] In 1947 two witnesses confirmed that the main reason Rixinger had wanted to deport the family was because he had promised their apartment to an acquaintance, and he himself wanted the stamp collection, books and some of the Mayers' furniture. These items were indeed found in Rixinger's possession after 1945.[122]

Only a small number of Jews who had been victims of the 'Jewish section' survived the Shoah and were able to testify in court after 1945. It is not therefore surprising that more people testified in Rixinger's favour after 1945 than against him, not least given that the questionees included former Gestapo officials who had themselves committed serious crimes and therefore wished to play down their involvement. Rixinger, Ebner and Zeitlberger denied that prisoners were brutally maltreated. Gertrude Pichler, a secretary in the 'Jewish section', also testified in the trial of Zeitlberger, one of the most brutal thugs in that unit, and denied that Jews were maltreated. She lied so brazenly that the public prosecutor's office applied for her to be charged on suspicion of perjury.[123]

Between 1943 and 1945, Unit IV B 4 also regularly checked whether 'mixed marriages' (between 'Aryans' and 'non-Aryans') still existed by summoning the spouses every fourteen days.[124] If the non-Jewish spouse died or divorced, the Jewish partner was deported. On 10 March 1944, for example, the Gestapo deported 'eighty-four Jews from no longer existing German–Jewish mixed marriages' to Theresienstadt.[125]

Apart from 'mixed marriages', Unit IV B 4 also checked up on 'first-degree Mischlings'. After 1942 they were exposed to growing persecution and were not allowed, for example, to live together with 'Aryans' other than their spouses or children. One of the Gestapo officials dealing with this was Alois Bucher. He had volunteered for the Gestapo in 1943 from the regular police with a view to earning more money and above all to being promoted more rapidly. Bucher was not only brutal but also underhand. He promised to help prisoners' relatives, and was paid by them in cash or with food and cigarettes – but he did not keep his promises. In one case he went as far as forcing the non-Jewish girlfriend of a 'first-degree Mischling' to have sexual intercourse with him. Bucher is the only Gestapo official to have been proven to date to have committed a sexual assault. Such assaults were doubtless frequent occurrences but were extensively hushed up after 1945.[126]

Between 1943 and 1945, the Vienna Gestapo 'Jewish section' deported 1,350 people to Theresienstadt, and between March 1943 and October 1944 around 350 people to Auschwitz. Most of the deportees did not survive.[127]

Looting of Jewish Assets by the Gestapo in Vienna

Together with the Vermögensverkehrsstelle (property transaction office), the central office for Jewish emigration in Vienna, and the finance administration, the Vienna Gestapo played a leading role in the systematic expropriation and looting of Jewish assets. On 17 March 1938 the Vienna Gestapo was authorized through a decree of Sipo chief Heydrich not only to make arrests but also to 'seize' assets during house searches.[128] Eight days later, a further decree designated the Vienna Gestapo as the sole authority in the Nazi administrative structure in Austria entitled to 'seize and confiscate assets belonging to enemies of Volk and state'.[129] The legal basis for this activity was the Second Regulation to the Law on the Reunification of Austria with the German Reich of 18 March 1938, whose content corresponded to Section 1 of the 'Regulation of the Reich President for the Protection of Volk and State' of 28 February 1933. It authorized the Reichsführer-SS and chief of the German police to take 'necessary measures' to 'maintain security and order, even outside the relevant legal framework', and to 'transfer his authority to other offices'. Through the decree of 23 March 1938, Himmler transferred authority pursuant to Section 1 to the chief of the security police, who on 25 March 1938 empowered the Gestapo to seize and confiscate 'assets belonging to enemies of Volk and state'. The decree further forbade personal enrichment, and ordered seizures by other authorities or NSDAP offices to be reported to the Gestapo and confirmed by it by means of seizure and confiscation orders.[130] This latter provision was aimed particularly at the NSDAP and its departments and followers. As Walter Stahlecker, inspector of the Sipo and SD in Austria, stated quite bluntly a few weeks later, directly after the annexation these people had 'attempted to an extent that went beyond any bounds to acquire assets from Jews and enemies of Volk and state'. In spite of the decree and Heydrich's letter, for example to Gruppenführer Mappies of the Vienna SA group on 28 March 1938, in which he explicitly stated that seizures were to be carried out exclusively by the Gestapo, unauthorized seizures and 'Aryanizations' continued repeatedly until the November Pogrom. Stahlecker estimated that 'the assets seized by these bodies had triple the value of those seized by the Gestapo'.[131]

In the weeks following the annexation, the Vienna Gestapo seized 'assets belonging to enemies of Volk and state', above all from Jews who had either fled or who were accused of an offence 'hostile to Volk or state', such as deliberate bankruptcy (Krida), unpaid taxes or 'suspicion of asset smuggling'.[132] Although the mere suspicion of such an offence was sufficient for arrest and seizure of assets, the Gestapo attempted to find 'evidence', as in the case of the industrialist David Goldmann, for example. Goldmann fled to Pressburg (Bratislava) with his wife and child directly after Schuschnigg's speech. As the family was not permitted to cross the border by car, they crossed on foot. Their chauffeur returned the car to Vienna and handed it over immediately to SS-Standarte 11. Both the family's apartment and all the furniture, shares, art treasures, jewellery and cash were seized by the Gestapo on 7 April 1938. According to the Gestapo, a picture of Stalin, issues of the *Rote Fahne* and monarchist leaflets were also found in the twenty-room apartment on Hermann Göring-Platz (now Roosevelt-Platz, 9th district).[133] The Gestapo did not even bother with this absurd 'argumentation' when they seized the apartment and furnishings of Isaak Demant, who had 'fled the Reich'. Demant's 'hasty departure' had been reported to the Gestapo by the Lichtenwerd NSDAP group. Demant's furniture was 'given to Ing. Woitsche, housing consultant of the city of Vienna', who transferred the 'proceeds', RM 570.33, to the Gestapo account.[134] The Vienna Gestapo had opened accounts for this purpose with both the Länderbank and the Creditanstalt, to which the balances of seized and closed accounts were also transferred. Franz Josef Huber, head of the Vienna Gestapo, and Viktor Siegel were authorized signatories. Siegel worked directly after the annexation in Section II H/SO, which – in close cooperation with Unit II B 4 – was responsible for 'securing Jewish assets'. The heads of this section were Josef Meisinger and Kurt Christmann, both from Germany.[135]

The Gestapo seized and confiscated all kinds of assets, ranging from furniture, property, cash, securities, savings books, stamp collections and warehouse contents to cars, works of art, silverware and insurance policies. According to a list drawn up by the Vienna Gestapo, by 21 June 1938 it had seized assets (such as jewellery and savings books) worth RM 3,902,391. This sum did not include the value of real estate property, mostly confiscated in favour of the 'Land of Austria' (Land Österreich), such as the three buildings belonging to the Ephrussi family at Dr Karl Lueger-Platz 14, Kärntnerring 8 and Schottengasse 12. The list also contains only a few objects confiscated in favour of the German Reich, such as the Hotel Metropole and the two buildings owned by Friedrich and Mathilde Georgi at Gusshausstrasse 28–30 in Wieden (4th district). These latter buildings, which included a garage and a clothing store, were also used by the Gestapo.[136] The seizures and confiscations of assets were lucrative for the Vienna Gestapo, and both the authority itself and its individual members profited from them. Apart from the properties mentioned above, the Gestapo acquired seized items such as furniture, typewriters and vehicles for its offices. The individual Gestapo officials also had plenty of opportunity for personal enrichment, not only through the misappropriation of seized objects and cash but also through blackmail and abuse of authority. These offences were rarely prosecuted, because few victims dared to complain about a 'house search', much less to accuse a Gestapo official of personal enrichment. One exception was the case of Gestapo official Friedrich Kosmath. Born in 1894, Kosmath was a jurist and worked as such in the security office of Vienna police headquarters from 1934 to 1938. After the annexation he joined the Gestapo, where he worked in the unit dealing with returnees from Russia and Spain. When his fiancée sought to purchase a house belonging to two arrested Jewish brothers, Kosmath had them summoned from the prison on Rossauer Lände and forced them to sell the house to his fiancée at a low estimated price. The case became known, and Kosmath was arrested on 1 July 1938 for abuse of authority.[137]

Rivalry between Authorities

The Gestapo had considerable discretionary powers regarding the seizure and confiscation of assets during the first months after the annexation. However, the confiscations had no legal basis, as the corresponding legal provisions regulating access to Jewish assets in the 'Altreich' had first to be extended to Austria. This legal limbo and the extensive powers of the Sipo very soon attracted the attention of various authorities within the Nazi state, first and foremost Minister President (of Prussia) Hermann Göring. As the person responsible for the Four-Year Plan, he endeavoured to acquire as many seized assets as possible for the state treasury. Massive confiscations in favour of the Austrian NSDAP or the Land of Austria would have meant that the central Reich authorities would no longer have had access to these assets. Göring therefore informed Himmler in a letter on 27 April 1938 that the Gestapo in Austria was entitled to seize assets but that there was no corresponding legal basis for confiscation, as had existed in the 'Altreich' since 1933. Three days later, on 30 April, he informed Heydrich's deputy Werner Best quite explicitly by telephone that he did not want the Gestapo in Austria to confiscate assets, and it should confine itself for the time being to seizures, as confiscations 'would be made possible and carried out in future under provisions currently being drafted'. Göring's objections had rapid consequences. On 3 May 1938, Sipo chief Reinhard Heydrich wrote to the head of the Vienna Gestapo informing him that in future the Gestapo was not to confiscate assets but merely to seize them.[138] The Reich authority was also taxed by the fact that in spite of several orders issued by Heydrich, the Vienna Gestapo did not keep a record of assets seized and confiscated in Austria until that summer. It was only on 14 July 1938 that Kurt Christmann, head of Section II H/SO of the Vienna Gestapo, travelled to Berlin with such a list.[139]

The question of the future disposal of Jewish assets seized in Austria proved to be extremely complex. Apart from Göring, the Reich ministry of the interior, and Reichsführer-SS and chief of the German police Heinrich Himmler, the bodies and individuals involved also included the Reich chancellery, the Reich ministries of economic affairs, finance and justice, and in Vienna Reichskommissar Bürckel and Reichsstatthalter Seyß-Inquart. Until November 1938, various negotiations between these authorities took place, and legislation was drafted in some cases. Bürckel and Seyß-Inquart in particular attempted to maintain control of the seized assets, not least to finance 'reparations' for Austrian 'Alte Kämpfer'.[140]

On 30 July 1938, the Reichsführer-SS authorized the Gestapo in Austria 'to auction in a suitable manner' vehicles, furniture and other movable seized Jewish assets. At the same time, he prohibited it with immediate effect from using the proceeds of these auctions and seized cash 'for any purpose' or to transfer them 'to other accounts', and ordered that these assets be place in a 'special fund'. These provisions, and Himmler's order that the Gestapo should draw up a precise list of the disposal to date of seized and confiscated cash,[141] would suggest that the Gestapo headquarters had previously been quite free in its handling of seized Jewish assets.

The extremely patchy source material does not permit any reliable statements as to the amount of the proceeds from auctions, which the Gestapo commissioned the Dorotheum to hold, but it must have been considerable. The value of the auctioned furniture owned by David Goldmann alone was estimated at RM 25,000.[142]

Not least on account of the uncontrolled looting after the annexation, Heydrich, by agreement with Göring, determined directly after the November Pogrom what was to be done with the assets seized during the 'protest action against the Jews'. The Gestapo played an important role in this regard, because it was tasked with drawing up lists of securities, cash, jewellery and valuable objects such as vehicles and furs, and, if 'the owner could no longer be determined', to deliver them on issuance of a receipt to the offices of the Oberfinanzpräsident.[143] If the owners could be determined, the seized assets were meant to be returned to them, although this never occurred in practice. According to Hildegard Rock, secretary of Karl Ebner, long-standing head of the 'Jewish section', 'after the November Pogrom the Vienna Gestapo transferred jewellery worth RM 1,000,000 to Berlin', where it was auctioned off cheaply.[144] However, Rock's statement can be neither verified nor disproved.

The 'Regulation on the Confiscation of Assets belonging to Enemies of the Volk and State in Austria' of 18 November 1938, which entered into force on 20 November and was to be applied retroactively to all assets already seized, created a legal basis for the confiscation of Jewish assets. The regulation authorized the Reichsstatthalter or agencies designated by him to confiscate assets belonging to people or groups 'who had promoted activities hostile to the Volk or state, and objects and rights used or intended for the promotion of such activities'. The ministry of internal and cultural affairs was entrusted with handling the seizure and confiscation orders.[145] The regulation did not, however, cover the future disposal or administration of assets confiscated hitherto. On the basis of a regulation of the Reichsstatthalter of 12 December 1938, they were to be transferred for the time being to the agencies that had administered seized or confiscated objects until then, with an account given to the ministry.[146]

Minister of finance Hans Fischböck raised serious objections to this regulation in a letter to the Reichsstatthalter in early January 1939. Among other things, he criticized the Gestapo, stating that it did not always follow the order 'to transfer valuables such as cash, securities, silverware, etc., to the central state treasury', and in such cases 'failed to give reasons for not doing so'. Fischböck demanded that 'a suitable commercial and legal trustee be commissioned to administer and dispose of [the seized assets]'.[147] His objections were clearly accepted, because on 11 February 1939 the Reichsstatthalter commissioned the ministry of finance to administer the assets belonging to 'enemies of Volk and state' confiscated in favour of Austria on the basis of the regulation of 18 November 1938. Two days later, the Gestapo was ordered to transfer all file records regarding confiscation orders or administrative and disposal measures to the ministry of finance.[148] On 14 February 1939 a meeting took place between Georg Steinböck, from the ministry of finance, and Huber, head of the Vienna Gestapo, in which Huber reported how the Gestapo had dealt to date with the confiscated and seized assets. According to him, the Gestapo had issued 200 to 250 confiscation reports, auctioned movable assets such as furniture and interior fittings (using the proceeds to cover administrative costs), transferred cash and securities to Gestapo bank accounts, and assigned art objects to the Reichsstatthalterei, and all real estate confiscated by the Vienna Gestapo to the state building authority (Staatsgebäudeverwaltung). Huber also said, however, that it was not possible to provide the original documents relating to these transactions, and that it would take around three weeks to transcribe them.[149]

On 15 March 1939 a decree of the Reichsführer-SS and chief of the German police revoked the decree of 30 June 1938 authorizing the Gestapo to auction movable assets, and explicitly stated that the Gestapo in Austria was 'no longer entitled to dispose of seized or confiscated assets itself, by sale, auction or in any other way'.[150] Thereupon, the Gestapo attempted to retain control of the auction of the assets, in particular furniture, of Jews who had escaped.[151] Apart from power-mongering and material greed, the Austrian National Socialists no doubt wished to use the confiscated assets as 'reparations' for former 'illegals'.[152] Humbert Achamer-Pifrader, Huber's deputy, also practised this type of reparation on his own accord, as the example of the SS man Arthur Geckl illustrates. According to Geckl's own statement, he had been beaten up on 7 May 1934 by David Goldmann and other passers-by after he had exploded a bomb in front of Café 'City' at Porzellangasse 1 in the 9th district, which was allegedly frequented mostly by Jews. He had been sentenced to twelve years' imprisonment and now demanded RM 15,000 'reparation' from Goldmann's seized assets. In April 1939, at a time when the ministry of finance had already been commissioned to handle seized assets, Achamer-Pifrader instructed Karl Ebner to pay Geckl RM 2,000 'reparation' from the seized assets of the industrialist Goldmann.[153]

The collaboration between the ministry of finance and the Gestapo was far from smooth. For example, in March 1939 the ministry requested a list of the cash, securities and other movable assets held by the Vienna Gestapo, but they did not respond to this request until a year later, in March 1940.[154] Shortly afterwards, on 1 April 1940, the assets in the 'Ostmark' and hence responsibility for their administration passed to the Reich. On 5 July 1940 a decree of the ministry of finance transferred responsibility for handling seized movable assets to the Oberfinanzpräsidium in Vienna.[155]

In summary, it may be stated that because of the absence of regulations by the state directly after the annexation, the Vienna Gestapo, while not enjoying a monopoly, had considerable discretionary powers in dealing with assets seized from Jewish owners. However, with the increasing consolidation of Reich bodies such as the Reich ministry of finance and the Reich ministry of economic affairs in Austria, and through pressure from Göring, this authority was steadily eroded and economic interests were given precedence. Nevertheless, the Gestapo was very reluctant to cede its authority to the Oberfinanzpräsidium, especially in view of the fact that the corruption and personal enrichment possible through the looting of Jewish assets was also a welcome 'perk' of the persecution. However, through the establishment of the 'Gestapo office for the administration of removals goods of Jewish emigrants' ('Vugesta', short for Verwaltungsstelle für das Umzugsgut jüdischer Emigranten bei der Geheimen Staatspolizei), the Vienna Gestapo managed not only to stake a claim for itself with respect to the authorities in Berlin, but also to retain access to seized Jewish assets.

Vugesta as an Instrument for Looting

On 1 August 1940, the Reich ministry of the interior issued a decree applicable to the entire Reich that removals goods of (mostly Jewish) emigrants that could not be sent on to them on account of the outbreak of war, and that had therefore remained with transport companies and in warehouses, were to be inventoried by the Reich finance authority and then disposed of.[156] The tax office in Moabit, Berlin, which since 1933 had been 'increasingly the control centre for the looting of Jewish emigrants', was entrusted with seizing these assets.[157] The leading officials at the Vienna Gestapo, first and foremost Karl Ebner, quickly realized that if the decree were implemented correctly they would not only lose control but would also barely profit from the disposal of the removals goods.[158] Ebner travelled to Berlin and suggested to the officials responsible in the Reich ministry of the interior and the Moabit tax office that for practical purposes the Gestapo should be entrusted with the auction of stored goods, with the stipulation that it transfer the proceeds, after deduction of all administrative costs, to the Reichsfinanzverwaltung (Reich fiscal administration). The authorities in Berlin immediately agreed to Ebner's proposal, probably because the management of the seized assets was already stretching the capacities of the Reichsfinanzverwaltung to the limit. Ebner then contacted the head of the Reich department for haulage and warehousing (Reichsverkehrsgruppe Spedition und Lagerei, RSL), Karl Herber. Herber had apparently contacted Ebner before he left for Berlin, and pointed out that the continued storage of the removals goods left behind was a great financial burden for the transport companies, because it blocked their warehouses. Ebner commissioned Herber to establish a Gestapo administration office responsible for organizing the registration and sale of goods left behind, and to transfer the proceeds to the Gestapo after deduction of all personnel and administrative costs.[159] This became the aforementioned 'Vugesta',[160] which Ebner also authorized to issue orders for seizure. The Gestapo gave it the necessary forms, which had only to be signed by Ebner after being filled out. Herber became head of Vugesta, which had its offices at the RSL/Ostmark at Bauernmarkt 24 in the city centre. It officially began operating on 7 September 1940.[161] One of his first measures was to instruct all transport companies to return to Vienna all removals goods that had already left Austria. Herber not only had a personal share of 3 per cent of Vugesta profits, but he had also acquired from the Gestapo a pre-emptive right to purchase the seized tangible assets to be auctioned, thereby acquiring – according to his own admission – paintings worth around RM 100,000.[162] Apart from four valuers, around twenty Jewish employees worked for Vugesta, albeit with minimal salaries. The goods seized, including valuable furniture, clothes, linen, carpets, paintings and other art objects, were sold in the Messehalle (trade fair hall) and the Sophiensäle (a historic event location, notably for balls) after their worth had been estimated by the valuers working independently on behalf of the Gestapo and also managing the sales. The estimates were meant to be kept low so as to make the objects accessible to large families, and later to those whose homes had been bombed.[163] It did not turn out quite like that in reality. Before the sales, the valuers, who received RM 50 per day, and the Gestapo officials and those close to them who had been invited to the sales, had the possibility of acquiring the best items very cheaply. In 1945, the valuer and antique dealer Bernhard Witke[164] – who was a close friend of Gestapo official Johann Rixinger – still had warehouses in 1945, the size of which 'had to be seen to be believed'.[165] Herber also possessed savings books in 1945 with a value of well over RM 200,000.[166] Among the Gestapo officials, Ebner and Rixinger in particular made purchases through Vugesta.[167] After 1945, numerous objects from Vugesta were found during a search of Ebner's home. Rixinger also obtained all the valuable interior furnishings, such as furniture, carpets and pictures, for his 'Aryanized' villa in Hinterbrühl from Vugesta.[168] In 1940, Ebner supervised the seizure of industrialist Phillip Gomperz's extremely valuable collection. Hilde Glücksmann, who worked for several years as a clerk for Vugesta and the furniture disposal office for Jewish removals goods (Möbelverwertungsstelle für jüdisches Umzugsgut), stated after 1945 that the Gestapo had stored the most valuable paintings from this collection for a time in the rooms of a former Jewish school in Castellezgasse, to which only Ebner had keys, and sold them to leading National Socialists.[169] A letter from Ebner documents the purchase by Gauleiter and Reichsstatthalter Baldur von Schirach of a painting by Lucas Cranach from the Gomperz collection for the bargain price of RM 30,000. In the same letter, Ebner noted that an invoice 'on the pattern of the enclosed model' was to be sent to 'Inspector of the Sipo and SD SS-Brigadeführer and Generalmajor der Polizei Huber', but did not mention what objects Huber acquired from the Gomperz collection.[170] According to Hilde Glücksmann's statement in June 1945, the Gestapo also had depots in the Landhaus (historic seat of the government of Lower Austria) in Herrengasse, in which valuable paintings were stored and sold. She stated that all documentary evidence had been 'completely destroyed' by the Gestapo.[171]

After the start of the deportation of the Jews to ghettos and extermination camps in the East, the Möbelverwertungsstelle für jüdisches Umzugsgut (furniture disposal office) was founded to 'dispose of' the household goods left behind by the deportees by selling them cheaply to antique dealers and private individuals. As well as being controlled by the Gestapo and headed by Karl Herber, the furniture disposal office also employed the same valuers and Jewish workers (more precisely, forced labourers) as Vugesta. The task of the valuers and Jewish workers was now to obtain the deportees' apartment keys from the central office for Jewish emigration or the Gestapo, and to clear the apartments. The proceeds were to be transferred to the Vienna Gestapo and the Oberfinanzpräsident of Vienna.[172]

Even after the start of deportations, the Gestapo was still able to get its hands on very valuable objects. In 1944, for example, it obtained the art collection belonging to Ernst Egger, which contained not only paintings but above all tapestries, silver, and old Vienna porcelain. Egger, who lived in a 'mixed marriage', had hidden these items with various friends, some items at the castle of Eisgrub (Lednice, Moravia) belonging to the Prince of Liechtenstein. Just before his deportation to Theresienstadt on 28 June 1944, during the 'takeover' at the collection point, the Gestapo found the list of hidden artworks and objets d'art, and immediately took steps to seize them. According to Hilde Glücksmann, Karl Ebner 'acquired' numerous pieces from Egger's porcelain collection.[173]

It is not possible to determine from the sources exactly how much the Gestapo earned through Vugesta from the sale of seized assets. There are only brief memos to give an idea of the extent. For example, the Vienna Gestapo daily report of 1–2 September 1941 mentions that a 'revenue of RM 4,046,285.75 … was achieved as at 31 July 1941'. This report referred only to 'furniture and carpets disposed of'. It also mentions that 'tangible assets with a total estimated value of around RM 2.5 million remain to be disposed of'.[174] In his plea for clemency to Reichsführer-SS Himmler on 24 March 1945, Karl Ebner, who had been sentenced to death by an SS court, stated that thanks to the organization he had 'nurtured', in other words Vugesta, around RM 1 billion worth of tangible assets had been 'earned for the Reich'.[175] After 1945 he disputed this amount.

Vugesta was specific to Vienna. Although Gestapo offices in the 'Altreich' also auctioned the assets of emigrated or deported Jews from 1941, from which officials, experts, transport companies, warehouse managers and others all profited, the scale was much smaller than in Vienna. Nowhere else was there a special organization like Vugesta. The 'disposal' of seized tangible assets from Jewish owners was managed in a highly 'professional' way thanks to the cooperation between the Gestapo, which represented the state power monopoly, and Karl Herber, who operated according to the criteria of private enterprise and represented the interests of an entire professional sector. In Herber's trial at the VG, Ernst Weber, one of his most trusted employees, claimed that Herber had founded Vugesta to 'rescue' the transport industry, which was 'suffering and illiquid' because of the high cost of storing the removals goods left behind. This was a crude assertion to protect him: Vugesta was founded because the transport companies, valuers, antique dealers, auction houses and others cooperating with it could look forward to healthy profits – and the Gestapo officials not only to material advantages but also to professional prestige.

Everyday Looting

The daily work of the Vienna Gestapo, more specifically the 'Jewish section', included the implementation and supervision of all decrees and regulations aimed at the complete looting of the assets of Jewish inhabitants. With the outbreak of war, Jews had to hand in wirelesses, typewriters, calculators, warming pads, irons, brushes, ski boots, bicycles, mountain boots, woollens, and much more. The Gestapo not only supervised the proper handing in of these tangible assets but also made a note of it in the daily reports;[176] it also carried out house searches to hunt for 'forbidden' objects or clothing.

Even after the closure of the central office for Jewish emigration, which had put together the transports to the extermination camps, the Gestapo officials in the 'Jewish section' gathered the asset waiver declarations and cash and jewellery at the collection points from the victims, who were allowed to keep only their wedding rings, and searched their baggage for hidden valuables.[177]

The Gestapo and the individual officials also profited from the cheap labour of Jews, who were paid only a fraction of the wages of non-Jews. For example, Rixinger and others had their coats, suits and shoes repaired in the IKG clothing department.[178] At best they paid the small amount due to Jews in wages and the material costs, and in many cases nothing at all. Quite a few Gestapo officials had joinery and plumbing work in their own homes carried out free of charge by members of the IKG technical department. Rixinger did at least pay a modest wage to the Jewish skilled workers who carried out the extensive renovation of his villa in Hinterbrühl. When he was asked at his trial in 1947 about the furnishings acquired cheaply through Vugesta, he gave the following justification: 'I found nothing untoward about purchasing individual items from amongst such Jewish assets [i.e. belonging to deportees], because if I had not bought them, someone else would have'.[179]

Notes

1. Aronson, *Heydrich*, 178; BA Berlin, R 1501, 207081.
2. Wildt, *Judenpolitik des SD*, 80–81.
3. Ibid., 39, 32.
4. BA Berlin, R 58/982, according to a memo by Sonderkommando II 112 of 9 Apr 1938, signed by Herbert Hagen, Freytag spent several weeks in Vienna to 'take care of business'.
5. Hachmeister, *Gegnerforscher*, 193.
6. Stadlbauer, 'Ehrlinger', 35.
7. Wildt, *Judenpolitik des SD*, 52.
8. See WStLA, Vienna LG Vg 4c Vr 1223/47, statement by Hildegard Rock at the Vienna police headquarters, 28 Jan 1946. From 1 Apr 1938, Rock was the secretary of Karl Ebner, who became a case-handler in the 'Jewish section' immediately after the annexation and headed Section II B from 1939 to 1942.
9. Mallmann, 'Menschenjagd und Massenmord', 292.
10. BA Berlin, R 58/6558, undated list of names of Viennese (Jewish) lawyers.
11. BA Berlin, R 58/982, memo by Herbert Hagen with the letterhead 'SD-Hauptamt, Sonderkommando II 112' and dated 'Vienna, 9 April 1938'.
12. BA Berlin, R 58/9811, letter from Department II 112 to Department II 1, 15 Jul 1938.
13. Klamper, 'Der schlechte Ort zu Wien', 33–42.
14. Rux, born on 3 Sep 1907 in Bromberg, studied law in Jena, joining the anti-democratic and antisemitic fraternity Germania in 1926. After joining the NSDAP, SS and SD in 1933, he served from 1935 in the Gestapo in Münster/Westphalia, Königsberg (now Kaliningrad) and Elbing, and was transferred in 1937 to the Gestapa.
15. DÖW 532 and Neugebauer/Schwarz, *Stacheldraht, mit Tod geladen*, 2.

16. From July 1938, Haselbacher headed the Gestapo office in Kiel, and from September 1939 the Gestapo regional headquarters in Düsseldorf. In summer 1940 he was promoted to BdSuSD in Brussels. On 13 Sep 1940 he died in an accident while on an official visit to France. See BA Berlin, 1501/207081 and R 9361-III/529284, also Klee, *Personenlexikon*.
17. BA Berlin, R 58/982, letter from Department II 112 in Vienna to SD Department II 1, 9 Apr 1938.
18. WStLA, Vienna LG, Vg 4c Vr 1223/47, statement by Karl Ebner, 26 Jul 1947.
19. BA Berlin, R 3012/354; Klein, 'Rudolf Lange', 99.
20. WStLA, Vienna LG, Vg 4c 1223/47, statement by Karl Ebner, 12 Jul 1947.
21. WStLA, Vienna LG, Vg 11g Vr 1866/46 (copy: DÖW 19 859), testimony of Othmar Trenker in the VG trial of Johann Rixinger, 1 Oct 1947.
22. WStLA, Vienna LG, 20a Vr 731/55 (resumption of LG Wien Vg 4 Vr 5597/47), statement by Emil Tuchmann, 20 Nov 1956.
23. DÖW 1456; WStLA, Vienna LG, Vg 12c Vr 1223/47, statement by Karl Ebner, 26 Jul 1947.
24. DÖW 12800, copy of Dachau admissions book 1938.
25. See Kapralik, 'Erinnerungen', 57.
26. See, e.g., DÖW reference library, Vienna Gestapo daily report no. 13 of 25 and 26 Oct 1938, recording the arrest of two male doctors and one female doctor on 'suspicion of performing abortions for gain'.
27. WStLA, Bundespolizeidirektion Wien: Staatspolizeiliche Abteilung, A1-Polizeiliche Erhebung: Gestapo Wien, list by Section II G-Dauerdienst (24-hour duty office) of the events of 12–13 Jul 1938.
28. DÖW reference library, Vienna Gestapo daily report no. 11 of 20–21 Oct 1938.
29. DÖW 19400/154 and 20100/8950.
30. Rosse-Blaschko was dismissed from his position as deputy head of the Litzmannstadt (Łódź) Gestapo in April 1942; see also Chapter 15.
31. NARA, microcopy T 84 R 13 (DÖW Film 68/2), 39 810, Vienna Gestapo daily report no. 9 of 19–21 Nov 1938.
32. RGBl. I, no. 115, 26 Jul 1938; RGBl. I, no. 1044, 17 Aug 1938.
33. RGBl. I, 1938, 969–70.
34. DÖW 1456, circular from Vienna Gestapo II B 4, 22 Mar 1938.
35. WStLA, Vienna LG, Vg 4c 1223/47, statement by Karl Ebner, 12 Jul 1947; DÖW 20333/7.
36. WStLA, ibid.
37. Wildt, *Judenpolitik des SD*, 12.
38. Herbert, *Best*, 211.
39. Wildt, *Judenpolitik des SD*, 27–28, 104.
40. Ibid., 12, 27–28, 104.
41. Stangneth, 'Otto Adolf Eichmann', 52.
42. BA Berlin, R 58/956, annual report of SD Central Department II 1, signed by Herbert Hagen.
43. Rabinovici, *Eichmann's Jews*, 40 (*Instanzen der Ohnmacht*, 82). Hereafter, the 'Jewish Community of Vienna' and its successor organization the 'Council of Elders of the Jews in Vienna' will still be referred to by the acronym IKG.
44. See Rosenkranz, *Verfolgung und Selbstbehauptung*; Moser, *Judenverfolgung*.
45. Safrian, *Eichmann's Men*.
46. Alois Brunner did not officially become head of the Central Office for Jewish Emigration until 1941, but he was already its unofficial head in 1939, after Eichmann had been ordered to establish an emigration authority in Prague based on the Vienna model.
47. BA Berlin R 58/956, activity report of Herbert Hagen.
48. WStLA, Vienna LG, Vg 4c 1223/47, statement by Karl Ebner, 12 Jul 1947.

49. Gemeinsame Anordnung für den Sicherheitsdienst des Reichsführers SS und die Geheime Staatspolizei (joint regulation for the security service of the Reichsführer-SS and the Gestapo) issued by Heydrich, chief of the Sicherheitshauptamt and Sipo, 1 Jul 1937, quoted in Wildt, *Judenpolitik des SD*, 118.
50. Wildt, *Judenpolitik des SD*, 40.
51. The refugee transports were 'illegal' to the extent that they sidestepped the British mandate's immigration restrictions.
52. From 1940, Erich Rajakowitsch, later Erich Raja (born 23 November 1905 in Trieste, died 14 August 1988 in Graz), was one of Eichmann's close collaborators. As such he was strongly involved in the deportation of Jews from the occupied Netherlands from 1942.
53. Kapralik, 'Erinnerungen', 54–55.
54. See the section 'Repression of Nonconformist Youth' in Chapter 13.
55. IKG Vienna archive, Bestand Wien, A/VIE/IKG/II/AD/3/7.
56. DÖW 8496, express letter from the Vienna Gestapo to Gauleiter Bürckel regarding the central office for Jewish emigration, 2 Jun 1941.
57. BA Berlin, R 58/276, telex from Reinhard Heydrich to all Gestapo regional headquarters and offices and all SD Ober- and Unterabschnitte, 10 Nov 1938.
58. WStLA, Vienna LG, Vg 4c Vr 1223/47, statement by Hildegard Rock, 28 Jan 1946.
59. [Jedenfalls würden überraschende Haussuchuchungen (sic) in den SA- und NSKK-Heimen und bei deren Führern Erstaunliches an den Tag bringen.] Report by (Josef) Trittner, head of SD Unterabschnitt Vienna on the *Judenaktion* from 9 to 11 November 1938, quoted in DÖW, *Widerstand Wien*, vol. 3, 281ff. The NSKK (Nationalsozialistisches Kraftfahrkorps – National Socialist Motor Corps) was a paramilitary sub-organization of the NSDAP.
60. WStLA, Bundespolizeidirektion Wien: Staatspolizeiliche Abteilung, A1-Polizeiliche Erhebung: Vienna Gestapo, list by Section II G-Dauerdienst (24-hour duty office) of the events of 12–13 July 1938.
61. WStLA, Vienna LG, Vg 4c Vr 1223/47, statement by Hildegard Rock, 28 Jan 1946.
62. See DÖW, *Widerstand Wien*, vol. 3, 217.
63. See Klamper, 'Situation der jüdischen Bevölkerung', 165, 169–70.
64. WStLA, Vienna LG, Vg 4c Vr 1223/47, trial of Karl Ebner, Wilhelm Bienenfeld, report on the IKG during the Nazi era.
65. DÖW 2529, letter from the IKG to the Vienna Gestapo regarding the release of stateless Jews arrested in Vienna, 12 Sep 1939.
66. Moser, *Judenverfolgung*, 9–10. Some 440 of the imprisoned Jews were exploited for 'racial science' research before their transfer to Buchenwald by a commission headed by Josef Wastl, head curator of the anthropology department of the natural history museum in Vienna; see Klee, *Personenlexikon*.
67. Between 6 a.m. and 8 p.m. in winter and 5 a.m. and 9 p.m. in summer.
68. Wilhelm Bienenfeld, report on the IKG (see n. 64).
69. Walk, *Das Sonderrecht für die Juden*, 305.
70. WStLA, Vienna LG Vg 4c Vr 1223/47, statement by Hildegard Rock at the Vienna police headquarters, 29 Jan 1946.
71. Kapralik, 'Erinnerungen', 56, 67.
72. The IKG informed the Jewish population either by means of the *Jüdisches Nachrichtenblatt*, or through notices posted in the office issuing food ration cards. See WStLA, Vienna LG Vg 11g Vr 1866/46 (copy: DÖW 19 859), testimony of Karl Ebner in the VG trial of Johann Rixinger, 1 Oct 1947.
73. Löwenherz could only reply that the Jewish population was highly intimidated, and that since the start of the war many Jews had been importuned on the street and often beaten up by passers-by. Wilhelm Bienenfeld, report on the IKG (see n. 64).

74. Wilhelm Bienenfeld, report on the IKG (see n. 64).
75. Rolf Günther, born 8 January 1913 in Erfurt, worked in the central office for Jewish emigration from July 1938. In 1941 he became Adolf Eichmann's deputy in Section IV B 4 (Emigration and Jewish affairs) in the RSHA.
76. Alois Brunner, born 8 April 1912 in Nádkút, Austria-Hungary, worked from November 1938 in the central office for Jewish emigration, and headed it from 1941. He was heavily involved in the deportation of Austrian Jews to the ghettos and extermination camps in the East.
77. Wilhelm Bienenfeld, report on the IKG (see n. 64).
78. The IKG and Zionist organizations permitted by the Gestapo to resume their activities conducted various retraining courses to increase emigration and immigration chances.
79. Klamper, 'Situation der jüdischen Bevölkerung', 289.
80. IKG Vienna archive, Bestand Jerusalem, A/W 165, 1–7.
81. Wilhelm Bienenfeld, report on the IKG (see n. 64).
82. See Rabinovici, *Eichmann's Jews*, 78 (*Instanzen der Ohnmacht*, 173–74). Sponer was paid RM 1,032.10 per month, while the average salary of IKG employees was only RM 125.
83. WStLA, Vienna LG, Vg 11g Vr 1866/46 (copy: DÖW 19 859), testimony of Karoline Schwarz to the Austrian state police, 5 Jan 1946.
84. After the November Pogrom, the British government relaxed the conditions for immigration, allowing Jewish children up to the age of 17 to immigrate, provided that a guarantor or foster family could be found for them. From 2 December 1938 to 22 August 1939, 2,262 children selected by the IKG were sent to Great Britain in twenty-three transports. Many of these children were the only members of their families to survive the Shoah. See DÖW, *Österreicher im Exil: Großbritannien 1938–1945*, 6ff.
85. On 31 December 1942 there were only 7,989 Jews remaining in Vienna; most were so-called *Geltungsjuden* (persons deemed to be Jews according to the Nuremberg Laws), *Mischehepaare* (partners in mixed marriages) or IKG employees; see Klamper, 'Situation der jüdischen Bevölkerung', 175–76.
86. Mang, *Die Unperson*, 136.
87. Wilhelm Bienenfeld, report on the IKG (see n. 64).
88. WStLA, Vienna LG, Vg 11g Vr 1866/46 (copy: DÖW 19 859), statement by Rixinger in the main proceedings, 1 Oct 1947.
89. WStLA, Vienna LG Vg 11g Vr 1866/46 (copy: DÖW 19 859), final report of the Austrian state police, 21 Jan 1946.
90. For the Nisko transports, see Moser, *Nisko*.
91. DÖW 8911, memo of the central office for Jewish emigration, 17 Oct 1939.
92. Moser, *Nisko*, 79ff.
93. Copy of a letter from Reich minister and head of the Reich chancellery, Berlin, 3 Dec 1940, to the Reichsstatthalter in Vienna, Gauleiter v. Schirach, 3 Dec 1940, Yad Vashem, 018/213, quoted in Safrian, *Eichmann's Men*, 68 (*Eichmann-Männer*, 97); see also Mang, 'Gestapo-Leitstelle Wien', 245ff; Rabinovici, *Eichmann's Jews*, 99–100 (*Instanzen der Ohnmacht*, 224).
94. DÖW, *Widerstand Wien*, vol. 3, 292; Mang, 'Gestapo-Leitstelle Wien', 251.
95. DÖW 2562, memo by Josef Löwenherz, head of the IKG Vienna, 1 Feb 1941.
96. See, e.g., DÖW 5733a, Vienna Gestapo daily report no. 4 of 9–10 Feb 1942.
97. Wilhelm Bienenfeld, report on the IKG (see n. 64).
98. See the section 'Looting of Jewish Assets', this chapter.
99. DÖW 19 400/69, letter from the Reichsstatthalter in Vienna to the Vienna Gestapo, 10 Apr 1941.
100. DÖW and the Institut Theresienstädter Initiative, *Theresienstädter Gedenkbuch*, 478.
101. Weisz, 'Gestapo-Leitstelle Wien', 260–61; WStLA, Vienna LG, Vg 11g Vr 1866/46 (copy: DÖW 19 859), statement by Johann Rixinger at the main proceedings, 1 Oct 1947.

102. RGBl. I, 547, police regulation on the (self-)identification of Jews (Polizeiverordnung über die Kennzeichnung der Juden), 1 Sep 1941. From 1 Apr 1942, Jews had to stick a paper 'Jewish star' on the front door of their apartments.
103. DÖW 5733e, Vienna Gestapo daily report no. 4 of 8–9 Sep 1941.
104. https://www.doew.at/personensuche (last accessed on 29 Oct 2017).
105. DÖW 5733a, Vienna Gestapo daily report no. 8 of 19–20 Jan 1942. On these two days alone, twenty-six people were arrested for 'infringing the police regulation on the identification of Jews'.
106. DÖW 5733a, Vienna Gestapo daily report no. 2 of 5–6 Jan 1942. Kurt Löwidt was deported to Riga on 11 January 1942.
107. DÖW 5733f, Vienna Gestapo daily report no. 4 of 10–12 Nov 1942. Flora Schön was deported on 5 January 1943 to Theresienstadt, where she died on 19 August 1943.
108. DÖW 5733a, Vienna Gestapo daily report no.12 of 27–28 Feb 1942. Schireno was deported on 9 April 1942 to Izbica.
109. DÖW E 21 708, report on the activity of the IKG Vienna and the council of elders of the Jews in Vienna in 1942.
110. Nazi jargon designated anyone with two 'full-Jewish' grandparents and who were members of the Jewish community on the 'effective date' (15 September 1935, adoption of the Nuremberg Laws) as *Geltungsjuden*. See Klamper, 'Situation der jüdischen Bevölkerung', 171ff.
111. See, e.g., WStLA, Vienna LG, Vg 3e Vr 1955/45, statement by Emil Tuchmann, 27 Sep 1945.
112. WStLA, Vienna LG Vg 11g Vr 1866/46 (copy: DÖW 19 859), statement by Karl Ebner, 3 Oct 1947.
113. WStLA, Vienna LG, Vg 11g Vr 1866/46 (copy: DÖW 19 859), statement by Wilhelm Bienenfeld, 2 Oct 1947.
114. See, e.g., Dams/Stolle, *The Gestapo*, 108 (*Die Gestapo*, 121).
115. Statement by Wilhelm Bienenfeld, see n. 113.
116. WStLA, Vienna LG, Vg 11g Vr 1866/46 (copy: DÖW 19 859), statement by Karl Ebner, 1 Oct 1946.
117. See the section 'Looting of Jewish Assets', this chapter.
118. For details, see Senekowitsch, *Feldmarschalleutnant Johann Friedländer*.
119. See the section 'Looting of Jewish Assets', this chapter.
120. Weisz, 'Gestapo-Leitstelle Wien', 2270.
121. WStLA, Vienna LG, Vg 11g Vr 1866/46 (copy: DÖW 19 859), testimony of Otto Butka, 7 Oct 1947.
122. Ibid., testimony of Otto Butka and Ernst Kleinert, 7 Oct 1947.
123. WStLA, Vienna LG, 20a Vr 731/55 (resumption of LG Wien Vg 4 Vr 5597/47), record of the main proceedings, 21 Nov 1956.
124. WStLA, Vienna LG, Vg 11g Vr 1866/46 (copy: DÖW 19 859), testimony of Hermann Kohout, 4 Dec 1947.
125. DÖW 8479, Vienna Gestapo daily report no. 5 of 14–16 Mar 1944.
126. WStLA, Vienna LG, Vg 1d Vr 442/45, writ by Vienna's state prosecutors, 28 Dec 1945.
127. See Moser, 'Deportation', 500.
128. DÖW 19400/177, decree of the chief of the security police, 17 Mar 1938.
129. DÖW 19400/177, decree of the chief of the security police, 25 Mar 1938.
130. Ibid.; Pfeifer, *Die Ostmark*, 36–37.
131. DÖW 19400/177, letter from Walter Stahlecker, 7 May 1938.
132. 'Krida' is the fraudulent or grossly negligent declaration of insolvency by a debtor. Alleged offences such as 'asset smuggling' and 'violations of the foreign currency law' were based on the German foreign exchange law, which entered into force in Austria on 23 March 1938. See Kuller, *Bürokratie und Verbrechen*, 241.

133. DÖW 19000/50, letter from the Vienna Gestapo, Unit II B 4, to the ministry of internal and cultural affairs regarding the seizure of assets belonging to David Goldmann, 5 May 1939.
134. DÖW 19000/51, letter from the Vienna Gestapo, II H/SO, to the inspector of the security police, 5 Jul 1939.
135. Ibid., for Meisinger, see Chapter 3.
136. DÖW 19400/170, list of assets confiscated and seized in the Ostmark, 22 Jul 1938.
137. DÖW 30 049/2295. Arnold and Rudolf Kolb had been detained since 13 March 1938 at the police prison on Rossauer Lände on suspicion of Krida. Kosmath was sentenced on 5 June 1939 to eight months' imprisonment. After release he worked as an insurance clerk.
138. DÖW 19 400/177.
139. ÖStA, AdR, BMF, seized assets (Juva) 1938–39, general files and detailed seizure records, part 1, letter from the office of the Reichsstatthalter, 18 Jul 1938.
140. See Kuller, *Bürokratie und Verbrechen*, 357ff. 'Reparation' was understood as compensation for damage that individual National Socialists had suffered from 1933 to 1938, when the NSDAP was illegal in Austria.
141. DÖW 19 400/182.
142. DÖW 19 000/50.
143. After the annexation, the provincial tax offices (Landesfinanzämter) in Austria were renamed 'Oberfinanzpräsidien'; see Kuller, *Bürokratie und Verbrechen*, 85.
144. WStLA, Vienna LG, Vg 4c Vr 1223/47, statement by Hildegard Rock at the Vienna police headquarters, 29 Jan 1946.
145. ÖStA, AdR, BMF, seized assets (Juva) 1938–39, general files and detailed seizure records, part 1, letter from the ministry of internal and cultural affairs to the Reich ministry of finance, Austria department, 1 Dec 1938.
146. Ibid., Regulation of the Reichsstatthalter of 12 Dec 1938.
147. Ibid., letter from the minister of finance to the Reichsstatthalter in Austria, 17 Jan 1939. Fischböck had previously drafted the law for the regulation on the registration of Jewish assets, and had also participated as an economic expert on 12 November 1938 in the interministerial conference at the Reich ministry of aviation, in which the exclusion of Jews from the German economy was decided.
148. Ibid., letter from the ministry of finance to the Vienna Gestapo and Gestapo offices in Austria, 13 Feb 1939.
149. Ibid., memo on the meeting of Hofrat Dr Steinböck with Franz Josef Huber, 14 Feb 1939.
150. DÖW 19 400/182.
151. ÖStA, AdR, BMF, seized assets (Juva) 1938–39, general files and detailed seizure records, part 1, letter from the Vienna Gestapo ('Jewish section') to the Reich ministry of finance, Austria department, 4 Apr 1939.
152. The Reich authorities vigorously rejected this appropriation of seized assets; see Kuller, *Bürokratie und Verbrechen*, 359.
153. DÖW 19 000/50.
154. ÖStA, AdR, BMF, seized assets (Juva) 1938–39, general files and detailed seizure records, part 1, letter of the ministry of finance to the Reich minister of finance in Berlin, 16 Mar 1940.
155. Kuller, *Bürokratie und Verbrechen*, 372–73.
156. WStLA, Vienna LG, Vg 4c Vr 1223/47, statement by Karl Ebner, 30 Jul 1947.
157. Kuller, *Bürokratie und Verbrechen*, 126–27.
158. WStLA, Vienna LG, Vg 4c Vr 1223/47, questioning of Karl Ebner, 30 Jul 1947.
159. In a letter of 1 Nov 1940 to the Vienna employment office, Herber described his function as follows: 'By order of the Vienna Gestapo, I am responsible as the administrative department of the Vienna Gestapo for the seizure and sale of removals goods'.

160. In most documents, Vugesta (sometimes 'Vugestap') is called 'Verwaltungsstelle für jüdisches Umzugsgut der Geheimen Staatspolizei'.
161. WStLA, Vienna LG, Vg 3c Vr 272/48, report of the Vienna police headquarters, 10 Feb 1948.
162. WStLA, Vienna LG, Vg 3c Vr 272/48, reports of the Linz police headquarters, 21 Feb 1948, and Vienna police headquarters, 10 Feb 1948.
163. WStLA, Vienna LG, Vg 2b Vr 2331/45, statement by Karl Ebner at the main proceedings against Bernhard Witke, 12 Jan 1949.
164. Witke joined the NSDAP on 20 Jun 1932. After the NSDAP was banned in 1933, he housed several National Socialist dynamiters and helped them to escape to Germany. After the annexation, together with the former agricultural worker Michael Oberhuber, Witke 'Aryanized' the antiques firm Josef Berger & Sohn, where Oberhuber was now working as a menial assistant. See WStLA, Vienna LG, Vg 2b Vr 2331/45, judgment against Bernhard Witke, 12 Jan 1949.
165. WStLA, Vienna LG, Vg 2b Vr 2331/45, expert opinion, cited in the judgment against Bernhard Witke, 12 Jan 1949.
166. WStLA, Vienna LG, Vg 3c Vr 272/48, report of the Vienna police headquarters, 9 Mar 1948.
167. WStLA, Vienna LG, Vg 2b Vr 2331/45, testimony of Hilde Glücksmann to the Polizeilicher Hilfsdienst for the Kommandantur of the city of Vienna, 8 Jun 1945.
168. WStLA, Vienna LG, Vg 3c Vr 272/48, report of the Linz police headquarters, 21 Feb 1948.
169. WStLA, Vienna LG, Vg 2b Vr 2331/45, testimony of Hilde Glücksmann to the Polizeilicher Hilfsdienst for the Kommandantur of the city of Vienna, 8 Jun 1945. This episode was also described by the witness Emil Gottesmann in the main proceedings against Johann Rixinger, WStLA, Vienna LG, Vg 11g Vr 1866/46. The school at Castellezgasse 35, Leopoldstadt (2nd district), was later used as a collection point for Jews intended for deportation.
170. WStLA, Vienna LG, Vg 4b Vr 1223/47, letters to the Vienna Gestapo regarding the Gomperz collection, 30 Jun and 16 Aug 1943, quoted in DÖW, *Widerstand Wien*, vol. 3, 246–47.
171. WStLA, Vienna LG, Vg 2b Vr 2331/45, testimony of Hilde Glücksmann to the Polizeilicher Hilfsdienst for the Kommandantur of the city of Vienna, 8 Jun 1945.
172. WStLA, Vienna LG, Vg 2b Vr 2331/45, testimony of Karl Ebner, 31 Mar 1947.
173. WStLA, Vienna LG, Vg 2b Vr 2331/45, testimony of Hilde Glücksmann to the Polizeilicher Hilfsdienst for the Kommandantur of the city of Vienna, 8 Jun 1945. See Lillie, *Was einmal war*, 291ff. Egger died in Theresienstadt on 9 December 1944.
174. DÖW 5732e, Vienna Gestapo daily report no. 1 of 1–2 Sept 1941.
175. WStLA, Vienna LG, Vg 4b Vr 1223/47, plea for clemency of Karl Ebner to Himmler, 24 Mar 1945.
176. See, e.g., DÖW 5733d, Vienna Gestapo daily report no. 8 of 17–19 July 1942.
177. WStLA, Vienna LG, Vg 11 g Vr 1866/46, statement by Wilhelm Bienenfeld at the main proceedings against Johann Rixinger, 3 Oct 1947.
178. In the IKG clothing department, old clothes were collected and repaired to provide the Jewish population with the most urgently required clothing, as Jews were not allowed to purchase clothes or fabrics.
179. [Ich habe aber nichts Bedenkliches daran gefunden, von solchem Judenvermögen einzelne Gegenstände zu kaufen, denn hätte ich diese nicht gekauft, so hätte sie eben jemand anderer erworben.] WStLA, Vienna LG, Vg 11 g Vr 1866/46, statement by Johann Rixinger at the main proceedings, 1 Oct 1947.

Chapter 11

PERSECUTION OF THE CATHOLIC CHURCH AND OTHER RELIGIOUS BODIES

Persecution of the Catholic Church

After the annexation of March 1938, the Catholic Church – until that point an important pillar of the 'Christian corporate state' – attempted to come to an arrangement with the new powers, through negotiations and by ingratiating itself with the National Socialist regime (notably in the appeal of the bishops for Catholics to vote 'yes' in the NS plebiscite of 10 April 1938).[1] Far from reciprocating this demonstration of goodwill, however, the Nazi regime proceeded to implement a series of harsh anti-Catholic measures. This put the church into a very difficult situation, as the Nazis paid no heed either to the existing Vatican concordats (with the German Reich and with Austria) or to long-established rights and ancient traditions. On the contrary, the new rulers were determined to use all means to break the ideological power of the Catholic Church; they lusted after church property, expropriated monastic communities and large religious foundations, destroyed Catholic education and journalism, and harassed the clergy, members of religious orders and lay people alike.

As the executive body responsible for carrying out the anti-Catholic measures decided upon at the political level, the Gestapo had an essential role to play in the repression of the Catholic Church. Particularly in the phase immediately following the annexation, preliminary work was done, in cooperation with the Gestapo, by the security service of the SS (SD), which was responsible for dealing with National Socialism's 'ideological opponents'. The SD main office sent several special commando units to Austria, which immediately went into operation in agreement with the Vienna Gestapo, which was still being built up at the time.[2]

The Gestapo was responsible for the seizure and confiscation of church assets, the obstruction of Catholic journalism and writing, the restriction of church activities, and most especially the persecution of individuals. However, as the Catholic Church was a legal institution and Hitler did not wish to enter into open conflict with it during the war, the Gestapo did not generally proceed with the same ruthless severity as it did against Jews and resistance activists. In very many cases, the Gestapo did not imprison priests or send them to concentration camps but, rather, imposed a kind of fine by setting bail. It is clear that this relative 'leniency' had its source at the highest level, where there was no wish for an escalation of conflict on the 'home front' during the war; at a lower level, by contrast, local and regional Nazi functionaries, many of whom were fanatically anti-Catholic, pressed for a more radical approach.

The office of the Vienna Gestapo responsible for the Catholic Church was Unit II B 1 (from 1942 IV B 1, and in 1944–45 IV 4a) in the important Section II B (Ideological opponents, from 1942 IV B), which also contained the offices responsible for Jews, sects and Freemasons, and the Lutheran Church. Between autumn 1938 and March 1945, the daily reports of the Vienna Gestapo – in which by no means all arrests were listed – recorded 301 arrests of individuals associated with the Catholic Church, or 2.1 per cent of a total of 14,367; in addition, there were a further 930 arrests from the Catholic-conservative camp, or 6.5 per cent.[3] For the year 1943, Franz Weisz has identified 52 arrests carried out by Unit IV 4a (Catholic and Lutheran churches, sects), or 0.24 per cent of all arrests in that year, which are complemented by the much higher figure of 89 reprimands, 16 referrals to the state prosecutors, and 43 bail payments; in 1943 there were no committals to concentration camps. In 1944, Unit IV 4a made 23 arrests.[4]

A key role in the Vienna Gestapo's activity in this field was played by the police jurist Karl Ebner, who himself grew up in a Catholic milieu and was a member of the Austrian Cartellverband (union of Catholic university fraternities for students and graduates, CV) and the Fatherland Front until 1938. Even before the annexation in March of that year, however, Ebner had made contact with the illegal Nazi movement. Subsequently he left the Catholic Church – like many other members of the police who were transferred to the Gestapo – and on the strength of his organizational abilities he rose from being an assistant adviser and case-handler in Unit II B 1 to become head of Section II B. As deputy head of the Vienna Gestapo from 1942 through to his arrest on 9 January 1945 – and de facto head for many months on account of Franz Josef Huber's extended absences – Ebner had broad scope for action. Once the signs appeared that the downfall of the Nazi regime was only a matter of time, he used this freedom to pursue a shrewd policy of *Rückversicherung* ('reinsurance', i.e. contingency planning), which also benefited a number of churchmen carefully selected by Ebner for that purpose.⁵

Seizure and Confiscation of Ecclesiastical Assets

In the period after the events of March 1938, the Vienna Gestapo was made responsible for the seizure and confiscation of ecclesiastical assets urgently demanded by local and regional Nazi functionaries, in particular from the great monasteries with their large buildings and extensive estates. The 'legal basis' for the confiscations was provided by the 'regulation concerning the confiscation of assets inimical to Volk and state in the land of Austria' of 18 November 1938,⁶ the beneficiaries for the most part being the German Reich or individual local municipalities or Nazi organizations, as specified by the political authorities. As Karl Ebner stated at the Vienna VG in 1947: 'Between 1939 and 1941, the Vienna Gestapo was many times urgently called upon to carry out confiscations of church assets, some of which had been submitted for approval in Berlin; in most cases, the applications to Berlin were accompanied by statements intended to prove that members of the monasteries and religious foundations had acted in a manner inimical to state and Volk'.⁷

'The first major ecclesiastical property to be seized', Ebner continued, 'was the Benedictine abbey of Göttweig, which was confiscated for the benefit of the nearby autonomous town of Krems.' Although he laid the responsibility for this confiscation on Humbert Achamer-Pifrader and Rudolf Lange, which was correct insofar as they were his superiors at the time, the application to Heydrich as chief of the Sipo and SD had in fact been drawn up by Ebner himself, who backed it up with allegations of 'economic abuses' in the administration and sexual offences on the part of members of the monastery.⁸ After Heydrich's deputy Werner Best had established the 'Volks- und Staatsfeindlichkeit' of Göttweig as an institution and had approved the confiscation, the notification to the Vienna Gestapo was issued on 15 September. The complaints and interventions made by ecclesiastical bodies were to no avail. Prior to the confiscation, in April and May 1939 Abbot Hartmann (Augustin) Strohsacker and six further monks of the community were arrested and interrogated by the Gestapo in connection with allegations of subversive statements and actions. The Gestapo submitted applications for two Benedictines to be put into 'protective custody'. From 1943, Göttweig was used to house a 'national-political' boarding school, or 'Napola'.⁹

The next religious establishments to be expropriated by the Vienna Gestapo were the Missionshaus Sankt Gabriel in Mödling, and the large and historic religious foundation of Klosterneuburg, both in May 1941. Two employees of the mission house were arrested for having removed items to the value of

RM 2,000 before the expropriation took place. Stift Klosterneuburg was subjected to a thorough search on 6 March 1941, and on 30 April the Gestapo moved the Augustinian canons to the religious house of the Piarists in Josefstadt (8th district). On 22 March 1941, the Reichsstatthalter of Vienna, Baldur von Schirach, had instructed Regierungspräsident Hans Dellbrügge that the Klosterneuburg archive should be transferred to the Gau archive, and that care should be taken to see that 'the Holy Joes don't walk off with anything'. A letter written by Dellbrügge to Huber on 27 March concerning the archive, library and art treasures indicates that 'the general instruction of the Führer in person' had to be obtained for the actual confiscation of seized property.[10] The buildings of Stift Klosterneuburg were put at the disposal of the Reichsstatthalter of Vienna, department of municipal administration, with the (unfulfilled) intention of an 'Adolf Hitler School' being founded there.[11] Finally, in March 1942, on the basis of directives of the Reich ministry of the interior, the entire assets of the Missionshaus Sankt Gabriel and of Stift Klosterneuburg were confiscated by the Vienna Gestapo for the benefit of the German Reich.[12]

These interventions were followed by similar proprietary measures against numerous other religious foundations and church institutions. The assets of the Benedictine abbey of Altenburg, for example, were confiscated by the Vienna Gestapo for the benefit of the German Reich, following which the Reich minister of finance transferred the assets to the Reichsgau Lower Danube. In the case of other religious communities, buildings were confiscated to accommodate ethnic German refugees (*Volksdeutsche*). In addition – without the involvement of the Gestapo – other Nazi organizations carried out 'wild' (i.e. unauthorized) seizures, which were often accompanied by assaults on representatives of the respective church bodies.[13]

In 1938–39 the Nazi regime implemented a number of measures intended to inflict a serious financial blow upon the Catholic Church: closing down the Religious Fund (established by Joseph II in 1782 with assets from his dissolution of religious foundations), abolishing state support, and in 1939 imposing a tax to be paid by church members (*Kirchensteuer*). As a result, the parishes had to distribute forms for the registration of those liable for the tax, which they did with the assistance of many voluntary helpers. This caused the Vienna Gestapo considerable concern, as they saw that this communal activity was hindering 'the party's ideological education work', and at the same time prompting the spread of 'covert propaganda against the party and state authorities'.[14] The Vienna Gestapo responded by reprimanding and in some cases arresting those involved, as they did with Catholic men and women who had sought to influence former church members to return to the fold.[15] Furthermore, the intense Nazi propaganda in Austria against church membership was also directed at Catholic members of the Gestapo, who found themselves under massive pressure to fall into line in this way.

Dissolution of Catholic Organizations

A great number of Catholic associations were dissolved or forced into political conformity (*Gleichschaltung*) by the liquidation commissioner for organizations, societies and associations (Stillhaltekommissar für Organisationen, Vereine und Verbände), who was appointed for the territory of annexed Austria in 1938.[16] The Gestapo was called upon to take the leading role in larger measures undertaken against organizations. On 6 September 1938, for example, all Vienna's six Kolping houses (hostels for young working people) were occupied without warning by Gestapo officials, SD men, and agents of the liquidation commissioner, and all the cash and documents found on the premises seized. Further items were confiscated from the secretariat of the Kolping House at Gumpendorferstrasse 39 in Mariahilf (6th district) and from the private apartments of Kolping functionaries.[17]

On 20 June 1939, in a bid to guarantee the monopoly of the Hitler Youth on youth and education work outside of schools in Austria, Himmler in his capacity as Reichsführer-SS issued a decree prohibiting a number of associations of the Bündische Jugend (a broad movement with many different youth groups, notably the 'Wandervogel' groups) and scouts, also criminalizing activities connected with them. The Vienna Gestapo arrested numerous activists from this milieu, and referred them to the relevant courts.[18]

Seizure and Confiscation of Writings and Printed Matter

Catholic publishing, which until 1938 was an extensive and thriving field of activity, was a particular thorn in the side of the Nazi authorities. For the Vienna Gestapo, a useful guideline was provided by the 'list of harmful and undesired writings' regularly issued by the Reich literature chamber (Reichsschrifttumskammer, one of the seven 'chambers' of the Reich chamber of culture founded by Goebbels in 1933),[19] which in addition to naming left-wing, pacifist and Jewish authors also included Catholic and other Christian publications. Many of the Gestapo daily reports mention confiscation raids on churches and church buildings. In December 1939, for example, at the printing works of Karl Gerolds Sohn, the Gestapo seized five thousand copies of the brochure 'Vespers for the four Sundays of Advent, Roman rite' ordered for publication by the Volksliturgischer Verlag Klosterneuburg, the reason being that sayings from the Old Testament were 'nothing but a glorification of Judaism'.[20] In April 1941 the Gestapo carried out several raids on printing works, seizing a total of thirty-one thousand copies of six different publications commissioned by Karl Rudolf, head of the department of pastoral care of the archdiocese of Vienna.[21] In May 1942, even the official gazette of the archdiocesan offices was seized because it contained an 'appeal from the Holy Father Pius XII for prayer on present matters of concern', which the Gestapo regarded as defeatist.[22]

Finally, a decree of the Reich literature chamber of 26 October 1940 was used to put an end to literature stands in churches. In February 1941, on the basis of this regulation, the Gestapo carried out a check on the stands in Vienna's churches and reported fifteen priests to the chamber, resulting in fines of RM 1,000 and an order to the archdiocese of Vienna to have all literature stands removed.[23]

The Arbeitsgemeinschaft für den religiösen Frieden (working group for religious peace) had developed out of the National Socialist union of priests (NS-Priesterbund) as an attempt on the part of the regime to influence and split the Catholic Church. In October 1938 it closed down after Cardinal Innitzer had prohibited all the priests in his jurisdiction from being members, whereupon the Gestapo, at the request of SD-Oberabschnitt 'Danube', conducted a house search, seized all the association's papers and sealed its rooms.[24]

In January 1939 it came to the Vienna Gestapo's attention that, on the strength of press cards issued by the Reich press chamber (Reichspressekammer), Catholic priests and members of religious orders (both priests and lay brothers) were disseminating Catholic writings with the aim of 'spreading anti-National Socialist propaganda amongst the general public'. Thereupon, the Gestapo instructed the authorities in 'Lower Danube' to confiscate the press cards and send them in to Morzinplatz.[25]

In February 1941, on the orders of the RSHA and 'in cooperation with SD-Leitabschnitt Wien', the Vienna Gestapo raided the publishing house that issued the Catholic periodical *Schönere Zukunft* 'in search of subversive material', and closed it down. The editor of the periodical, Joseph Eberle, a leading figure in political Catholicism and a proponent of a Christian antisemitism, was arrested and interned in a concentration camp for a number of months.[26]

Further Restrictions on Religious Life

The Gestapo repeatedly took action against religious instruction given outside schools, where it was prohibited. In March 1943, Herbert Heiny, curate of the parish of Gerasdorf, was reprimanded by the Vienna Gestapo for having taken twelve altar boys or young servers to Vienna on an outing to the circus at his own expense in order to make them 'more amenable to the interests of his parish church'.[27] Even handicraft lessons for children were prohibited, as is shown by the warning issued in May 1943 to the curate of the parish of Schwechat, Dominik Poppen, and to the bookkeeper Hermine Martin, who was in charge of giving the lessons.[28]

On 28 February 1939, Herbert Friedl, deputy district administrator (Landrat) of Baden and a member of the NSDAP, telephoned the Vienna Gestapo in order to request action against the parish priest of Pottendorf, Arnold Dolezal, so that 'the danger of self-help on the part of the national population' might be promptly averted. What the local Nazis objected to was that Father Dolezal, after various Catholic associations had been prohibited, had taken matters into his own hands by transferring 'Bible study groups, meetings of the parish church council and liturgical evenings' to the presbytery, thus engaging in 'clandestine club-like activity'.[29]

Therese Dümler, Margarethe Hofmann and Sophie Pick, sisters of a religious order and all from the 'Altreich', were compelled by the Vienna Gestapo to return to the principal convent of their province because, 'since the prohibition of confessional schools, they have held unauthorized sewing and music classes for young people in a private house, and spread unrest among the people through their clerical-propagandistic behaviour'. Similarly, Sister Gertrude Arlet of the institute of the Blessed Virgin Mary ('Mary Ward sisters' or 'Englische Fräulein') was accused by the Gestapo of spreading 'clerical propaganda' and of being 'a constant source of unrest among the people'. She was ordered to leave Rohrendorf near Krems, and return to her mother house. For the same reason, the parish priest of Felling, Heinrich Schultehinrichs, who had already received a warning from the Gestapo, was banned from the Alpine and Danube Gaus.[30] Franz König, priest on the staff of the cathedral of Sankt Pölten (and from 1956 Archbishop of Vienna), had to make a bail payment of RM 1,000 because he had 'organized prohibited leisure activities by arranging gatherings of young people'.[31]

In many places the Gestapo intervened on account of parish priests and curates' resistance to the limitations on religious feast days imposed by the Nazi regime. The parish priest Milo Offenberger from Göpfritz was reprimanded for having appealed to Catholics 'to continue to observe the abolished Marian holidays as liturgical feast days'.[32] On 23 May 1941, the parish priests Erich Pastor of Waldeck-Wopfing, Matthias Schneider of Rohr im Gebirge, Erich Baumann of Hochwolkersdorf and Albin Formanns of Theresienfeld were arrested by the Vienna Gestapo branch office of Wiener Neustadt 'for not observing the regulation concerning the transferral of Ascension Day'.[33] The Gestapo took similar measures – issuing warnings or setting bail – against Karl Pfeifer, parish priest of Obritzberg, Hubert Anton Rudolf, dean of the Augustinian canonry of Herzogenburg, and Ludwig Kessler, parish priest of Zlabern, who had encouraged parishioners, in particular agricultural labourers, not to work on the feast of Corpus Christi, which had been abolished as a holiday.[34]

Church events scheduled at the same time as Nazi activities tended to arouse particular wrath in NSDAP functionaries, who regarded them as deliberate attempts to cause disturbance or create competition.[35] Josef Sturm, for example, parish priest of Sankt Andrä vor dem Hagentale, was reprimanded for having organized an extraordinary Advent blessing at the same time as an NSDAP event. As the Gestapo daily report noted, also referring to earlier penalties imposed on the parish priest: 'The event in the church resulted in attendance at the party function leaving much to be desired'.³⁶ Even pilgrimages prompted the Gestapo to take action, as they caused 'an unjustifiable increase in the number of rail travellers at a time when the Reichsbahn is already overstretched because of the war'. Subsequently a Gestapo order resulted in the archdiocese of Vienna appealing to its parish priests to refrain from organizing pilgrimages.³⁷

Certain important anti-church measures were taken without the involvement of the Gestapo, notably those directed at the destruction of Catholic education: abolition of school prayers, removal of crucifixes from classrooms, dismissal of those responsible for pastoral work in the parishes, and other limitations on religious education in schools imposed by the relevant administrative and political authorities.³⁸ However, if there were protests against these measures, the Gestapo intervened immediately. When Karl Ramharter, a Catholic teacher of religion in Haag (Lower Danube), was prohibited from giving religious instruction because of having 'repeatedly made subversive and anti-NSDAP statements', sixty to seventy people demonstrated in front of the school to demand that he be reinstated. After the Vienna Gestapo had identified three men and two women as the instigators of the demonstration, these 'ringleaders' were referred to the public prosecutors at the regional court (Landgericht) of Sankt Pölten. A similar episode took place in the parish of Sindelburg, where the curate Franz Herzog had been banned by the regional education authority (Landesschulrat) from giving religious instruction, and Dean Johann Mayerhofer announced in church on Whitsunday 1940 that the celebration of first communion would have to be indefinitely postponed. On the following day around forty women responded by going to the mayor and demanding that the children should once again receive their religious instruction. On 18 May 1940 the Vienna Gestapo arrested four women as the 'ringleaders', three smallholders and an agricultural labourer, and kept them in 'protective custody' for ten days.³⁹ In another incident, the Gestapo arrested Josef Buchta, parish priest of Niederabsdorf, who had organized a petition against dismissals of teachers, and with him the parish church councillor and farmer Franz Fembeck.⁴⁰ After the Benedictine fathers Alois Baresch and Franz Lohrmann and the diocesan priest Josef Seywald had conducted ballots amongst pupils of schools in Kilb and Mank on the retention of school prayers, and had allegedly sought to 'incite the local population to a rally', they were suspended from giving religious instruction and reprimanded by the Gestapo.⁴¹

Surveillance and Spying

'The unit in question [II B 1, 'Catholic Church']', wrote Lambert Leutgeb, head of the Vienna Gestapo's Section II N (Intelligence), in the report he composed when imprisoned after the war in Yugoslavia, 'was responsible for monitoring the Catholic Church and its institutions.'⁴² However, only in isolated cases was this surveillance actually carried out by Gestapo members. The Gestapo daily report on the reading of the first pastoral letter of the Austrian bishops in Austria's churches on Sunday, 4 September 1938, stated: 'In Vienna, 128 churches were monitored by Gestapo officials. ... Thanks to informants, it was also possible to obtain the original text of the pastoral letter'. A meeting of the leaders of Catholic Action in the archdiocese of Vienna held on 3 and 4 September at the abbey of Heiligenkreuz also aroused the interest of the Gestapo; some of the participants were photographed, and five individuals identified by name.[43] The provost of Klosterneuburg, Alipius Josef Linda, was spied on by an NSDAP member by the name of Tischler, who obtained information from the provost's chauffeur and passed it on to the local NSDAP district leader (Kreisleiter), Karl Kleemann, a German on the staff of Reichskommissar Bürckel.[44]

In March 1941 the Vienna Gestapo demanded the names of all parish church councillors (together with their occupations and places of employment). When the archdiocesan offices declined to reveal these details, the request was made to the individual parish offices. At the same time, all Vienna's municipal employees were required to reveal whether they were active in a parish council and, if so, to resign from their church function.[45]

In its battle against the Catholic Church no less than in its political and racial persecution, the Gestapo used informants, who usually came from the milieu of the organization that the Gestapo wanted to spy on. Of no less importance were the – often malicious – denunciations that came from NSDAP units and comrades. For example, the local NSDAP group leader (Ortsgruppenleiter) of Sankt Anton an der Jessnitz gave the Vienna Gestapo branch office of Sankt Pölten technically detailed suggestions as to how it could use an air duct in the school at Wohlfahrtsschlag to eavesdrop on the new parish priest Johann Grießer without compromising either the Ortsgruppenleiter or the school. As the Gestapo clearly did not send anyone to do the job, the task was given to the 'Blockleiter und Parteigenosse' (block leader and party comrade) Josef Reßl, a local teacher. On 10 October 1940, as a result of this intervention, the special court (Sondergericht, SG) of Vienna sentenced the parish priest to eighteen months' imprisonment for offences under the 'Heimtückegesetz' (law against 'insidious utterances').[46] In at least three cases, priests whose sermons had allegedly contained 'subversive' (*staatsfeindlich*) statements were reported to the police by the local mayors. However, as the statements were clearly not sufficiently subversive to warrant court proceedings, the Gestapo contented itself with reprimands.[47]

Vienna Gestapo Toleration of Anti-Catholic Aggression by Nazi Organizations

Although the Gestapo had nothing to do with the many acts of aggression and excesses carried out, particularly in 1938 by NSDAP members and formations, the Vienna Gestapo commonly ignored the appeals of victims for action to be taken and refrained from proceedings against the culprits, who were commonly recorded as 'unknown offenders'. On 20 November 1938, for example, SS men fired shots from a car at the presbytery of the parish of Schwechat, but the Gestapo report claimed – in spite of the car registration number being known – that 'it was not possible to ascertain the identity of the car owner or of the SS men likely to have been involved'.[48]

Likewise, on 8 October 1938 during the storming of the archbishop's palace by the Hitler Youth, an act of revenge for the large demonstration of young Catholics in front of St Stephen's cathedral the day before, the police and Gestapo were called in to assist but again failed to take action. The Gestapo daily report contents itself with two short, one-sided assertions: 'On 8 October 1938 there was an attack on the archbishop's palace in Vienna in which certain valuable objects were damaged and one priest injured. The offenders could not be identified'. The blame was put on the victim: 'The excesses were due to the inflammatory sermon delivered by Cardinal Innitzer on 7 October 1938'. Subsequently, when Gauleiter Bürckel delivered a genuinely inflammatory speech to two hundred thousand 'Volksgenossen' at Heldenplatz on 13 October, the Gestapo styled the Nazi rally a 'people's mass demonstration against Cardinal Archbishop Innitzer'. On the periphery of the Catholic youth demonstration, Gestapo officials arrested several participants; amongst those committed to concentration camps was the 18-year-old Hermann Lein and the Catholic student Ferdinand Habel, who perished at Mauthausen on 3 February 1940.[49]

Church accounts of these events were suppressed, and the NS media, being 'aligned' (*Gleichschaltung*), did not report on them. After giving an interview about the occurrences to a French newspaper, the Dominican priest and Swiss citizen Emil Broglie was summoned to Morzinplatz at Bürckel's behest and ordered to leave the German Reich within twenty-four hours.[50]

In early December 1938, the Jesuit Johannes Maria Lenz, who had been under investigation by the Gestapo since late autumn that year, was arrested for 'insulting the Führer and spreading unsettling rumours', and was accused, among other things, of making multiple copies of a report on the 'attack on the archbishop's palace in Vienna' and of 'misusing the confessional to spread misinformation concerning alleged political atrocities'. The Gestapo transferred Lenz to Dachau, where he was interned until the liberation in April 1945.[51]

A further serious incident occurred at St Stephen's during the evening liturgy on 8 December 1941 (Solemnity of the Immaculate Conception), when twenty to thirty Nazi youths barged into the cathedral, harassed members of the congregation, insulted the Church and clergy in foul terms, and prevented Innitzer from leaving the building. The police were called but came too late, and the only person to be arrested was a Catholic woman who had called out to the youths: 'A decent Jew is better than you Bolsheviks'.[52]

Suppression of Individual Catholic Resistance

As is clear from the statistics quoted at the head of the present chapter, the Gestapo in many cases let priests off with reprimands or with setting bail; further customary sanctions were curfews combined with a ban on public speaking or expulsion from the Danube and Alpine Gaus. Only when the misdemeanour was a serious one did the Gestapo apply for 'protective custody' or refer the case to the public prosecutors. The Gestapo reserved these harsher measures particularly for Catholics who had stood up publicly against the Nazi regime and its deeds, or who were members of resistance groups. On 1 December 1938, for example, the Gestapo took Alois Hanig, parish priest of Stillfried an der March, into 'protective custody' and had legal proceedings initiated against him because 'he continually issued incomplete birth certificates to Jews who had had themselves baptized by him'. For the same kind of offence – 'falsifying baptism papers to obtain an Aryan certificate [Ariernachweis]' – the parish priest of Korneuburg Vinzenz Oskar Ludwig and his sacristan Leopold Frühlinger were arrested and referred to the public prosecutors, as was the parish priest Wilhelm Suchet of Vienna.[53]

On 8 September 1941, on the instructions of the Vienna Gestapo, Hubert (Ernst) Trompeter, curate of Margarethen am Moos and member of a religious order, and Peter Wolf, administrator of the parish of Mönchhof, were arrested by the border police at Bruck an der Leitha because they had sought 'to influence the local people in a manner inimical to National Socialism' and had stood up against regulations of the state and the NSDAP. To punish several children for attending a Hitler Youth roll-call one Sunday instead of going to church, Wolf had allegedly 'beaten them with a stick during religious instruction'. The Gestapo applied for a 'protective custody' order on the two priests, who were interned at Dachau until April 1945.[54]

Particularly by means of informants and denouncers, the Gestapo paid very close attention to sermons, which they feared would enable priests to influence a wider circle of listeners and spread 'propaganda inimical to the state and the NSDAP' ('staats- und parteifeindliche Propaganda'). The deterrents and penalties used by the Gestapo ranged from reprimands and bans on public speaking or expulsion from the Gau to prosecution under the 'Heimtückegesetz'; or, alternatively, 'protective custody' with committal to a concentration camp.

As director of the archdiocese of Vienna's pastoral ministry department, Karl Rudolf was one of the most important representatives of Catholicism in the city; on 8 August 1943, in the parish church of Hainburg an der Donau, he preached a sermon that was assessed as being an 'attack on the National Socialist worldview and state', for which the Gestapo banned him from the Gau of Vienna.[55] Furthermore, the Gestapo prohibited Johann Vetter, provincial of the Dominican order, from preaching anywhere in the German Reich because he 'made use in his mission sermons of parables from Holy Scripture eminently likely to have a defeatist effect on his listeners'. Similarly, the Salvatorian provincial Franz Xaver Bader was penalized by the Gestapo for spreading a rumour and criticizing the pro-euthanasia propaganda film *Ich klage an* ('J'accuse').[56]

Raimund Weißensteiner served as a curate in Hollabrunn, Lower Austria, in the parish of St Brigitta in Brigittenau (20th district), and at the Votivkirche. After being reprimanded in November 1938 for a 'subversive statement', he was arrested by the Gestapo on 16 September 1943 for making defeatist statements and was later deprived of his professorship at the Vienna academy of music. He was sentenced to three years' imprisonment on 27 October 1943, and interned until 15 April 1945.[57]

In 1943, Johann Ecker, parish priest of Sankt Margarethen (Burgenland), was sentenced to two months' imprisonment for attempting 'to prevent young people who had attended an obligatory roll-call on a Sunday from serving in the Hitler Youth'. On 16 December 1943 he was arrested once again by the Gestapo because he had given French civilian workers wishing to escape to Hungary instructions about how to realize their plan, and also gave them shelter in the presbytery.[58]

Numerous arrests and convictions were related to the prohibited practice of listening to foreign radio stations. On 10 December 1942, for example, the priest and Catholic teacher of religion Michael Molecz was arrested by the Gestapo; on 21 May 1943 he was sentenced to four years and six months' imprisonment with hard labour for 'radio crime', and he remained in prison until the end of April 1945. In September and October 1939, Anton Pauk, priest and member of a religious order, repeatedly listened to the prohibited Vatican radio station; likewise, he was arrested by the Vienna Gestapo and sentenced to fifteen months' imprisonment on 18 July 1940.[59]

On 30 May 1941, Theresia Steinbauer, superior of the home for religious sisters at Lainz hospital, and three members of the Franciscan Sisters of Christian Charity ('Hartmann Sisters'), Aloisia and Anna Fröhlich and Josefa Kammermayer, were arrested by the Vienna Gestapo for disseminating a 'Catholic polemic' in which 'the racial philosophy of National Socialism is criticized and presented as the work of the devil'. On 16 December 1941, the Vienna SG imposed prison sentences on the four nuns ranging from six to eight months for offences under the 'Heimtückegesetz'.[60]

The most outstanding example of courageous and steadfast resistance in this field was that of Sister Maria Restituta of the Franciscan Sisters of Christian Charity. As a surgical nurse at the public hospital in Mödling, Lower Austria, she disseminated an anti-war and Austrian-patriotic poem, and was denounced at the Mödling SD field station by Dr Lambert Stumfohl, who was on the hospital staff and was also an SS-Untersturmführer. Following her arrest by the Vienna Gestapo on 18 February 1942, she was subjected to intensive interrogation in order to force her to reveal the origin of this widely disseminated poem. The death sentence imposed on her by the VGH on 29 October 1942 was carried out on 30 March 1943 – in spite of interventions in her favour on the part of Cardinal Innitzer and others – because the Nazi leadership wanted to set an example and demonstrate the regime's anti-Catholic position.[61]

The Vienna Gestapo's suppression of priests and members of religious orders who belonged to resistance groups is dealt with in the section 'Catholic-Conservative and Legitimist Resistance' in Chapter 12.

Jehovah's Witnesses

Although prohibited in Austria after 1935–36, the international Bible students' association (Internationale Bibelforschervereinigung, IBV) resolutely continued its illegal activities following the events of March 1938, despite the much harsher repressive measures under the Nazi regime. Known in NS jargon as 'Bibelforscher' (Bible students), the members of this small Christian group referred to themselves as 'Zeugen Jehovas' (Jehovah's Witnesses). They not only propagated their religious teachings in widely distributed publications but also adopted clear political positions. They categorically rejected the National Socialist state and refused to use the salutation 'Heil Hitler!' or join the Hitler Youth. Most particularly, as principled pacifists, they refused to perform military service or to work in the armaments industry. In addition, they actively opposed other totalitarian forms of government and dictatorial systems such as Italian Fascism, the Franco regime in Spain, and Communism in Russia; furthermore, within the German Reich, they not only protested against the persecution of their own members but also raised their voices on behalf of Jews and others. The Jehovah's Witnesses, whom the Nazis slanderously claimed to be working 'in the service of Jewish plans to conquer the world', were persecuted by the regime no less systematically and brutally than the political opposition. The community of faith and its will to resist were to be broken by means of imprisonment, concentration camps and death sentences.[62]

The Vienna Gestapo office responsible for the investigation and arrest of Jehovah's Witnesses and for referring them to the special court (or otherwise committal to a concentration camp) was Unit II B 3 (Sects and Freemasons), which was headed by Kriminalobersekretär Johann Zisterer and divided into the subunits II B 3a ('Bibelforscher') and II B 3b (Freemasons, fortune-tellers, astrologers, occult societies). After the organizational reform of 1942, Unit II B 3 became Section IV B 3, before finally being merged with Section IV B 2 (Lutheran Church) to form IV B 2/3. Its superior was the head of Section II B (Ideological opponents) Karl Ebner, who was also deputy head of the entire Vienna Gestapo. With only four members, the unit had a low status in the overall organizational structure.[63]

The Vienna Gestapo set its sights particularly on the IBV's organizational network, especially its leaders in the former Austrian federal provinces, and the infrastructure underlying its extensive publishing activities. Following the arrest and committal to a concentration camp of August Kraft, the illegal head of the IBV for former Austria, this function was performed from May 1939 by the Vienna greengrocer Peter Gölles until he too was arrested by the Gestapo.[64] On 8 June 1940 the RSHA issued an order that on 12 June all members of the IBV should be taken into 'protective custody' at once, expressly specifying that the women should not be excluded. This mass arrest, which was accompanied by interrogations, house searches and seizures of 'Bibelforscher' material, was also carried out in Austria.[65] In the course of this measure, the head of Vienna's illegal Jehovah's Witnesses was arrested together with forty-four further 'Bibelforscher' and sentenced on 2 May 1941 to ten years' imprisonment with hard labour for 'undermining military morale'. Gölles was only spared the death sentence because he 'abjured the ideas of the "Bibelforscher"'.[66]

Even after the mass round-up, Jehovah's Witnesses were still arrested on a regular basis. In 1941, the large-scale circulation of leaflets by the cashier Alois Kasperkowitz aroused the Gestapo's particular interest after the Vienna Gestapo head Huber found leaflets and the brochure 'Harmageddon' in his personal mail. On 24 October 1941, Kasperkowitz was arrested by the Gestapo and on 5 March 1942 he was sentenced by the Vienna SG to ten years' imprisonment with hard labour for 'participation in an anti-military association'. In September 1943 he was transferred from Waldheim prison to Buchenwald concentration camp, where he remained until the liberation.[67]

Unlike the Jews and Roma, who were persecuted on racist grounds, the Jehovah's Witnesses were given some opportunity to avoid persecution by 'recanting' the teachings of the IBV and thereby earning themselves a milder sentence or release from internment in a concentration camp. That only a small number succumbed to this temptation is a testimony to the strength of conviction of the Jehovah's Witnesses generally. For example, Antonie Schneider was arrested by the Gestapo on 24 June 1940 but released after making a declaration of loyalty, assuring the officials that she would 'turn away from the teaching of the IBV and in the future perform all services required of her by the state'. However, when she appeared at the Vienna SG, she changed her tune, as recorded in the Gestapo daily report: 'At the main hearing Schneider confessed in passionate terms to being a True Christian ... that is to say, a Jehovah's Witness ... and proved entirely unrepentant'. The courageous woman was arrested once again while still in the courtroom and led off to start serving her sentence immediately.[68] On 12 February 1942, Johanna Grübling was convicted at Vienna SG of 'participation in an anti-military association' and sentenced to 'only' six months' imprisonment because she had 'abjured the teachings of the IBV'. After serving her sentence, she was remanded to the Gestapo, who proceeded to check the validity of her 'abjuration'. The relevant Gestapo daily report contains the following record: 'At her more recent interrogation, she stated ... that she had only abjured in order not to be given a sentence of imprisonment with hard labour. As she persists in pronouncing herself to be a "Jehovah's Witness", the application was made for her to be committed to a concentration camp'. She was sent to Ravensbrück.[69] The Vienna Gestapo dealt in the same way with Marie Herforth, Ferdinanda Kraupa and Olga Besenböck, who were sentenced to two years' imprisonment with hard labour on 6 February 1941 for 'participation in an anti-military association'. In July 1942, having served their sentences, they were remanded to the Gestapo, where they declared themselves to be loyal Jehovah's Witnesses and refused 'any kind of work that was necessary for the defence of the Reich'. They were sent to Ravensbrück concentration camp, where they remained until the liberation.[70]

With its focus on war and territorial gains, the Nazi regime was naturally highly sensitive to any refusal to carry arms, engage in active service or take the oath of allegiance. Consequently, the conscientious objectors from the ranks of the Jehovah's Witnesses were punished with particular severity. Although the prosecution of conscripts or those subject to conscription was primarily the responsibility of the military authorities, it was frequently the Gestapo that carried out the arrests. On 5 October 1940, for example, after the manual labourer Wilhelm Puschmann had refused to put on a military uniform, he was taken by the Gestapo to the local military prison 'Heeresstandortarrest Wien X'. According to the Gestapo report, he adopted the 'position that he would rather suffer death than take up arms for the Third Reich'.[71] After refusing to comply with the call-up order, Karl August Haas hid in an allotment shed from June 1940 until his arrest by the Gestapo on 27 September 1941. On 5 March 1942 he was sentenced to death by the Reich military court for 'undermining military morale', and was executed on 11 April 1942 at the prison of Brandenburg-Görden.[72]

Almost all the Austrian conscientious objectors sentenced to death were Jehovah's Witnesses. According to statistics provided by their official body, of the 550 members of the Jehovah's Witnesses in Austria, 445 were interned, of whom 154 were put to death, 54 of these for refusing to perform military service or for 'undermining military morale'.[73] According to Thomas Walter, however, the NS military courts sentenced 51 Austrian Jehovah's Witnesses to death for refusing to perform military service and carried out the sentences in 42 instances; five conscientious objectors died in prisons or concentration camps.[74] The daily reports of the Vienna Gestapo record 230 arrests of Jehovah's Witnesses ('Bibelforscher'), that is to say, 1.4 per cent of total arrests. While only 19 per cent of all those arrested by the Vienna Gestapo were women, in the case of the Jehovah's Witnesses, women made up more than half of the total of 230 arrested.[75]

Other Small Religious Groups

The Seventh Day Adventist reform movement, which was also against the performance of military service and had broken away from the Seventh Day Adventist Church over that very issue, continued its religious practice and was persecuted by the Nazi authorities in very much the same way as the Jehovah's Witnesses.[76]

On 23 April 1942, for example, the bodice-maker Stefanie Obhlidal was arrested by the Vienna Gestapo; found in her possession was a farewell letter from the conscientious objector Julius Ranacher, who had been executed in March that year. Although Obhlidal was released on account of serious illness, she was referred to the Vienna SG, which on 29 May 1942 sentenced her to fifteen months' imprisonment with hard labour for 'undermining military morale'. Likewise in April 1942, the artist Josef Holzbauer, a member of the Seventh Day Adventists since 1936, was arrested by the Vienna Gestapo; on 30 June 1942 he was sentenced to five years' imprisonment with hard labour, also for 'undermining military morale', and remained in prison until the end of the war.[77]

The daily reports of the Vienna Gestapo indicate that a number of religious or quasi-religious groups in Vienna were persecuted, even though they had little influence and were more or less harmless to the Nazi regime. Most especially, house searches led to the seizure of religious writings, publicity material and books; to a large extent, detention for a short period and reprimands were the most severe measures undertaken against members of such groups, amongst whom were Rudolf Weymelka (October 1938), a contracted municipal worker and member of the prohibited sect Christliche Versammlung (Christian assembly), and Emil Sekot and Rudolf Stief, who were planning to organize a Vienna branch of the Grail association Abd-ru-shin Sect of Vomperberg. The Gestapo also took measures against publications and promotional activities of the authorized association (sect) Deutsche Volksmission/Volksgemeinschaft entschiedener Christen (German mission/community of staunch Christians).[78] Between June and September 1941 the Gestapo put a total of thirty-five members of the prohibited 'First Church of Christ, Scientist' under temporary arrest, and seized a number of their publications. The detainees were released after being reprimanded and prohibited from further activities.[79] Emma Scheffler, a home worker and member of the prohibited sect Menschenfreundliche Versammlung (Philanthropic assembly), was put into 'protective custody', having already been reprimanded before. Furthermore, certain individuals were put under arrest for 'spiritualist' activities – for example, Johann Malik, founder and president of the Christophorusbund.[80]

Freemasons

Freemasonry – noted for its humanistic orientation, neutral stance on politics and religion, hierarchical structure and division into lodges – occupied an important position in National Socialist ideology and propaganda.[81] Its influence and sheer size were hugely overestimated by the Nazis, for whom the Freemasons were an internal enemy to an extent only exceeded by Jews and Communists, even being seen as part of the 'Jewish world conspiracy'. As such they were prohibited and persecuted, from 1933 in Germany and from March 1938 in annexed Austria.

At the time of the annexation in March 1938 the Freemasons only had around eight hundred members in Austria. Furthermore, there were no longer any lodges outside Vienna, because discrimination on the part of the corporate state, which was Catholic in its ideology and thus in principle against the Freemasons, had led to a considerable fall in membership. The members came principally from the worlds of business, culture, the human and natural sciences, medicine and law. Around 70 to 80 per cent of the brethren of the grand lodge in Vienna were of Jewish descent. Among the most prominent members were the Nobel Peace Prize winner Alfred Hermann Fried, the cabaret artist Fritz Grünbaum, who was murdered at Dachau, and Richard Coudenhove-Kalergi, founder of the Pan-Europa Movement.[82]

The leading role in the persecution was initially taken by the SD, with the SD main office in Berlin having a special section (II 111) devoted to the Freemasons. The goal of the SD officials sent to Vienna immediately after the annexation of Austria (led by SS-Sturmführer Erich Ehlers) as part of SD-Einsatzkommando 'Österreich' was to suppress the lodges as rapidly as possible and seize their entire assets. In pursuing these ends they had recourse to detailed information about the lodges and their premises, functionaries and members; the lists that they brought with them contained 925 names of Freemasons, some of whom were to be taken into 'protective custody'.[83]

On 13 March 1938, right after the annexation, the Grand Master Richard Schlesinger was arrested and compelled to hand over the financial assets of the Grand Lodge of Vienna. In a commando raid on 16 March, forty SD men headed by Ehlers took control of the lodge's house at Dorotheergasse 12 in the centre of Vienna, and carted off the movable goods to the SD premises at Theresianumgasse 16–18. The following days witnessed further summonses, house searches and seizures at other lodges, though some of the premises had already been plundered by other Nazi organizations. A total of 200,000 schillings (the equivalent of around 950,000 euros today) in cash, savings books and securities were seized. In a further move, the Rotary Club was compelled to disband and to hand over its furniture; and searches were carried out at the premises of publishing houses such as Amalthea and Saturn, which had published Masonic writings.[84]

As part of the task-sharing with the SD, the detentions[85] and bureaucratic handling of the seizures and subsequent confiscations were the responsibility of the Gestapa, or rather – especially once the SD men from Berlin had been withdrawn from Vienna – of the Vienna Gestapo established on 15 March 1938. Following his arrest, the 77-year-old Richard Schlesinger – Grand Master since 1919 and now seriously ill – was so badly treated while in detention in the police prison on Elisabethpromenade (now Rossauer Lände) that he died on 5 June 1938, shortly after being released. Posthumously, the SS weekly *Der Stürmer* exposed Schlesinger to the mockery and hatred of its readers with a humiliating photograph, entitled the 'Jewish bastard Dr Schlesinger', taken a few weeks before his death.[86]

The names of several Freemasons appear on a list of Jewish lawyers to be interned at Dachau, drawn up in spring 1938 by SD-Leitabschnitt 'Vienna'; amongst the summary grounds quoted for concentration camp internment are such formulas as 'dangerous Freemason', 'malicious Freemason' and 'communist Freemason'.[87]

There were numerous further arrests of Freemasons, particularly in the course of the November Pogrom of 1938. Many left the country, and a significant number were interned at Dachau or Buchenwald. However, in most cases individual Freemasons were persecuted not because of their membership of a masonic lodge but as part of the Nazi regime's general persecution of the Jews. The names are known of around one hundred Austrian Freemasons who fell victim to the Nazi regime; some six hundred sought and found refuge in exile.[88]

The Vienna Gestapo dissolved the grand lodge of Vienna with effect from 15 April 1938, expropriating its assets for the benefit of the German Reich. Until August 1939, the Freemasons' premises at Dorotheergasse 12 served as an 'NS-Bücherverwertungsstelle' (book-processing office), where 'Aryanized' libraries were stored before being transported elsewhere.[89]

After the seizures and confiscations of assets and the neutralization of freemasonry as a power in society, its numbers being drastically reduced through voluntary emigration, forced emigration and deportations, the relevant unit of the Vienna Gestapo – until 1942, II B 3 (Sects and Freemasons) – no longer had very much to do with the Freemasons. After the organizational reform of 1942, Unit II B 3 with a staff of just four mutated into IV B 3 or IV B 2/3, which was responsible for the Lutheran Church, sects and Freemasons.[90]

As membership of a lodge disqualified applicants from becoming members of the NSDAP after 1933, only a small number of Freemasons were able to find their way into the party (and these only by 'gracious favour of the Führer'), one of whom was the writer Franz Karl Ginzkey.[91] One special case was that of Kurt Reichl, a high-ranking Freemason who had been expelled in 1932 on account of financial irregularities. Subsequently he published anti-Masonic writings, and from mid-1935 he offered his services to the SD (Department II 111) as an informant. While the information provided by Reichl was very useful to the SD during its operations of March 1938, it ultimately rebounded on Reichl himself. On 15 March, on the basis of material seized during the raids in Vienna, Reichl was taken into 'protective custody' by the Gestapa in Berlin. As one result of his interrogations, Department II 112 of the SD offered to provide the head of the SD for SS-Oberabschnitt 'Danube' with 'information about leading Jews in Vienna and Jewish organizations', and subsequently sent extracts from interrogation records to Vienna.[92] Released from detention after eleven months, Reichl returned to work for the SD, in Vienna and other places. Marcus G. Patka describes him as having been 'the most evil opportunist and traitor in the history of Austrian Freemasonry'.[93]

Notes

1. See Liebmann, 'Kirche und Anschluss', 137.
2. For a detailed account, see Stadlbauer, 'Ehrlinger', 174–200.
3. DÖW 20 333/7, Sections of the Vienna Gestapo with their heads and members, n.d., no author/compiler (a listing most likely compiled by the Austrian state police in the course of proceedings against members of the Vienna Gestapo); Neugebauer, *Austrian Resistance*, 32–33. On the daily reports and arrests, see also Chapter 6, this volume.
4. Weisz, 'Gestapo-Leitstelle Wien', supplement no. 164, 232, and table no. 31, 37.
5. For details, see Mang, *Die Unperson*, 115–30, and the section 'Reinsurance' in Chapter 5, this volume.
6. 'Verordnung über die Einziehung volks- und staatsfeindlichen Vermögens im Lande Österreich'. RGBl. I 1938, pp. 1620–21; GBlÖ. Nr. 589/1938. For details, see Bandhauer-Schöffmann, *Entzug und Restitution*.
7. WStLA, Vienna LG, Vg 4c 1223/47 (copy: DÖW 8919), statement by Karl Ebner, 29 July 1947.
8. Ibid.; BA Berlin, R 5101, express letter Vienna Gestapo II B 1 (Pifrader) to Reichsführer-SS Himmler, 23 May 1939; ibid., letter of the Reichsführer-SS, signed by Best, to the Reich minister for churches (Reichskirchenminister), 16 Aug 1939.
9. NARA, microcopy T 84 R 16 (DÖW Film 78), 43 146 and 43 136, Vienna Gestapo daily reports, no. 8 of 25–26 Apr 1939 and no. 1 of 29 Apr – 30 May 1939. 'Napola' stood for 'Nationalpolitische Erziehungsanstalt'.
10. [dass die Pfaffen nichts mitschleppen / generelle Weisung des Führers] ÖStA, AdR, Reichsstatthalter Wien, Organisationsreferat, Karton 193.
11. WStLA, Vienna LG, Vg 4c 1223/47 (copy: DÖW 8919), statement by Karl Ebner, 29 July 1947; DÖW 5732 c, Vienna Gestapo daily report no. 5 of 9–11 May 1941; DAW, Bischofsakten Innitzer 19, Vienna Gestapo confiscation order; Stiftsarchiv Klosterneuburg, K. 493, no. 1, letter from the Reichsstatthalter in Vienna to the provost of Stift Klosterneuburg, Alipius Josef Linda, 22 Feb 1941.
12. DÖW 5733 b, Vienna Gestapo daily report no. 8 of 18–19 Mar 1942.
13. DÖW, *Widerstand Niederösterreich*, vol. 3, 118–35.

14. NARA, microcopy T 84 R 16 (DÖW Film 71), 43 420, Vienna Gestapo daily report no. 11 of 24–25 Oct 1939.
15. See extracts from Gestapo reports in *Widerstand Wien*, vol. 3, 76–80.
16. For details, see Pawlowsky/Leisch-Prost/Klösch, *Vereine, Organisationen und Verbände*.
17. NARA, microcopy, T 84 R 13 (DÖW Film 68/2), 40 059, 40 035, Vienna Gestapo daily reports no. 6 of 7 Sep 1938 and no. 11 of 13 Sep 1938.
18. DÖW, *Widerstand Wien*, vol. 3, 18–19; Neugebauer, *Austrian Resistance*, 152–56.
19. 'Liste des schädlichen und unerwünschten Schrifttums', see reprint Vaduz, 1979.
20. NARA, microcopy T 84 R 16 (DÖW Film 78), 43 572 ff., Vienna Gestapo daily report no. 4 of 7–18 Dec 1939.
21. DÖW 5732 b, Vienna Gestapo daily report of 28–29 Apr 1941.
22. DÖW 5733 c, Vienna Gestapo daily report no. 7 of 17–18 May 1942.
23. DÖW 5732 b, Vienna Gestapo daily report no. 3 of 4–6 Apr 1941; DAW, Bischofsakten Innitzer 19, report of the archbishop's office concerning restrictive measures affecting religious and church life, 1941.
24. NARA, microcopy T 84 R 13 (DÖW Film 76), 40 024ff, Vienna Gestapo daily report no. 13 of 15 Sept 1938; ibid., 39 797, Vienna Gestapo daily report no. 10 of 22–23 Nov 1938; *Wiener Diözesanblatt*, 76/10 (30 Sep 1938), and 76/11 (15 Oct 1938).
25. NÖLA/ZR, 253, I/1a, 1939 (copy: DÖW E 19 284), express letter from the Vienna Gestapo to the authorities of the Reichsgau Lower Danube, 14 Jan 1939.
26. DÖW 5732 a, Vienna Gestapo daily report no. 3 of 5–6 Feb 1941.
27. DÖW 5734 b, Vienna Gestapo daily report no. 7 of 19–22 Mar 1943.
28. DÖW 5734 c, Vienna Gestapo daily report no. 8 of 22–26 May 1943.
29. NARA, microcopy T 84 R 16 (DÖW Film 78), 43 221, Vienna Gestapo daily report no. 2 of 2–3 Mar 1939.
30. DÖW 5733 e, Vienna Gestapo daily report no. 7 of 21–24 Aug 1942.
31. DÖW 5734 c, Vienna Gestapo daily report no. 7 of 21–24 May 1943.
32. NARA, microcopy T 84 R 13 (DÖW Film 76), 39 948, Vienna Gestapo daily report no. 1 of 1 Oct 1938.
33. Ascension Day was transferred from the Thursday to the following Sunday. DÖW 5732 c, Vienna Gestapo daily reports no. 11 of 26–27 May 1941 and no. 12 of 28–29 May 1941.
34. DÖW 5733 f, Vienna Gestapo daily report no. 7 of 20–23 Nov 1942, and DÖW 8475, no. 9 of 27–31 Aug 1943.
35. NARA, microcopy T 84 R 14 (DÖW Film 99), 40 837, daily inland situation report of the IdSuSD to the Reich commissioner for the reunification of Austria with the German Reich, 3 Nov 1939.
36. DÖW 5734 c, Vienna Gestapo daily report no. 1 of 1–3 May 1943.
37. DÖW 5733 e, Vienna Gestapo daily report no.1 of 29 Sep – 1 Oct 1942.
38. DAW Bischofsakten Innitzer, 18 (copy: DÖW 16 345), letter of protest from Bishop Michael Memelauer and Archbishop Innitzer to the Reichsstatthalter of Lower Danube concerning the provision of religious instruction by lay teachers, 22 Sep 1941.
39. NARA, microcopy T 84 R 16 (DÖW Film 78), 43 101, Vienna Gestapo daily report no. 11 of 23–24 May 1939.
40. NARA, microcopy T 84 R 16 (DÖW Film 78), 43 630, Vienna Gestapo daily report no. 10 of 25–24 Nov 1939.
41. NARA, microcopy T 84 R 16 (DÖW Film 78), 43 036, Vienna Gestapo daily report no. 12 of 27–28 May 1939.
42. Archives of the Republic of Slovenia, AS 1931, 809, sheets 640–81, Lambert Leutgeb, 'Die Organisation der Geheimen Staatspolizei-Staatspolizeileitstelle Wien nach dem März 1938 bis zur Gründung des Reichssicherheitshauptamtes 1941', 7 and 26 (composed 1947–48

while in Yugoslavian detention). The incorrect date for the foundation of the RSHA (1941 instead of 1939) was most likely a slip of the pen or a dictation error.
43. NARA, microcopy T 84 R 13 (DÖW Film 76), 40 066, Vienna Gestapo daily report no. 5 of 6 Sep 1939.
44. BA Berlin, R 5101, letter from Kreisleiter Arnhold to Kreisleiter Kleemann, 9 Mar 1939.
45. DAW, Bischofsakten Innitzer, report of the archdiocesan offices (Erzbischöfliches Ordinariat), 1941.
46. DÖW 14 111, letters of the NSDAP-Ortsgruppenleiter of Sankt Anton an der Jessnitz to the Vienna Gestapo branch office of Sankt Pölten, 15 and 24 Jan 1940, judgment of the Vienna SG against Johann Grießer, 10 Oct 1940. The 'Heimtückegesetz' was, in full, the Gesetz gegen heimtückische Angriffe auf Staat und Partei und zum Schutz der Parteiuniformen (Law against insidious attacks on state and party and for the protection of party uniforms) of 20 Dec 1934; see the section 'Anti-regime Utterances' in Chapter 13, this volume.
47. NARA, microcopy T 84 R 13 (DÖW 76), 39 799, 39 770, Vienna Gestapo daily reports no. 10 of 22–23 Nov 1938 and no. 1 of 1–2 Dec 1938, and T 84 R 16, 43 466, Vienna Gestapo daily report no. 4 of 10–11 Jan 1939.
48. NARA, microcopy T 84 R 13 (DÖW Film 76), 39 804, Vienna Gestapo daily report no. 9 of 20–21 Nov 1938.
49. Lein, *Innitzergardist*, 27ff.; http://www.doew.at/erinnern/personendatenbanken/gestapo-opfer (last accessed on 30 Jun 2017).
50. NARA, microcopy T 84 R 13 (DÖW Film 76), 39 895, 39 913 f., 39 833, Vienna Gestapo daily reports no. 6 of 8–10 Oct 1938, no. 8 of 13–14 Oct 1938 and no. 10 of 18–19 Oct 1938. Later, Lenz wrote the books *Als Priester in den Ketten der Gestapo* (Salzburg, 1945) and *Christus in Dachau* (Loosdorf bei Melk, 1956), translated into English as *Christ in Dachau* (Roman Catholic Books, 1960), both of which became bestsellers of their kind.
51. [den Beichtstuhl zu politischer Gräuelpropaganda missbraucht] NARA, microcopy T 84 R 13 (DÖW 76), 39 813, 39 754, 39 703, T 84 R 16 (DÖW Film 78), 43 473, Vienna Gestapo daily reports no. 8 of 17–18 Nov 1938, no. 3 of 6–7 Dec 1938, no. 10 of 22–23 Dec 1938, no. 3 of 5–9 Jan 1939.
52. [Ein anständiger Jude ist besser als ihr Bolschwiken.] DÖW 5732 g, Vienna Gestapo daily report no. 4 of 8–9 Dec 1941.
53. NARA, microcopy T 84 R 13 (DÖW 76), 39 938, 39 753, T 84 R 16 (DÖW Film 78), 43 262, Vienna Gestapo daily reports no. 3 of 4 Oct 1938, no. 3 of 6–7 Dec 1938, no. 5 of 9–10 Feb 1939, no. 12 of 22–24 Oct 1938.
54. DÖW 5732 e, Vienna Gestapo daily report no. 5 of 10–11 Sep 1941; www.doew.at/erinnern/personendatenbanken/gestapo-opfer (last accessed on 2 Jul 2017).
55. DÖW 8478, Vienna Gestapo daily report no. 2 of 7–10 Jan 1944. See also Rudolf, *Aufbau im Widerstand*.
56. DÖW 8479, Vienna Gestapo daily reports no. 2 of 4–6 Apr 1944 and no. 1 of 1–4 May 1944.
57. www.doew.at/erinnern/personendatenbanken/gestapo-opfer (last accessed on 2 Jul 2017); DÖW 8476, Vienna Gestapo daily report no. 5 of 14–16 Sep 1943.
58. www.doew.at/erinnern/personendatenbanken/gestapo-opfer (last accessed on 3 Jul 2017).
59. Ibid.
60. DÖW 5732 c, Vienna Gestapo daily report no. 1 of 30 May – 3 June 1941; DÖW 8597, judgment of the SG at the Vienna LG, 16 Dec 1941.
61. Beinhauer, 'Sr. M. Restituta Kafka', 119–34; Liebmann, 'Schlussvortrag im Seligsprechungsprozess', 13–19; Kempner, *Priester vor Hitlers Tribunalen*, 469–81; Maimann, 'Schwester Restituta', 201–12. Stumfohl was sentenced to five years' imprisonment (*schwerer Kerker*) for

denunciations and illegality; see WStLA, Vienna LG, Vg 12g V2 1096/46, judgment of 20 Aug 1948.
62. See, among others, Garbe, *Between Resistance and Martyrdom*; Beaurain, 'Die Kinder von Zeugen Jehovas'; Jakli, 'Die Verfolgung der ZeugInnen Jehovas', 347–67.
63. DÖW 20 333/7, Sections of the Vienna Gestapo (see n. 3); Weisz, 'Gestapo-Leitstelle Wien', 243ff. and 610ff.
64. WStLA, Vienna LG, Sondergericht SHv 6350/47, concluding memo of the Vienna Gestapo concerning the leaders of the 'Bibelforscher' organization in the Ostmark, 17 Dec 1941.
65. WStLA, Vienna LG, Vg 4 b Vr 1223/47, statement by Karl Ebner at the Vienna LG, 28 June 1947; WStLA, Vienna LG, Sondergericht SHv 4575/47.
66. DÖW 5732 e, Vienna Gestapo daily report no. 4 of 7–9 Feb 1941; WStLA, Vienna LG, Sondergericht SHv 207/47, Vienna Gestapo record of the interrogation of Ernst Bojanowsky, 1940. Gölles remained in prison until April 1945.
67. WStLA, Vienna LG, Sondergericht SHv 6272/47, Vienna Gestapo report on IBV flyer propaganda, 12 Dec 1941; www.doew.at/erinnern/personendatenbanken/gestapo-opfer (last accessed on 9 May 2017).
68. DÖW 5732 a, Vienna Gestapo daily report no. 4 of 7–9 Feb 1941.
69. DÖW 5732 a, Vienna Gestapo daily report no. 13 of 29–30 Jun 1942; www.doew.at/erinnern/personendatenbanken/gestapo-opfer (last accessed on 9 May 2017).
70. DÖW 5733 d, Vienna Gestapo daily report no. 8 of 17–19 Jul 1942; www.doew.at/erinnern/personendatenbanken/gestapo-opfer (last accessed on 9 May 2017).
71. DÖW 5731, Vienna Gestapo daily report no. 11 of 24–25 Oct 1940.
72. DÖW 5733 b, Vienna Gestapo daily report no. 12 of 27–28 Apr 1942; www.doew.at/erinnern/personendatenbanken/gestapo-opfer (last accessed on 9 May 2017).
73. On the numbers of victims see Jakli, 'Die Verfolgung der ZeugInnen Jehovas', 360–61 and n. 118.
74. Walter, 'Standhaft bis in den Tod', 342–57.
75. Bailer/Ungar, 'Die Zahl der Todesopfer politischer Verfolgung', 12; Neugebauer, *Austrian Resistance*, 33–34.
76. DÖW, *Widerstand Wien*, vol. 3, 186ff.
77. DÖW reference library, Vienna Gestapo daily report no. 9 of 20–21 Apr 1942 and no. 1 of 1–2 July 1942; www.doew.at/erinnern/personendatenbanken/gestapo-opfer (last accessed on 9 May 2017).
78. NARA, microcopy T 84 R 13 (DÖW Film 68/2), Vienna Gestapo daily reports no. 3 of 4 Oct 1938, no. 8 of 14 Oct 1938, no. 1 of 1–2 Dec 1938; DÖW 5732 d, Vienna Gestapo daily report no. 7 of 15–17 Aug 1941.
79. DÖW 5732 d, Vienna Gestapo daily report no. 1 of 30 Jun – 1 Jul 1941; DÖW 5742 c, Vienna Gestapo daily report no. 10 of 23 Sep 1941.
80. DÖW 8476, Vienna Gestapo daily report no. 1 of 1–2 Sep 1943 and no. 7 of 25–27 Jan 1944.
81. The persecution of Freemasons, Jehovah's Witnesses and other small religious groups happened to be the responsibility of one and the same office of the Vienna Gestapo (II B 3, from 1942 IV B 3). It is not the intention of the author to equate the groups in any way.
82. This section follows the detailed account by Patka, *Österreichische Freimaurer*, see 7ff. and 18ff. See also 'Freimaurer im Exil und Widerstand', *Zwischenwelt* 34/3 (Oct 2017), a special edition on Freemasons in exile and resistance.
83. Ibid., 39ff.
84. Ibid., 45ff.
85. For details, see Stadlbauer, *Ehrlinger*, 188 and n. 984.
86. *Der Stürmer* 9/1938 (special issue), 6; Patka, *Dr Richard Schlesinger*, 167–95.

87. BA Berlin, R 58/6558, files of SD-Oberabschnitt 'Donau' and SD-Leitabschnitt 'Vienna', 1938–41, document headed 'Betr: Unterbringung von Juden im Konzentrationslager Dachau' [Re: Accommodation of Jews in the concentration camp of Dachau], undated and unsigned.
88. Patka, *Freimaurer*, 54ff., 67ff.
89. Ibid., 56ff.
90. DÖW 20 333/7, Sections of the Vienna Gestapo (see n. 3).
91. Patka, *Freimaurer*, 74.
92. BA Berlin, R 58/982, correspondence between the SD Dept II 112 with the head of SD-Oberabschnitt 'Donau', Jul–Sep 1938.
93. Patka, *Freimaurer*, 87ff., 105 and 113..

Chapter 12

SUPPRESSION OF ORGANIZED RESISTANCE

Catholic-Conservative and Legitimist Resistance

In addition to having to combat Communist and Socialist resistance, the Vienna Gestapo also faced opposition from Catholic-conservative and legitimist groups. For the Nazi regime, the goals common to these groups – the downfall of the National Socialist regime and the re-establishment of an independent Austria; or even, for some, a 'greater Austria' with a Habsburg as head of state – constituted a threat of the first order. The central figure in these conservative (and in some cases reactionary) endeavours and aspirations was the 'pretender' Otto Habsburg, who lived in Belgium and took refuge in the United States in 1940. Accordingly, from 20 March 1938 a warrant was issued for his arrest under charges of high treason, his assets were seized by order of Hitler in person, and his followers were pursued by the Gestapo.[1] When the Vienna Gestapo organized its first deportation of Austrians on 1 April 1938, the internees included a leading representative of Austrian legitimism, Hans Karl (Freiherr von) Zeßner-Spitzenberg, a professor at the Vienna agricultural college, who was tortured to death at Dachau, perishing on 1 August 1938.[2]

Until 1942, the Vienna Gestapo office responsible for legitimists was Unit II C 1. Headed for a time by Johann Sanitzer, who was notorious for his brutality, it had a staff of around twenty-five to thirty; after the structural reform of 1942 the legitimists became the responsibility of Section IV A 3, which had a staff of around fourteen and also dealt with cases under the 'Heimtückegesetz' (law against 'insidious utterances').[3] In the period from autumn 1938 to March

1945, the Vienna Gestapo daily reports (which by no means recorded all arrests) document the arrests of 930 people from the conservative-Catholic camp, that is to say, 6.5 per cent of the 14,367 arrests cited in the daily reports, though it should be noted that the latter figure does not include the detainees of March/April 1938, or the priests and nuns arrested.[4]

Particularly dangerous from the point of view of the Gestapo was the legitimist resistance group led by Hauptmann Karl Burian, firstly because Burian, by way of the landowner Josef Krinninger, was in direct contact with Otto Habsburg, and secondly because the group's plans were aimed directly at the Gestapo headquarters on Morzinplatz. One of the (expropriated) co-proprietors of Hotel Metropole (now the Vienna Gestapo headquarters) was the staunch legitimist Karl Friediger, who took the Hotel Metropole floor plans with him when he fled to Prague after the annexation of March 1938. He subsequently leaked them to the resistance group and joined them in planning a bomb attack on the hotel. When Burian got in touch with a supposed contact man from the Polish secret service in order to pass on important military information, he was betrayed by the Gestapo spy Josef Materna, who was also an informant of the Vienna office of the Abwehr, and arrested by the Gestapo on 13 October 1938. His fellow activists also fell into the hands of the Gestapo. On 9 December 1943, after five years of internment, Burian was sentenced to death and executed in Vienna on 13 March 1944.[5]

The most important resistance groups in the period 1938–40 were the three Austrian freedom movements led by the Augustinian canon Karl Roman Scholz, the junior lawyer Jakob Kastelic, and Karl Lederer, a civil servant dismissed from the office of the financial procurator in 1939. Their aim was the re-establishment of a Greater Austrian monarchy following the overthrow of the Nazi regime, to which end they gathered together several hundred activists, a good number of whom were pupils of the grammar school in Klosterneuburg. The groups were on the point of a political and organizational merger when the Gestapo broke up the organization in a series of mass arrests in July 1940. In its daily report for 12–13 February 1941, it stated that 121 of those arrested had been reported to the VGH, and 22, all members of the Wehrmacht, to the Reich military court (Reichskriegsgericht). The arrests of around 300 further members in the Reichsgaus of Vienna, Lower Danube and Upper Danube 'had to be postponed on account of shortage of space in suitable prisons'.[6] The resistance group led by Karl Roman Scholz and with it the Lederer and Kastelic groups fell victim to the treachery of the Burgtheater actor Otto Hartmann, who had of his own free will become a Gestapo informant and had acted as an agent provocateur, inciting the groups to engage in terrorist activities. It is said that Hartmann received 'blood money' of RM 30,000. As the historian Hans Schafranek has recently established, the legitimist and conservative resistance groups were no less thoroughly infiltrated by informants than the Communist and Socialist groups; and ultimately, it was these informants who enabled the Gestapo to crush them.[7]

The legal proceedings against the members of the three freedom movements and other Catholic and legitimist resistance were not started until 1943 – and the defendants were held in investigative or 'protective' custody for more than three years – on account of an order by Hitler, probably issued in 1939, to the effect that no legal proceedings should be instituted against Austrian 'separatists'. A report of 3 January 1944 submitted to the Reich minister of justice by an unnamed 'ministerial court observer' indicates that the Führer's order had been rescinded about four months before – that is to say, in September 1943. From November onwards, VGH trials in Regensburg, Salzburg and Vienna of around three hundred Austrian 'separatists and legitimists' led to numerous sentences of death or to imprisonment with hard labour. It is not known why Hitler, with his intense hatred for the house of Habsburg, should have put off legal proceedings against these groups for so long, nor indeed why he finally rescinded his order.[8]

Between 1938 and 1940 the Vienna Gestapo succeeded in crushing a number of other Catholic-conservative resistance groups, in particular groups of youths from the banned Österreichisches Jungvolk (the youth organization of the corporate state) and the former youth group movement Bündische Jugend.[9] That young people of Catholic and legitimist orientation were treated with considerably greater leniency by the NS judiciary than were the activists of the

Figure 12.1. Burgtheater actor and Gestapo informant Otto Hartmann facing charges at the Vienna Volksgericht, 1947. © Österreichische Nationalbibliothek, Bildarchiv und Graphiksammlung. Used with permission.

Communist youth league (Kommunistischer Jugendverband, KJV), who were invariably charged with 'preparation for high treason' (*Vorbereitung zum Hochverrat*) and sentenced to death in large numbers, is evident from the sources and related to the order mentioned above. Clearly, the Nazi judiciary, because they could not apply the high treason paragraphs to the conservative youths, resorted to the milder provisions of the law against the formation of new parties (Gesetz gegen die Neubildung von Parteien); similarly, the Gestapo tended to allow young people from the right-wing camp to be let off with reprimands after short periods of detention, usually having them conscripted into the Wehrmacht. For example, having been active in the resistance from as early as March 1938, a group of pupils from the Schopenhauerstrasse grammar school, Währing (18th district), were reported to the Gestapo by their Nazi-minded German teacher Ernst Wilmersdorf, arrested from June 1938 onwards, but then released after only short periods of detention. One of their number, Hugo Pepper, who was in fact a left-winger, rose to become an officer and was the leader of a military resistance group in 1945.[10]

After the Vienna Gestapo had crushed this first large wave of young Catholic and legitimist resistance, it was not until 1942 that two further substantial Catholic-conservative resistance groups were formed: the Antifaschistische Freiheitsbewegung Österreich (anti-Fascist freedom movement of Austria), which was principally active in Carinthia, Styria and (the former) Burgenland; and, secondly, an organization in Vienna led by Heinrich Maier, curate of a parish in Währing, Franz Josef Messner, chairman of the board of the rubber manufacturing company Semperit, and Walter Caldonazzi, a forestry engineer from Tyrol. In 1943 and 1944, the Gestapo succeeded in crushing both groups through the use of informants and the extraction of confessions by means of torture. On 6 July and 23 August 1943, the Gestapo arrested the Franciscan fathers Eduard Steinwender, provincial of the Franciscan province of Austria, and Johannes Kapistran Pieller, guardian and rector of the Franciscan church in Eisenstadt, along with their fellow-activists the parish priest Anton Granig and the retired teacher Franz Bernthaler. They were among forty prisoners sentenced to death who were compelled to undertake a forced march from Vienna to Stein an der Donau, where they were executed by firing squad on 15 April 1945.[11]

The Maier-Messner group was of considerable politico-military importance on account of the contacts it established, by way of Switzerland and Istanbul, with the US wartime secret service OSS, which it supplied with important information about the armaments industry in eastern Austria, for the purpose of bombing missions.[12] The importance of this contact for the OSS is illustrated by the fact that no less than RM 100,000 (roughly €360,000 in present-day terms) were placed at Franz Josef Messner's disposal for resistance activities in Austria. The sum was confiscated when Messner was arrested in Budapest on 29 March 1944.[13] Similarly, Messner's Vienna villa at Hasenauerstrasse 61 (Währing, 18th district) was seized by the Gestapo and used by Section IV A 2, headed by Johann Sanitzer, for the detention of British, American and Soviet radio and parachute agents.[14] The Gestapo investigated and tracked down this resistance network between February and April 1944 with the assistance of Semperit employee Sigismund Romen, an informer and staunch Nazi, and the Czech multiple agent Bedrich Laufer of the Prague office of the Abwehr, SD/Gestapo, and later an OSS (dis)informer.[15] On 28 October 1944, eight members of the group were sentenced to death by the VGH for 'preparation for high treason' through 'participation in a separatist group'; on 23 April 1945, Franz Josef Messner was one of the last prisoners to be gassed at Mauthausen.[16]

The last phase of Nazi rule in 1944–45 saw the formation of further resistance groups, which recruited their members from the conservative-bourgeois social milieu that had been largely associated with the establishment under the corporate state. However, far from having legitimist or monarchist goals, these groups directed their activities at the restoration of the Republic of Austria in accordance with the Allies' Moscow Declaration of 1 November 1943. The Vienna Gestapo daily reports contain numerous records of the seizure of handbills and newsletters produced by groups such as Free Austria (Freies Österreich) and the Austrian freedom movement (Österreichische Freiheitsbewegung), appealing to their readers to join the struggle against Nazi rule and fight for a free Austria. The Gestapo did not succeed in tracking down all these groups, some of which are only documented through the preservation of their illegal publications. Free Austria, however, led by Karl Gruber, a writer also employed full-time in another capacity, was crushed by the Gestapo between September and December 1944, with the members arrested remaining in Gestapo detention until 6 April 1945.[17]

Figure 12.2. The resistance activist Franz Josef Messner, who was arrested by the Vienna Gestapo on 29 March 1944 and murdered at Mauthausen on 23 April 1945. Gestapo identification photos. © Dokumentationsarchiv des österreichischen Widerstandes. Used with permission.

Between September 1944 and February 1945, at least eighteen members of the Austrian freedom front (Österreichische Freiheitsfront) resistance group founded by Johann Knoll were arrested by the Vienna Gestapo, after the group had been infiltrated and betrayed by the Gestapo informant Bobby Biel. The 16-year-old schoolboy Herbert Baumann and a number of his fellow activists were brutally maltreated in October 1944 by Johann Sanitzer and other Gestapo officials from units IV 2a and 2b. The Gestapo committed Knoll to Dachau, where he had already been interned once in 1938–39, and transferred Franz Herbert, formerly a captain in the Hungarian army, to Mauthausen concentration camp.[18]

The most important and best-known resistance group from this milieu was O5, which was initiated by the former Fatherland Front director of propaganda Hans Becker and succeeded in establishing contact with the Western Allies through Fritz Molden, who had deserted from the Wehrmacht in summer 1944. In December 1944, O5 formed the Provisorisches Österreichisches Nationalkomitee (provisional Austrian national committee, POEN) and collaborated with the military resistance group led by Carl Szokoll in Military District XVII. However, in the months January to March 1945 the Vienna Gestapo succeeded in putting an end to the POEN through numerous arrests of activists such as Hans Becker, Otto Spitz and Alfons Stillfried, so that O5 was unable to play its intended leading role in the Vienna area as a major political force in the liberation and restoration of Austria.[19]

Communist Resistance

Founded in 1918, the Kommunistische Partei Österreichs (Austrian Communist party, KPÖ) was a largely insignificant political force during the First Republic. However, in the course of the events of 1933–34 – suppression of democracy, establishment of the Austro-Fascist dictatorship, prohibition of social democracy – the KPÖ experienced a considerable upswing when its ranks were joined by large numbers of disillusioned and radicalized Social Democrats. Furthermore, following the annexation of March 1938, the KPÖ immediately raised the cry of active resistance, stood up for the restoration of Austria's independence, and gave its resistance struggle an emphatically Austrian-patriotic orientation, thereby succeeding – in spite of the immediate onslaught of Nazi terror – in winning over many more Social Democrats for its organizations, especially municipal employees, factory workers and clerical staff. As a result, in numerical terms the KPÖ became the strongest sector of the Austrian resistance.[20]

The brunt of the Vienna Gestapo's work countering political resistance was borne by Section II A, which was responsible for the suppression of Socialists, Communists and other left-wingers. Within Section II A, the Communist movement was until 1942 the responsibility of Unit II A 1, which from 1942 to 1944 was renamed Section IV A 1 and in 1944–45 Unit IV 1 a, both of which were responsible not only for Communism and Socialism but also for 'radio crimes'. Responsibility for parachute agents – who were largely Communist-minded – was borne by Section IV A 2 (1942–44) and subsequently Section IV 2 (1944–45). The head of Section II A (1938 to end of 1941) was SS-Sturmbannführer Wilhelm Bock, from the 'Altreich', and the head of its successor Section IV A was SS-Sturmbannführer Othmar Trnka (Trenker); within Section IV A, the head of Unit IV A 1 was SS-Sturmbannführer Fritz Mayer, and the head of Unit IV A 2 (from 1942, IV 2) was SS-Obersturmführer Johann Sanitzer.[21] The intelligence office (Group IV N, for 'Nachrichten') headed by Lambert Leutgeb was also involved in important cases and even carried out arrests, for example, of the high-ranking KPÖ functionary Leo Gabler.[22]

Franz Weisz cites Section II A (1938–42) as having 92 staff members (67 executive, 25 administrative), Section IV A 1 (1942–44) as having 64, and IV 1 a (1944–45) as having 40. From 1942 to 1945, Section IV A 2, subsequently IV 2, had between 16 and 20 staff.[23] The units responsible for countering left-wing resistance were thus among the most amply staffed of the entire Vienna Gestapo, as is reflected above all in the enormous number of arrests.

At the centre of Communist activities, the goal of which was mass resistance, was the dissemination of illegal printed matter aimed at breaking the Nazi regime's monopoly on public opinion. Innumerable small leaflets, flyers and newsletters were produced and distributed under the greatest difficulty and danger. As a Vienna Gestapo situation report for the period January to March 1939 noted: 'Since the beginning of the year there has been a far from insignificant increase in Communist pamphlet propaganda'.[24] While in the 'Altreich' the RSHA noted a 'further decrease in the production and propaganda of inflammatory Communist writings', and at the same time saw 'an intensification of pamphlet propaganda on the part of the KP in the Ostmark,' where in the year 1939 alone the Gestapo offices seized 127 flyers, 1,005 brochures, some 5,000 leaflets and 1,000 copies of resolutions of the KPÖ central committee. At the beginning of December 1939, the Vienna Gestapo raided the technical apparatus of the KPÖ, arresting 119 resistance activists and seizing eight typewriters, three duplicating machines and a quantity of other material used for the production of leaflets.[25]

As it did against other resistance groupings, the Vienna Gestapo used informants and cell spies against the Communist organizations – with an extremely high degree of success. The majority of spies, it can be assumed, were only induced to betray their former fellow-activists through the use of physical violence or psychological pressure. The brutal and devious methods used to 'turn' them are described more closely in Chapter 6 on Gestapo methods and Chapter 7 on Gestapo informants.

One major factor that enabled the Gestapo to infiltrate and crush almost all of the Communist organizations was the KPÖ's centralistic structure, reflecting Lenin's principle of 'democratic centralism'. Although the KPÖ leadership in Moscow repeatedly flew emissaries to Austria for the purpose of rebuilding party organizations and orientating them according to the party line, these representatives were regularly arrested on landing, or shortly thereafter. While it is not possible to go into greater detail here, the arrests and extortion of confessions led to the crushing of regional, local and factory groups with considerable numbers of activists.[26]

A key role in these developments was played by the former KJV functionary Kurt Koppel (code name 'Ossi', Gestapo cover names 'Glaser' and others), who had been recruited as a Gestapo spy by Lambert Leutgeb and subsequently rose to become the right-hand man of the top KPÖ functionary Erwin Puschmann, sent from Moscow to Austria in 1940. Through 'Ossi', who acted as a go-between for several central functionaries and maintained contacts abroad, the Gestapo was kept informed about all the important developments, contacts and individuals in the KPÖ. By means of tailing, arrests and brutal interrogations, the Gestapo acquired further information that resulted in massive waves of arrests. According to a Vienna Gestapo record from October 1941, no fewer than 536 Communists had been arrested, including 42 top functionaries and 105 regular functionaries. A total of 112 detainees were handed over to the VGH, which sentenced most of them to death for 'preparation for high treason'. Only in the course of 1941 did it gradually dawn upon Communists imprisoned in Vienna that Koppel had been a traitor and spy; Puschmann, too, had repeatedly dismissed warnings about Koppel's reliability. Whereas Puschmann was executed in Vienna on 7 January 1943, in 1945 Koppel succeeded in going into hiding.[27]

All in all, by 1943 the Gestapo had succeeded in crushing the great majority of the KPÖ's factory, local and district groups, handing their activists over to the Nazi courts or committing them to concentration camps. The same is true of the extremely active KJV (Communist youth league), which had attracted the Gestapo's attention by spreading anti-war propaganda and infiltrating the Hitler Youth. Within this milieu, the KJV suffered devastating losses through the treachery of Koppel's life-partner and co-informant Margarete Kahane (code name 'Sonja').[28]

Furthermore, the activities of the traitor 'Ossi' in the central apparatus of the KPÖ led to the uncovering of the large KPÖ group in the former federal province of Styria built up by Herbert Eichholzer, Karl Drews and Franz Weiß, as a result of which more than 250 suspects were targeted by the Gestapo.[29] Similarly, with the help of the informant Koppel, the resistance group known by the Vienna Gestapo as the 'Czech section of the KPÖ' was tracked down when it established contact with the central directorate of the KPÖ. At least twenty-six members of the group were arrested, twenty of whom were summarily shot on

26 November 1941 at Mauthausen in accordance with the order for *Sonderbehandlung* ('special treatment', code term for extrajudicial killing) issued by Reichsführer-SS Himmler.

According to the research findings of Hans Schafranek, more than eight hundred activists fell prey to the Gestapo on account of the Koppel–Kahane informant duo.[30] Even after Koppel had been exposed and transferred to Zagreb in the middle of 1941, the Vienna Gestapo was able to use other turncoats to continue its systematic spying in the Communist milieu. One newly formed five-person group, which the Gestapo incorrectly dubbed the 'central committee of the KPÖ', only survived for three months, from April to July 1942. By means of informants it was in fact steered, controlled and monitored by the Vienna Gestapo. All the leading members were executed, tortured to death or committed suicide.[31] In February 1943, in connection with this group, the members of a Communist 'group of intellectuals' were arrested by the Vienna Gestapo. Their leading thinker, the staff doctor Adalbert von Springer, who had composed several anti-war KPÖ flyers, was sentenced to death by the Reich military court for 'preparation for high treason' and 'undermining military morale', and was executed on 18 September 1943.[32]

Among those who acted as cell spies for the Vienna Gestapo were Karl Zwifelhofer, formerly domestic head of the KPÖ, and Fritz Schwager; in both cases, the Vienna Gestapo put pressure on the Reich ministry of justice not to carry out the death sentences already passed. Instead, they were instructed to get on good terms with fellow internees, sound them out and pass on information gathered to the Gestapo.[33]

As a result of the permeation of the central KPÖ apparatus with Gestapo spies and informants, the commando units parachuted in from the Soviet Union on party-related or intelligence missions were doomed to failure from the outset. Johann Sanitzer, the Gestapo official responsible for countering parachute agents, operated with particular 'success' in this field. By means of brutal torture, arrests and mistreatment, even of uninvolved family members, he succeeded in 'turning' numerous Allied parachutists (not only from the Communist side), forcing them to transmit false information to their intelligence officers at home, principally related to military matters. Newly arrived parachutists were usually arrested immediately after landing – or, after a period of observation, together with their contacts.[34] In 1947, Sanitzer stated before the Vienna LG that during his time as head of Section IV A 2 he had brought about the arrest of around a hundred Allied agents and five hundred hosts.[35]

In 1942 the task of countering Communist resistance became so great that there were no longer sufficient detention facilities for all the arrests planned. As the chief Reich prosecutor at the VGH stated in a report submitted to the Reich minister of justice: 'According to information from the headquarters of the Vienna Gestapo, there are a further 1,500 persons in Vienna strongly suspected of Communist activity, whom the Gestapo can only arrest gradually for lack of sufficient detention space and staff'.³⁶

'From the very beginning of its existence in 1938, the Vienna Gestapo directed particular attention to combating Communist and Marxist efforts.' This entirely correct observation was the first sentence of a report of a Gestapo official with responsibility in this field at the 'Meeting of the [IV]N and IV A 1 section heads in the Ostmark' (Tagung der N- und IV A 1-Referenten der Ostmark) held in Vienna on 28 March 1944. After giving an account of the most important measures taken against the KPÖ and the arrest of its leading functionaries, the speaker presented an overall balance including the numbers of detentions: 742 in 1938; 1,132 in 1939; 837 in 1940; 1,507 in 1941; 881 in 1942; and 1,173 in 1943 – that is to say, 'all in all around 6,300 arrests of Communist functionaries and party members to date'. Finally he noted that 'in this duty sector, 364 death sentences have been pronounced upon Communist party members, of which 293 have been carried out'.³⁷

Of the 14,367 arrests recorded in the Vienna Gestapo daily reports – although they do not record all arrests made – 4,202 (29.2 per cent) can be categorized as being related to members of the workers' movement (Communists, Socialists and others).³⁸ The Vienna Gestapo figures largely match those established by the DÖW and Marburg University on the basis of NS judicial records. Of the 2,137 people who faced charges of high treason at the VGH, 1,106 (52 per cent) were associated with the KPÖ; and of the 4,163 defendants at the OLGs of Vienna and Graz, it was 1,930 (46 per cent).³⁹ In addition, a large number of Communist resistance fighters were sent without trial to concentration camps, where many more perished than did defendants who faced judicial proceedings.

Nevertheless, the devastating blows struck by the Gestapo and the demise, by 1943, of the KPÖ's regional and local network by no means meant the end of Communist resistance in Austria, as new politico-military strategies were conceived and organizational structures created in the form of armed combat groups and partisan units (in Styria, Carinthia and Slovenia). These, however, fell outside the Vienna Gestapo's geographical area of competence.⁴⁰

In the final phase of Nazi rule in 1945, Communist activists once again built up organizational structures in Vienna – one such activist being the top party functionary Josef Lauscher, who had escaped from the Saurer-Werke satellite camp (Simmering, 11th district) – or became involved in cross-party resistance groups such as O5. Although Vienna Gestapo informants (Josef Koutny, Georg Weidinger, Josef Lochmann) succeeded in infiltrating certain Communist groups and O5 (and bringing about a number of arrests), these resistance activities were only partially detected by the Vienna Gestapo, not least because the Gestapo organizational units had already been moved westwards, and certain important officials were seeking to save their skins through 'reinsurance' practices.⁴¹

Socialist Resistance

Although by 1938 the Revolutionary Socialists (RS), successors to the Sozialdemokratische Arbeiterpartei (Social Democratic workers' party, SDAP), had been operating underground for four years and possessed sound illegal cadres and considerable conspiratorial experience, the events of March 1938 were a severe political and organizational setback for them. The central committee of the RS, aware of the fact that the repressive measures of the National Socialists would be a great deal more severe than those of the corporate state, ordered its members to cease all illegal activities for three months. This order from the party leadership, the arrests of many Socialists in the wake of the annexation, and the emigration of many functionaries (in particular those of Jewish origin) combined to bring about a marked organizational decline. Failure to observe the order to exercise caution and the resumption of organizational activities in summer 1938 very soon enabled the Gestapo, with its network of informants and spies, to track down and arrest a great number of activists.[42] In their preventive arrests, the Vienna Gestapo initially concentrated on the RS functionaries such as Friedrich Hillegeist, Franz Olah and Bruno Kreisky who had stood up against the Nazi threat before March 1938 and could be expected to continue their opposition to the Nazi regime; by contrast, the former Social Democratic politicians were largely spared, one of the few exceptions being the former mayor of Vienna, Karl Seitz. The Nazis applied their repressive measures with full force to a group they particularly hated, namely, the Social Democrats of Jewish origin. One of these was the Vienna city council finance expert Robert Danneberg, whom the Gestapo detained when he was crossing the border into Czechoslovakia; he was in the first Austrian transport to Dachau of 1 April 1938, and murdered at Auschwitz in 1942.[43] The relative restraint in dealing with (non-Jewish) Social Democrats was consistent with the Nazi propaganda policy of using social demagogy to gain the allegiance of those who had fought in the civil hostilities of February 1934. For example, as pointed out by Gestapo official Lambert Leutgeb in the account he wrote while imprisoned in Yugoslavia, the Nazi mayor of Vienna Hermann Neubacher made a great show of reinstating the municipal workers and employees who had lost their jobs for taking part in the 1934 uprising.[44]

Until 1942, Unit II A 2, which had a staff of around twenty-three and was headed for a time by Josef Auinger, was responsible for combating Socialist resistance. From 1942 to 1944 the office was part of the new Unit IV A 1, which was headed by SS-Sturmbannführer Fritz Mayer and was also responsible for Communist resistance and investigating 'radio crime'; it had sixty-four members of staff. In the final phase of the war, 1944–45, the office was called IV 1a and had a staff of forty.[45] The office responsible for combating Socialist resistance cooperated closely with Section IV N (Intelligence, headed by Lambert Leutgeb) and with the office responsible for parachute agents, Unit IV A 2 (Johann Sanitzer), which resulted in a considerable increase in the striking power and effectiveness of all offices involved.

The painstaking research of Hans Schafranek has revealed that the Vienna Gestapo deployed a total of seven informants against the RS. The organization of Socialist resistance suffered a fateful blow in this first phase (1938–39) through the betrayal of the RS by one of their leading functionaries, the former sports editor of the *Arbeiter-Zeitung* Hans Pav. After his arrest in March 1938 along with other members of the RS, Pav soon succumbed to psychological pressure applied by the Gestapo and agreed to act as a spy and informant, for which the VG sentenced him to fifteen years' imprisonment in 1947. As an agent provocateur (spy number 'S 20'), Pav made contact with numerous comrades for the purpose of building up the RS, and went abroad to meet leading RS functionaries such as Josef Buttinger, ignoring their warnings not to engage in further activities. The entire central organization of the RS fell victim to his treachery.[46] The only leading figure who avoided arrest at the hands of the Gestapo was Muriel Gardiner, who was a US citizen and later married Buttinger. Described by the VGH as a 'zealous Marxist agent', she returned to Austria a number of times and saved many endangered RS members by supplying them with fake passports and affidavits or financial support, thus enabling them to escape from the Reich.[47]

Among the comrades betrayed by Pav was Käthe Leichter, formerly head of the women's department of Vienna's chamber of labour, who did not want to leave her aged mother alone in Vienna and was arrested by the Gestapo on 30 May 1938. On 14 October 1939, following the suspension of proceedings on a charge of high treason, the Vienna LG sentenced her to seven months' imprisonment with hard labour, together with the RS functionary Friederike Nödl and the prison warden Pauline Nestler, who had helped her. After serving her sentence, Leichter was remanded to the Vienna Gestapo (*Rücküberstellung*) and in December 1939 was sent to the women's concentration camp of Ravensbrück. One of the most outstanding women of Austrian Social Democracy, Käthe Leichter was gassed in the '14f13' operation of March 1942 at the NS 'euthanasia' facility of Bernburg.[48]

As early as 27 September 1938, having received a report of the Vienna Gestapo 'on the increase in Communist and Marxist propaganda activities, strikes etc.', Heydrich as chief of the security police ordered all the Gestapo offices in Austria 'to devote particular attention to the preventive suppression of Communism and Marxism' and 'to take all leading KPD and SPD functionaries into protective custody … until further notice'. In a telex of 30 September 1938 sent in response to the order, Franz Josef Huber, head of the Vienna Gestapo, reported that through the deployment of informants it had been possible to identify '80 higher- and middle-ranking functionaries and a further 150 individuals engaging in illegal activities', clearly Communists and Revolutionary Socialists. As soon as an order had been issued for the 'mass arrest of the A 1 people' (meaning those dealt with by Unit II A 1), he continued, they should be arrested immediately, but he advised against any arrests being made before the official instruction.[49] The large-scale wave of arrests did not take place until 22 August 1939, shortly before the beginning of the war, when forty-seven RS and sixty-seven Communist activists were taken into detention.[50] The Vienna Gestapo first interrogated them and then in many cases tortured them in order to force them to divulge the names of other resistance fighters, to make confessions or to agree to act as spies. Then the detainees were either reported to the courts or transferred to concentration camps.

The traitor par excellence was the informant 'Edi', whom Schafranek has identified as the teacher Eduard Korbel. In February 1934, Korbel, who had been Schutzbund leader for the Vienna zone 'West', defected to the Dollfuß regime; shortly after the annexation of March 1938 he entered the service of the Gestapo as a spy and informant. Preserved at the DÖW are forty-seven of Korbel's reports dating from May 1938 to October 1940, in which prominent RS functionaries such as Manfred Ackermann, Roman Felleis and Josef Pleyl are mentioned. Korbel's reports led to the arrests of numerous Socialists, including the youth group activist Josef Staribacher (later federal minister of trade), who was arrested on 22 August 1939 and interned for one year at Buchenwald concentration camp.[51] Ludwig Leser, former deputy governor of Burgenland, who was revealed a number of years ago to have been a (paid) Gestapo informant (cover name 'Lederer', 'S 26'), was in contact with RS officials abroad, but as the reports he submitted to the Gestapo from October 1939 were very generally formulated, it is not clear that anyone was actually harmed as a result.[52]

The RS members who remained active concentrated on supporting the families of those who had been arrested, and the Sozialistische Arbeiterhilfe (Aid to Socialist Workers, SAH) founded in 1934 in effect became a substitute for the RS party organization. However, these activists, amongst them Friederike Nödl, Karl Holoubek, Wilhelmine Moik and Erwin Scharf, were arrested by the Vienna Gestapo between May and July 1938; but on 9 June 1939 – at the first VGH trial in Vienna, which made front-page news in the *Völkischer Beobachter* – they were given relatively mild prison sentences of between eighteen and thirty months.[53]

A second set of leaders, who rebuilt the SAH and maintained contacts with the Socialist representation in exile in Brno (Brünn) and the one in Paris, was uncovered by the Vienna Gestapo in July 1939. Subsequently, the Vienna OLG gave nine defendants prison sentences ranging from one year to twenty-seven months. After serving his sentence, Franz Pfannenstiel from the Vienna RS leadership was transferred by the Gestapo to Dachau. In 1944 he was conscripted into a Wehrmacht penal unit from which he deserted to the Red Army with other concentration camp internees before finally perishing as a Soviet prisoner of war. The RS resistance fighter Hans Gmeiner, who was arrested on 22 August 1939 and charged with 'preparation for high treason' (*Vorbereitung zum Hochverrat*), died on 21 July 1940 in the prison hospital of the Vienna LG.⁵⁴

In the first years the defendants got off with relatively light sentences, but this was no great advantage as once they had served their time in prison they were normally transferred to concentration camps or conscripted into Wehrmacht penal units. The toolmaker Josef Nagl from Perchtoldsdorf, for example, was charged with 'preparation for high treason' for working for the SAH, and on 6 November 1940 was sentenced by the Vienna OLG to 'only' eighteen months' imprisonment; after serving his sentence, however, he was remanded to the Vienna Gestapo and transferred in December 1941 to Auschwitz, where he was murdered on 29 June 1942.⁵⁵

Many Social Democratic politicians and activists perished in the Holocaust, amongst them the members of the Austrian parliament Karl Klimberger, Johannes Paul Schlesinger, Robert Danneberg and Viktor Stein, the lawyers Heinrich Steinitz, Hugo Sperber and Oswald Richter, and the youth functionaries Otto Felix Kanitz and Hans and Steffi Kunke. In all these cases, by arresting them the Gestapo had done the preparatory work that paved the way for their deaths.⁵⁶

As a result of the rigorous suppression of the RS and the breaking off of contact with the groups in exile following the outbreak of war, the Socialist resistance disintegrated into a number of isolated groups. Under the Nazi regime it proved impossible to sustain a centrally led party organization covering the whole of Austria; where this was attempted, as in the case of the KPÖ, there were massive losses. Individual Socialist functionaries such as Felix Slavik and Alfred Migsch made attempts to rebuild organizations. In 1939 – through the mediation of the prelate Jakob Fried – Slavik made contact with the Müller-Thanner resistance group (Johann Müller being a legitimist, Erich Thanner a Catholic activist), which was betrayed by the Gestapo spy Josef Alge, the owner of a textile company in Vorarlberg, and crushed by the Vienna Gestapo in November 1939.⁵⁷

From autumn 1942, Alfred Migsch, who after the war was to be a member of Leopold Figl's cabinet, established links with former Socialist youth functionaries (Ludwig Kostroun, Franz Pfeffer, Karl Mark), and during 1943 worked closely with the widely ramified pro-Communist resistance group led by the Slovenian Communist Karl Hudomalj under the name Anti-Hitler-Bewegung Österreichs (anti-Hitler movement of Austria), which published the illegal newspaper *Wahrheit* (Truth). After operating for a relatively long time, the group was finally infiltrated by the Vienna Gestapo through the deployment of two informants, Georg Weidinger and Josef Lochmann, who claimed they were members of the KPÖ central committee. Along with Hudomalj and others, Migsch was arrested in January 1944 and interned at Mauthausen.⁵⁸

Similarly, in 1940 the RS group of Meidling (12th district) led by Johann Cäsar was infiltrated by a Gestapo spy with the cover name 'Vogel', whom Hans Schafranek has identified as the group's former leader Max Vozihnoj. Vozihnoj had been interned at Buchenwald in the centrally ordered mass arrest of August 1939, and was morally broken when he was released in March 1940. He acted as an agent provocateur, seeking to radicalize the Meidling resistance group and incite it to acts of violence. In January and February 1943, the Gestapo arrested nine of its activists. Paul Grabatsch was interned at Dachau until the end of the war, and Cäsar survived at the Flossenbürg concentration camp.[59]

Of the other still existing Socialist resistance groups, the most significant was that led by the Viennese secondary schoolteacher Johann Otto Haas. Until its exposure in July 1942 it had bases in Vienna, Salzburg (province) and Tyrol, and among railway workers; futhermore, it was in close contact with the German resistance group 'Neu Beginnen' (which had close links with the RS) and with the Bavarian Social Democrat Waldemar von Knoeringen, who was active abroad. After being arrested by the Vienna Gestapo on 20 July 1942, Haas was sentenced to death by the VGH for 'preparation for high treason' and executed on 30 August 1944 at the Vienna LG. His mother Philomena Haas, until 1934 a functionary of the SDAP and member of Vienna city council, was arrested on 23 September 1942 on suspicion of having aided 'the subversive efforts of her son through active participation'; on 15 December 1943 she was sentenced to four years' imprisonment with hard labour for 'preparation for high treason' and 'radio crime'. Another member of Haas's group, the teacher Eduard Göth from Hinterbrühl, was arrested on 7 August 1942. On 3 February 1943 he wrote the following to his family in a secret message smuggled out of prison: 'Because I have professed non-violence I have to die. I therefore accuse: (1) Adolf Hitler, (2) the Gestapo, room 223, where I was forced to sign documents with confessions that were untrue'.[60] Göth was sentenced to death by the VGH and executed on 13 March 1944 at the Vienna LG.

Even such acts as professing publicly to being a Social Democrat, the use of Socialist symbols, the *Freundschaft* ('Friendship') salute, the singing of workers' songs, or any form of anti-Nazi utterance were prosecuted by the Gestapo and the special courts. In most cases, those who publicly manifested their political position – in spite of the likelihood of prosecution – were former SDAP functionaries. The machine fitter Franz Lux was taken into temporary custody on 14 December 1939 for declaring, as was recorded, 'I sh** on the [Nazi] party, I'm a Social Democrat'. The joiner's assistant Emanuel Sedlaczek, described in a Gestapo report as 'formerly a Social Democratic trade unionist', was arrested on 18 October 1940 because he disturbed a public meeting of the NSDAP by heckling; on 18 December 1941 he was sentenced to one year's imprisonment for 'an offence under the Heimtückegesetz'. On 30 April 1940, the Vienna tram attendant Franz Speihs was arrested by the Gestapo because, according to the daily report of 3–4 May 1940, he had uttered the following words in a restaurant: 'No one can convince me. I'm not a National Socialist and I'll never become one. I'm a 1934 barricade fighter, and that's what I'll always be. I won't allow myself to be converted. When the regime is overthrown we'll come and smash up your restaurant, which is only patronized by Nazis'.[61]

The baker's assistant Franz Staudinger was arrested on 29 July 1939 by the Vienna Gestapo, 'because after the burial of the former Schutzbund leader Wilhelm Swatosch he took his leave of some colleagues with the *Freundschaft* salutation and a raised clenched fist'. Although he got off with a reprimand, he was arrested again in mid-December 1941, and on 7 May 1942 the Vienna SG sentenced him to nine months' imprisonment for 'an offence under the Heimtückegesetz'. On 11 February 1943, Emmerich Kadanik, a tailor's assistant working in the military clothing office in Brunn am Gebirge and a 'long-time member of the Social Democratic party and trade union treasurer', was arrested for having used the *Freundschaft* greeting, which the Gestapo qualified as 'Marxist word-of-mouth propaganda', *Mundpropaganda* being a term used to cover all kinds of utterances right down to casual remarks or offhand comments.[62]

In the Social Democratic milieu, instead of full-fledged organizations there developed loose circles of like-minded friends. Such groups, made up mainly of well-known Social Democrats, played a not insignificant role in connection with the 20 July 1944 plot, when the German resistance activists sought the collaboration of Austrian Social Democrats and Christian Socials. After the failure of the anti-Hitler putsch, numerous Social Democratic functionaries were arrested, amongst them Adolf Schärf, Johann Böhm, Theodor Körner and Karl Seitz.[63]

The final phase of the war saw a number of Socialists becoming active in cross-party resistance groups. One was Robert Hutterer, who represented the RS in the cross-party Österreichische Freiheitsfront (Austrian freedom front); he was arrested by the Vienna Gestapo on 14 October 1944 and interned at Dachau from November 1944 until the camp was liberated. While Franz Fischer, active in the same group, was likewise arrested in October 1944 and interned at Dachau, Rudolf Fiedler was arrested on 8 November 1944 and remained in pre-trial custody for 'high and state treason' (*Hoch- und Landesverrat*) until 6 April 1945.[64]

Other Left-Wing Resistance Groups, Spanish Civil War Fighters and Returnees from Russia

Vienna League of Mischlings

Within the Jewish population in Vienna, which was constantly shrinking on account of forced emigration and deportation, a resistance group was formed under the name Mischlingsliga Wien (Vienna league of Mischlings, MLW).

While its members were mainly 'first-degree Mischlings' (having two Jewish grandparents), they also included – to use the terminology of the chief Reich prosecutor at the VGH[65] – 'Volljuden' (full Jews) and 'Geltungsjuden' ('first-degree Mischlings' who 'counted as full Jews' on account, for example, of having been members of the Jewish community when the Nuremberg Laws entered into force on 15 September 1935). The MLW numbered around a hundred activists, mainly young people who as 'Mischlings' were subject to discrimination at school or in their work. Although the MLW had links to the KPÖ and was led by a Communist – the KJV functionary Otto Ernst Andreasch, who had already been temporarily detained by the Gestapo in 1940 – it also had Socialists and conservatives among its members.

The MLW became very active in the field of leaflet propaganda, and it established links with the Yugoslav Partisans under Tito.[66] On the basis of information from the counter-intelligence section of Military District XVII and the confession of the first MLW member to be arrested, Robert Pollak, the Vienna Gestapo succeeded in tracking down the group and arrested most of the activists between January and March 1944.[67] Those arrested were interrogated in the 'Jewish section' (IV B 4) by the Gestapo official Karl Zeitlberger, who forced them to make confessions with threats, insults such as 'Saujud' (Jewish swine) and 'Judenbub' (Jewboy), and face-slapping, though stopping short of severe maltreatment.[68] Although those who were put on trial got off relatively lightly because their contacts with the KPÖ and the Partisans remained secret – the sentences at the VGH ranged from one year in a juvenile prison to six years' imprisonment with hard labour – the Gestapo deported the 'full Jews' and *Geltungsjuden* without trial to Auschwitz, where they perished. The *Geltungsjude* Alexander Pick, a diabetic, was denied his insulin and not allowed to be taken to the Jewish hospital while in Gestapo detention, with the result that he died after fourteen days in custody, as his mother Maria Pick testified in the VG

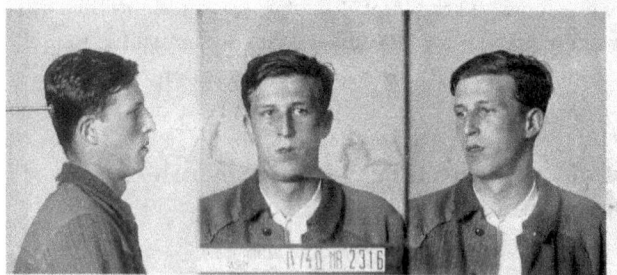

Figure 12.3. Otto Ernst Andreasch, leader of the Vienna league of Mischlings. He lost his life in an air raid while serving a prison sentence. Gestapo identification photos. © Wiener Stadt- und Landesarchiv. Used with permission.

proceedings against Zeitlberger.⁶⁹ When serving his six-year prison sentence, Otto Ernst Andreasch was put to work clearing mines and lost his life in an air raid on 6 November 1944.⁷⁰

Trotskyists, Anarchists, NS Dissidents

Unlike the highly activist Communists, the various small groups in the tradition of the Russian revolutionary and leading Communist dissident Leon Trotsky largely operated in isolation. The publications of the Kampfbund zur Befreiung der Arbeiterklasse (Combat league for the liberation of the working class), Proletarische Internationalisten (Proletarian internationalists), Organisation Proletarischer Revolutionäre (Organization of proletarian revolutionaries) and the group 'Gegen den Strom' (Against the current) were distributed with remarkable regularity but in restricted circles, so that the organizations were largely able to keep operating until 1945. The only one to be broken up by the Gestapo was the group 'Gegen den Strom', in 1943. Its leading figures – the commercial clerk Josef Friedrich Ernst Jakobovits and the lathe operator's assistant Franz Kascha – were arrested in April 1943, sentenced to death by the VGH on 10 December 1943 for 'preparation for high treason', and executed on 13 March 1944 at the Vienna LG.⁷¹

That there was an anarchist group at all is only apparent from the existence of illegal pamphlets bearing insulting statements about Hitler, who in connection with his years in Vienna is called a 'shirker', 'pimp' and 'Adolf the syphilitic'. The pamphlets appeared in several issues in 1941 but the Vienna Gestapo never ran their authors to ground.⁷²

The left-wing NSDAP splinter groups that were the Austrian counterparts of the Strasser brothers' Schwarze Front (Black Front) in Germany were entirely insignificant. They were regarded by the Gestapo as 'national-Bolshevist' and were treated no better than any other opponents of the regime. The Nazi party was the area of responsibility of Units II H 1 and 2 (from 1942 Unit IV A 4).⁷³ The factory manager Franz Hager, who had been a member of the NSDAP splinter group 'Kampfgemeinschaft revolutionärer Nationalsozialisten' since 1930 and was in contact with Otto Strasser in Berlin, was taken into 'protective custody' for a number of months by the Vienna Gestapo in spring 1938. On 1 August 1941, Hager was arrested once again for distributing two to three hundred leaflets, signed 'Pacifex', 'Copacifex' or 'Cocopacifex', which contained 'extremely hateful attacks on the Führer and the National Socialist regime and ideology', and appealed to readers to 'join the Communist party and form revolutionary committees'. On 13 June 1942, Hager was sentenced to death for 'preparation for high treason', 'aiding and abetting the enemy' and 'undermining military morale'; he was executed on 30 September 1942 at the Vienna LG. Furthermore, the commercial employee Karl Tuch was arrested by the Gestapo for activity on behalf of the Black Front and for 'betraying the party', and met his end in obscure circumstances, most likely in 1943.⁷⁴

Spanish Civil War Fighters

Within Section II A, a separate unit, II A 3, headed by SS-Unterscharführer Kriminalrat Franz Morawetz, was responsible for monitoring Spanish Civil War fighters who had returned (or had been returned), and returnees from the Soviet Union ('Russia returnees'); according to Rosa Friedl of that unit, the official responsible for the Russia returnees was Theodor Thellmann.⁷⁵ In 1940 the unit was for a short time headed by Otto Heger, who later moved to the Orpo and was deployed in the Baltic region.⁷⁶ Following the German invasion of the Soviet Union in June 1941, the unit's official activities largely came to an end; in the organization reform of 1942, it was incorporated into Section IV A 1.

In the Spanish Civil War of 1936–39, at least fourteen hundred Austrians – former members of the Schutzbund, Communists, Socialists and other left-wingers, amongst them thirty-four women – fought for the Spanish Republic.⁷⁷ After the defeat of the Spanish Republic they were compelled to flee to France, where they were interned. After the events of March 1938 these Austrians were targeted by the Gestapo. In July 1938, the Vienna Gestapo published a decree of the Gestapa in Berlin ordering that 'all Reich Germans returning to the Reich after fighting on the side of the Reds ... are to be transferred to the Gestapa in a joint transport'. Furthermore, all earlier Austrian returnees from Spain were to be registered, as were others still living in 'Red Spain'.⁷⁸

In spite of assurances of immunity from punishment on the part of the German armistice commission and the RSHA, the Spanish Civil War fighters who fell into German hands were, following a decree of 25 September 1940 issued by Heydrich as head of the RSHA, arrested by the Gestapo and taken into 'protective custody' – that is to say, sent to concentration camps – 'for the duration of the war at least'. In the power struggle between the Gestapo and the NS judiciary over who should deal with the Spanish Civil War fighters, the RSHA had clearly prevailed.⁷⁹

Moreover, as a result of misjudgement of the 1939–41 Molotov–Ribbentrop non-aggression pact (and the German–Soviet treaty of friendship), the KPÖ representatives in France had committed the fatal mistake of recommending the – non-Jewish and non-incriminated – Spanish Civil War fighters to return voluntarily from France to the German Reich.⁸⁰ These, whether interned or free, were handed over to the German authorities and either transferred directly from the border to a concentration camp, in most cases Dachau, or transported to their local Gestapo office, whence they followed their comrades to the camps. In a 'protective custody' order against Michael Eichinger issued by the RSHA at the request of the Vienna Gestapo in 1942, it is stated that by fighting 'in the

Spanish Civil War on the side of the Reds' – and later in the French Foreign Legion – Eichinger had jeopardized 'the existence and security of Volk and state', and 'had committed treason in respect of Germandom [Deutschtum], and gives rise to the fear that if set free he will once again become active to the detriment of the Reich'.[81]

Judicial proceedings already initiated were terminated and Civil War fighters already sentenced were reprieved, released from detention and transferred by the Gestapo to concentration camps. The medical student Josef Schneeweiß, who fought for the republic from September 1936 in the Centuria Thälmann and the 11th International Brigade, and was arrested in Paris in December 1940, was transferred to the Vienna Gestapo. After being sentenced by the Vienna OLG to two-and-a-half years' imprisonment with hard labour on 11 November 1941 for 'preparation for high treason', he was remanded to the Vienna Gestapo and sent to Dachau. The procedure subsequently followed is a clear case of juridical deviousness. In 1942 Schneeweiß was formally reprieved and the remaining sentence was waived. The reprieval decision, which was communicated to him at Dachau by the camp commandant, contained the following request: 'I ask for the condemned man to be informed that the reprieval decision has been made on the basis of guarantees undertaken by the repatriation officer of the German armistice commission on the treatment of Spanish Civil War fighters'. The 'reprieval decision' notwithstanding, Schneeweiß was kept interned until the liberation of Dachau on 29 April 1945.[82]

Hans Landauer (b. 1921) of Oberwaltersdorf, Lower Austria, was the youngest Austrian to fight for the Republicans in the Spanish Civil War. After being repatriated following internment at the camps of Argelès, St Cyprien and Gurs, and in Toulon prison, Landauer was detained for a number of weeks by the Vienna Gestapo. There, by his own account, he was not maltreated, for the simple reason that he, along with other Spanish Civil War fighters, was in any case destined for internment in a concentration camp. Similarly, the cartwright's assistant Franz Kasteiner, who was taken prisoner by Franco's forces in March 1938, was handed over to the German authorities and transferred to the Vienna Gestapo in December 1941. Kasteiner was then sent to the concentration camp of Groß-Rosen, where he perished on 22 November 1942.

The Socialist writer and International Brigades fighter Benedikt Fantner was repatriated to the Vienna Gestapo in October 1940 and sent to Dachau, where he arrived on 22 February 1941. As an internee no longer capable of hard labour, on 19 January 1942 he was transferred in the '14f13' operation to the 'euthanasia' centre of Hartheim, where he was gassed.[83] Further Spanish Civil War fighters such as Josef Meisel, Ludwig Beer, Lisa Gavric and Anna Peczenik fell into the hands of the Vienna Gestapo as members of the Communist resistance group that returned from France to Vienna, and ended up in various concentration camps.[84] Julius Günser, a member of this group and likewise a former civil war fighter, was arrested on 26 August 1943 by the Vienna Gestapo, who by means of serious maltreatment succeeded in 'turning' him and forcing him to betray numerous comrades (see also the section 'Cell Spies' in Chapter 7, this volume); he perished in February 1945 at Mauthausen. Another member of the group, Josef Pazdernik, who had lost a leg in Murcia, also became a Gestapo informant.[85]

'Russia Returnees'

Many Germans and Austrians who had gone to the Soviet Union in the 1920s and 1930s as workers or political refugees now returned to the German Reich, either voluntarily or under compulsion. They were regarded with great distrust by the Nazi authorities, who feared that they would pursue political contacts or have intelligence tasks to fulfil. A series of decrees issued to the Gestapo offices by the chief of the Sipo and SD and by the Gestapa/RSHA regulated the modalities for the treatment of the 'Russia returnees' (*Russlandrückkehrer*) precisely. In the most important one, a 24-page decree issued by the Gestapa on 5 August 1939, it was laid down that if there was no warrant out or police requests for the arrest of a given Russia returnee, he or she should be allowed to continue the homeward journey, on the condition that on arrival they should immediately register with the local Gestapo office. The regular Gestapo offices and regional headquarters were instructed to open files on all the returnees in their area, and 'to interrogate them as exhaustively as possible'. Divided into twelve points, the interrogation instructions were aimed at ascertaining personal data, and gaining political, economic and military data and information about individuals, instances of repression, and tasks imposed by the NKVD (People's commissariat for internal affairs). In the case of pending penal proceedings, notably for Communist activity in the USSR, the returnee was to be arrested, as were stateless 'Russian returnees of German blood' and emigrants. Jewish returnees were in general to be taken into *Schulungshaft* (sic, schooling custody); foreigners were to be taken into deportation custody and deported.[86] In a further decree of 31 August 1940, the RSHA laid down the procedure to be followed by Gestapo offices with respect to returnees possibly having NKVD duties to perform – the NS authorities were clearly afraid of the possibility of their being infiltrated into the German Reich as Soviet secret agents.[87]

These strict regulations resulted in the Vienna Gestapo taking action on numerous occasions. According to information provided to the DÖW by the German researcher Wilhelm Mensing, around 150 records of interrogations of Austrian Russia returnees are preserved.[88] The Vienna Gestapo created identification files on 68 Russia returnees.[89] However, given the incompleteness of the identification card index, it can be assumed that the actual number of returnees was considerably higher.

The Gestapo very likely gained little important information from their many interrogations. While the returnees were intimidated and threatened with penalties if they gave false information, they were as a rule not maltreated, and the information they provided was correspondingly meagre. On 3 October 1939, for example, the upholsterer's assistant Ferdinand Blahut from Vienna was interrogated by an official of Unit II A 3; he claimed not to have belonged to a political party, taken part in gatherings, or met any other German or Austrian workers in the Soviet Union; nor did he have anything to report on industrial plants or military sites. Although he had been offered Soviet citizenship, he had refused it out of lack of sympathy for the system and had solely worked as an upholsterer in various companies. He had returned to Germany voluntarily because of the bad economic situation, and had undertaken no obligations to the NKVD on leaving the Soviet Union.[90]

On 27 May 1938 the Vienna Gestapo interrogated the lathe operator's assistant Johann Karigl, who had fought in the Schutzbund in February 1934 and had arrived in the USSR on 1 December 1934 by way of Czechoslovakia. Karigl was more communicative than Blahut, providing information about his work at a munitions factory in Kharkov, revealing the names of four NKVD victims, and giving detailed information about twenty-six Austrians in Kharkov and four members of the Schutzbund who had gone to Spain. Furthermore, he severely incriminated a Jewish Communist named Turnheim as an NKVD confidential agent and denouncer. The conscientious Gestapo official Thellmann recorded all his statements, adding on the memo that Karigl had been interrogated 'in accordance with all the points of the decree' and had provided 'no useful or relevant information'. Like all others interrogated, Karigl had to sign a commitment to secrecy; if he did not keep his word, or 'in the case of Communist activity or acting in any other way inimical to the state', he would have to 'reckon with being taken into protective custody for an indefinite period of time'.[91]

The machine fitter Ludwig Kern, who had gone to the USSR in 1926 as one of five hundred Austrians engaged in the 'Uhlfeld-Aktion' (a project to build up an Austrian colony in the Kazakh steppe), was deported to Austria in December 1937 for not taking Soviet citizenship. His interrogation by Unit II A 3 of the Vienna Gestapo in February 1939 yielded as little in the way of new knowledge and information as numerous others carried out along the same lines.[92]

Gestapo documents indicate that Russia returnees were put under surveillance once they had been released. On 27 February 1940, for example, Unit II A 3 requested the NSDAP offices for the Gau of Vienna to monitor Franz Krapez and to report back after five months. After this period, the NSDAP office for District VI of Vienna confirmed that the returnee had given no cause for political concern, and declined to continue the surveillance.[93]

The Vienna Gestapo also monitored returnees through the deployment of informants. In his most recent study on the informants of the Vienna Gestapo,

Hans Schafranek gives the names of two women who spied for the Gestapo in this milieu: Marie Zoder, a long-standing member of the KPÖ, and Anna Mönch, a founder member, who received a monthly payment of RM 250.[94]

Not all returnees entered the German Reich voluntarily. In many cases, individuals categorized as politically unreliable were expelled from the Soviet Union or taken out of NKVD prisons or camps and – until the launching of the German attack on 22 June 1941 – handed over to German authorities at the border (Brest-Litovsk, Lublin and other crossing points). For many this was tantamount to a death sentence, as was vividly described by Margarete Buber-Neumann, widow of the top KPD functionary Heinz Neumann murdered in 1937.[95] Amongst the prisoners handed over to the Gestapo by the NKVD was Franz Koritschoner, a co-founder of the KPÖ. Like others, he was transferred to the Vienna Gestapo, where he was interrogated, a file being opened on him on 17 April 1941.

On the same day, a file was opened on the young Spanish Civil War fighter Hans Landauer. For about two weeks, Landauer and a number of other 'Spanienkämpfer' (Spain fighters) shared Cell 44a at the police prison on Rossauer Lände with Franz Koritschoner, who was in very poor health after detention at a Soviet camp, and still bore the signs of maltreatment (most likely at the hands of the NKVD). While the returnees from Spain were transported to Dachau on 6 June 1941 and survived the war, Koritschoner was deported around the same time to Auschwitz, where he was murdered on 8 or 9 June 1941.[96] The handing over of Koritschoner, who as a Jew and a Communist was doubly endangered, was no isolated case; others like him were handed over to the Gestapo, such as Wilhelm Brainin and Paul Meisel, both Viennese, who were not transported to Vienna, however, but to the Lublin ghetto and Buchenwald concentration camp respectively, where they both perished. The diplomat Gerhard von Walther, at the time posted to the German Embassy in Moscow, later reported that 'two to three hundred German Communists were transferred against their will'.[97]

Repression of Foreign Forced Labourers

In the course of the imperialistic war begun by Nazi Germany in 1939, millions of people from the conquered, occupied and plundered European lands and territories, principally those in eastern and south-eastern Europe, were deported, largely by force, to the German Reich, where they were put to work, mostly in the armaments industry and on large building sites, but also in agriculture. In 1944, 5,295,000 'foreign workers' (*Fremdarbeiter*) were registered in the German Reich, including some 580,000 on the territory of present-day Austria, where they were augmented by more than 200,000 POWs and Hungarian Jewish forced labourers and concentration camp internees.[98] The forced labourers were not only exploited as workers but also subjected to a strict regime with racist gradations. Soviet citizens, including Ukrainians and others – who were known as 'Ostarbeiter' (workers from the East) – were treated worse than workers from west European countries; in particular, harsh punishments were imposed in order to prevent contact with the local population. A general decree of the Reichsführer-SS of 20 February 1942 laid down the following with respect to the *Ostarbeiter*: 'The aim is to stop Communist thought penetrating the German population by preventing any contact that is not immediately related to work, and as far as possible to forestall any solidarity between German people and the workhands from the former Soviet Russian territory. The state police should proceed against Germans who act contrary to this aim in accordance with the nature of the individual case'.[99]

Reichsführer-SS Himmler ordered particularly severe penalties for sexual relations between *Ostarbeiter* and locals: 'Every case of sexual intercourse with comrades from the German Volk should be dealt with through application for *Sonderbehandlung* ['special treatment'] in the case of male workers from the former Soviet Russian territory, and for committal to a concentration camp in the case of female workers'.[100]

In the eyes of the NS leadership, however, the millions of forced labourers transferred to the Reich also represented a great source of potential uncertainty. It is no coincidence that the general staff plan 'Walküre' that Oberst Stauffenberg adapted for his attempted putsch on 20 July 1944 had originally been devised for the eventuality of unrest and uprisings on the part of concentration camp internees, POWs and foreign labourers.[101]

The Gestapo was responsible for implementing the strict regulations, penalizing offences and countering acts of resistance by foreign workers. It took action even in simple cases of labour disputes or in order to stiffen discipline at the workplace.[102] In her seminal work on the AELs, however, Gabriele Lotfi notes that in none of the cases she investigated did the Gestapo take measures on its own initiative, but always followed reports from firms or NSDAP formations.[103] This was the case, for example, when on 18 July 1941, the Vienna Gestapo intervened at the DAF (Deutsche Arbeitsfront) camp at Laaerbergstrasse 68, Favoriten (10th district), where 660 Italian workers employed by various firms as dyke-diggers and brickyard hands refused to start work for various reasons, including poor food. After the arrest of the ringleaders Nikola Danolfi and Ferdinando D'Angio and a general Gestapo admonition, work was resumed on the following day.[104]

Firms were also subjected to spot checks by arrangement with the DAF. After an inspection of this kind on 22 February 1943 at the mechanical engineering factory Alexander Friedmann at Handelskai 134, Leopoldstadt (2nd district), three Croatian civilian workers were arrested and committed to Oberlanzendorf AEL and three other Croats were reprimanded. The Vienna Gestapo daily report explained the measures as follows: 'The intervention took place directly on the company premises, in order to set a cautionary example to the other members of their group'.[105]

By contrast, the large numbers of POWs, who were strictly guarded and exploited for forced labour, were not the responsibility of the Gestapo – even following offences such as sabotage or prohibited sexual relations – but of their respective POW camps (Stalags), which were administered and headed by the Wehrmacht. Following Einsatzbefehl (operational order) No. 9 issued by Sipo chief Heydrich on 21 July 1941, Soviet POWs were set apart by the Sipo and SD, and for the most part murdered (*Sonderbehandlung*) in concentration camps.[106] However, there is no evidence that the Vienna Gestapo – unlike other Gestapo regional headquarters – was involved in such actions.

The innumerable instances of offences such as 'breach of work contract' (leaving the workplace without permission, refusing to work, and the like) led to a shift of the Gestapo's focus from local resistance fighters to foreign forced labourers, and thus to a change in its fields of activity. Another result was that the Gestapo's methods became more brutal, with the *Ostarbeiter*, who were considered *Untermenschen* (subhuman) and *fremdvölkisch* (foreign, alien), being treated even less humanely than German/Austrian resistance fighters and regime opponents. Disciplinary offences, escape attempts and sexual relations with Germans (or Austrians) were punished with extreme measures – severe maltreatment, shootings, executions and murders by Gestapo officials were no rare occurrences.

At the Vienna Gestapo headquarters, offences by foreign workers and POWs were dealt with by Group IV D (1938–42, II E), with the constantly growing task complex 'breach of work contract and asocials' being allotted to Section IV D 6. From 1942, Group IV D was headed by SS-Sturmbannführer Regierungsrat Dr Viktor Siegel, who from 1943 to 1944, under the new GVP, became responsible for all matters related to foreigners and, from 1944, the *Ostarbeiter* also.[107] His deputy and right-hand man was SS-Sturmbannführer Kriminalrat Oskar Wendzio, a Reich German who had been transferred from the Brünn (Brno) Gestapo to Vienna as a punishment. Wendzio, who was older than Siegel and is said to have thought he should have been head of Group IV D (later IV 5), headed Section IV D 5 (Ostarbeiter). He made a significant contribution to the exacerbation of interrogation procedures by spurring on his subordinates – notably the NSDAP 'Alter Kämpfer' Rudolf Hitzler – to achieve 'successes'. According to the judgment delivered by the Vienna VG in 1948, Hitzler was the 'the most feared Gestapo thug at Morzinplatz'. Hitzler's assaults upon foreign workers (as well as his maltreatment of resistance fighters) were considered in detail in the VG proceedings, and confirmed on the basis of witness statements and his own admissions. To quote the judgment:

According to the testimony of Eduard Eckhardt, formerly senior administrator of the police prison, the number of *Ostarbeiter* detainees maltreated by Hitzler in this way ran into the hundreds. The witness Gustav Hübner, who had been employed as the baths' attendant at the police prison, described the dreadful sight of the detainees when they undressed to wash after their extremely brutal maltreatment: faces swollen and smeared with dried blood, backs bleeding and covered with weals, arms pulled out of joint.[108]

In Section IV D 5 (Ostarbeiter) there were several instances of death following maltreatment. At least one case was reported to the state prosecutor by the police prison director Stefan Palmer; however, the proceedings at the SS- und Polizeigericht (SS and police court) against Hitzler were discontinued, in particular because Siegel and Wendzio stood up for him. Shortly after, Hitzler was transferred to Section IV A 1, in which he continued his brutality, most notably in the Reichsgau Lower Danube in the final phase of the Nazi regime.[109] While the few deaths recorded at Morzinplatz were the result of vicious interrogations, they were not executions; however, a number of Gestapo officials were involved in extra-legal executions of Poles and *Ostarbeiter*, mostly in connection with prohibited sexual relations. When the Gestapo wanted a detainee to be disposed of, the murder was carried out through *Sonderbehandlung* at Mauthausen or another concentration camp.

As a rule, the Vienna Gestapo did not waste much time on forced labourers brought to Morzinplatz for 'breach of work contract', unless there was some kind of political background. The detainees were usually despatched, without the creation of identification files or records in the daily reports, to the Vienna Gestapo AEL of Oberlanzendorf or to Mauthausen or one of its many satellite camps. First-time offenders were let off with reprimands, which were roughly the same in number as committals to camps.[110] In the entire period 1938–45, the Vienna Gestapo daily reports record the arrests of only 2,251 forced labourers and POWs, listed with name and offence-related data; however, these were clearly only a fraction of the total because, as we know from Vienna Gestapo statistics, even in one single month, July 1943, as many as 1,576 foreign workers were arrested for refusing to work (albeit not recorded by name).[111]

By contrast, foreign workers belonging to resistance groups were interrogated at Morzinplatz with the most brutal methods – as described in connection with Austrian resistance fighters – in order to force them to reveal names of fellow activists. The Vienna Gestapo daily reports record large numbers of arrests of resistance fighters from the ranks of the foreign workers. Among others, French, Dutch, Slovene, Croat, Serb, Polish, Russian and Ukrainian resistance organizations were uncovered and crushed.[112]

The most important resistance group of this kind was the Eastern workers' anti-Hitler movement (Anti-Hitler-Bewegung der Ostarbeiter). It cooperated closely with the anti-Hitler movement of Austria founded at the end of 1942 by the Slovenian Karl Hudomalj, a Communist party functionary, the history of which has been described in several publications by Hans Schafranek.[113] In a number of important armaments factories in and around Vienna, it established a network of resistance committees which were not discovered by the Vienna Gestapo until the end of October 1943.[114] The investigations and subsequent measures were carried out with the greatest brutality by the 'Ostarbeiter section' under Rudolf Hitzler, and Section IV A 2 (Sabotage, radio and parachute agents) under Johann Sanitzer.[115] The crushing of the organization, in the course of which a large number of Soviet Russian and Austrian activists were arrested, succeeded largely because of the deployment of informants who led the parachutist Gregor Kersche into a trap when he was flown in from the Soviet Union.[116]

The Gestapo identified and tracked down the leader of this Communist *Ostarbeiter* organization, the Russian Iwan Schelasko, who was employed at the Felsinger tarboard factory in Oyenhausen and was arrested in January 1944 along with numerous other activists. They were accused by the Gestapo not only of pursuing Socialist/Communist political goals but also of carrying out acts of sabotage and forming partisan squads; and it was indeed the case that at the Maier knitwear factory in Meidling (12th district), the worker Igor Truskowski deliberately caused two steam boilers to explode, creating damage to the tune of between RM 30,000 and RM 40,000. Similarly, Iwan Miseluk, a *Hilfswilliger* (non-German military volunteer) employed at the Waffen-SS automotive training facility near Schönbrunn Palace in Vienna, was instructed by the organization to steal arms and ammunition from his place of work. By this time, the Croat Alexander Rankov (Rankow) had organized a group of *Ostarbeiter*, who were to have joined up with the Croatian (Tito) partisans. A key role in the movement was played by the printer Ilja Kirnosow, employed at the Elektron company in the Siebenhirten area of Vienna, who was a member of the Communist party of the Soviet Union and a sergeant in the Red Army. According to the Gestapo, he was a 'full Jew' who had managed to avoid being taken prisoner and had infiltrated the German Reich as an *Ostarbeiter*; as such, the Gestapo claimed, he was preparing a 'shockwave of acts of sabotage with the aim of reducing German arms production'. Almost all the *Ostarbeiter* involved in the organization of their anti-Hitler movement were sent to Mauthausen and murdered there (or at Hartheim) in August 1944.[117] Apart from Hans Schafranek's admirable studies on this *Ostarbeiter* organization, the resistance activities of foreign forced labourers – which were considerable, particularly on the part of Soviet POWs – remain a little-researched field.[118]

In at least one case, the Vienna Gestapo itself documented the maltreatment of a Soviet worker in an identification card index photographic record. On

4 January 1944, the Russian assistant lathe-operator Nikolaj Baran, member of the Anti-Hitler-Bewegung der Ostarbeiter, was arrested under the cover name 'Konstantin Dombrowsky' and perished in that month as a result of maltreatment in the course of interrogations lasting whole days. Even that, however, did not bring his ill treatment by the Gestapo to an end: his corpse became the object of a further identification file, which was created under the correct name Baran.[119]

Hundreds of thousands of forced labourers suffered under the repressive measures implemented in the German Reich. In the course of six months in 1944, a total of 205,949 arrests were recorded in the Reich and occupied territories. According to the cautious estimate ventured by Gabriele Lotfi, around 5 per cent of all foreign civilian workers received punishments in the form of detention in an AEL.[120]

The Vienna Gestapo's area of competence saw enormous increases in the numbers of arrests for labour-related offences. While the first half of 1941 saw 1,667 arrests for such offences (including 1,208 Poles and 126 citizens of the German Reich), in the single month of July 1943 the Vienna Gestapo recorded no fewer than 1,654 arrests, mostly of *Ostarbeiter*, for refusing to work.[121] In 1943–44, the arrests for refusing to work or breach of work contract accounted for 77 per cent of total arrests in that period.[122] On some days the Vienna Gestapo took more than fifty foreign workers into detention for labour-related offences.[123] There were 2,143 arrests in August 1943; of the 892 *Ostarbeiter*, 264 Poles, and 250 south-east Europeans who were arrested for refusing to work, 451 were interned at Oberlanzendorf AEL and 465 were let off with a reprimand.[124] The terror inflicted upon the forced labourers by the Vienna Gestapo peaked in March 1944, when out of a total 2,656 arrestees – 2,024 of whom (76 per cent) were foreign workers – 561 were transferred to AELs, 69 committed to concentration camps and 509 reprimanded. The overwhelming majority of those arrested for refusing to work were foreign civilian workers: 1,074 *Ostarbeiter*, 292 Poles, 285 south-east Europeans, 157 from the Protectorate (Bohemia and Moravia), and 125 French; only 47 were (ethnic) Germans (including Austrians).[125] In the years 1943–44, between 96 and 98 per cent of those arrested every month for refusing to work were foreign workers, and more than half of the arrestees were Soviet forced labourers.[126]

Figure 12.4. Tortured to death by the Gestapo: Soviet civilian forced labourer Nikolaj Baran. Gestapo identification photos. © Wiener Stadt- und Landesarchiv. Used with permission.

Franz Weisz has established the following figures for arrests in the sector 'Wirtschaftsangelegenheiten, Straftaten ausländischer Arbeiter' (economic affairs, criminal offences by foreign workers) in the years 1940 to 1944: 649 in 1940; 2,225 in 1941; 5,194 in 1942; 18,785 in 1943; and 7,949 in 1944. Not including 1945, this amounts to around 35,000 arrests – that is to say, around 75 per cent of the 47,000 arrests statistically recorded (however, as noted elsewhere, the latter figure does not included the even greater number of Jews taken into detention and deported).[127] These figures indicate that – alongside the combating of organized and non-organized resistance and the persecution of the Jews – the repression of the eastern and south-eastern European workers compelled to engage in forced labour in the wake of the extension of the war in 1941 was clearly one of the Vienna Gestapo's principal fields of activity.

Notes

1. See *Kleine Volkszeitung*, 20 Apr 1938, 2; but almost all newspapers contained similarly worded reports. For a general account of the legitimist-monarchist resistance, see Moll, *Habsburg gegen Hitler*, 133–44; Walterskirchen, *Blaues Blut*.
2. Neugebauer/Schwarz, *Stacheldraht, mit Tod geladen*, 52–53; in greater detail: Welan/Wohnout, 'Hans Karl Zeßner-Spitzenberg', 21–41; Walterskirchen, *Blaues Blut*, 68–87.
3. DÖW 20 333/7, Sections of the Vienna Gestapo with their heads and members, n.d., no author (probably compiled by the Austrian state police in the course of proceedings against members of the Vienna Gestapo).
4. DÖW 20 333/7, Sections of the Vienna Gestapo (see n. 3); Neugebauer, *Widerstand*, 35–36. On the daily reports and the arrests, see also Chapter 6, this volume.
5. DÖW 4150; Luza, *Resistance*, 30, 40; DÖW, *Widerstand Wien*, vol. 3, 129–30; for greater detail, see Prosl, 'Karl Burian', 375–91; www.doew.at/erinnern/personendatenbanken/gestapo-opfer (last accessed on 29 Jul 2017). Schafranek, *Widerstand und Verrat* (2017), 161–80, reasonably claims that the contact with the Polish intelligence agent Gabrynovicz was a fiction and provocation on the part of the Vienna Gestapo.
6. DÖW 5732a, Vienna Gestapo daily report no. 6 for 12–13 Feb 1941; Neugebauer, *Austrian Resistance*, 145–51.
7. Schafranek, *Widerstand und Verrat* (2017), 161–248.
8. DÖW 21 432 (copy, original at BA, Berlin), report of an unnamed 'ministerial court observer' to the Reich minister of justice, 3 Jan 1944.
9. DÖW, *Widerstand Wien*, vol. 3, 82ff.; Neugebauer, *Austrian Resistance*, 152–56.
10. DÖW 11 482, Vienna Gestapo memo concerning the illegal youth group; see section regarding Hugo Pepper, 2 Aug 1938.
11. DÖW 5734 d, Vienna Gestapo daily reports no. 2 of 4–8 July 1943 and no. 8 of 24–26 Aug 1943; Neugebauer, *Austrian Resistance*, 164–69.
12. Luza, *Resistance*, 170–71, 175; Beer, 'Arcel/Cassia/Redbird', 75–100.
13. DÖW 51 617, Vienna Gestapo record of the interrogation of Heinrich Maier, 7 Apr 1944; DÖW 21 299, bill of indictment of the chief Reich prosecutor at the VGH against Heinrich Maier et al., 5 Oct 1944. Our thanks go to Hans Schafranek for putting documents at our disposal.

14. According to the 1941 'Lehmann' (directory of Vienna addresses), Messner lived at Hasenauerstraße 61. A later owner of the house, Dr Homa Jordis, supplied the information (email to Wolfgang Neugebauer, 3 Jan 2018) that the land register cites Franz Josef and Franziska Messner as proprietors from 29 July 1938. As early as 1938, Hasenauerstraße 12 (quoted in Weisz, 'Gestapo-Leitstelle Wien', 925) was already being used by the Gestapo for the accommodation of higher-ranking officials; see DÖW 20 333/8.
15. For greater detail, see Schafranek/Hurton, 'Im Netz der Verräter'; DÖW 8479, Vienna Gestapo daily reports no. 3 of 7–9 Mar 1944 and no. 7 of 21–23 Mar 1944.
16. Schafranek/Hurton, 'Im Netz der Verräter'; *Rot-Weiß-Rot-Buch*, 138–39.
17. http://www.doew.at//erinnern/personendatenbanken/gestapo-opfer (last accessed on 29 Jul 2017); DÖW, *Widerstand Wien*, vol. 3, 444–51.
18. DÖW reference library, Vienna Gestapo daily report no. 2 of 8–14 Dec 1944; WStLA, Vienna LG, Vg 11 c Vr 586/47, record of the main hearing in the VG proceedings against Johann Sanitzer, 13 Jan 1949.
19. Luza, *Resistance*, 158–66; Molden, *Ruf des Gewissens*, 166ff.; Neugebauer, *Austrian Resistance*, 216–20; Rathkolb, 'Raoul Bumballa', 295–317. There are no extant Vienna Gestapo daily reports for this phase of the war.
20. Neugebauer, *Austrian Resistance*, 79–114.
21. DÖW 20 333/7, Sections of the Vienna Gestapo (see n. 3); Archives of the Republic of Slovenia, AS 1931, 809, sheets 640–81, Lambert Leutgeb, 'Die Organisation der Geheimen Staatspolizei-Staatspolizeileitstelle Wien nach dem März 1938 bis zur Gründung des Reichssicherheitshauptamtes 1941', 7 and 26 (composed 1947–48 while in Yugoslavian detention).
22. Schafranek, *Widerstand und Verrat* (2017), 100.
23. Weisz, 'Gestapo-Leitstelle Wien', Tables, table no. 129, 136.
24. DÖW 1578, Vienna Gestapo situation report concerning Communism, Jan–Mar 1939, no precise date.
25. DÖW 1453, report of the RSHA concerning inflammatory Communist propaganda, 20 Feb 1940; DÖW 2505, 441; DÖW, *Widerstand Wien*, vol. 2, 214ff.
26. For a detailed account, see Schafranek, *Widerstand und Verrat* (2017). Letters penned by activists from detention offer profound insights into the catastrophic situation they faced at the hands of the Gestapo; see Rizy/Weinert, *'Mein Kopf wird euch auch nicht retten'*.
27. DÖW, *Widerstand Wien*, vol. 2, 103; Schafranek, 'V-Leute und "Verräter"'; idem, *Widerstand und Verrat* (2017), esp. 417–27; Schütte-Lihotzky, *Erinnerungen*, 61–74.
28. For greater detail on Koppel and Kahane, see Cezanne-Thauss, 'Lambert Leutgeb'. Kahane perished in detention in Yugoslavia.
29. Knoll, *Widerstand in der Provinz*, 78.
30. 'Verräter und politisches Werkzeug', *Der Standard*, 10 Feb 2009; DÖW, *Widerstand Wien*, vol. 2, 107; Neugebauer, *Austrian Resistance*, 87ff.; Schafranek, *Widerstand und Verrat* (2017), 422–23, comes to the conclusion that his earlier estimate requires 'considerable upward correction'.
31. Schafranek, *Widerstand und Verrat* (2017), 110–26; idem, 'V-Leute', 328–29.
32. DÖW, *Widerstand Wien*, vol. 2, 113ff.; www.doew.at/personensuche (last accessed on 18 Nov 2017).
33. Schafranek, *Widerstand und Verrat* (2017), 363–91; idem, 'V-Leute', 336–37; Meisel, *'Jetzt haben wir Ihnen'*, 118ff. See Chapter 7 this volume, and the brochure of the Reich propaganda office, Vienna, published in Geppert, *Im Namen des Volkes*. Whereas Zwifelhofer disappeared after he had been taken into custody by the Austrian state police in 1945, Schwager, in spite of KPÖ protests, was subsequently active as a functionary in the SED (GDR).

34. Schafranek, 'V-Leute', 336–67; Albu and Weisz, 'Spitzel und Spitzelwesen der Gestapo', 169–208; Neugebauer, *Austrian Resistance*, 106ff. After being sentenced to life imprisonment by a Vienna VG in 1945, Sanitzer was taken to the USSR by the Soviet occupying powers, where he was compelled to make extensive confessions about his activities and his staff, contacts and victims. Hans Schafranek kindly donated a translation of the Russian interrogation records to the DÖW.
35. DÖW 8912, statement by Johann Sanitzer at the Vienna LG, 15 Feb 1947; Schafranek, 'Im Hinterland des Feindes', 33–34.
36. DÖW 4935, report of the chief Reich prosecutor at the VGH to the Reich minister of justice following a tour of duty in the 'Ostmark', 28 May 1942.
37. DÖW 5080, Vienna Gestapo report, 28 Mar 1944.
38. Bailer/Ungar, 'Die Zahl der Todesopfer politischer Verfolgung', 114–15; with reference to the relevant organizational entities II A, IV A 1 and IV 1a, Weisz, 'Gestapo-Leitstelle Wien', table no. 2, 193, cites 4,654 arrests for the period 1938–45, but draws attention to the incompleteness of the Gestapo reports on which his findings are based.
39. Neugebauer, 'Widerstand', 67–68.
40. For a summary account, see Neugebauer, 'Mit der Waffe in der Hand', 383–96.
41. For a detailed account, see Mugrauer, 'Eine "Bande von Gaunern"', 101–40; Schafranek, *Widerstand und Verrat* (2017), 126–31. The daily reports of the Vienna Gestapo are only extant until March 1945, and even in these the records of the arrests are far from complete. In particular, the decentralized Gestapo units operating in the Reichsgau Lower Danube, which were involved in numerous crimes right up until the last day of the war (for example, in Stein, Krems and Sankt Pölten, and in the Gloggnitz area), did not bother to compose written reports.
42. Neugebauer, *Austrian Resistance*, 69ff.
43. See Chapter 9 this volume, and Neugebauer/Schwarz, *Stacheldraht mit Tod geladen*.
44. Lambert Leutgeb, 'Die Organisation der Geheimen Staatspolizei-Staatspolizeileitstelle Wien' (see n. 21), 16, in the archives of the Republic of Slovenia.
45. DÖW 20 333/7, Sections of the Vienna Gestapo (see n. 3); Weisz, 'Gestapo-Leitstelle Wien', Tables, table no. 129, 136.
46. Schafranek, *Widerstand und Verrat* (2017), 55.
47. Gardiner/Buttinger, *Damit wir nicht vergessen*, 73ff.
48. DÖW 7006; *Austrian Labor Information*, 20 May 1942. For details, see Steiner, *Käthe Leichter*. Käthe Leichter's two sons succeeded in fleeing to the United States, where Franz Leichter became a New York state senator.
49. DÖW 1576, telex from security police chief Heydrich to the Vienna Gestapo headquarters concerning the preventive combating of Communism and Marxism, 27 Sep 1938; telex from the Vienna Gestapo to Heydrich concerning Communist and Marxist subversive activities, 30 Sep 1938.
50. DÖW 1580, report of the Vienna Gestapo, Unit II A 2, concerning operations against the RS, 3 Sep 1939. See also Chapter 9, this volume.
51. DÖW 5796; Schafranek, *Widerstand und Verrat* (2017), 136–51.
52. For the controversy on this point, see Feymann, 'Das Deutschnationale im politischen Denken Ludwig Lesers'; Leser, 'Ludwig Leser. Pionier des Burgenlandes'.
53. DÖW 3675, Vienna Gestapo daily report of 26 Jul 1938 (the document is a rough handwritten copy); DÖW 7256, VGH judgment against Friederike Nödl and others, 11 Jun 1939; *Völkischer Beobachter*, Vienna edition, 10 and 11 Jun 1939.
54. DÖW, OLG Wien OJs 24/40, Vienna OLG judgment against Franz Pfannenstiel and others, 20 Jan 1940; www.doew.at/erinnern/personendatenbanken/gestapo-opfer (last accessed on 9 Oct 2017)

55. www.doew.at/erinnern/personendatenbanken/gestapo-opfer (last accessed on 9 Oct 2017).
56. See Neugebauer/Steiner, *Widerstand*, 98ff.
57. Schafranek, *Widerstand und Verrat* (2017), 221ff.
58. For details, see Schafranek, 'Das "Anti-Hitler-Komitee"', 7–20.
59. Schafranek, *Widerstand und Verrat* (2017), 55, 151–60, 470–74; DÖW, *Widerstand Wien*, vol. 2, 7ff.; DÖW E 19592; www.doew.at/erinnern/personendatenbanken/gestapo-opfer (last accessed on 9 Oct 2017).
60. www.doew.at/erinnern/personendatenbanken/gestapo-opfer (last accessed on 2 Oct 2017); Paul Schärf, *Otto Haas*; DÖW, *Widerstand Wien*, vol. 2, 63ff.
61. www.doew.at/erinnern/personendatenbanken/gestapo-opfer (last accessed on 3 Oct 2017).
62. Ibid.
63. See the section, Mass Arrest after 20 July 1944: Operation 'Gitter', in Chapter 9, this volume; and the account of the conversation between Adolf Schärf and Wilhelm Leuschner in Schärf, *Österreichs Erneuerung*, 19ff.
64. www.doew.at/erinnern/personendatenbanken/gestapo-opfer (last accessed on 3 Oct 2017). The 'Österreichische Freiheitsfront' in Vienna is not to be confused with the group of partisan fighters of the same name in Styria.
65. DÖW 989, indictment of the chief Reich prosecutor at the VGH against Otto Ernst Andreasch and others for 'constitutional high treason' (*Verfassungshochverrat*), 5 Jun 1944.
66. DÖW reference library, Vienna Gestapo daily report no. 2 of 3–4 May 1940; DÖW 7162, record from memory of the interrogation of Otto Horn, 10 Mar 1971; https://www.doew.at/erinnern/biographien/erzaehlte-geschichte/widerstand-1938–1945/otto-horn-wiener-mischlingsliga; http://www.doew.at/personensuche (last accessed on 5 Oct 2017).
67. DÖW reference library, Vienna Gestapo daily report no. 1 of 1–2 Mar 1944, no. 5 of 14–16 Mar 1944; WStLA, Vienna LG, 20a Vr 731/55, statement by Karl Zeitlberger in the main proceedings, 19 Nov 1956.
68. WStLA, Vienna LG, Vg 4c 5597/47, statement by Otto Horn at the Vienna police headquarters, 5 Jul 1947.
69. WStLA, Vienna LG, Vg 4c 5597/47, statement by Maria Pick, 20 Nov 1947.
70. http://www.doew.at/personensuche (last accessed on 6 Oct 2017).
71. DÖW 5734 b, Vienna Gestapo daily reports no. 2 of 2–5 Apr 1943, no. 4 of 9–12 Apr 1943, no. 5 of 13–15 Apr 1943; DÖW 8477, Vienna Gestapo daily report no. 5 of 14–16 Dec 1943; DÖW, *Widerstand Wien*, vol. 2, 418ff.; www.doew.at/erinnern/personendatenbanken/gestapo-opfer (last accessed on 23 Aug 2017); *Trotzkistische Opfer des NS-Terrors*.
72. DÖW Bibliothek 4063/6 and 4063/7.
73. DÖW 20 333/7, Sections of the Vienna Gestapo (see n. 3); Lambert Leutgeb, 'Die Organisation der Geheimen Staatspolizei-Staatspolizeileitstelle' (see n. 21).
74. DÖW reference library, Vienna Gestapo daily report no. 1 of 1–3 Aug 1941; DÖW, *Widerstand Wien*, vol. 2, 437; www.doew.at/erinnern/personendatenbanken/gestapo-opfer (last accessed on 10 Mar 2017). According to information provided by the WStLA, Tuch was declared dead in the 1950s with the statement that he 'certainly did not survive the year 1943'. It is unclear whether this Karl Tuch was the same person as the Karl Tuch whose name was on the list of those deported in the first Austrian transport to Dachau in 1938 (subsequently deleted).
75. DÖW 20 333/7, Sections of the Vienna Gestapo (see n. 3); DÖW 19 685, record of the interrogation of Rosa Friedl, 5 Oct 1945, quoted from Schafranek, *Zwischen NKWD und Gestapo*, 102–3.
76. WStLA, Vienna LG, Vg 26d Vr 5331/47, Vienna police headquarters, report concerning Otto Heger, 11 Jun 1946.

77. DÖW, *Für Spaniens Freiheit*; Landauer/Hackl, *Lexikon*; Filip, 'Voluntarias Internacionales', 1–4.
78. DÖW 8049, letter from the Vienna Gestapo regional headquarters to the authorities of the Reichsgau Lower Danube concerning the transfer of returnee Spanish Civil War fighters, 7 Jul 1938.
79. BA Berlin, R 58/265, decree of the chief of the Sipo and SD to all Gestapo offices and regional headquarters concerning the treatment of former (red) Spanish Civil War fighters, both Reich-German and foreign, 25 Sep 1940. For detail on the conflict between the NS judiciary and the RSHA, see Form/Kirschner, 'Verfahren gegen ehemalige Spanienkämpfer', 751–65.
80. DÖW, *Für Spaniens Freiheit*, 295–96, 361–67; Landauer/Hackl, *Lexikon*, 38.
81. OF NÖ 1313 (copy: DÖW E 19 285), protective custody order against Michael Eichinger of Vienna, 1 Jun 1942.
82. www.doew.at/erinnern/personendatenbanken/gestapo-opfer (last accessed on 25 May 2021); DÖW, *Widerstand Wien*, vol. 2, 431–32; Form/Kirschner, 'Verfahren gegen ehemalige Spanienkämpfer', 752–53; Schneeweiß, *Keine Führer*; DÖW Mitteilungen, no. 157 (Jul 2002), see under http://www.doew.at/cms/download/3kehs/157.pdf (last accessed on 15 Dec 2014).
83. Landauer/Hackl, *Lexikon*, 131 and 84. For details, see Exenberger, 'Der österreichische Arbeiterschriftsteller Benedikt Fantner', 45–60
84. See the section 'Vienna Gestapo Officials in France' in Chapter 15, this volume.
85. Schafranek, *Widerstand und Verrat* (2017), 335, 338, 364ff.; Landauer/Hackl, *Lexikon*, 103, 136, 242.
86. BA Berlin, R 58, 9113, Gestapa decree concerning Russia returnees, 5 Aug 1939.
87. Ibid.; RSHA decree concerning Russia returnees, 31 Aug 1940.
88. Information supplied by Josef Vogl (DÖW), who provided us with a number of interrogation records photocopied by Wilhelm Mensing at the PAAA.
89. Printout of the Vienna Gestapo's identification card index (Erkennungsdienstliche Kartei), digitized by the DÖW.
90. PAAA, RZ 211 R150277, Vienna Gestapo record of the interrogation of Ferdinand Blahut, 3 Oct 1939.
91. PAAA, RZ 211, R 151.612, Vienna Gestapo record of the interrogation of Johann Karigl, 27 May 1938.
92. PAAA, RZ 211, R 151.671, Vienna Gestapo record of the interrogation of Ludwig Kern, 24 Feb 1939.
93. PAAA, RZ 211, letter from the Vienna Gestapo to the NSDAP headquarters for the Gau of Vienna concerning the monitoring of Franz Krapez, 27 Feb 1940; letter from the NSDAP office for District VI of Vienna to the Gau personnel office of the Vienna NSDAP, 7 Nov 1940.
94. Schafranek, *Widerstand und Verrat* (2017), 50–51.
95. Buber-Neumann, *Under Two Dictators*.
96. DÖW collection 'Erzählte Geschichte', interview no. 46, Hans Landauer, part II, 108–10; DÖW, Spanish Civil War fighters archive, 25 000/I402, Hans Landauer, 'Zelle 44a' (manuscript); Steiner, 'Franz Koritschoner', 2; Schafranek, 'Franz Koritschoner', 17–18; Schafranek, *Zwischen NKWD und Gestapo*, 76–77; Mugrauer, 'Franz Koritschoner', 33–37. Dr Manfred Mugrauer provided us with the recording of an interview of 1976 with the Spanish Civil War veteran Eduard Buchgraber, who was also detained with Koritschoner at the police prison.
97. Schafranek, *Zwischen NKWD und Gestapo*, 113 and 149. The figure quoted presumably also included Austrians.

98. Freund, 'Zwangsarbeit', 217.
99. [Es kommt darauf an, ein Eindringen kommunistischen Gedankengutes in die deutsche Bevölkerung durch Unterbindung jedes nicht unmittelbar mit der Arbeit zusammenhängenden Umganges zu verhindern und nach Möglichkeit jede Solidarität zwischen deutschen Menschen und den Arbeitskräften aus dem altsowjetrussischen Gebiet zu vermeiden. Gegen Deutsche, die dem zuwiderhandeln, ist mit den nach der Lage des Einzelfalles gebotenen staatspolizeilichen Maßnahmen vorzugehen.] BA Berlin, RD 19/3, RdErl. des RFSSuChDtPol. im RMdI, 20 Feb 1942, quoted from Schafranek, 'Die "Anti-Hitler-Bewegung Österreichs"', 231.
100. [Für jeden Geschlechtsverkehr mit deutschen Volksgenossen oder Volksgenossinnen ist bei männlichen Arbeitskräften aus dem altsowjetrussischen Gebiet Sonderbehandlung, bei weiblichen Arbeitskräften Einweisung in ein Konzentrationslager zu beantragen.] BA Berlin, RD 19/3, RdErl. des RFSSuChDtPol. im RMdI, 20 Feb 1942, quoted from Schafranek, 'Die "Anti-Hitler-Bewegung Österreichs"', 234–35.
101. See amongst many others, Ueberschär, 'Der militärische Umsturzplan "Walküre"', 489ff.
102. See the Vienna Gestapo daily reports in DÖW, *Widerstand Wien*, vol. 3, 363–74.
103. Lotfi, *KZ der Gestapo*, 129.
104. DÖW 5732d, Vienna Gestapo daily report no. 9 of 18–20 Jul 1941.
105. DÖW 5734b, Vienna Gestapo daily report no. 1 of 26 Feb to 1 Mar 1943.
106. Heusler, 'Prävention durch Terror'; Otto, 'Die Gestapo und die sowjetischen Kriegsgefangenen', 201–21.
107. Sections of the Vienna Gestapo with their heads and members, n.d., no author/compiler (a listing most likely compiled by the Austrian state police in the course of proceedings against members of the Vienna Gestapo); WStLA, Volksgericht Wien, Vg 1h Vr 2179/49, statement by Viktor Siegel before the Vienna LG, 24 Jul 1947.
108. WStLA, Vienna LG, Vg 12a 612/46 (copy: DÖW 20 642), judgment against Rudolf Hitzler, 19 Mar 1948. Principally on account of his confession, Hitzler escaped a death sentence and was given life imprisonment. Like many other Nazi war criminals he was amnestied in 1955.
109. Ibid., testimony by Stefan Palmer in the main proceedings, 10 Mar 1948.
110. WStLA, Vienna LG, Vg 12a 612/46 (copy: DÖW 20 642), statement by Rudolf Hitzler in the main proceedings, 8 Mar 1948.
111. DÖW reference library (also DÖW 5734d), Vienna Gestapo statistics for Jul 1943.
112. See DÖW, *Widerstand Wien*, vol. 3, 375–93.
113. Schafranek, 'Die "Anti-Hitler-Bewegung Österreichs"', 229–58.
114. DÖW 8476, Vienna Gestapo daily reports no. 19 of 1–4 Nov 1943 and no. 25 of 23–25 Nov 1943.
115. The reports of the VG proceedings against Sanitzer and Hitzler contain numerous testimonies by victims of maltreatment; see WStLA, Vienna LG, Vg 11c Vr 586/47, judgment against Johann Sanitzer for the crimes of high treason and of torture and maltreatment, 17 Jan 1949, and Vg 12a Vr 612/46 (copy: DÖW 20 642).
116. Schafranek, 'Das "Anti-Hitler-Komitee"', 7–20.
117. Russian names transliterated in accordance with the archival sources. DÖW 8476, Vienna Gestapo daily report no. 6 of 19–21 Oct 1943; DÖW 8477, no. 1 of 1–4 Nov 1943, no. 3 of 7–9 Dec 1943; DÖW 8478, no. 3 of 11–13 Jan 1944, no. 8 of 28–31 Jan 1944, no. 4 of 11–14 Feb 1944; DÖW, *Widerstand Wien*, vol. 3, 388ff. For detail see Schafranek, 'Die "Anti-Hitler-Bewegung Österreichs"', 229–58.
118. See Spoerer, *Zwangsarbeit*, 171ff.
119. http://www.doew.at/erkennen/ausstellung/gedenkstaette-salztorgasse/verschleppt-und-verfolgt-auslaendische-zwangsarbeiterInnen (last accessed on 16 Feb 2017). It is not clear

whether it was the maltreatment of Baran that led to Rudolf Hitzler's trial at the SS and police court. See also the identification photos of Baran at Figure 12.4.
120. Lotfi, *KZ der Gestapo*, 317 and 323; Tech, *Arbeitserziehungslager*, 40.
121. DÖW 5732a, Vienna Gestapo daily report no. 8 of 16–17 July 1941.
122. Prinz, 'Oberlanzendorf', 209.
123. DÖW reference library, Vienna Gestapo daily report no. 11 of 24–25 July 1943.
124. DÖW reference library (also DÖW 5734d), Vienna Gestapo statistics for Aug 1943.
125. DÖW reference library (also DÖW 21 027), Vienna Gestapo statistics for Mar 1944.
126. DÖW reference library: Vienna Gestapo daily report, 27–29 Jul 1943, annex; Vienna Gestapo daily reports, 1 Jan to 28 Feb 1944, annex; Vienna Gestapo statistics for Sep 1943; Vienna Gestapo statistics for Mar 1944.
127. Weisz, 'Gestapo-Leitstelle Wien', Tables, tables no. 2 and 3, synopsis no. 2, 192.

Chapter 13

SUPPRESSION OF NON-ORGANIZED RESISTANCE

'Anti-regime Utterances'

Along with organized resistance, which was classified as 'preparation for high treason' (*Vorbereitung zum Hochverrat*), 'anti-regime utterances' (*regime-feindliche Äußerungen*) were one of the most frequent offences for which people were arrested by the Gestapo and tried by the NS courts. Amongst the many offences punishable under the 'Heimtückegesetz' ('insidious utterances law', see below) were not only defeatist statements, spreading rumours and making jokes about or insulting leading NS functionaries, but also pro-Communist or pro-Catholic utterances, the singing of prohibited songs, standing up for Jews, foreigners and others, or refusing to make contributions to NSDAP collections or use the 'Deutscher Gruß' (i.e. 'Heil Hitler!'). To a certain extent, anti-regime utterances were a barometer of the general public mood, because in most cases such statements – far from being consciously 'insidious' or 'treacherous', or intended to 'undermine military morale'– were simply spontaneous expressions of disillusionment, embitterment and hatred for the Nazi regime. It was not the committed resistance fighter who would fall foul of the Gestapo and courts on this account, but rather the perfectly ordinary citizen – even members of the Nazi party. A situation report sent to Reichsstatthalter Baldur von Schirach on 4 September 1944 by Eduard Frauenfeld, who as head of the NS propaganda office in Vienna will certainly have known what he was talking about, ran as follows: 'At present, tendentially defeatist statements ... can be heard coming from thoroughly decent party and Volk comrades [Partei- und Volksgenossen]'.¹ Nor can it be dismissed as purely coincidental that at this point such statements were becoming increasingly anti-Prussian or anti-German and pro-Austrian in tone.²

However, the Nazi authorities allowed no outlets for this kind of discontent; the Gestapo and NS judiciary followed a policy of zero tolerance, consistently taking action against harmless jokes about Hitler and other prominent Nazis. Usually, the law applied was the one 'against insidious attacks on state and party and for the protection of party uniforms' (Gesetz gegen heimtückische Angriffe auf Staat und Partei und zum Schutz der Parteiuniformen) of 20 December 1934, known as the 'Heimtückegesetz'; in the Gestapo jargon, such offences were referred to as 'heimtückische Äußerungen' (insidious utterances) – or simply *Heimtücke* (insidiousness, malice, treachery). The clause that was used, § 2 (1), ran as follows: 'Whoever, with reference to leading figures in the state or NSDAP, their directives or the institutions established by them, makes statements that are hateful, inflammatory or indicative of a base cast of mind, and are likely to undermine the confidence of the Volk in their political leadership, shall be punished with imprisonment'.³

By Nazi standards, the short prison sentences imposed were a relatively mild punishment. In more serious cases, however, the offence was categorized as 'Wehrkraftzersetzung' (undermining military morale) under the special wartime penal code of 17 August 1938 (Verordnung über das Sonderstrafrecht im Kriege und bei besonderem Einsatz), in which § 5 (1) stated: 'Undermining military morale shall be punished with death: 1. Whoever openly challenges or incites others to refuse to fulfil their duty to serve in the Wehrmacht or allied armed forces, or otherwise openly tries to weaken or undermine the military will of the German Volk or an allied people'.⁴ If the offence was described as 'kommunistische Mundpropaganda' (Communist word-of-mouth propaganda), which was sometimes the case even when the offender had no links to a Communist group, the high treason paragraph of the Reich Penal Code (RStGB) could be applied. Although the prerogative of making the legal distinction between 'undermining military morale' and 'high treason' theoretically lay with the state prosecutor, the Gestapo, as the body responsible for investigations, tracking, interrogations and referrals, often determined the outcome of the judicial proceedings through its referral, and could also opt for other procedures and sanctions – for example, committal to a concentration camp. In short, when it came to 'political offences', the Gestapo had not only the first word but also the last.⁵

From 1938 to 1942, the Vienna Gestapo office responsible for offences under the 'Heimtückegesetz' was Unit II C 2, headed by Polizeisekretär Oskar Schmidt. It was part of Section II C ('National opposition', headed by Regierungsrat Dr Otto Heger), which was also responsible for combating legitimism and resistance groups. When listening to foreign radio broadcasts (or 'radio crime', *Rundfunkverbrechen*) was prohibited at the beginning of the war in 1939, this offence was added to the tasks of Unit II C 2. From 1942 to 1944, according to the GVP, the office responsible for *Heimtücke* and legitimism was Section IV A 3 (headed by SS-Sturmbannführer Kriminalrat Christian Nicoll); in 1944–45, after the restructuring, the office was known as IV 1 b.[6]

While there were any number of cases of 'insidious utterances' and listening to foreign radio broadcasts, they were of secondary importance for the Gestapo in comparison with the task of combating political opponents or the persecution of Jews and (later) foreign forced labourers. In a post-war statement, the head of Section IV N, 'Intelligence', Lambert Leutgeb, patronizingly described offenders under the 'Heimtückegesetz' as mere 'moaners' ('Meckerer'). Unit II C 2 (until 1942) had a staff of only nine, including two women; from 1942, its successor Section IV A 3, which now had the additional responsibility for legitimism, was allocated an additional five men.[7]

In the areas of 'insidious utterances' and 'radio crime', the Gestapo could not follow a proactive strategy, given its limited personnel resources and the large number of cases; on the contrary, for its investigations and the tracking down of offenders it had to rely on denunciations from the general public.[8] According to Lambert Leutgeb, 'the unit received innumerable anonymous letters'.[9]

Although the Gestapo was obliged by law to refer all cases it dealt with to the public prosecutor's office and the courts, it did not always do so, especially if it was not clear what the outcome of proceedings would be. While in minor cases offenders were let off with a reprimand, in more serious cases the Gestapo could also resort to sending offenders to a 'labour education camp' (*Arbeitserziehungslager*, AEL) or a concentration camp. In addition, the Gestapo was usually able to have offenders remanded to them after they had served their sentences (*Rücküberstellung*), so that it once again had them in its power.

From May 1943 to March 1944, up to ninety people per month were arrested by the office responsible for insidious utterances and legitimism, Unit IV A 3 (out of a total of 2,000 to 2,600 arrests by the Vienna Gestapo in the same period), leading to about a hundred criminal charges and seventy to a hundred reprimands per month. However, the number of committals to Oberlanzendorf AEL averaged only two or three per month, and committals to concentration camps were even rarer.[10]

One of the Gestapo's principal goals in taking measures against these trivial instances of resistance and opposition was certainly to intimidate the general population and to deter people from making any kind of anti-regime statements whatever. The following cases demonstrate not only the harshness of the laws and the severity of the Gestapo and the Nazi judiciary but also the diversity of expressions of opinion penalized; furthermore, there is no mistaking that the penalties imposed became increasingly severe in the course of the war.

On 31 December 1938, for example, the sewer worker Ignaz Markisch was released with a reprimand after only a brief period of detention; he had been arrested for singing the Social Democratic workers' youth organization song 'Wir sind jung und das ist schön' ('We are young and that is great') and declaring 'I am a Red and always will be'.[11] Similarly, the baker's assistant Franz Staudinger was let off with a reprimand after being arrested by the Gestapo on 29 July 1939 for taking leave of his comrades after the burial of a Schutzbund leader 'with the *Freundschaft* salutation and a raised clenched fist'; however, he was arrested again in mid-December 1941, and on 7 May 1942 was sentenced by the Vienna SG to nine months' imprisonment for 'violation of the Heimtückegesetz'.[12] The tailor's assistant Franz Brom was arrested on 22 February 1940 for declaring in a tavern: 'I'm a Communist and we're fighting for England and France. We will shoot a lot more Germans before we're finished. You Nazis with your swastikas can all go to hell, and your Führer too'. What became of Brom is not known.[13]

Johanna Bihary trampled on a picture of Goebbels, saying: 'He's a scoundrel and that's the only way he deserves to be treated'. She was arrested on 28 May 1943, and after being transferred to Vienna general hospital remained in detention without trial until 12 April 1945. On 21 May 1943, her husband, the lawyer Napoleon Bihary, a member of the SA and the NSDAP from before March 1938 until his expulsion in July 1943, was arrested for 'preparation for high treason' on account of his connections with a group of parachutists coming from the Soviet Union, and – likewise without trial – was interned at Dachau until liberation.[14] The manual labourer Franz Wrba was arrested by the Gestapo on 23 March 1943 because, at the E.F. Teich works in Alsergrund (9th district), he had 'engaged in Communist word-of-mouth propaganda, thus strongly diminishing the staff's joy in their work and confidence in victory'. He was sentenced to death by the VGH on 23 April 1944 and executed in Brandenburg an der Havel (at the prison of Brandenburg-Görden) on 5 June 1944.[15]

On 15 November 1943, the medical student Gustav Ziegler was arrested by the Gestapo 'on account of statements he made to an officer of the German Wehrmacht that were calculated to undermine military morale'; among other things, he had declared that the war was 'as good as lost'. The Gestapo's pre-emption of a court judgment led to a death sentence from the VGH, which was carried out at the Vienna LG on 30 August 1944.[16]

While the penalties for a first offence under the 'Heimtückegesetz' were relatively light, the Gestapo could send persistent offenders to a concentration camp or report them to the courts, where they would face charges for 'undermining military morale'. For example, the commercial employee Ludwig Staszyszyn was reprimanded for subversive statements in April 1939, and on 25 November 1940 he was sentenced to six months' imprisonment for 'violation of the Heimtückegesetz'. One month after serving his sentence, when at a tavern, he declared: 'The Germans are potato-eating barbarians. The one-party system cannot last, because it was built at the point of the bayonet. I'm an Austrian, and an Austrian

I will stay!' On 19 September 1941, Staszyszyn was arrested again by the Vienna Gestapo, who clearly considered the sentence expected from the courts would be insufficient, as on 18 August 1942 he was committed to Auschwitz, where he perished on 2 September 1942.[17]

In April 1944, the Gestapo took the tram driver Franz Groll into 'protective custody' for twenty-one days for an 'offence against the regulation on radio broadcasts'. After being released he was arrested once again, this time for 'subversive statements'; according to the Gestapo daily report for 12–18 May 1944, he 'subjected his NS-minded family members to serious threats, claiming that they had better believe what he was saying, namely, that by September 1944 Germany would have lost the war. As G. is an unrepentant and fanatical Marxist, he is being committed to a concentration camp'. Groll perished on 15 November 1944 at Flossenbürg.[18]

After being detained in 1940, the waiter Friedrich Hauptvogel was arrested again on 1 August 1941 for 'violation of the Heimtückegesetz' and interned until 10 November 1943 at Dachau. According to the Vienna Gestapo daily report for 1–3 August 1941 he had made the following statements: 'Heil England! Heil America! Heil Moscow! The worst bloody German of them all ['der größte Marmeladesaubruder', see endnote] is Adolf Hitler, but this time he is losing his battle, because we are well organized. Hitler is also the biggest whoremonger, so I give my life for Communism!'[19]

In the case of Catholic priests who openly or indirectly criticized regime measures, the Gestapo often resorted to reprimands, expulsions from the Gau (or from all the Alpine and Danube Gaus), bans on public speaking, bail or committal to concentration camps when there was no prospect of their being sentenced by the courts.[20]

Some individuals fell foul of the Gestapo for speaking positively about Jews or criticizing the anti-Jewish measures. On 8 May 1944, for example, Olga Groh was arrested by the Vienna Gestapo, and on 5 January 1945 was sentenced to two years' imprisonment with hard labour for 'undermining military morale' on account of things she had said about, for example, the gas vans used for the extermination of the Jews. According to the 5 January 1945 judgment of the Vienna OLG, based on the document with which the Gestapo had reported her to the courts, she had said: 'The Jews were loaded into vans and the SS did this all on their own, as drivers and as other necessary assistants. Once they were under way, a nozzle was opened to let out the gas, and by the time the vehicles reached their destination the Jews were done for'.[21]

Similarly, Maria Gerhardt was arrested on 2 September 1941, and on 28 March 1942 was sentenced to one year's imprisonment for 'violation of the Heimtückegesetz'. The indictment of 18 February 1942 recorded that she had made pro-Jewish statements:

Maria Gerhardt voiced her agreement with these inflammatory speeches and outbursts of hatred, confessing frankly that she hated National Socialism. She too referred to the NSDAP and regime leaders with expressions such as 'this rabble, dogs, beasts, criminals, this shitty government'. She also expressed negative opinions about the treatment of the Jews, for whom she felt sorry: 'The Jews are having to leave their beautiful apartments and are being assigned to miserable quarters in Vienna-Leopoldstadt. When the Gestapo do their house searches they steal everything they can. They are riff-raff – in fact, they are the ones who should be exterminated'.[22]

The Gestapo responded rigorously to the numerous rumours circulating about leading Nazis. For example, the warehouse worker Rudolf Hansmann is recorded as having said, among other things, that 'after a personal argument with Himmler, the Führer shot him [Himmler] dead, and that as a consequence Göring fired at Hitler'. Hansmann was arrested on 18 August 1941, and on 17 November 1941 was sentenced to nine months' imprisonment for 'violation of the Heimtückegesetz'.[23]

The farmer Richard Kaysenbrecht was arrested by the Vienna Gestapo on 10 November 1943 for 'subversive statements', sentenced to death by the VGH on 25 April 1944 for 'undermining military morale', and executed on 19 June 1944 at the prison of Brandenburg-Görden. As stated in the death sentence based on the Gestapo report: 'The claim that high-ranking NSDAP members from Berlin had their wives, children and jewellery taken to Switzerland in regularly overcrowded trains, and that even Reichsleiter von Schirach did the same, is – it goes without saying – liable to undermine the German people's faith in their cause and their determination to fight for victory'.[24]

In this connection it may be noted that in July 1942 the Vienna Gestapo applied to the RSHA for the opera singer Lotte Lehmann (married name Charlotte Krause) to be deprived of her citizenship. The internationally famous soprano, formerly Kammersängerin of the Vienna state opera, had said to a French journalist that 'although she was of German blood, she would not return to Germany because she wasn't going to put up with being told what music to put on her recital programmes'.[25]

In cases of anti-regime statements, the measures taken by the Gestapo and judiciary naturally became known to family members, neighbours and colleagues and thus also achieved their intended goal of intimidation and deterrence. Most people were extremely wary of making critical statements about the regime, not least because one could never assess the risk of being denounced.

'Radio Crime', Seizures of Foreign Newspapers

On 1 September 1939, significantly the very day on which war broke out, the Verordnung über außerordentliche Rundfunkmaßnahmen (regulation on extraordinary measures related to radio broadcasts) made it a criminal offence to listen to foreign radio stations (§ 1) and to disseminate news contained in their broadcasts (§ 2).[26] While the Gestapo and Nazi judiciary referred to these offences as 'radio crime' (*Rundfunkverbrechen*), the popular term was *Schwarzhören* (black listening).[27] The intention behind enshrining this prohibition in law was to prevent access to information and propaganda stemming from enemy or neutral states, and to consolidate the Nazi regime's monopoly on news broadcasting. However, the exclusively Nazi orientation of all German radio stations and their obviously mendacious propaganda led more and more people to doubt the truth of the news broadcasts, especially as the war went on. Consequently, in spite of the threat of severe penalties, many people took to listening to 'enemy radio stations'. The most important of these, the BBC and Radio Moscow, transmitted detailed German-language programmes and news broadcasts; however, these foreign stations could not be received with the conventional *Volksempfänger* (people's receiver) wireless, but only with higher-quality sets. The Nazi perspective on the matter was expressed succinctly by Eugen Hadamovsky, national programming director of German radio from 1933 to 1942: 'When the fight for the life of the Volk is in progress, nobody has the right to listen to the enemy or to spread enemy news'.[28]

As long as *Schwarzhören* was not combined with other, graver offences such as 'preparation for high treason' or 'undermining military morale', the trials were held before the special courts (SGs) established at the regional courts (LGs). In the course of the war, the Vienna SG, by far the most important NS tribunal for this offence, conducted a total of 290 trials for cases of 'radio crime' and passed judgments on 400 individuals, as a rule imposing sentences of between one and two years' imprisonment with hard labour. In very serious cases the court could pronounce the death sentence, which the Vienna SG did five times.[29] The severity of the penalties increased when mere listening to foreign broadcasts was compounded by then disseminating the news, this element of the offence being categorized by the Nazi courts as 'undermining military morale' or 'preparation for high treason'. In these cases, the VGH, the Vienna OLG and other Nazi courts sometimes imposed the death sentence; at the VGH, almost half of the Austrians tried for 'undermining military morale' were condemned to death.[30]

The scope of the Gestapo's competence was more extensive in 'radio crime' than in other offences. Not only was it responsible for tracking down offenders but it also determined how they were to be penalized, because it alone decided whether an application for prosecution should be submitted to the courts or whether some other kind of sanction should be applied.[31] Guidelines on this matter had been laid down by the RSHA on 7 September 1939, the day when the regulation on radio broadcasts was promulgated in the *Reichs-Gesetzblatt* (Reich law gazette). As RSHA chief Reinhard Heydrich wrote, 'in practical terms, the impact of the whole regulation [was made] dependent upon the decision of the state secret police ... whose conscientious examination of each and every case' was to ensure 'that only real vermin [Volksschädlinge] were brought before the special court'. As proceedings before the SGs had 'a deterrent effect for the general population' and should therefore lead to 'penalties with as exemplary a character as possible ... the Gestapo regional headquarters [Leitstelle] should in general only apply for criminal prosecution in appropriate cases'. The regional headquarters was not only to consider what broadcasts had been listened to; the most important criteria were 'the offender's general attitude and particular motivation'.

Initially it had been specified that the Gestapo regional headquarters had to obtain permission from the RSHA before submitting an application for charges to be brought by the public prosecutor.[32] However, this arrangement did not stand the test of time, and an RSHA decree of 1 March 1940 gave the heads of the regional headquarters authority to 'decide at their own discretion and responsibility whether to file for prosecution'. In cases of doubt, the RSHA was to be consulted.[33]

At the Vienna Gestapo, the task of dealing with this offence was allotted to Unit II C 2, headed by Polizeisekretär Oskar Schmidt and responsible for 'insidious utterances'. In the restructuring of 1942, 'radio crime' was added to the main areas of responsibility of Section IV A 1 (Communism, Marxism), headed by SS-Sturmbannführer Kriminalrat Fritz Mayer. In the 1944–45 structural reform, this office received the new designation Unit IV 1 a.[34]

Statistics for the Vienna Gestapo indicate that the number of people arrested for listening to foreign radio stations in 1943–44 was less than 20 per month, out of an overall monthly total of around 2,200 arrests. In the thirteen months for which statistics are available, the Vienna Gestapo submitted 112 applications for prosecution under § 5 of the regulation on radio broadcasts, and let 110 off with a reprimand. Committals to camps were quite rare: in February 1944, thirteen people were transferred to Oberlanzendorf AEL, and one sole committal to a concentration camp is recorded for March 1944. In certain months of 1941, between three and five arrests are reported (with Vienna Gestapo detentions ranging between two and three hundred at that point). In all, between 1938 and 1944 the Vienna Gestapo made 488 arrests for 'radio crime'; as mentioned above, of those referred to the courts, 400 were convicted and sentenced.[35]

Although there was a limit of twenty-one days on the period between arrest and referral to the judiciary following an application for prosecution, extensions could easily be obtained from the RSHA, and detainees sometimes remained in investigative custody for up to two years.[36] Such periods were usually sufficient for the extraction of confessions, commonly achieved through maltreatment in the form of punching, kicking or threats (for example, that family members would be arrested); prolonged, systematic torture of the kind deployed on political detainees was not generally used, especially as typical *Schwarzhörer* were not associated with the political organizations under investigation, and nor did they have the endurance that political resistance fighters displayed. Furthermore, as the likely penalties for listening to foreign radio broadcasts were less severe than those faced by defendants accused of high treason, a confession was not liable to have such serious consequences. Christian Müllner's doctoral thesis on this subject records a number of cases of maltreatment of *Schwarzhörer*, the principal culprits being the infamous Vienna Gestapo thugs Rudolf Hitzler, Armin Kraupatz and Johann Röhrling, who were sentenced to lengthy terms of imprisonment by the Vienna VG for the crimes of torture and maltreatment under the War Criminals Act (KVG) of June 1945, § 3, paras 1 and 2.[37]

In cases of 'radio crime', while the Gestapo had to submit an application for prosecution to the court, it was also at liberty to send defendants to an AEL or a concentration camp, or to let them off with a reprimand. The consequences of this situation for individual detainees are vividly demonstrated by a letter dated 12 September 1944 from the lawyer Konrad Zembaty to the wife of the master builder Alexander Grasel, who had been arrested by the Vienna Gestapo on 17 July 1944 for 'dissemination of news heard on foreign radio stations':

> Concerning the above matter, I made an enquiry with the Gestapo at Room 280, where I was informed that your husband's case is one of malicious dissemination of foreign news broadcasts, which constitutes an offence tantamount both to high treason and to undermining military morale. The decision concerning the case has already been made in Berlin and will determine whether, assuming that the offence is subject to court proceedings, your husband:
>
> (1) Will be tried by the Volksgerichtshof (high treason), or
> (2) Will be tried by the special court in Vienna (undermining military morale), or
> (3) Will be deported to a concentration camp.

Shortly afterwards, on 22 September 1944, Grasel was transferred to Dachau, where he perished on the day before liberation, 28 April 1945.[38]

Committal to a concentration camp had incomparably harder consequences than a prison sentence. That the denunciation of 'radio crime' sometimes had a racist background and that the treatment of offenders had racist-based gradations is made clear by the example of the family of Anton ('Toni') Birkmeyer, first solo dancer in the ballet of the Vienna state opera. Because his wife Jolanthe was of Jewish origin, Birkmeyer had been expelled from the Reichstheaterkammer (Reich theatre chamber) and had lost his position at the state opera. Between November 1939 and February 1940, together with several friends, Birkmeyer and his wife listened to foreign broadcasts in their apartment. In April 1940, Toni and Jolanthe Birkmeyer and four others were arrested by the Gestapo after being denounced by their daughter Susanne and her friend Edith Prandstetter (a member of the NSDAP). On 3 September 1940, Anton Birkmeyer was sentenced by the Vienna SG to eighteen months' imprisonment with hard labour for 'violation of the regulation on radio broadcasts', and after serving the sentence (reckoned from the time of his arrest) was released from Stein prison in October 1941. His wife, by contrast, was sentenced to three years' imprisonment with hard labour but was remanded to the Vienna Gestapo in December 1942 from the women's prison of Aichach and deported to Auschwitz, where she perished on 2 January 1943. Their friends Walter Fischer and Bela Bernhard Basch were likewise sentenced, but then remanded to the Gestapo and deported to the Włodawa ghetto and Auschwitz respectively. Neither survived.[39]

When individuals serving or having served prison sentences were remanded to the Gestapo, it was left up to the Gestapo to decide between release, extended detention, or committal to a concentration camp. On 29 June 1942, Emma Steininger, owner of the Eden Bar in the centre of Vienna, was arrested because she had 'repeatedly made subversive statements concerning the Führer and the German Reich', and had allowed Jews to use her apartment and wireless set to listen to enemy radio stations. She was sentenced to three years' imprisonment with hard labour for 'radio crime'. After her conditional release from the women's labour prison of Aichach on 27 September 1944 she was detained by the Gestapo until the beginning of November.[40]

If listening to foreign radio broadcasts was compounded by association with a resistance group, the consequences became very much more severe. As the offence 'preparation for high treason' was punished with lengthy sentences of imprisonment with hard labour (and increasingly with death sentences), it was of secondary importance whether a charge also included 'radio crime'. For example, on 5 October 1942, the Vienna Gestapo arrested the master baker Oskar Blie for – in spite of being a member of the NSDAP – making a donation of RM 10 to the KPÖ functionary Anton Gajda; on 25 March 1943, Blie was sentenced to fifteen years' imprisonment with hard labour for 'preparation for high treason' and 'radio crime', and was finally interned at Sachsenhausen concentration camp from 11 November 1943 until the end of April 1945.[41]

The monopoly on information and news held by the Nazi regime had implications not only for foreign radio stations but also for foreign newspapers and periodicals. In this field no specific legal prohibitions or sanctions were promulgated; instead, the censorship was carried out through rigorous controls on the foreign news media legally distributed in the German Reich. After the outbreak of war in 1939, these primarily affected the press organs of neutral states, because there was no longer any possibility of media exchange with states at war.

While the press office of the Vienna police president monitored the domestic newspapers, which were in any case Nazi-oriented and controlled by Reich minister of propaganda Joseph Goebbels, the Gestapo was responsible for monitoring the foreign press. In the period 1938–42 this was done by Section II P (for 'Presse'), initially headed by Ernst Weimann, who had come from the Munich

Gestapo, and then by SS-Sturmbannführer Regierungsassessor Alfons Blaschke (who changed his name to Rosse); from 1942 this office was called Section IV C 3 (Press), and from 1945 Section IV 6 b. In all these periods, SS-Untersturmführer Kriminalkommissar Johann Hoi is named as a member of staff. Initially, the office was also responsible for 'prohibited and undesirable books', primarily meaning books of Jewish – and later also of Catholic – provenance. From the outbreak of war in September 1939 the office's competence was restricted to foreign printed matter in circulation within the borders of the Reich. The repression of local illegal publishing, in particular of producers and distributors, was taken over by sections II A, B and C.[42]

As reported by Lambert Leutgeb when detained in Yugoslavia, the section head had given 'several women with knowledge of foreign languages the job of reading the foreign newspapers. The other tasks were carried out by four Kripo officials'. Passages of relevance to the Gestapo had to be translated into German.[43] Franz Weisz has established that the section had a staff of twenty in 1938–42, seventeen in 1942–44, and fifteen in 1944–45.[44]

When print media were seized, justification was given using the blanket formula 'endangering public security and order' (*Gefährdung der öffentlichen Sicherheit und Ordnung*). As was stated in a daily report concerning the seizure of no fewer than 362 issues of foreign newspapers: 'All the papers listed are anti-German in character, containing articles against Germany and in some cases Greek and English military reports'.[45] If an official complaint was submitted, the Gestapo ordered the general seizure of the newspaper, which was then carried out by police officials at newsagents' shops and elsewhere. In 1941, of the 5,118 newspapers seized, 1,862 were Turkish-language, 573 Bulgarian, 553 Croatian, 462 Romanian, 428 Greek, 364 Serbian, 363 Hungarian, 315 Slovene, 180 Slovak, and 18 in other languages. After the occupation of Yugoslavia in April 1941, the Gestapo targeted press organs from neutral Turkey in particular. Amongst the numerous different newspapers seized were many issues of the well-respected Turkish newspaper *Cumhuriyet*.[46]

The Vienna Gestapo daily reports contain regular references to the seizure of foreign newspapers. In one daily report from the beginning of January 1941, for example, nine of the fourteen pages are devoted to lists of newspapers seized. This extensive reporting on a field of activity of lesser importance to the Gestapo lasted until the end of May 1942; thereafter, the daily reports no longer contained any references to foreign newspapers, even though reporting to the superior office in Berlin continued.[47]

In the reporting period from 18 December 1940 to 5 January 1941 no fewer than 362 newspapers were seized, mostly Yugoslavian, with 'newspapers' meaning not just single copies but whole issues for a particular day.[48] As the actual offenders were as a rule abroad and thus not within reach, the offensive measures taken by the Vienna Gestapo were limited. While in 1939 there were ten arrests, in 1941 there were five; furthermore, in that year twenty-three individuals were reported to the state prosecutor, with one receiving a reprimand and fifteen having bail set. In the entire period 1938–45 there were only fifteen arrests related to press and cultural matters (as compared with fifty thousand arrests in all).[49]

Repression of Individuals Rendering Assistance to Jews, Forced Labourers or POWs

Assistance to Jews

The persecution of the Jews also extended to non-Jews who rendered assistance to Jews fleeing or suffering from persecution or discrimination. This help, usually profoundly humanitarian in motivation, was not infrequently based on family relations or friendship, and it took a large number of different forms. As it ran counter to one of the Nazis' central political and ideological objectives, such help constituted a major challenge to the regime. The non-Jewish ('Aryan') population was systematically stirred up against the Jews and prohibited from all dealings with them; such dealings were treated by the Gestapo as 'judenfreundliches Verhalten' (friendly behaviour to Jews). In the daily reports of the Vienna Gestapo, the category 'Jewish affairs' (Judenangelegenheiten), which included not only detentions of Jews for offences against the anti-Jewish regulations but also 1,532 arrests of 'Judenhelfer' (Jew-helpers), accounted for more than 10 per cent of all recorded arrests.[50]

In such cases – with the exception of 'defilement of the race' (*Rassenschande*), which had been defined in the Nuremberg Laws of 1935, and prohibited marriages and sexual relations between Jews and persons 'of German blood' (*deutschblütig*)[51] – there were no legal provisions for judicial proceedings; as a result, the related offences, in particular providing accommodation for Jews who had gone into hiding, were penalized with Gestapo detention or concentration camp internment. On 24 October 1941, the RSHA circulated a decree threatening any 'citizens of German blood' who were seen engaging in 'friendly relations with Jews in public' with 'protective custody' of up to three months.[52] As a rule, most detentions exceeded three months by far, which brought with it the risk of death during internment in a concentration camp.

At the Vienna Gestapo, the repression of *Judenhelfer* was carried out by Unit II B 4 (from 1942, Section IV B 4, 'Jews'), which was part of Section II B headed by SS-Obersturmbannführer Regierungsrat Karl Ebner (from 1942, Group IV B). The 'Judenreferat' ('Jewish section') was one of the most important offices of the Vienna Gestapo, and for a certain time (1938–39) had the most staff.[53]

Although until the outbreak of war in 1939 it was still possible for Jews to emigrate legally from the German Reich (albeit under difficult conditions, in particular having to leave their entire wealth and property behind – 'Aryanization'), the Gestapo took measures against illegal, uncontrolled emigration. In such cases the principal aim was to prevent Jews from taking assets with them (for example, currency or jewellery). From February 1941, when systematic deportations began, the Gestapo increasingly targeted Jews who were aiming to escape or had gone into hiding. They and their helpers were to be tracked down, arrested and – through the central office for Jewish emigration – allocated to deportation transports. In pursuing these aims the Gestapo used the methods they typically employed in countering opponents: on the one hand, deploying (Jewish) informants, principally recruited with the prospect of being spared deportation themselves, to assist in the tracking down of Jews in hiding or seeking to flee;[54] and on the other hand, maltreating detainees to coerce them into giving information about other fugitives or hosts.

One of the most important and dangerous forms of assistance was the provision of accommodation – that is to say, hiding Jews who had gone underground. Without this help it was practically impossible for Jews to escape deportation in the longer term, because they were otherwise unable to obtain food, which was strictly rationed. Providing accommodation, an extremely risky undertaking, was principally done for Jews within the helpers' families or circles of friends. The retired senior civil servant Josef Gurtner, for example, hid his sister-in-law Camilla Zwerger in order to save her from deportation. On 29 April 1943 the Gestapo opened an identification file on him for *judenfreundliches Verhalten*, and on 13 November 1943 he was transferred to Dachau; both Camilla Zwerger and his own wife Gisela Gurtner perished at Auschwitz. The antique and second-hand dealer Josef Kriz and his wife Anna Kriz hid her sister-in-law in an attempt to save her from deportation, but on 2 October 1942 he was arrested by the Gestapo and was interned from November 1942 to 1 December 1943 at Auschwitz, where his wife perished. For six months, the lathe operator Anton Friedrich Matejka took in Leopold Blechner, who was hiding in Vienna; Matejka was arrested on 20 April 1943 and interned at Flossenbürg concentration camp until 27 February 1944. On 21 January 1943 the Gestapo opened an identification file on the businessman Karl Wewerka for *judenfreundliches Verhalten*; together with his wife Riza Wewerka, he had given accommodation to Jews threatened with deportation. The Gestapo had him taken into 'protective custody'; his wife perished at Auschwitz.[55] The commercial employee Leonore Rollig was arrested for *judenfreundliches Verhalten* on 19 November 1942 and transferred to Ravensbrück women's concentration camp on 20 February 1943; the Vienna Gestapo's daily report for 17–19 November 1942 recorded her activities as follows: 'In spite of a reprimand issued by the Gestapo on 14 February 1942 for associating with Jews, she once again gave a Jewess accommodation in her apartment for several days, in order to protect her from evacuation to the East. Furthermore, she was in contact with

Jews who escaped to near Warsaw from the collection point in Vienna, and had provided them with underwear'.[56]

Another important form of assistance was the procuring of (forged) documents, especially ones testifying to 'Aryan' descent. On 28 June 1943 the Gestapo opened an identification file on the driver Josef Boes 'on suspicion of forging documents'; he had assisted two Jews in 'attempting to forge certificates of descent' and had appended his own signature, identifying himself as a Gestapo official. He was sentenced to death on 10 November 1943 and executed on 9 December 1943 at the Vienna LG. In April 1942 the businessman Curt (Kurt) Meisel – formerly of the Austrian Legion and a member of the NSDAP until he was expelled in 1943 – obtained forged certificates of descent for his wife, and took his family to Switzerland. He was arrested in Berlin on 26 October 1942, and on 24 April 1943 he was sent by the Vienna Gestapo to Dachau, where he remained until liberation.[57]

A left-wing resistance group in Vienna centring on the medical student Ella Lingens and her husband the junior doctor Kurt Lingens, the psychoanalyst Karl (Graf von) Motesiczky and the lawyer Aladar Döry von Jobbahaza embarked on a more far-reaching assistance campaign with a distinct political background. With tragic consequences, they engaged the most important Gestapo informant in the Jewish milieu, Rudolf Klinger, to help Jews to flee. Although Klinger helped the banker Ernst (Baron von) Lieben, an uncle of Motesiczky's, by getting him out of a collection point and over the border to Hungary, he subsequently betrayed a sizeable group of refugee Polish Jews who had been hidden on Motesiczky's estate at Hinterbrühl near Vienna, and were to have been brought to Switzerland.[58]

Ella and Kurt Lingens, Motesiczky and Döry were arrested by the Vienna Gestapo on 13 October 1942 for attempting to assist individuals to flee, as was reported in Vienna Gestapo daily report no. 5 of 13–15 October 1942:

> Dr Ella Lingens is charged with having given financial aid to Jakob Israel and Bernhard Israel Goldstein – Polish Jews already arrested on 4 September 1942 in Feldkirch – and their wives Pepi Sara G., née Mandelbaum, and Helene Sara G., née Rapaport, who are strongly suspected of belonging to the Polish resistance movement, and with having supported them in their illegal efforts to emigrate. In addition, it has been proven that an unidentified person from Poland delivered valuable jewellery to her, to be used in financing the emigration of the Jews.

Following the arrest of Döry von Jobbahaza, the same Gestapo daily report stated that 'a Jewish woman was apprehended in his apartment, where she had been hidden for quite some time; she was transferred to the Jewish collection point'.[59] While Kurt Lingens was transferred to a military penal unit, in February 1943 the Gestapo sent Döry, Motesiczky and Ella Lingens to Auschwitz, where Motesiczky perished on 25 June 1943. Ella and Kurt Lingens and Karl

Motesiczky were later honoured by Yad Vashem as 'Righteous Among the Nations'.⁶⁰

The farmer Franz Mersits from Nikitsch (Burgenland) helped persecuted individuals to cross the border into Hungary; he was arrested on 28 May 1942 and transferred to Groß-Rosen concentration camp, where he perished on 18 November 1942. Theresia Lichtblau was arrested on 9 December 1942 for 'assisting Jews to leave the country illegally' and then transferred to Ravensbrück in February 1943. Her children Gisela, Kurt and Harry Lichtblau were also arrested; as they were *Geltungsjuden* (considered 'full Jews'), they were deported to Auschwitz, where they all perished.⁶¹

After being arrested for 'smuggling Jews' (*Judenschmuggel*) by the Vienna Gestapo in 1942, on 3 March 1943 the police sergeant Ferdinand Gürth was sentenced by SS and Police Court VII (Vienna) to four years' imprisonment with hard labour for 'abuse of official authority', and was interned at Mauthausen until 1945. The coal merchant Camilla Plaschka gave accommodation to the victim of racial persecution Sure Mehler-Bergmann and was going to help her to escape to Hungary. Plaschka was arrested on 17 February 1943 and interned at Auschwitz from April 1943 to 13 January 1944; Mehler-Bergmann was also deported to Auschwitz, but did not survive. On 21 August 1943 the Vienna Gestapo opened an identification file on Johanna Frühwirth for 'smuggling Jews and taking assets out of the country'; she perished at Auschwitz on 7 December 1943.⁶²

Jews on the run or in hiding could only survive through support in the form of money, clothes and food. The penalty for giving this kind of help was also internment in a concentration camp. In May 1942 Rosa Franziska Jung was arrested for 'unauthorized provision of food to work education internees' and 'close relations with Jews', and was deported to Ravensbrück on 7 August 1942.

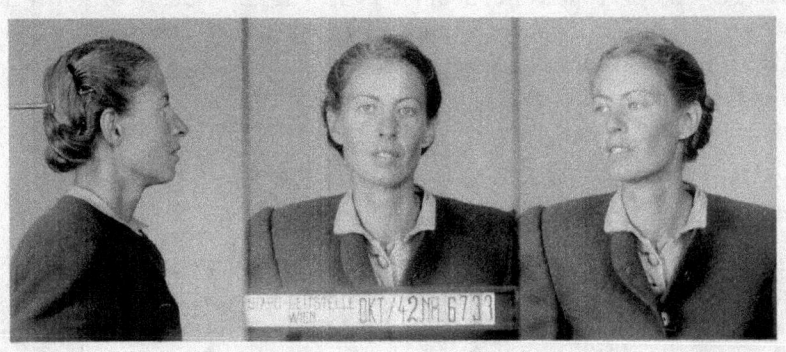

Figure 13.1. The socialist resistance activist Ella Lingens following her arrest. Gestapo identification photos. © Wiener Stadt- und Landesarchiv. Used with permission.

On 24 April 1942 the tobacconist Stefanie Reiß was arrested for *judenfreundliches Verhalten* (accepting jewellery for safekeeping) and transferred to Auschwitz, where she died on 12 January 1943.⁶³ The Vienna Gestapo daily report for 20–21 February 1942 records the arrest of the writer Marcell 'Israel' Klang, who had received monthly donations of between 5 and 10 RM from around fifty people; although fourteen of these were members of the NDSAP, the entry does not indicate whether there was an investigation to identify them. Klang died on 25 June 1942, five days after arriving at Mauthausen.⁶⁴

In addition to the many cases of assistance being rendered out of idealism, there were also a considerable number of cases in which the motivation was principally financial. These mostly involved professional assistance to people fleeing the Reich. However, if these professionals fell foul of the Gestapo, they were not treated any differently from the idealists and were as a rule interned in concentration camps. Franziska Bauer, for example, was arrested for 'smuggling Jews' in September 1942, together with her husband Rudolf Bauer and their son Othmar; she died on 18 March 1943 in the Vienna police prison. The businessman Ludwig Drapal was arrested in 1942 for 'assisting in smuggling Jews', and perished at Dachau on 20 November 1943.⁶⁵

The Gestapo also proceeded with the utmost severity against shopkeepers and business people who sold food to Jews. The businessman Georg Engelhardt, for example, was arrested on 13 November 1941 because he had 'sold goods to Jews on the black market'; an application was made for him 'to be taken into protective custody and committed to a concentration camp for behaviour harmful to the Volk'. Engelhardt perished on 7 May 1942 at Groß-Rosen. In July 1940 the street vendor Barbara Gollosch was arrested and kept in detention for a time for having repeatedly offended against the 'price regulations' and having sold fruit to Jews 'in spite of a previous reprimand'.⁶⁶

By the end of 2018, Israel's Holocaust memorial centre Yad Vashem had accorded the title 'Righteous Among the Nations' to 27,362 individuals from over fifty countries. The fact that only 110 of these were from Austria is aptly reflected in the title of Erika Weinzierl's book on this subject: *Zu wenig Gerechte* ('Too Few Righteous').⁶⁷

Prohibited Contact with Prisoners of War and Foreign Forced Labourers

The Gestapo and NS judiciary were also active in countering assistance given to POWs and to the forced labourers who were brought in great numbers to the German Reich (including Austria) from the occupied countries of Europe. While the help given was often motivated by humanitarian considerations and compassion for these people, who were mostly undernourished and subject to discrimination in many forms, it also testified to a conscious rejection of the regime with its racist ideology and norms. As a result, the NS authorities applied a variety of penal sanctions in order to prevent contact with POWs and to ensure they were not treated in too friendly a manner. The Wehrkraftschutzverordnung (Regulation on the protection of military morale) of 25 November 1939 contained a special paragraph (§ 4) on 'verbotener Umgang mit Kriegsgefangenen' (prohibited contact with prisoners of war) specifying that gross violation of 'das gesunde Volksempfinden' (literally, healthy Volk feeling) was to be punished with imprisonment, with or without hard labour. A further regulation of 1940 prohibited any contact or relations with POWs, except when necessary for work.[68] In an express letter of 31 January 1940, Reichsführer-SS Heinrich Himmler instructed the Gestapo offices to deal with German women violating the regulation by 'taking [them] into protective custody until further notice and interning them in a concentration camp for at least one year'. Social relations such as meeting at dances were considered a 'gross violation' of *das gesunde Volksempfinden*.[69] In May 1940, Himmler ordered that German women arrested for becoming involved with POWs should be reported to the state prosecutor immediately, and only taken into 'protective custody' once released by the courts.[70]

While contact with foreign civilian workers was not prohibited by law, the Gestapo and SGs extended the restrictions on contact with POWs on their own initiative to contact with Polish, Russian and Ukrainian women. Prohibited relations with female civilian workers from Eastern Europe could result in 'protective custody' and committal to a concentration camp, or trial before an SG.[71] Conversely, Polish, and later Soviet Russian, POWs who had sexual relations with a woman 'of German blood' could be executed by the Gestapo – *Sonderbehandlung* ('special treatment'), as it was known in SS and Gestapo jargon.[72] While numerous such murders were committed by 'Reich-German' Gestapo offices, only two cases are known within the Vienna Gestapo area, by members of the branch offices of Sankt Pölten and Wiener Neustadt.

No particular section at the Vienna Gestapo had specific responsibility for these offences. Arrests were made by sections II A, B, C and E (from 1942, IV A, B and D), although the total number of arrestees was small in comparison with those in other offence categories. Between June and August 1941, when the Vienna Gestapo were taking around three hundred people into detention per month, there were only seven arrests for 'prohibited contact' (0.7 per cent); similarly, in the whole of 1943 only a slightly larger percentage fell into this category, 166 out of a total of 8,725 arrests (1.9 per cent).[73] In 1943 and 1944 the number of arrests per month ranged between 0 and 56, the number of reprimands exceeded referrals to the courts, and only in two recorded cases was an offender committed to an AEL.[74] In her degree dissertation on 462 trials at the Vienna SG for 'prohibited contact', Dagmar Weitz states that of 571 defendants – all arrested and reported by Gestapo – 332 were convicted.[75] These figures indicate that the Vienna Gestapo attached less importance to this field than the 'Reich-German' Gestapo offices did,[76] and clearly preferred to focus their human resources on more important targets – namely, Jews, resistance fighters, and foreign civilian workers. Many arrests, detentions and convictions for 'prohibited contact' were based on denunciations from the general public or from Nazi offices and organizations.[77]

Under the Nazi regime, this prohibited contact with POWs (and foreign workers) came in various forms, ranging from friendly conversation or gifts to sexual intercourse or assistance to individuals seeking to flee. Even quite harmless acts sufficed to provoke a response by the Gestapo and could lead to judicial proceedings; however, the sentences were generally relatively lenient by Nazi standards – so long as the contact had not been compounded by a graver offence such as high treason or helping individuals to flee (*Fluchthilfe*). On 31 March 1942, for example, the waitress Angela Jahn was arrested by a regular policeman because she had thrown bread, pastries and an orange to Russian POWs. Because her husband had been a member of the SDAP for many years, the Vienna Gestapo accused her of having acted out of 'political conviction', and on 28 May 1942, the Vienna SG sentenced her to three months' imprisonment for 'prohibited contact with POWs'.[78] On 18 March 1942, the assistant barman Johann Bauer was arrested by officials of the Sauerbrunn (Burgenland) border police post, which was under the Vienna Gestapo, because he had thrown cigarettes out of a train to Russian POWs; he too was tried by the Vienna SG.[79] The locksmith's assistant Adolf Lampl, who had been interned for several months for having participated (as a Social Democrat) in the February Uprising of 1934 and was a member of the SA from 1938 to 1942, was arrested on 1 May 1942 because he had passed on food to Soviet POWs at his place of work; on 16 July 1942, the Vienna SG sentenced him to three months' imprisonment for 'prohibited contact'. On 6 January 1943, the toolmaker Anton Hietler was arrested for 'insulting the Führer' and 'prohibited contact with Russian POWs', to whom he had given jam sandwiches; he too was dealt with relatively leniently by the Vienna SG, which sentenced him to two months' imprisonment on 5 May 1943.[80] The ticket inspector Franz Schramek had likewise distributed food to Soviet Russian POWs; however, as he was an active member of the KPÖ at the time, he received a far harsher sentence, ten years' imprisonment with hard labour, imposed by the VGH on 12 February 1943 for 'preparation for high treason'. Schramek remained in prison until the end of the war.[81]

When the Vienna OLG sentenced Alfred Strotzka and Johann Suppinger, both workers at the Wiener Lokomotivfabrik (Vienna locomotive factory), to three and five years' imprisonment with hard labour, the mere fact of their collecting food for Soviet POWs was categorized as 'preparation for high treason'. As stated in the court judgment delivered on 10 November 1942: 'In Vienna on 1 May 1942 the accused demonstrated their solidarity with Communism by collecting and then distributing food and other things such as alcoholic drinks and cigarettes to Bolshevist prisoners of war, thereby committing the crimes of preparing high treason and prohibited contact with prisoners of war'. While Strotzka was released after serving his sentence, Suppinger was a victim of the massacre at Stein labour prison on 6 April 1945.[82]

Johann Michalek, an employee at the ironwork construction firm Wiener Brückenbau und Eisenkonstruktions-AG, received an even more severe sentence because he had not only provided French POWs with bread, chocolate and the like but had also helped a total of twenty Frenchmen to escape to Hungary in 1942–43. Michalek was arrested by the Gestapo on 13 February 1943 for helping individuals to flee, condemned to death by the VGH on 10 July 1943 for 'aiding and abetting the enemy', and executed on 9 September 1943 in Berlin.[83] A remarkable operation for the benefit of a Soviet Russian POW was undertaken by a group of workers from the firm Strohmayer in Margareten (5th district); according to the relevant Gestapo report, 'on 24 March 1942 they mounted a demonstrative public protest against the treatment of a Soviet Russian prisoner of war by a military guard unit' and were arrested by the Gestapo 'on the instructions of the warehouse manager of the firm Austria in Vienna-Simmering'. The carpenter Karl Ressek got off very lightly for his part in this offence, as on 17 September 1942 he was sentenced to four weeks' imprisonment for 'insulting public officials'.[84]

Harsh measures were taken against prison and police officials who were found to have helped prisoners or detainees. For example, the police official Johann Grausam accepted letters from internees at the police prison on Rossauer Lände (at that time Elisabethpromenade, hence the prison's nickname 'Liesl') and passed them on to recipients. On 11 July 1939 he was arrested by the Gestapo for 'abuse of his authority as a former police official' and interned under a 'protective custody' order at Buchenwald, where he remained until 17 April 1940.[85] Within the Vienna Gestapo's area of authority, in the years 1941 to 1944 only four instances are recorded of trials of Gestapo officials at the Vienna SS- und Polizeigericht (SS and police court) for assisting prisoners; however, nothing is known of their outcomes.[86]

The provisions concerning 'prohibited contact with prisoners of war', in particular concerning gross violation of *das gesunde Volksempfinden*, were principally aimed at women who had relationships with POWs or foreign civilian workers. Even harmless contact could lead to Gestapo intervention. For example, the Vienna Gestapo branch office in Wiener Neustadt tracked down the 16-year-old schoolgirl Martha Laschitz and extracted a confession from her after she had thrown letters to and had a rendezvous with a French POW, which the Wiener Neustadt LG saw as a serious violation of the 'honour of a German girl' ('Ehre eines deutschen Mädchens'), sentencing her to a month's juvenile detention for an offence under the Wehrkraftschutzverordnung.[87] In his function as

Vienna inspector of the Sipo and SD, Franz Josef Huber complained in a weekly situation report to Reichskommissar Bürckel about the 'unworthy behaviour of the German population with regard to Polish civilian workers taken prisoner in the course of the war', which had necessitated an 'intervention on the part of the police or SA': 'At Etshof [correctly: Etsdorf] am Kamp it was established that a farmhand engaged to a soldier on the Western front had become involved with a Polish agricultural worker. She was fetched by the SA, her hair was shorn, and in the afternoon she was paraded through the town.'[88]

It goes without saying that the police took no steps to prevent such acts of racist humiliation, which on the contrary were applauded even by the head of the Vienna Gestapo.

Persecution of Homosexuals

As with the persecution of the Jews, the driving force behind the persecution of homosexuals was Reichsführer-SS Heinrich Himmler, whose rise to power in the Nazi movement stemmed not least from the elimination of the homosexual SA chief of staff Ernst Röhm in June 1934. Fearing that the 'numbers of homosexual men unwilling to procreate' would lead to the downfall of the German Volk, Himmler pleaded for 'hangers-on' (*Mitläufer*) and 'seducees' to be guided back into the *Volksgemeinschaft* (ethnic community) through re-education measures applied by the police and judiciary, while 'inveterate' homosexuals, after serving terms of imprisonment, were to be committed to 'preventive police custody' (i.e. concentration camps).[89]

While homosexual acts had been criminal offences in Austria before 1938 (and remained so until the penal reform of 1971), the persecution of homosexuals intensified, both in quantity and in character, under the Nazi regime. In § 129 of the old Austrian penal code (StG), sexual activity 'with persons of the same sex' was described as an 'unnatural sexual act' ('Unzucht wider die Natur') and penalized accordingly; and the paragraph, along with other penal provisions, remained in force on Austrian territory after the annexation of March 1938.[90] As a result, lesbian acts were still subject to prosecution, while in the 'Altreich', under § 175 RStGB, homosexuality between women was not a criminal offence. However, prosecutions of lesbians and transgender people had no significant place in the activities of the Vienna Gestapo. As a rule, cases of lesbianism, transvestism and transsexuality were passed on to the Kripo. As regards transsexuality, recent research by Ilse Reiter-Zatloukal and Rainer Herrn has prompted Andreas Brunner and Hannes Sulzenbacher, who conducted a project to record by name homosexual and transgender victims in Vienna in the years 1938–45, to question whether 'specific persecution of transsexuals by the Nazis' existed at all.[91] As regards lesbianism, at least one arrest is documented in the Vienna Gestapo daily reports: 'The bar singer Franziska Stefanie F. ... was brought in on account of alleged homosexual activity with an unknown female. After interrogation she was transferred to the Vienna Kripo to be dealt with by the appropriate department, as was the waiter Franz O., who had reported her, as he was strongly intoxicated'.[92]

Within the Vienna Gestapo, Unit II S 1 dealt with prostitution and a whole complex of offences including homosexuality, abortion, secret prostitution, pornography and public indecency. In parallel with the Gestapo, homosexuals were also prosecuted by the Kripo, which had been responsible for them before 1938, so that in a significant number of cases it had arrestees transferred to it by the Gestapo. Finally – for the obvious purpose of freeing up Gestapo resources for tasks regarded as more urgent for the regime – an instruction issued by the chief of the Sipo and SD specified that from September 1939 all newly reported cases of homosexuality should be handed over to the Kripo. From that point onwards until the end of 1940, the Gestapo only handled cases already under investigation.[93] On 15 October 1940, for example, Gottfried G. was arrested for an 'unnatural sexual act' following a report from the Innsbruck Gestapo, but he was then transferred to the Kripo.[94]

Regarding the relatively low numbers of arrests in this area, it should thus be remembered that the Vienna Gestapo was only responsible for dealing with homosexuals for around eighteen months. The Vienna Gestapo daily reports evaluated by the DÖW record 207 arrests of homosexuals – that is to say, 1.6 per cent of all those arrested.[95]

Not only the Gestapo but also the Kripo applied the methods and procedures described in Chapter 6 to homosexuals: spying and surveillance, informants and agents provocateurs, brutality during interrogations, the practice of having defendants remanded after acquittal or release from prison (*Rücküberstellung*), and committal to concentration camps. As with the prosecution of political opponents, the fact that the Gestapo and Kripo had access to police records from the years of the corporate state had devastating consequences. The Sipo files for Vienna and the federal province of Lower Austria were scoured for names and data on suspected or convicted individuals; contacts and informants continued to be used, and details concerning bars, night clubs, meeting places, public conveniences and the like were used to facilitate undercover surveillance, in some cases leading to raids and arrests.[96]

Homosexuals were subjected to maltreatment during interrogations no less than political detainees. On 9 December 1938, Rudolf R., a post office savings bank employee under arrest at Morzinplatz for homosexuality, after making a confession and revealing the names of four further people, committed suicide by jumping out of a lavatory window and down a light well.[97] After the war, the homosexual victims of the Gestapo – unlike those who had suffered political or racial persecution – did not come forward with information, act as witnesses at trials, or compose reports of their experiences, because at that time they still lived in fear of being prosecuted for their sexual orientation.

The numbers of persecuted homosexuals cited in older literature, often based on rough estimates, are not supported by more recent and more detailed research. The earlier estimates of the total number of homosexual concentration camp victims, which range from five to fifteen thousand,[98] would suggest that the number from Austria (the population of which was 9 per cent of that of the German Reich) was between 450 and 1,350, which is unrealistically high. Brigitte Bailer and Gerhard Ungar, the researchers principally responsible for the DÖW project aimed at recording by name the victims of political persecution, state in their project summary: 'At least seventy-one men were murdered because of their sexual orientation or perished on account of conditions in internment'. This figure represents around 1 per cent of all Austrian victims.[99]

Brunner and Sulzenbacher have studied and evaluated around eight hundred relevant trial records preserved at the Wiener Stadt- und Landesarchiv. Amongst the defendants were 1,400 men and 79 women; the Vienna SG pronounced only three death sentences.[100] In a further project on military jurisdiction it was established that 48 Viennese/Austrians were charged and convicted by military courts operating on Austrian territory. The prison sentences imposed (some with hard labour) ranged from one to ten years at the very most; there were no death sentences.[101]

However, the courts' relative leniency towards homosexuals (in comparison with political offenders) was counteracted by the Gestapo and Kripo practice of applying to the respective court for remand, with which the court was obliged to comply. In such cases, defendants were returned after being acquitted or having served their sentence, and could thus still be committed to a concentration camp under 'preventive' or 'protective' custody, though this only happened in a small fraction of the cases, of which Brunner and Sulzenbacher identified forty-nine. A much more frequent measure was *Frontbewährung* (probation at the front), under which convicted homosexuals were called up for service in particularly dangerous theatres of war, where there was a high risk of their being killed or returning home as invalids.[102] The bare numerical information provided in this section is naturally not intended to make light of the gravity of the discrimination, the suffering of the victims, or the anxiety and terror that a whole section of society experienced as a result.

Repression of Nonconformist Youth: 'Schlurfs' and 'Swing-Jugend'

In Vienna as in other cities throughout the German Reich, the strictly regimented official organization of young people in the Hitler-Jugend (HJ, Hitler Youth) and the Bund Deutscher Mädel (BDM, League of German girls) did not prevent informal nonconformist youth groups forming – unpermitted and undesired – outside the state bodies.[103]

The rejection of the norms and demands of the Nazi system, through consciously different habits and behaviour in such respects as clothing, hairstyle and music, was a particularly important phenomenon amongst working-class youth. In Vienna these young dissenters were known as 'Schlurfs'. Not all, of course, necessarily had a genuinely anti-Nazi political orientation, and Schlurfs in fact continued to be a feature of working-class youth until well into the 1950s.[104] They were spurred into resistance above all by the regimentation of the Hitler Youth (enforcing participation in events and social gatherings at Hitler Youth centres, for example, or the wearing of uniform and the sporting of short haircuts). In spite of threats and repressive measures, a considerable number of young people refused to serve in the Hitler Youth or went absent without leave. Ernst Nedwed from Rudolfsheim (15th district) reported on the opposition to the Hitler Youth in his area: 'In our working-class district there were many young people who, with the support of their parents, used various tricks and excuses to get out of serving in the HJ. In addition, there was a broad opposition movement, which gained in strength especially from 1943 onwards, and rejected the HJ's military drill, coercion and cropped haircuts'.[105]

This rejection of the NS youth organizations led to numerous attacks on HJ centres and functionaries, and even on those of the BDM. These acts of aggression were a response to the Hitler Youth's street patrols and to the raids in which the Schlurfs were humiliated by having stripes shaved into their haircuts or having their hair shaved off entirely.[106]

The daily reports of the Vienna Gestapo in the years 1941–43 contain numerous records of Hitler Youth functionaries being attacked by other youths. A few representative examples are given here.[107] The report for 14–16 March 1941 contains the following passage: 'In recent days we have received various reports of members of the Hitler Youth being picked on by adolescent boys when on their way home from their meeting place, and in some cases also being maltreated. On 13 March 1941, for instance, a group of HJ members were attacked and beaten up in Vienna-Alsergrund, with a shot being fired by an unidentified person'.[108]

The Vienna Gestapo daily report for 1–3 December 1942 recorded that four girls and four boys attacked a 13-year-old grammar school (Gymnasium) girl on Mariahilfergürtel, and called her an 'HJ-Trampel' (Hitler Youth floosie). In Landstrasse (3rd district), a 16-year-old BDM girl had her pigtails cut off; and in Favoriten (10th district) three secondary school boys aged between 12 and 14 were arrested for having set upon three Hitler Youth members.[109] On 18 March 1943 there was a more important case in the HJ centre at Längenfeldgasse 19, Meidling (12th district), where the Hitler Youth boys refused to obey their leaders' orders. As recorded in the report for 23–25 March 1943: 'The young lads then proceeded to throw the hostel chairs around and break them up, and then to use the broken chairs as weapons'. The boys arrested by the Gestapo were put into 'protective custody'.[110]

Many of the youths, mostly aged between 12 and 15, were tracked down by the Gestapo and sentenced by the courts, despatched to camps, or recruited into penal units of the Wehrmacht. In the guidelines on youth groups (Richtlinien zur Bekämpfung jugendlicher Cliquen) of 25 October 1944 issued by RSHA chief Ernst Kaltenbrunner, the monitoring and suppression of such 'cliques' was declared to be 'important to the war effort' (*kriegswichtig*), and the respective competences of the Kripo and Gestapo were clearly defined. While the Kripo was responsible for everyday youth criminality, 'cliques with marked or predominantly political or subversive goals' became the responsibility of the Gestapo.[111]

Non-appearance or unpunctuality at the workplace and lack of working discipline were common offences in this milieu, as also were attempts to avoid recruitment into the Wehrmacht by feigning illness at the medical examinations; all such offences were categorized as 'asocial' by the regime.[112] It was to counter such forms of behaviour that the city of Vienna established the 'labour education camp' (AEL) of Oberlanzendorf, to which hundreds of nonconformist youths were sent, and which was taken over by the Vienna Gestapo in 1941.

Young people from other social classes, mainly grammar school pupils, defied the demands of the Nazis through their enthusiasm for popular music from the United States, notably jazz and swing. The regime prohibited these musical genres, which they saw as a threat to its vision of the good and *völkisch* German upbringing and vilified as 'Negermusik'. Despite or perhaps even because of this, jazz and swing attracted considerable interest, which was also, however, an expression of rebellion against the older generation. Although the 'Swing-Jugend' movement was initially somewhat unpolitical, the repressive measures of the Nazis had the effect of politicizing many of its members and shifting them closer to the resistance, as happened with the 'Edelweiss pirates' in Cologne and other towns in western Germany.[113]

'Swing-Jugend' groups also formed in Vienna. The daily report of the Vienna Gestapo for 9–12 April 1943 records the arrest of Otto Finke, Walter von Perko and Hermann Toth, all grammar school pupils, stating that they 'intended to found an association with the goal of overthrowing the NS regime. They attended "Swing-Jugend" gatherings'.[114] One enthusiastic swing fan was Günther Schifter, who later became well known in Austria as the radio broadcaster and jazz expert 'Howdy' Schifter. After being interrogated by the Gestapo, Schifter was conscripted into the Wehrmacht and then transferred at the end of 1944 to Oberlanzendorf AEL, which he escaped from towards the end of the war.[115]

For the Gestapo, nonconformist and rebellious youths were of only secondary importance. They are not even specifically mentioned amongst the tasks allotted to the various departments and units of the Vienna Gestapo on their organization charts (GVPs). We may assume that recalcitrant young people were dealt with by members of departments II E and later IV D 6, which were responsible for 'asocials', 'slackers', and Oberlanzendorf AEL. The Vienna Gestapo report for 2–5 October 1942, which recorded that the uniformed police had arrested thirty-eight young people in Vienna-Atzgersdorf in August 1942, and a further twenty-one the following month, states 'that none of the actions [of the Schlurfs] were politically motivated'.[116] However, this did not save the young people from coming up against the Gestapo in all its severity; they were simply categorized as 'asocial' and interned at Oberlanzendorf AEL.

In any case, these manifestations of a specific youth culture demonstrate that even a totalitarian regime possessing all possible means of indoctrination and repression was still unable to exert ideological and political control over all members of the younger generation.

Notes

1. DÖW 8570.
2. Hanisch, *Widerstand*, 168–69; see also Frei, *Der kleine Widerstand*.
3. [Wer öffentlich gehässige, hetzerische oder von niedriger Gesinnung zeugende Äußerungen über leitende Persönlichkeiten des Staates oder der NSDAP, über ihre Anordnungen oder die von ihnen geschaffenen Einrichtungen macht, die geeignet sind, das Vertrauen des Volkes zur politischen Führung zu untergraben, wird mit Gefängnis bestraft.] *Strafgesetzbuch für das Deutsche Reich*, 195–96.
4. [Wegen Zersetzung der Wehrkraft wird mit dem Tode bestraft: 1. Wer öffentlich dazu auffordert oder anreizt, die Erfüllung der Dienstpflicht in der deutschen oder einer verbündeten Wehrmacht zu verweigern, oder sonst öffentlich den Willen des deutschen oder verbündeten Volkes zu wehrhaften Selbstbehauptung zu lähmen oder zersetzen sucht.] Ibid., 259–60.
5. For details, see Dörner, 'Heimtücke', 325–42.
6. DÖW 20 333/7, Sections of the Vienna Gestapo with their heads and members, n.d., no author/compiler (a listing most likely compiled by the Austrian state police in the course of proceedings against members of the Vienna Gestapo); Archives of the Republic of Slovenia, AS 1931, 809, sheets 640–81, Lambert Leutgeb, 'Die Organisation der Geheimen Staatspolizei-Staatspolizeileitstelle Wien nach dem März 1938 bis zur Gründung des Reichssicherheitshauptamtes 1941', 7 and 26 (composed 1947–48 while in Yugoslavian detention).
7. Ibid.
8. Dörner, 'Heimtücke', 341.
9. Leutgeb, 'Die Organisation der Geheimen Staatspolizei-Staatspolizeileitstelle Wien' (see n. 6 above); see also Chapter 8, this volume.
10. DÖW reference library, Vienna Gestapo statistics (appended to the last daily report of each month).
11. www.doew.at/erinnern/personendatenbanken/gestapo-opfer (last accessed on 30 Mar 2017).
12. Ibid.
13. DÖW reference library, Vienna Gestapo daily report no. 11 of 24–26 Feb 1940; www.doew.at/erinnern/personendatenbanken/gestapo-opfer (last accessed on 10 Mar 2017).

14. http://www.doew.at/personensuche?gestapo (last accessed on 9 Mar 2017); DÖW, *Widerstand Wien*, vol. 2, 459–60, statement by Johann Sanitzer, Salzburg district court (Bezirksgericht), 15 Jun 1956.
15. http://www.doew.at/personensuche?gestapo (last accessed on 9 Mar 2017); DÖW reference library, Vienna Gestapo daily report no. 8 of 23–25 Mar 1943; Vienna Gestapo daily report no. 3 of 12–18 May 1944.
16. DÖW reference library, Vienna Gestapo daily report no. 8 of 26–30 Nov 1943; www.doew.at/erinnern/personendatenbanken/gestapo-opfer (last accessed on 10 Mar 2017)
17. DÖW reference library, Vienna Gestapo daily report no. 9 of 19–20 Sep 1941; www.doew.at/erinnern/personendatenbanken/gestapo-opfer (last accessed on 10 Mar 2017).
18. DÖW reference library, Vienna Gestapo daily report no. 3 of 12–18 May 1944; www.doew.at/erinnern/personendatenbanken/gestapo-opfer (last accessed on 9 Mar 2017).
19. DÖW reference library, Vienna Gestapo daily report no. 1 of 1–3 Aug 1941; www.doew.at/erinnern/personendatenbanken/gestapo-opfer. In the eastern part of Austria, *Marmeladinger* or *Marmeladebrüder* was (and still is) used as a pejorative term for Germans.
20. For more detail, see the section 'Persecution of the Catholic Church' in Chapter 11, this volume.
21. www.doew.at/erinnern/personendatenbanken/gestapo-opfer (last accessed on 11 Mar 2017).
22. Ibid.
23. DÖW reference library, Vienna Gestapo daily report no. 8 of 18–19 Aug 1941; www.doew.at/erinnern/personendatenbanken/gestapo-opfer (last accessed on 10 Mar 2017).
24. www.doew.at/erinnern/personendatenbanken/gestapo-opfer (last accessed on 31 Mar 2017).
25. DÖW 5733 d, Vienna Gestapo daily report no. 13 of 29–31 Jul 1942.
26. RGBl., I, 1683.
27. Reuband, "Schwarzhören", 374–98.
28. Klingler, *Nationalsozialistische Rundfunkpolitik*; see also Hensle, *Rundfunkverbrechen*.
29. For detail, see Müllner, 'Schwarzhörer und Denunzianten'.
30. Kirschner, 'Wehrkraftzersetzung', 403–48 (esp. 427ff.), 497ff.
31. RGBl., I, 1683, § 5 Rundfunkverordnung.
32. BA Berlin, R 3001/25009, express letter from chief of the Sipo and SD Heydrich to all Gestapo offices and other recipients concerning the Verordnung über außerordentliche Rundfunkmaßnahmen of 7 Sep 1939.
33. BA Berlin, R 58/268, 220, RSHA decree to all Gestapo regional headquarters ('Leitstellen'), 1 Mar 1940.
34. DÖW 20 333/7, Sections of the Vienna Gestapo (see n. 6); Lambert Leutgeb, 'Die Organisation der Geheimen Staatspolizei-Staatspolizeileitstelle Wien' (see n. 6).
35. The Vienna Gestapo monthly statistics were usually appended to the last daily report of the respective month and can be consulted in the DÖW reference library. See also Weisz, 'Gestapo-Leitstelle Wien', Tables, tables no. 3/1 and 3/2, 3–4.
36. DÖW 20 421, record of the interview of Franz Weisz with the former Gestapo officer Heinrich Wohl, 11 Apr 1984.
37. Müllner, 'Schwarzhörer und Denunzianten', 96–99; WStLA, Vienna LG, Vg 11 Vr 1265/46 (copy: DÖW 19 824), judgment against Johann Röhrling and Adolf Swoboda, 19 Dec 1947; WStLA, Vienna LG, Vg 12a 612/46 (copy: DÖW 20 642), judgment against Rudolf Hitzler, 19 Mar 1948; WStLA, Vienna LG, Vg 11d Vr 428/46, judgment against Armin Kraupatz, 15 Jun 1947.
38. www.doew.at/erinnern/personendatenbanken/gestapo-opfer (last accessed on 16 Mar 2017).
39. DÖW reference library, Vienna Gestapo daily report no. 7 of 16–17 Apr 1940 and no. 8 of 18–19 Apr 1940; WStLA, SHv 8711/47, *Gnadenheft* and *Vollstreckungsheft* concerning

Jolanthe Birkmeyer; www.doew.at/erinnern/personendatenbanken/gestapo-opfer (last accessed on 16 Mar 2017).
40. DÖW reference library, Vienna Gestapo daily report no. 1 of 1–2 July 1942; www.doew.at/erinnern/personendatenbanken/gestapo-opfer (last accessed on 16 Mar 2017); see also Höfferer, 'Emmy Stein', 67–82.
41. DÖW reference library, Vienna Gestapo daily report no. 3 of 6–8 Oct 1942; www.doew.at/erinnern/personendatenbanken/gestapo-opfer (last accessed on 16 Mar 2017).
42. Weisz, 'Gestapo-Leitstelle Wien', 444ff. In 1942–43, Alfons Rosse was the deputy head of the Gestapo office of Litzmannstadt (Łódź).
43. DÖW 20 333/7, Sections of the Vienna Gestapo (see n. 6); Lambert Leutgeb, 'Die Organisation der Geheimen Staatspolizei-Staatspolizeileitstelle Wien' (see n. 6). Further, Weisz, 'Gestapo-Leitstelle Wien', 446ff.
44. Weisz, 'Gestapo-Leitstelle Wien', Tables, table no. 129, 136.
45. DÖW reference library, Vienna Gestapo daily report no. 2 of 6–7 Jan 1941.
46. Weisz, 'Gestapo-Leitstelle Wien', chart no. 44/1, 80.
47. DÖW reference library, Vienna Gestapo daily report no. 1 of 1–2 Jun 1942.
48. DÖW reference library, Vienna Gestapo daily report no. 2 of 6–7 Jan 1941.
49. Weisz, 'Gestapo-Leitstelle Wien', Tables, synopsis no. 2, 193.
50. Bailer et al., 'Die Gestapo', 173. As noted elsewhere, not all arrests were recorded in the daily reports.
51. RGBl. I, 1146, Gesetz zum Schutze des deutschen Blutes und der deutschen Ehre, 15 Sep 1935. The 'Blutschutzgesetz' was one of the two Nuremberg Race Laws.
52. Longerich, *'Davon haben wir nichts gewusst!'*, 181.
53. Lambert Leutgeb, 'Die Organisation der Geheimen Staatspolizei-Staatspolizeileitstelle Wien' (see n. 6). On II B 4 (later IV B 4), see Chapter 10, this volume.
54. See Tausendfreund, *Erzwungener Verrat*, 252ff.; Rabinovici, *Eichmann's Jews*, 131–32 (*Instanzen der Ohnmacht*, 288ff.).
55. www.doew.at/erinnern/personendatenbanken/gestapo-opfer (last accessed on 22 Apr 2017).
56. DÖW 5733f, Vienna Gestapo daily report no. 6 of 17–19 Nov 1942; www.doew.at/erinnern/personendatenbanken/gestapo-opfer (last accessed on 22 Apr 2017).
57. www.doew.at/erinnern/personendatenbanken/gestapo-opfer (last accessed on 22 Apr 2017).
58. DÖW 7245b, written testimony of Ella Lingens; Tausendfreund, *Erzwungener Verrat*, 254.
59. DÖW 5733f, Vienna Gestapo daily report no. 5 of 13–15 Oct 1942.
60. For detail, see Rothländer, *Karl Motesiczky*.
61. www.doew.at/erinnern/personendatenbanken/gestapo-opfer (last accessed on 22 Apr 2017).
62. Ibid.
63. Ibid.
64. DÖW, *Widerstand Wien*, vol. 3, 508; www.doew.at/personensuche (last accessed on 22 Apr 2017).
65. www.doew.at/erinnern/personendatenbanken/gestapo-opfer (last accessed on 22 Apr 2017).
66. Ibid.
67. Weinzierl, *Zu wenig Gerechte*, esp. 140ff.; Meisels, *Die Gerechten Österreichs*, 2; https://www.jewishvirtuallibrary.org/statistical-breakdown-of-the-righteous-gentiles (last accessed on 26 May 2021).
68. RGBl. I, 2319, Verordnung zur Ergänzung der Strafvorschriften zum Schutz der Wehrkraft des Deutschen Volkes, 25 Nov 1939; RGBl. I, 769, Verordnung über den Umgang mit Kriegsgefangenen, 11 May 1940.
69. Hesse et al., *Topographie des Terrors*, 265.
70. BA Berlin, express letter from the Reichsführer-SS to all Gestapo offices, 7 May 1940, quoted from Paul/Primavesi, 'Die Verfolgung der "Fremdvölkischen"', 389.

71. Wüllenweber, *Sondergerichte*, 193–94.
72. Paul/Primavesi, 'Die Verfolgung der "Fremdvölkischen"', 394–401.
73. Weisz, 'Gestapo-Leitstelle Wien', supplements 28/2–4 and 164.
74. DÖW reference library, Vienna Gestapo statistics for the months May 1943 to March 1944 (appended to the last daily report of each month).
75. Weitz, 'Verbotener Umgang'.
76. According to Diewald-Kerkmann, *Politische Denunziation*, 119, there were 4,345 convictions for 'prohibited contact' in 1940, and 5,763 in the first half of 1943.
77. Ibid., 122.
78. DÖW, *Widerstand Wien*, vol. 3, 520–21.
79. DÖW, *Widerstand Wien*, vol. 3, 520; www.doew.at/erinnern/personensuche (last accessed on 22 Apr 2017).
80. www.doew.at/erinnern/personendatenbanken/gestapo-opfer (last accessed on 22 Apr 2017).
81. Ibid.
82. DÖW, *Widerstand Wien*, vol. 3, 521; www.doew.at/erinnern/personendatenbanken/gestapo-opfer (last accessed on 22 Apr 2017).
83. DÖW reference library, Vienna Gestapo daily report no. 6 of 16–18 Feb 1943; DÖW 4045, VGH judgment against Johann Michalek, 10 Jul 1943.
84. DÖW, *Widerstand Wien*, vol. 3, 520; www.doew.at/erinnern/personendatenbanken/gestapo-opfer (last accessed on 22 Apr 2017).
85. www.doew.at/erinnern/personendatenbanken/gestapo-opfer (last accessed on 22 Apr 2017).
86. Weisz, 'Gestapo-Leitstelle Wien', Tables, table no. 35.
87. NÖLA, KG Wiener Neustadt, 8 E 734/42 (copy: DÖW E 19 279), judgment against Martha Laschitz for an offence under the Wehrkraftschutzverordnung, 29 Sep 1942.
88. ÖStA, AVA, Reichsstatthalter, Reichskommissar, Stimmungsberichte ('mood reports'), 387 (copy: DÖW E 18 036).
89. [Ausfall zeugungsunwilliger, homosexueller Männer] Jellonnek, 'Staatspolizeiliche Fahndungs- und Ermittlungsmethoden gegen Homosexuelle', 345ff.
90. Quoted from: https://de.wikisource.org/wiki/Strafgesetz_1852_(%C3%96sterreich)#.C2.A7._129._Verbrechen_der_Unzucht._I._wider_die_Natur (last accessed on 13 Nov 2016).
91. Brunner/Sulzenbacher, 'Das Projekt der Namentlichen Erfassung der homosexuellen und transgender Opfer', 114–15.
92. NARA, microcopy T 84 R 13, 40074 (copy: DÖW Film 68/2), daily report no. 4 of 5 Sep 1938, 3.
93. BA Berlin, R 58 243–276, express letter from the chief of the Sipo and SD, 31 Aug 1939; Weisz, 'Gestapo-Leitstelle Wien', 451–53.
94. DÖW 5732f, Vienna Gestapo daily report no. 7 of 15–16 Oct 1940.
95. Bailer et al., 'Die Gestapo', 174.
96. DÖW 19 795, statement by the Gestapo official Alfred Bodenstein at the Vienna police headquarters, 7 Jul 1945; see also Weisz, 'Gestapo-Leitstelle Wien', 455–58.
97. NARA, microcopy T 84, R 13, 39 744f. (copy: DÖW Film 68/2), Vienna Gestapo daily report of 10–12 Dec 1938.
98. Jellonnek, 'Staatspolizeiliche Fahndungs- und Ermittlungsmethoden gegen Homosexuelle', 356.
99. Bailer/Ungar, 'Die Zahl der Todesopfer politischer Verfolgung', 112–13.
100. Brunner/Sulzenbacher, 'Das Projekt der Namentlichen Erfassung der homosexuellen und transgender Opfer', 106.
101. Bauer/Sulzenbacher, 'Schlussbericht' (Final Report), 5–6.

102. Brunner/Sulzenbacher, 'Das Projekt der Namentlichen Erfassung der homosexuellen und transgender Opfer', 109ff.
103. See, among many others, Peukert, *Die Edelweißpiraten*.
104. For detail, see Gerbel/Mejstrik/Sieder, 'Die "Schlurfs"', 523–48.
105. *Der sozialdemokratische Kämpfer*, 1-2-3 (2008), 8–9 ('Jugendwiderstand: Wien 1944/45').
106. Gerbel/Mejstrik/Sieder, 'Die "Schlurfs"', 540ff.
107. DÖW, *Widerstand Wien*, vol. 3, 525ff.
108. DÖW 5732b, Vienna Gestapo daily report, 14–16 Mar 1941.
109. DÖW 5733f, Vienna Gestapo daily report no. 1 of 1–3 Dec 1942.
110. DÖW 5734b, Vienna Gestapo daily report no. 5 of 12–15 Feb 1943.
111. Quoted from: http://shoahproject.net/widerstand/kids/shkids4.htm (last accessed on 26 May 2021).
112. Gerbel/Mejstrik/Sieder, 'Die "Schlurfs"', 534–38.
113. Otto Klambauer, 'Mit "Swing Heil" gegen Hitler', *Kurier*, 15 Apr 2007, 34.
114. DÖW 5743b, Vienna Gestapo daily report no. 4 of 9–12 Apr 1943.
115. *Kurier*, 15 Apr 2007, 34.
116. DÖW 5733f, Vienna Gestapo daily report no. 1 of 2–5 Oct 1942.

Chapter 14

OBERLANZENDORF 'LABOUR EDUCATION CAMP'

Origins and Function of the AELs

The '(forced) labour education camp' (*Arbeitserziehungslager*, AEL) constituted a specific category of Nazi detention centre, and in the course of its development it became increasingly similar to the concentration camp.[1] The AELs originated following the outbreak of war in 1939 and served for the disciplining of so-called 'asocials', particularly amongst the young. Offences such as refusal to work, breach of work contract and slacking were sanctioned – primarily to serve the interests of large industrial concerns – with limited periods of harsh camp internment. Unlike the concentration camps, the AELs were not answerable to the Inspektion der Konzentrationslager (concentration camps inspectorate department) or, later, its successor Amtsgruppe D of the SS-Wirtschafts- und Verwaltungshauptamt (SS head office for the economy and administration); on the contrary, they were under the command of the regional Gestapo offices, which were paid by the firms for the forced labour performed by the inmates. In the course of the deportation of huge numbers of foreign workers from the occupied territories in eastern and south-eastern Europe, the *Fremdarbeiter* (foreign workers) became by far the largest group interned in the AELs, and roughly 5 per cent of foreign workers were interned in an AEL at some point in the war.

Committals to AELs took place on the basis of applications submitted by Gestapo offices without the involvement of the judiciary, and had no foundation in law. Unlike *Schutzhaft* ('protective custody') in concentration camps, which had no time limit, internment in an AEL was normally restricted to a few weeks, though as with *Schutzhaft* there was no legal recourse against committal. There were around two hundred AELs, in which cautious estimates reckon a total of at least half a million people were interned. As Gabriele Lotfi, the first historian to publish a comprehensive account of this kind of camp, has observed: 'The AELs proliferated from below into the Nazi terror system, where they established themselves as the Sipo's third level of repression, beyond the arm of the judiciary and independent of the concentration camps'.[2]

Foundation of Oberlanzendorf AEL – Takeover by the Vienna Gestapo in 1941

Oberlanzendorf AEL was not created by the Gestapo but, rather, was founded by Vienna city council in September 1940 as a 'work institute' (*Arbeitsanstalt*) for men over eighteen years of age in the grounds of Schloss Oberlanzendorf, which after serving as a home for handicapped children and then for 'problem kids' became the property of the city of Vienna after the annexation of Austria in 1938.[3]

For the Nazi regime, the 'asocials' problem came to a head in autumn 1940 when there was anti-German rioting at a football match between the Vienna team Admira and the German champions Schalke 04.[4] Consequently, an 'asocials commission' was formed in the Reichsgau of Vienna in which members of the city's welfare and legal departments, NSDAP, police, employment exchange and other bodies worked together and took responsibility for committals to the AEL. From 1941 to the end of July 1944, the 'Asozialenkommission' had 420 men interned at the AEL, which was only a fraction of the total number of internees, and few in comparison with the many thousands sent there by the Vienna Gestapo.[5]

As organizing a camp was a task beyond the capacity of the municipal administration, the AEL was taken over by the Vienna Gestapo at the city's request, even before it went into operation in March 1941. The Gestapo employed very different and more radical means of guarding and handling the internees than the city had at its disposal. From now on, the camp's official name was: 'Geheime Staatspolizei, Staatspolizeileitstelle Wien, Arbeitserziehungslager Oberlanzendorf'.[6] This development brought fundamental structural changes. In particular, the competence to make committals to the AEL passed into the hands of the Gestapo; from now on, the city of Vienna could only submit proposals. As Viktor Siegel, the Gestapo official responsible, made absolutely clear in a letter to the 'racial-political office' (Rassenpolitisches Amt) of the Vienna NSDAP at the end of 1942: 'Oberlanzendorf is an *Arbeitserziehungslager*. It is no longer a work institution'.[7]

While Schloss Oberlanzendorf housed the offices of the camp administration and was the official seat of Section IV D 6 of the Vienna Gestapo, the internees were housed in nine newly erected wooden huts in the grounds. The property was officially leased to the Vienna Gestapo on 8 July 1941. The camp was designed to house around 400 internees; in 1944, however, it was holding over 900 and by the end of the war more than 2,000 – so overcrowding alone meant the living conditions steadily deteriorated. The camp was surrounded by a barbed wire fence with several watchtowers bearing machine gun emplacements; it also contained a 'barracks' for the guards, and a number of other camp facilities.[8]

Commandant and Guards

After being taken over by the Vienna Gestapo, the AEL was dealt with by Section IV D 6, which was responsible for 'breaches of work contract' and 'asocials'. From 1942 to 1944 the overall head of Group IV D was Viktor Siegel, who under the 1944 GVP was responsible for all aliens, including the *Ostarbeiter*. Siegel, born in 1908, who had been an NSDAP member since 1932 and an SS-Sturmbannführer since 1942, was made head of Department IV in December 1944 and was one of the Vienna Gestapo's leading functionaries. In addition to having supervisory authority over the camp (monitoring the camp, the camp commandant, and the guards), the section head was also responsible for approving punishments administered to internees.[9] The character and extent of punishments for internees were regulated by the RSHA decree of 12 December 1941.[10]

The camp commandant – according to the official rubber stamp 'Lagerkommandant'[11] – was answerable to the head of the Vienna Gestapo (until December 1944 Franz Josef Huber), to whom he was obliged to report all important actions and events (e.g. deaths), as well to the section head. The head of the Vienna Gestapo could have individuals interned at the AEL without consulting his official superior body; every six months, however, he had to submit a report to the RSHA with information about the number of internees, committals, escapes, deaths and other matters.[12]

The AEL was intended to be manned by staff of the Vienna Gestapo, but it turned out they had insufficient capacity for this purpose. As a result, the camp guard was supplemented with a number of Waffen-SS members who were not fit for service at the front ('Gv. H.-Leute') and from 1943 with *Volksdeutsche* (ethnic Germans), mostly from Romania. Altogether the camp guard numbered around forty to fifty.[13]

The first camp commandant – initially still under the aegis of the city of Vienna – was the (high-ranking) SS-Sturmbannführer Leopold Köberl, who remained in office until 1942. Born in 1904, Köberl had been a member of the SA since 1922, the NSDAP since 1929, and the SS since 1934; in 1938, however, he did not join the Gestapo but was a municipal employee from November of that year. In the years 1935–38 he was for a time leader of the infamous SS-Standarte 89, and demonstrated his qualities as a dyed-in-the-wool Nazi during the November Pogrom of 1938, when he gave the commands for the destruction of four Vienna synagogues. He is said to have been dismissed as commandant of Oberlanzendorf in 1942 on account of incompetence; thereafter, by his own account, he did active service as a 'Partisanenjäger' (partisan-hunter). In 1945 he took off to West Germany and returned to Vienna unchallenged in 1957. Köberl's successor, SS-Obersturmführer Karl Schmidt, joined the Gestapo in 1938, having been a rural police officer and a Kripo official, and an illegal SS and NSDAP member since 1937. Schmidt's collaborator, deputy and (from 1944) successor, SS-Untersturmführer Karl Künzel (b. 1907), followed a similar career – police officer/official, illegal Nazi, entry into the Gestapo in 1938.[14]

Change of Function and Categories of Internee

When the AEL was taken over by the Gestapo, its character and structure as a camp changed fundamentally, as did the composition of the internees. While the city of Vienna only wanted to use it to penalize local 'work-shirkers' and 'asocials' with 'reformatory internment', under the Gestapo the reasons for committals became primarily economic in character. Now, the majority of the internees were foreign forced labourers alleged to have committed 'breaches of work contract'.[15] Many were transferred to the AEL by Gestapo border police posts after being caught attempting to flee the Reich, or by the regular uniformed police (Orpo) or factory security guards (Werkschutz). More than half of the Oberlanzendorf internees were *Ostarbeiter* (from the Soviet Union), and there were large contingents of French, Greeks, Poles and people from the Protectorate of Bohemia and Moravia.

With the exception of those under protective custody, the majority of the internees were put to work on farms in the vicinity, or in construction, armaments or other firms; the Gestapo received appropriate remuneration for the internees' labour and set a wage (50 pfennig per day) for the workers themselves, which the evidence indicates was not paid out. The internees had to make their way on foot to their often distant places of work, where they toiled from 7 A.M. to 6 or 7 P.M. In the camp itself, cleaning, gardening and other manual tasks were carried out by internees. One particularly dangerous task outside the camp was clearing bomb damage; during an Allied raid on the Matzleinsdorf freight railway station on 11 October 1944, for example, thirty-three forced labourers from the AEL lost their lives, in addition to the civilian fatalities.[16]

In 1943, a women's camp for around a hundred internees was set up, separated from the rest of the AEL by a high wall and guarded by women, mainly

Volksdeutsche. In addition to 'asocials' and foreigners, the internees also included women under 'protective custody' orders, one of whom was the former (and later) Social Democrat member of the Austrian parliament Gabriele Proft, arrested by the Gestapo in January 1945.[17]

From 1943, and in particular as the front came nearer, the Vienna Gestapo increasingly used the AEL to intern local and foreign 'protective custody' detainees, amongst whom were many resistance fighters. The reason was that the prisons in Vienna no longer had the capacity to cope with the large number of arrests, court cases and 'protective custody' orders; as a result – contrary to RSHA orders – Oberlanzendorf was used to hold those under investigative detention or 'protective custody' whose transfer to a concentration camp had been delayed.[18] For example, in October 1944, Julia Färber and Magdalena Sticker – both Jews who had gone underground and were arrested by the 'Jewish section' in Vienna and Rams (near Gloggnitz) respectively – were interned at the AEL, where they survived.[19]

Oberlanzendorf also served as a provisional place of internment for those detained by Nazi bodies. At the end of 1944, for example, the Wehrmacht used the AEL to intern around three hundred Romanians, most of whom were so debilitated by their previous experiences that they did not leave the camp alive. In the spring of 1944, after the occupation of Hungary by German troops, many members of the Hungarian political and social elite who were suspected of being anti-German, including Jewish bankers and entrepreneurs, were arrested and brought to Oberlanzendorf. While this group was on the whole left undisturbed, many individuals from it were transported to Mauthausen.

Oberlanzendorf was also used for the temporary detention of members of the Communist-Socialist resistance group led by Johann (Hans) Strohmer, who had been tracked down and arrested in mid-March 1945 by Johann Sanitzer's section; the group was particularly well established in the Vienna police and had connections with the O5 resistance group. They were put into specially built single cells, where they were seriously maltreated by Vienna Gestapo officials under the direction of Franz Straub, head of Section IV 1.[20] Hans Strohmer, brother of the Communist resistance fighter Franz Strohmer executed in 1943, was shot by the SS at Katzelsdorf (near Tulln) on 4 April 1945 when he was unable to keep going on the evacuation march to Mauthausen.[21]

It often happened that members of the political opposition who had served prison sentences or been released from concentration camps were subjected – without any legal basis – to further internment at the AEL after being remanded to the Gestapo on the basis of an application for *Rücküberstellung*. For example, Wilhelmine Artner had been interned in Vienna and at Ravensbrück from March 1938 to the end of January 1943 'on account of the hostile attitude she displayed towards the NS movement in the years 1933–38'; when she was released from prison on 17 January 1945 after serving her sentence for 'undermining military morale', she was interned by the Vienna Gestapo at Oberlanzendorf but was fortunate enough to be released when the camp was closed down at the beginning of April 1945.[22] Similarly, the Communist resistance fighter Katharina Smudits (later, by marriage, Sasso) arrested in 1942 was interned for a number of weeks at Oberlanzendorf in summer 1944 after serving her judicial sentence and the expiry of her 'protective custody' order; she was subsequently transferred by the Gestapo to Ravensbrück.[23]

The establishment of the AELs – and most especially their repurposing as camps for disciplining foreign forced labourers – gave the Gestapo considerable additional power in the war, and significantly greater threat potential.[24] The historian Josef Prinz, in his study on Oberlanzendorf, comes to the conclusion that the AEL acquired 'the character of an interim station and short-term custody location for detainees of very different kinds', and that the 'labour education camp' in fact became a 'police prison'.[25] With Oberlanzendorf AEL, the Vienna Gestapo effectively had a concentration camp of its own readily available on its very doorstep.

Conditions and Atrocities in the AEL, and Transfers to Concentration Camps

In most AELs, the living and working conditions deteriorated steadily and tended to become increasingly like those in concentrations camps. One major difference, however – apart from the absence of the mass murder facilities that existed in camps such as Mauthausen and Auschwitz – was the fact that internment was limited to eight weeks. At Oberlanzendorf AEL the conditions got progressively worse and were appallingly bad by the last phase of the war, when up to fifty internees were crammed into unheated, vermin-infested and filthy huts designed for a maximum of eighteen. The washing facilities and latrines were entirely inadequate for the increased number of internees, who also suffered from a lack of proper clothing and shoes. The food worsened as the war progressed, consisting solely of bread with soup or root vegetables served in bowls without eating utensils. Furthermore, the situation was aggravated by the camp authorities and guards helping themselves to large quantities of the food intended for internees.

The sole provider of medical care was the Rannersdorf village doctor Hans Cihak, later supplemented by an internee, the resistance fighter Dr Fritz Gerscha. Given the general conditions in the camp, the lack of necessary medical supplies, and the spread of infectious diseases, the doctors were constantly fighting a losing battle.[26]

At the AELs, chronic overcrowding, undernourishment and associated illnesses had a devastating effect on the death rate, which increased sharply from

1943. With the internment of more and more *Ostarbeiter* – who were treated badly enough as it was – many AELs effectively developed into death camps, with the death toll being driven up by starvation and typhus.[27]

At Oberlanzendorf as in many other AELs, the death rate amongst internees rose dramatically: while at the beginning of 1943 an average of ten deaths per month were registered, in the second half of that year the average was fifteen per *week*, and in 1944 it was ten to twelve per *day*. Until mid-1943 the dead were buried at the local cemetery; thereafter the corpses were transported by lorry to the nearby Vienna central cemetery, to be buried in mass graves.[28] The following are just a few examples of the huge loss of human life for which the Vienna Gestapo was responsible at Oberlanzendorf. The labourer Alois Luchesi, on whom the Gestapo opened an identification file on 29 December 1942 for being 'work-shy', perished at Oberlanzendorf on 11 February 1943.[29] On 8 January 1943 the Vienna Gestapo opened an identification file on Dimitrius Margaritis, who died at Oberlanzendorf on 4 March 1943.[30] On 6 July 1941, the Jewish internee Ernst Schwed was shot dead. He had been arrested on 19 June and transferred to the AEL on 3 July 1941 after being reported to the Gestapo for 'non-appearance at work' by a Vienna waste disposal firm; unable to continue performing the hard labour imposed on him – shifting rocks with a wheelbarrow – he attempted to escape and was shot in the back of the head by a certain SS-Rottenführer Meyer.[31]

Franz Weisz has established that from the second half of 1943 onwards internees were increasingly often subjected to penalties, including deprivation of food, being locked in the air-raid shelter and corporal punishment, or even hanging on the gallows. As the proportion of foreigners in the AELs rose and the war situation became more critical, the guards increasingly shed their inhibitions. They habitually administered punishments and maltreatment without obtaining the requisite approval from the camp commandant, and their superiors did not forbid or intervene against such actions.[32] While the brutality of Gestapo officials at Morzinplatz was primarily applied in order to extract confessions, the tormenting of internees at Oberlanzendorf was of a different order in that it was often intended simply to humiliate the victims or to satisfy the sadistic tendencies of camp staff. One particularly frequent penalty was the flogging, with twenty-five strokes on the bare buttocks. Known as the 'Polenstrafe' because it was the punishment instituted by Reichsführer-SS Himmler exclusively for Poles, it was theoretically only to be applied at the order of the respective Gestapo office head, but it was also used arbitrarily by SS guards on internees of other nationalities. As the political detainee Ludwig Radosch, interned at Oberlanzendorf in 1944, put in his testimony before the Vienna VG on 21 January 1947:

> They hit or beat us at every opportunity – it was all the same to the guards whether there was a reason or not. Sometimes they did it out of sheer boredom. Once they hit

an internee simply for looking at them 'stupidly'. I think the man was a foreigner, but in any case, he was so badly maltreated that he collapsed. Immediately afterwards, the same SS man drove everyone except the kapos into the middle of the room. I was also excepted because I was a political internee. Then he ordered them all to sing, and he beat time by hitting them over the head with a riding crop.[33]

Particularly feared for his brutality and unpredictability was the *Volksdeutscher* from Romania SS-Unterscharführer Adam Milanovicz, known to the internees as the 'bloodhound of Oberlanzendorf'. As stated in the Vienna state prosecutor's bill of indictment of 12 March 1952, 'Milanowitz [sic] struck the internees not only with his hands and fists but also with sticks, canes and other objects, also kicking them for the slightest reasons. ... He was particularly fond of letting a large and powerful boxer dog loose on the prisoners, which dragged them down onto the ground'. Both the indictment and the judgment delivered by the Vienna LG operating as a VG on 14 May 1952 list numerous specific cases in which he maltreated or tormented internees. Particularly cruel were the baths alternating between extremes of hot and cold water, and in winter the spraying of internees with ice-cold water in the open air.[34]

Günther Schifter (b. 1923) was a fan of the American popular music that was prohibited by the authorities and vilified as 'Negermusik'; at a dance in December 1944, he was arrested with more than thirty others and interned until 2 April 1945 at Oberlanzendorf. There he witnessed numerous instances of maltreatment, about which he testified in detail as a witness at the Vienna LG on 13 March 1947:

> I observed that these internees [Serbian partisans] were the worst treated of all. There were days when they were given nothing to eat. The accused, Milanovicz, and other guards subjected them to extreme maltreatment. ... The duty guards beat them so hard that they were unable to get back on their feet. ... Immediately after my committal to the camp I saw from my window a group of the protective custody internees having to line up on the parade ground and being given twenty-five strokes each with a truncheon on their outstretched hands. ... Then they had to take off their shoes and were given twenty strokes on the soles of their feet. ... They [the men of the camp guard] could beat the internees whenever they wanted, which is why every one of them had a truncheon. ... They delivered the strokes with all the strength they could muster.[35]

This account is confirmed by, among other sources, the statement of the Dutch civilian worker Johannes Jacobs, who was an interpreter in Section IV D from August 1943. The Vienna police transcription of his statement of 28 July 1945 describes conditions at the AEL: 'When food was being distributed, I personally witnessed camp guards (mostly *Volksdeutsche* and members of the SS) indiscriminately lashing out with truncheons at the internees, some of whom were physically injured. Shortly afterwards a Frenchman showed me his spectacles smashed into many pieces and a serious wound on his head'. When Jacobs reported such occurrences to the camp commandant, Künzel, and the head of the 'Ostarbeiter' unit, SS-Sturmbannführer Oskar Wendzio, he was yelled at and threatened; however, the section head Viktor Siegel promised to have the matter investigated.[36]

Given that the Vienna Gestapo carried out no executions at the headquarters on Morzinplatz – not counting the cases of detainees perishing as a result of torture – those destined to be executed were transferred to Mauthausen or other concentration camps with their files marked 'Rückkehr unerwünscht' (return undesired). But as an alternative, executions were carried out at Oberlanzendorf, by hanging on the gallows or by shooting, the victims mainly being Polish or Soviet Russian internees. When internees attempted to escape, they were shot at, leading to regular fatalities. Any escapees who were brought back to the camp alive were severely punished.[37]

Large numbers of internees, in particular foreign workers, were transferred from Oberlanzendorf to concentration camps, which for many was tantamount to a death sentence. The Greek citizen Banajotis Samaropoulos, for example, on whom the Vienna Gestapo opened an identification file on 8 January 1943, was committed to Flossenbürg concentration camp on 6 April, where he perished on 5 May of that year. At the end of July 1941, the commercial clerk and labourer Otto Zeillinger (Zeilinger), who had already spent two years interned at Buchenwald, was arrested for being 'work-shy' and sent to Oberlanzendorf AEL, where he was maltreated. After being released, he was detained once again in September 1942 for 'breach of work contract' and finally transferred to Mauthausen, where he died on 30 June 1943. The Russian farm labourer Ivan Worobjew was arrested by the Vienna Gestapo at the end of February or beginning of March 1944 under suspicion of belonging to a 'band' of 'Ostarbeiter', and was already interned at Oberlanzendorf when the Gestapo opened his identification file on 23 March; on the following day he was transported to Mauthausen, where he perished on 26 June 1944.[38] Similarly, in August 1944 the Italian labourer Sebastiano Pizzo was already interned at Oberlanzendorf for being found 'without fixed address or identity papers' when the Vienna Gestapo created his identification file, which is marked 'Schutzhaftabgabe' (for protective custody); he was subsequently transferred to Flossenbürg, where he perished on 5 December 1944.[39]

Evacuation of the Camp in 1945 – Total Numbers of Internees and Fatalities

While most of the internees were released when Oberlanzendorf AEL was closed down in April 1945, those not released were compelled to undergo an evacuation march in the direction of Mauthausen, during which there were numerous acts of barbarity: of the roughly four hundred 'protective custody' internees on the march, some forty to fifty were shot by SS guards, and others died of exhaustion along the way. The camp commandant Künzel had issued the order that all internees no longer able to walk were to be shot, for which purpose a special firing squad was formed, headed by the SS man Adam Milanovicz. Of the internees who made it to Mauthausen on 16 April 1945, many were murdered there.[40]

Given the facts of the case, Künzel's statement before the Vienna police in 1946 that his superior officer Viktor Siegel had given the order 'to liquidate the Lanzendorf camp inmates' is not plausible, and was clearly intended to minimize his own responsibility and suggest that he was 'simply obeying orders'. In fact, Siegel transmitted to Künzel an order of the RSHA or, rather, of the commander of the Sipo in Military District XVII, Mildner, to the effect that 'if the enemy is approaching', foreign and 'protective custody' internees' from the AEL were to be transported to Mauthausen. On forced marches, it was normal practice for the SS men to shoot internees who could not keep going; for this, no orders were required.[41]

In his thorough study of Oberlanzendorf AEL, Josef Prinz concludes that it is no longer possible to establish the exact number of internees who passed through the camp. As a decree specified that the duration of internment should not exceed fifty-six days (in theory – in practice it was a different matter), there was a high turnover at the AEL. Prinz estimates a total of 'considerably more than 10,000 internees', and points out that the internee index cards were numbered serially and went up to over 17,400.[42]

In present-day terms, the response of the post-war judiciary to these Gestapo crimes can only be described as inadequate. In 1950 the Vienna VG passed sentences on two former camp commandants: Karl Künzel was condemned to life imprisonment and Karl Schmidt to twelve years. Like many other Nazi criminals, they were soon amnestied: Schmidt was released from prison in 1954 and Künzel in 1955. Adam Milanovicz, the 'bloodhound of Oberlanzendorf', was sentenced to twenty years' imprisonment in 1952 but was granted amnesty in 1956.[43] He remained in the neighbouring village of Maria Lanzendorf, worked as a petrol station assistant and became chairman of the local football club.[44]

Notes

1. Broszat, 'Nationalsozialistische Konzentrationslager', 101ff.
2. Lotfi, 'Stätten des Terrors', 255–69, quotation from p. 260; for detail see Lotfi, *KZ der Gestapo*.
3. Letter from the mayor of Vienna to the Reichsstatthalter in Vienna concerning the establishment of a work institution, 17 Mar 1941, quoted in DÖW, *Widerstand Niederösterreich*, vol. 2, 574. In 1938 the locality of Oberlanzendorf was made part of Schwechat, then in the

23rd district of (greater) Vienna; since 1954 it has belonged to the commune of Lanzendorf (Lower Austria) not to be confused with the neighbouring Maria Lanzendorf.
4. https://de.wikipedia.org/wiki/SK_Admira_Wien#cite_note-8 (last accessed on 28 Mar 2016).
5. Czech, *Selektion und 'Ausmerze'*, 127–29.
6. DÖW 16 851, communication of the camp commandant to Section II P of the Vienna Gestapo, 12 Oct 1941.
7. [Oberlanzendorf ist ein Arbeitserziehungslager, nicht mehr eine Arbeitsanstalt.] Prinz, 'Oberlanzendorf', 205–6.
8. Weisz, 'Gestapo-Leitstelle Wien', vol. 3, 654–55; Prinz, 'Oberlanzendorf', 204, 251ff.
9. WStLA, Vienna LG, Vg 1h Vr 2179/49, statement by Viktor Siegel to the Vienna LG, 24 Jul 1947; BA Berlin, SSO Viktor Siegel; Weisz, 'Gestapo-Leitstelle Wien', vol. 3, 656–57.
10. BA Berlin, R 58, 1027/6/220-237, decree of the Reichsführer-SS, 12 Dec 1941.
11. DÖW 16 851, communication of the camp commandant to Section II P of the Vienna Gestapo, 12 Oct 1941.
12. Weisz, 'Gestapo-Leitstelle Wien', vol. 2, 306.
13. Ibid., vol. 3, 656–57, and Notes III, 512, nn. 96, 97; Prinz, 'Oberlanzendorf', 252–54. 'Gv. H.' stood for 'Garnisonverwendung Heimat' (barracks deployment: homeland).
14. BA Berlin, SSO 190 A Leopold Köberl; ibid., SSO 226 A Karl Künzel; http://www.profil.at/history/novemberpogrom-wien-keiner-taeter-gericht-369003; http://rundgang.blogsport.de/images/Broschuere_November2014.pdf; http://www.forum-der-wehrmacht.de/index.php/Thread/34518-89-SS-Standarte/ (all last accessed on 14 Apr 2016); Prinz, 'Oberlanzendorf', 250.
15. Prinz, 'Oberlanzendorf', 243.
16. Ibid., 254–56.
17. http://www.doew.at/result; http://www.dasrotewien.at/seite/proft-gabriele-geb-jirsa (both last accessed on 9 Apr 2016).
18. Weisz, 'Gestapo-Leitstelle Wien', vol. 3, 656; Prinz, 'Oberlanzendorf', 238.
19. WStLA, Vienna LG, Vg 5a Vr 884/47 against Karl Bergauer (copy: DÖW 18 961/1), testimony of Heinrich Schwarzstein to the Vienna LG, 22 Jul 1947.
20. Prinz, 'Oberlanzendorf', 279–81. SS-Sturmbannführer Franz Straub, a Reich German, was deployed in autumn 1944 as a special agent of the RSHA at the Vienna Gestapo.
21. DÖW E 20 019, record from memory of the interrogation of Alfred Pollak of Vienna, formerly interned at Oberlanzendorf, n.d.; see also Sainitzer, 'Die Gruppe Strohmer', 71ff.
22. http://www.doew.at/suche?query=oberlanzendorf&newsearch=10 (last accessed on 11 Apr 2016).
23. Prinz, 'Oberlanzendorf', 240–41, n. 227.
24. Lotfi, 'Stätten des Terrors', 269.
25. Prinz, 'Oberlanzendorf', 240–41.
26. Ibid., 262–65.
27. Mark Spoerer, review of Lotfi, *KZ der Gestapo*, in 'H-Soz-Kult', 1 May 2000, http://www.hsozkult.de/publicationreview/id/rezbuecher-284 (last accessed on 9 Apr 2016).
28. Weisz, 'Gestapo-Leitstelle Wien', vol. 3, 658.
29. http://www.doew.at/erinnern/fotos-und-dokumente/1938–1945/das-arbeitserziehungslager-oberlanzendorf#oberlanzendorf (last accessed on 17 Apr 2016).
30. Ibid.
31. DÖW reference library, Vienna Gestapo daily report of 4–6 July 1941, also to be found under http://www.doew.at/cms/download/52ke6/tb3_juli41.pdf (last accessed on 17 Apr 2016).
32. Weisz, 'Gestapo-Leitstelle Wien', vol. 3, 658.

33. WStLA, Vienna LG, Vg 1 Vr 4750/46, testimony of Ludwig Radosch, 21 Jan 1947.
34. WStLA, Vienna LG, Vg 1a Vr 350/50, bill of indictment of the Vienna public prosecutors and judgment of the Vienna LG as VG of 14 May 1952 (against Adam Milanowitz/Milanovicz).
35. http://www.doew.at/cms/download/76sv4/22994_7_aussage_schifter.pdf (last accessed on 17 Apr 2016), statement by Günther Schifter to the Vienna LG in the proceedings against Karl Künzel, 13 Mar 1947.
36. DÖW 20 333/12A, transcription of the statement made to the Vienna police by the Dutch interpreter Johannes Jacobs, 28 Jul 1945.
37. Prinz, 'Oberlanzendorf', 268–69.
38. http://www.doew.at/suche?query=oberlanzendorf&newsearch=10 (last accessed on 17 Apr 2016).
39. Ibid.
40. For detail see Prinz, 'Oberlanzendorf', 282–96.
41. DÖW 20 333/34, statement by Karl Künzel at the Vienna police headquarters, 16 Feb 1946; WStLA, Vienna LG, Vg 1e Vr 4750/46, judgment of the Vienna LG as VG against Karl Künzel and Karl Schmidt, 26 Jun 1950.
42. Prinz, 'Oberlanzendorf', 243–44.
43. http://www.doew.at/erinnern/fotos-und-dokumente/1938–1945/das-arbeitserziehungslager-oberlanzendorf#oberlanzendorf (last accessed on 9 Apr 2016).
44. http://www.tenhumbergreinhard.de/1933-1945-taeter-und-mitlaeufer/1933-1945-biografien-m/milanovicz-adam.html (last accessed on 9 Apr 2016).

Chapter 15

VIENNA GESTAPO OFFICIALS ON 'EXTERNAL DEPLOYMENT'

Nazi Germany's expansionist policy broadened the Gestapo's area of deployment and tasks considerably. In all the territories occupied by the German Reich, Sipo offices were established in which the Gestapo, Kripo and SD were conflated and to which Gestapo officials from all over the Reich were posted for what was known as 'Auswärtiger Einsatz' (external deployment). These offices were headed by a 'Befehlshaber der Sipo und des SD' (BdSuSD, commander-in-chief of the Sipo and SD), with authority over several officers with the title 'Kommandeur der Sipo und des SD' (KdSuSD, commander of the Sipo and SD). The KdSuSD offices were structured in very much the same way as the RSHA – that is to say, with the Gestapo allocated to Department IV.[1] They developed out of the mobile 'Einsatzgruppen' (EGs, deployment groups) or 'Einsatzkommandos' (EKs), which operated in almost every theatre of war and in which – as Himmler had always intended – the Gestapo and Kripo were fused with the SS and SD to form a single Sipo/SD complex.[2] EGs and EKs, which also included Orpo officials, followed the fighting troops and had the task of securing and 'pacifying' (*Befriedung*) the territory behind the advancing Wehrmacht. In other words, they were to eliminate anything going on that was 'hostile to state and Reich' and to use all possible means to crush any form of resistance. In order to achieve this, the EKs had the right to act on their own initiative with unlimited executive powers vis-à-vis the civilian population.[3] While Heydrich instructed the EGs and EKs operating in Western countries to 'behave entirely irreproachably and with restraint' towards the local population,[4] in the East 'the ground was laid for mass murder' only shortly after the invasion of

Poland.⁵ In accordance with the racist policy of *völkische Flurbereinigung* (literally, 'ethnic land cleansing'),⁶ the Gestapo repressed and eliminated not only all opponents but also all potential opponents of the Nazi regime in Poland and the Soviet Union. In addition to the Jews, this included the cultural elites (in Poland particularly the nobility and Catholic clergy), Communists, Communist functionaries, Sinti and Roma, POWs, partisans, and the mentally handicapped. The Gestapo was thus involved not only in mass executions of hostages, partisans (real or merely supposed), POWs and Jews, but also in the murder of disabled people, the guarding of ghettos and forced labour camps, and the deportation of Jews to the extermination camps.⁷ The staff not only of the EGs and EKs but also of the BdSuSD and KdSuSD stations were recruited from officials and general staff of the Kripo, Waffen-SS, SD and Gestapo. Among this last group were numerous members of the Vienna Gestapo, whose 'external deployment' this chapter will describe, at least in outline, without making any claim to presenting a comprehensive account.

The Vienna Gestapo appears to have been exceptional in that some of its highest-ranking officials, notably Franz Josef Huber and Karl Ebner, were never redeployed or transferred elsewhere. This may have been in part due to personal connections, as Huber had good contacts to the RSHA, which his friend Ebner was also no doubt able to take advantage of. All those below this top echelon were subject, as elsewhere, to what has been called the 'redeployment and transferral merry-go-round' that Himmler and Heydrich made a priority in the Gestapo generally.⁸ Because of the paucity of the sources, which are fragmentary and, for example, entirely lacking in staff files, it is very difficult to establish whether Vienna Gestapo officials sought and welcomed redeployments and transfers as a career move or, on the contrary, regarded them with fear and trepidation. However, as far as the really fanatical Nazis were concerned – such as Armin Kraupatz and Felix Landau (both considered in greater detail below) – there is no doubt that they saw 'Auswärtiger Einsatz' as an opportunity to put their inhumane and racist views into practice, and to satisfy their sense of superiority and lust for power. Furthermore, they could also expect – as could all members of the EK and Sipo outposts and offices – many diverse opportunities for financial gain. Towards the end of the war, however, numerous Vienna Gestapo officials were transferred to BdSuSD and KdSuSD posts in Hungary, Yugoslavia or Slovakia, where confrontation with real armed partisans probably made 'external deployment' a good deal less attractive.

The first 'Auswärtiger Einsatz' of Vienna Gestapo officials took place with the invasion of 'rump Czechoslovakia' by German troops in March 1939, when, among others, Josef Brunnhölzl (b. 1907), Karl Glück (1900), Johann Hoi (1901), Franz Morawetz (1887), Johann Rixinger (1899) and Franz Rudischer (1904) were deployed to build up Gestapo offices at Znaim (Znojmo), Olmütz (Olomouc), Mährisch-Ostrau (Ostrava) and elsewhere, after the Gestapo offices and regional headquarters all over the German Reich had been instructed to select reliable officials for this operation. Nor can there have been any doubt about the 'reliability' of these particular ones, as they had all been 'illegals' between 1933 and 1938; Glück was a holder of the Blood Order (Blutorden), a Nazi party medal for members who had suffered persecution or injuries in what they called the 'Kampfzeit' (in Austria, 1933–38). In all probability they belonged to EG II, which was formed in Vienna by its commander Walter Stahlecker, and consisted of around 250 men. The Vienna Gestapo officials later testified that they had served in various sections of the new Gestapo offices and regional headquarters, though without giving any more detailed information about their activities. According to the research findings of Oldřich Sládek, immediately after the annexation, the Gestapo offices were principally occupied with mass arrests and the seizure of documents to enable them to track down further opponents.[9] Apart from Franz Rudischer, who until July 1942 headed the Vienna Gestapo branch office of Znaim/Znojmo, all those mentioned returned to Vienna before the end of 1939.[10]

Two Vienna Gestapo officials, Heinrich Berger and Josef Auinger, both jurists with doctorates, were appointed to high-level posts in the Protectorate of Bohemia and Moravia. Berger (b. 1896) had been deputy head of Department II under Wilhelm Bock as early as October 1938, and was head from June 1941; in the spring of 1942 he was posted to the Gestapo regional headquarters ('Leitstelle') of Prague, where he headed various sections. After the assassination of Heydrich, he acted as assessor at summary courts and personally supervised the SS when they burned down the village of Ležáky as an act of retribution on 10 June 1942, shooting all the male inhabitants and transporting the women and children to concentration camps. In 1943 Berger became deputy head of the Prague Gestapo; from February 1944 to May 1945, he was head of the Klagenfurt Gestapo. On 17 August 1948 he was sentenced to twenty-two years' imprisonment by the Klagenfurt external senate of the Graz VG, but was released in June 1950 on account of 'poor health'.[11]

From July to December 1942, Josef Auinger was acting head of Special Commando Unit 7b, which was involved in the Holocaust in the Soviet Union. At the beginning of 1943 he was transferred to the office of the BdSuSD in Prague, where on 26 February 1943 Karl Hermann Frank, HSSPF in the protectorate, appointed him inspector of the plain-clothes police in Bohemia. The sources available to the present authors do not make it clear whether Auinger personally committed atrocities in Smolensk or Prague. However, a number of fragmentary files permit the conclusion that his duties in Prague included the supervision of the 'gypsy camp' of Lety, in which the conditions were appalling; and evidence shows he visited it.[12] In spring 1944, Auinger was transferred to a KdSuSD outpost in Hungary, and in October 1944 to the RSHA. In May 1945 he was taken prisoner by the French occupying forces, who in 1947 handed him over to the Soviet Union, where he was sentenced to twenty-five years' hard labour. After initially serving the sentence in East Germany and from 1950 in a prison near Irkutsk, he was allowed to return to Austria in 1955. He died in 1960 without ever facing charges in an Austrian court.[13]

Another Vienna Gestapo official active in 'external deployment' was Alfons Rosse-Blaschko (b. 1905), who was likewise a doctor of law and had been made head of Section II P (Press) following the annexation. From April 1942 until the end of 1943, he was deputy head of the 'Litzmannstadt' (Łódź) Gestapo, which was a branch office of the Gestapo regional headquarters of Posen (Poznań) in the Reichsgau Wartheland ('Warthegau').[14] In addition to the repression of any oppositional activity whatsoever, the Litzmannstadt Gestapo was involved in systematically clearing the new Reichsgau of Poles and Jews, who were to be replaced by newly settled *Volksdeutsche*. It also had the tasks of controlling the Łódź ghetto and the Jewish council established by the occupying authorities; in these capacities, it settled up with the German Reich railways for the costs of the 'special trains' that arrived at the ghetto from the Reich or occupied territories, supervised deportations from the ghetto to Chełmno extermination camp, and recorded details concerning the arrivals and departures of deportation trains in the situation reports drawn up for the RSHA.[15] Furthermore, the Gestapo was responsible for penalizing 'criminal offences' by inmates of the ghetto, such as food-smuggling and attempts to escape, though it was unable to suppress either activity entirely. On 10 May 1943, Rosse, obviously mindful of the Warsaw ghetto uprising that had broken out in the previous month, wrote to Department A 5 of the Forschungsamt ('research office', the intelligence agency operating under the aegis of the Reich air ministry) concerning the difficulties faced in guarding the ghetto: 'If there should at some point be serious unrest, it would lead to a worrying situation, as the guard can only be described as weak in comparison with the relatively large population of the ghetto. The Jews might succeed in overwhelming the guards, particularly if there were also unrest on the part of the Polish population of Litzmannstadt'.[16] At the end of 1943, Rosse was transferred to the RSHA, where he worked until 1945. In two post-war trials before the Vienna VG, he denied having had anything to do with the Łódź ghetto or the deportations. In the early 1960s he remained in denial even when seriously incriminating documents surfaced during proceedings against the head of the Litzmannstadt Gestapo, Otto Bradfisch, at the LGs of Munich and Hanover. Finally, the later proceedings against Alfons Rosse were terminated, and in all he only spent a few weeks in detention.[17]

The German invasion of Poland in 1939 was from the very beginning accompanied by atrocities, perpetrated above all by members of EGs or KdSuSD units. As well as Jews, their victims included not only Polish politicians, clergy, teachers and doctors but also workers and trade unionists. As a result of the existence of this 'specific milieu of violence',[18] even officials in relatively lowly positions acquired summary power over life and death. Two such men were Armin Kraupatz and Karl Macher, both of the Vienna Gestapo.

Kraupatz (b. 1911) had been sentenced to fifteen years' imprisonment for participating in the July 1934 putsch, but was amnestied in July 1936; in 1937 he found employment at the Kripo head office in Berlin. After the annexation of Austria in 1938 he worked at the Vienna Gestapo in Department III (Counter-intelligence, espionage). In 1939 he was posted to the Gestapo office of Oppeln, Silesia (now Opole, Poland). There, EG II was formed,[19] and in its ranks he marched into Poland. Between 1940 and July 1943 he was under the command of the Radom KdSuSD, who was responsible for the guarding and supervision of Radom ghetto established in the spring of 1941. Kraupatz committed numerous crimes in the ghetto, which numbered around thirty thousand inmates. After the war, several witnesses stated in court that during the evacuation of the ghetto in August 1942 – in which around twenty thousand Jews were deported to Treblinka extermination camp – Kraupatz threw babies and infants out of windows onto the streets, and fired at random at people being driven out of the houses.[20] In 1943, Kraupatz was transferred back to the Vienna Gestapo. On 16 June 1947 he was sentenced by the Vienna VG to fifteen years' imprisonment but only for offences under §§ 3, 4, 10 and 11 of the KVG. As Poland submitted an extradition request, further investigations were initiated in 1949 but finally terminated in accordance with a decision by the Vienna OLG of 25 January 1956.[21]

Karl Macher (b. 1911 in Vienna) was already a long-standing member of the NSDAP when he joined the Vienna Gestapo in June 1938. In autumn 1941 he was posted to serve under the Radom KdSuSD at the outpost of Tomaszów-Mazowiecki, where he was involved in the murder of many Jews. From 1942, he taught at the Sipo school in Drögen (Fürstenberg an der Havel). In November 1943 he was transferred to the BdSuSD in Athens, where by his own account he worked in various sections, allegedly ending up in the intelligence section. However, a letter of 26 May 1956 from the Greek war crimes office to the chief state prosecutor at Bonn LG asserts that Macher not only participated in mass executions, torture, the killing of hostages and other atrocities in and around Athens and Piraeus but was also responsible for numerous cases of maltreatment of internees at Chaidari concentration camp near Athens. Another name that appears in the same letter is 'Klendorfer', also referred to as 'Partisanen-Franz'. The entry actually refers to Franz Kleedorfer, likewise a member of the Vienna Gestapo, who during his deployment in Greece boasted of having murdered two thousand people with his own hands in Russia.[22] At the end of the war, Macher was directly subordinate to the leader of the EK in Krems/Stein, Rudolf Mildner. After 1945 he was accused of having participated in the execution of forty-two prisoners at Stein prison. On 1 March 1949, he was sentenced to thirty months' imprisonment by the Vienna LG functioning as a VG. On 10 May 1970 he was sentenced by a jury at the Graz LG to a further thirty months for his activities in Poland.[23]

After the invasion of the Soviet Union, EGs advanced into East Galicia, which was made part of the Generalgouvernement on 1 August 1941 as the district 'Galicia'. In their ranks were the Vienna Gestapo officials Erwin Linauer and Felix Landau. Linauer (b. 1905) of Department III of the Vienna Gestapo was posted to the Oppeln Gestapo in 1939 and to the KdSuSD of Lemberg (Lviv, Ukraine) in 1941, to serve at the outpost of Stanislau (Stanisławów).[24] He was involved in many murders in the Stanisławów ghetto; survivors described him as one of the 'worst ghetto officials' and as someone who took pleasure in murder. He was transferred back to the Vienna Gestapo at the end of 1943. In November 1947 he was arrested for the crimes he committed in Stanisławów and, with the agreement of the American occupying forces, handed over to the Soviets. He died in a Soviet camp in 1952.[25]

At the beginning of July 1942, the Vienna Gestapo official Felix Landau entered the eastern Galician county town of Drohobycz with EK Lemberg. A member of the NSDAP since 1931 and a holder of the Blood Order, Landau had fled to the German Reich after participating in the July 1934 putsch; following the annexation of Austria in 1938 he joined the staff of the Vienna Gestapo as a member of Section II E, which at the time dealt principally with offences such as 'relocation of assets and foreign currency' by Jews. In 1939 Landau voluntarily enrolled in an EK in Olmütz (Olomouc, Moravia), then moved to the Radom KdSuSD and in June 1941 to EK Lemberg, of which Drohobycz was an outpost.[26] Shortly after arriving on 12 July 1941 he was in the firing squad at the murder of twenty-three Jews, as he recorded in his diary: 'At 6 A.M. I am suddenly woken up from deep sleep. Report for an execution. OK, now it's my turn to play the executioner and then gravedigger, why not'.[27] Landau was given the task of organizing and directing the work of the Jewish population, in which function he committed numerous atrocities – for example, shooting twenty men for not having appeared punctually at work.[28] In 1947 he succeeded in escaping from the US Army Camp Marcus W. Orr in Salzburg ('Lager Glasenbach'), but was again arrested in West Germany in 1958. On 16 March 1962, Landau (see also Figure 15.1) was sentenced to life imprisonment by the Stuttgart LG, but he was reprieved in 1973.[29]

Another member of the Vienna Gestapo to be posted to the district of Galicia was the jurist Richard Ulbing (b. 1897), who joined Department III after the annexation. From 12 September 1942 he was deputy KdSuSD in Lemberg, whence he was redeployed to the Bromberg (Bydgoszcz) Gestapo on 1 April 1943, to the Paris BdSuSD on 20 June 1943 and to the Danzig (Gdansk) IdSuSD in October 1944. Until now no evidence of abuses or criminal offences on Ulbing's part has been found. Nevertheless, after 1945 he chose to live with 'friends' in Germany and did not return to Austria until 1957.[30]

Relatively few documents have been found relating to the activity of the jurist Otto Heger, who was redeployed in May 1942 as commander of the Orpo in Riga, where by his own account he was involved in criminal law cases and in Latvian economic and administrative affairs until March 1944. Prior to his redeployment, Heger (b. 1898) had headed various units of Department II of the Vienna Gestapo. That he was well connected is indicated by his Gau file, which contains the memo, 'personal friend of deputy mayor [Thomas] Kozich and city councillor Sepp Mayer'. It has not yet been established what function Heger performed in Riga. After 1945 he was re-employed in the police.[31]

Staff of the Vienna Gestapo were also redeployed to Gestapo offices in Western countries such as the Netherlands, Italy or Greece. Friedrich Kranebitter (b. 1903), a jurist and member of the NSDAP since 1931, was appointed head of the Gestapo office under the BdSuSD in Verona on 25 January 1943.[32] Previously he had been deputy head of the Vienna Gestapo branch office of Wiener Neustadt, and for short periods head of the branch office of Sankt Pölten and head of Sections II G and II K in Vienna. In March 1942, Kranebitter was moved to the RSHA, whence in April 1942 he was posted to serve under the BdSuSD in Kiev (Kyiv), where he was made KdSuSD in Kharkov (Kharkiv). According to Soviet sources, in this function he was responsible for mass executions and the use of a gas van.[33] As head of the Verona Gestapo he ordered not only barbaric reprisals against the partisan movements that were strong in

Figure 15.1. Shooting of Jewish men in eastern Europe (photograph found in the possession of Felix Landau when he was arrested). © Dokumentationsarchiv des österreichischen Widerstandes. Used with permission.

northern Italy, such as the shooting of hostages, but also the deportation to Auschwitz of the Jews interned at Fossoli concentration camp.[34] After being captured and interned by American soldiers in May 1945, Kranebitter was handed over to the Austrian authorities in 1948. On 17 January 1949 he was sentenced by the Vienna VG to one year's imprisonment – for illegal membership of the NSDAP.[35]

SS-Oberführer Humbert Achamer-Pifrader (b. 1900) and SS-Standartenführer Rudolf Mildner (b. 1902) were the highest-ranking Vienna Gestapo officials to complete their careers with 'external deployment'. They were two of a number of Austrians who rose to influential positions in the Sipo having worked before the 1938 annexation at the Gestapa, where they were able to build up good personal contacts, in particular with Himmler and Heydrich.[36] Both occupied posts at the highest level of the Vienna Gestapo at a critical period in its history: Achamer-Pifrader was deputy head from March to November 1938 and thus formatively involved in the building up of the Vienna Gestapo; and Mildner occupied leading positions in 1944–45 as deputy head under Huber, then KdSuSD.[37]

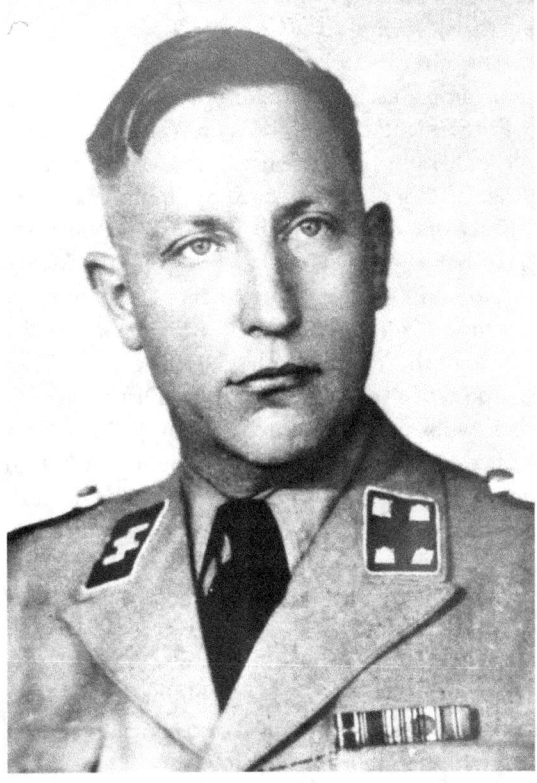

Figure 15.2. Vienna Gestapo official Friedrich Kranebitter, head of the Verona Gestapo from January 1943. © Dokumentationsarchiv des österreichischen Widerstandes. Used with permission.

After serving in Vienna, Humbert Achamer-Pifrader was made head of the Darmstadt Gestapo on 1 December 1939 and given the additional function of IdSuSD with headquarters in Wiesbaden in 1940. In 1942, in the latter capacity, he personally organized the first deportation to the East of Jews from Hesse. In September 1942 he was appointed BdSuSD for the Reichskommissariat 'Ostland', and in autumn 1943 IdSuSD for Berlin and Stettin (Military Districts III and II). In March 1944 he was made head of Department IV A 5 of the RSHA and shortly afterwards leader of Einsatzgruppe F, to which Josef Auinger also belonged. EG F was deployed in Hungary and was – in cooperation with Adolf Eichmann and his staff – involved in the deportation of the Jews of Hungary.[38] After the failure of the 20 July 1944 plot, Achamer-Pifrader played a leading role in tracking down and prosecuting the resistance fighters involved. He was killed in January 1945 during an air raid while on a journey of inspection in Linz.[39]

Rudolf Mildner became deputy head of the Linz Gestapo after the annexation of Austria in 1938, and from August 1939 was for a short time deputy head of the Salzburg Gestapo. In December 1939 he was made head of the Chemnitz Gestapo, and in March 1941 of the Gestapo regional headquarters of Kattowitz (Silesia, now Katowice, Poland). In this capacity he was responsible for the deportation of Silesian Jews and from summer 1942 for presiding over the police and summary court (Polizei- und Standgericht) that held sessions in Block 11 of the main camp Auschwitz I and, in accordance with a regulation issued by Gauleiter Fritz Bracht, sentenced defendants to death for acts of resistance (actual or alleged), right down to listening to foreign radio broadcasts or black marketeering. Mildner was described by the SS man Pery Broad, who served at Auschwitz, as 'one of the most bloodthirsty ... butchers of the Third Reich'. From September 1943 Mildner was BdSuSD in Copenhagen, and from February 1944 IdSuSD in Kassel. After being redeployed for a short period to the RSHA, in June 1944 he was appointed to take over the duties of Franz Josef Huber as head of the Vienna Gestapo; in December 1944 he was given the newly created post of 'KdSuSD in Military District XVII', thus effectively replacing Huber, who had fallen into disfavour with RSHA chief Kaltenbrunner. In this function, Mildner ordered the public execution of the resistance fighters Major Karl Biedermann, Hauptmann Alfred Huth and Oberleutnant Rudolf Raschke on 8 April 1945 in Floridsdorf, and was ultimately responsible for numerous crimes committed in 'Lower Danube' by displaced Gestapo offices in the final phase of the Nazi regime. After the war, Mildner succeeded in downplaying his important role in the Sipo, with the result that his only appearance at the Nuremberg trial of major war criminals was as a witness against Ernst Kaltenbrunner. After going into hiding in 1949, he escaped – to Argentina, according to Simon Wiesenthal – thus putting himself beyond the reach of the German and Austrian post-war judiciary.[40]

Deployment of a Group of Vienna Gestapo Officials in France, 1943–44

In 1943–44, a group of Vienna Gestapo officials were involved in an operation in France that was different in character from the activities of individual Gestapo officials who were involved in mass crimes as members of Sipo units in the occupied territories of Europe. The task of the Gestapo officials in France was to track down and crush an important resistance group with activities also extending to Austria. The group's members were Austrian Communists in exile in France, of whom there were many. They cooperated with the Parti Communiste Français (PCF) and the French Resistance and built up a widely ramified resistance network with bases in Paris and the occupied territories of southern France. The group developed a remarkable range of resistance activities, including infiltration and undermining of German military formations, sabotage, and the production and dissemination of the illegal German-language newspapers *Soldat im Westen* (Soldier in the West) and *Soldat am Mittelmeer* (Soldier on the Mediterranean). The foremost activity of the 'Travail Anti-Allemand' (TA, a section of the Resistance)[41] was anti-war in its orientation, and designed to subvert the morale of German/Austrian soldiers in the Wehrmacht. This form of agitation, known as 'Mädelarbeit' (girl work) because it was carried out by young women, was extremely dangerous and led to considerable losses. In 1942, in view of the (for Nazi Germany) catastrophic course taken by the Battle of Stalingrad (August 1942 to February 1943), the leaders of this Austrian resistance group considered the time ripe to extend their struggle outside France and give a boost to the resistance in Austria. To that end, from November 1942 a considerable number of activists (at least forty, including women) were sent disguised as French civilian workers, mostly with forged Alsatian identities, to Vienna and other places in Austria, where they were soon able to establish contacts with resistance groups in industrial firms.[42]

The Vienna Gestapo did not recognize the size or specific structure of this resistance group until the summer of 1943, after their attention had been drawn to illegal flyers signed by the new Vienna leadership of the Austrian Communist Party: 'Neue Wiener Stadtleitung der KPÖ'. This development was recorded in the Vienna Gestapo daily report of 27–31 August 1943:

> Since around May 1943 ... the Vienna Gestapo has gained knowledge of a number of new Communist leaflets which ... suggest the rebuilding of a central Communist literature apparatus. Extensive investigations, observation and the deployment of new informants have now led to the identification of a smaller circle of leading functionaries and of a number of persons in contact with large industrial firms in Vienna. Interestingly, this new attempt at reorganizing the central leadership of the KPÖ, which has so far always been crushed, appears to have been carried out on the

orders of an unspecified functionary of the illegal PCF in Paris. To that end, Austrian émigrés and red Spanish Civil War fighters [Rotspanienkämpfer] who succeeded in evading the German authorities in France have been provided with completely bogus French identification papers and infiltrated into the Reich in a transport of French workers.[43]

The Vienna Gestapo's investigations led to the arrests of four activists from this group – Ludwig Beer, Julius Günser, Walter Greif and Frieda Günzburg – all carrying forged French identity documents. They were brutally tortured, enabling the Gestapo to become party to the names and details of other participants; under the greatest pressure, the Spanish Civil War veteran Julius Günser finally gave in and collaborated.[44] As a result, other activists were arrested and the Gestapo gained knowledge of the involvement of Josef Meisel, who had been among the returnees of November 1942 and had been arrested in May 1943 but had not made any confessions.[45]

Following a wave of arrests by the French police in late autumn 1943, the Vienna Gestapo found out that the arrestees included members of the KPÖ and KPD. On the instructions of the BdSuSD for France in Paris (SS-Standartenführer Helmut Knochen), the Vienna Gestapo sent several officials with experience in the suppression of Communist resistance to Paris, under the leadership of Eduard Tucek, who had held the relatively lowly position of a Kriminalsekretär in the Section IV A 1 (Communists, Marxists) with the SS rank of Sturmscharführer since 1941. It was not for nothing that he was recruited for this task, as he had a reputation for extorting confessions by means of torture, gained not least through his part in the crushing of the KJV and a Communist cell in the Vienna police. Although the Vienna Gestapo officials did not initially make any further arrests, this period saw the first instances of maltreatment of detainees.[46] On 19 November 1943, for example, the Viennese Friederike Weitzenbaum and her brother Max were handed over by the French police to the Vienna Gestapo officials, who savagely maltreated them. In her testimony to the Austrian police in 1946, Friederike Weitzenbaum said of her brother: 'When I saw him [for the last time], his face was swollen and deformed, and he could hardly stand on his own two feet'. On 31 July 1944, Max Weitzenbaum was deported from Drancy assembly camp to Auschwitz and then transferred to the Mauthausen satellite camp of Ebensee, where he perished on 24 March 1945.[47]

Following a further instruction from the BdSuSD France at the end of April 1944, a Gestapo group once again led by Eduard Tucek succeeded in tracking down numerous Communist resistance fighters in Paris, Lyon and elsewhere. The large number of victims of this wave of arrests was not least the result of one of the KPÖ leaders in France, Leopold Hagmüller – in an incredible breach of the rules of underground political activity – being caught with a highly revealing list of the names, cover names and addresses of the resistance activists that the illegal organization had smuggled into Austria disguised as French civilian workers, who as a result were tracked down and arrested in Austria. The operation of the Vienna Gestapo officials in France, however, had to be terminated, as Tucek later put it, 'on account of enemy action, that is to say, the imminent prospect of Paris being taken by the Americans'.[48]

The arrestees were interrogated with Vienna Gestapo's customary brutal methods in order to compel them to make confessions and reveal the names and addresses of co-resistance fighters. The TA activist Selma Steinmetz arrested in June 1944 in Lyon, later a long-standing DÖW librarian, said of her maltreatment by Vienna Gestapo officials:

> I was interrogated a number of times in Lyon by the Gestapo official Eduard Tucek and another one whose name I don't know. Tucek was intent on getting me to reveal the names of addresses of all those I had been in contact with who had been active in the resistance movement. As we were living there illegally and acted in strict accordance with the rules of underground political activity, I knew neither the real names nor the addresses of most of these persons, so that I could not have revealed them even if I had wanted to. After tying me up in chains, Tucek first punched me with his bare fists. Then he resorted to using a horsewhip with which he gave me such a beating over my whole body that I ended up covered with bleeding weals, and the skin was hanging in shreds off my body. On the next day he used the bath method. After having to undress down to my underwear, I was tied hand and foot and laid in a cold bath. My head was repeatedly plunged into the water and when I raised my head out of the water the shower was held in my face so that I could hardly draw breath. I thought I would suffocate at any moment. ... This was how I was interrogated by Tucek for five days.

On 7 August 1944, Steinmetz was transferred to Drancy assembly camp, which was the point of departure for transports of Jews to Auschwitz and other extermination camps, but she was liberated there by Allied soldiers on 17 August.[49] Her partner Oskar Grossmann, a member of the KPÖ central committee and political leader for southern France, was likewise arrested in Lyon, where he was most likely murdered in the course of Gestapo interrogations.[50] Paul Kessler, arrested on 22 April 1944 in Lyon, was likewise severely maltreated for days on end by Tucek and his assistants, with methods similar to those used on Selma Steinmetz; nor did they even spare his wife or 15-year-old daughter.[51] A similar fate was suffered by the resistance fighter Ida Margulies, arrested in August 1944 in Paris, who reported on her maltreatment to the state police in Vienna: 'He gave me such a beating on my backside that when I was put into detention, the prison doctor was outraged. When – by chance, it was the day we were taken away in a transport – I came face to face with my husband, he didn't recognize me because I was so disfigured from repeated maltreatment'.[52]

The Gestapo official Karl Künzel, formerly commandant of Oberlanzendorf AEL, worked together with Tucek, and in 1945 was also interned with him at Camp Marcus W. Orr in Salzburg. There, as Künzel told the state police in 1946, Tucek boasted about the Gestapo operation in France, recounting how he had severely maltreated detainees during interrogations; one Frenchwoman, he bragged, had even jumped out of the window with the intention of committing suicide in order to get away from him.[53]

The resistance fighters arrested by the Gestapo in Austria were treated in the same way. Josef Gradl, for example, a Spanish Civil War fighter and returnee from France who had been tracked down by Tucek to Ptuj (Slovenia, in German Pettau), was arrested by the Vienna Gestapo official sent there for that purpose, Karl Wolf, and immediately subjected to severe maltreatment on the spot, before succeeding in escaping from detention.[54] While the Gestapo deported most of the arrestees to concentration camps (on account of their Jewish origins) – mainly to Auschwitz and Ravensbrück – Gottfried Kubasta, who was one of the first to return to Vienna in November 1942, was sentenced to death by the VGH and executed in Vienna on 5 December 1944.[55]

The statement made by Tucek before the state police that no arrestees were 'transferred by us into the territory of the Reich' was clearly a deliberate attempt to mislead the authorities. As most of the members of this resistance group in France and Austria were – according to the Nazis – Jews, they were not brought to trial but in most cases deported from Drancy to Auschwitz, and from there in some cases to other camps.[56] The rapid liberation of Paris by the French Resistance and Allied troops in August 1944 saved many internees and prisoners from imminent deportation. A small number, among them Egon Kodicek, Emanuel Edel, Paul Kessler and Moritz Fels-Margulies, succeeded in escaping from prisons or transports, and thus survived.[57]

Eduard Tucek was interned at Camp Marcus W. Orr in 1945, and from 1946 detained by the state police in Vienna. In 1947, at the request of the French occupying forces, he was handed over to the French military courts; in 1949 he was sentenced to five years' imprisonment but was released in 1950. After his return to Austria, the proceedings suspended in 1947 were not resumed until 1956, but were then terminated under the amnesty towards former Nazis in 1957.[58] The crimes committed by Tucek as a member of the Gestapo in Austria were thus never brought before a court of law – not only the innumerable cases of maltreatment of detainees but also, among other things, his role as executioner at a summary court in Krems in April 1945.

Notes

1. See, among others, Mallmann/Böhler/Matthäus, *Einsatzgruppen in Polen*, 101.
2. Dams/Stolle, *Die Gestapo*, 134–35 (*The Gestapo*, 120).
3. Rüter/de Mildt, *Justiz und NS-Verbrechen*, vol. XLIV, serial no. 864, pp. 249ff.
4. Mallmann, 'Menschenjagd und Massenmord', 300.
5. [Weichen in Richtung Massenmord (gestellt)] Mallmann/Böhler/Matthäus, *Einsatzgruppen in Polen*, 57.
6. Mallmann, 'Menschenjagd und Massenmord', 294.
7. See, for example, Alberti, *Die Verfolgung und Vernichtung der Juden*, 71.
8. [Abordnungs- und Versetzungskarussell] Paul/Mallmann, *Die Gestapo – Mythos und Realität*, 13. The frequent redeployments were, for example, quoted by the jurist Friedrich Mayer as the reason for his having no children. In a 'Statement concerning the present childlessness of my marriage', dated 30 September 1943, he explains that as he had been posted to the BdSuSD in Metz from September 1942 to May 1943 and thereafter to the Prague Gestapo he had spent 'only a few days' with his wife. See BA Berlin, R 9361-III/125016 and R 9361-III/542555.
9. Sladek, 'Standrecht und Standgericht', in Paul/Mallmann, *Die Gestapo im Zweiten Weltkrieg*, 318ff; for details, see WStLA, Vienna LG, Vg 4d Vr 4465/45 (Josef Brunnhölzl), LG Wien, Vg 1 Vr 5331/46 (Karl Glück), LG Wien, Vg 2b Vr 4466/47 (Johann Hoi), LG Wien, Vg 5a Vr 5261/46 (Franz Morawetz), LG Wien, Vg 11g Vr 1866/46 (Johann Rixinger), LG Wien, Vg 1 Vr 2216/51(Franz Rudischer). Stahlecker was appointed BdSuSD in the Protectorate of Bohemia and Moravia on 2 June 1939. The protectorate was considered to be an integral part of the German Reich ('unmittelbares Reichsgebiet') and thus had Gestapo offices and a regional headquarters in Prague; in addition it had its own BdSuSD, which also gave it a security police structure characteristic of the occupied territories.
10. On Karl Glück, see BA Berlin, Berlin Document Center, Personenbezogene Unterlagen der NSDAP/Parteikorrespondenz, R 9361-II/299532, and Personenbezogene Unterlagen der SS und SA: R9361-III/55125 and 9361-III/526509.
11. WStLA, Vienna LG, Vg 8b Vr 9144/46; BA Berlin, Berlin Document Center, Personenbezogene Unterlagen der Reichskulturkammer, R 9361-VI/13911.
12. DÖW 19826.
13. Gafke, *Heydrichs Ostmärker*, 270ff.; WStLA, Vienna LG, Vg 8e Vr 177/55; BA Berlin, Berlin Document Center, Personenbezogene Unterlagen der SS und SA: R 9361-III/514956, R 9361-III/4082; RGVA 500k/1/32, 1372k/5/81, 1372k/5/89; ÖSTA, AdR, Gau file Josef Auinger, no. 4346; 'Meldungen aus den besetzten Ostgebieten', no. 25 (16 Oct 1942), in Mallmann et al., *Deutsche Berichte aus dem Osten*, vol. 3, 475ff.
14. Alberti, *Die Verfolgung und Vernichtung der Juden*, 72. The Warthegau was an administrative district artificially created in 1939, following the conquest of Poland, out of the western and central part of the occupied country. Łódź was renamed 'Litzmannstadt' in 1940 after the Prussian general and NSDAP politician Karl Litzmann (1850–1936).
15. Diamant, *Ghetto Litzmannstadt*, 120ff.
16. Alberti, *Die Verfolgung und Vernichtung der Juden*, 170.
17. ÖStA, Gau file no. 48956, Alfons Rosse; WStLA, Vienna LG, Vg Vr 1827/49 and 27 d Vr 1279/63.
18. Mallmann/Paul, *Karrieren der Gewalt*, 15.
19. Mallmann/Böhler/Matthäus, *Einsatzgruppen in Polen*, 25.
20. Testimony of Amzel Warschauer, Rachmil Wajsbord and Leon Daeyer before the Jewish committee in Stuttgart on 2 Sep 1946, quoted from: http://www.nachkriegsjustiz.at/service/gesetze/kvg.php (last accessed on 2 May 2018).

21. ÖStA, AdR, Gau file Armin Kraupatz, no. 266 854; WStLA, Vienna LG, Vg 11d Vr 428/46 and Vg 6d Vr 3066/47; BA Berlin, Deutsche Dienststellen in Polen: R 70-Polen/781, and Berlin Document Center, Personenbezogene Unterlagen der NSDAP/Parteikorrespondenz R 9361-II/573711.
22. DÖW 19 051; Mazower, *Inside Hitler's Greece*, 221 (*Griechenland unter Hitler*, 265).
23. Ferihumer/Garscha, 'Der "Stein-Komplex"', 75–81; ÖStA, AdR, Gau file Karl Macher, no. 69 668; WStLA, Vienna LG Vg 6d Vr 7463/46; BA Berlin, Berlin Document Center, Personenbezogene Unterlagen der SS und SA: R 9361-III/123827, R 9361-III/541622; http://www.nachkriegsjustiz.at/prozesse/geschworeneng/35prozesse56_04.php (accessed on 2 May 2018); see also Chapter 16.
24. BA Berlin, ZR 816A.07.
25. WStLA, Vienna LG, Vg 6d 428/46; GARF, R-9474/1a/9694, Bestand: Oberster Gerichtshof der UdSSR, Akt 114s-11, Linauer Erwin, Rabara Ernst, Dunkl Josef, Kohaut Franz; RGVA, microfilm 1525k/1/482, fols. 40–41.
26. Staatsarchiv Ludwigsburg, Bestand EL 317 III Bü 1103, record of the interrogation of Felix Landau before the Landeskriminalamt Baden-Württemberg, Stuttgart, 1 Dec 1959.
27. Rüter/de Mildt, *Justiz und NS-Verbrechen*, vol. XVIII, serial no. 531, p. 359.
28. Ibid., 364.
29. Pohl, *Nationalsozialistische Judenverfolgung*, 417.
30. ÖStA, AdR, Gau file no. 38 653, Richard Ulbing; WStLA, Vienna LG, Vg 4c Vr 648/48; BA Berlin, Berlin Document Center, Personenbezogene Unterlagen der SS und SA: R 9361-III/560700; Pohl, *Nationalsozialistische Judenverfolgung*, 421.
31. ÖStA, AdR, Gau file Otto Heger, no. 5352; WStLA, Vienna LG, Vg 3c Vr 9010/45; BA Berlin, Berlin Document Center, Personenbezogene Unterlagen der SS und SA: R 9361-II/377940.
32. BA Berlin, R/9361-III 537525.
33. See *Deutsche Greuel in Russland*.
34. BA Berlin, R 70-Italien/11.
35. WStLA, Vienna LG, Vg 12 Vr 6171/48, judgment against Friedrich Kranebitter, 17 Jan 1949.
36. See the section 'Planning, Preparation and Measures' in Chapter 2, this volume.
37. See the section 'Personnel Continuity and Rotation' in Chapter 5, this volume.
38. On 13 March 1944, Joseph Goebbels noted in his diary: 'Hungary has 700,000 Jews; we will see to it that they do not slip through our fingers'. Quoted from Gafke, *Heydrichs Ostmärker*, 129.
39. ÖStA, AdR, Gau file 336 120, Humbert Achamer-Pifrader; Gafke, *Heydrichs Ostmärker*, 103ff. and 269–70; Graf, *Österreichische SS-Generäle*, 308ff.; Klee, *Personenlexikon*, 10.
40. ÖStA, AdR, Gau file 180169, Rudolf Mildner; Gafke, *Heydrichs Ostmärker*, 144ff. and 294–95; https://www.donau-uni.ac.at/dam/jcr:af3509d2-5a3f-4c8c-bee8-e3ac60db62cf/ns-fl__chtlinge_blaschitz.pdf (last accessed on 26 May 2021).
41. The designation 'Travail Allemand' is also found in the sources and used in the literature. See, for example, DÖW, *Österreicher im Exil: Frankreich*, 177–238 and especially 26ff., and Neugebauer, *Austrian Resistance*, 94–98.
42. See Bailer, 'Tatort Frankreich', 397–406, and DÖW, *Österreicher im Exil: Frankreich*, 29.
43. DÖW 8475, Vienna Gestapo daily report no. 9 of 27–31 Aug 1943.
44. The account by Franz Marek, one of the TA leaders, to the effect that 'Jula Günser, much praised as a hero in the party' had 'begun to spill the beans straight after his first slap in the face' [nach der ersten Ohrfeige zu 'singen' begonnen hatte] must – given the brutal torture that Günser is known to have suffered under the Vienna Gestapo – be regarded as factually incorrect and furthermore – given that he was murdered at Mauthausen on 19 Feb 1945 – inappropriate in its tone. See Franz Marek, 'Erinnerungen' (typescript, Vienna, n.d. (1979)),

quoted from DÖW, *Österreicher im Exil: Frankreich*, 181–82; http://www.doew.at/erinnern/biographien/spanienarchiv-online/spanienfreiwillige-g/guenser-julius (last accessed on 26 Mar 2017).
45. DÖW 8475, Vienna Gestapo daily report no. 9 of 27–31 Aug 1943.
46. WStLA, Vienna LG, Vg 4c Vr 1438/47 (copy: DÖW 19 224), VG proceedings against Eduard Tucek, statement by Tucek to the Staatspolizei, Polizeidirektion Wien (state police, Vienna police headquarters), 2 Jan 1946; ibid., statement by Eduard Rabofsky, 3 Dec 1946; ibid., report of the Vienna police headquarters, Department I (state police), 13 May 1946.
47. Ibid., statement by Friederike Weitzenbaum, 7 Jan 1947; www.doew.at/erinnern/personendatenbanken/gestapo-opfer (last accessed on 25 Mar 2017).
48. WStLA, Vienna LG, Vg 4c Vr 1438/47 (copy: DÖW 19 224), statement by Eduard Tucek, 2 Jan 1946. Hagmüller ended up at Dachau, where he survived. His partner Paula Draxler perished in the course of Gestapo interrogations in Paris in 1944. Hagmüller's failure to observe the rules is also documented through statements of co-resistance fighters (e.g. in a DÖW interview with Gerti Schindel); see DÖW, *Erzählte Geschichte*, vol. 1, 248.
49. WStLA, Vienna LG Vg 4c Vr 1438/47 (copy: DÖW 19 224), statement by Selma Steinmetz at the Vienna police headquarters, 28 Jun 1946.
50. http://www.klahrgesellschaft.at/KaempferInnen/Grossmann.html (last accessed on 26 Mar 2017).
51. WStLA, Vienna LG,Vg 4c Vr 1438/47 (copy: DÖW 19 224), statement by Paul Kessler at the Vienna police headquarters, 3 Dec 1946.
52. Ibid., statement by Ida (Judith) Margulies at the Vienna police headquarters, 5 Jul 1946.
53. Ibid., statement by Karl Künzel at the Vienna police headquarters, 4 Jan 1946.
54. WStLA, Vienna LG Vg 11h Vr 2016/47 (copy: DÖW 19 193), record of the main proceedings, 14 May 1948.
55. DÖW reference library, Vienna Gestapo daily report no. 4 of 10–13 Sept 1943; http://www.doew.at/personensuche?lastname=kubasta&gestapo=1&politisch=1&lang=de (last accessed on 25 Sep 2020).
56. WStLA, Vienna LG Vg 4c Vr 1438/47 (copy: DÖW 19 224), statement by Eduard Tucek, 2 Jan 1946.
57. DÖW, *Österreicher im Exil: Frankreich*, 177–81, 200ff.
58. WStLA, Vienna LG Vg 4c Vr 1438/47 (copy: DÖW 19 224), letter from the Vienna LG to the French high commissioner in Austria, 13 Jun 1947; judgment of the Tribunal Militaire Permanent de Paris, 14 Nov 1949 (extract and translation); communication of the ministry of justice to the Vienna LG, 9 Mar 1951; petition of the state prosecutor of the Vienna LG to the investigating judge, 3 Sep 1957. On the financial assistance provided by the Republic of Austria for Tucek's legal costs and homeward travel expenses, and on the republic's waiver of repayment, see Bailer, *Tatort Frankreich*, 404–5.

Chapter 16

END-PHASE CRIMES

The Nazi regime's tendency towards 'cumulative radicalization', particularly in its anti-Jewish policy and its persecution of resistance fighters and the inhabitants of the occupied territories, has long been a subject of historical research.[1] The crimes committed during the period when it was clear that the Nazi regime was falling apart, involving not only the Gestapo but also the Wehrmacht, Waffen-SS, Volkssturm, judiciary, NSDAP and other Nazi formations, as well as some of the population, have come to be known in academic literature as 'end-phase crimes' (*Endphaseverbrechen* or *Kriegsendphaseverbrechen*).[2] It is not clear whether there was a general decree or order by Himmler or the RSHA, or whether the crimes were committed independently by lower-level units as a result of the decentralization of decision-making competences. At all events, in this declining phase of the Nazi regime, the will to destroy and demolish existed at both the higher and lower levels. The primary targets of this radicalization process were deserters and 'traitors', suspicious foreign workers and POWs, political opponents, Jews, and prison and concentration camp inmates.[3]

The extent and intensity of these atrocities at regional and local levels were extremely diverse, however, depending on the attitude and behaviour of the respective authorities. Whereas the Nazi terror in the Reichsgaus Lower Danube, Carinthia and Styria remained unabated until these areas were liberated (and, in some cases, even after the capitulation on 8 May 1945), the Salzkammergut was relatively spared, although it was intended to be part of the planned (but never realized) 'Alpine fortress', and was sought out as a refuge by senior Nazi functionaries, including RSHA chief Ernst Kaltenbrunner and

Adolf Eichmann. In the face of the looming defeat of Hitler's Germany, quite a few incriminated Nazis, including Gestapo officials, prepared to flee, go into hiding or defect to the Allies.[4]

Numerous end-phase crimes involving Gestapo officials were committed in the Vienna Gestapo's area of competence. Above all, Huber's short-term deputy and successor from 1 December 1944, SS-Standartenführer Rudolf Mildner, now commander of the Sipo and SD in Military District XVII, ensured that orders to kill were ruthlessly carried out. Not all of the murders at this time were the result of orders from above or out of fear of the consequences of disobedience. On the contrary, countless criminal acts were committed by fanatical local and regional NSDAP functionaries, members of the SA, SS, Hitler Youth and other Nazi formations. That killings did not have to be ordered from above is shown by the massacre of 170 Hungarian Jews in Rechnitz on 25 March 1945, which was initiated and carried out by local NSDAP functionaries. The driving force was not obedience, a 'sense of duty', or the fact that disobeying the order would have risked life and limb (*Befehlsnotstand*), but it was a desire to destroy and terrorize, which was a fundamental component of the Nazi ideology.[5] This chapter looks at some of the most important types of end-phase crime in the Vienna Gestapo's jurisdiction.

Murders of Downed Allied Airmen and Members of Allied Commando Operations

The German (and Austrian) population were hard hit by the Allied air raids, which started in Austria in 1943 and intensified towards the end of the war. The bombardments, as the historian Georg Hoffmann from Graz has written, 'were regarded as the ultimate Allied crime. The Nazi propaganda image of the "terror bombing" remains fixed in people's minds, even today'.[6] The Nazi regime, first and foremost Reich propaganda minister Joseph Goebbels, consistently stirred up the population to take revenge on British and American 'terror bombers' forced to land and to resort to lynch justice. In practice, however, it was usually local NSDAP, Hitler Youth or Reichsarbeitsdienst (RAD, Reich labour service) functionaries or members of the SS or Volkssturm who were most active, encouraging or forcing underlings to carry out these murderous tasks. Where it was not possible to foment, organize or orchestrate public anger, the killing was carried out in many cases by the Gestapo. According to Hoffmann's detailed research, at least seventy murders were committed on Austrian soil, and over ninety if the non-Austrian territories incorporated into the Alpine and Danube Gaus are included. Some 169 members of the US Air Force are listed as missing. In the German Reich as a whole, as many as one thousand Allied soldiers are thought to have been murdered.[7]

Whereas US airmen in Luftwaffe POW camps were interrogated but not usually in danger of their lives, the Gestapo had a particular (and deadly) interest in those members of the Allied military suspected of intelligence operations, sabotage or combat activities. For example, several American airmen and agents who had been shot down in Slovakia in 1944 and had fled to partisan groups were brought to the Vienna Gestapo in November 1944 after their arrest and brutally maltreated there for a number of weeks. Several soldiers were then transferred to Mauthausen; amongst these, Sergeant Richard G. Moulton survived.[8]

The American bomber pilot Lieutenant Robert M. Hyde, who landed by parachute in Sulz im Wienerwald (Vienna Woods) on 16 July 1944, resisted arrest by the police and killed the forester Karl Neubauer in the struggle. After his imprisonment by the police, the injured pilot was brought by two Gestapo officials from the field hospital to the Gestapo headquarters on Morzinplatz, where he was severely maltreated for several days. According to testimony by the Gestapo officials Johann Sanitzer and Viktor Siegel before the Vienna LG, Reichsführer-SS Himmler was informed of the case and ordered the prisoner's execution. SS-Standartenführer Rudolf Mildner, deputizing for Gestapo head Huber, ordered two subordinate officials, Lambert Schneider and N. Bernauer, to carry out the execution. A fictitious report was issued stating that Lieutenant Hyde had been shot at close quarters in Sulz on 11 August 1944 'while trying to escape'. The trial for murder of Lambert Schneider was discontinued by the Volksgericht in Vienna on 26 January 1948 after the Vienna public prosecutor's office could see no reason for further judicial proceedings. Schneider was sentenced to merely three years' imprisonment on 20 March 1948 for 'illegal activity' for the NSDAP (§§ 10, 11, Prohibition Act). Mildner and Bernauer could not be traced by the Austrian judiciary.[9]

Whereas most of the murders of Allied airmen were initiated or carried out by NS functionaries, the murders of two US airmen on 22 March 1945 were committed by a crowd of people angered by a massive air raid when the men were paraded through Vienna for propaganda purposes; in addition, numerous other US soldiers were maltreated.[10] The Vienna Gestapo does not appear to have been involved.

The hard course of action by the Gestapo against Allied parachutists – members of commando units carrying out military, intelligence and political missions on German territory – was based on an order from Hitler. The 'Commando Order' of 18 October 1942 stated that members of Allied commando operations were to be 'slaughtered' ('niedergemacht', 'mown down') immediately, or after they had been captured.[11] This order was not followed to the letter by the Vienna Gestapo, because – with the agreement of the RSHA – the responsible Section IV 2 headed by Kriminalrat Johann Sanitzer preferred to brutally interrogate the parachutists arrested, on landing or afterwards, and then turn them for *Funkspiele* (disinformation by means of fake radio messages). While the majority of those held in Sanitzer's headquarters on Hasenauerstrasse in the 18th district survived, most of the parachutists, contacts and those providing shelter who were transferred to concentration camps perished.[12]

When four parachutists landed near Schützen im Gebirge in October 1944 as part of the OSS operation 'Dupont' and went into hiding there, the SD informant number 120, gendarmerie post leader Andreas Mikler, notified Heinrich Kunnert, SD chief in Eisenstadt, who 'reported the same day to the SDLA Vienna on the basis of information by the said person and the Gestapo'. The report named those who had sheltered the parachutists before their arrest. On the basis of Kunnert's report, the Vienna Gestapo arrested the four parachutists – US Captain Jack Taylor and three Austrian ex-POWs who had volunteered for service in the US forces, Ernst Unger, Fritz Gertner and Johann Pascher – and their supporters and shelterers in November and December 1944. Josef Prieler, head of Schützen municipal office, who had been told about the OSS mission, was shot by Gestapo official Heinrich Knoth when being arrested, while Unger, Gertner and Pascher were sentenced to death by a military court for 'undermining the war effort' (*Kriegsverrat*), espionage and desertion. They were able to escape, however, before their scheduled execution by firing squad at Döllersheim. Captain Taylor was interrogated at Sanitzer's headquarters and then transferred to Mauthausen where he was fortunate enough to survive. His detailed report written on 30 May 1945 gives an insight into the sophisticated but brutal methods used by Sanitzer against Allied parachutists.[13]

Murders of Resistance Fighters, Mostly on the Basis of Summary Trials

After the fall of Vienna in early April 1945, the Gestapo, now deprived of its headquarters on Morzinplatz, withdrew west without a fight to various decentralized posts in the Reichsgau Lower Danube, and then continued its murderous activities as before.

A large resistance group had formed in 1944 in the Moosbierbaum area consisting of workers from Werk Moosbierbaum (formerly Donau-Chemie), prisoners at the labour camp of the same name (an external unit of Stein prison), foreign workers, POWs and some local farmers. Through the perfidious activity of the Gestapo informant and agent provocateur Walter Ehart (cover name 'Paul Wiesmayer'), an ethnic German from Yugoslavia, over two hundred men and women were arrested in an operation in January 1945 led by Johann Röhrling of the Sankt Pölten Gestapo; from March 1945, between 120 and 140 of them were transferred to Mauthausen. Of these, 47 were gassed on 27 April 1945, shortly before the camp was liberated by US troops. While the Gestapo official Röhrling, born in 1907 and a member of the illegal NSDAP and SS since 1937, was sentenced by the Vienna VG to fifteen years' imprisonment and remained in prison until 1954, the trial of Ehart by Sankt Pölten district court (Kreisgericht) was discontinued in 1957, and he was not deported to Yugoslavia because he had applied for asylum.¹⁴

A large non-aligned resistance group had also formed in Sankt Pölten around deputy police director Otto Kirchl, landowner Graf (Count) Josef Trauttmansdorff and their respective wives Hedwig Kirchl and Gräfin Helena Trauttmansdorff, as well as local farmers, who planned 'sabotage and combat operations as the Russian troops approached'. They were betrayed, and on 9 April 1945 several officials in the Sankt Pölten police and other members of the resistance group were arrested by the Gestapo. Röhrling in particular went about the ensuing interrogations with extreme brutality. Police lieutenant Johann Schuster committed suicide in his cell. On the instruction of Gauleiter Hugo Jury, a summary trial was held on 13 April 1945, at which twelve resistance fighters were sentenced to death for high treason and shot by a Waffen-SS firing squad. Sankt Pölten Gestapo officials supervised the trial, the transport to the execution site and the execution itself.¹⁵

The Gestapo official Rudolf Hitzler, notorious for his brutal maltreatment of prisoners, was transferred in April 1945 to Stein an der Donau together with a fortystrong Sipo EK. While he was there, he tracked down an Austrian resistance group formed at the turn of 1945 around the future Stein mayor Josef Diewald, the doctor Gustav Kullnig and the hairdresser Josef Czeloth. After the brutal interrogation of Kullnig and Czeloth, Hitzler prepared the brief for the summary trial, at which the resistance fighters were sentenced to death; on 15 April 1945, they were executed by firing squad at Stein prison. Therese Diewald, wife of the mayor, who had escaped, was arrested by Hitzler as a member of the family, and was severely maltreated in an attempt to make her reveal her husband's whereabouts.¹⁶

The summary trial of three Wehrmacht soldiers from Gneixendorf POW camp was also 'rigged' in similar fashion by Hitzler. At Stalag (Stammlager, main camp) XVII B Krems-Gneixendorf, where a pro-Austrian resistance group made up of officers and other ranks had been formed, the commandant Hauptmann Franz Schweiger had sent forty guards led by Oberleutnant Kilian and Feldwebel N.N. Zelenka on a march westward to escape the hopeless prospect of combating the approaching Red Army. The plan was betrayed by a Gestapo informant, and the members of the Wehrmacht unit were disarmed and arrested on 17 April 1945 by a Volkssturm unit led by Leo Pilz, organizer of the major massacre at Stein prison on 6 April 1945. Hitzler extracted confessions, and Schweiger, Kilian and Zelenka were sentenced to death on 21 April 1945 by a summary court headed by Oberlandesgerichtsrat Viktor Reindl, and publicly hanged.¹⁷ No further executions were carried out, because members of the EK refused to act, and the Waffen-SS unit meant to replace it was transferred to the front.

A number of further executions by summary courts took place in the Reichsgau Lower Danube in April 1945, carried out by local and regional Nazi functionaries and members of the SS, Wehrmacht and judiciary, but with no evident involvement of the Gestapo.[18]

Murder of Jews and Inmates of Concentration Camps and Prisons

In June 1944, Reichsführer-SS Himmler had already ordered that as the enemy approached, camp inmates should be transferred to concentration camps further away from the front. If this was not possible, they were to be killed. Within the Vienna Gestapo jurisdiction, this order affected Oberlanzendorf AEL, and many inmates were killed when it was being cleared.[19]

The Gestapo was also involved in the massacre of some two hundred Hungarian Jewish forced labourers in Rechnitz (Burgenland) on 25 March 1945. During a party given by Graf (Count) Ivan and Gräfin Margareta Batthyany at Schloss Rechnitz, Franz Podezin, a Gestapo official and local NSDAP group leader who was working with the Rechnitz border police ordered the shooting of around two hundred Hungarian Jewish forced labourers who were too debilitated to work. The atrocity was committed by around ten local members of the NSDAP and other Nazi formations, including Joachim Oldenburg, the estate manager at the castle. Despite intensive searches, most of the corpses still remain undiscovered today. The principal offender, Franz Podezin, was able to flee abroad, allegedly with the assistance of Countess Margareta Batthyany-Thyssen.[20]

The massacre at the end of March 1945 of over one hundred Hungarian Jewish forced labourers in the Slovakian territory of Engerau/Petržalka, which was incorporated into Reichsgau Lower Danube in 1938, was mainly the work of the SA camp guards. Also involved in the crime – although it is no longer possible to determine the extent of their participation – were members of the Vienna Gestapo border police station of Engerau, established at the end of 1944, and led by SS-Untersturmführer Anton Hartgasser. In the trial, Hartgasser was accused by police witnesses of having himself shot inmates who could no longer be transported, at the cemetery in Engerau. The SA man Rudolf Kronberger, one of the principal offenders, who was sentenced to death by the Vienna VG (and executed) in the first Engerau trial in 1945, claimed to have received the liquidation order from Hartgasser. Hartgasser himself stated that the order was given by the Vienna Gestapo official Franz Kleedorfer. The historian Claudia Kuretsidis-Haider, who has been studying the Engerau case for many years, is not convinced by this shifting of blame, and suspects that the SA camp guards were mainly responsible for the mass murder. The trial in

Germany of Hartgasser, who was once again serving in the police force, was discontinued in 1953 on extremely spurious grounds.[21]

The large-scale massacre at Stein prison on 6 April 1945 and the murders in the surrounding area were mainly organized by local Nazi functionaries and carried out by members of the Volkssturm, Wehrmacht, SA, SS and Hitler Youth. In April 1945, the Gestapo unit stationed in Stein, known as 'Kommando Macher' after its leader SS-Hauptsturmführer Karl Macher, was involved in maltreatment of inmates and in extrajudicial executions, at least by cordoning off the area and escorting the victims. In 1949, Macher was acquitted by the Vienna VG of the charge of issuing a liquidation order; even back in 1947, a trial had been discontinued by the public prosecutor's office on the grounds that Macher 'had had to assume that the executions were legal'.[22]

On 28 or 29 March 1945, two days before the arrival of the Red Army in Eisenstadt, the local Gestapo official SS-Oberscharführer Heinrich Scharff, a long-standing NSDAP member, is said to have taken six inmates from detention in the Landhaus – five men and one woman – and shot them in the back of the head. As Scharff died on 20 February 1946, his trial was discontinued, and the underlying facts remained unexplained.[23]

In 1945, a series of further murders and massacres of Hungarian Jewish forced labourers building the Südostwall (a system of fortifications in Burgenland) were committed by local guards without Gestapo involvement.[24]

With the exception of the crimes committed during the forced march of inmates of Oberlanzendorf AEL, the Vienna Gestapo was not among the main perpetrators of end-phase crimes. They were committed for the most part by fanatical local or regional Nazi functionaries, members of various Waffen-SS Jagdkommandos, and (Nazi-oriented) leaders of the Volkssturm, RAD and Südostwall construction works. Members of the Vienna Gestapo headquarters and branch offices nevertheless proceeded with great brutality in their task of combating resistance and all other actual or imagined opponents; in particular, they provided considerable assistance in the numerous trials by summary courts.

Notes

1. The expression 'cumulative radicalization' was coined by the historian Hans Mommsen (with reference to the Holocaust), but also applies to other Nazi crimes, e.g. criminal justice; see Mommsen, *NS-Regime*.
2. This term is said to have been coined by the Dutch penologist C.F. Rüter; see Garscha/Kuretsidis-Haider, 'Rüter-Kategorien', 73–117.
3. Paul, 'Erschießungen', 543–68; Wolfrum, 'Widerstand', 430–46.
4. See the section 'Reinsurance' in Chapter 5, and Chapter 17, this volume.
5. WStLA, Vienna LG, Vg 11g Vr 190/48 (DÖW 21 585), indictment by Vienna Staatsanwaltschaft of Stefan Beiglböck and others, 27 Nov 1947; DÖW, *Widerstand Burgenland*, 336ff.

6. Quoted from *Profil*, 14 Mar 2015, in: http://www.profil.at/history/sadistischer-schlussakkord-endkriegsverbrechen-zweiter-weltkrieg-5556219 (accessed on 23 Aug 2017).
 7. Hoffmann, *Fliegerlynchjustiz*, 383.
 8. Ibid., 148, n. 75, 233–34.
 9. WStLA, Vienna LG, Vg 4c Vr 1300/48 and Vg 12g Vr 3650/47; LG Vienna, 27g Vr 9547/60, report by the Landesgendarmeriekommando für Niederösterreich to the STA Vienna against Lambert Schneider and Bernauer, 20 Nov 1946, testimonies of Johann Sanitzer and Viktor Siegel; ZStL, 110 AR-Z 4/196, vol. 1, sheets 1–180, letter by the Vienna public prosecutor's office, 17 Nov 1960; Hoffmann, *Fliegerlynchjustiz*, 198–99. Hoffmann gives the location as Klausen-Leopoldsdorf.
10. Hoffmann, *Fliegerlynchjustiz*, 226ff.
11. Ibid., 167.
12. Weisz, 'Gestapo-Leitstelle', 925; for Sanitzer's interrogation methods, see the section 'Radicalization, Interrogation and Maltreatment' in Chapter 6, this volume.
13. WStLA, Vienna LG, Vg 4c 202/46, testimony of Johann Sanitzer, 13 Nov 1946; DÖW, *Widerstand Burgenland*, 398ff.; Neugebauer/Schwarz, *Der Wille zum aufrechten Gang*, 128; Lt. Jack Taylor, text of debriefing on 30 May 1945, in https://www.jewishvirtuallibrary.org/the-dupont-mission-october-1944-may 1945 (last accessed on 27 May 2021).
14. BA Berlin, RS 5507, Hans Röhrling; Mitterrutzner, 'Gestapoaktion Moosbierbaum', 460ff; for the operations of Gestapo informants in this area, see Schafranek, *Widerstand und Verrat* (2017), 249–93.
15. DÖW, *Widerstand Niederösterreich*, vol. 3, 310ff, and vol. 2, 516ff; Schafranek, *Widerstand und Verrat* (2017), 279–93.
16. WStLA (copy: DÖW 20 642), Volksgericht Wien Vg 12a 612/46 (DÖW 20 642), judgment against Rudolf Hitzler, 19 Mar 1948; DÖW, *Widerstand Niederösterreich*, vol. 2, 531–32; for informants, see Schafranek, *Widerstand und Verrat* (2017), 274–79.
17. DÖW, *Widerstand Niederösterreich*, vol. 2, 517, 532–33, 620; for more details, see Ferihumer/Garscha, 'Stein-Komplex', 51–82.
18. See, e.g., the execution of three deserters in Amstetten on 3 May 1945 by the summary court of Luftgau-Kommando XVII: Roth, 'Widerstand am Fliegerhorst Markersdorf'; see also Zellhofer, 'NS-Morde'; DÖW, *Widerstand Niederösterreich*, vol. 2, 520–29.
19. See the section 'Evacuation of the Camp' in Chapter 14, this volume.
20. See, e.g., Manoschek, *Der Fall Rechnitz*; Holpfer, 'Der Umgang der Burgenländischen Nachkriegsgesellschaft'; DÖW, *Widerstand Burgenland*, 336ff. The Rechnitz massacre has been the subject of films and plays, by Elfriede Jelinek and others.
21. Kuretsidis-Haider, *'Das Volk sitzt zu Gericht'*, 263ff; telephone conversation with the author on 25 Jan 2015.
22. Ferihumer/Garscha, 'Stein-Komplex', 75–81.
23. WStLA, Vienna LG, Vg 4c 4398/45, charge from Eisenstadt police station to Eisenstadt district court against Heinrich Scharff, 27 Nov 1945; DÖW, *Widerstand Burgenland*, 413–14.
24. DÖW, *Widerstand Burgenland*, 333ff.

Chapter 17

THE END OF THE VIENNA GESTAPO

The imminent collapse of the Nazi regime in Europe and the approaching front in the East also had a significant impact on the Vienna Gestapo. In early December 1944, by order of the RSHA, the Sipo was restructured and all forces concentrated by combining the Gestapo, SD and Kripo into a single unit headed by a commander of the Sipo and SD in Vienna, to which post the RSHA appointed SS-Standartenführer Rudolf Mildner (b. 1902 in Moravia), who had also been active in Austria for a time.[1] Franz Josef Huber, the long-serving Gestapo head who had been 'sick' since Easter 1944, was promoted to become commander-in-chief of the Sipo and SD in Military District XVII – in theory a higher-ranking position, but of lesser importance in practice. In effect, Mildner, who had been deputizing for Huber since July 1944, now replaced Huber as head of the Vienna Gestapo.[2] This restructuring was also formally reflected in the daily reports and the Vienna Gestapo news sheet, both issued from December 1944 by the 'Commander of the Sipo' in Vienna.[3]

To protect the building at Morzinplatz 4 from attack by rebels or Allied units, a defence unit was formed, arms and ammunition stores installed, members of the Gestapo given military training in Bruck an der Leitha, and alarm drills carried out.[4] On 28 March 1945, the supreme head of the Gestapo and commander of the Ersatzheer (reserve army), Reichsführer-SS Heinrich Himmler, inspected the measures and visited the Gestapo headquarters on Morzinplatz for the last time, meeting high-level Nazi, SS and Sipo functionaries there.[5] Neither the Gestapo defence unit nor the regrouped Sanitzer EK were involved in fighting, however, because as the Red Army approached in April 1945, the Vienna Gestapo preferred to beat a hasty retreat (via Floridsdorf to Strebersdorf) without fighting, and to continue to concentrate on fighting the 'enemy within'. The instruction to avoid 'contact with the [actual] enemy' during the 'withdrawal' came from Sipo commander Mildner, who claimed that he did not wish to 'sacrifice his people' for the city of Vienna.⁶

The Vienna Gestapo suffered severely from Allied air raids. On 15 January 1945, the headquarters were hit for the first time, and the rooms on the fourth and fifth floors were heavily damaged. Further hits around 20 March 1945 destroyed large parts of Morzinplatz 4, resulting in the transfer of the remaining files and records to the law courts building at Riemergasse 1, likewise in the city centre. Staff were housed in alternative quarters: for example, the intelligence section was transferred to Rossau barracks, while Unit IV A 2, headed by Johann Sanitzer and responsible for Allied parachutists, was installed at Hasenauerstrasse 61 in the 18th district, the villa of Semperit director Franz Josef Messner, who had been arrested by the Gestapo in March 1944 for high treason.

Before the building and rooms of the Vienna Gestapo were abandoned, from mid-March 1945 the files were moved elsewhere or destroyed, in particular because the Allies had announced severe reprisals against Nazi criminals and so these documents put the Gestapo men in grave danger. The vast majority of the files and records were burned between 3 and 6 April 1945 in the courtyard of the law courts building on Riemergasse and at Schloss Rappoltenkirchen in Lower Austria. The Waffen-SS unit tasked with blowing up the Gestapo headquarters was unable to complete its mission on account of the rapid advance of the Soviet troops. The ruins were finally dynamited by Red Army pioneers after Vienna had been liberated.⁷ In the 1950s, the housing block Leopold Figl-Hof was built on the site; for many years it contained Simon Wiesenthal's office, and since 2011 it has been the venue of a DÖW exhibition dedicated to the victims of the Vienna Gestapo.⁸

The Gestapo headquarters in the former Hotel Metropole was evacuated between 6 and 9 April 1945. The fate of the sixteen hundred or so Gestapo detainees in Viennese prisons was completely uncertain. In 1945, countless inmates from concentration camps, camps and prisons in territories under German rule perished in the course of the many evacuation marches, mostly shot by SS guards when they were no longer able to walk. These victims also included inmates of the Vienna Gestapo-run AEL of Oberlanzendorf, and Jewish and political inmates and detainees were also massacred at Engerau, Rechnitz, Hadersdorf, Stein and other places. It is unclear whether a general order was given to liquidate prisoners of the police and courts scheduled for transport (in the case of contact with the enemy); there is no evidence of one, and that it existed at all is only claimed in defence statements of Gestapo officials to the Austrian authorities.⁹

The original plan of transporting or marching the detainees from Vienna westward towards Mauthausen could not be carried out because of the shortage of guards and the chaotic wartime conditions on the roads. The last detainee transport from Morzinplatz took place on 2 April 1945. By 5 April 1945, forty-five detainees from the Vienna LG prison had been taken to Stein prison,[10] where several hundred inmates – and four prison officers who wanted to free them – were murdered in mass executions on 6 and 15 April 1945. Among these victims were most of the detainees transferred there by the Vienna Gestapo, including eighteen members of the Polish resistance group 'Stragan'.[11] Although Mildner had left a bloody trail behind him in the East, he was reluctant or no longer had the capacity to order the murder of the fifteen hundred detainees remaining in Vienna. While prison inmates held by the judiciary, including future federal chancellor Leopold Figl, were released from 4 April 1945, the Vienna Gestapo leadership forbade the release of its detainees without Mildner's authorization. As those responsible in the police prison feared reprisals by the Gestapo, detainees only began to be released gradually from 6 April, after the Sipo had retreated to Strebersdorf. The last remaining Gestapo detainees were freed by the Red Army by 10 April 1945.[12]

The last major crime by the Gestapo in Vienna was its participation in the execution of the Austrian resistance fighters Major Karl Biedermann, Hauptmann Alfred Huth and Oberleutnant Rudolf Raschke on 8 April 1945 in Floridsdorf. They were members of the military resistance group around Major Carl Szokoll, which wanted to hand the city of Vienna over to the Red Army without a fight (Operation Radetzky). Although the death sentences were pronounced by a summary court, the SS and Gestapo were significantly involved in the tracking down and executions.[13] Around this time, SS-Obersturmbannführer Otto Skorzeny arrived in Vienna and was the driving force behind the harsh measures directed at resistance fighters in the Wehrmacht; Skorzeny was known for his participation in the freeing of Mussolini in 1943 and was head of the SS-Jagdverbände formed in the RSHA in October 1944 for sabotage and secret missions.[14]

After the resistance group had been betrayed by Obergefreiter Erich Roland, Sanitzer's unit arrested the officers and some other ranks, and brutally extracted confessions from them. Skorzeny managed to persuade General Rudolf von Bünau, commander of Vienna's defence, that the three officers should not be shot, as was usual for soldiers, but hanged. Bünau ordered the Gestapo to carry out the executions, and Mildner, Siegel and Sanitzer passed on this order to the Sanitzer EK headed by SS-Untersturmführer Franz Kleedorfer. Kleedorfer, who described himself as the 'bloodhound of Athens', having previously been involved in mass murders in Greece, carried out a gruesome execution with the aid of two assigned Italian POWs. When the rope broke on Hauptmann Huth, Kleedorfer stabbed him twice in the head with his knife before stringing him up again. Skorzeny, Mildner and Sanitzer watched this violence, which was also seen by several eyewitnesses in the surrounding area.[15]

The evacuation of the Gestapo headquarters in Vienna did not by any means signify the end of the Vienna Gestapo terror. The Gestapo offices and EKs retreating westward before the advancing Soviet army continued their repressive activities unabated in the Reichsgau Lower Danube. Under Sipo commander Mildner were around six hundred Kripo, Gestapo and SD officials.[16] In the Krems and Sankt Pölten area in particular, Vienna Gestapo officials, with their brutal methods of interrogation and sophistication in handling informants, provided important assistance in the trials of resistance fighters by Nazi summary courts.[17]

While the Vienna Gestapo continued to hunt, maltreat and murder resistance fighters, deserters, Jews and other enemies until the last days of Nazi rule in May 1945, it played no part in the military 'defence against Bolshevism' ordered by the Nazi leadership. As soon as the situation became dangerous and the front approached, the Gestapo units disbanded. Their members fled west, attempted to hide with forged papers and disguised uniforms, or else allowed themselves to be taken prisoner by the US Army – while at the same time youths were being sent to the slaughter at the front in SS and Volkssturm units. Some top functionaries such as Franz Josef Huber and Karl Ebner had previously made 'reinsurance' arrangements so as to safeguard their survival in defeat.[18] And that is how a criminal organization unique in the history of Vienna came to an end.

Notes

1. WStLA, Vienna LG, Vg 8b Vr 425/46 (DÖW 19 811), 'Professional curriculum vitae' written by Rudolf Mildner in 1936.
2. On the restructuring of the departments and sections, see Chapter 4, this volume; further details in Weisz, 'Gestapo-Leitstelle Wien', 853–54, 858–59, 950ff.
3. DÖW reference library, Vienna Gestapo daily report no. 2 of 8–14 Dec 1944; 'Nachrichtenblatt des Kommandeurs der Sicherheitspolizei in Wien' 3(24), 15 Dec 1944.
4. Weisz, 'Gestapo-Leitstelle Wien', 854.
5. Schirach, *Ich glaubte an Hitler*, 311–12.
6. WStLA, Vienna LG, Vg 8b Vr 425/46 (DÖW 19 811), file annotation, Vienna police headquarters, I/StB, 30 Mar 1947.
7. Weisz, 'Hauptquartier', 264.
8. The Gedenkraum für die Opfer des österreichischen Freiheitskampfes 1938 bis 1945 (memorial room for the victims of the Austrian freedom struggle 1938–45), on Salztorgasse, was installed by victims' associations in 1968. In 2011 the DÖW enlarged the space to include a history of the Gestapo; see DÖW, *Jahrbuch 2012*.
9. Weisz, 'Gestapo-Leitstelle Wien', 947, n. 186, is in 'no doubt' that such a liquidation order existed.
10. Weisz, 'Hauptquartier', 256.
11. For details, see Jagschitz/Neugebauer, *Stein, 6. April 1945*; Neugebauer, *Austrian Resistance*, 248.

12. Weisz, 'Gestapo-Leitstelle Wien', 967ff.; Weisz, 'Hauptquartier', 257; Neider, 'Strafvollzug', 12–13.
13. DÖW 4623, record of the SS summary trial of Hauptmann Alfred Huth and Oberleutnant Rudolf Raschke, 8 Apr 1945; DÖW 6384b, judgment of special summary trial of Major Karl Biedermann, 6 Apr 1945; for Major Biedermann's role as commander of the 'Heeres-Streife Groß-Wien' (i.e. army patrol in the Gau of greater Vienna), see critical comments in Lichtenwagner, *Leerstellen*, 194ff.
14. WStLA, Vienna LG, 27a Vr 7604/61. The trial record does not give a clear indication of Otto Skorzeny's precise role. According to the department head Viktor Siegel, Skorzeny did not have any authority over the Gestapo, but given that he was an SS officer with special authorization from Hitler, this did not prevent him from playing a dominant role. Information on the SS-Jagdverbände and Skorzeny can be found on the extreme right-wing website http://de.metapedia.org/wiki/SS-Jagdverb%C3%A4nde (last accessed on 7 Nov 2017).
15. WStLA, Vienna LG, Vg 11 Vr 5887/48. In this VG trial of Franz Kleedorfer, the facts of the case are described at length and in detail by the defendants and other Gestapo officers, and through the testimony of uninvolved eyewitnesses. According to his superior Johann Sanitzer (16 Mar 1948), disciplinary proceedings had been instigated against Kleedorfer for posing as an SS-Obersturmführer.
16. Weisz, 'Gestapo-Leitstelle Wien', 994ff.
17. See Chapter 16, this volume.
18. See the section 'Reinsurance' in Chapter 5, this volume.

Chapter 18

PROSECUTION OF VIENNA GESTAPO OFFICIALS

Arrests and Administration of Justice by Allied Courts

In 1945, the victorious Allies were all interested in the complete eradication of the National Socialist regime and its organizations and institutions, and in the prosecution of Nazi criminals. It was announced at the Yalta Conference in February 1945: 'We are determined … to wipe out the Nazi Party, Nazi laws, organizations and institutions'.[1] Even before Yalta, a manual had been drafted at the end of 1944 by the Supreme Headquarters Allied Expeditionary Force (SHAEF), the joint headquarters of the armies of the United States and Great Britain operating in Europe, defining the groups of people to be arrested and interned, including 'all officials and other employees of the Gestapo'.[2] The Gestapo officials arrested after the capitulation of the Nazi regime were first interned in camps run by the Allied powers. For example, Othmar Trenker and Viktor Siegel were interned at the US Marcus W. Orr camp in Salzburg, and Karl Ebner at the British camp of Wolfsberg in Carinthia. In the Soviet occupation zone, most of the internees were handed over to the Austrian authorities. As the Allies had already agreed to have Nazi perpetrators tried in the countries where they had committed the crimes, some members of the Austrian Sipo were tried in countries in eastern and south-eastern Europe – Lambert Leutgeb in Yugoslavia and Johann Sanitzer in the Soviet Union, for example. In most cases, Austria did not extradite Nazi perpetrators to other countries, even when applications to that effect were made.

At the Nuremberg trials, the Gestapo and SD as a whole was declared to be a criminal organization on account of the numerous crimes (extermination of the Jews, murders in concentration camps, killing and maltreatment of forced labourers and POWs), setting international standards in this way.[3]

After their arrest, the Vienna Gestapo heads Franz Josef Huber and Rudolf Mildner were transferred to the US camp at Nuremberg-Langwasser. Whereas Mildner escaped from the camp and fled to Argentina after testifying before the International Military Tribunal in Nuremberg, Huber was protected because of the US interest in his expert knowledge, and he was therefore able to await the hearings without too many worries. Although on terms of confidence with Heydrich and Müller, he claimed (when questioned by Robert M.W. Kempner on 9 February 1948)[4] to have been informed about the deportation of Jews only at 'the end of August 1944' by Ebner – his 'deputy, who dealt with Jewish affairs insofar as they involved the Gestapo'. Huber's brazen cynicism comes through clearly in the record of the questioning:

Kempner:	What did you know about the elimination of the Jews? What were you in 1942?
Huber:	In 1942 I was inspector of the security police in Vienna and head of the Vienna Gestapo.
Kempner:	Now, the Jews were rounded up from Vienna.
Huber:	In Austria there was a central office for the Jewish emigration [sic], which was not under my command.
Kempner:	The Jews were taken away.
Huber:	They were sent to the East. I cannot tell you how many. Near Riga. They were ordered to work for the Wehrmacht. As far as I recall, postcards from Jews were sent from there to Vienna.
Kempner:	Did you believe that was really the case?
Huber:	Yes.
Kempner:	Did you ever hear that they were being exterminated?
Huber:	Yes.
Kempner:	When was this?
Huber:	Possibly at the end of 1944.

While at the camp in Wolfsberg, Ebner composed a dense twenty-page dossier typed with single-spaced lines which was to work fatefully against him in his later trial before the Volksgericht (VG) in Vienna. Rudolf Merkel, the Gestapo defence counsel at the Nuremberg trials, had turned to Ebner as the 'highest-ranking and most senior [Vienna Gestapo] official available after 1945'. Merkel was collecting arguments for his ultimately unsuccessful defence strategy, and sought the advice of experienced jurists who had been in the Gestapo. Ebner wrote pages about the Vienna Gestapo's personnel and organization structures, but as former head of the 'Jewish section' did not forget to shift the entire blame to the central office for Jewish emigration. He wrote that for the deportation of

Vienna's Jewish population, the central office 'was superior to the Gestapo' and 'could avail itself of the Gestapo's services at any time for its purpose'.[5]

Trenker and Siegel in the Marcus W. Orr camp prepared a written statement at Merkel's behest. Entitled 'Reply to the charge against the Gestapo', it was more official than Ebner's dossier, and the authors described themselves as 'authorized representatives of former Gestapo officials'. The statement systematically denied that the Gestapo was guilty of or bore any responsibility for crimes in the Nazi regime, particularly the deportation and murder of the Jewish population. The Gestapo was described as a 'police service under public law', whose officials were 'seconded' to it from the Austrian police and gendarmerie, just like, for example, 'railway or post office officials'. The authors pointed out that, in contrast to Germany, 'where Hitler came to power legally, all Austrian governments from 1933 to 1938 … were illegal'; the concentration camps were also 'not invented by the Gestapo but were institutions of a legitimate government', and 'the torture supposedly carried out by the Gestapo was grossly misrepresented'. The central defence strategy related to the 'accusation of murdering hundreds of thousands of Jews in concentration camps'. It was later to become part of the standard repertoire of all Gestapo defendants: 'Only the central office for Jewish emigration was entitled to evacuate the Jews. … When Jews were transferred to concentration camps, it was not the action of an individual Gestapo official but a response to central instructions from a legitimate government'.[6]

All former Vienna Gestapo officials having to explain their involvement in the deportation of Vienna's Jewish population to an Austrian Volksgericht resorted to this defence strategy: the planning, organization and carrying out of the deportations were the sole responsibility of the central office, which received its orders directly from the RSHA in Berlin, and the Gestapo and Kripo only performed occasional auxiliary policing services on the instructions of the central office.[7] In assessing the truthfulness of these statements, it should not be forgotten that in view of the death sentence demanded by the prosecution, a defendant such as the former head of the 'Jewish section' was literally talking to save his neck.

Police Arrests of Nazi Functionaries and Perpetrators in Vienna in 1945

Already on 8 May 1945, while the fighting was still going on in Austria, the provisional government under Karl Renner passed a constitutional law to inaugurate measures against the NSDAP and the prosecution of Nazi crimes.[8] 'While the cities were still in ruins and the memory above all of Nazi massacres taking place before the eyes of the population was still fresh, ostracization and stigmatization of the Nazis was thoroughly popular.'[9] On 26 June 1945 the Prohibition Act was supplemented by the War Criminals Act (KVG), creating an irrefutable legal basis for prosecuting Nazi crimes.[10] The aim was clearly to demonstrate to the world that Austria was making a determined and decisive contribution to the rapid elimination of the ideological and organizational basis of the Nazi regime, and to the prosecution of the crimes of its supporters.

Because of the particular situation at the end of the war – extensive authority held by the occupying powers, difficulty in rebuilding the administration and judiciary after the collapse of the Nazi regime – the initial prosecution of regime supporters was carried out not by the judiciary, which had not yet been restored, but by the Vienna police force, already established in April 1945. In Vienna, which was occupied first by the Soviets (the Western Allied forces did not arrive until 1 September 1945), the police began arresting Nazis immediately after the liberation of the city. On 17 April 1945 the Soviet commandant Lieutenant-General Alexei Blagodatov ordered the establishment of an 'auxiliary police service [Polizeilicher Hilfsdienst] for the headquarters of the commandant of the city of Vienna'. This institution of the Soviet occupying power was staffed by Austrians and it operated until the restoration of the Bundespolizeidirektion Wien (Vienna federal police headquarters) on 17 June 1945. It was headed by the Communist anti-Fascist Rudolf Hautmann, who thus acted as Vienna's chief of police. This police unit contained a considerable number of Communists, including former concentration camp inmates, partisans and Spanish Civil War and resistance fighters. On 25 April 1945 the Fahndungsdienst (investigation department), the forerunner of the Staatspolizeiliches Büro (state police bureau), was created to investigate, identify and track down active National Socialists, in coordination with the Soviet regional commandant's headquarters.[11] On 28 May 1945, Hautmann ordered the arrest of 'Nazi holders of public office, leading Nazis, SS men, SA men, Gestapo officials, and informants and denouncers. Simple [NSDAP] members who are loyal [to the new authorities] are to be left alone'. According to Hautmann, 2,000 suspected Nazis had been arrested by the end of May 1945;[12] others put the figure at 5,500. Most of the arrestees were detained at the police prison on Rossauer Lände; in addition, there were twelve temporary camps for Nazi internees in greater Vienna.[13]

Under § 14 of the Public Authorities Transfer Act (Behörden-Überleitungsgesetz) of 20 July 1945, the Gestapo and its offices were disbanded, but the infelicitous wording stated that insofar as the Gestapo's 'affairs were being continued, [they] ... would be conducted by the security service with substantive and local authority'.[14] It was not until the constitutional law of 13 December 1945 that this wording was changed so that police work could be carried out only in the service of the judiciary.[15]

The regular police took over 6,500 members of the auxiliary police service, of whom a significant number were soon discharged. On 13 June 1945, the Communist Spanish Civil War fighter and concentration camp inmate Heinrich Dürmayer became chief of the state police (official title: head of Department I of the Vienna police). Other top positions were also occupied by members of the KPÖ. These officials, most of whom had a resistance and partisan background or had been interned in concentration camps, had strong personal reasons for prosecuting Nazi criminals, particularly Gestapo officials: 'A central task and one of the greatest achievements of Dürmayer's State Police', wrote the historian Hans Hautmann, 'was the investigation and tracking down of Nazi criminals and the securing of evidence (Nazi card files and records, 'Aryanization' files, etc.)'. For this purpose, a state police department was created in the VGs, which liaised with the public prosecutor's office.[16] The documents and secured original Gestapo files collected by the Vienna police, including the organizational chart of the Vienna Gestapo with the names of officials working in the different departments, sections and units, were of great assistance to the authors of the present book.[17]

In November 1945 there were 1,340 Nazis in the work and detention camps, some of whom were soon released because of the triviality of the offences or for lack of evidence. The rest were transferred to the Allies or to the Austrian VGs for sentencing. In this way, the numbers had dwindled to 590 at the end of 1945 and 418 in January 1946.[18] During 1946 the police arrested a further 1,370 Nazi criminals, 1,161 of whom were handed over to the courts. By 31 December 1946 there were only thirty-five inmates, after which the work and detention camps run by Department I of the Vienna police were closed.[19] In an increasingly anti-Communist climate, Dürmayer was relieved of his duties by minister of the interior Oskar Helmer, and transferred to Salzburg, to be replaced by the police lawyer Oswald Peterlunger, who had been interned by the Nazi regime in 1938 and dismissed from the civil service in 1939.

Despite this, the police continued to carry out extensive and valuable investigations for the VGs, leading to the conviction of Gestapo officials. Every two weeks the police compiled wanted lists, on the basis of which the Austrian government published four lists of war criminals. A special commission was founded for that purpose, consisting of police and ministerial officials, judges and public prosecutors.[20]

Austria's People's Courts (VGs), 1945–55

Heavily incriminated former officials of the Vienna Gestapo appeared before Austrian Volksgerichte (People's Courts, VGs) established on the basis of the KVG of 26 June 1945. The VGs had the status of special panels of criminal judges, and were involved in prosecuting Nazi crimes from 1945 to 1955. The Vienna VG started working from August 1945. The name 'Volksgericht' – deliberately chosen as being similar to the Nazi term 'Volksgerichtshof' (VGH), and sometimes even confused with it – was meant to signal that the Nazi perpetrators would be punished with the same severity as former opponents of the National Socialists had been by the terrifying VGH. VGs were established on the premises of the Oberlandesgerichte (higher regional courts) of Vienna, Linz, Graz and Innsbruck. The officials of the Vienna Gestapo were tried before the 'Landesgericht für Strafsachen Wien als Volksgericht' (Vienna regional criminal court as Volksgericht).

The VGs had three lay judges and two career judges, one of whom was the presiding judge. Legal remedies such as appeals and nullifications were suspended, leading them to be disparaged as 'Standgerichte' (summary courts) by the defendants. The severe shortage of personnel was a problem, because over fifteen hundred judges and public prosecutors were regarded as incriminated on account of their activity under the Nazi regime. In early 1948, trials of Nazi perpetrators in Vienna were being conducted by seven panels of judges daily, which accounted for half of the entire judiciary. Between 1945 and 1955, preliminary investigations were initiated in 139,829 cases, charges were brought in 28,148, and sentences pronounced in 23,477. There were 13,607 convictions, including 43 death sentences, 30 of which were carried out.[21]

The four war criminal lists drawn up by the police and courts were particularly important for identifying perpetrators in Austria. On the first list, published on 4 December 1945, there were eighty-three names.[22] Apart from Kaltenbrunner, Seyß-Inquart, von Schirach, Globocnik, Brunner I, Brunner II, Portschy and Eigruber, there were also four leading protagonists of the Vienna Gestapo – Franz Josef Huber, Karl Ebner, Othmar Trnka [Trenker] and Rudolf Mildner – along with Christian Nicoll 'for severe maltreatment of detainees' and Rudolf Hitzler 'for most severe maltreatment of numerous detainees'. In the second list,[23] there were thirteen Vienna Gestapo officials among the fifty-five wanted persons, including the Gestapo officials Ferdinand Schmidt, 'Gestapo head, major Aryanizer'; Josef Auinger 'for brutal persecution of political opponents in March 1938 in Vienna'; Johann Rixinger 'for deportation of Jews [and] seizure of and self-enrichment with Jewish assets'; Lambert Leutgeb, 'the leading agent provocateur in the Vienna Gestapo intelligence service'; and Johann Sanitzer 'for brutal persecution of the resistance movement and involvement in the execution of Major Biedermann'.[24]

Other Vienna Gestapo officials wanted for arrest were: Adolf Anderle 'for brutal suppression of the Vienna resistance movement'; Franz Gerstl 'for participation in the shooting of forty-six inmates of Stein prison'; Josef Handl 'for most severe maltreatment of detainees'; Erwin Linauer 'for the murder of inmates at Stein prison by shooting in the back of the head'; Emil Marchart 'for incitement to murder around three hundred Wehrmacht members and foreigners ... at Stein prison by shooting in the back of the head'; Anton Perger 'for most severe maltreatment of political detainees'; Karl Prieler 'a leading figure in the July revolt of 1934'; and Eduard Tucek 'for the execution of three Wehrmacht members by hanging on the main square in Krems'.

The VG and the Vienna public prosecutor's office showed considerable vigour and determination in prosecuting officials of the Vienna Gestapo – at least in the initial years after 1945. The assistance of the population was sought in rooting out Gestapo officials. A composite file entitled 'UT Gestapo' – UT standing for 'Unbekannte Täter' (unknown offenders) – was compiled with a view to systematically registering and identifying Gestapo officials, and it included photos of as many of the suspects – around a thousand in all – as possible.[25] These photos and the accompanying information were formed into a public exhibition with the confusing title 'Tausend Gestapohelfer gesucht' (Wanted: 1,000 Gestapo helpers) from 7 to 21 September 1947 at the Vienna LG (the 'Graues Haus'). The idea was to enable everyone who had had contact with Gestapo officials in Vienna to identify individuals. As the rooms in the former headquarters had neither inscriptions nor nameplates, a model of the building on Morzinplatz was created on the basis of original plans. It was intended to help those who had come to inspect the photos to get their bearings, and thus to identify individuals.[26] Thanks to these efforts and intensive investigations, many important Gestapo officials, including Karl Ebner, Othmar Trenker, Viktor Siegel and Johann Sanitzer, were brought to trial and convicted in the following years.

The work of the judiciary at the time faced considerable difficulties. Little research had been carried out, and there was sparse knowledge of the full extent of the Nazi crimes in Europe or the structure of Nazi repression. Moreover, the destruction of files in March–April 1945 meant that incriminating written material was hard to come by. The former Gestapo members appearing as witnesses generally spoke in each other's defence, and potential witnesses for the prosecution – the Gestapo's victims – had in many cases been either killed or forced to flee. Even when victims were present, they were often treated unfairly by the defence lawyers so as to undermine their credibility. In particular, the crimes committed in other countries were difficult to prove and were not generally pursued. The paucity of evidence regarding particularly serious crimes such as mass murder meant that the less serious crime – as it would appear today – of 'illegality' (i.e. membership of and involvement with the prohibited Nazi movement between 1933 and 1938) was assigned a disproportionately high level of importance in VG trials and sentencing.[27]

After the Austrian judiciary's intensive prosecution of Nazi crimes in 1946 and 1947, the number of convictions dropped considerably. With the start of the Cold War, the Allies eased their pressure on the VGs and their sentencing practice. The at times dramatic events in connection with the trial of Ebner, both in the courtroom and in public, were a clear indication of the ambivalent attitude towards the VGs and their verdicts that was beginning to form. There were fierce criticisms of the VGs in parliament and some of the media, and calls for the VGs to be closed and for a line to be drawn under the whole business. Although the fateful utterance by Minister of the Interior Oskar Helmer, 'I am in favour of drawing matters out',[28] referred to the restitution of looted Jewish property, it can also be applied to the diminishing willingness of the judiciary to pronounce rapid judgments on Nazi perpetrators. There was already an unashamed movement to quietly reintegrate former Nazis into society so as to gain their votes. This development was also to the advantage of former Vienna Gestapo staff.

The following sections feature some selected cases in order to illustrate the judicial prosecution of Vienna Gestapo officials in the first years after the war.

Franz Josef Huber and the Protecting Hand of the US Secret Service

On 29 April 1948 the camp jurisdiction at the US internment camp in Nuremberg-Langwasser asked the Vienna police headquarters to 'conduct an urgent … and intensive investigation of the activities of [Huber in Vienna] … between 1938 and 1945 … and to send details of the investigation results as soon as possible'.[29] Not until 31 August 1948 did the Vienna police send information from Huber's Gau file, with only an extremely sparse 'investigation report' containing personal statements by just one former Gestapo official and the commandant of the Vienna Gestapo in-house guard. Huber was released by the Americans a short time afterwards, and the court of cassation in Munich took over the task of asking the Austrian authorities for information about Huber's work in Vienna. On 14 December 1948 it determined that 'in spite of several requests to provide the required details … the Austrian authorities have not yet sent any material about Huber'. This had an impact on the trial to the extent that, as was explicitly noted in the grounds for the verdict of 13 January 1949, only the incriminating material seen by the court about Huber's activity in Vienna could be taken into account in the proceedings; furthermore, 'although the public prosecutor had requested further information from Vienna on 28 July, 4 October and 16 November 1948, no answer had been received, much less a request by the government for extradition.[30] The court therefore refrained from taking account of this point [Huber's activities in Vienna] as an incriminating consideration in the judgment against the defendant'.

The judgment delivered by the 'Spruchkammer Nürnberg, Sitzgruppe Garmisch' stated: 'The defendant is classified in group III, "lesser offenders" [Minderbelastete]. He is sentenced to one year's probation … No special labour is ordered ... A single payment of DM 500 to the reparation fund is ordered'. It is questionable whether incriminating material from Vienna would have affected the sentence. Captain Haig, 301 Military Intelligence Co APO 403 US Army, testified that 'in investigations concerning individuals active in Austria ... he had received good information about Huber's activities ... He fulfilled his police duties as fairly and justly as possible'.

On 2 February 1949, the public prosecutor filed an appeal with the court of cassation in Munich. Seven days later, Austria issued an arrest warrant for Huber and requested his extradition. The ministry of justice sent records of the questioning of Ebner, Trenker and Sanitzer, and mentioned in a letter that 'the legal department of the American headquarters in Vienna has been asked repeatedly to arrange for Huber's extradition to Austria'. Huber did not appear at the appeal hearing, having 'cut off links with his family and was on the run'. The initial verdict was reversed, and he was classified as a major offender (*Hauptschuldiger*) and sentenced in his absence to five years in a work camp. The grounds referred explicitly to the fact that 'material that seriously incriminated him had been obtained from Vienna, his former duty station'.

In a clemency appeal of 17 December 1951, Huber's counsel stated that he had disappeared because of the extradition request by the Austrian government: 'It is understandable that the defendant should fear falling into the hands of the Russians, as his former department head ... Sanitzer ... had been released by the Russians from prison, and works today for the Volkspolizei [of the GDR]'.[31] After the arrest warrant for Huber was withdrawn on 6 September 1954, the case was reopened and the verdict of the appeal court rescinded.

The grounds for the rescission verdict largely exonerate one of the central figures in the Nazi terror in Austria: 'Apart from his long membership of the Gestapo, his career, in spite of the extremely rapid rise, was that of a particularly hardworking police officer ... The court reached the conclusion that this brilliant career was the result not of membership of the party but primarily of the defendant's expert skills'. Until his retirement, the man who for almost seven years had headed the largest Gestapo regional headquarters in the entire German Reich was apparently the warehouse bookkeeper for an office machine company in Munich. However, the US secret service's interest in Huber had continued in the background. He was recruited by the Bundesnachrichtendienst (BND) in Pullach, from 1956 the successor to the Gehlen organization, which was full of former members of the SS, SD and Sipo – in some cases, highly incriminated ones. Following the release of classified BND documents, it has transpired that Huber was a 'full-time member with a fixed salary and department head of the BND from 1 April 1957'.[32] Under political pressure, the possible Nazi past of BND members was reviewed in 1963, and Huber was suspended and ultimately retired on 31 July 1967.

Karl Ebner – 'Grey Eminence' or 'Angel of Morzinplatz'?

Ebner was handed over to the Austrian authorities by the British occupying powers on 20 February 1947 and transferred to the Vienna LG, where his trial by the VG began on 6 December 1948.[33] It was accompanied by a political scandal and media spectacle indicative of the by now ambivalent attitude to the VGs and their verdicts. A few days previously, Othmar Trenker, former head of the Vienna Gestapo department responsible for the left-wing movement, had been sentenced to a mere eighteen months' imprisonment, for 'illegality',[34] which further stoked up the atmosphere before Ebner's trial.

Ebner was charged not only with illegal NSDAP and SS membership before the annexation, but also and above all with having functioned as Huber's deputy and as head of the department (Group IV B) that included the 'Jewish section'. While the International Military Tribunal in Nuremberg left undefined the function of 'deputy Gestapo head', all 'leading officials of the Gestapo or SD from department head upwards who did not have exclusively administrative functions' were threatened with the death sentence.[35] Still without knowledge of the nature of the charge against the Gestapo, Ebner unwittingly wrote his own (potential) death sentence in the Wolfsberg dossier referred to earlier: 'In early 1942 [various] sections were divided up amongst three departments: Department IV A (Left-wing movements) headed by Dr Trenker; Department IV B (Ideological opponents) headed by Dr Ebner; and Department IV C headed by Dr Siegel'.[36]

As the function of 'deputy Gestapo head' was not mentioned in the Austrian KVG either,[37] the charge would have had to focus on proving Ebner's function as a 'department head'. Public prosecutor Wolfgang Laßmann determined instead that the Gestapo did not have any department heads, and that the 'group headed at the time by Dr Ebner ... was not an independent department and is not regarded as such by the prosecution'.[38] Laßmann did not even address the question of whether the responsibility of the permanent deputy head should possibly be considered greater than that of a department head.

Laßmann, who had already been more of a defence counsel than a prosecutor in Trenker's trial, then got into a war of words with the presiding judge. The issue was so serious that, with much media coverage, Laßmann was recalled, another public prosecutor appointed and, on the initiative of the Allied Council, twelve representatives of the occupying powers were seconded to the main proceedings as observers.[39]

The trial focused on the testimony of twenty-three witnesses, nineteen of whom spoke in Ebner's defence, including high clergymen such as the prelates Josef Wagner and Jakob Fried, and above all members of the Austrian Cartellverband (union of Catholic university fraternities for students and graduates, CV). In addition, a number of testimonies, including those of prominent personalities such as the actor Hans Moser and the conductor Josef Krips, were read out, which – with few exceptions – also served to exonerate Ebner. Ebner's strategy of carefully orchestrated reinsurance had proved highly successful.⁴⁰

In his closing statement, the new public prosecutor concentrated on proving that as deputy Gestapo head, Ebner had occupied a position superior to a department head. He called for conviction according to § 3/3 KVG (Torture and maltreatment) and the death sentence. He also demanded conviction under § 34 of the Penal Code, 'because the accused will also be convicted of illegality'. The charge pursuant to § 5 KVG (Participation in the expulsion of Vienna's Jews), on account of Ebner's involvement in the looting and deportation of the Jewish population of Vienna, had already been dropped before the start of the trial. In his emotional closing statement, Ebner's defence counsel called for acquittal of the charge under § 3/3 KVG: 'Not all Gestapo officials were inhuman and criminal. There were also those who felt and acted with humanity ... The VG is asked to treat his case as a special one, and to let the heart speak, as he [Ebner] often did himself'.⁴¹

On 11 December 1948, Ebner was sentenced to twenty years' imprisonment after allowance had been made for his time in camp internment and pre-trial custody. The sentence that saved Ebner from the death penalty read: 'The court was unanimously agreed that the fact that the defendant saved the lives of many people made him into a case worthy of special consideration, and justified his being spared the death penalty. However, in view of the large number of victims of the methods employed by the Gestapo, of which he was a leading official, the sentence of twenty years is deemed a reasonable atonement'.⁴²

After he was pardoned by the federal president in 1953, Ebner was initially unemployed. He received a small civil service pension and worked as a caretaker in a subsidiary firm of the Creditanstalt bank. His academic title, which had been revoked, was restored in the 1960s.⁴³

Othmar Trenker, Jurist with Qualification as a Thug

On 15 January 1947, Othmar Trenker (formerly Trnka)⁴⁴ was transferred by the US authorities from the Marcus W. Orr internment camp to the Vienna LG, where his trial before the VG started on 1 December 1948.⁴⁵ Like Ebner after him, he was charged as an 'illegal' under §§ 10, 11 and under § 3 KVG. As a Gestapo 'department head', he also came under the definition of the Nuremberg tribunal, with the possibility of being sentenced to death for collective responsibility.⁴⁶

From the outset, Trenker, who made no statement about his Gestapo functions in the run-up to the trial, pursued a strategy of denying an official appointment as department head. After evidence was presented (and confirmed in writing by Ebner) that he was appointed head of the department named Group IV A (Combating opponents) in May 1942, he claimed in court that the 'real' department head was Huber, who at that time in fact performed mainly representative functions. Furthermore, under the last GVP of 1944–45, Trenker was a genuine 'department head' as he was in charge of Department IV, and at the same time head of Section IV 1 (Opposition).[47]

Prosecutor Laßmann, who – as in the subsequent trial of Ebner – was more of a defence counsel than a prosecutor, 'summoned only a few prosecution witnesses, and confused them with leading questions'.[48] Trenker also had the support of a series of witnesses in his defence, including prominent personalities such as the former and present Vienna mayors, Karl Seitz and Theodor Körner. Trenker too had 'saved others in order to save himself', using his leading position in good time to provide himself with personal reinsurance. Trenker's defence counsel even went as far as stating that 'his client Dr Trenker and his colleague Dr Ebner were the true "angels of the Gestapo"'.[49]

Trenker was then sentenced to a mere eighteen months' imprisonment, for 'illegality', but with allowance for the time already spent in prison he was released from custody. The critical charge under § 3 KVG (Torture and maltreatment) was dropped, although prosecution witnesses accused him of having personally used violence. The verdict gave rise to fierce media criticism and debates in parliament, which were further fuelled by the leniency of the sentence compared with the sentence imposed a short time afterwards on Ebner.

On 16 December 1948, the public prosecutor's office applied for the case to be reopened under § 3/1 KVG. Trenker was arrested two days later, and charged on 8 July 1949 with, 'as a senior official, passing on [responsibility for] approval of enhanced interrogations to higher offices but, on the other hand, also of actively taking part himself in enhanced interrogations'.[50] The question dealt with intensively in Ebner's trial as to whether he had been a department head was also taken up again.

In the second trial beginning on 2 October 1949, several witnesses once again spoke in Trenker's defence, but this time there were also Gestapo arrestees who reported having been maltreated by Trenker in person. Trenker denied both his active participation in torture and his function as department head. He was nevertheless sentenced to five years' imprisonment on 22 October 1949 under § 3/1 KVG for ordering 'enhanced interrogation' and for personal maltreatment of Gestapo arrestees. As for the critical charge under § 3/3 KVG regarding his position as a Gestapo department head, he was once again acquitted in accordance with *in dubio pro reo* (in doubt, for the accused): the 'VG was not entirely satisfied that the accused had actually been a department head, even if there remain grounds of varying degrees of seriousness for suspecting this was the case'.[51]

This verdict was also criticized in some sectors of public opinion as being too lenient in comparison with Ebner's sentence of twenty years' imprisonment. It is striking that in both cases the court was hesitant to apply § 3/3 KVG and the concept of collective responsibility with its demand for the death penalty. Ebner too was not convicted for his function as department head, which he himself admitted, but as deputy Gestapo head. The Nuremberg tribunal had not defined any particular punishment for the latter function as it was by definition at a higher hierarchical level than a department head.

Trenker was released from prison on probation in 1950, and after the amnesty in 1957 he received a civil service pension, with his time in the Vienna Gestapo from 1938 to 1945 being counted towards it.[52]

Karl Silberbauer and the Long Arm of the Law

There are two striking features connected with the case of Karl Silberbauer. First is the degree of international attention paid to an otherwise inconspicuous Vienna Gestapo Kriminalsekretär, who through an accident of history happened to be in charge of the arrest of Anne Frank and her family in Amsterdam on 4 August 1944. Second is the intensity of the judicial prosecution of Nazi perpetrators still in evidence in the early post-war years – even if, as in Silberbauer's case, the charge was based on few and conflicting testimonies, and ultimately resulted in acquittal.

Silberbauer returned to Vienna in April 1945 from his posting to the SD office in Amsterdam. He was arrested by the Soviet secret police on 8 May and handed over to the Austrian police. He was accused by three witnesses of having maltreated them during interrogations at the Vienna headquarters by punching, slapping and 'strangling with a chain'. On 30 June 1945, however, he was released from detention. After one of the three witnesses produced new evidence, Silberbauer was arrested again on 13 September 1945 but released once again five days later. Following a statement by one of the other three witnesses with new information about maltreatment, Silberbauer was arrested yet again on 2 October 1945. In the subsequent trial before the Vienna VG he was charged under § 11 VG ('Illegality') and § 3 KVG ('Torture and maltreatment'). He relativized his 'illegality' with the usual reference to the 'backdating' of his membership to before 1938, although he had in fact confirmed his status as an NSDAP 'Alter Kämpfer'. With the arguments 'I wasn't in the SS: the SD is now incorrectly equated with the SS' and 'The SD was a voluntary activity ... we only played football and handball', he was clearly counting on the court being entirely ignorant about these matters.

After joining the Vienna Gestapo in 1942, Silberbauer had worked in Section IV A 1 (Communism, Marxism) before being transferred on 10 November

1943 to the BdSuSD The Hague (to work for the Kripo in Amsterdam). Before 1938, as a Kripo official in Favoriten (10th district), he had been involved in the suppression of left-wing opposition, and he now claimed that the prosecution witnesses were hostile to him because they were former Communists. In his defence, Kripo colleagues and also people interrogated by Silberbauer emphasized above all his proper conception of duty. In spite of incriminating documents, Silberbauer was acquitted of 'illegality' on 13 July 1946, but sentenced to one year's imprisonment under § 3 KVG, which he served until his release on 1 July 1947.[53] After Silberbauer applied in 1952 for the case to be reopened to obtain compensation for his time in prison, the verdict in the first trial was reversed in a new hearing before the Vienna VG on 22 January 1954, and Silberbauer was acquitted. Compensation for the time served was refused because the acquittal had only been pronounced on account of a lack of evidence.[54] The arrest of the Frank family in Amsterdam was not an issue in these trials.

On 15 November 1963, Simon Wiesenthal informed the Austrian ministry of the interior that he had found the name Silberbauer in an Amsterdam telephone book of Section IV A 4 (Personal surveillance) of the BdSuSD Holland. He had mistakenly been sought in the Netherlands under the name 'Silbernagel'. Silberbauer, who had rejoined the Vienna police in 1954, was suspended from duty and charged, but the case was dropped in 1964 on the grounds that Silberbauer had merely been carrying out an order. Anne Frank's father Otto also later confirmed that, in his official capacity, Silberbauer had acted properly.[55]

Anton Brödl, Abnormal Criminal or Simulator?

The former metalworker and professional musician Anton Brödl, who held the rank of Kriminalsekretär and SS-Scharführer, was one of the most brutal thugs in the Vienna Gestapo. Testimonies described him as violent-tempered and irascible, and also devious, sometimes starting interrogations by pretending to be a Gestapo arrestee or, more specifically, a member of a resistance group. He was notable for his extreme violence towards women, as in the case of Rosa Grossmann, who jumped down the stairwell from the fourth floor of the Gestapo building in an attempt to avoid further maltreatment, but survived.[56]

Brödl gave himself up and was remanded in custody on 8 January 1947. After thirteen witnesses had been summoned, he was charged under § 11 ('Illegality'), in conjunction with § 8 VG ('Registration fraud'), and under § 3 ('Torture and maltreatment') and § 4 KVG ('Crimes against humanity and human dignity'). When questioned on 17 February 1947, Brödl admitted being an NSDAP 'Alter Kämpfer' with the Ostmark medal, and pleaded guilty to the charges of illegality, maltreatment and crimes against humanity.[57]

After the charges were brought, seventeen witnesses were summoned, including Brödl's superior Johann Sanitzer, most of whom strongly incriminated him. Josef Sasso and Rupert Grissinger testified to having suffered 'severe' and 'brutal' maltreatment at Brödl's hands.[58] As Sanitzer's former right-hand man in Section IV A 2 (Sabotage and parachutists), Brödl claimed that he had been carrying out orders, and attempted to justify the use of torture by arguing that information extracted from agents prevented targeted enemy air raids, or at least reduced their severity.

Brödl was not brought to trial, however, as a psychiatric assessment at the end of 1947 stated that he was not fit to face trial, and he was transferred to Steinhof psychiatric hospital on 2 June 1948 on account of 'paranoid depression … as a form of prison psychosis'. At the end of November 1948 his defence counsel applied to the Vienna LG for Brödl's release, as he would otherwise be 'confined for life in Steinhof', which was worse than life imprisonment. He included a list of witnesses in his defence, and mentioned 'fifteen to twenty' priests for whom his client had intervened through personal contact with Cardinal Innitzer. In March 1950, however, the application for release was refused because Brödl 'was suspected and accused of an offence carrying the death penalty'.

On 18 March 1950, Brödl wrote a 'blackmail letter' from Steinhof to the minister of justice, Otto Tschadek, evidently with the intention of having the case dropped on account of insanity. He threatened to take the police president and his family hostage with his '5,000-strong combat and sabotage group … without consideration for life or property', and demanded compensation for imprisonment in Swiss gold francs. Even before then, Brödl had urged Karl Renner, Leopold Figl and other politicians 'to do everything to settle my demand [to Tschadek] as rapidly as possible', because 'as a virtuoso violinist … I am currently preparing for a concert tour'.

Shortly afterwards, a medical assessment came to the conclusion that Brödl had not been 'mentally disordered' during his time in the Gestapo and that his condition only 'started to develop … after 1947'. Another psychiatric assessment on 28 January 1951 stated that Brödl was not mentally ill but that he was still not fit to face trial on account of a psychopathic 'querulous paranoia'. On 7 February 1951 the Vienna LG finally revoked the court detention, and on 14 December 1951 he was 'legally incapacitated on account of mental illness' by the Vienna city centre district court. The defence counsel's request for the case to be dropped was rejected by the public prosecutor's office in Vienna, however, and a new health examination ordered.

Brödl was 'given leave of absence' four times from Steinhof, and temporarily readmitted every six months. When he was finally discharged on 7 September 1954, after almost six years, he worked as a sales representative. A test on 21 June 1955 stated that he had 'good intellectual capacities, [and] no signs of insanity'. In October 1955, in an assessment conducted by the medical faculty of Vienna University, Brödl was diagnosed with chronic mental illness with systematic delusional ideas (paranoia), and the report recommended 'permanent confinement ... of this extremely dangerous mental patient'. Following a request for pardon by his wife to Federal President Adolf Schärf so as to put an end to the case, Brödl's prosecution was lifted by way of a decision of the Vienna LG of 12 November 1957 (under the Nazi amnesty of 1957).[59]

In view of the diverging psychiatric assessments, it is not possible to determine whether Anton Brödl was a 'mentally abnormal criminal' or whether he simulated a mental illness to escape the threatened death penalty. One way or the other, this was how one of the most brutal thugs in the Vienna Gestapo was able to escape responsibility for his actions.

Johann Sanitzer, the Gestapo 'Intelligence Beast'

Johann Sanitzer, an NSDAP 'Alter Kämpfer', Kriminalrat and SS-Hauptsturmführer, was one of the main figures within the Vienna Gestapo. He represented a highly 'efficient' combination of intelligence and violence. One after another, witnesses accused him and his underlings, above all his 'right-hand man' Brödl, of carrying out interrogations with extreme brutality. Questioned by the public

Figure 18.1. Johann Sanitzer as defendant before the Vienna Volksgericht, January 1949. © Dokumentationsarchiv des österreichischen Widerstandes. Used with permission.

prosecutor, several parachutists and persons who sheltered them confirmed that torture was almost always applied in his sections.

Sanitzer, who headed west towards the end of the war, was arrested on 7 June 1945 by the Americans, interned at Marcus W. Orr camp in Salzburg and handed over to the Austrian authorities in October 1946. In his trial before the Vienna VG (11–14 January 1949), Sanitzer, who had studied German, history and philosophy for five semesters at Vienna University, defended himself aggressively and eloquently. He pleaded guilty to the charge under § 10 VG ('Illegality'), but not guilty to § 3 KVG ('Torture and maltreatment') because he had always obtained authorization for 'enhanced interrogation' from his superiors Trenker or Huber.[60]

The almost obligatory charge of 'illegality' paled into insignificance compared with the charges of excessive personal violence. As Karl Ebner stated, in the sections headed by Sanitzer – IV A 2 (Aiding and abetting the enemy, Sabotage) and later IV 2 (Sabotage, *Funkspiele*) – the use of torture was 'a matter of course … I believe six, twelve or twenty-four blows with a stick were used to achieve the desired result'.[61]

Sanitzer justified the routine use of 'enhanced interrogation' by stating that it enabled other parachute agents to be captured quickly and thereby prevent radio guidance of Allied bombers: 'I would not claim to have saved a city of a million inhabitants, but I prevented many air raids'. In any case, there was no scope for mercy in the handling of parachute agents, as ordered in an express letter from Heydrich: 'Parachutists who are arrested are to be handcuffed and gagged immediately after arrest. Immediate search of body, clothing and bags … because experience has shown that the captured parachutist is under instructions to commit suicide with a handgun or cyanide pills'.[62]

Sanitzer testified in court that he had 'interrogated hundreds of people, arrested over one hundred agents, and had around twenty enhanced interrogations carried out'. However, he had only taken part in person if 'specialist knowledge' was required. In such cases he in fact often took action himself: surviving Gestapo detainees have stated that 'in some interrogations he wore an oilcloth apron so as not to bloody his uniform'.[63] Sanitzer nevertheless trivialized his brutality afterwards in a quite cynical manner: 'I cannot imagine how these people testifying against me are still alive if it's really true that I wanted to kill them'. He also claimed to have told his superior Trenker that 'it can't go on like this – the people are being beaten stupid', which was a telling claim to make, even if it was an argument in his own defence.

That Sanitzer was also adept in the strategy of reinsurance is also shown by the testimony of the former Vienna mayor Karl Seitz,[64] who stated – with explicit mention of Sanitzer – that he had been correctly handled at Morzinplatz following the 20 July 1944 plot. This possibly saved the Gestapo thug from the death penalty.

Sanitzer was sentenced to life imprisonment on 17 January 1949 for illegality (§§ 10, 11 VG), torture and maltreatment (§ 3 KVG), and crimes against humanity and human dignity (§ 4 KVG).[65] Two months after the verdict he was removed from Stein prison by Soviet officers and taken to Moscow, where he was interrogated at length – probably being put under physical and mental pressure – and produced a full confession of his activity in the Gestapo.[66] Sanitzer came back from the Soviet Union in 1955 in one of the last returnee transports. The ministry of justice ordered the 'temporary suspension of the prison sentence interrupted by the intervention of the former Soviet occupying power': 'In view of the particularly harsh conditions … of the time spent in Russia … it would be unduly hard to imprison him immediately on his return'.[67] On 17 December 1956, Sanitzer was finally pardoned by Federal President Theodor Körner.[68] The fact that he was amnestied in spite of his life sentence gave rise to fierce public protests.

In the course of the reintegration of former NSDAP members into Austrian society pursued by the ÖVP and SPÖ, the major parties of the time, the prosecution of Nazi perpetrators gradually abated. Charges were dropped, lenient sentences or acquittals were pronounced, and the cases of those already convicted were reopened. The generous pardons by the federal presidents and the legal amnesties ensured that convicted perpetrators were released ahead of time. After the jurisdiction of the VGs ended and jury trials were reintroduced, there were only isolated legal proceedings. Former Vienna Gestapo officials also benefited from this leniency. Even existing sentences were no longer carried out, such as Johann Sanitzer's life sentence (after his return from Soviet imprisonment). Ferdinand Obenfeldner, a member of the Innsbruck Gestapo, was even able to make a political career with the SPÖ.[69]

Notes

1. https://de.wikipedia.org/wiki/Konferenz_von_Jalta#cite_ref-1 (last accessed on 31 Mar 2018).
2. Garscha, 'Entnazifizierung und gerichtliche Ahndung', 856.
3. Dams/Stolle, *The Gestapo*, 157–61 (*Die Gestapo*, 173–77).
4. IfZ München, ZS 735, sheets 1ff. Robert M.W. Kempner, assistant US chief counsel at the Nuremberg trials, expert and adviser to the US government; before 1933 he was chief legal adviser in the Prussian ministry of the interior.
5. For details, see Mang, *Die Unperson*, 178ff.
6. WStLA, Vienna LG, Vg 12g Vr 1223/47, Karl Ebner, 'Erwiderung auf die Anklageschrift gegen die Geheime Staatspolizei'.
7. Thus, Ebner testified before the Vienna VG that 'the central office for Jewish emigration … was a pure party office answerable to the RSHA and affiliated to the inspector of the Sipo and SD in Military District XVII [Huber], who was responsible for accommodation and the provision of resources but did not have any further authority to give orders. The leading figures

in the central office were Eichmann, and later Brunner. We [the Gestapo] were a completely separate office and had no direct influence' (WStLA, Vienna LG, Vg 12g Vr 1223/47 – Hv 1337/48 sheet 80–81).
8. StGBl. Nr. 13/1945, constitutional law of 8 May 1945 on the prohibition of the NSDAP (Prohibition Act).
9. Garscha, 'Entnazifizierung und gerichtliche Ahndung', 852ff.
10. StGBl. Nr. 32/1945, constitutional law of 26 June 1945 on war crimes and other National Socialist misdeeds (War Criminals Act).
11. Hautmann, 'Polizeilicher Hilfsdienst', 281ff.
12. Report entitled 'Bisherige Maßnahmen gegen Nationalsozialisten' and report of the auxiliary police service, end of May 1945, quoted from Hautmann, 'Kommunisten und Kommunistinnen'; see also the project report 'Die Rolle der österreichischen Sicherheitsverwaltung bei der Wiederherstellung eines demokratischen und unabhängigen Staates nach 1945' by Winfried R. Garscha and Claudia Kuretsidis-Haider (Vienna, December 2000), and the comments on the involvement of the police in the investigation of Nazi violent crimes in the years 1945 to 1948. The project report can be consulted at the DÖW, Vienna.
13. Sabitzer, 'Schwieriger Neubeginn', 73ff; Mang, 'Juristen in der Gestapo', 138–46.
14. StGBl., year 1945, no. 94, Law of 20 July 1945 on the transfer of administrative and judicial institutions of the German Reich to the legal order of the Republic of Austria.
15. StGBl., year 1945, no. 232/1945.
16. Hautmann, 'Kommunisten und Kommunistinnen'.
17. These documents, with the label 'Bundespolizeidirektion Wien: Abteilung I, Staatspolizeiliche Abteilung' are in the WStLA; a few files are also in the DÖW, e.g. the list of sections and heads/employees of the Vienna Gestapo, n.d., DÖW 20 333/7 (see Chapter 11, n. 3, this volume).
18. Theimer, 'Staatspolizei', 85.
19. Hautmann, 'Polizeilicher Hilfsdienst', 281ff; see also Theimer, 'Staatspolizei'.
20. *Neues Österreich*, 192, 4 Dec 1945.
21. See Kuretsidis-Haider, *'Das Volk sitzt zu Gericht'*; Garscha, 'Entnazifizierung und gerichtliche Ahndung'; Butterweck, *Nationalsozialisten vor dem Volksgericht*.
22. *Neues Österreich*, no. 192, 4 Dec 1945.
23. Ibid., no. 225, 13 Jan 1946.
24. It is interesting to note the absence of Viktor Siegel, one of the leading Vienna Gestapo officials, head of the department for 'foreigners' and 'Eastern workers', and responsible for the notorious Oberlanzendorf AEL; see Chapter 14, this volume.
25. WStLA, Vienna LG, Vg 4c Vr 5840/1947.
26. See https://www.geschichtewiki.wien.gv.at/Gestapoleitstelle_Wien (last accessed on 27 May 2021).
27. For details, see Butterweck, *Nationalsozialisten vor dem Volksgericht*.
28. Statement by Oskar Helmer in the ministerial council, 9 Nov 1948, quoted from Knight, *Wortprotokolle*, 197.
29. This section (including quotes) is based on the denazification file of Franz Josef Huber held at the central office of the state justice administrations for the investigation of National Socialist crimes (ZStL, KHN/HKM).
30. However, a memo regarding the VG trial of Siegel, Sanitzer, Trnka, Garhofer and Ebner states: 'On the occasion of the report of the visit to Nuremberg presented today to the federal minister of justice, the minister suggested that in parallel to the current request for extradition of Franz Josef Huber – and until the request is finally dealt with – a request for temporary extradition [Ausleihbegehren] for the purpose of questioning Huber be made by the federal ministry of justice to the legal division in Vienna. … For technical reasons, it was not possible

to question Huber in the camp in Garmisch-Partenkirchen where he is interned' (WStLA, Vienna LG, Vg 4c Vr 586/47, 15 Dec 1947). Note: At this time Huber was not in the US camp at Langwasser but in the hospital of the Garmisch-Partenkirchen internment and work camp – presumably the 'technical reasons' why the questioning could not take place.
31. See the section on Johann Sanitzer later in this chapter. That he was working for the Volkspolizei (of the GDR) was only a rumour.
32. Nowack, *Sicherheitsrisiko NS-Belastung*, e-book location 1108.
33. WStLA, Vienna LG, Vg 4 c 1223/47 (DÖW 8919), VG proceedings against Karl Ebner; see Mang, *Die Unperson*, 181ff.
34. §§ 10, 10 VG 1947: 'illegality' referred to membership of the NSDAP or one of its affiliated bodies during the prohibition period (1933–38) and was considered 'high treason'. Ebner joined the NSDAP in 1936 and the SS in 1937; for Trenker, see the section later in the present chapter.
35. Marschall, *Volksgerichtsbarkeit und Verfolgung*, 2ff. The Nuremberg tribunal was well aware of the problem of collective responsibility: 'If the court is convinced of the criminal responsibility of an organization or group, it should not hesitate to call it criminal on the grounds that the theory of "group criminality" is new or because it could be used unfairly by future courts' (*Der Nürnberger Prozess*, 857).
36. WStLA, Vienna LG, Vg 4 c 1223/47 (DÖW 8919), VG proceedings against Karl Ebner, 'Wolfsberger Dossier'.
37. StGBl. Nr. 32/1945, constitutional law of 26 Jun 1945 on war crimes and other National Socialist misdeeds.
38. *Neues Österreich*, 7 Dec 1948. As can be observed from the section 'Vienna Gestapo GVPs' in Chapter 4, this volume, the position of department head was not easy to determine. In the 2nd GVP (1942–44), which Ebner referred to in his dossier, there were departments called 'groups', headed by Ebner, Trenker, Siegel and others. However, as Ebner also confirmed in his dossier, they had the same areas of responsibility as 'departments'.
39. *Volksstimme*, 10 Dec 1948.
40. See the section 'Reinsurance' in Chapter 5, this volume.
41. *Wiener Zeitung*, 11 Dec 1948.
42. WStLA, Vienna LG, Vg 4 c 1223/47, judgment against Karl Ebner, 11 Dec 1948.
43. Mang, *Die Unperson*, 231–49.
44. Himmler only approved Trnka's promotion to SS-Sturmbannführer if he would change his name (NARA, Washington, SS-Personalhauptamt A 3343 880-189 B 8.05). In a circular of 18 Mar 1940, Heydrich noted that it was 'not compatible with the honour of a German man for him to have a Polish or Czech ... surname', and that it was desirable for 'members of the Sipo and SD to change such names to German ones' (BA Berlin, R 58/261, sheet 70).
45. For details, see Pichler, 'Dr Othmar Trenker'.
46. Only those who had left such a position before 1 Sep 1939 – i.e. the start of the war – were excluded from this *praesumptio juris et de jure* (fact that according to the law cannot be denied).
47. Trenker claimed to have occupied the position of department head on a 'temporary basis' only, and referred to the absence of an appointment document from the RSHA. This claim is refuted both by Ebner's dossier and Huber's circular of 1 May 1944; see the section on 'Vienna Gestapo GVPs' in Chapter 4, this volume.
48. Pichler, 'Trenker', 114.
49. *Neues Österreich*, 2 Dec 1948.
50. [die Genehmigung für verschärfte Vernehmungen als leitender Beamter an höhere Dienststellen weitergeleitet zu haben, andererseits aber auch aktiv an der Durchführung von verschärften Vernehmungen beteiligt gewesen zu sein] Pichler, 'Trenker', 137. For details on *verschärfte Vernehmung* (enhanced interrogation) – the Gestapo term for maltreatment and

torture – see the section 'Radicalization, Interrogation and Maltreatment' in Chapter 6, this volume.
51. Pichler, 'Trenker', 144.
52. Ibid., 169–71.
53. WStLA, Vienna LG, Vg 2a Vr 432/46 (DÖW 19 920), judgment against Karl Silberbauer, 13 Jul 1946.
54. WStLA, Vienna LG, Vg 8e Vr 288/52, judgment against Karl Silberbauer, 22 Jan 1954.
55. http://www.simon-wiesenthal-archiv.at (last accessed on 31 Aug 2017); https://de.wikipedia.org/wiki/Karl_Josef_Silberbauer#Verhaftung_Anne_Franks (last accessed on 25 Nov 2017).
56. See https://www.doew.at/erkennen/ausstellung/gedenkstaette-salztorgasse/sie-gingen-den-anderen-weg-organisierter-widerstand-in-oesterreich-6 (last accessed on 27 May 2021).
57. WStLA, Vienna LG, Vg 4d Vr 1251/47 (DÖW 20 503), statement by Anton Brödl.
58. See the section 'Radicalization, Interrogation and Maltreatment' in Chapter 6, this volume.
59. All details and quotes from WStLA, Vienna LG, Vg 4d Vr 1251/4 (DÖW 20 503).
60. WStLA, Vienna LG, Vg 4c Vr 586/47 (DÖW 8912), VG trial of Johann Sanitzer.
61. ZStL 110 AR-Z 4/1961 II, sheets 214–13, testimony of Karl Ebner in the trial of Johann Sanitzer.
62. BA Berlin, R 58/3366, express letter from Heydrich (ppa. Müller), 6 Jun 1942. As Heydrich had already died of his injuries following the attack in Prague, the letter was signed by Gestapo chief Müller.
63. Schafranek, *Widerstand und Verrat* (2017), 465.
64. WStLA, Vienna LG, Vg 4c Vr 586/47 (DÖW 8912), testimony of Karl Seitz, 9 Jan 1948.
65. Ibid., judgment against Johann Sanitzer, 17 Jan 1949.
66. See Schafranek, *Widerstand und Verrat* (2017), 461–66. Schafranek had access to Sanitzer's investigation and prosecution file at the central archive of the FSB in Moscow. He had the interrogation records translated from Russian, and gave a copy to the DÖW.
67. Butterweck, *Nationalsozialisten vor dem Volksgericht*, 753.
68. WStLA, Vienna LG, Vg 4c Vr 586/47 (DÖW 8912).
69. See Neugebauer/Schwarz, *Der Wille zum aufrechten Gang*, 151–60.

Summary and Conclusion

The Gestapo regional headquarters in Vienna (Gestapo-Leitstelle Wien) was – if one discounts the central office in Berlin, the Gestapa (from 1939 Amt/Department IV of the RSHA) – the largest Gestapo office in the entire German Reich. Its important position in the Nazi machinery of repression derived not only from its numerical size – nine hundred staff, competence over an area amounting to 24,000 km² with a population of more than 3.6 million – but also from the fact that the head of the Vienna Gestapo, Franz Josef Huber, was also in charge of border police: as border inspector II (south-east) for military districts XVII and XVIII he was responsible for border control at the frontiers to Slovakia, Hungary, Yugoslavia, Italy and Switzerland. Furthermore, as inspector of the security police and SD (IdSuSD) for Military District XVII, Huber was also (formally) the superior of the Zentralstelle für jüdische Auswanderung in Wien (Central Office for Jewish Emigration in Vienna), which was in practice headed by Adolf Eichmann and Alois Brunner. The expulsion and deportation of the Viennese Jews was carried out by the central office in close complicity and cooperation with what came to be known as the 'Judenreferat' ('Jewish section') of the Vienna Gestapo. In short, the Vienna Gestapo was the most important instrument of Nazi terror in Austria.

In the 'Altreich' (i.e. the German Reich within its pre-1938 borders), the Gestapo developed over a period of several years out of the police machinery of the Weimar Republic. At the Vienna Gestapo, by contrast, the practices and organizational and staff structures of the already fully formed German Gestapo were adopted within a very short time in March and April 1938 – or, to be more precise, were imposed and set into operation by the central authorities in Berlin (at this point, Himmler as Reichsführer-SS and Heydrich as chief of the security police and SD). Although the top positions at the newly created Vienna Gestapo were initially occupied by officials from the 'Altreich', there is no denying that Austrians played a far from insignificant role in its establishment, as indeed they did in the whole process of the annexation of March 1938 ('Anschluss'). Austrian police officials who had fled to Germany to avoid imprisonment for Nazi activities were amongst those who worked at the Gestapa and at the main office of the SS security service (Sicherheitsdienst, SD) on preparing the police operations to be carried out during and following the annexation. Furthermore, when the Nazi party was illegal in Austria (1933–38), Austrian Nazis and Nazi sympathizers had for months and years before March 1938 systematically been supplying Berlin with information and documents that were used to draw up card indexes and lists, on the basis of which large numbers of Austrian Jews and opponents of Nazism were later arrested, and many subsequently interned in concentration camps. These thoroughly Nazi-oriented Austrian police officials soon occupied important positions at the Vienna Gestapo.

Austria was the first territory outside the 'Altreich' in which a new police apparatus was built up on the basis of the 'Reich-German' organizational structures. The experience gained through this process turned out to be very useful to the heads of the central offices in Berlin (not only Himmler and Heydrich but also Heinrich Müller at the Gestapa) in their implementation of the Nazi system of terror in other countries. Similarly, for the German officials who initially dominated the Vienna Gestapo, such as Karl Haselbacher, Kurt Christmann and Rudolf Lange, working in Vienna was just a springboard for their further careers in the German police in the occupied territories.

With regard to the repression exercised by the Gestapo and Nazi judiciary, the overall situation in the 'Alpine and Danube Gaus' – as annexed Austria was known until 1945 – differed in a number of important respects from that in the 'Altreich', where the years of peace up to 1938–39 had enabled the Nazi regime to continuously build up and expand its power structures, score certain successes on the economic and foreign fronts, indoctrinate German society with its political ideology, and largely eliminate opposition to the regime. In annexed Austria, the span of time in which total rule was established was shorter by five years. Thereafter, the war and its consequences for the general population steadily diminished the Austrians' initial enthusiasm of 1938. Furthermore, in a factor that should not be underestimated, there developed a growing consciousness of Austria as a land in its own right. This factor could not be ignored by the Nazi authorities, including the Gestapo, and among other things resulted in an increase in anti-German feeling.

Although these tendencies manifested themselves most especially in the resistance and in some parts of the population, they also extended into the ranks of the Nazi movement, where a certain latent dissatisfaction developed over the dominant position held by 'Reich Germans'. Nevertheless, the friction between

German and Austrian officials within the Vienna Gestapo should not be overemphasized, especially as the latter were no less virulent as National Socialists and believers in 'Greater Germany' than their German colleagues, and were quite their equals in brutality and violence. They had not the slightest interest in Austrian independence or opposition to the Nazi regime: their priorities were to get the best possible jobs, pursue their careers and acquire power within the system. The effectiveness and efficiency of the Gestapo were not impaired by rivalries such as those between Reich Germans and 'Ostmärker'. Nevertheless, the rivalry was one of the reasons why Franz Josef Huber, the (Bavarian) head of the Vienna Gestapo, succeeded in bringing about a certain reduction in the number of Reich Germans in leading positions. In addition, Himmler's pursuit of the amalgamation of the SS and Sipo resulted in the Gestapo/SD complex becoming the area of the Nazi state with the greatest proportion of NSDAP and SS members, and the area most profoundly imbued with the Nazi ideology.

The view held by Franz Weisz that the Gestapo in Austria was, 'in terms of its staff, a police force of the corporate state' ('personell ein ständestaatlicher Polizeikörper') is not shared by the present authors. Although almost all Austrian Gestapo officials had been in the police of the corporate state, they had not been supporters or upholders of that regime but, rather, fanatical opponents: they took part in the Nazis' attempted putsch of July 1934 and betrayed state secrets to the central authorities in Berlin; they fled to the 'Altreich' when under threat of prosecution, and assisted there in the preparations for the annexation; and from 11 March 1938, it was future Gestapo officials who organized the Nazi coup in the Vienna police, immediately arresting high-ranking officials of the corporate state police.

According to information provided by Franz Weisz, in the period of the first organizational plan (GVP, 1938–42), around 80 to 85 per cent of Gestapo officials had come from the Austrian police. In the first weeks after the annexation of March 1938, around 320 officials from the former Austrian state police (Staatspolizei, a section of the federal police) or criminal investigation police were taken into the Gestapo, where they formed almost 50 per cent of the overall staff. Of the remainder, somewhat less than 40 per cent had been recruited from the Vienna security guard (Sicherheitswache). Only a relatively small proportion of the staff had come from the rural police (Gendarmerie) or from non-police occupations. Immediately after the annexation, many Austrian police officials claimed to have been 'illegal Nazis' – that is to say, they claimed the status 'Alter Kämpfer' (literally 'old fighter', veteran). They hoped to make quick careers and also to profit materially from the introduction of the Reich remuneration law (Reichsbesoldungsgesetz). To this end, the office of the Vienna NSDAP Gauleiter issued hundreds of Austrian Gestapo officials with 'Alter Kämpfer' certificates. Most of the Gestapo officials who had not declared themselves 'illegals' immediately after the annexation very quickly joined not only the NSDAP but also the SS, although membership of these organizations was by no means obligatory for security police (Sipo) staff. While there was doubtless strong group pressure within the Vienna Gestapo to join the NSDAP and SS, this was primarily generated by the fear on the part of individual Gestapo staff members that if they did not join they would face difficulties at the workplace, miss out on possible career opportunities, and end up as outsiders amongst their colleagues.

The great majority of Vienna Gestapo officials with a rank lower than section head – heads or members of units, usually with the police rank of Kriminalsekretär, Kriminaloberassistent or Kriminalassistent – were born between 1900 and 1910. Almost all had lower-middle-class backgrounds and had originally trained for different occupations before joining the police.

One striking feature of the Vienna Gestapo was that it had a disproportionately large number of jurists. Originally its staff included around twenty Austrian and ten German jurists, while even large Gestapo regional headquarters in the 'Altreich' only had two or at the most three. The high number of personnel with special and in particular juristic qualifications was necessitated by a number of challenges, notably setting up such a large Gestapo office, dealing with the introduction of Reich-German laws, rules and practices, and not least such complex matters as the expropriation of religious foundations and the looting of the Jewish population. Later, the number of jurists steadily diminished, mainly on account of officials being deployed elsewhere.

It is estimated that between 1938 and 1942, 17 per cent of the Vienna Gestapo staff were women. In the course of the war the percentage grew – as a result of male staff being transferred or deployed elsewhere – to over 30 per cent; but in absolute figures, the number of women employed between 1938 and 1944 only rose from around 140 to around 170. The great majority of female Gestapo staff were taken on from the Austrian state police immediately after the annexation. Female Gestapo staff exclusively performed office tasks to support the male officials who were their superiors. They managed the extensive card indexes and files, typed interrogation records dictated to them by the male officials, and operated the telex machines and telephone system. Furthermore, cleaning work was also done by women. As well as always being subordinate to male officials, female Gestapo staff could neither acquire civil servant status nor rise to positions of authority.

The persistently high number of personnel and strikingly low staff turnover at the Vienna Gestapo in comparison with other Gestapo regional headquarters can be attributed to the intentions of the Vienna Gestapo head Franz Josef Huber, who set great store by continuity and loyalty amongst his staff. In this he benefited from the awareness of the Gestapo leadership in Berlin of how geopolitically exposed, and thus how important, the Vienna Gestapo office was, as evidenced by certain objective factors: considerably greater resistance to the Nazi regime than in the 'Altreich' (in particular on the part of the Communists), pro-Habsburg separatist tendencies in conservative social circles, and the situation on the Reich's borders to states such as Czechoslovakia and Yugoslavia (which were on the list to become the next victims of annexation); and later, the increasing number of forced labourers from the East, who were considered dangerous, the operations of allied commando units, and in 1945 the approach of the front.

Until 1944, the Vienna Gestapo staff roster displayed a higher level of continuity than other regional headquarters at the level of the head and deputy head (Huber and Ebner), and in terms of the overall number of staff. However, there was not the same continuity at lower levels, where there were constant changes of section and unit heads, not least because of the implementation of the new, centrally ordered organizational structures in the GVPs of 1942 and 1944.

While the Vienna Gestapo, with a staff of around nine hundred, was the largest regional headquarters in the German Reich, it was by no means oversized for the great number of its tasks – the persecution of the Jews, the suppression of organized resistance and all manifestations of individual opposition, the oppression of hundreds of thousands of foreign forced labourers, the running of its own concentration camp (Oberlanzendorf AEL), and extensive border control. Furthermore, there were specific goals behind the vast quantity of routine bureaucracy. Above all, in the pre-digital age, the maintenance of the Erkennungsdienstliche Kartei (identification card index, with photos and descriptions of persons arrested) was an absolute prerequisite for state police measures; as emphasized in the study by Dams and Stolle, it was the 'bureaucratic linchpin of the persecution'. Daily and monthly reports, correspondence with central offices, the composition of often lengthy documents substantiating referrals of detainees to the state prosecutors and courts, and the administration of large numbers of 'protective custody' orders (required for committals to concentration camps) – all this called for a host not only of (mainly female) typists but also of trained police staff, a considerable number of whom had to be jurists.

In Gestapo interrogations, maltreatment of detainees was a matter of course, but although there were officials with sadistic tendencies, as a rule torture was used with the specific and conscious intention of extracting confessions and compelling detainees to betray their fellow resistance fighters. The forms of maltreatment ranged from, at the mildest, protracted and frequently repeated interrogations, with long periods of standing, doing knee bends and the like, through threats, humiliations, insults and deprivation of food, fluids and (for smokers) cigarettes, to brutal violence (beatings, hanging on chains, and more refined methods) for days or even weeks, in full awareness of the fact that it would result in serious damage to the victim's health or even death. Torture was given a semblance of (pseudo-)legality through central directives concerning 'enhanced interrogation' (*verschärfte Vernehmung*), which were of course ignored in practice, with the tacit consent of the perpetrators' superiors.

Although there were no murders as such on the Vienna Gestapo premises at Morzinplatz, a number of detainees perished as a result of torture, or committed suicide in order to escape further torment or ensure that they did not betray fellow activists. When the Gestapo wished an individual to be killed, it as a rule did this by having him or her committed to a concentration camp.

The 'radicalization spiral' identified by Gerhard Paul and Klaus-Michael Mallmann in the activities of the Gestapo can also, in a modified form, be observed in Austria. While the mass arrests and violent attacks on Jews and political opponents that immediately began during the annexation were largely carried out by local Austrian Nazis, from 15 March 1938 onwards the newly established Gestapo offices made targeted arrests (on the basis of lists prepared in Berlin) and deported detainees to concentration camps. The invasion of the Soviet Union in June 1941 was accompanied by a further harshening of Gestapo procedures, particularly against Communist activists, with the NS judiciary displaying its ongoing radicalization in a massive increase in death sentences. There is no doubt that the intensification of the NS regime's brutality and barbarity evident in the mass murder of Jews in the East from 1941 – in which a leading role was played by Sipo and SD units – also had a knock-on effect on the workings of the Gestapo within the Reich. Furthermore, the activities of the Gestapo were changed – not only quantitatively but also qualitatively – by the huge increase in forced labour performed by deported foreign workers and POWs throughout the German Reich (and thus also in Austria). As the Soviet forced labourers ('Ostarbeiter') in particular were considered 'Untermenschen' (subhuman) and a danger to security, they were mercilessly punished for the slightest offences at the workplace, maltreated in large numbers in interrogations, and committed to concentration camps. However, only in a few cases – by contrast with the many cases associated with Reich-German Gestapo offices – were there extra-legal executions of *Ostarbeiter* and Poles, and these were on account of sexual relations with locals.

The Gestapo's strongest weapon against resistance groups was the use of informants. At the Vienna Gestapo, under the direction of section heads Lambert Leutgeb and Johann Sanitzer, a huge undercover agents system was built up which succeeded in infiltrating, investigating and crushing the great majority of organized resistance groups. Most of the informants were recruited from within the resistance milieu and – mostly under physical and psychological pressure – compelled to collaborate, and even certain top KPÖ functionaries ended up acting as 'cell spies'. Sanitzer, as the official responsible for dealing with parachute agents, succeeded in arresting the majority of Allied parachutists in his area of competence and compelling them to engage in *Funkspiele* (literally 'radio games'), that is, transmitting military and intelligence-related disinformation to the Allies.

In the light of decades spent studying the repression of resistance fighters and oppositionals, we consider it necessary to relativize – at least partially (and for the Vienna Gestapo) – the critique of the 'Gestapo myth' presented by Gellately, Paul, Mallmann and others, because this approach tends to underestimate the Gestapo. It is true that the Gestapo with its – in comparison with the Stasi of the GDR – relatively small apparatus did not have the omnipotence or omnipresence that were attributed to it both by the regime and by its opponents, and which were the foundation of its 'myth'. It could not have worked with such success or efficiency without the assistance of 'Partei- und Volksgenossen' ('comrades of party and Volk'). Above all, the Gestapo benefited greatly from the dense network of Nazi organizations – NSDAP, SA, SS, SD, DAF, NSBO (NS factories organization) and others – that covered the entire Reich, including Austria, and existed in all strata of the population.

However, the denunciations were essentially confined to the sphere of individual resistance, that is, acts of the kind categorized as 'insidious utterances' or 'undermining military morale' and 'radio crime', or economy-related offences and violations of the NS anti-Jewish regulations – in Austria, there were practically no denunciations of or in the organized political resistance. The Communist works groups were not denounced (as would have been quite feasible) by fellow-workers, and the same was true of the Catholic-conservative and legitimist resistance and rural resistance. The extensive crushing of the organized resistance was not based on reports from the population or internal betrayal: on the contrary, the 'success' of the Gestapo was due to the systematic use of informants ('V-Leute'), the extraction of confessions by force, and other police methods characteristic of dictatorships.

Our research does not indicate that denouncers were in the majority or that there was such a thing as a 'denunciation society', as proposed by Paul and Mallmann with reference to Robert Gellately. While the number of people arrested by the Vienna Gestapo on account of denunciations was high, it remained markedly lower than the numbers recorded for German cities. Most denunciations to the Vienna Gestapo were made by NSDAP members or organizations, though admittedly the organizations often first received the denunciation from non-party members. Nevertheless, in our view it would be an exaggeration and inappropriate, at least for Austria, to conclude from the large number of denunciations that the Nazi regime was not a regime or dictatorship but (to quote the historian Götz Aly) a 'National Socialist people's state' 'nationalsozialistischer Volksstaat').

Because of its relatively low number of personnel, the Gestapo was dependent on the collaboration of other police formations, authorities and bodies, and the NSDAP offices. While the criminal investigation police (Kriminalpolizei, Kripo), as the second principal sector of the Sipo, was on the same hierarchical level as the Gestapo, the distribution of tasks meant that the

Gestapo was the dominant partner, especially as the Kripo was also subordinate to Vienna Gestapo head Huber (and later, his successor Mildner) as inspector of the Sipo and SD. In accordance with a directive of September 1939 from Heydrich, the persecution of homosexuals was made the responsibility of the Kripo, in order to relieve the Gestapo. Likewise, the regular uniformed police (Ordnungspolizei, Orpo), including the 'protection police' (Schutzpolizei, Schupo) and the rural police (Gendarmerie), performed auxiliary tasks for the Gestapo – for example, in the larger-scale mass arrests, in the encircling of suspicious buildings, and in detainee transports. Schupo policemen were also used to guard detainees at the in-house prison at Morzinplatz; in 1938–39, to quote a prominent example, the Schupo was given responsibility for guarding the 'special detainees' Kurt Schuschnigg and Louis Rothschild. From 1937 onwards, the border police was directly subordinate to the Gestapo, for the logical reason that border control had very important functions on account of such problems as 'subversives' seeking to flee the Reich, foreign agents, and smuggling.

On the basis of the Funktionsbefehl (function order) issued in July 1937 by Heydrich as chief of the Sipo and SD (to demarcate the responsibilities of the two bodies), the Gestapo and SD cooperated more closely, particularly in March and April 1938, on house searches, seizures, and the arrest and detention of political opponents, Jews and Freemasons, especially because only the Gestapo had executive (i.e. police) authority within the Reich. In the persecution of the Jews there was, in spite of occasional squabbles over competence, an efficient division of tasks between the Gestapo and the SD, with the SD managing to acquire a leading role in driving Jews into emigration and in the deportations (until the end of 1942) through the 'Central Office for Jewish Emigration in Vienna', established by Adolf Eichmann, which was formally answerable to Huber as IdSuSD. Nevertheless, the Vienna Gestapo had many important tasks in the persecution of the Jews, such as the supervision and instrumentalization of the Israelitische Kultusgemeinde (Jewish community of Vienna, IKG), the issuing and implementation of innumerable discriminatory regulations, the punishment of individual Jews, and looting deportees' assets.

The relations of the Gestapo and SD with Abwehr Office XVII (Military District XVII, 'Vienna') were more competitive in character. Occasionally, exchange of information led to arrests of resistance fighters, as in the case of the resistance groups led by Hauptmann Karl Burian and the Semperit board chairman Franz Josef Messner. However, the Gestapo never got wind of the fact that Oberst Rudolf von Marogna-Redwitz, the official head of the Vienna office of the Abwehr from 1938 to February 1944, belonged to the inner circle of plotters around Oberst Stauffenberg, and was involved in the resistance operation in Vienna.

The Vienna Gestapo engaged in functional cooperation with the municipal and state administration in the Reichsgau of (greater) Vienna, which was of particular significance in connection with the first deportations from Vienna, namely, the 'Nisko transports' of 1939 and the initial deportations to the Generalgouvernement from February 1941.

For National Socialism (and thus also for the Gestapo), the Jews were the main enemy. Although the Vienna Gestapo was not in charge of the forced emigration and deportation of the Jews, having to cede this function to the central office for Jewish emigration, the Vienna Gestapo's 'Jewish section' (headed for most of the period by Karl Ebner) played an important and at times critical role. The Vienna Gestapo organized the first large-scale deportations of Jews to concentration camps (Dachau, Buchenwald), and in February 1941 did the groundwork for the first large-scale transport of Viennese Jews to the Generalgouvernement – for which Gauleiter Schirach had obtained Hitler's approval. Furthermore, from 1943 to 1945, following the closing down of the central office, the Vienna Gestapo had full responsibility for the deportations of Jews. Through its 'Jewish section', the Vienna Gestapo was instrumental in applying innumerable Nazi measures designed to discriminate against, harass and rob those Jews still remaining in Vienna, with the enforced cooperation of functionaries of the Jewish community. In particular, 'Vugesta' (Gestapo office for the administration of the removals goods of Jewish emigrants), an institution unique to Vienna, developed into a major source of financial gain for staff of the 'Jewish section' and their favoured friends, and also for NSDAP and state functionaries, up to and including Reichsstatthalter Baldur von Schirach.

The Vienna Gestapo also played a leading role in the expropriation of religious foundations and looting of church property, especially as it was the authority that issued the seizure and confiscation orders. In this field, however, the Vienna Gestapo had to take account of strong influence exerted by local and regional NSDAP offices wishing to remove the religious personnel and take possession of church buildings and land for their own purposes; for example, it was intended that the Augustinian religious foundation of Stift Klosterneuburg should be used for an 'Adolf Hitler School'.

The Vienna Gestapo scored its greatest 'successes' in the suppression of resistance, in which its most powerful weapons were the deployment of informants for tracking down opponents and the use of the most brutal interrogation methods. It managed to crush practically all organized resistance groups – until 1943–44 at least. This was particularly true of what was numerically by far the largest Austrian resistance group, namely, the Communists, amongst whom the Vienna Gestapo had made around 6,300 arrests by the end of 1943. According to the research findings of Hans Schafranek, more than 800 of these arrests had resulted from the undercover activities of the informants Kurt Koppel, a former KJV functionary, and his helpmate Margarete Kahane. While former Spanish

Civil War fighters who returned from France, a number of whom were detained for periods of time (1939–40) by the Vienna Gestapo, were deported to concentration camps, returnees from Russia very largely remained undetected – with the exception of some Jewish expatriates transferred back to Austria by the NKVD, and of some arrests resulting from interrogations and surveillance.

The Socialist organizations – which had earlier set their sights on revolution in a 'greater Germany' – likewise fell victim to Vienna Gestapo informants. The mass arrest operation against Communists and Revolutionary Socialists ordered by Sipo chief Heydrich and carried out by the Vienna Gestapo on 22 August 1939 took place on the basis of proscription lists already drawn up in 1938, combined with information systematically collected through the work of informants.

The Catholic, conservative and legitimist resistance groups – mostly Habsburg-minded and aiming at the restoration of a 'greater Austria' – were likewise crushed by the Gestapo, which was however confronted with one obstacle in that a mysterious instruction of Hitler's from 1939 had specified that (Austrian) 'separatists' could not be prosecuted by the courts or judiciary, as a result of which the arrestees were kept interned in prisons for several years under 'protective custody' orders. Only in autumn 1943 was Hitler's instruction revoked and the court proceedings were completed – leading to numerous death sentences.

The small religious group of the Jehovah's Witnesses was persecuted by the Nazi regime particularly on account of its members' refusal to perform military service or work in armaments factories. The mass round-up of 8 June 1940 ordered by the RSHA, which was accompanied by interrogations, house searches and the seizure of Bible study materials, was carried out to the letter by the Gestapo in Austria as elsewhere. Of the 550 active Jehovah's Witnesses in Austria, 445 were imprisoned, 230 of these by the Vienna Gestapo, and 154 perished.

While the Freemasons were a major enemy in the eyes of the NS regime, almost on a level with the Jews and the Communists (as shown by the laborious preparations made at the SD main office in preparation for the annexation of Austria in March 1938), they were of practically no significance for the Vienna Gestapo after their elimination in March and April 1938.

Although individual acts of resistance – such as 'insidious utterances' (i.e. anti-regime statements), listening to foreign radio stations, and helping Jews or POWs – were reported in large numbers, they were only of secondary importance for the Gestapo. Both the suppression of homosexuality and the persecution of persons categorized as 'asocials' was left up to the Kripo, which was also responsible for the persecution of Roma and Sinti. Particularly as the war progressed, the Gestapo accorded absolute priority to combating organized resistance, partisans and enemy agents, and to the repression of non-compliant foreign forced labourers. Monitoring the general population for anti-regime statements, 'radio crime' or the infringement of NS regulations would have far exceeded their human resources; in these areas, the Gestapo was very largely dependent on denunciations by 'comrades from Volk and party'.

With the massive increase in foreign forced labour, the Gestapo's principal field of activity shifted to the foreign labourers, in particular the *Ostarbeiter* (from the Soviet Union) and the Poles, both of whom were regarded as potential sources of danger to the NS regime. Of the fifty thousand people arrested in the Vienna Gestapo's area of competence, thirty thousand were foreign civilian workers, who were committed to concentration camps for the slightest infringements of work discipline or other NS regulations. Although the 'work education camp' (Arbeitserziehungslager, AEL) of Oberlanzendorf was originally established by the city of Vienna as a reformatory camp for 'asocial' youths, it was soon taken over by the Vienna Gestapo, which thus effectively had a concentration camp readily available near Vienna. Increasingly, the internees included, besides resistance activists and recalcitrant youths, more and more *Ostarbeiter*; furthermore, the living conditions there deteriorated steadily until they were comparable with those in concentration camps. Finally, many Oberlanzendorf inmates perished on the 'evacuation march' to Mauthausen ordered by the Vienna Gestapo at the beginning of April 1945.

Numerous Vienna Gestapo officials spent periods of time on duty outside the Reich, serving in 'Einsatzgruppen' ('deployment groups', EGs) and Sipo offices in the occupied territories, where they were involved in serious crimes (mass murders of Jews and Roma, partisans and civilians). These extraterritorial crimes and the part played in them by Austrian Sipo officials constitute such a vast thematic field that the present volume cannot offer anything approaching a complete account, which would call for a number of specialized research projects. Chapter 15 on the 'external deployment' of Vienna Gestapo officials thus merely describes a number of cases, such as the head of the Verona Gestapo responsible for deportations of Jews, Friedrich Kranebitter, and Armin Kraupatz as a perpetrator of atrocities in the Radom ghetto. On another front, the Vienna Gestapo carried out a special operation in 1943–44, combating a widely ramified Communist resistance group in occupied France, which in 1942–43 had sent a large number of activists to support the resistance in Austria.

The last stage in the radicalization of NS repression was characterized by what have come to be known as the 'end-phase crimes'. In the Vienna Gestapo area, for example, there were murders of Allied pilots who had been shot down. Furthermore, Vienna Gestapo officials played a significant part in the operations of various NS summary courts through investigations and manhunts, brutal interrogations, and assistance at executions, including those of three Austrian officers of the Wehrmacht on 8 April 1945 in Floridsdorf (21st district of Vienna), and executions in Sankt Pölten and Krems in the Reichsgau 'Lower Danube'. However, the more than fifteen hundred detainees and prisoners still held by the Vienna Gestapo were not liquidated, as had been feared, not least because of the rapid collapse of NS rule in the Vienna area. Nevertheless, even after the fall of Vienna, the westward-displaced Vienna Gestapo continued its brutal repression in 'Lower Danube' until the last days of the war. The end of the Vienna Gestapo was marked by retreat without a fight in the face of the advancing Red Army, by officials taking flight or going underground with fake identities and forged papers, and by measures to destroy evidence of the Vienna Gestapo's deeds.

The prosecution of perpetrators from the Vienna Gestapo was initiated immediately after the liberation of Vienna in April 1945, in the first instance by state police organs, which included Communist resistance fighters and committed anti-Fascists. Several thousand people suspected of being Nazis were taken into police custody, and in the summer of that year the task of punishing NS crimes was taken over by the Volksgerichte (VGs) created through the War Criminals Act of 26 June 1945.

When the leading Gestapo officials Karl Ebner, Othmar Trenker and Viktor Siegel were in Allied internment camps, they composed lengthy exoneratory documents for the Gestapo's defence lawyer at the Nuremberg trials, Dr Rudolf Merkel. Central to these documents was the consistent denial of any guilt or co-responsibility on the part of the Gestapo for the crimes of the NS regime, in particular the deportation and extermination of the Jews. The Gestapo was referred to as a 'police duty station recognized in public law' ('öffentlich-rechtlich anerkannte Polizeidienststelle'), whose staff, it was claimed, had been transferred to the Gestapo from the Austrian police and Gendarmerie, just like, for example, 'railway or post office officials'.

From 1946, numerous Gestapo officials were tried by the Vienna VG, where they pursued this strategy of self-justification. As a rule, the former Gestapo officials spoke out in favour of each other when called as witnesses, while the victims of the Gestapo – as a result of forced emigration or murder – were not around to make statements as witnesses for the prosecution. As a result of the paucity of concrete evidence, the trials and judgments of the VGs attached greater importance to the (from today's point of view) less serious charge of 'illegality' – that is, membership and activity in the Nazi movement during its prohibition in Austria from 1933 to 1938.

As is shown by the cases considered in the present volume (Franz Josef Huber, Karl Ebner, Othmar Trenker, Johann Sanitzer and others), the judgments against leading officials of the Vienna Gestapo were lenient – in spite of the War Criminals Act allowing for the death sentence. The defendant punished most leniently of all was the principal perpetrator, Franz Josef Huber, who was not extradited to Austria and – thanks to the intervention of the US secret service and the protection of the German authorities – got off with a fine of 500 DM. From 1943, Huber and his deputy Ebner had implemented a strategy of 'reinsurance' – giving preferential treatment to selected detainees, in particular from the Catholic-conservative milieu – in order to lay the ground for their post-war survival. In the course of the reintegration of former NSDAP members into Austrian society pursued by the major political parties of the time, the ÖVP and the SPÖ, the late 1940s and 1950s saw a constant decline in the prosecution of Nazi perpetrators. Former Vienna Gestapo officials also benefited from federal presidents' liberality in issuing pardons, and from legal amnesties. After the jurisdiction of the VGs ended and jury trials were reintroduced, there were only isolated legal proceedings against former Gestapo staff.

BIBLIOGRAPHY

Archival Sources
Archiv der Israelitischen Kultusgemeinde Wien
Archive of the Jewish Community of Vienna
Vienna holdings, A/VIE/IKG/II/AD/3/7
Jerusalem holdings, A/W 165, 1–7

Archives of the Republic of Slovenia
SI AS 1931, 811, sheets 2107–2324

Bundesarchiv Berlin

Federal Archives, Berlin
NS-Archiv des Ministeriums für Staatssicherheit der DDR
NSDAP-Mitgliederkartei
NS 5 Deutsche Arbeitsfront
NS 19 Persönlicher Stab Reichsführer SS
NS 33 NS-Führungshauptamt
R 35 Deutsche Umsiedlungs-Treuhand-Gesellschaft
R 19 Hauptamt Ordnungspolizei
R 43 Reichskanzlei
R58 Reichssicherheitshauptamt
R 75 Umwandererzentralstelle Posen
R 901 Auswärtiges Amt
R 1501 Reichsministerium des Innern
R 2301 Rechnungshof des Deutschen Reiches
R 3001 Reichsjustizministerium
R 3012 Reichsjustizprüfungsamt

Sammlung Berlin Document Center: Personenbezogene Unterlagen der SS und SA, Personenbezogene Unterlagen der Reichskulturkammer (RKK), Personenbezogene Unterlagen der NSDAP, Personenbezogene Unterlagen der NSDAP/Parteikorrespondenz
R 70 – Polen Deutsche Polizeidienststellen in Polen
R 70 – Italien Deutsche Polizeidienststellen in Italien
ZB II: Juristen, Wissenschaftler, NSDAP und Gliederungen, Gestapo, SD, V-Männer, KZ
ZC: Verfahrensakten VGH und andere Gerichte, RJM, Staatsanwaltschaften
ZC I: Verfahrensakten VGH und andere Gerichte
ZC II: Verfahrensakten VGH, Reichsgericht
ZR: RSHA, Gestapo, SD, Polizei, SS, militärische Abwehr, V-Männer

Diözesanarchiv Wien
Archive of the Archdiocese of Vienna
Bischofsakten Innitzer (Archbishop Innitzer, files)

Dokumentationsarchiv des österreichischen Widerstands
Documentation Centre of Austrian Resistance
Akten des Volksgerichts beim Landesgericht für Strafsachen Wien (records of the VG at the Vienna LG)
Akten des Sondergerichts beim Landgericht Wien (records of the SG at the Vienna LG)
Akten der Besonderen Senate des OLG Wien (records of the Special Senates of the Vienna OLG, classification: OJs)
Tagesberichte, -rapporte Gestapo Wien (Vienna Gestapo daily reports) 1938–1945 (online edition now only available under licence and to institutions)
Unterlagen des 1948 aufgelösten Bundesverbands ehemaliger politisch verfolgter Antifaschisten – KZ-Verband
Akten des Opferfürsorgereferates des Magistrats der Stadt Wien
Interviews, 'Erzählte Geschichte' collection, transcripts
Splitterakten der Bundespolizeidirektion Wien: Abteilung I, Staatspolizeiliche Abteilung (Vienna Police Headquarters: Department I, State Police)

Hessisches Hauptstaatsarchiv Wiesbaden
Hessian State Archives, Wiesbaden
518/8586, Verfahren vor der Wiedergutmachungskammer des LG Frankfurt am Main in der Rückerstattungssache Robert Feix

Institut für Zeitgeschichte München
Leibniz Institute for Contemporary History, Munich
ZS 735, 7738/89, sheets 24–51, interview with Franz Josef Huber

National Archives and Records Administration (NARA), Washington DC
SS-Personalhauptamt
Microcopies T 84, R 13, R 14, R 16, Vienna Gestapo daily reports (copies at DÖW)

KV2/2656, Detailed interrogation report of Johann Sanitzer, Gestapo, Vienna

Niederösterreichisches Landesarchiv
Archive of the Federal Province of Lower Austria
ZR, 253, I/Ia, 1939
Kreisgericht Wiener Neustadt

Österreichisches Staatsarchiv
Austrian State Archives
AdR, Bundesministerium für Finanzen, beschlagnahmte Vermögen, Judenvermögensabgabe (JUVA)
AdR 04, 'Bürckel' material
AdR, Gauakten (Gau files)
AdR, Bestand Liegenschaften, box 388
AdR, Reichsstatthalter Wien, Organisationsreferat, box 193
AVA Reichsstatthalter, Staatspolizeileitstelle Wien, Asservate Dr. Schuschnigg
AVA, Reichsstatthalter, Reichskommissar, Stimmungsberichte

Politisches Archiv des Auswärtigen Amts
Political Archive of the Federal Foreign Office, Germany
RZ211

Private archive Doris (Dymia) Schulze, Vienna

Private archive Thomas Mang
Dr Karl Ebner, Statement on the structure and operations of the Vienna Gestapo 1938–45
Interview by Thomas Mang with Ebner's daughter Ingrid Leierer-Ebner, 23 July 1998

Russian State Military Archive (RGVA), Moscow
'Special Archive', holding 1525k (no title, central collected card indexes of all Gestapo regional headquarters)

State Archive of the Russian Federation (GARF), Moscow
Holding R-7523: Supreme Soviet
Department (Opis) 76a: Decisions of the Presidium of the Supreme Soviet of the USSR on petitions for pardon of persons condemned to death (1951–54)
File 89: Statements of the Supreme Court of the USSR in matters concerning persons condemned to death
Holding R 9474: Supreme Court of the USSR
Department (Opis) 1a: Plenum of the Supreme Court. Materials for permanent preservation
File 9694: Supreme Court of the USSR. Subject 114s-1951 Linauer Erwin, Rabara Ernst, Dunkl Josef, Kohout Franz

Wiener Stadt- und Landesarchiv (WstLA)
Archive of the City and Federal Province of Vienna
Bundespolizeidirektion Wien: Abteilung I, Staatspolizeiliche Abteilung (Vienna Police Headquarters: Department I, State Police)
Gebäudeakt Wien 1, Morzinplatz 4, Innere Stadt Einlagezahl 306
Handelsgericht Wien, A44-B-Registerakten: A44-B-Registerakten: B1, 42 Hotel Metropole
Verfahren des Volksgerichts beim Landesgericht für Strafsachen Wien (proceedings of the VG at the Vienna LG)
Verfahren des Sondergerichts beim Landgericht Wien (proceedings of the SG at the Vienna LG)

Yad Vashem
'Österreich-Sammlung' / 'Austria Collection'

Zentrale Stelle der Landesjustizverwaltungen zur Aufklärung nationalsozialistischer Verbrechen / Central Office of the State Justice Administrations for the Investigation of National Socialist Crimes (ZStL)
110 AR-Z 70/76, Entnazifizierungsakten (denazification files) Franz Josef Huber

Printed Sources (see also Books and Articles)
Austrian Labor Information (New York, 1942–45)
Reichsgesetzblatt (German Reich)
Strafgesetzbuch für das Deutsche Reich
Staatsgesetzblatt für die Republik Österreich (1945)
Völkischer Beobachter
Wiener Diözesanblatt
Neues Österreich, 1945, 1946, 1948
Volksstimme, 1948
Wiener Zeitung, 1948
Der Spiegel
Nachrichtenblatt des Kommandeurs der Sicherheitspolizei in Wien (1945)

Internet Sources
http://www.doew.at/erinnern/personendatenbanken/gestapo-opfer
'Deutsche Geschichte im 20. Jahrhundert Online' (2009, access now only possible under licence and to institutions)
https://de.wikipedia.org
https://en.wikipedia.org
www.simon-wiesenthal-archiv.at
http://www.dasrotewien.at
http://www.gdw-berlin.de/nc/de/vertiefung/biographien/
www.klahrgesellschaft.at/Mitteilungen
DÖW yearbooks and certain other titles can be downloaded under: https://www.doew.at/erforschen/publikationen/downloads

Books and Articles

Alberti, Michael. *Die Verfolgung und Vernichtung der Juden im Reichsgau Wartheland 1939–1945*. Wiesbaden, 2006.

Albu, Diana, and Franz Weisz. 'Spitzel und Spitzelwesen der Gestapo in Wien von 1938 bis 1945'. *Wiener Geschichtsblätter* 54(3) (1999), 169–208.

Améry, Jean. *At the Mind's Limits: Contemplations by a Survivor on Auschwitz and its Realities*, trans. Sidney Rosenfeld and Stella P. Rosenfeld. Bloomington, IN, 1980. (*Jenseits von Schuld und Sühne, Bewältigungsversuche eines Überwältigten*. Munich, 1966)

Angetter, Daniela. *Gott schütze Österreich. Wilhelm Zehner (1883–1938). Porträt eines österreichischen Soldaten* (Österreichisches Biographisches Lexikon – Schriftenreihe, vol. 10). Vienna, 2006 (2nd printing).

Aronson, Shlomo. *Reinhard Heydrich und die Frühgeschichte von Gestapo und SD*. Stuttgart, 1971.

Bailer, Brigitte. 'Tatort Frankreich: Widerstand von ÖsterreicherInnen und ein "Experte" der Gestapo-Leitstelle Wien', in L. Dreidemy, R. Hufschmied and A. Meisinger (eds), *Bananen, Cola, Zeitgeschichte. Oliver Rathkolb und das lange 20. Jahrhundert*, vol. 1 (Vienna, 2015), 397–406.

Bailer, Brigitte, and Wolfgang Form (eds). 'Tagesrapporte der Gestapo-Leitstelle Wien 1938–1945', in 'Deutsche Geschichte im 20. Jahrhundert Online' (2009, access now only possible under licence and to institutions).

Bailer, Brigitte, and Gerhard Ungar. 'Die Zahl der Todesopfer politischer Verfolgung – Ergebnisse des Projekts', in DÖW, *Jahrbuch 2013*, 111–24.

Bailer, Brigitte, et al. 'Die Gestapo als zentrales Instrument des NS-Terrors in Österreich', in DÖW, *Jahrbuch 2013*, 163–90.

Banach, Jens. *Heydrichs Elite. Das Führungskorps der Sicherheitspolizei und des SD 1936–1945*. Paderborn, 1998.

Bandhauer-Schöffmann, Irene. *Entzug und Restitution im Bereich der Katholischen Kirche* (Veröffentlichungen der Österreichischen Historikerkommission, 22/1). Vienna, 2004.

Bauer, Manuela, and Hannes Sulzenbacher. 'Schlussbericht zum Forschungsprojekt "Die Strafverfolgung homosexueller Handlungen durch die NS-Militärgerichtsbarkeit in Wien 1938–1945"' (made available to the authors by the Zukunftsfonds der Republik Österreich / Future Fund of the Republic of Austria).

Beaurain, Carine. 'Die Kinder von Zeugen Jehovas unter dem Dritten Reich. Verfolgung von Kindern und Jugendlichen in Europa'. Doctoral thesis, Vienna, 2004.

Beer, Siegfried. '"Arcel/Cassia/Redbird". Die Widerstandsgruppe Maier–Messner und der amerikanische Kriegsgeheimdienst OSS in Bern, Istanbul und Algier 1943/1944', in DÖW, *Jahrbuch 1993*, 75–100.

Beinhauer, Edith. 'Sr. M. Restituta Kafka SFCC. Selige, Krankenschwester, Demokratin', in Mikrut, *Martyrologium*, vol. 1, 119–34.

Benz, Wolfgang, Hermann Graml and Hermann Weiß (eds). *Enzyklopädie des Nationalsozialismus*. Munich, 1997.

Best, Werner. 'Die Geheime Staatspolizei', *Deutsches Recht* 6(7/8) (15 April 1936).

———. 'Rechtsbegriff und Verfassung', *Deutsches Recht* 9(24) (29 July 1939).

Birn, Ruth Bettina. *Die höheren SS- und Polizeiführer. Himmlers Vertreter im Reich und den besetzten Gebieten*. Düsseldorf, 1986.

Black, Peter R. *Ernst Kaltenbrunner: Ideological Soldier of the Third Reich*. Princeton, NJ, 1984.

Boberach, Heinz (ed.). *Meldungen aus dem Reich. Auswahl aus den geheimen Lageberichten des Sicherheitsdienstes der SS 1939–1944*. Neuwied, 1965.

Broszat, Martin. 'Nationalsozialistische Konzentrationslager 1933–1945', in Martin Broszat et al. (eds), *Anatomie des SS-Staates* (5th printing, Munich, 1989).

Brunner, Andreas, and Hannes Sulzenbacher. 'Das Projekt der Namentlichen Erfassung der homosexuellen und transgender Opfer des Nationalsozialismus in Wien', in Andreas Brunner, Hannes Sulzenbacher and Wolfgang Wilhelm (eds), *Zu spät? Dimensionen des Gedenkens an homosexuelle und transgender Opfer des Nationalsozialismus* (Vienna, 2015), 98–122.

Buber-Neumann, Margarete. *Under Two Dictators: Prisoner of Stalin and Hitler*, trans. Edward Fitzgerald. London, 2008. (*Als Gefangene bei Stalin und Hitler*. Stuttgart, 1968)

Buchheim, Hans. 'Die Höheren SS- und Polizeiführer'. *Vierteljahreshefte für Zeitgeschichte* 11(4) (October 1963), 362–91.

Buchheit, Gert. *Der deutsche Geheimdienst. Geschichte der militärischen Abwehr*. Munich, 1966.

Bukey, Evan Burr. *Hitler's Austria: Popular Sentiment in the Nazi Era, 1938–1945*. Chapel Hill, NC, 2000.

Butterweck, Hellmut. *Nationalsozialisten vor dem Volksgericht Wien. Österreichs Ringen um Gerechtigkeit 1945–1955 in der zeitgenössischen öffentlichen Wahrnehmung*. Innsbruck, 2016.

Cezanne-Thauss, Christine. 'Lambert Leutgeb. Ein Wiener Gestapobeamter und seine Spitzel. Zur Biographie und Tätigkeit Lambert Leutgebs, Leiter des Nachrichtenreferats der Gestapo-Leitstelle Wien'. Degree dissertation, Vienna University, 2003.

Crankshaw, Edward. *Gestapo: Instrument of Tyranny*. New York, 1956.

Czech, Herwig. *Selektion und 'Ausmerze'. Das Wiener Gesundheitsamt und die Umsetzung der nationalsozialistischen 'Erbgesundheitspolitik' 1938 bis 1945*. Vienna, 2003.

Dahm, Volker. 'Der Terrorapparat', in *Die tödliche Utopie. Bilder, Texte, Dokumente, Daten zum Dritten Reich*. Munich, 1999.

Dams, Carsten, and Michael Stolle. *The Gestapo: Power and Terror in the Third Reich*, trans. Charlotte Ryland. Oxford, 2014. (*Die Gestapo. Herrschaft und Terror im Dritten Reich*. Munich, 2008)

Davy, Ulrike. *Die Geheime Staatspolizei in Österreich, Organisation und Aufgaben der Geheimen Staatspolizei im 'Dritten Reich' und die Weiterführung ihrer Geschäfte durch österreichische Staatsbehörden*. Vienna, 1990.

Deutsche Greuel in Russland. Gerichtstag in Charkow. Vienna: Sternverlag, n.d. (ca. 1946).

Diamant, Adolf. *Ghetto Litzmannstadt. Bilanz eines nationalsozialistischen Verbrechens*. Frankfurt am Main, 1986.

Diewald-Kerkmann, Gisela. 'Denunziantentum und Gestapo. Die freiwilligen "Helfer aus der Bevölkerung"', in Paul and Mallmann, *Die Gestapo – Mythos und Realität*, 288–305.

———. *Politische Denunziation im NS-Regime*. Bonn, 1995.
Dohmen, Herbert, and Nina Scholz. *Denunziert*. Vienna, 2003.
Dokumentationsarchiv des österreichischen Widerstandes (DÖW). *'Anschluß' 1938. Eine Dokumentation*. Vienna, 1988.
DÖW. *Erzählte Geschichte. Berichte von Widerstandskämpfern und Verfolgten* (vol. 1 in the series 'Erzählte Geschichte') Vienna, 1986.
DÖW. *Für Spaniens Freiheit. Österreicher an der Seite der Spanischen Republik 1936–1939*. Vienna, 1986.
DÖW. *Jahrbuch* (Vienna, 1986–2020).
DÖW. *Österreicher im Exil: Frankreich 1938–1945. Eine Dokumentation*. Vienna, 1984.
DÖW. *Österreicher im Exil: Großbritannien 1938–1945. Eine Dokumentation*. Vienna, 1992.
DÖW. *Widerstand und Verfolgung im Burgenland 1934–1945*. Vienna, 1979.
DÖW. *Widerstand und Verfolgung in Niederösterreich 1934–1945*, 3 vols. Vienna, 1987.
DÖW. *Widerstand und Verfolgung in Tirol 1934–1945*, 2 vols. Vienna, 1984.
DÖW. *Widerstand und Verfolgung in Wien 1934–1945*, 3 vols. 2nd printing, Vienna, 1984.
DÖW and the Institut Theresienstädter Initiative. *Theresienstädter Gedenkbuch. Österreichische Jüdinnen und Juden in Theresienstadt 1942–1945*. Prague, 2005.
Dörner, Bernward. 'Gestapo und "Heimtücke". Zur Praxis der Geheimen Staatspolizei bei der Verfolgung von Verstößen gegen das "Heimtücke-Gesetz"', in Paul and Mallmann, *Die Gestapo – Mythos und Realität*, 325–42.
———. *'Heimtücke'. Das Gesetz als Waffe. Kontrolle, Abschreckung und Verfolgung in Deutschland 1933–1945*. Paderborn, 1998.
———. 'NS-Herrschaft und Denunziation. Anmerkungen zu Defiziten in der Denunziationsforschung'. *Historical Social Research* 26(2/3) (2001), 55–69.
Eckert, Rainer. 'Gestapo-Berichte. Abbildungen der Realität oder reine Spekulation?', in Paul and Mallmann, *Die Gestapo – Mythos und Realität*, 204–7.
Evans, Richard J. *The Third Reich in Power, 1933–1939*. London, 2005.-
Exenberger, Herbert. 'Der österreichische Arbeiterschriftsteller Benedikt Fantner – ermordet im Jänner 1942 in der Gaskammer von Hartheim', in Bund sozialdemokratischer Freiheitskämpfer, Opfer des Faschismus und aktiver Antifaschisten, *Jahrbuch 2007* (Vienna, 2007), 45–60.
Ferihumer, Konstantin, and Winfried Garscha. 'Der "Stein-Komplex"', in DÖW, *Jahrbuch 2016*, 51–82.
Feymann, Walter. 'Das Deutschnationale im politischen Denken Ludwig Lesers', in Wolfgang Gürtler and Gerhard Winkler (eds), *Forscher – Gestalter – Vermittler. Festschrift Gerald Schlag* (Eisenstadt, 2001), 87–106.
Filip, Irene. 'Voluntarias Internacionales de la Libertad. 34 Österreicherinnen gegen Franco'. *Mitteilungen der Alfred Klahr Gesellschaft* 23(3) (September 2016), 1–4.
Fischer, Erica. *Das Wichtigste ist, sich selber treu zu bleiben. Die Geschichte der Zwillingsschwestern Rosl und Liesl*. Vienna, 2005.
Form, Wolfgang, and Albrecht Kirschner. 'Verfahren gegen ehemalige Spanienkämpfer', in Form, Neugebauer and Schiller, *NS-Justiz und politische Verfolgung in Österreich 1938–1945*, 751–65.

Fraenkel, Ernst. *The Dual State: A Contribution to the Theory of Dictatorship*, trans. E.A. Shils in collaboration with Edith Lowenstein and Klaus Knorr. Oxford, 2017. (*Der Doppelstaat*. Frankfurt am Main, [1984] 1941).
Frei, Bruno. *Der kleine Widerstand*. Vienna, 1978.
Freihammer, Nina. 'Dem NS-Regime nicht untergeordnet. Biographische Stationen des österreichischen Widerstandskämpfers Josef Sasso bis 1945'. Degree dissertation, Vienna University, 1999.
'Freimaurer im Exil und Widerstand'. *Zwischenwelt* 34(3) (October 2017).
Freund, Florian. 'Zwangsarbeit von zivilen Ausländern und Ausländerinnen in Österreich 1938 bis 1945', in Ingrid Böhler and Rolf Steininger (eds), *Österreichischer Zeitgeschichtetag 1993, 24. bis 27. Mai 1993 in Innsbruck* (Innsbruck, 1995), 216–24.
Gafke, Matthias. *Heydrichs Ostmärker. Das österreichische Führungspersonal der Sicherheitspolizei und des SD 1939–1945*. Darmstadt, 2014.
Garbe, Detlef. *Between Resistance and Martyrdom: Jehovah's Witnesses in the Third Reich*, trans. Dagmar G. Grimm. Madison, WI, 2008. (*Zwischen Widerstand und Martyrium. Die Zeugen Jehovas im 'Dritten Reich'*. Munich, 1999)
Gardiner, Muriel, and Joseph Buttinger. *Damit wir nicht vergessen. Unsere Jahre 1934–1947 in Wien, Paris und New York*. Vienna, 1978.
Garscha, Winfried R. 'Entnazifizierung und gerichtliche Ahndung von NS-Verbrechen', in Talos et al. (eds), *NS-Herrschaft in Österreich. Ein Handbuch*, 852–83.
———. 'Organisatoren und Nutzniesser des Holocaust, Denunzianten, "Illegale"', in DÖW, *Jahrbuch 2001*, 91–123.
Garscha, Winfried R., and Claudia Kuretsidis-Haider. 'Der Export der "Rüter-Kategorien". Eine Zwischenbilanz der Erfassung und Analyse der österreichischen Gerichtsverfahren wegen nationalsozialistischer Gewaltverbrechen', in Dick de Mildt (ed.), *Staatsverbrechen vor Gericht. Festschrift für Christiaan Frederik Rüter zum 65. Geburtstag* (Amsterdam, 2003), 73–117.
'Gedenkstätte für die Opfer der Gestapo Wien', pictures and texts from the exhibition curated by Elisabeth Boeckl-Klamper, Thomas Mang and Wolfgang Neugebauer, in DÖW, *Jahrbuch 2012*, 11–85.
Gellately, Robert. 'Allwissend und allgegenwärtig? Entstehung, Funktion und Wandel des Gestapo-Mythos', in Paul and Mallmann, *Die Gestapo – Mythos und Realität*, 47–70.
———. *The Gestapo and German Society: Enforcing Racial Policy 1933–1945*. Oxford, 1990.
Geppert, W. *Im Namen des Volkes. 25 Jahre Bedrohung der Welt*. Vienna, 1942.
Gerbel, Christian, Alexander Mejstrik and Reinhard Sieder. 'Die "Schlurfs". Verweigerung und Opposition von Wiener Arbeiterjugendlichen im Dritten Reich', in Talos et al. (eds), *NS-Herrschaft in Österreich. Ein Handbuch*, 523–48.
Glaubauf, Karl. *Robert Bernardis. Österreichs Stauffenberg*. Privately printed, 1994.
Graf, Wolfgang. *Österreichische SS-Generäle. Himmlers verlässliche Vasallen*. Klagenfurt, 2012.
Grode, Walter. *Die 'Sonderbehandlung 14f13' in den Konzentrationslagern des Dritten Reiches. Ein Beitrag zur Dynamik faschistischer Vernichtungspolitik*. Frankfurt am Main, 1987.

Hachmeister, Lutz. *Der Gegnerforscher. Die Karriere des SS-Führers Franz Alfred Six*. Munich, 1998.
Halbrainer, Heimo. *'Der größte Lump im ganzen Land, das ist und bleibt der Denunziant'. Denunziation in der Steiermark 1938–1945 und der Umgang mit den Denunzianten in der Zweiten Republik*. Graz, 2007.
Handbuch Reichsgau Wien 63/64. Vienna, 1941.
Hanisch, Ernst. 'Gibt es einen spezifisch österreichischen Widerstand', in Peter Steinbach (ed.), *Widerstand. Ein Problem zwischen Theorie und Geschichte* (Cologne, 1987), 163–76.
Hautmann, Hans. 'Kommunisten und Kommunistinnen in der Wiener Polizei'. *Mitteilungen der Alfred Klahr Gesellschaft* 19(2) (June 2012), 2–25.
———. 'Der Polizeiliche Hilfsdienst für die Kommandantur der Stadt Wien im Jahr 1945', in *Quellen & Studien 2000. Die Alfred Klahr Gesellschaft und ihr Archiv. Beiträge zur österreichischen Geschichte des 20. Jahrhunderts* (Vienna, 2000), 277–346.
Heimann-Jelinek, Felicitas. 'Die "Arisierung" der Rothschildschen Vermögen in Wien und ihre Restituierung nach 1945', in Georg Heuberger (ed.), *Die Rothschilds. Beiträge zur Geschichte einer europäischen Familie* (Frankfurt, 1994), 355–68.
Hensle. Michael. *Rundfunkverbrechen. Das Hören von 'Feindsendern' im Nationalsozialismus*. Berlin, 2003.
Herbert, Ulrich. *Best. Biographische Studien über Radikalismus, Weltanschauung und Vernunft, 1903–1989*. Bonn, 1996.
Hesse, Klaus, Pamela Eve Selwyn and the Stiftung Topographie des Terrors. *Topographie des Terrors. Gestapo, SS und Reichssicherheitshauptamt in der Wilhelm- und Prinz-Albrecht-Straße – eine Dokumentation*. Berlin, 2010.
Heusler, Andreas. 'Prävention durch Terror. Die Gestapo und die Kontrolle der ausländischen Zwangsarbeiter am Beispiel München', in Paul and Mallmann, *Die Gestapo im Zweiten Weltkrieg*, 222–36.
Heydrich, Reinhard. 'Aufbau und Entwicklung der Sicherheitspolizei im Lande Österreich'. *Das Schwarze Korps. Zeitung der Schutzstaffeln der NSDAP – Organ der Reichsführung SS*, 21 April 1938, 3–4.
———. 'Die Bekämpfung der Staatsfeinde'. *Deutsches Recht* 6(7/8) (15 April 1936), 121–23.
Höfferer, Christina. 'Emmy Stein – Operettenstar und Gründerin der Eden-Bar'. *Wiener Geschichtsblätter* 61(2) (2006), 67–82.
Hoffmann, Georg. *Fliegerlynchjustiz. Gewalt gegen abgeschossene alliierte Flugzeugbesatzungen 1943–1945*. Paderborn, 2015.
Holpfer, Eva. 'Der Umgang der Burgenländischen Nachkriegsgesellschaft mit NS-Verbrechen bis 1955. Am Beispiel der wegen der Massaker von Deutschschützen und Rechnitz geführten Volksgerichtsprozesse'. Degree dissertation, Vienna University, 1998.
'Homosexuellenverfolgung in Österreich. Geschichte und Nachgeschichte'. *Zeitgeschichte* 43(2) (March–April 2016).
Höttl, Wilhelm. *Einsatz für das Reich*. Koblenz, 1997.
Indelárová, Lenka. *Finale der Vernichtung. Die Einsatzgruppe H in der Slowakei 1944/1945*. Darmstadt, 2013.

Jagschitz, Gerhard, and Wolfgang Neugebauer (eds). *Stein, 6. April 1945. Das Urteil des Volksgerichts Wien (August 1946) gegen die Verantwortlichen des Massakers im Zuchthaus Stein.* Vienna, 1995.

Jakli, Timon. 'Die Verfolgung der ZeugInnen Jehovas in Österreich 1938–1945'. *Zeitgeschichte* 42(6) (Nov/Dec 2015), 347–67.

Jedlicka, Ludwig. *Der 20. Juli 1944 in Österreich.* Vienna, 1965.

Jellonnek, Burkhard. 'Staatspolizeiliche Fahndungs- und Ermittlungsmethoden gegen Homosexuelle', in Paul and Mallmann, *Die Gestapo – Mythos und Realität*, 343–56.

Johnson, Eric A. *Nazi Terror: The Gestapo, Jews, and Ordinary Germans.* New York, 1999.

Kapralik, Charles J. 'Erinnerungen eines Beamten der Wiener Israelitischen Kultusgemeinde 1938/39'. *LBI-Bulletin* 58 (1981), 52–78.

Kempner, Benedicta Maria. *Priester vor Hitlers Tribunalen.* Munich, 1966.

Kirschner, Albrecht. 'Wehrkraftzersetzung', in Form, Neugebauer and Schiller, *NS-Justiz und politische Verfolgung in Österreich 1938–1945*, 403–748.

Klamper, Elisabeth. 'Der schlechte Ort zu Wien. Zur Situation der Wiener Juden vom "Anschluß" bis zum Novemberpogrom 1938', in Tino Erben (ed.), *Der Novemberpogrom 1938. Die "Reichskristallnacht" in Wien. 116. Sonderausstellung des Historischen Museums der Stadt Wien. 10. Nov. 1988 bis 29. Jänner 1989.* (Vienna, 1988), 33–42.

———. 'Die Situation der jüdischen Bevölkerung in Wien vom Ausbruch bis zum Ende des Krieges', in DÖW. *Jüdische Schicksale. Berichte von Verfolgten* (vol. 3 in the series 'Erzählte Geschichte'; Vienna, 1992), 164–301.

Klee, Ernst. *Personenlexikon zum Dritten Reich. Wer war was vor und nach 1945.* 2nd printing, Frankfurt am Main, 2007.

Klingler, Walter. *Nationalsozialistische Rundfunkpolitik 1942–1945. Organisation, Programm und die Hörer.* University of Mannheim, 1983.

Knight, Robert (ed.). *Ich bin dafür, die Sache in die Länge zu ziehen. Wortprotokolle der österreichischen Bundesregierung von 1945–1952 über die Entschädigung der Juden.* Frankfurt am Main, 1988.

Kohlhaas, Elisabeth. 'Die Mitarbeiter der regionalen Staatspolizeistellen', in Paul and Mallmann, *Die Gestapo – Mythos und Realität*, 219–35.

———. 'Weibliche Angestellte der Gestapo 1933–1945', in Krauss, *Sie waren dabei*, 148–65.

Koop, Volker. *In Hitlers Hand. 'Sonder- und Ehrenhäftlinge' der SS.* Cologne, 2010.

Krausnick, Helmut, and Wilhelm Hans-Heinrich. *Die Truppe des Weltanschauungskrieges. Die Einsatzgruppen der Sicherheitspolizei und des SD 1938–1942.* Stuttgart, 1981.

Krauss, Marita (ed.). *Sie waren dabei. Mitläuferinnen, Nutznießerinnen, Täterinnen im Nationalsozialismus.* Göttingen, 2008.

Kreisky, Bruno. *Erinnerungen. Das Vermächtnis eines Jahrhundertpolitikers*, ed. Oliver Rathkolb. Vienna, 2007.

Kuller, Christiane. *Bürokratie und Verbrechen. Antisemitische Finanzpolitik und Verwaltungspraxis im nationalsozialistischen Deutschland.* Munich, 2013.

Kuretsidis-Haider, Claudia. *'Das Volk sitzt zu Gericht'. Österreichische Justiz und NS-Verbrechen am Beispiel der Engerau-Prozesse 1945–1955.* Innsbruck, 2006.

Landauer, Hans. 'Zelle 44a'. Manuscript, DÖW Spanish Civil War fighters archive, 25 000/I402.

Landauer, Hans, in collaboration with Erich Hackl. *Lexikon der österreichischen Spanienkämpfer 1936–1939*. 2nd printing, Vienna, 2008.
Lein, Hermann. *Als Innitzergardist in Dachau und Mauthausen*. Vienna, 1988.
Lenz, Johannes Maria. *Als Priester in den Ketten der Gestapo*. Salzburg, 1945.
Leser, Norbert. 'Ludwig Leser. Pionier des Burgenlandes'. *Österreich in Geschichte und Literatur* 4(1991), 194–205.
Lichtenwagner, Mathias. *Leerstellen. Zur Topographie der Wehrmachtsjustiz in Wien vor und nach 1945*. Vienna, 2012.
Liebmann, Maximilian. 'Kirche und Anschluss', in Liebmann, Hans Paarhammer and Alfred Rinnerthaler (eds), *Staat und Kirche in der 'Ostmark'* (Frankfurt am Main, 1998), 207–30.
———. 'Schlussvortrag im Seligsprechungsprozess Maria Restituta (Helene Kafka)', in DÖW, *Jahrbuch 1991*, 13–19.
Lillie, Sophie. *Was einmal war. Handbuch der enteigneten Kunstsammlungen Wiens*. Vienna, 2003.
Linck, Stephan. *Der Ordnung verpflichtet. Deutsche Polizei 1933–1949. Der Fall Flensburg*. Paderborn, 2000.
'Liste des schädlichen und unerwünschten Schrifttums'. Reprint of the issues 1938–1941, Vaduz, 1979.
Longerich, Peter. *'Davon haben wir nichts gewusst!' Die Deutschen und die Judenverfolgung 1933–1945*. Munich, 2006.
Lotfi, Gabriele. *KZ der Gestapo. Arbeitserziehungslager im Dritten Reich*. Stuttgart, 2000.
———. 'Stätten des Terrors. Die "Arbeitserziehungslager" der Gestapo', in Paul and Mallmann, *Die Gestapo im Zweiten Weltkrieg*, 255–69.
Lustiger, Arno. *Rettungswiderstand. Über die Judenretter in Europa während der NS-Zeit*. Göttingen, 2011.
Luza, Radomir. *The Resistance in Austria 1938–1945*. Minneapolis, 1984.
Maimann, Helene. 'Schwester Restituta. Versuch über eine Unbequeme', in Helmut Konrad and Wolfgang Neugebauer (eds), *Arbeiterbewegung. Faschismus. Nationalbewußtsein* (Vienna, 1983), 201–12.
Mallmann, Klaus-Michael. 'Menschenjagd und Massenmord. Das neue Instrument der Einsatzgruppen und -kommandos 1938–1945', in Paul and Mallmann, *Die Gestapo im Zweiten Weltkrieg*, 291–316.
———. 'Die V-Leute der Gestapo. Umrisse einer kollektiven Biographie', in Paul and Mallmann, *Die Gestapo – Mythos und Realität*, 268–87.
Mallmann, Klaus-Michael, and Gerhard Paul. 'Allwissend, allmächtig, allgegenwärtig? Gestapo, Gesellschaft und Widerstand'. *Zeitschrift für Geschichtswissenschaft* 41(1993), 984–89.
———. 'Die Gestapo. Weltanschauungsexekutive mit gesellschaftlichem Rückhalt', in Paul and Mallmann, *Die Gestapo im Zweiten Weltkrieg*, 599–650.
———. *Herrschaft und Alltag. Ein Industrierevier im Dritten Reich*. Bonn, 1991.
——— (eds). *Karrieren der Gewalt. Nationalsozialistische Täterbiographien*. Darmstadt, 2004.
Mallmann, Klaus-Michael, Jochen Böhler and Jürgen Matthäus. *Einsatzgruppen in Polen. Darstellung und Dokumentation*. Darmstadt, 2008.

Mallmann, Klaus-Michael, et al. (eds). *Deutsche Berichte aus dem Osten. Dokumente der Einsatzgruppen in der Sowjetunion*, vol. 3. Darmstadt, 2014.
Mang, Thomas. '"Er brachte sehr gute und schöne Nachrichten". Leutgebs V-Leute der Gestapo. Das Verhörprotokoll, Belgrad 1947/48', in DÖW, *Jahrbuch 2014*, 165–94.
———. *'Gestapo-Leitstelle Wien – Mein Name ist Huber' Wer trug die lokale Verantwortung für den Mord an den Juden Wiens?* Münster, 2004.
———. 'Juristen in der Gestapo und der Sonderfall Leitstelle Wien', in Helmut Gebhardt (ed.), *Polizei, Recht und Geschichte* (Graz, 2006), 138–46.
———. '"Nicht in der Lage, die Judenfrage in Österreich zu lösen": Gestapo, Gauleitung und "Zentralstelle" – falsche Mythen und echte Verantwortung'. Doctoral thesis, Vienna, 2001.
———. 'Retter, um sich selbst zu retten. Die Strategie der Rückversicherung. Dr. Karl Ebner, Leiter-Stellvertreter der Staatspolizeileitstelle Wien 1942–1945'. Degree dissertation, Vienna University, 1998.
———. *Die Unperson. Karl Ebner, Judenreferent der Gestapo Wien. Eine Täterbiografie*. Bozen/Bolzano, 2013.
Manoschek, Walter (ed.). *Der Fall Rechnitz. Das Massaker an Juden im März 1945*, with a text by Elfriede Jelinek, 'Im Zweifelsfalle'. Vienna, 2009.
Marschall, Karl. *Volksgerichtsbarkeit und Verfolgung von nationalsozialistischen Gewaltverbrechen in Österreich*. 2nd printing, Vienna, 1987.
Matthäus, Jürgen. 'Konzept als Kalkül. Das Judenbild des SD 1934–1939', in Michael Wildt (ed.), *Nachrichtendienst, politische Elite und Mordeinheit. Der Sicherheitsdienst des Reichsführers SS* (Hamburg, 2003), 118–43.
Mazower, Mark. *Inside Hitler's Greece: The Experience of Occupation 1941–1944*. Hartford, CT, 2001. German translation: *Griechenland unter Hitler. Das Leben während der deutschen Besatzung 1941–1944* (Frankfurt am Main, 2016).
Meisel, Josef. *'Jetzt haben wir Ihnen, Meisel!' Kampf, Widerstand und Verfolgung des österreichischen Antifaschisten Josef Meisel (1911–1945)*. Vienna, 1985.
Meisels, Moshe. *Die Gerechten Österreichs. Eine Dokumentation der Menschlichkeit*. Tel Aviv, 1996.
Mikrut, Jan. *Blutzeugen des Glaubens. Martyrologium des 20. Jahrhunderts*, vol. 1. Vienna, 1999.
Mitterrutzner, Christa. 'Gestapoaktion Moosbierbaum', in DÖW, *Widerstand Niederösterreich*, vol. 2, 460ff.
Molden, Otto. *Der Ruf des Gewissens. Der österreichische Freiheitskampf 1938–1945*. Vienna, 1958.
Moll, Martin. 'Habsburg gegen Hitler. Legitimisten und Monarchisten im Widerstand', in Karner/Duffek, *Widerstand in Österreich 1938–1945*, 133–44.
Mommsen, Hans. *Das NS-Regime und die Auslöschung des Judentums in Europa*. Göttingen, 2014.
Moser, Jonny. 'Deportation – der Weg in den Tod', in DÖW, *Jüdische Schicksale. Berichte von Verfolgten* (vol. 3 in the series 'Erzählte Geschichte'; Vienna, 1992), 495–500.
———. *Die Judenverfolgung in Österreich 1938–1945*. Vienna, 1966.
———. *Nisko. Die ersten Judendeportationen*. Vienna, 2012.

Mugrauer, Manfred. 'Eine "Bande von Gaunern, Schwindlern und naiven Leuten". Die Widerstandsbewegung O5 und die Kommunistische Partei Österreichs', in DÖW, *Jahrbuch 2016*, 101–40.

———. 'Franz Koritschoner (1892–1941)'. *Volksstimme* (July 2014), 33–37.

Müllner, Christian. 'Schwarzhörer und Denunzianten. Vergehen nach §§ 1, 2 der Verordnung über außerordentliche Rundfunkmaßnahmen vor dem Sondergericht Wien'. Doctoral thesis, Vienna, 2011.

Neider, Michael. 'Der Strafvollzug auf dem Staatsgebiet von Österreich 1938–45'. Manuscript held at DÖW.

Neugebauer, Wolfgang. *The Austrian Resistance 1938–1945*, trans. John Nicholson and Eric Canepa. Vienna, 2014. (*Der österreichische Widerstand 1938–1945*. Revised edn, Vienna, 2015)

———. 'Mit der Waffe in der Hand. ... PartisanInnen in Österreich 1938–1945', in Lucile Dreidemy et al. (eds), *Bananen, Cola, Zeitgeschichte. Oliver Rathkolb und das lange 20. Jahrhundert*, 2 vols (Vienna, 2015), vol. 2, 383–96.

———. 'Repressionsapparat und -maßnahmen 1933–1938', in Emmerich Tálos and Wolfgang Neugebauer (eds), *Austrofaschismus. Politik, Ökonomie, Kultur* (Vienna, 2005), 298–321.

———. 'Widerstand von Jugendlichen gegen das NS-Regime', in Bundesjugendvertretung, *Geraubte Kindheit. Kinder und Jugendliche im Nationalsozialismus* (Vienna, 2010), 159–70.

Neugebauer, Wolfgang, and Peter Schwarz. *Stacheldraht, mit Tod geladen ... Der erste Österreichertransport in das KZ Dachau 1938*. Vienna, 2008.

———. *Der Wille zum aufrechten Gang. Offenlegung der Rolle des BSA bei der gesellschaftlichen Reintegration ehemaliger Nationalsozialisten*. Published under the aegis of the Bund sozialdemokratischer AkademikerInnen, Intellektueller und KünstlerInnen (BSA). Vienna, 2004.

Neugebauer, Wolfgang, and Herbert Steiner. 'Widerstand und Verfolgung in Österreich (im Zeitraum vom 12. Februar 1938 bis zum 10. April 1938)', in *Anschluß 1938. Protokoll des Symposiums am 14. und 15. März 1978* (Vienna, 1981), 86–108.

Nitschke, Peter. 'Polizei und Gestapo. Vorauseilender Gehorsam oder polykratischer Konflikt?' in Paul and Mallmann, *Die Gestapo – Mythos und Realität*, 306–24.

Nowack, Sabrina. *Sicherheitsrisiko NS-Belastung: Personalüberprüfungen im Bundesnachrichtendienst in den 1960er Jahren* (Veröffentlichungen der Unabhängigen Historikerkommission 4). Berlin 2016.

Der Nürnberger Prozess. Das Protokoll des Prozesses gegen die Hauptkriegsverbrecher vor dem Internationalen Militärgerichtshof 14. November 1945 – 1. Oktober 1946. Digitale Bibliothek, vol. 20 (Berlin, 1999), vol. 16 (Frechen, 2000). (The Nuremberg Trials: The Complete Proceedings, 22 vols, Avalon Project online: https://avalon.law.yale.edu/subject_menus/imt.asp, last accessed 27 May 2021.

Otto, Reinhard. 'Die Gestapo und die sowjetischen Kriegsgefangenen', in Paul and Mallmann, *Die Gestapo im Zweiten Weltkrieg*, 201–21.

Patka, Marcus G. 'Gedanken einer Epoche. Dr Richard Schlesinger, Großmeister der Großloge von Wien von 1919 bis 1938', in *Quatuor Coronati Berichte* 36 (2016), 167–95.

———. *Österreichische Freimaurer im Nationalsozialismus. Treue und Verrat*. Vienna, 2010.
Paul, Gerhard. '"Diese Erschießungen haben mich innerlich gar nicht mehr berührt". Die Kriegsendphaseverbrechen der Gestapo 1944/45', in Paul and Mallmann, *Die Gestapo im Zweiten Weltkrieg*, 543–68.
———. 'Ganz normale Akademiker', in Paul and Mallmann, *Die Gestapo – Mythos und Realität*, 236–54.
———. 'Kämpfende Verwaltung', in Paul and Mallmann, *Die Gestapo im Zweiten Weltkrieg*, 42–81.
———. 'Kontinuität und Radikalisierung. Die Staatspolizeistelle Würzburg', in Paul and Mallmann, *Die Gestapo – Mythos und Realität*, 161–77.
Paul, Gerhard, and Klaus-Michael Mallmann (eds). *Die Gestapo – Mythos und Realität*. Darmstadt, 1995.
——— (eds). *Die Gestapo im Zweiten Weltkrieg. 'Heimatfront' und besetztes Europa*. Darmstadt, 2000.
Paul, Gerhard, and Alexander Primavesi. 'Die Verfolgung der "Fremdvölkischen"', in Paul and Mallmann, *Die Gestapo – Mythos und Realität*, 388–401.
Pawlowsky, Verena, Edith Leisch-Prost and Christian Klösch. *Vereine im Nationalsozialismus. Vermögensentzug durch den Stillhaltekommissar für Vereine, Organisationen und Verbände und Aspekte der Restitution in Österreich nach 1945. Vereine, Stiftungen und Fonds im Nationalsozialismus* (Veröffentlichungen der Österreichischen Historikerkommission, vol. 21/1). Vienna, 2004.
Peukert, Detlev. *Die Edelweißpiraten. Protestbewegung jugendlicher Arbeiter im 'Dritten Reich'. Eine Dokumentation*. Cologne, 1988.
Pfeifer, Helfried. *Die Ostmark. Eingliederung und Neugestaltung*. Vienna, 1941.
Pfundtner, Hans (ed.). *Dr. Wilhelm Frick und sein Ministerium*. Munich, 1937.
Pichler, Ulrike. 'Dr. Othmar Trenker (Trnka) 1905–1986. Aufstieg, Tätigkeit und Verurteilung eines Wiener Gestapobeamten'. Degree dissertation, Vienna University, 2010.
Pirker, Peter. *Subversion deutscher Herrschaft. Der britische Kriegsgeheimdienst SOE und Österreich* (Zeitgeschichte im Kontext, ed. Oliver Rathkolb, 6). Göttingen, 2012.
Pohl, Dieter. *Nationalsozialistische Judenverfolgung in Ostgalizien 1941–1944. Organisation und Durchführung eines staatlichen Massenverbrechens*. Munich, 1996.
Prinz, Josef. '"Erziehung durch Arbeit – Arbeit durch Erziehung?" Ein Beitrag zur Geschichte des Arbeitserziehungslagers Oberlanzendorf bei Wien 1940–1945', in Willibald Rosner and Reinelde Motz-Linhart (eds), *Forschungen zur NS-Zeit in Niederösterreich 1938–1945* (Sankt Pölten, 2007), 185–312.
Prosl v. Chodelbach, Christian. 'Karl Burian und das Corps Ottonen', in Sebastian Sigler (ed.), *Corpsstudenten im Widerstand gegen Hitler* (Berlin, 2014), 375–91.
Rabinovici, Doron. *Eichmann's Jews*, trans. Nick Somers. Cambridge, 2011. (*Instanzen der Ohnmacht. Wien 1938–1945. Der Weg zum Judenrat*. Frankfurt am Main, 2000).
Ramme, Alwin. *Der Sicherheitsdienst der SS*. Berlin, 1970.
Rathkolb, Oliver. 'Raoul Bumballa. Ein politischer Nonkonformist 1945. Fallstudie zur Funktion der O5 im Widerstand und in der Parteirestauration', in *Unterdrückung und Emanzipation. Festschrift für Erika Weinzierl* (Vienna, 1985), 295–317.

Reuband, Karl-Heinz. 'Denunziation im Dritten Reich. Die Bedeutung von Systemunterstützung und Gelegenheitsstrukturen'. *Historical Social Research* 26(2/3) (2001), 219–34.

———. '"Schwarzhören" im Dritten Reich. Verbreitung, Erscheinungsformen und Kommunikationsmuster beim Umgang mit verbotenen Sendern'. *Archiv für Sozialgeschichte* (2001), 374–98.

Rizy, Lisl, and Willi Weinert (eds). *'Mein Kopf wird euch auch nicht retten'. Korrespondenzen österreichischer WiderstandskämpferInnen aus der Haft*. Vienna, 2016.

Röder, Werner. *Sonderfahndungsliste UdSSR*. Erlangen, 1976.

Röll, Wolfgang. *Sozialdemokraten im Konzentrationslager Buchenwald 1937–1945*. Göttingen, 2000.

Rosenkranz, Herbert. *Verfolgung und Selbstbehauptung. Die Juden in Österreich 1938–1945*. Vienna, 1978.

Roth, Stephan. '"Da ich heute um 5 Uhr erschossen werde …". Widerstand am Fliegerhorst Markersdorf', in DÖW, *Jahrbuch 2016*, 83–99.

Rothländer, Christiane. *Karl Motesiczky 1904–1943. Eine biographische Rekonstruktion*. Vienna, 2010.

Rot-Weiß-Rot-Buch. Darstellungen, Dokumente und Nachweise zur Vorgeschichte und Geschichte der Okkupation Österreich (nach amtlichen Quellen), part 1. Vienna, 1946.

Rudolf, Karl. *Aufbau im Widerstand. Ein Seelsorgebericht aus Österreich 1938–1945*. Salzburg, 1947.

Rürup, Reinhard (ed.). *Topographie des Terrors. Gestapo, SS und Reichssicherheitshauptamt auf dem 'Prinz-Albrecht-Gelände'. Eine Dokumentation*. Berlin, 2001.

Rüter, C.F., and D.W. de Mildt (eds). *Justiz und NS-Verbrechen. Sammlung Deutscher Strafurteile wegen Nationalsozialistischer Tötungsverbrechen 1945–2012*, 49 vols. Amsterdam, 1968–2012.

Sabitzer, Werner. 'Schwieriger Neubeginn. Im Mai 1945, kurz nach Kriegsende, gab es in Wien vier Polizeiorganisationen, drei von ihnen waren unter kommunistischem Einfluss'. *Öffentliche Sicherheit* 2005(5–6), 73ff.

Safrian, Hans. *Eichmann's Men*, trans. Ute Stargedt. Cambridge, 2010. (*Die Eichmann-Männer*. Vienna, 1993)

Safrian, Hans, and Hans Witek. *'Und keiner war dabei'. Dokumente des alltäglichen Antisemitismus in Wien 1938*. New printing, Vienna, 2008.

Sainitzer, Lukas. 'Die Gruppe Strohmer und der Todesmarsch von Oberlanzendorf nach Mauthausen', in *Jahrbuch der KZ-Gedenkstätte Mauthausen* 7 (2013), published under the aegis of the Austrian Federal Ministry of the Interior (Vienna, 2013), 71–84.

Schafranek, Hans. 'Die "Anti-Hitler-Bewegung Österreichs" und die "Anti-Hitler-Bewegung der Ostarbeiter" im Widerstand gegen das NS-Regime 1942-1944', in DÖW, *Jahrbuch 2015*, 229–58.

———. 'Das "Anti-Hitler-Komitee" und die Fallschirmagenten-Gruppe um Gregor Kersche'. *Journal for Intelligence, Propaganda and Security Studies* 6(1) (2012), 7–20.

———. 'Drei Gestapo-Spitzel und ein eifriger Kriminalbeamter. Die Infiltration und Zerschlagung des KJV Wien-Baumgarten (1940) und der KPÖ-Bezirksleitung Wien-Leopoldstadt (1940/41) durch V-Leute der Gestapo', in DÖW, *Jahrbuch 2009*.

———. 'Franz Koritschoner (1892–1941)'. Manuscript (Vienna, 1995) held at DÖW.

———. 'Im Hinterland des Feindes. Sowjetische Fallschirmagenten im Deutschen Reich 1942–1944', in DÖW, *Jahrbuch 1996*, 10–40.

———. *Söldner, für den Anschluss. Die österreichische Legion 1933–1938*. Vienna, 2010.

———. 'V-Leute und "Verräter". Die Unterwanderung kommunistischer Widerstandsgruppen durch Konfidenten der Wiener Gestapo'. *IWK. Internationale wissenschaftliche Korrespondenz zur Geschichte der deutschen Arbeiterbewegung* 3 (2000), 300–349.

———. *Widerstand und Verrat. Gestapospitzel im antifaschistischen Untergrund*. Vienna, 2017, reprinted 2020.

———. *Widerstand und Verrat. Die Unterwanderung der illegalen Arbeiterbewegung in Österreich (1938–1944) durch die Gestapo*. Vienna, 1996.

———. *Zwischen NKWD und Gestapo. Die Auslieferung deutscher und österreichischer Antifaschisten aus der Sowjetunion an Nazideutschland 1937–1941*. Frankfurt am Main, 1990.

Schafranek, Hans, and Andrea Hurton. 'Im Netz der Verräter'. *Der Standard*, 4 June 2010.

Schärf, Adolf. *Österreichs Erneuerung 1945–1955*. Vienna, 1955.

Schärf, Paul. *Otto Haas. Ein revolutionärer Sozialist gegen das Dritte Reich*. Vienna, 1967.

Schellenberg, Walter. *Aufzeichnungen. Die Memoiren des letzten Geheimdienstchefs unter Hitler*. Wiesbaden, 1979. (*The Labyrinth. The Memoirs of Hitler's Secret Service Chief*. London, 1956.)

Schirach, Baldur von. *Ich glaubte an Hitler*. Munich, 1967.

Schmidl, Erwin A. *Der 'Anschluss' Österreichs. Der Deutsche Einmarsch im März 1938*. Bonn, 1994.

Schmiechen-Ackermann, Detlef. 'Der "Blockwart". Die unteren Parteifunktionäre im nationalsozialistischen Terror- und Überwachungsapparat'. *Vierteljahrshefte für Zeitgeschichte* 48(4) (October 2000), 575–602.

Schneeweiß, Josef. *Keine Führer. Keine Götter. Erinnerungen eines Arztes und Spanienkämpfers*. Vienna, 1986.

Schubert, Helga. *Judasfrauen. Zehn Fallgeschichten weiblicher Dominanz im Dritten Reich*. Frankfurt am Main, 1990.

Schuschnigg, Kurt von. *Austrian Requiem*, trans. Franz von Hildebrand. New York, 1947. (*Ein Requiem in Rot-Weiß-Rot*. Vienna, 1978)

Schütte-Lihotzky, Margarete. *Erinnerungen aus dem Widerstand*. Hamburg, 1985.

Schwager, Irma. 'Zum hundertsten Geburtstag von Selma Steinmetz'. *Mitteilungen der Alfred Klahr Gesellschaft* 14(3) (September 2007), 21.

Schwarz, Peter. 'Der Ballhausplatz 2 im Brennpunkt der NS-Diktatur 1938–1945: Die Kontextualisierung eines Herrschafts- und Machtzentrums aus politik-, struktur-, verwaltungs- und personengeschichtlicher Perspektive'. Doctoral thesis, Vienna, 2017.

Senekowitsch, Martin. *Feldmarschalleutnant Johann Friedländer, 1882–1945. Ein vergessener Offizier des Bundesheeres*. Vienna, 1995.

Sládek, Oldřich. 'Standrecht und Standgericht. Die Gestapo in Böhmen und Mähren', in Paul and Mallmann, *Die Gestapo im Zweiten Weltkrieg*, 317–39.

Spoerer, Mark. *Zwangsarbeit unter dem Hakenkreuz. Ausländische Zivilarbeiter, Kriegsgefangene und Häftlinge im Dritten Reich und im besetzten Europa 1939–1945*. Stuttgart, 2001.
Stadlbauer, Peter. 'SS-Einsatzgruppenführer Erich Ehrlinger. Eine Studie zu NS-Gewaltverbrechen und deutscher Nachkriegsjustizgeschichte'. Doctoral thesis, Vienna, 2017.
Stadler, Karl. *Adolf Schärf. Mensch, Politiker, Staatsmann*. Vienna, 1982.
———. *Österreich 1938–1945 im Spiegel der NS-Akten*. Vienna, 1966.
Stangneth, Bettina. 'Otto Adolf Eichmann. Reichssicherheitshauptamt. Der Organisator', in Hans-Christian Jasch and Christoph Kreutzmüller, *Die Teilnehmer. Die Männer der Wannsee-Konferenz* (Berlin, 2017), 45–62.
Steinbach, Peter, and Johannes Tuchel (eds). *Widerstand gegen die nationalsozialistische Diktatur 1933–1945*. Berlin, 2004.
Steiner, Herbert (ed.). *Die Erhebung der österreichischen Nationalsozialisten im Juli 1934. Akten der Historischen Kommission des Reichsführers SS*. Vienna, 1984.
———. 'Franz Koritschoner – Biographische Bemerkungen'. Manuscript (n.d.) held at DÖW.
———. *Käthe Leichter. Leben und Werk*. Vienna, 1973.
Steiner, John M., and Jobst Freiherr von Cornberg. 'Willkür in der Willkür. Befreiungen von den antisemitischen Nürnberger Gesetzen'. *Vierteljahrshefte für Zeitgeschichte* 46(2) (April 1998), 143–87.
Stolle, Michael. *Die Geheime Staatspolizei in Baden*. Konstanz, 2001.
Szita, Szabolcs. *Verschleppt, verhungert, vernichtet. Die Deportation von ungarischen Juden auf das Gebiet des annektierten Österreich 1944–1945* (with a foreword by György Konrád). Vienna, 1991.
Tausendfreund, Doris. *Erzwungener Verrat. Jüdische 'Greifer' im Dienst der Gestapo 1943–1945*. Berlin, 2006.
Tech, Andrea. *Arbeitserziehungslager der Gestapo in Nordwestdeutschland 1940–1945*. Göttingen, 2003.
Theimer, Gerald. 'Die Wiener Staatspolizei in den Jahren 1945–1947'. Doctoral thesis, Vienna, 1995.
Tidl, Georg. 'Marie Hofmann-Tidl. Zehn Jahre im Leben einer antifaschistischen Widerstandskämpferin (1935–1945)'. *Mitteilungen der Alfred Klahr Gesellschaft* 23(4) (December 2016), 30–33.
Ueberschär, Gerd R. (ed.). *Trotzkistische Opfer des NS-Terrors in Österreich. Eine Dokumentation*. Vienna, 2001.
———. 'Der militärische Umsturzplan "Walküre"', in Steinbach and Tuchel, *Widerstand gegen die nationalsozialistische Diktatur 1933–1945*, 353–62.
Ungar, Gerhard. 'Die Konzentrationslager', in DÖW, *Jahrbuch 2013*, 191–209.
Walk, Joseph. *Das Sonderrecht für die Juden im NS-Staat, Eine Sammlung der gesetzlichen Maßnahmen und Richtlinien – Inhalt und Bedeutung*. Heidelberg, 1981.
Walter, Thomas. 'Standhaft bis in den Tod. Die Zeugen Jehovas und die NS-Militärgerichtsbarkeit', in Walter Manoschek (ed.), *Opfer der NS-Militärjustiz. Urteilspraxis, Strafvollzug, Entschädigungspolitik in Österreich* (Vienna, 2003), 342–57.

Walterskirchen, Gudula. *Blaues Blut für Österreich. Adelige im Widerstand gegen den Nationalsozialismus*. Vienna, 2000.

Weinert, Willi. '"Er starb für Österreichs Freiheit". Zur 65. Wiederkehr des Todes von Josef Angermann'. *Mitteilungen der Alfred Klahr Gesellschaft* 16(1) (March 2009), 5–6.

Weinzierl, Erika. *Zu wenig Gerechte. Österreich und Judenverfolgung 1938–1945*. 4th printing, augmented, Graz, 1997.

Weisz, Franz. 'Die Geheime Staatspolizei, Staatspolizeileitstelle Wien 1938–1945. Organisation, Arbeitsweise und personale Belange' (reference: Weisz, 'Gestapo-Leitstelle Wien'). Unpublished doctoral thesis, Vienna University, 1991.

———. 'Das Hauptquartier der Wiener Gestapo – das Haus am Morzinplatz Nr. 4', in *Jahrbuch des Vereins für Geschichte der Stadt Wien, Jahrgang 51* (1995), 243–64.

———. 'Personell vor allem ein "ständestaatlicher Polizeikörper". Die Gestapo in Österreich', in Paul and Mallmann, *Die Gestapo – Mythos und Realität*, 439–62.

———. 'Steinhäusl Otto', in *Österreichisches Biographisches Lexikon 1815–1950* (ÖBL), vol. 13 (Vienna, 2007–10), 184.

———. 'Die V-Männer der Gestapo-Leitstelle Wien. Organisation, Personalstruktur, Arbeitsweise'. *Zeitgeschichte* 40(6) (2013), 338–57.

Weitz, Dagmar. '"Verbotener Umgang mit Kriegsgefangenen" vor dem Sondergericht Wien'. Degree dissertation, University of Vienna, 2006.

Welan, Manfried, and Helmut Wohnout. 'Hans Karl Zeßner-Spitzenberg – einer der ersten toten Österreicher in Dachau', in DÖW, *Forschungen zum Nationalsozialismus und dessen Nachwirkungen in Österreich. Festschrift für Brigitte Bailer* (Vienna, 2012), 21–41.

Wildt, Michael (ed.). *Die Judenpolitik des SD 1935 bis 1938. Eine Dokumentation*. Munich, 1995.

Wildt, Michael. *An Uncompromising Generation: The Nazi Leadership of the Reich Security Main Office*, trans. Tom Lampert. Madison, WI, 2010. (*Generation des Unbedingten. Das Führungskorps des Reichssicherheitshauptamtes*. Hamburg, 2002)

Wilhelm, Friedrich. *Die Polizei im NS-Staat. Die Geschichte der Organisation im Überblick*. Paderborn, 1999.

Wilhelm, Marianne. 'SD-Hauptaußenstelle und Volkstumsstelle Eisenstadt'. Doctoral thesis, University of Vienna 2004.

Wolfrum, Edgar. 'Widerstand in den letzten Kriegsmonaten und Endphasenverbrechen', in Steinbach and Tuchel, *Widerstand gegen die nationalsozialistische Diktatur 1933–1945*, 430–44.

Wüllenweber, Hans. *Sondergerichte im Dritten Reich*. Frankfurt am Main, 1990.

Zehner, Hanspeter. 'Mord oder Selbstmord? Neue Erkenntnisse zum gewaltsamen Tod des Generals der Infanterie Wilhelm Zehner (1938)'. *Truppendienst* 271(4) (2003), http://www.bundesheer.at/truppendienst/ausgaben/artikel.php?id=77 (last accessed on 11 May 2016).

Zellhofer, Martin. 'Die NS-Morde und -Standgerichtsfälle in Schwarzau im Gebirge und Umgebung im April/Mai 1945 im Lichte des Volksgerichtsverfahrens 1945–1948'. Degree dissertation, University of Vienna, 2008.

INDEX

*Page numbers in **bold** refer to figures and charts.*

A

Abd-ru-shin sect (Grail association), 224
Abwehr (Wehrmacht counter-intelligence service), 71–72, 103, 170, 233, 236, 365
Achamer-Pifrader, Humbert, **cover photo**, 25–26, 28, 32–35, 37, 53–59, **75**–76, 86, 120, 180, 198, 211, 315–16
Ackermann, Manfred, 244
Adam, Walter, 165
Aichach, women's labour prison, 276
'Aktion 14f13'. Operation '14f13'
'Aktion Gitter'. Vienna Gestapo, arrests, July 1944
Albacete, cadre office, 145
Albrecht, Karl, 118
Alge, Josef, 245
Allied soldiers, murders of, 325–27
Altaus, looted art, 103
Altenburg, monastery, 212
Aly, Götz, 154, 364
Améry, Jean, 121
Amler, Karl, 89–91
amnesties, 265n108, 305, 312, 354, 370
Amsterdam, 349–50
Anderle, Adolf, 171, 342
Andreanczik, Stefan, 128, 138n67
Andreasch, Otto Ernst, **248**–49
Angermann, Josef, 127, 138n64
anti-Fascist freedom movement of Austria (Antifaschistische Freiheitsbewegung Österreichs), 125, 235
anti-Hitler movement of Austria (Anti-Hitler-Bewegung Österreichs), 245, 257–58
applications for 'remand' ('Rücküberstellung'), 121, 138n73, 129–30, 154, 243, 251, 269, 276, 287, 300
Arbeitserziehungslager ('labour education camp', AEL) Oberlanzendorf, 94, 134, 257, 269, 274, 290–91, 296–307, 368; commandant and guards, 94, 298–99; evacuation march, 304–5, 333, 368; foundation 1940/41, 297–98; internee mortality rate, 304–7
Argelès, camp, 251
Arlet, Gertrude, 215
Armster, Otto, 72
Artner, Wilhelmine, 300
Aryanization. *See under* Jews
(young) 'asocials'. *See* Arbeitserziehungslager
Athens, BdSuSD, 312; mass murder, 334
Auer, Josef, 125
Auinger, Josef, 32, 89, 91–**92**, 97, 120, 154, 242, 310, 316, 342
Auschwitz (Oswiecim), concentration camp, 39, 43n28, 112n99, 126, 166, 191, 193, 242, 248, 254, 280–82, 315–16, 320
Austrian freedom front (Österreichische Freiheitsfront), 237, 247
Austrian freedom movement/s (Österreichische Freiheitsbewegung/en), 141, 233–34, 236

B

Baden, 41, 142; district administrator of, 214–15

Bader, Franz Xaver, 220
Baran, Nikolaj, 136n8, **259**, 266n119
Baresch, Alois, 216
Basch, Bela Bernhard, 276
Batthyany: Ivan Graf, Margareta Gräfin, 329
Bauer: Franziska, Rudolf, Othmar, 282
Bauer, Johann, 284
Baumann, Erich, 215
Baumann, Herbert, 237
Bavarian political police, 24–25, 33–36, 61n24
Beck, Oskar, 158–59
Becker, Hans, 237
Beer, Ludwig, 251–52, 318
Belgrade, military tribunal, 139n105, 142, 145
Berchtesgaden agreement, 162
Berger, Heinrich, **75**–76, 310
Berlin, 184–85, 196–98, 249; Center for Research on Antisemitism, 151; Gestapo regional headquarters, 39–40, 50; Federal Archives (BA), ix, 6–7, 86; Moabit tax office, 199; 20 July 1944, 168–71. *See also* Gestapa, RSHA and SD main office
Bernadotte, Folke Graf, 102
Bernardis, Robert, 170–71
Bernatzik, Hugo, 132
Bernau, 174
Bernauer, first name unkn., 326
Bernburg, NS 'euthanasia' centre, 131, 243
Bernstein, James, 186
Bernthaler, Franz, 235
Besenböck, Olga, 223
Best, Werner, 11–12, 16, 29, 69, 71, 84, 99, 140, 174, 195, 211
Biedermann, Karl, 316, 334, 336n13, 342
Biel, Bobby, 237
Bienenfeld, Wilhelm, 187, 191
Bihary: Johanna, Napoleon, 270
Birkmeyer: Anton, Jolanthe, Susanne, 275
Black, Peter R., 18
Blagodatow, Alexej, 340
Blahut, Ferdinand, 253
Blaschek, Josef, 146
Blaschke, Alfons, 277
Blechner, Leopold, 279
Blie, Oskar, 276

Blum, Leon, 54
Bock, Fritz, 131, 165
Bock, Wilhelm, **75**–76, 86, 99, 238, 310
Bodenstein, Alfred, 156
Boes, Josef, 280
Böhm, Annemarie (nee Klein), 51, 60n9
Böhm, Johann, 247
Bonn, regional court, 312
border police (Grenzpolizei), 2, 7, 38–40, 68, 180, 299, 358, 365; Bruck an der Leitha, 124, 219; Eisenstadt, 29, 124, 156–57; Engerau (Petržalka), 124–25, 329; Kittsee, 124; Rechnitz, 329; Sauerbrunn, 124, 284
Bormann, Martin, 72
Bovensiepen, Otto, 29
Bracht, Fritz, 316
Bradfisch, Otto, 311
Brainin, Wilhelm, 254
Brand, Joel, 102
Brandenburg-Görden (prison), executions, 223, 270, 272
Bratislava, 145, 194
Bremen, Kripo, 133
Brenner, Josef, 126
Brest-Litovsk, extradition of political prisoners, 254
Broad, Pery, 316
Brödl, Anton, 350–52
Broglie, Emil, 218
Brom, Franz, 270
Bromberg (Bydgoszcz), Gestapo office, 313
Brünn (Brno), Gestapo office, 45n76, 97–98, 256; Socialist representation in exile, 244
Brunner, Alois, 135, 182, 186, 188, 203n46, 205n76, 342, 358
Brunner, Andreas, 286
Brunner, Anton, 342
Brunner, Heinrich, **75**–76, 86
Brunner, Johann, 124–25, 127
Brunnhölzl, Josef, 309
Brussels, Gestapo, 45n72, 98
Buber-Neumann, Margarethe, 254
Buchenwald, concentration camp, 127, 194–95, 167, 177, 179, 185, 204n66, 222, 226, 244, 246, 254, 285, 304, 366
Bucher, Alois, 192–93

Buchsbaum, Leopold, 31
Buchta, Josef, 216
Bünau, Rudolf von, 334
Bürckel, Josef, 27, 53–54, 134, 158, 163, 183, 188, 196, 217–18, 286
Burian, Karl, 50, 233, 365
Buttinger, Josef, 243

C
Cailleau, Alfred, 54
Caldonazzi, Walter, 124, 235
Canaris, Wilhelm, 71
Cartellverband (Austrian union of Catholic university fraternities, CV), 107, 210, 346
Cäsar, Johann, 246
Catholic Church, Nazi dissolution of Catholic organizations, 213; restrictions on religious life, 214–16; seizure and confiscation of ecclesiastical assets, writings and printed matter, 211–12; suppression of individual Catholic resistance, 219–21; surveillance and spying, 216–17; Vienna Gestapo toleration of anti-Catholic aggression by Nazi organizations, 217–18
Catholic-conservative and legitimist resistance, 232–37
cell spies (Zellenspitzel), 145–47, 238, 240, 363
Central Office for Jewish Emigration (Zentralstelle für jüdische Auswanderung), 4, 37, 70–71, 104, 119, 135, 180–183, 185, 188–190, 194, 200, 202, 279, 338–39, 358, 365–66
Chaidari, concentration camp, 312
Chelmno, extermination camp, 311
Chemnitz, Gestapo office, 316
Christelly, Josef, 155
Christian: Gustav, Vinzenz, 131
Christmann, Kurt, 38, 45n73, 194, 196, 359
Cihak, Hans, 301
Cologne, 50; Edelweiß-Piraten, 290; Gestapo regional headquarters, 159; Opekta company, 49–50

Communist resistance, 118, 124, 131, 137n45, 147, 237–42, 251, 318, 368–69; Czech section, 127–28, 141, 239; parachutists, 240; Styria, 141, 239, 241; Communist youth league (KJV), 122, 141, 235, 239, 248
concentration camp committals, 11, 120, 130–32
Copenhagen, BdSuSD, 316
Coudenhove-Kalergi, Richard von, 225
Crankshaw, Edward, 84
Cumhuriyet, seized newspaper, 277
Czeloth, Josef, 328

D
Dachau, concentration camp, 50, 59, 130–32, 163, 175–78, 219, 226, 232, 247, 250–51, 366; first transport of Austrians ('VIP transport'), 32, 44n65, 164–67, 177, 263n74
Daluege, Kurt, 20, 26, 35, 100
Dams, Carsten, 2, 115, 151
D'Angio, Ferdinando, 255
Danneberg, Robert, 166, 242, 245
Danolfi, Nikola, 255
Danzig (Gdansk), Sipo, 313
Darmstadt, Gestapo office, 316
Dellbrügge, Hans, 212
Delphin, first name unkn., 28
Demant, Isaak, 194
Demschik, Heinrich, 30, 34
denunciations, 4–5, 134, 140, 151–61, 179, 184, 217, 269, 284, 364, 368
Deutschkreutz, resistance group in, 124
Diels, Rudolf, 10
Diewald: Josef, Therese, 328
Dlabaja, Albert, 127
Dohmen, Herbert, 158
Dolezal, Arnold, 214–15
Döllersheim, Wehrmacht training ground, 327
Dollfuß, Engelbert, 36, 165–66, 244
Dombrowsky, Konstantin. *See* Baran, Nikolaj
Dörhage, Hans, 77–78, 187
Dörner, Bernward, 74, 151, 153, 155
Döry von Jobbahaza, Aladar, 280

Döry von Jobbaháza, Ladislaus, 157
Drancy, collection camp, 318–20
Drapal, Ludwig, 282
Drasche-Wartinberg, Nadine Freifrau von, 157
Draxler, Ludwig, 165
Draxler, Paula, 323n48
Draxler, Therese, 159
Drews, Karl, 141, 239
Drohobycz, Einsatzkommando Lemberg, 313
Dubsky, Adolf Graf, 47
Dulles, Allen W., 103, 112n100
Dümler, Therese, 215
Dürmayer, Heinrich, 341
Düsseldorf, Gestapo regional headquarters, 40
Dworak, Josef, 89, 97

E

Ebensee, concentration camp, 318
Eberle, Joseph, 214
Ebhardt, Franz, 73
Ebner, Karl, 19–20, 66, 71, 73, **77**, **79**, 85–87, 89–90, 92–93, 94–98, **96**, **107**, 122–23, 135, 146, 152, 309, 335–37; 'business distribution plan' (GVP), 74, 76–79; churches intelligence service, 73; demotion, 97–98; denunciations, 153, 155; deportation of Jews, 191–92; Jehovah's Witnesses, 221–22; head of 'Jewish section', 175, 177–78, 180, 182, 184–89, 278, 366; leaving Catholic Church, 91; maltreatment, 147, 353; plot of July 1944, 168–70; 'reinsurance', 2–3, 5, 105–8, 210; seizure and confiscation of ecclesiastical assets, 210–12; seizure of Jewish assets, 196; total number of arrests, 116; trial at Vienna Volksgericht, 342–44, 346–47, 369; Vugesta as instrument for looting, 199–201; Wolfsberg dossier, 100, 338–39
Ebreichsdorf, 157
Ecker, Johann, 220
Eckhardt, Eduard, 257
Edel, Emanuel, 320
Egger, Ernst, 200–1, 208n173

Ehart, Walter, 327–28
Ehlers, Erich, 225
Ehrlich, Jakob, 166
Ehrlinger, Erich, 175
Eichholzer, Herbert, 141, 239
Eichinger, Michael, 250
Eichmann, Adolf, 4, 21, 25, 37, 39, 70–71, 82n41, 103–4, 177, 180–83, 185, 188, 203n46, 204n52, 205n75, 316, 325, 354–55n7, 358, 365
Eifler, Alexander (von), 166
Einsatzkommandos (EKs), xvi, 20, 308; EK Austria, 20, 36, 132, 225; EK Lemberg (Lviv), 313; EK Olmütz (Olomouc), 313; EK Sanitzer, 331, 334; EK Sipo, Stein, 328; EK 2, 45n7, 75
Eisenhower, Dwight David, 102
Eisenstadt, 156, 235; border police station, 38, 124, 133, 330; Gestapo office, 26, 29, 42n16; SD, 133, 327
Engelhardt, Georg, 282
Engerau (Petržalka), border police post, 38, 124–25, 133; massacre, 329, 333
Ephrussi, family, 195
Esebeck, Hans-Karl Freiherr von, 170
establishment of the Gestapo in Austria, 24–29
Etsdorf am Kamp, racial humiliation, 286
Evans, Richard J., 152
exposé on establishment of the Sipo in Austria, 24, 35

F

fake radio messages (*Funkspiele*), 51, 127, 326
Fantner, Benedikt, 251
Färber, Julia, 300
Fechner, Kurt, 72
Feigenbaum, Rudolf, 183
Feix, Robert, 48–50
Feldkirch, 280
Felleis, Roman, 244
Felling, Catholic priest of, 215
Fels-Margulies, Moritz, 320
Fembeck, Franz, 216
Ferstel, Heinrich von, 47
Fey, Emil, 163

Fiedler, Rudolf, 247
Figl, Leopold, 32, 131, 165, 333–34, 351
Finke, Otto, 290
Fischböck, Hans, 197, 207n147
Fischer, Franz, 247
Fischer, Herbert, 42n25
Fischer, Walter, 276
Flesch, Hermann, 47
Flossenbürg, concentration camp, 59, 127, 165, 246, 271, 279, 304
Fohringer, Josef, 127
foreign forced labour(ers), 4, 72, 116–17, 119–20, 126, 128, 130, 135, 152, 171, 184–85, 200, 254–60, 269, 282, 296, 299, 301, 309, 329–30, 338, 362–63, 368
foreign newspapers, seizure of, 276–78
Formanns, Albin, 215
Forschungsamt der Luftwaffe (Luftwaffe research office), 72–73, 311
Forster, Stefanie, 164
Fossoli, camp for Jews, 315
Fraenkel, Ernst, 9, 11–12
Frank: Anne, Otto, 349–50
Frank, Karl Hermann, 310
Frankfurt am Main, Gestapo regional headquarters, 40
Frankfurt an der Oder, 28
Frauenfeld, Alfred, 170
Free Austria (Freies Österreich), resistance group, 236
Freemasons, 14, 97, 33, 174, 225–28, 230n81, 367
Freytag, Horst, 175, 202n4
Frick, Wilhelm, 10, 16, 26, 65
Fried, Alfred Hermann, 225
Fried, Jakob, 245, 346
Friedell, Egon, 164, 176
Friediger: Hedwig, 50, Karl, 50, 233, Markus, 48, 50
Friedl, Herbert, 214
Friedl, Rosa, 93–**95**, 250
Friedländer, Johann, 191
Friedmann, Desider, 166, 176, 255
Fritsch, Hildegard, 93
Fritzl, first name unkn., 122
Fröhlich: Aloisia, Anna, 220

Frühlinger, Leopold, 219
Frühwirth, Johanna, 281
Führer, Erich, 112n285
Fürer, Erwin, 156
fusion/amalgamation of police/Sipo and SS/SD, 3, 15–20, 66, 90–91, 132

G

Gabler, Leo, 238
Gabriel, Ernst, 124
Gabrynovicz, first name unkn., 260n5
Gajda, Anton, 276
Gallop, Heinrich, 182
Gardiner, Muriel (from 1939 Gardiner-Buttinger), 243
Garhofer, Josef, 33–34
Garmisch-Partenkirchen, 344, 356n30
Garscha, Winfried, 154, 158
Gavric, Lisa, 251
Geckl, Arthur, 198
Gehlen, Reinhold, 345
Gellately, Robert, 5, 17, 151–52, 157, 364
Gendarmerie (rural police), 15, 20, 26, 88, 128, 134, 327, 339, 360, 365; Geheime Feldgendarmerie, 134
Georgi: Friedrich, Mathilde, 194
Gerasdorf, parish of, 214
Gerhardt, Maria, 271–72
Gerö, Josef, 165
Gerscha, Fritz, 94, 301
Gerstl, Franz, 342
Gertner, Fritz, 327
Geschäftsverteilungspläne (GVPs), Gestapo Vienna, 3, 13, 23n38, 74–80 (**75**, **77**, **79**), 82n85, 100, 160n20, 187, 256, 269, 298, 348, 356n38, 362
Gestapa, 27, 29, 34–35, 71–72, 76, 86, 100–1, 114, 116–17, 130, 153, 175–78, 183, 226, 250, 252, 315, 359; appointment of head and deputy head of the Vienna Gestapo in 1938, 85–86; arrest of Austrian Communists and Socialists in 1939, 168–69, 243–44; 'germ cell' of the Gestapo, 9–11; GVPs, 19–21, 24, 73; personnel structure of the German Gestapo, 83–85; preparations for the annexation of Austria, 24–26,

33–35; 'protective custody' order, 130–31, **169**; 'special detainees' Kurt Schuschnigg and Louis Rothschild, 54–56, 58–60. *See also* Humbert Achamer-Pifrader and Rudolf Mildner
Gestapo laws, 9–12, 71
Ginzkey, Franz Karl, 226
Glasenbach. *See* Salzburg
Globocnik, Odilo, 35, 44n62, 342
Gloggnitz, arrest of hidden Jews, 262n41, 300
Glück, Karl, 309–10
Glücksmann, Hilde, 200–1
Gmeiner, Hans, 245
Gneixendorf, POW camp, 328
Goebbels, Joseph, 72, 183, 213, 270, 276, 325
Goldmann, David, 194, 196, 198
Goldstein: Bernhard 'Israel', Helene 'Sara', Jakob 'Israel', Pepi 'Sara', 280
Gölles, Peter, 222, 230n66
Gollner, Franz, 127
Gollosch, Barbara, 282
Gomperz, Philip, 200
Göpfritz, Catholic priest of, 215
Goppelt, Hugo, 77–**79**, 180
Gorbach, Alfons, 165
Göring, Hermann, 9–10, 31, 37, 43n41, 57, 72–73, 105, 195–96, 198, 272
Göth, Eduard, 246
Gottesmann, Georg, 190
Göttweig, Benedictine abbey, 211
Gotzmann, Leo, 168, 188
Grabatsch, Paul, 246
Gradl, Josef, 320
Granig, Anton, 113n118, 235
Grasel, Alexander, 275
Grausam, Johann, 285
Graz, Gestapo office, 26, 28, 39–40, 42n16, 69, 171; regional court, 241, 342
Greif, Walter, 131
Grießer, Johann, 217
Grissinger, Rupert, 123–24, 351
Groh, Olga, 271
Groll, Franz, 271
Groß-Rosen, concentration camp, 147, 251, 281–82

Grossmann, Oskar, 319
Grossmann, Rosa, 127, 350
Gruber, Josef, 131
Gruber, Karl, 236
Grübling, Johanna, 222
Grünbaum, Fritz, 225
Grünn, Franz, 31
Grynszpan, Herschel, 183
Gubsch, Erwin, **75**
Günser, Julius, 147, 252, 318, 322n44
Günther, Rolf, 186, 205n75
Günzburg, Frieda, 318
Gurs, camp, 251
Gürth, Ferdinand, 281
Gurtner: Josef, Gisela, 279
Güttl, Karl, 191–92

H

Haag, demonstration at, 216
Haas: Johann Otto, Philomena, 246
Haas, Karl August, 223
Habel, Ferdinand, 218
Habsburg, Otto (Erzherzog/Archduke), 50, 60n16, 232–33
Hackl, first name unkn., 164
Hadamovsky, Eugen, 273
Hadersdorf, massacre at, 333
Hagen, Herbert, 175–76
Hager, Franz, 249
Hagmüller, Leopold, 318, 323n48
Haig, first name unkn., 345
Hainburg, anti-Nazi preaching at, 219; communist resistance group, 125–26
Hamann, Hans, **75**, 77
Handl, Josef, 342
Hanig, Alois, 219
Hansmann, Rudolf, 272
Harster, Wilhelm, 28
Hartgasser, Anton, 329–30
Hartheim, NS 'euthanasia' centre, 129, 132, 251, 259
Hartmann, Otto, 141–42, 144, 149n5, **234**
Harwich, Kindertransport, 187
Haselbacher, Karl, 38, 45n72, 86, 97, 99, 174–75, 177, 180, 203n16, 359
Hasenauer, Karl von, 47
Hauptvogel, Friedrich, 271

Hautmann, Rudolf, 340
Hecht, Robert, 165–66
Heger, Otto, 250, 269, 314
Heigelmayr, Franz, 131
Heigl, Paul, 132
Heiligenkreuz, surveillance at abbey of, 217
Heiny, Herbert, 214
Helia, Aloisia, 156
Hellenbach, Lazar Freiherr von, 47
Helmer, Oskar, 171, 344
Hemetsberger, Karl, 25, 41n4, 164, 172n6
Herber, Karl, 199–201
Herbert, Franz, 237
Herbert, Ulrich, 16
Herforth, Marie, 223
Herrn, Rainer, 286
Herzog, Franz, 216
Herzog, Johann, 164
Hess, Josef, 177
Heydrich, Reinhard, 5, 29, 35, 53–54, 63, 83, 85–86, 99, 104, 114, 117, 175, 184, 338, 347n44, 353n62, 358–59, 365, 367; competence for concentration camp committals, 130; decree on the seizure and confiscation of assets of 'enemies of Volk and state', 193, 196, 211; denunciations, 153; detention of over a thousand Jewish men at the Prater football stadium in 1939, 185; ensuring the Gestapo's power monopoly, 163; establishment of a 'Jewish reservation' in Nisko, 188; establishment of Vienna Gestapo, 26–27n21; Funktionsbefehl (function order), 69–70, 182, 365; fusion of police and SS, 15–19; fusion of Sipo and SD, 132; historical commission of the Reichsführer-SS, 53; inspectors of the Sipo and SD, 65–66, 68–69; instruction concerning 'radio crimes', 273; on the 'enemy of the Volk' ('Volksfeind'), 13; operational order concerning 'special treatment' for Soviet POWs, 256; order for mass arrests in Austria, 167; orders arrest of General Zehner, 164; orders Spanish Civil War fighters to be taken into 'protective custody', 250; orders 'special treatment' for 'underminers of military morale', 127; orders arrest of Austrian Communists and Socialists, 243; persecution of homosexuals, 133; 'protective custody', 10

Hietler, Anton, 284
higher SS and police leaders (Höhere SS- und Polizeiführer, HSSPFs), 17, 64–67, 98
Hillegeist, Friedrich, 167, 242
Himmler, Heinrich, 5, 31–32, 66, 74, 83, 85–86, 94, 98, 114, 213, 347, 358–59; chief of the German police, 10–12; establishment of Vienna Gestapo, 26–27, 35–36; fusion of police and SS, 3, 17; higher SS and police leaders, 64–65; historical commission of the Reichsführer-SS, 53–54, 59–60; on two types of 'enemy of Volk and state' ('Volksfeind'), 13; order to evacuate or kill camp inmates, 329; orders execution of POW Lieutenant Hyde, 326; orders 'special treatment' for Czech resistance fighters, 240; persecution of homosexuals, 286; plot of 20 July 1944, 170–71; 1940 prohibition of contacts and relations with prisoners of war and foreign forced labourers, 283; punishment exclusively for Poles ('Polenstrafe'), 302; 'reinsurance', 102; RSHA, 19–20; SD, 69, 71–72; seizure and confiscation of assets in Austria, 193, 195–96, 201, 211; 'special detainees' Kurt Schuschnigg and Louis Rothschild, 52–55, 58
Hinker, Walter, 125
Hinterbrühl, 200, 202, 246, 280
Hirt, Karl, 33
historical commission of the Reichsführer-SS (Historische Kommission des Reichsführers SS), 53–54, 58–60
Hitler, Adolf, 9–10, 71, 73, 246, 336n14; approves the deportation of Vienna's Jews, 188, 366; Austrian police sworn in under allegiance to Hitler in 1938, 26; Berchtesgaden Agreement of 1938, 29, 162; decree on Himmler's

appointment as chief of the German police, 12; decree on 'protective custody', 15; 'extraordinary constitutional court' against Schuschnigg, 53, 58–59; 'insidious utterances' against Hitler, 156–58, 249, 271; mistrust of the judiciary and of jurists, 85; orders seizure of Otto Habsburg's assets, 232; orders the 'slaughter' of allied parachute agents, 327–28; plot of 20 July 1944, 168–171; prohibits legal proceedings against Austrian 'separatists', 234

Hitler Youth (Hitler-Jugend, HJ), 14, 134, 163, 184, 213, 218–19, 221, 239, 288–89, 325, 334

Hitzler, Rudolf, 122–24, 256–58, 265n108, 275, 328, 342

Hoep(p)ner, Erich, 171, 172n25

Hoffmann, Georg, 325

Hoffmann, Hugo, 50

Hoffmann von Fallersleben, August Heinrich, 153

Höfler, Karl, 122

Hofmann, Margarethe, 215

Hofmann, Marie, 118, 121, 137n30

Hoi, Johann, 33, 89, 101, 277, 310

Holoubek, Karl, 244

Holzbauer, Josef, 224

homosexuals, 13, 21, 117, 133, 286–88, 365

Höttl, Wilhelm, 21, 74, 103

Huber, Franz Josef, **cover photo**, 7, 32, 53, **75**, **77**, **79**, 86, 91, **96**, **104**, 114, 117, 134–35, 144, 168, 194, 200, 212, 222, 286, 309, 315–16, 325–26, 339n7, 342, 348n47, 361, 365, 369; AEL Oberlanzendorf, 298; border police inspector II (South-East), 39; 'business distribution plans' (GVPs), 75–80; commander-in-chief of the Sipo and SD in Military District XVII, 332; cooperation with SD and central office for Jewish emigration, 70–71, 183; demotion, 98; deportation of Vienna's Jews, 188–89; dual function as head of the Vienna Gestapo and inspector of the Sipo and SD, 63, 65–69, 133, 358; 'enhanced interrogation', 122; establishment of Vienna Gestapo, 24–28; exoneration by US secret service and German Spruchkammer, 344–46; full-time member of BND, 345; German-Austrian conflict potential, 99, 100–1; Gestapa office II C ('Austrian Affairs'), 34; Hotel Metropole (headquarters), 37, **49**, 51; interrogation by Robert M. W. Kempner, assistant US chief counsel at the Nuremberg trials, 338; Luftwaffe research office (Forschungsamt der Luftwaffe), 73; personnel continuity and rotation, 96–98; 'reinsurance', 2–7, 103–7, 108, 148, 335; seizure and confiscation of Jewish assets, 197–98; 'special detainees' Kurt Schuschnigg and Louis Rothschild, 54–56; 'special operation against leading Communists and Revolutionary Socialists', 167, 243

Hübner, Gustav, 257

Hudomalj, Karl, 245, 258

Hurdes, Felix, 171

Huth, Alfred, 316, 334–35

Huttary, Albert, 125, 131

Hutterer, Robert, 247

Hüttl, Heinrich, 31

Hyde, Robert M., 326

I

identification card index (Erkennungsdienstliche Kartei), 115–16, 119, 258–59, 362

Ilitsch, Danitza, 113n107

illegal Nazis in Austrian police, 34–35, 50, 88, 360

incorporation of Gestapo officials into SS, rank alignment, 4, 11, 17, 90–91

informants (V-Leute), 21, 73, 95, 100, 118, 121–22, 129, 132–33, 140–47, 152, 217, 234–35, 238–40, 242–43, 245, 253–54, 258, 279, 287, 318, 340, 363–64, 366–67

Innitzer, Theodor, 52, 214, 218, 221, 351, 354

Innsbruck, Gestapo office, 26–29, 39–40, 42n16; regional court, 342; Reichenau, Gestapo prison, 132

inspectors of the security police and SD (IdSuSDs), 17, 27–28, 42n25, 43n27, 65–67, 71, 81n22, **96**, 104, 135, 182, 358, 365
interrogations. *See* Vienna Gestapo, maltreatment
Irkutsk, prison, 311
Isselhorst, Erich, 28
Istanbul, OSS, 235
Izbica, 206n108

J
Jacob, Gustav, **77**
Jacobs, Johannes, 303
Jahn, Angela, 284
Jakobovits, Josef Friedrich Ernst, 249
Jehovah's Witnesses, 114, 122, 221–24, 230n61, 367
Jelinek, Elfriede, 331n20
Jews, 'Aryanization' (looting), 49–51, 57–58, 163, 176, 193–202; ; discrimination and maltreatment, 178–80, 185–87, 192–93, 366; dissolution of IKG, 181, 187; expulsion/forced emigration, 70–71, 180–83, 347; forced labour, 184–85, 200; Kindertransport, 187; Vienna Gestapo 'Jewish section', 174–202; mass arrests and deportations, 70–71, 163–67, 178–80, 185, 187–193; November Pogrom, 183–185; transports to Palestine, 102; Righteous Among the Nations, 280–82; Vugesta, 198–202, 208n160, 366. *See also under* central office for Jewish emigration
Jirousek, Rudolf, 31–32
Jochmann, Rosa, 168–**69**
Johnson, Eric A., 154, 159
Jokl, Fritz, 190
Joksch, Ferdinand, 73
Jung, Rosa Franziska, 281
Junker, Josef, 164
Jury, Hugo, 328

K
Kadanik, Emmerich, 247
Kafka, Helene. *See* Restituta, Sister
Kahane, Grete ('Sonja'), 141, 239–40, 261n28, 366

Kaltenbrunner, Ernst, 18, 27, 31, 33, 35–36, 42, 42n18, 46n94, 54, 58, 63–66, 68, 98, 102–3, 105, 290, 316, 324, 342
Kamba, Franz, 33, 89, 101
Kammermayer, Josef, 220
Kämpf, Walter, 122
Kanitz, Otto Felix, 245
Kaphengst, Hans Karl, 67
Kapralik, Charles J., 182, 187
Karigl, Johann, 253
Kascha, Franz, 249
Kasperkowitz, Alois, 223
Kasteiner, Franz, 251
Kastelic, Jakob, 124, 141, 233
Kattowitz (Katowice), public execution of Polish resistance fighters, 98; Gestapo regional headquarters, 43n28
Katzelsdorf, execution at, 300
Kaysenbrecht, Richard, 272
Kempner, Robert M. W., 338, 355n4
Kennerknecht, Georg, 131
Keppler, Wilhelm, 31, 38, 43n41
Kern, Anton, 25
Kern, Hubert, 25, 154
Kern, Ludwig, 253
Kersche, Gregor, 124, 127, 258
Kerssenbrock, Elisabeth Gräfin, 56
Kersten, Felix, 171
Kessler, Ludwig, 215
Kessler, Paul, 319–20
Ketteler, Wilhelm-Emanuel Freiherr von, 132
Kharkov, 253; KdSuSD, 314
Kiev, BdSuSD, 43n27, 314
Kilb, conflict over school prayers at, 216
Kilian, first name unkn., 328
Kirchl: Otto, Hedwig, 328
Kirnosow, Ilja, 258
Klagenfurt, Gestapo office, 26–29, 39–40, 42n16, 69, 310
Klang, Marcell 'Israel', 282
Klausner, Hubert, 36
Kleedorfer, Franz, 312, 330, 334–35, 336n15
Kleemann, Karl, 217
Klein: Ernst A., Elisabeth, Gottlieb, 48–49, 51, 60n9

Klein, Oswald, **77**
Klekner, Oskar, 122
Klemperer, Victor, 102
Klimberger, Karl, 245
Klinger, Rudolf, 142, 280
Klosterneuburg, 233; Augustinian religious foundation, 211, 217, 366; Volksliturgischer Verlag, 213
Knochen, Helmut, 318
Knoeringen, Waldemar von, 246
Knoll, Johann, 237
Knoll, Kurt, 132
Knoth, Heinrich, 327
Köberl, Leopold, 298–99
Kodicek, Egon, 320
Kodré, Heinrich, 170
Köhl, Siegfried, 121
Köhler, Hermann, 123–24
Kolb: Arnold, Rudolf, 207n137
Kolb, Otto, 101
Kolisch, Siegfried, 189
König, Franz, 215
Koppe, Wilhelm, 53, 61n32
Koppel, Kurt ('Ossi'), 136n21, 141, 145–46, 239–40, 366
Korbel, Eduard, 141, 244
Koritschoner, Franz, 254
Körner, Theodor, 108, 171, 247, 348, 354
Korneuburg, arrest of Catholic priest of, 219
Kosmath, Friedrich, 195, 207n137
Kostroun, Ludwig, 245
Kotanyi, Johann, 166
Koutny: Josef, Leopold, 144, 241
Kozian, Rudolf, 158
Kozich, Thomas, 156, 161n32, 314
KPÖ (Communist Party of Austria). *See under* Communist resistance
Kraft, August, 222
Kranebitter, Friedrich, 86, 91, 109n19, 214–15, **315**, 368
Krapez, Franz, 253
Kraupa, Ferdinanda, 223
Kraupatz, Armin, 275, 309, 312, 368
Krause, Charlotte. *See* Lehmann, Lotte
Krefeld, Gestapo office, 154, 159
Kreisky, Bruno, 50, 242
Krems, 41, 262n41; resistance group, 328; summary court, 120, 320, 335, 343
Kriminalpolizei (Kripo, criminal investigation police), 15–17, 20, 26, 322, 40, 66–67, 76, 85, 87, 89–90, 132–33, 164, 184, 277, 286–88, 308–9, 312, 332, 335, 340, 350, 364–65, 367
Krinninger, Josef, 233
Krips, Josef, 105, 107, 347
Kriz: Anna, Josef, 279
Kronberger, Rudolf, 329
Kubasta, Gottfried, 320
Kubs, Stella, 159
Kuchmann, Otto, 175, 178, 181, 183, 185–88
Kullnig, Gustav, 328
Kunke: Hans, Steffi, 245
Kunnert, Heinrich, 133, 139n90, 327
Kunschak, Leopold, 57
Künzel, Karl, 94, 299, 304–5, 320

L

'labour education camp'. *See* Arbeitserziehungslager (AEL)
Lackenbach, gypsy camp, 133
Lahousen, Erwin von, 72
Lampl, Adolf, 284
Landau, Felix, 309, 313–**14**
Landauer, Hans, 251, 254
Lang, Johann, 126
Lange, Rudolf, 38, 45n75, 54, 86, 97, 99, 177–78, 211, 359
Laschitz, Martha, 285
Laßmann, Wolfgang, 346, 348
Laufer, Bedrich, 236
Lauscher, Josef, 241
Lederer, Karl, 141, 233
left-wing resistance groups, 249–50
Lehmann, Lotte, 105, 272
Leichter, Franz, 262n48
Leichter, Käthe, 243, 262n48
Lein, Hermann, 218
Lemberg (Lviv). *See* Einsatzkommandos, Lemberg
Lenz, Johannes Maria, 218
Leopold, Josef, 34
Leser, Ludwig, 244
Lety, gypsy camp, 310

Leutgeb, Lambert, 7, 13, 99, 118, 141–45, 217, 238–39, 242, 269, 277, 337, 342, 363
Lezaky, massacre, 310
Lichtblau: Theresia, Gisela, Kurt, Harry, 281
Lieben, Ernst (Freiherr von), 280
Linauer, Erwin, 313, 342
Linda, Alipius Josef, 217
Lingens: Ella, Kurt, 280–**81**
Linz, 100, 171; Eichmann, 25; Gestapo office, 25–26, 28, 39–40, 42n16, 69, 316; regional court, 342
Lippmann, Alexander, 47
'Litzmannstadt' (Łódź), 321n14; Gestapo office, 203n30, 311, 293n42
Ljubljana, archives of the republic of Slovenia, 7
Lochmann, Josef, 241
Łódź. *See* 'Litzmannstadt'
Lohrmann, Franz, 216
Lotfi, Gabriele, 255, 259, 297
Löwenherz, Josef, **181**, 184–88, 204n73, 206n106
Löwidt, Kurt, 190
Lublin, 254
Luchesi, Alois, 302
Ludwig, Vinzenz Oskar, 219
Lundenburg (Břeclav), border police post, 38, 41, 45n80, 133
Lux, Franz, 246
Lviv. *See* Einatzkommandos, Lemberg
Lyon, Gestapo, 318–19

M

Macher, Karl, 88, 109n28, 312, 330
Mährisch-Ostrau (Ostrava), Gestapo office, 97, 309
Maier, Heinrich, 124, 235, 258
Maier-Messner resistance group, 235
Maisel, Karl, 167
Malik, Johann, 225
Mallmann, Klaus-Michael, 2, 5, 119–20, 134, 143, 151–52, 157, 363–64
maltreatment. *See* Vienna Gestapo, maltreatment
Maly Trostinec, extermination camp, 158
Manda, Rudolf, 31

Mank, conflict over school prayers at, 216
Mantler, Karl, 167
Mappies, first name unkn., 193
Marchart, Emil, 342
Marchegg, border police post, 38, 45n77, 133
Marek, Franz, 322n44
Margaritis, Dimitrius, 302
Margulies, Ida, 319
Mark, Karl, 245
Markisch, Ignaz, 269
Marogna-Redwitz, Rudolf Graf, 72, 170, 365
Martin, Hermine, 214
mass arrests in Austria, 114, 119–20, 134, 162–73, 178–79, 233, 310, 363, 365
Matejka, Friedrich, 279
Materna, Josef, 233
Matzner, Maria, 148
Mauthausen, concentration camp, 126, 129, **236**, 257–58, 300–1, 304–5, 326–27, 332, 368; Einsatzgruppe F, 39, 97, 316; 'Sonderbehandlung', 127–28, 240, 257
Mauthner, Josef, 60n4
Mayer, Friedrich (Fritz), 238, 242, 274, 321n8
Mayer, Gerda, 192
Mayer, Sepp, 314
Mayerhofer, Johann, 216
Mayr-Melnhof, Franz Freiherr von, 60n4
Mehler-Bergmann, Sure, 281
Meisel, Curt (Kurt), 280
Meisel, Josef, 137n45, 146–47, 251, 318
Meisel, Paul, 254
Meisinger, Josef, 38, 52, 64n24, 194
Meller, Theresia, 125
Merkel, Rudolf, 82n63, 112n94, 338–39, 369
Mersits, Franz, 281
Messner, Franz Josef, 124, 149, 235–**36**, 261n14, 333
Metropole, Hotel (Vienna Gestapo headquarters), 4, 37, 47–51, **49**, **92**, 175, 194, 233, 333
Meyer, first name unkn., 302
Michalek, Johann, 285
Michall, Emil, 30

Migsch, Alfred, 245
Mikler, Andreas, 133, 327
Miksch, Josef, 89
Milanovicz, Adam, 303–5
Mildner, Rudolf, 120, 338, 342; commander of the Sipo and SD in Military District XVII, 43n28, 332; deputy and successor of Huber as head of Vienna Gestapo, 67, 98; deputy head of Linz Gestapo, 25, 28, 81n21; 'end-phase crimes', 312, 325–26, 332–35; 'enhanced interrogation', 122; escape to Argentina, 316, 338; plot of July 1944, 168, 170; stations in his Gestapo career, 316
Miseluk, Iwan, 258
Mittelbau-Dora, concentration camp, 146
Mödling, Missionshaus Sankt Gabriel, 211, 220
Moik, Wilhelmine, 244
Molden, Fritz, 237
Molecz, Michael, 220
Mommsen, Hans, 330n1
Mönch, Anna, 254
Moosbierbaum, resistance group, 327
Morawetz, Franz, **79**, 250, 309
Moscow, 354; Comintern secretariat, 145; German embassy, 254; Moscow Declaration on Austria, 236; FSB, 357n66; KPÖ, 127, 145, 239, 271; Radio Moscow, 126, 273
Moser, Hans, 105, 107, 347
Mösslacher, Johann, 164
Motesiczky, Karl (Graf), 280–81
Moulton, Richard G., 326
Muhr, Rudolfine, 168
Müller, Heinrich, 52, 63, 71, 83, 104, 114, 117, 167, 338, 353, 359; 'enhanced interrogation', 121; establishment of Vienna Gestapo, 27–28, 35–37; IdSuSD in SS-Oberabschnitt 'Danube', 68; 'special detainees' Kurt Schuschnigg and Louis Rothschild, 54, 57–59; November Pogrom, 183
Müller, Herbert, 134–35
Münch, Walter, 126
Munich, 1939 assassination attempt on Hitler, 4, 22, 162; court of cassation (Kassationshof), 344–45; Munich Agreement, 38; Schuschnigg's transfer to, 54, 58–59; SS and police court, 98. *See also* Bavarian political police
murders, extrajudicial executions (('Sonderbehandlung'), 85, 126–29, 239–40, 256, 283, 313, 325–26, 330, 334, 338, 363, 368
'Mythos Gestapo' ('Gestapo myth'), 5, 120, 152, 364

N
Nagl, Josef, 245
Nagy, Franz, 31
Nazi dissidents, 249–50
Nazi networks in pre-war police machinery, 24–26, 32–35
Nazi putsch in Vienna police, March 1938, 30–35
Nedwed, Ernst, 289
Nestler, Pauline, 243
Neubacher, Hermann, 242
Neubauer, Karl, 326
Neuffer, Johann, 171
Neulengbach, extrajudicial execution at, 128
Neumann, Heinz, 254
Neustädter-Stürmer, Odo, 164
Nicoll, Christian, 97–98, 154, 269, 342
Niederabsdorf, conflict over religious education in, 216
Niemöller, Martin, 54
Nikitsch, 281
Nisko, deportations, 188, 366
Nitsche, Adele, 125
Nödl, Friederike, 243
non-conformist youths ('Schlurfs'), 288–91
Norde, Inge, 73
Nosske, Gustav Adolf, 28
Nuremberg, civilian denazification court ('Spruchkammer'), 106, 344–45; International Military Tribunal, 78, 8n63, 93, 102, 112n94, 140, 316, 338, 344, 346–47; Nuremberg Laws, 13, 48–49, 142, 165, 179, 190, 205n85, 206n110, 248, 278, 243n51; US Internment Camp Nuremberg-Langwasser, 106, 338, 356n30

O

Obenaus, Erwin, 156
Obenfeldner, Ferdinand, 354
Oberhuber, Michael, 208n164
Oberlanzendorf. *See* Arbeitserziehungslager (AEL)
Obernosterer, Elisabeth, 93
Obhlidal, Stefanie, 224
Odessa, 158
Offenberger, Milo, 215
Olah, Franz, 242
Olmütz (Olomouc), Gestapo office, 309, 313
Operation '14f13', 131–32, 243, 251
Oppeln (Opole), Gestapo office, 312–13
Ordnungspolizei (regular uniformed police, Orpo), 3, 20, 25–26, 100, 134, 365
Osio, Alois, 165
OSS, 236, 300; Allen W. Dulles, 103, 112n100; commando unit Dupont, 103, 133, 327
Oyenhausen, 258
O5, 237, 241

P

Paheimer, Maria, 73
Painsi(e)pp, Margarete (Grete), 105, 113n107
Palmer, Stefan, 123, 257
parachute agents, 73, 103, 106, 123, 127, 129, 147–48, 236, 238, 240, 243, 258, 353, 363
Paris, 62n56, 145, 168, 181, 183, 251, 318–20; Socialist representaton in exile, 244
Pascher, Johann, 327
Pastor, Erich, 215
Pauk, Anton, 220
Paul, Gerhard, 2, 83–84, 119–20, 134, 139n91, 151, 363–64
Paul, Josef, 32
Pav, Hans, 141, 243
Pazdernik, Josef, 252
Peczenik, Anna, 251
Pelzer, Robert, 176
Pepper, Hugo, 235
Perchtoldsdorf, 245
Perger, Anton, 343
Perger, Karl, 93
Perko, Walter von, 290
Peterlunger, Oswald, 341
Petržalka. *See* Engerau
Pettau (Ptuj), 320
Pfannenstiel, Franz, 244
Pfeffer, Franz, 245
Pfeifer, Karl, 215
Pichler, Gertrude, 94, 192
Pick: Alexander, Maria, 126, 248
Pick, Sophie, 215
Pieller, Wilhelm, 113n118, 235
Pifrader, Humbert. *See* Achamer-Pifrader, Humbert
Pilz, Leo, 329
Pius XII, Pope, 213
Pizzo, Sebastiano, 304
Plaschka, Camilla, 281
Plaue, 171
Pleyl, Josef, 244
Ploi, Emilia, 94
plot of 20 July 1944, 4, 54, 67, 72, 99, 102, 114, 122, 130, 162, 168, 170, 247, 255, 316, 353
Podezin, Franz, 329
police preparations for March 1938 annexation, 24–27
Pollak, Paul, 179
Pollak, Robert, 248
Pöllhuber, Johann, 33
Polte, Friedrich, 135, 139n105
Popelka, Adolf, 32
Poppen, Dominik, 214
Posen (Poznan), Gestapo regional headquarters, 311
post-war prosecutions, 2, 337–54; Allied courts, 337–39; arrests by Vienna police, 339–41; Vienna Volksgericht (people's court), 341–44
Potetz, Helene, 168
Pottendorf, Catholic priest, 214
Potzinger, Johann, 119, 148
Prague, 181, 203n46, 236, 357n62; Gestapo regional headquarters, 1, 40, 310, 321n8–9
Prandstetter, Edith, 275
Preiss, Fritz, 180

Prieler, Josef, 133, 327
Prieler, Karl, 89, 343
Prinz, Josef, 301, 305
Probst, Otto, 131, 167
Proft, Gabriele, 300
prohibited contacts with POWs, 282–86
'protective custody' ('Schutzhaft'), 10, 14–15, 21, 78, 100, 117, 130–31, 153–54, 163, 168–**169**, 183, 211, 216, 219, 222, 224–25, 227, 243, 249–50, 253, 271, 278–79, 282–83, 285, 290, 296, 299–301, 303–5, 362, 367
provisional Austrian national committee (Provisorisches Österreichisches Nationalkomitee, POEN), 237
Puhl, Hermann, **77**
Puschmann, Erwin, 136n21, 239
Puschmann, Wilhelm, 223

Q
Querner, Rudolf, 68, 168, 170

R
Rack, Rolf, 78-**79**, 189
'radio crimes', 129, 153, 220, 268–69, 272–76, 364, 367–68
Radler, Georg, 190
Radom, ghetto, 88, 312, 368
Radosch, Ludwig, 302
Rainer, Friedrich, 35
Rajakowitsch, Erich, 182, 204n52
Rakwetz: Theodor sen., Theodor jun., 129, 148
Ramharter, Karl, 216
Ranacher, Julius, 224
Rankow, Alexander, 258
Rannersdorf, village doctor of, 301
Rappoltenkirchen, Schloss, 333
Rasch, Otto, 28, 42n25, 43n27
Raschke, Rudolf, 316, 334
Rath, Ernst vom, 183
Ravensbrück, concentration camp, 131, 167–68, 171, 223, 243, 279, 281, 301, 320
Rechnitz, massacre at, 325, 329, 333
records and card indexes, 2–3, 21, 115–16, 361

referrals to state prosecutors and courts, 129–30, 362
Regensburg, VGH, 234
Reich defence commissioner (Reichsverteidigungskommisssar), 65, 68, 80n9, 134
Reich security main office (Reichssicherheitshauptamt). *See* RSHA
Reichl, Kurt, 227–28
Reindl, Viktor, 328
'reinsurance', 102–8, 148, 171, 346–48, 353
reintegration of former Nazis, 7, 354, 370
Reiß, Stefanie, 282
Reither, Josef, 165, 170–71
relationship between Kaltenbrunner and Huber, 27, 63, 98
Rennau, Heinz, **75**, 339, 351
Renner, Karl, 339, 351
research questions and status, 2–3, 5–7
Ressek, Karl, 285
Reßl, Josef, 217
Restituta, Sister, 113n118, 220
returnees from Russia, 95, 252–54, 367
returnees from Spanish Civil War/France, 250–52, 254
Reuband, Karl-Heinz, 151
Richter, Karl, 129
Richter, Oswald, 245
Riehl, Walter, 137n30
Riese, Josef, 157
Riga, ghetto, 45n75, 50, 190, 338; Ordnungspolizei, 314
Righteous Among the Nations. *See under* Jews
Rixinger, Johann, 89, 98, 178, 186, 188, 191–92, 200, 202, 309, 342
Rock, Hildegard, 93–94, 184
Rogowoj, Leo, 158
Röhm, Ernst, 10, 58, 286
Rohrendorf, Institute of the Blessed Virgin Mary ('Mary Ward sisters'), 215
Röhrling, Johann, 124, 275, 327–28
Roland, Erich, 334
Rollig, Leonore, 279–80
Roma, 18, 21, 133, 165, 222, 309, 367–68
Romen, Sigismund, 236
Ronge, Maximilian, 30, 36, 44n65, 165

Rosse-Blaschko, Alfons, 179, 203n30, 311
Rossmanith, Ernst, 31
Rothschild: Alphonse Freiherr von, Eugene Freiherr von, 62n56
Rothschild, Louis Freiherr von, 4, 51–54, 56–59, 134
Rothschild Hospital, 178, 186–87, 192, 365
Rotter, Konrad, 33
RSHA (Reich security main office, Reichssicherheitshauptamt), 3, 16–20, 45n21, 63–64, 66–68, 71–74, 76, 78, 80, 84, 98–99, 103–4, 114, 117–18, 132, 145–46, 185, 188, 191, 214, 222, 238, 252, 272–74, 278, 290, 298, 300, 305–6n20, 308–11, 314, 316, 324–25, 332, 334, 339; higher SS and police leaders, 17–18, 27, 63–68, 80n6, 168, 170; organizational structure, 20–22; plot of 20 July 1944, 170; 'protective custody' order, 130; prototype of Heydrich's 'fighting administration', 18–19; suppression of Spanish Civil War fighters, 250
Rudischer, Franz, 33, **128**, 309–10
Rudolf, Hubert Anton, 215
Rudolf, Karl, 219
Rüter, C. F., 330n2
Rux, Karl-Heinz, 38, 45n74, 177, 202n14

S

SA, 10, 30, 57, 176, 286, 329
Sachsenhausen, concentration camp, 59, 276
Salzburg, 341; Gestapo office, 26, 28, 39–40, 42n16, 43n27, 28, 45n73, 74, 68–69, 246, 316; Camp Marcus W. Orr (Glasenbach), 313, 320, 337, 353; VGH, 234
Samaropoulos, Banajotis, 304
Sanitzer, Johann, **79**, 98–99, 103, 118, 123–25, 127, 147–48, 232, 236–38, 240, 243, 258, 262n34, 326–27, 332–34, 337, 342–43, 345, 351–54, **352**, 357n66, 363, 369
Sankt Andrä, parish priest of, 215
Sankt Anton an der Jessnitz, surveillance of parish priest, 217
Sankt Margarethen, arrest of Catholic priest of, 220
Sankt Pölten, priest at cathedral, 215; Vienna Gestapo branch office, 38–39, 120, 124, 128, 217, 262n41, 283, 327–28, 335
Sasso: Josef, Katharina (Smudits), 119, 148, 301, 351
Schärf, Adolf, 108, 171, 247, 352
Scharf, Erwin, 244
Scharff, Heinrich, 330
Scharizer, Karl, 168, 170
Scheffler, Emma, 224
Schelasko, Iwan, 258
Schellenberg, Walter, 34–35
Schifter, Günther ('Howdy'), 290, 303
Schindler, Josef, 97
Schirach, Baldur von, 4, 65, 68, 71, 105, 134–35, 139n102, 188, 200, 212, 267, 272
Schireno, Alfred, 190, 206n108, 342, 366
Schleiffer, Otto, 91, 97
Schlesinger, Johannes Paul, 245
Schlesinger, first name unkn., 105
Schlesinger, Richard, 225–26
Schmidt, Ferdinand, 31, 36–37, **75**–76, 86, 342
Schmidt, Karl, 299, 305
Schmidt, Oskar, 154, 268, 274
Schmitz, Richard, 165
Schneeweiß, Josef, 251
Schneider, Antonie, 222
Schneider, Johann, 155
Schneider, Lambert, 326
Schneider, Matthias, 215
Schneidmadl, Heinrich, 171
Scholz, Karl Roman, 113n118, 141, 233
Schön, Flora, 190, 206n107
Schramek, Franz, 284
Schultehinrichs, Heinrich, 215
Schulz, Erwin, 28
Schumann, Carl, 47
Schuschnigg: Kurt, 4, 29–30, 32, 51–60, 60n41, 114, 134, 162, 167, 186; Vera, 55, 62n41; Arthur, 62n41
Schussnig, Bruno, 157
Schuster, Johann, 328

Schütte(-Lihotzky), Margaret(h)e, 130
Schützen, shooting of an officer at, 133, 327
'Schutzhaft'. *See* 'protective custody'
Schutzpolizei ('protection police', Schupo), 15, 20, 26, 134, 365
Schwager, Friedrich, 146–47, 240, 261n33
Schwarz, Karoline, 187
Schwarz: Rosa, Michael, 159
Schwechat, 163, 214; gunfire directed at presbytery, 218
Schwed, Ernst, 302
Schweiger, Franz, 328
Schwertführer, Ernst, 89
SD (SS-Sicherheitsdienst, SS security service), Eisenstadt, 132–33, 327; Vienna, 65–71, 135, 335
SD main office (SD-Hauptamt), 24, 35, 225, 367; 'Einsatzkommandos' (task units) in Austria, 36–37, 209–10, 225; exposé 'The Austrian security system and its integration into the security police of the Reich', 24, 35; foreign intelligence service, 72; 'Meldungen aus dem Reich', 21, 72; persecution of Freemasons, 37, 225–26, 365
Sedlaczek, Emanuel, 246
Seetzen, Heinrich, 27, 86
Seilern, Paul Graf, 157
Seitz, Karl, 102, 170–71, 242, 247, 348, 354
Sekot, Emil, 224
Seventh Day Adventist Reform Movement, 224
Seyß-Inquart, Arthur, 29, 52, 162
Seywald, Josef, 216
Siegel, Viktor, 58, 62n61, **77**–80, 92, 99, 179, 194, 256–57, 297–98, 304–5, 326, 334, 336n14, 337, 339, 343, 346, 355n24, 369
Siegelberg (Siglberg), Mark, 166
Sindelburg, conflict over religious education in, 216
Sinzinger, Adolf, 170
Six, Franz Alfred, 53, 132, 176
Skorzeny, Otto, 334, 336n14
Skubl, Michael, 30, 35
Slavik, Felix, 245

Slezak, Leo, 105, 112n107
Smudits, Katharina. *See* Sasso
Socialist resistance, 142, 148, 167–68, 171, 237–38, 242–47, 269–70, 280–**81**, 300
'Sonderhäftlinge'. *See* Schuschnigg and Rothschild
'Sonderbehandlung'. *See* murders
Sonnenschein, Fritz, 134
Soswinski, Ludwig, 164
Spanish Civil War fighters. *See* returnees
Spann, first name unkn., 29
Speihs, Franz, 246
Sperber, Hugo, 245
Spindelberger, Josef, 155
Spitz, Otto, 237
Sponer, Eduard, 186–87, 205n82
Springer, Adalbert von, 240
Springer, Paul, 32, 44n47
SS and police court (SS- und Polizeigericht), 99, 115, 122, 257, 266n119, 281, 285
SS security service. *See* SD
Stachelberger, Josef, 49, 51–52
Stahlecker, Walter, 42n25, 58, 182, 193–94, 310, 321n9
Stalingrad, 105–6
Stanicz, Gisela, 156–57
Stanislau (Stanisławów), 313
Staribacher, Josef, 244
Staszyszyn, Ludwig, 270–71
Staud, Johann, 165
Staudinger, Franz, 247, 270
Stauffenberg, Claus Schenk Graf, 168, 170, 255, 365
Stauffenberg, family, 54
St Cyprien, camp, 251
Stein, Viktor, 245
Stein an der Donau, prison, 113n118, 235, 276, 285, 312, 328, 330, 342–43, 354
Steinbauer, Theresia, 220
Steinböck, Georg, 197
Steinhäusl, Otto, 25, 33, 36, 53, 85, 89–90, 101
Steininger, Emma, 276
Steinitz, Heinrich, 245
Steinmetz, Selma, 319
Steinwender, Eduard, 113n118
Stern, Michael, 106

Stern, Wilhelm, 186
Sticker, Magdalena, 300
Stief, Rudolf, 224
Stillfried an der March, protective custody for Catholic priest, 219
Stillfried, Alfons, 237
Stillfried, Emanuel, 165
Stockau, Georg Graf, 47
Stolle, Michael, 2, 11, 83, 115, 134, 151, 362
Strasser, Otto, 249
Straub, Franz, **79**, 98, 300, 306n20
Strauss, Alice, 105, 112n107
Strauss, Richard, 112n107
Strecha, Georg, 147
Stricker, Robert, 166
Strohmer: Johann (Hans), Franz, 300
Strohsacker, Hartmann (Augustin), 211
Strotzka, Alfred, 284–85
Stuckart, Wilhelm, 13
Stumfohl, Lambert, 221 229n61
Sturm, Josef, 215
Stuttgart, regional court, 313
Suchet, Wilhelm, 219
suicides, 45n74, 51, 54–55, 124, 126–27, 129, 147, 163–66, 184, 240, 287, 320, 328, 353, 363
Sulz, murder at, 326
summary courts, 329–30, 335, 342, 368
Suppinger, Johann, 284–85
surveillance, 14, 38, 117–18, 121, 136n21, 141, 151–52, 216–17, 253, 287, 367
Swatosch, Wilhelm, 247
swearing in of the Austrian police, 26
Swing-Jugend, 289–90
Szokoll, Carl, 170, 237, 334

T
Taylor, Jack, 327
Thaler, Josef, 32
The Hague, BdSuSD, 350
Thellmann, Theodor, 250
Theresienstadt (Terezin), ghetto, 159, 189, 191–93, 202, 208n173; Kleine Festung, 132, 148
Thierack, Otto Georg, 145
Tischer, Leopold, 127
Tischler, Ludwig, 47
Tomaszów, liquidation of 'Jewish council' of, 88
torture. *See* Vienna Gestapo, maltreatment
Toth, Hermann, 290
Toulon, prison, 251
Towin, Franz, 57
Toyfl, Franz, 33–34
Traunstein, supreme SS- and police court (Munich) in session at, 98
Trauttmansdorff: Josef Graf, Helena Gräfin, 328
Trenka, first name unkn., 28
Trenker (Trnka), Othmar, 2, 52, 54, **77**–80, 82n63, 92, 99, 148, 154, 238, 337, 339, 342–43, 345–49, 353–54, 356n38, 356n47, 369
Trittner, Josef, 184
Trnka, Othmar. *See* Trenker, Othmar
Trompeter, Hubert (Ernst), 219
Trotsky, Leo, 249
Trotzkyists and anarchists, 249
Truskowski, Igor, 258
Tschadek, Otto, 351
Tucek, Eduard, 318–20, 323n58, 343
Tuch, Karl, 249
Tuchmann, Emil, 178, 187, 192
Turnheim, first name unkn., 253
Twain: Mark, Clara, Jean, 48

U
Ulbing, Richard, **75**, 77, 90, 100, 123, 313
Unger, Ernst, 327
'insidious utterances' ('Heimtücke'), **77**, 129, 153, 156–57, 217. 219–20, 229n46, 232, 246–47, 267–72

V
Verona, Gestapo office, 86, 109n19, 314–**315**, 368
Vetter, Johann, 219
Vienna Gestapo, air raids, 147–48, 325, 333, 351, 353; arrests: 1, 4, 30, 37, 114, 117–20, 223, 130, 133–34, 137n45, 138n71, 141, 162–63, 167–68, 171, 177–78, 193, 210, 220, 226, 227n3, 233, 237–42, 244, 257, 259–60,

262n38,n41, 269, 274, 277–78, 283–84, 287, 293n50, 300, 310, 318, 337, 339, 363, 365–67; arrests of March/April 1938, 32, 162–63, 141, 226, 233, 358; arrests of August 1939, 167–68, 244–45, 252, 367; arrests after July 1944 plot, 4, 54, 67, 72, 99, 102, 114, 122, 162, 168, 232, 247, 255, 316, 353; card indexes, 21, 30, 36–37, 115, 167, 359, 361, 373; competencies, regional and supraregional, 38; counter-intelligence, 21, 30, 39, 71–72, 76, 78, 86, 103, 106, 132, 135, 248, 353; counter-intelligence officers in industry, 132, 135; daily reports, 3, 6, 7, 86, 114, 116–17, 119, 157, 189–90, 201, 210, 213, 223–24, 233, 236, 241, 255, 257, 277–78, 287, 289, 332, 362; end of (1945), 332–35, 369; end-phase crimes, 4, 120, 324–25, 330, 368; establishment, 24, 30, 33, 35–36, 117, 174–75, 183, 359; evacuation and destruction of Gestapo building, 4, 333, 335; 'external deployment', 308–9, 311, 315, 368; in France, 97, 317–20, 368; female employees, 91, 93–95; final extrajudicial executions, 127–28, 330; German-Austrian conflict potential, 99; Hotel Metropole (headquarters), **cover photo**, 4, 37, 47, **49**–51, **92**, 175, 233, 333; key research issues, 5; maltreatment, 93–94, 115, 119, 121, 124–27, 129, 137n47, 138n63, 163, 166, 176, 178, 180, 184, 248, 252, 254, 256–57, 259, 265n115, 274–75, 287, 302, 312, 318–320, 328, 331n12, 338, 342–43, 347–351, 353–354, 356n50, 357n58, 362; methods, 1, 4, 6, 85, 102, 114–15, 120–22, 127, 145, 238, 257, 319, 331n12, 362, 366; organizational structure, 6, 13, 19–20, 30, 74, 83, 221, 241, 358, 362; personnel: continuity and rotation, 96, 322n37; first measures, 35, 164–65, 182, 366; recruitment, 4, 73, 85, 142–44; structure, 3–4, 6, 63, 74–77, 79, 81n18, 20, 86–87, 91, 221, 338, 358, 362; publications and research, 2, 4, 258; radicalization, 119–21, 324–25, 330n1, 363, 368; 'reinsurance', 5, 98, 102–4, 105–8, 148, 160n12, 171, 173n27, 211, 227n5, 241, 330n4, 335–36n18, 347–48, 353, 356n40, 370; restructuring 1944/45, 332–34; source material, 2, 6, 50, 80, 87, 93, 99–100, 118, 143, 175, 178, 196; 'special detainees' Kurt Schuschnigg and Louis Rothschild, 52, 54, 59, 365. *See also* Geschäftsverteilungspläne (GVPs)

Vienna league of Mischlings (Mischlingsliga Wien), 126, 247–49, **248**

Vinzenz: Christian, Gustav, Theresia, 131

Vogel, Wilhelm, 97

Volters, Eduard, 132

Vomperberg. *See* Abd-ru-shin (Grail association)

Vozihnoj, Max, 246

Vugesta. *See under Jews*

W

Wagner, Josef, 347

Waldheim, prison, 222

Walther, Gerhard von, 254

Wanner, Karl, 125

War Criminals Act (Republic of Austria), 95, 111n73, 154, 156, 265n108, 275, 340, 369

Warsaw, 280

Wartha, Anton, 91

Wastl, Josef, 204n66

Weber, Ernst, 201

Weber, Max, 16

Wehofschitz, Otto, 127

Weidinger, Georg, 241, 245

Weidinger, Josef, 32, 91

Weimann, Ernst, 179, 276

Weinberger, Lois, 171

Weiser, Ludwig, 31, 43n39

Weiss, Maximilian, 47

Weißensteiner, Raimund, 220

Weisz, Franz, 2, 91, 119, 121–22, 127, 142, 154, 360

Weitschacher, Johann, 97

Weitzenbaum: Friederike, Max, 318

Weizsäcker, Ernst von, 117

Wendl, Josef, 86

Wendzio, Oskar, 123, 137n37, 256–57, 304
Wertheim, Franz Freiherr von, 47
Wewerka: Karl, Riza, 279
Weymelka, Rudolf, 224
Wiener Neustadt, Vienna Gestapo branch office, 38, 40, 124, 128, 167, 215, 283, 285, 314
Wiesbaden, deportation of Jews, 316
Wiesenthal, Simon, 316, 333, 350
Wild, Josef, 124
Wildt, Michael, 18–19, 84
Wilmersdorf, Ernst, 235
Winzendorf, crossfire with Gestapo officials at, 119
Witke, Bernhard, 200, 208n164
Witkowitzer Bergbau- und Eisenhüttenwerk (mining and iron works), 56–57
Włodawa, ghetto, 276
Wobisch, Helmut, 132
Wohl, Emil, 49, 51
Wohl, Heinrich, 137n34
Wohlmuth, first name unkn., 128
Woitsche, Fritz, 194
Wolff, Karl Friedrich Otto, 58, 62n60
Wolf, Karl, 125, 171, 320
Wolf, Peter, 219
Wolfsberg, British internment camp, 82n63, 112n94, 337–38
Wöllersdorf, internment camp, 145, 165
Worobjew, Ivan, 304
Wottawa, Karl, 179
Wrba, Franz, 270
Würzburg, Gestapo, 139n91

Y

Yalta, conference, 337
youth movements, 234–35

Z

Zagreb, 145, 240
Zehner: Wilhelm, Maria, 117, 164
Zeillinger (Zeilinger), Otto, 304
Zeitlberger, Karl, 94, 126, 192, 248–49
Zelburg, Franz, 165
Zelenka, first name unkn., 328
Zembaty, Konrad, 275
Zeßner-Spitzenberg, Hans Karl Freiherr von, 232
Ziegler, Gustav, 270
Zisterer, Johann, 221
Znaim (Znojmo), Vienna Gestapo branch office, 38, 41, 309–10
Zoder, Marie, 254
Zwerger, Camilla, 279
Zwettl, Vienna Gestapo branch office, 38
Zwifelhofer: Karl, Leopold, 141, 145–46, 149n23, 240, 261n23

www.ingramcontent.com/pod-product-compliance
Lightning Source LLC
Chambersburg PA
CBHW072043110526
44590CB00018B/3017